The Bloomsbury Companion
to Stanley Kubrick

The Bloomsbury Companion to Stanley Kubrick

Edited by
Nathan Abrams and I.Q. Hunter

BLOOMSBURY ACADEMIC
NEW YORK • LONDON • OXFORD • NEW DELHI • SYDNEY

BLOOMSBURY ACADEMIC
Bloomsbury Publishing Inc
50 Bedford Square, London, WC1B 3DP, UK
1385 Broadway, New York, NY 10018, USA
29 Earlsfort Terrace, Dublin 2, Ireland

BLOOMSBURY, BLOOMSBURY ACADEMIC and the Diana logo are trademarks of
Bloomsbury Publishing Plc

First published in the United States of America 2021
This paperback edition published in 2022

Cover design by Namkwan Cho
Cover image © Collection Christophel / ArenaPAL

A catalog record for this book is available from the Library of Congress.

ISBN: HB: 978-1-5013-4362-9
PB: 978-1-5013-7395-4
ePDF: 978-1-5013-4365-0
eBook: 978-1-5013-4363-6

Typeset by Newgen KnowledgeWorks Pvt. Ltd., Chennai, India

To find out more about our authors and books visit www.bloomsbury.com
and sign up for our newsletters.

Contents

Illustrations

Notes on Contributors

Nathan Abrams is Professor in Film at Bangor University where he also directs the Centre for Film, Television and Screen Studies. His most recent books are *Stanley Kubrick: New York Jewish Intellectual* (2018) and (with Robert Kolker) *Eyes Wide Shut: Stanley Kubrick and the Making of His Final Film* (2019). He is currently editing *Kubrick's Mitteleuropa: The Central European Imaginary in the Films of Stanley Kubrick* (with Jeremi Szaniawski); *Alien Legacies: The Evolution of a Franchise* (with Greg Frame); and *New Wave, New Hollywood: Reassessment, Recovery, and Legacy* (with Greg Frame).

I.Q. Hunter is Professor of Film Studies at De Montfort University, Leicester, UK; author of *British Trash Cinema* (2013) and *Cult Film as a Guide to Life* (2016); and editor or co-editor of thirteen books, including *Pulping Fictions* (1996), *Trash Aesthetics* (1997), *British Science Fiction Cinema* (1999), *British Comedy Cinema* (2012), *Science Fiction across Media: Adaptation/Novelization* (2013), *The Routledge Companion to British Cinema* (2017), and *The Jaws Book: New Perspectives on the Classic Summer Blockbuster* (2020). He is currently writing *Psychomania* (2021) for Auteur's Devil's Advocates series.

Jerold J. Abrams is an associate professor of philosophy at Creighton University in Omaha, Nebraska. He is the editor of *The Philosophy of Stanley Kubrick* (2007). Recent publications include "*2001* as Philosophy: A Technological Odyssey" (2019); "The Philosophy of War in *Dr. Strangelove*" (forthcoming); and "Philosophy of Prehistoric Painting and Cinema: Werner Herzog's *Cave of Forgotten Dreams*" (2019).

Ernesto R. Acevedo-Muñoz is Professor of Cinema Studies and Chair in the Department of Cinema Studies and Moving Image Arts at the University of Colorado in Boulder. He is the author of the books *West Side Story as Cinema: The Making and Impact of an American Masterpiece* (2013), *Pedro Almodóvar* (2007/9), and *Buñuel and Mexico: The Crisis of National Cinema* (2003). His work has also appeared in numerous collections and journals including *Quarterly Review of Film & Video*; *Film & History*; *Lit*; *Letras peninsulares*; *Short Film Studies*; *Mise au point*; *After Hitchcock*; *Authorship in Film Adaptation*; *Contemporary Spanish Cinema and Genre*; *A Companion to Luis Buñuel*; *Genre Gender Race and World Cinema*; *El Impacto de la Metrópolis: La Experiencia Americana en Lorca*; *Dalí y Buñuel*; and *Hollywood at the Intersection of Race and Identity*.

Graham Allen is a professor in the School of English, University College Cork, Ireland. He has published numerous books, including *Harold Bloom: A Poetics of Conflict* (1994), *Intertextuality* (2000), *Roland Barthes* (2003), and *Mary Shelley* (2008). He researches and publishes on Romantic literature, literary theory, and film, and is currently completing a book on philosophies of education and Mary Shelley's *Frankenstein*. He has published extensively on Kubrick's films, including papers on *A Clockwork Orange*, *The Killing*, *The Shining*, *Dr. Strangelove*, and *A.I. Artificial Intelligence*, and is currently researching a book on Kubrick's contribution to Future Studies. Professor Allen is an award-winning poet. He has published poetry collections, *The One That Got Away* and *The Madhouse System*, as well as an ongoing e-poem *Holes* (www.holesbygrahamallen. org). His new collection, *No Rainbows Here*, will be published in 2020.

Mick Broderick is Associate Professor of Media Analysis in the School of Arts at Murdoch University, and from 2004 to 2018 was the deputy director of the National Academy of Screen & Sound. His scholarly writing has been translated into French, Italian, and Japanese with his major publications *Reconstructing Strangelove: Inside Stanley Kubrick's "Nightmare Comedy"* (2017) and *Trauma and Disability in Mad Max: Beyond the Road Warrior's Fury* (2019, co-authored with Katie Ellis); editions of the reference work *Nuclear Movies* (1988, 1991) and, as editor, *The Kubrick Legacy* (2019) and *Hibakusha Cinema: Hiroshima, Nagasaki and the Nuclear Image in Japanese Film* (1996, 1999, 2014). Co-edited collections (with Antonio Traverso) include *Interrogating Trauma: Collective Suffering in Global Art and Media* (2011) and *Trauma, Media, Art: New Perspectives* (2010). Under contract for publication in 2020 is the co-authored monograph *Virtual Realities: Case Studies in Immersion and Aesthetics* (with Stuart Bender).

Geoffrey Cocks is Professor Emeritus of History at Albion College. He is the author of *Psychotherapy in the Third Reich: The Göring Institute* (1985, 1997); *The Wolf at the Door: Stanley Kubrick, History, and the Holocaust* (2004); *The State of Health: Illness in Nazi Germany* (2012); and co-editor of *Depth of Field: Stanley Kubrick, Film, and the Uses of History* (2006). He lives in Carmel-by-the-Sea, California.

Richard Daniels was a senior archivist and Stanley Kubrick Archivist at the University of the Arts London Archives and Special Collections Centre for over ten years, beginning in 2007 when the Stanley Kubrick Archive arrived there. In that time he initiated protocols on the management and access of the universities collections, including the Kubrick Archive. He also planned and managed the cataloguing of a large proportion of the Kubrick Archive. He assisted researchers using the archive and frequently gave lectures and papers on the life and work of Stanley Kubrick and on his archive. He has presented at conferences and events in the UK and across Europe. He has also advised similar film-related archives, including the Ingmar Bergman Archive in Stockholm and the Cinemateca Distrital Bogota. He has written several journal articles and book chapters and is co-editor of the book *Stanley Kubrick: New Perspectives*.

James Fenwick is a senior lecturer in media and communications. He is the author of *Stanley Kubrick Produces* (2020) and editor of *Understanding Kubrick's 2001: A Space Odyssey: Representation and Interpretation* (2018). His research interests include the life and work of Stanley Kubrick and Kirk Douglas, urban media and the representation of Sheffield, and unmade American film.

Gregory Frame is Lecturer in Film Studies at Bangor University, Wales. His research interests relate primarily to the politics of mainstream American cinema and television. His first book, *The American Film in Television: Myth, Politics and Representation*, was a runner-up in the British Association of Film, Television and Screen Studies Best Monograph Awards in 2016. His recent published articles include work on Jennifer Lawrence's star image and contemporary dystopian film, both of which address the concerns of his current project that explores the impact of the 2008/9 financial crisis on film and television.

Christine Lee Gengaro has taught in the music department at Los Angeles City College for more than a dozen years. An avid writer and researcher, she often gravitates toward topics that address music and popular media, or music and literature. Dr. Gengaro has published two books, *Listening to Stanley Kubrick: The Music in His Films* (2013) and *Experiencing: Chopin* (2017), and has recently edited the Irwell Edition of Anthony Burgess's *This Man and Music* (2020). She has presented papers in the United States, Europe, and South East Asia, and her published work appears in numerous journals and books, including *The Encyclopedia of Hip Hop* and *The Worlds of Back to the Future*. Dr. Gengaro has been the program annotator for the Los Angeles Chamber Orchestra since 2008.

Marat Grinberg is Associate Professor of Russian and Humanities at Reed College. He received his PhD in comparative literature from the University of Chicago in 2006. He is a specialist in twentieth-century Russian literature and culture and teaches courses in Russian poetry and nineteenth-century novels, Russian and Jewish literature, Jewish modernisms, Soviet science fiction, and Comparative Literature. He is the author of *I Am To Be Read Not from Left to Right, But in Jewish: From Right to Left: The Poetics of Boris Slutsky* (2011, paperback 2013) and *Commissar* (2016). He is also co-editor of *Woody on Rye: Jewishness in the Films and Plays of Woody Allen* (2013). He has published extensively in both academic and journalistic venues on Russian and Jewish literature, culture, and cinema.

Rodney F. Hill, Associate Professor of Film in the Herbert School of Communication at Hofstra University, is co-author of *The Francis Ford Coppola Encyclopedia* and *The Encyclopedia of Stanley Kubrick*; co-editor of *Francis Ford Coppola: Interviews*; and a contributor to several other books, including *The Essential Science-Fiction Television Reader*; *The Stanley Kubrick Archives*; and *After Kubrick: A Filmmaker's Legacy*. His writing has also appeared in *Cineaste*; *Film Quarterly*; *Cinema Journal*; *Literature/Film Quarterly*; and elsewhere, and he has been featured in video essays for several DVD/Blu-ray releases by the Criterion Collection, including Kubrick's *Dr. Strangelove* and Coppola's *Rumble Fish*.

Robert P. Kolker is Professor Emeritus at the University of Maryland. He is the author of numerous books, including *A Cinema of Loneliness* (4th edn.); *Film, Form, and*

Culture; *The Extraordinary Image: Orson Welles, Alfred Hitchcock, Stanley Kubrick and the Reimagining of Cinema*; and, with Nathan Abrams, *Eyes Wide Shut: Stanley Kubrick and the Making of His Final Film*.

Peter Krämer is a senior research fellow in cinema and TV in the Leicester Media School at De Montfort University (Leicester, UK). He also is a senior fellow in the School of Art, Media and American Studies at the University of East Anglia (Norwich, UK) as well as a regular guest lecturer at Masaryk University (Brno, Czech Republic) and at the University of Television and Film, Munich (Germany). He is the author or editor of eleven academic books, including the BFI Film Classics on *Dr. Strangelove* and *2001: A Space Odyssey*; a volume on *A Clockwork Orange* in Palgrave's "Controversies" series; and *Stanley Kubrick: New Perspectives* (2015, co-edited with Tatjana Ljujić and Richard Daniels).

Dominic Lash is a film scholar and musician. He has taught at the Universities of Bristol and Reading, and at King's College London. He has published in journals including *Screen* and *Movie*, and his first monograph, *The Cinema of Disorientation*, was published in 2020. He is currently working on a book titled *Robert Pippin and Film* for the Bloomsbury Academic Film Thinks series.

Philippe Mather is Associate Professor of Film Studies at Campion College, University of Regina (Saskatchewan, Canada). His monograph on Kubrick's photojournalism is titled *Stanley Kubrick at Look Magazine: Authorship and Genre in Photojournalism and Film* (2013). He also co-edited the collection *Rediscovering French Science-Fiction in Literature, Film and Comics* (2016) and has published in journals including *Kinema*; *Cinémas*; *Science-Fiction Studies*; *Historical Journal of Film, Radio and Television*; *Extrapolation*; *Cinémathèque*; *The International Journal of the Image*; and the *Canadian Journal of Film Studies*. His areas of expertise include the cinema of Singapore, film music, the science fiction genre, and Stanley Kubrick. His current research focuses on Orientalism in film, using Singapore as a case study.

Catriona McAvoy is a writer and researcher at the University of the Arts London. "Discovering Kubrickism" is a research project that she began in 2009 as part of her master's degree. Her research has developed and continued, and it now encompasses conference papers, book chapters, journal articles, and talks that present a new perspective on the films and working methods of Stanley Kubrick. McAvoy has also worked as a post producer in the television and film industry and continues research with interest in film and filmmaking. Some of her publications include "In Conversation with Diane Johnson" and "In Conversation with Lisa and Louise Burns," in *Studies in the Horror Film: Stanley Kubrick's The Shining*, and "*The Shining*: Looking Beyond the Myths," in *Stanley Kubrick: New Perspectives*, ed. Tatjana Ljujić, Peter Krämer, and Richard Daniels (2015).

Joy McEntee is a senior lecturer in the Department of English and Creative Writing at the University of Adelaide. Her research focuses on adaptation studies, masculinities, and American Cold War film. Her work has been published in *Camera Obscura*;

Screening the Past; *Adaptation*; *Literature/Film Quarterly*; and *The Journal of Adaptation in Film and Performance*.

Kate McQuiston is Professor of Music at the University of Hawai'i at Mānoa. Her main research area is music in film, with foci on directorial and compositional style, auteur directors, preexisting music, musical quotation, and music in biopics. She is the author of *"We'll Meet Again": Musical Design in the Films of Stanley Kubrick* (2013) and has written articles and chapters for *Literature/Film Quarterly*; *The Routledge Companion to Screen Music and Sound*; and the *Journal of the Society for American Music*.

Matthew Melia is a senior lecturer in the School of Arts, Culture and Communication at Kingston University in London. He was awarded PhD from Kingston for *Architecture and Cruelty in the Writings of Antonin Artaud, Samuel Beckett and Jean Genet* in 2007. He is currently revising his PhD for possible publication. His ongoing research into the work of Stanley Kubrick and Ken Russell focuses on such areas as the unwritten production histories of *A Clockwork Orange* and the unmade and unreleased films of Ken Russell.

Dijana Metlić is Associate Professor of Art History at the Academy of Arts, University of Novi Sad. She received her PhD in modern art and film studies from the Faculty of Philosophy, University of Belgrade, in 2012. She has written three books: *Nedeljko Gvozdenović: In Pursuit of Absolute Painting* (2018), *The Images of Ephemeral World: Connections between French and Serbian Intimism* (2017), and *Stanley Kubrick: Between Painting and Film* (2013). Her recently published papers include "Zenitist Cinema: Influences of Marinetti and Mayakovsky" (2019), "Stanley Kubrick and Hieronymus Bosch: In the Garden of Earthly Delights" (2018), and "Unmasking the Society: Use of Masks in Kubrick's Films" (2017). Her primary area of research is modern art, with a particular focus on the interrelations between film, photography, and fine arts.

Rod Munday is a lecturer in digital culture and gaming at Aberystwyth University. He has also been the webmaster of The Kubrick Site (visual-memory.co.uk/amk) since the late 1990s. His recent Kubrick-related publications include a paper for the French journal *Essais* (2017). He is also the co-author (with Daniel Chandler) of the *Oxford Dictionary of Media and Communication* (2020) and the *Oxford Dictionary of Social Media* (2013). Before academia, he worked in television postproduction.

Elisa Pezzotta, PhD in film and television studies, is an assistant editor at *Cinergie. Il Cinema e le altre Arti* and a member of the international editorial board of *Zbornik radova Akademije umetnosti* (Collection of Papers of the Academy of Arts). She has participated in many international conferences. She is the author of *Stanley Kubrick: Adapting the Sublime*, and of several articles published in *Cinergie*; *Elephant & Castle*; *Adaptation*; *Offscreen*; the *Journal of Adaptation in Film & Performance*; and *Wide Screen*. She co-edited special issues in *Cinergie*; the *Historical Journal of Film, Radio and Television*; and *Elephant & Castle*.

Manca Perko has a PhD in film studies and currently teaches film production and documentary at the University of East Anglia and is an external marker at the University of York. Her research focuses on collaboration in film crews, problematizing the attribution of creative autonomy, and authorship in film industry. She is an associate member of the Slovene Association of Cinematographers and a member of the education board of The European Federation of Cinematographers (IMAGO), actively promoting the role of education in the art of filmmaking. She is also an international filmmaker.

Lawrence Ratna is an honorary consultant psychiatrist at Barnet Enfield and Haringey MHT and at Freedom from Torture. He has been Associate Professor of Psychiatry at St. Georges University Medical School, Grenada; secretary for the Campaign Against the Abuse of Psychiatry for Political Purposes; and medical advisor to the Manic-Depressive fellowship. He has been a practicing psychiatrist for fifty-two years. In 1971 he helped set up the first twenty-four-hour psychiatric crisis service in Britain and developed many programs that have become national policy, such as the role of the family in the elderly, computerized case records, and metabolic monitoring. He teaches and lectures all over the UK and the world. He has a life-long interest in the psychiatric aspects of art and film. His current project is the neurobiology of Stanley Kubrick.

Karen A. Ritzenhoff is a professor in the Department of Communication at Central Connecticut State University where she teaches classes on film and television studies, gender studies, and visual communication. She is co-chair of the Women, Gender, and Sexuality Studies Program. Ritzenhoff has co-edited numerous books, including *Screening the Dark Side of Love* (2012), *Border Visions: Diaspora and Identity in Film* (2013), *Selling Sex on Screen* (2015), *The Apocalypse in Film* (2015), *The Handmaid's Tale: Teaching Dystopia, Feminism, and Resistance across Disciplines and Borders* (2019), and *New Perspectives on the War Film* (2019). She is currently working on a co-edited volume, *Black Panther: Afro-Futurism, Gender, Identity and the Re-making of Blackness*, as well as a co-edited book, *Mediated Terror in the 21st Century*. Ritzenhoff is co-chair of the Special Interest Group on War and Media Studies at the Society for Cinema and Media Studies (SCMS) where she also served as co-chair of the Women's Caucus.

Jeremi Szaniawski is Assistant Professor in Comparative Literature and Film Studies and the Amesbury Professor of Polish Language and Culture at the University of Massachusetts, Amherst. He is the author and editor of several volumes, including *After Kubrick: A Filmmaker's Legacy* (2020).

Filippo Ulivieri is Italy's leading expert on Stanley Kubrick. His research on *2001: A Space Odyssey*, *A Clockwork Orange*, Kubrick's unrealized films, and the myths surrounding his persona have been presented in several international conferences and published in Italian and English. He is the author of *Stanley Kubrick and Me: Thirty Years at His Side* (2016), the biography of Emilio D'Alessandro, personal assistant to the director. He is co-writer of *S Is for Stanley* (2015), winner of the David di Donatello award for best documentary feature. His most recent book is *2001 Between Kubrick and Clarke: The Genesis, Making and Authorship of a Masterpiece*.

Serenella Zanotti is Associate Professor of English and Translation Studies at Roma Tre University, Italy. She has published widely in the fields of audiovisual translation, cross-cultural pragmatics, translator manuscript genetics, translingualism, and feminist translation theories. Her most recent work focuses on Stanley Kubrick and films in translation. She is the author of *Italian Joyce. A Journey through Language and Translation* (2013) and co-editor of numerous volumes, most recently *Linguistic and Cultural Representation in Audiovisual Translation* (2018), *James Joyce's Silences* (2018), *Donne in traduzione* (2018), and *Reassessing Dubbing: Historical Approaches and Current Trends* (2019). She has been awarded a Helm Fellowship to support research at the Lilly Library, Indiana University; and a Harry Ransom Center Research Fellowship in the Humanities to research at the Ransom Center, University of Texas at Austin (2019).

Acknowledgments

The editors would like to thank the team at Bloomsbury, especially Katie Gallof, for believing in this project from the outset and giving it the green light. It has been somewhat of a herculean task shepherding almost thirty chapters and their authors to this point. Along the way, we have received help from, among others, Georgia Hester, a final-year student at Bangor University, who, as an intern, assisted with the final preparations for delivering the manuscript. I.Q. Hunter wishes to thank the Leicester Media School and the Cinema and Television History Research Institute (CATHI) at De Montfort University for supporting this project.

Nathan Abrams would like to dedicate this book to his father who passed away before it was published.

Introduction

Nathan Abrams and I.Q. Hunter

Stanley Kubrick (July 26, 1928–March 7, 1999) completed a body of photographic works, three documentaries, and thirteen full-length films, the releases of which were increasingly widely spaced. Strikingly disparate, the films range from a symbolic war film (*Fear and Desire*, 1953, which he later dismissed as juvenilia), film noirs (*Killer's Kiss*, 1955; *The Killing*, 1956), historical epics (*Spartacus*, 1960; *Barry Lyndon*, 1975), and science fiction (*Dr. Strangelove or: How I Learned to Stop Worrying and Love the Bomb*, 1964; *2001: A Space Odyssey*, 1968; and *A Clockwork Orange*, 1971), to war films (*Paths of Glory*, 1957; *Full Metal Jacket*, 1987), a horror film (*The Shining*, 1980), and sexual dramas (*Lolita*, 1962; *Eyes Wide Shut*, 1999).

This remarkable body of films continues to attract worldwide scholarly, critical, and fan attention. Even though Kubrick died over twenty years ago, interest in him has neither declined nor abated. Indeed, the opposite is probably true. The films have been rereleased in 4K at cinemas and festivals and transferred to Blu-ray in lavish box sets. The touring exhibition of artifacts related to his life and work, beginning in Frankfurt in 2004, has gone all over the globe, attracting millions of visitors. The opening of the Stanley Kubrick Archive (SKA) in 2007 has encouraged new scholarship and cult appreciation. His photography has also been the subject of major exhibitions. Academic conferences about Kubrick have been held in Bangor, Bordeaux, Leicester, Leiden, London, Munich, and Paris, while fan groups are flourishing on social media (at the time of writing, The Stanley Kubrick Appreciation Society and The Kubrick Society on Facebook have a combined total of 57,000 members).

Kubrick is now one of the most written-about film directors in history. The scholarship surrounding him is large and still growing. The list of essays, journal special issues, books and monographs on his collected works, as well as his individual films, and biographies is too long to summarize here, though much of the work in English is cited in the bibliography at the end of this book, which provides an indication of the size and breadth of what is now referred to as "Kubrick Studies." None of the existing books on Kubrick, however, is organized thematically or works as a textbook introduction to the key approaches to his films. *The Bloomsbury Companion to Stanley Kubrick* is designed to fill this gap, offering a comprehensive introduction to and summary of the current scholarship in Kubrick Studies, with a thematic rather than film-by-film approach, that is informed throughout by primary research at the SKA.

Life and Work

Born in 1928 in New York City, Stanley Kubrick was a child prodigy. He excelled at chess and photography, but his interests were far wider than that. Even though his grades at high school were not great, he landed himself a part-time job as a photographer at *Look* magazine at the tender age of 17 in 1945. Not long thereafter, he was promoted to a full-time position and was sent out on various assignments during which he took thousands of pictures. His earliest photography, largely critically overlooked, tells us much about his emergent interests and style. He learned about light, composition, framing, and how to work as part of a team with a writer. As Philippe Mather shows in this book, Kubrick's photographic career is essential to understanding Kubrick the film director.

Kubrick was also an autodidact and avid reader throughout his life (as Catriona McAvoy shows in her chapter). Living in Greenwich Village with his first wife, Toba Metz, he viewed everything he could at the Museum of Modern Art and elsewhere; Kubrick soon decided he could make the transition from a stills photographer to a moving-image director with results no worse than those he saw on screen. His first film was the documentary, *The Day of the Fight* (1951), itself an adaptation of a photospread he did for *Look* on the twins Walter and Vincent Cartier. Walter was a boxer and Vincent was his manager, and the movie depicts a day in their life as Walter prepares for a big bout. The movie shows Kubrick's early interest in doubles, boxing, doctors (his father Jacques or Jack was a physician), food, and religion. It also featured friends and family on screen and as part of the crew. Kubrick's next film, *Flying Padre* (1951), was also a documentary, this time about an airborne priest who flew a small aircraft to minister to his congregation in New Mexico. Kubrick, who also trained as a pilot but later renounced flying, reflects his interest in fatherhood, absent fathers, children and childhood, and again religion. Kubrick's final documentary—this time in color—was *The Seafarers* (1953), a promotional film for the Seafarers International Union. Even though he was a gun-for-hire, providing images for another's narration (not unlike how he worked at *Look*), Kubrick was able to show his nascent style in terms of long tracking shots, interest in technology, as well as fatherhood, family, food, and even sex.

Meanwhile, Kubrick was considering moving into feature filmmaking. Borrowing money from a relative and renting a camera, Kubrick flew off to California with some friends and a skeleton crew (an experience that stayed with him throughout his mature filmmaking career) and shot *Fear and Desire*. An allegorical film about four soldiers trapped behind enemy lines in an unnamed country in an unnamed conflict, *Fear and Desire* was made at the time of the Korean War, though, as Geoffrey Cocks points out in this book, much of its iconography is drawn from the Second World War. Disappointed with the film and its critical reaction, Kubrick disowned *Fear and Desire* and destroyed every negative he could get hold of. Unbeknown to him, however, one copy survived and was restored and rereleased after his death, allowing us to understand much about the origins of the director's feature filmmaking career.

Fear and Desire was written by his high school friend, Howard Sackler, who later became famous in his own right as a Pulitzer Prize-winning playwright. Kubrick teamed up with him again to write *Killer's Kiss*, a film noir about a declining boxer and a "taxi dancer," a 1950s euphemism for a prostitute. Set in and shot on the sly in New York City, the film is an early version of "guerilla filmmaking." The boxing sequences built upon *Day of the Fight* and like his first film, which cameoed Toba Metz as a fisherwoman, *Killer's Kiss* featured his second wife, Vivian Sobotka, as a ballet dancer, the sister of the heroine. Both women also worked behind the camera on their respective films.

After *Killer's Kiss*, Kubrick teamed up with producer James B. Harris, and the two formed a key partnership as Harris-Kubrick Productions. As James Fenwick shows in his chapter, this partnership has been overlooked in the scholarly literature, but it was important because it allowed Kubrick to focus on the creative elements of production, while Harris worked on the more mundane aspects such as budgets, marketing, contracts, and so on. Following the amicable breakup of the partnership in the early 1960s, Kubrick increasingly took control on all aspects of preproduction, production, and postproduction—at the expense of the rate of his output, which declined drastically.

The first film Harris and Kubrick made together, *The Killing*, was what author, screenwriter, and dramatist David Mamet has called the best film of its genre: the "one last job" heist movie (2008: 149). Indeed, the fractured narrative, held together by a single omniscient narrator, was also much admired by Quentin Tarantino whose *Reservoir Dogs* (1991) and *Pulp Fiction* (1994) would be unthinkable without *The Killing*. Another film noir, shot in black and white, *The Killing* was made in California, Kubrick's first brush with Hollywood. Based on a novel by Lionel White, the plot involves a ragtag collection of men assembled to pull off an ambitious racetrack robbery. Fate and chance, in the minutest of ways—a very Kubrickian tic—intervene to foil its successful outcome. It was considered a very existentialist picture—one that very much fit into the prevailing postwar ethos in Greenwich Village at the time. *The Killing* was also the first of Kubrick's many adaptations, this time with hardboiled writer Jim Thompson, which Graham Allen discusses in his chapter. Like most filmmakers, Kubrick based his films on preexisting material—typically fiction—and his status as an auteur depended on the unique way that he made that material his own.

The Killing brought Harris and Kubrick to the attention of the major Hollywood studios. They were signed up by MGM with whom they wanted to make *Paths of Glory*. Their bosses, though, did not want another war movie. They sifted through the studio's properties and came across *Burning Secret*, an early-nineteenth-century Viennese novella by Stefan Zweig about a holidaying mother and son, whose vacation (and relationship) is disturbed by a philanderer. The project never came to fruition because they were fired from MGM, in part because they were working on adapting *Paths of Glory* with writers Jim Thompson and Calder Willingham. Peter Krämer and Filippo Ulivieri chart this and many other unmade projects of Kubrick's.

Harris and Kubrick were able to make *Paths of Glory* by teaming up with Kirk Douglas, then a major Hollywood star and independent producer. *Paths of Glory* was a bleak First World War tale, based on a true story, in which a pair of vainglorious generals attempt to take an impregnable German position but without success. Looking to scapegoat the soldiers, the generals court-martial three of them on trumped-up charges. *Paths of Glory* owed much to Kubrick's favorite director, Max Ophüls, especially its long tracking shots through the trenches and the way the camera glided through buildings, past walls. It is the first of many films in which Kubrick explores opposites and hierarchies. It was on this film that Kubrick met his third and final wife, Christiane Harlan, who plays the captured singer in the final scene.

Paths of Glory was Kubrick's breakthrough movie and cemented his growing reputation. He received an offer to work on what became *One-Eyed Jacks* with Marlon Brando, but also toyed with many other screenplay ideas, as Ulivieri and Krämer show in their chapter. Nothing came to fruition, and this was a barren period for Harris and Kubrick until 1959 when Kirk Douglas rescued them with an offer for Kubrick to helm his gladiator epic *Spartacus* after he fired the director Anthony Mann. Seeing an opportunity to break free of the contract they had signed with Douglas and given that he had not worked on a movie since 1957, Kubrick readily agreed. Douglas probably envisaged their relationship not unlike when Kubrick worked on *The Seafarers*—a gun-for-hire working on another's screenplay. But Kubrick had other ideas, and he injected far more of himself into *Spartacus* than perhaps he has been credited for.

Although Kubrick was negative about the finished product and his experience of working for a major Hollywood studio left him with a bitter taste in his mouth, he learned much on that production. As Matt Melia notes in his chapter, it created his appetite for working with classically trained British theater actors of the likes of Laurence Olivier, Charles Laughton, and Peter Ustinov. Only 30 at the time, Kubrick had to learn to navigate between various experienced Hollywood players and crew (at least one of whom was anti-Semitic), and all of whom were vying to "improve" the script, from the big-name actor and producer Douglas, and Dalton Trumbo the (blacklisted) screenwriter, to Howard Fast, who had written the bestselling source novel as well as a draft of the screenplay. Despite his youth, Kubrick emerged with his reputation intact, having helmed what is still considered one of the best movies of the epic genre. The Kubrick that many came to revere from the 1960s onwards was formed on that set.

Kubrick swore never to work in Hollywood again. He was no fan of living in Los Angeles and wanted to be as far away from the studios as possible. Britain promised a more relaxed lifestyle, first-rate production facilities and personnel, and generous tax breaks, and Kubrick moved there with his family. In Britain he could make the films he wanted with little direct Hollywood interference. Indeed, in 1971, Kubrick secured an unprecedented deal with Warner Bros. that gave him complete artistic control.

Following *Spartacus*, to demonstrate their newly won independence, Kubrick and Harris moved to make Vladimir Nabokov's bestselling novel, *Lolita*, as their next film. *Lolita* was highly controversial because it was about the "seduction" of a 12-year-old girl by a middle-aged man who then loses her to a similarly aged rival. Even though the Motion Picture Production Code in the United States was weakening in the early 1960s, *Lolita* was exceptionally transgressive. Childhood was sacred in Hollywood cinema, as Nathan Abrams shows in his chapter. Working with Nabokov but discarding his huge screenplay as unfilmable, Harris and Kubrick went about adapting the book themselves, though the film was enhanced by memorable improvisations from Peter

Sellers. Kubrick later said that if he had known how censorship would compromise the film, he would never have made it (see Gelmis 1970).

The theme of sex continued to interest Kubrick, and for his next project, he decided to marry it with the Cold War and the theme of Mutual Assured Destruction. Tapping into the New Left zeitgeist, which was questioning Cold War orthodoxies, as well as the newly emerging black, sicknik, and Beatnik humor of the likes of comedian Lenny Bruce, Kubrick worked on adapting Peter George's *Red Alert*, a serious novel about a mad general who orders a preemptive nuclear strike on the Soviet Union. Kubrick reworked it as black comedy, bringing on board novelist Terry Southern to assist with the humor, and casting Peter Sellers again, initially in four roles but in the end in only three. The result, *Dr. Strangelove*, has been hailed as possibly the first countercultural story. It also showcased Ken Adam's remarkable set design, Kubrick's cinema verité shooting, as well as the performances of Sellers and George C. Scott in particular. Before completion, Harris and Kubrick parted company on good terms over creative differences at the direction the film was taking. Kubrick thereafter would work as his own studio head.

Sticking with the science fiction "what if" question, Kubrick then wanted to make the "proverbially really good science fiction film" (see Krämer 2010: 18). He alighted upon Arthur C. Clarke's short story, "The Sentinel" (1951), and novel, *Childhood's End* (1953). Together they worked on the screenplay and a simultaneous novelization, which was published after the film was released. The movie took four years to come to screen. The doubling of the typical length it took Kubrick to make a movie perhaps owed to the lack of brake that Harris provided, but also his absence meant that Kubrick felt he had to pick up tasks that he had previously trusted Harris to handle. Another reason for the film's protracted production was Kubrick deciding to alter radically the style of film he was making. The original screen treatment was for a didactic narrated film about evolution, artificial intelligence, and alien life, with a preface featuring scientists. The final movie was near-abstract, with minimal dialogue, and relied far more on sound, found music, and symbolic images than he had risked before: "The feel of the experience is the important thing, not the ability to verbalize it. I tried to create a visual experience which directly penetrates the subconscious content of the material" (Kubrick in Phillips 2001: 153). Both of his previous features were marked by their talkativeness, but *2001: A Space Odyssey* became more of a silent prayer to the omniscient power that governed the universe. Kubrick transformed the science fiction genre. Before *2001* it was typically a B-movie genre. Even the better ones were still marred by bleeping flying saucers and clumsy special effects that did little to move it out of its niche and juvenile audience. By contrast, Kubrick innovated and experimented technologically—front projection for the Dawn of Man sequence coupled with humans mimicking apes that were considered so realistic that the Oscar panel did not realize they weren't apes; the rotating space station and shots of the Moon; HAL and the revolving centrifuge on the Discovery; the fractal effects for the Stargate sequence; Bowman's aging in the final section, all held together by a "found" score that rejected the composed soundtrack that was the Hollywood norm in favor of preexisting classical and modernist music from the likes of Johann and Richard

Strauss, Ligeti and Khachaturian (see the chapters by Kate McQuiston and Christine Lee Gengaro). So adept were the visual and aural effects of *2001*—another reason that the movie took longer to make—that they have pretty much influenced all of science fiction on film since (see Benson 2018).

The genius of *2001* was that it also spoke to a generation. It came in 1968—a critical year in US and world history—but only indirectly referred to those events with a brief mention of the Cold War and the continuing antagonism between the United States and the USSR. There was no direct mention of Vietnam, student protests, riots, political assassinations, or the Black Power movement. Compared to *Planet of the Apes*, which came out the same year, Kubrick's space epic was more philosophical than political.

Kubrick toyed with two other projects after completing *2001*—a biopic of Napoleon and an adaptation of Viennese-Jewish writer Arthur Schnitzler's 1926 *Traumnovelle* (*Rhapsody: A Dreamstory*). The story that won out was *A Clockwork Orange* , adapted from Anthony Burgess's 1962 novel. The film is set in London in a dystopian future in which a fascistic, near-totalitarian government rules but in which law and order has broken down. Its teenaged protagonist, Alex DeLarge, memorably played by Malcolm McDowell, leads a gang of Droogs who speak Nadsat—a blend of Cockney and Russian—as they commit heinous crimes of violence, theft, and rape. Imprisoned for murder but released so he can receive an experimental treatment, Alex is "reformed" as an instrument of the state.

In a rare departure, Kubrick worked on the screenplay alone. He also shot it quickly, on the cheap and on location, and exploited the latest technology in the form of radio mics. As befitting the early 1970s, *A Clockwork Orange* was violent. But perhaps what made it so shocking was that the violence was edited to Beethoven and Rossini, turning the violence into something artful, aesthetic, and even balletic. One can consider it almost as a musical in the vein of *The Producers* (1968), *Funny Girl* (1968), and *Fiddler on the Roof* (1971). *A Clockwork Orange* was commercially successful but caused outrage and was linked to copycat violence. Kubrick withdrew the film from circulation in the UK after his family was threatened and it was only viewable there again after his death.

Kubrick still wished to produce his Napoleon biopic and even began preproduction. Warner Bros., however, got nervy after the failure of *Waterloo* (1970) and he had to sink his hopes into *Barry Lyndon*, an obscure nineteenth-century novel by William M. Thackeray about a social-climbing Irishman in upper-class English society who receives his comeuppance and loses a leg. Again, Kubrick worked on adapting the screenplay on his own, but it was everything *A Clockwork Orange* was not. Over three hours long, *Barry Lyndon* was lavish and slow, with languid zooms and compositions based on eighteen-century paintings. The violence was ritualized and formulaic as befitting a society that still believed in dueling as a means to settle scores and slights. It was his least commercial film to date, one that lost him money, seemingly a film out of its time, and it is only in recent years that it has been reevaluated as one his masterpieces (see Pramaggiore 2015).

As the decade drew to an end, Kubrick discovered a ghost story with commercial possibilities, Stephen King's *The Shining* (1977). Working with novelist Diane Johnson, whose work he admired but ultimately felt was not right for him to adapt, Kubrick transformed King's supernatural story about a man who goes stir crazy in a haunted hotel to one of psychological trauma. While it came at the end of, and cashed in on, a decade of New Horror films that began with *Rosemary's Baby* (1968) and *Night of the Living Dead* (1968), *The Shining* was an unusual contribution to a genre associated, by the late 1970s, with teen slasher films. Longer than any previous horror film, *The Shining* was not a slasher film but a meticulous slow burning study in ambiguity. Little admired by critics on its original release, *The Shining* came to set the benchmark for horror thereafter with many of its tropes endlessly mimicked (and mocked) across a variety of media beyond film. There are a variety of reasons for this. Kubrick constructed an amazing hotel set in Elstree, a composite of many existing ones but which contained its own internal logic that made little structural sense in reality. He then infused the film with references to the Freudian uncanny, Bruno Bettelheim's psychology (see our chapter on psychoanalysis), fairy tales, popular culture and, so Geoffrey Cocks argues here, the Holocaust. This potent combination launched various conspiracy theories and speculative reasoning about the *real* meaning of *The Shining*, culminating in the documentary *Room 237* (2012). Very few other films can boast of such a lasting impact.

It took Kubrick seven years to complete his next film. Far from resting and taking a break, he was searching around for another project. Again, his interest in the Holocaust was piqued (see Cocks and Grinberg's chapters), as was his desire to make *Traumnovelle*. Neither came to fruition as he began to focus on another—and this time his final—war movie, *Full Metal Jacket*. In a sense, it allowed him to remake his first feature film, *Fear and Desire*, as well as those elements of *Spartacus* that disappointed him because of his lack of overall control. Working with Vietnam War correspondent Michael Herr, who had written the classic *Dispatches* (1977), as well as with Gustav Hasford, author of the source novel, *The Short-Timers* (1979), Kubrick produced a striking and eccentric contribution to the second cycle of Vietnam War movies. In the first half, a platoon of US Marine Corps recruits is put through a violent and humiliating basic training regime by a racist, homophobic, and sexist drill sergeant. The second half is a series of vignettes, partly set in the city of Hue, which Kubrick had recreated in a disused gasworks in East London, even importing palm trees to make it look more authentic.

Kubrick did not make another film for twelve years. One of the reasons for this was that he embarked on two further projects. *A.I. Artificial Intelligence*, an adaptation of Brian Aldiss's short story "Super-Toys Last All Summer Long" (1969) was to be an update of the Pinocchio story but this time featuring the special effects that he couldn't achieve with *2001* now that CGI had progressed sufficiently enough to achieve them. Kubrick worked with various writers—Aldiss, Ian Watson, Sara Maitland—but unhappiness with either the screenplay or the effects led him to abandon the project, which was eventually directed by his friend Steven Spielberg and released in 2001. The other project was a movie about the Holocaust. After a search that lasted some years, Kubrick discovered Louis Begley's semi-autobiographical novel *Wartime Lies* (1991) about a Jewish boy and his aunt who survive wartime Poland by posing as gentiles. Kubrick had drafted a screenplay with the title *Aryan Papers* and begun extensive preproduction, including sourcing locations and casting. But the imminent release of

Spielberg's *Schindler's List* (1993) put a stop to it. Burned by the proximity of *Platoon* (1986) to *Full Metal Jacket*—audiences won't typically see the same kind of film in the same month—Warner Bros. begged Kubrick to drop his film. According to Christiane Kubrick, Kubrick had grown depressed by the subject matter and he was probably relieved not to have to shoot a movie about such a traumatizing topic.

By the mid-1990s, and with his health ailing, Kubrick turned back to the one project he had been hoping to make since the 1950s, Schnitzler's *Traumnovelle*. After many stops and starts, particularly following the completion of *2001*, Kubrick was finally able to turn to the novella that had intrigued and troubled him since he first read it. Kubrick was now old enough and had been married long enough to tackle a film about the internal emotional life of a husband and father whose smug security and mental comfort is challenged by the revelations of his wife's independent sexual desires. Working initially with Frederic Raphael and then on his own, Kubrick produced a screenplay that led to the longest continuous shoot in cinematic history. Another challenge was recreating New York City in London, just as he had done with Hue in *Full Metal Jacket*. This time he used a combination of a Pinewood backlot coupled with some location shooting in and around London. The result was challenging, and many critics hated it and still hate it (see Frame's chapter on reception). Instead of the expected erotic thriller—admittedly promised in the advertising and trailer—*Eyes Wide Shut* was closer to a 1970s European art movie: a dreamlike study of what goes on inside a man's head during a fruitless quest for sexual fulfillment. Although considered a box office and critical disappointment on initial release, like so many of Kubrick's films, *Eyes Wide Shut* was subsequently critically assessed and has become a cult film. Kubrick himself declared it was to be his best movie. Whether it is or not—and the jury is still out over twenty years later—it was his final testament as he died shortly after its first screening but before its final release (leading many to question whether it was actually the film he wanted to show to cinema audiences).

By the time of his death Kubrick had gained a reputation as the consummate auteur, who had wrested control from the studios and operated with remarkable independence within the changing studio system of the 1960s–1990s. He became perhaps the most independent filmmaker working in commercial mainstream cinema in American film history. Who else would have been given nineteen years (1980–99) to make just two films?

Unusually for artists, Kubrick's reputation has not gone into steep decline since his death. He remains a popular director as well as a cult figure. In the wake of more and more scandalous revelations, *Eyes Wide Shut* is hailed to be prophetic. Every time some sort of international conflict is imminent another *Dr. Strangelove* meme is produced.

Kubrick's films have lasted and gained in reputation for two main reasons. First, they are films of ideas. Kubrick, as Nathan Abrams (2018) argues elsewhere and Jerold Abrams here, was an intellectual and philosophical filmmaker, who believed that "If it can be written, or thought, it can be filmed." He commented on the key issues of his time and did so with an almost uncanny ability to preempt the key discussion points of the day. His films straddled art house cinema and genre cinema, achieving both commercial success and critical acclaim through their distinctive visual language, innovative use of music, and repeated themes of dehumanization, madness, and determinism. Formally Modernist and experimental, they sought to communicate ideas through "pure cinema" enhanced by music: "Film operates on a level much closer to music and painting than to the printed word, and, of course, movies present an opportunity to convey complex concepts and abstractions without the traditional reliance on words," he said (in Gelmis 2001: 90). They were films that could appeal to both mainstream and art house audiences. Very few other directors can boast that reach. That he gave few interviews and refused to clarify the meaning of his provocative and ambiguous films allows audiences to come up with their own ideas and encourages them to search for deeper hidden meanings. Perhaps only Kubrick could inspire a film like *Room 237* in which *The Shining* is subjected to laser-like scrutiny to argue that it is not simply a horror movie about a man going stir crazy who then attempts to chop up his family with an ax.

The second reason that Kubrick's films have lasted is that he pushed the envelope technologically. Most obvious in the groundbreaking special effects in *2001*, Kubrick's technological mastery is evident in his virtuoso tracking and Steadicam shots, use of one-point perspective, innovative employment of found music, and experimental lighting techniques (as on *Barry Lyndon*, where a camera fitted with an ultrafast Zeiss lens developed by NASA allowed shooting in candlelight).

Kubrick was, however, a controversial director, and not only because films like *Lolita* and *A Clockwork Orange* challenged censorship rules and conventional mores. His detractors were and remain numerous, including such influential voices as Andrew Sarris, Pauline Kael, and David Thomson (though even he came to call *The Shining* Kubrick's "one great film"). The critical standing of his films has been remarkably changeable and uncertain, but his current reputation seems secure and *Paths of Glory*, *Dr. Strangelove*, and *2001* are regarded as canonical classics.

Kubrick himself became a mythologized figure, who was often depicted as a reclusive and misanthropic genius. Accusations include his films being "cold" and unemotional; pretentious; middlebrow; misanthropic; misogynistic, occasionally racist, and sexist (see the chapters by Broderick, McEntee, and Ritzenhoff). Such accusations, though, confuse the films with a misunderstanding of their maker, or more precisely his public image. The emergence of more memoirs about Kubrick show that he was a warm, loving, family man who enjoyed the company of friends, family, and his pets. Far from being cold and unemotional, he worked closely with trusted collaborators (see Perko's chapter), often relying on them on multiple occasions, pushing them to give him what he didn't know he was looking for in the first place. Kubrick was not a Hitchcock. He did not have everything planned and laid out in his head before shooting. He did impeccable preproduction research that made him a virtual master on whatever subject he was working on, but that did not mean he knew exactly what his films would look and sound like. He was open to ideas and often these came out during production itself hence leading to the protracted shoots and multiple takes. We now also know that he was a demanding, perfectionist director who insisted on one hundred per cent commitment over the duration of a project. Time zones and times of day meant nothing to Kubrick who, if he wanted something done, was to be completed as he requested. The family lives of collaborators no doubt suffered, as the documentary (*Filmworker* 2017) about Leon Vitali, his right-hand man from 1975 to 19, attests.

The Bloomsbury Companion to Stanley Kubrick cannot be wholly comprehensive but it attempts to introduce and summarize the state of the field of Kubrick Studies but also to provoke new work. There are still more angles to pursue and reams of new material in the SKA to read. Kubrick's status as a filmmaker may be fixed, but our understanding of him is not and is changing all the time. We hope that those who read this book will be inspired to add to it.

We have divided the book into five sections. "Industry" explores Kubrick in terms of production (Fenwick), authorship (Munday), adaptation (Allen), collaboration (Perko), Britain (Melia), translation (Zanotti), and critical reception (Frame). "Sound and Image" focuses on Kubrick's photography (Mather), his use of framing (Kolker), formalism (Hill), acting (Acevedo-Muñoz), art history (Metlić), musical composition (McQuiston) and use of preexisting music (Gengaro). Section Three, "Gender and Identity," explores the key issues of feminism (Ritzenhoff), gender and sexuality (Broderick), marriage and family (McEntee), Jewishness (Grinberg), and the Holocaust (Cocks). "Thematic Approaches" tackles such topics as optimism and pessimism in Kubrick's films (Lash), philosophy (J. Abrams), time (Pezzotta), madness (Ratna), psychoanalysis (Hunter and Abrams), childhood (Abrams), and genre (Szaniawski). The final section reflects on researching Kubrick in terms of the archive (Orgill and Daniels), research and reading (McAvoy), and his unmade films (Krämer and Ulivieri).

One final note: we have compiled all the references into one master bibliography at the end, which has necessitated citing multiple editions of the same text, reflecting the variety of Kubrick Studies.

Part One

Industry

Introduction

This opening section considers how Stanley Kubrick managed to carve out a distinctive place within the American film industry both as a powerful auteur but also one of its most independent figures. Emerging as the old studio system was dying, as a forerunner of New Hollywood cinema, Kubrick made highly personal films that cut across mainstream genre filmmaking and art cinema but were always designed for commercial success. He was fortunate in becoming a director at a transitional moment in Hollywood, when the classical studio system was weakening in favor of independent producers, stars, and directors who were gaining more power and creative autonomy.

In a rare move, James Fenwick focuses on Kubrick's role as a producer (rather than just as a director). He shows how becoming a producer was essential to Kubrick's achieving what he called "annihilating control" (Krämer 2015b: 50) over his films and career, an aspiration that followed his frustrating experience on *Spartacus*. Especially important was seizing control of publicity, which enabled Kubrick to promote what would become his brand. A deal with Warner Bros. in 1970 won him unprecedented leverage, which he increased through obfuscation, limiting information, and not cooperating with studio executives. This power, however, as Fenwick suggests, was ultimately a self-defeating strategy. It not only left Kubrick unable to decide among projects and caught up in micromanaging preproduction, but it also so engaged him in postproduction tasks (checking prints, managing marketing and publicity, translation) that his role as producer took over from that of director, which further increased the gaps between his films.

Kubrick's desire for autonomy and his vertically integrated oversight of his projects made him the very model of an auteur, a term popularized in the 1960s when directors were emerging as "superstars" (Gelmis 2001). Indeed, if Kubrick does not count as an auteur, it is hard to imagine any director who does. Rod Munday's chapter surveys how critics have judged Kubrick's claims as an auteur against the background of changing ideas of auteurism, noting that the first wave of auteurist critics, like Jean-Luc Godard (1968) and Andrew Sarris (1968a: 196), did not especially value his films. As auteurism became an aspect of marketing, Kubrick's auteur status enabled his films increasingly to be sold by his name. At the same time, Kubrick consciously promoted his public image as an all-powerful, perfectionist genius, and he became a legend without becoming a conventional celebrity or media figure.

The next two chapters modify the idea of auteur by emphasizing the importance of collaboration to Kubrick, even if creative decisions would always ultimately rest with him. Possibly undercutting the link between auteurism and originality, Kubrick's films from *The Killing* onwards were all adaptations of previously existing fictional material, usually novels or short stories (Jenkins 1997; Pezzotta 2013). (Only once did he plan a nonfictional film, *Napoleon*.) These sources were rarely classics with a significant cultural footprint (Nabokov's *Lolita* is an exception) and often quite obscure. Although *Traumnovelle* (*Rhapsody: A Dream Story*), the source of *Eyes Wide Shut*, was a passion project for Kubrick, most of his sources were seemingly chosen as representative of a genre or for their commercial possibilities rather than for their high qualities and exploitable profile. This is standard practice in filmmaking whereby most films, in both the mainstream and art cinema, are adaptations designed to repurpose presold intellectual property. What is significant about Kubrick, however, is that, like John Ford, Alfred Hitchcock, and Steven Spielberg, he was an auteur of adaptation. Unlike with many adaptations, the fact that his films are adaptations is not the most important discursive frame for understanding them—nor was it how they were promoted. They were generally promoted as the latest Kubrick film rather than as adaptations. Graham Allen's chapter shows how Kubrick often radically transformed his literary sources so that they worked as visual and aural experiences rather than imitations of the original. His later films in particular became postmodern reflections on the epistemology of cinema and film as dreamscape.

Typically, when adapting a source text, Kubrick worked closely with others, usually creative writers rather than professional screenwriters. In only two cases, *A Clockwork Orange* and *Barry Lyndon*, Kubrick adapted the books himself and is the only writer credited as the screenwriter. Manca Perko's chapter examines Kubrick's collaborative practices in detail. Like European directors such as Ingmar Bergman, Kubrick repeatedly employed the same personnel on his films, using small crews to keep costs down; it was almost an artisanal approach to filmmaking. Kubrick's co-workers commented on his openness to collaboration, which was part of his exploratory attitude towards production and direction. Encouraging creativity in others played the same role as allowing for multiple takes: it maximized the possibilities of generating choices. As Peter Krämer has said, he would "select collaborators and establish work procedures which were likely to produce results he could not have come up with on his own" (2015b: 61). Working for Kubrick was often difficult but rewarding, and he seemed to mentor some of his collaborators who regarded the experience as an apprenticeship in filmmaking. Many stuck with him for years, like Leon Vitali, whose time with Kubrick is recorded in *Filmworker* (2017). Numerous of Kubrick's collaborators won Oscars, too, generally for technical achievements (*Barry Lyndon* won four), though Kubrick was accused of stealing credit, for example from Douglas Trumbull for the special effects on *2001* (Child 2014).

Matthew Melia looks at the relationship between Kubrick and Britain, where he moved with his family in the early 1960s to make *Lolita* and maintain an independent distance from the studios. This enabled Kubrick to make use of British talent, and to take advantage of tax breaks such as the Eady Levy, which used box office takings to subsidize production (Fenwick 2017). As Melia shows, Kubrick was only one of several expatriate directors and other film workers who, in a significant transatlantic exchange of talent, moved to the UK in the 1950s and 1960s, some because of the blacklist in Hollywood. Melia also considers whether Kubrick's films were "British" in a wider sense. Though none was set in contemporary Britain, *A Clockwork Orange*, with its location shooting at such places as Thamesmead and Brunel University, and *Barry Lyndon*, mostly set and filmed in England and Ireland, are arguably the most British in their themes and references to British science fiction and television, exploitation cinema, colonialism, and class. Because Britain often stands in for somewhere else, as in *Lolita*, *Full Metal Jacket*, and *Eyes Wide Shut*, the films' "trans-Atlanticism" results in a sense of dislocation, which further enhances their dreamlike qualities. Much of the films' Britishness rests with their use of British character actors, often familiar from television; Kubrick showed a preference for British actors as early as *Spartacus*.

Serenella Zanotti considers how Kubrick's control over his films extended to translation of dialogue, dubbing, and subtitling. Kubrick had a varying but often close involvement with the production of foreign language versions. He selected translators and dubbing directors, giving them notes and setting out his intentions. As with his input into marketing, the aim was to aid box office success. He saw translation as intrinsic to the creative process, and often chose outsiders to the dubbing and subtitling industries to bring a freshness of approach. His preference for hiring voice actors with no previous experience of dubbing and established film directors rather than dubbing specialists helped to ensure that their work was not routinized.

One aspect Kubrick didn't have control over was the critical response to his films. Gregory Frame looks at what was the often difficult reception of his films, many of which did not initially meet with universal critical acclaim (though it is a myth that *2001* was poorly received (Krämer 2010: 92–3)). There has been a continuous process of reevaluation of the films by critics and academics. Once marginalized films like *Lolita* and *Barry Lyndon* have become more central to his reputation, and scholars and critics have begun relooking at his earliest efforts. Archival research into Kubrick's input into *Spartacus* has prompted reevaluation of a film often seen as marginal (Radford 2015). Frame argues that the expectations raised by Kubrick's brand as an auteur came to suffocate the response to his films. There still remains critical disagreement about his films, especially *Eyes Wide Shut*, though that has achieved academic and some popular critical acclaim years after its initial release (Chion 2008; Kolker and Abrams 2019). The enthusiastic reception of *Barry Lyndon* on its 2016 may even have been influenced by academic reappraisal (Pramaggiore 2015a).

1

Kubrick and Production

James Fenwick

Across the thirteen feature films that Stanley Kubrick directed, he received the credit of producer on nine of them. Moreover, if one considers the partnership with James B. Harris between 1955 and 1963, during which Harris produced three films as part of their Harris-Kubrick Pictures Corporation, Kubrick was arguably involved as a producer on twelve of his own feature films. He was very much his own producer throughout most of his career, though with varying degrees of creative and business control at specific time periods. In the earliest years as a producer, Kubrick operated at a low-budget level of independence, with little influence over the way his films were handled by the studios to which he sold them. By the late 1960s, following the critical and commercial success of *2001: A Space Odyssey*, Kubrick had established himself as one of the most powerful and potent producing brands in Hollywood. However, Kubrick's output slowed considerably in the ensuing decades and, despite the extent of the producing control he had managed to obtain, he seemingly found it harder to produce and release a feature film.

Consider the fact that Kubrick directed and produced nine feature films in the twenty-two-year period between 1953 and 1975, in contrast to directing and producing only three feature films in the twenty-three-year period between 1976 and 1999. Kubrick's output significantly reduced during his Warner Bros. (WB) years, a company with which he had struck a three-picture contract in 1970 and a further three-picture contract in 1984. During these years Kubrick apparently had unprecedented levels of producing authority, with almost total executive control of his films, but he was somehow unable—maybe even struggling—to move his pictures out of development and into production. Kubrick worked on various projects that consumed his energy in the 1980s and 1990s, including *A.I. Artificial Intelligence* and *Aryan Papers* among others, only to abandon them despite extensive research and financial investment.

This chapter explores Kubrick's role as a producer, analyzing how he was able to secure the levels of autonomy that he did by the 1970s, before moving on to evaluate his role as a producer during the years. The chapter will argue that Kubrick's success in obtaining the levels of producing control that he did was ultimately self-defeating, with WB enabling Kubrick's decline in output by the levels of autonomy they granted him. The chapter serves as a comprehensive overview of Kubrick as a producer, but by no means discusses in-depth every facet of his career. Instead, the chapter argues that there are three key phases to understanding Kubrick's career as a producer. First, the phase between 1951 and 1961 in which Kubrick sought to obtain autonomy as a producer. Second, the phase between 1962 and 1968 in which Kubrick sought to consolidate his autonomy. And third, his career from 1970 onwards when he worked exclusively with WB and was allowed unyielding levels of control to the point it crippled his ability to operate. Taken together, these three phases begin to reveal the industrial contexts of producing autonomy and the impact they had on Kubrick's creative output.

Obtaining Autonomy

Throughout the 1950s Kubrick was a producer operating with various forms of independence from the major studios, which provided spaces of autonomy, particularly over areas of creative control. This allowed Kubrick to develop an innovative aesthetic approach to his work between his first feature, *Fear and Desire*, and his final collaboration with producing partner James B. Harris, *Lolita*. Across this roughly decade-long period, from the early 1950s to the early 1960s, Kubrick directed six feature films, making it one of the most productive periods of his career, with nearly half of all his feature films produced during this time frame. Yet, ironically, this is the period that Kubrick was most restricted in his powers as a producer, at least when it came to his position as a producer in relation to the studios financing his productions.

Postwar Hollywood was undergoing rapid transformations in its mode of production, moving toward a form of semi-independent producing, in which independent producers were subcontracted for one-off projects, or on nonexclusive contracts. These producers formed their own production companies, sourced a script or story material, brought together a cast and crew, and sought a budget. The number of independent production companies incorporated in the United States rose rapidly throughout the 1950s. Actors, writers, and directors were looking to become their own producers and take control of their own careers. This is not to suggest that Hollywood studios no longer had any creative control, but rather that levels of control and autonomy were now open for negotiation.

Kubrick's first forays as a feature film producer, working as a low-budget independent producer on *Fear and Desire* and *Killer's Kiss*, both largely financed by private sources, demonstrate how he was exploiting these spaces of autonomy to gain control over his productions. *Killer's Kiss* also involved Kubrick learning what he later described as the, "Kafka-esque nature of making, closing, breaking, etc., film deals" (Kubrick to James B. Harris, November 19, 1962, SK/1/2/2/2, SKA). With *Killer's Kiss*, Kubrick formed his first professional production company, Minotaur Productions, and turned to a number of businesses for additional funding—on top of the investment from his uncle, Martin Perveler—negotiating promissory notes, loan agreements, and deferments with companies such as Deluxe Laboratories, Titra Sound Corp, and the Camera Equipment Company. In the process of making these deals, Kubrick sacrificed the rights to the profits of *Killer's Kiss* but retained creative control of the production. These companies were not interested in the aesthetic product, but rather in ensuring a return on their investment. At the same time, Kubrick's key concern with these first two features—while ostensibly beginning to explore his aesthetic and intellectual interests—would seem to have been about gaining the attention of mainstream Hollywood, with an eye to securing larger budgets as an independent producer. Indeed, Kubrick reputedly quipped to Chris Chase (stage name Irene Kane) on the set of *Killer's Kiss* that, "honey, nobody's going to get anything out of this movie but me" (Phillips 2005: 287).

Kubrick was demonstrating his abilities, at least with *Killer's Kiss*, at being able to produce a relatively commercial-orientated genre picture on a modest budget. His attempts were certainly successful in respect of gaining the attention of United Artists (UA), which bought the film with the aim of encouraging Kubrick to produce further pictures for the company. UA's business strategy in the 1950s was to develop new and innovative producers, providing them with large degrees of creative control. This opened yet another space of producing autonomy for Kubrick, who produced his next two features, *The Killing* and *Paths of Glory*, for UA. The deals struck with UA were nonexclusive picture-by-picture contracts. Having teamed up with James B. Harris to form the Harris Kubrick Pictures Corporation in 1955, Kubrick would not receive a producing credit again until *Dr. Strangelove*. However, Harris and Kubrick's partnership was, according to Harris himself, one of an equal decision-making process. Harris's role was to obtain the rights to potential future property the company could adapt, to obtain funding, and to obtain time and space for Kubrick to focus on the creative choices of the films being produced.

Yet, while Harris Kubrick Pictures had relative autonomy of the creative aspects of the actual production, it had little producing autonomy over the promotion and distribution of its films between 1955 and 1962. For example, on *Paths of Glory* both Harris and Kubrick found they were working against the publicity department of UA, which was intent on selling the picture as an "all-out action campaign with no projection whatsoever of unusualness" (Stan Margulies to Myers P. Beck, February 25, 1958, Box 23, Folder 25, Kirk Douglas Papers [KDP]). Kubrick and Harris had protested to UA about this approach, believing that the film could appeal beyond a masculine audience to a young, liberal, metropolitan base in cities such as New York. Kubrick wanted to include images of Susanne Christian—his future wife and the only significant female character in the film—in adverts and in the film's trailer. UA ignored Kubrick's suggestions, despite publicly stating that their contracts with independent producers had an inbuilt space for autonomy over promotional strategies. It seems that this space for autonomy amounted to a producer being able to voice concerns, but not to have any further input over the promotional strategies. Control over publicity would form the key battleground for Kubrick in the ensuing decade.

The final key aspect to understanding Kubrick's approach to producing in this period, indeed, to understanding his view of producing control for the remainder of his career, is the contract Harris Kubrick Pictures agreed with Kirk Douglas's Bryna Productions in January 1957. In return for appearing in *Paths of Glory*, Douglas signed Harris Kubrick Pictures to a four-picture deal, two of which were to star Douglas, and the first of which needed to enter production within fifteen months of the completion of *Paths of Glory*. The contract allowed Douglas to pick the properties that Harris Kubrick

Pictures would have to produce. In addition, Harris Kubrick Pictures had to forfeit any of the literary properties it owned should either of its business partners, Harris or Kubrick, default on the contract. The contract amounted to Harris and Kubrick surrendering substantial producing autonomy, but they had agreed to the contract out of a desire to have Douglas star in their film. What followed was a key approach by Kubrick to obtaining producing control in the future: a process of noncooperation. The contract underwent renegotiation during the production of *Paths of Glory*, but Kubrick refused to sign the revised contract as he did not want to hand over creative control to Douglas, something that he felt would be fatal to his independence (Fenwick forthcoming).

Harris and Kubrick's attempts to terminate the contract included violating its terms by collaborating with other production companies and by considering dissolving Harris Kubrick Pictures in May 1957. This threat forced Douglas to realize that Harris and Kubrick were intent on protecting their producing autonomy. A Termination and Release Agreement replaced the contract in May 1958, but this was even more brutal in its terms and conditions, including enforced fees on future Harris Kubrick Pictures features and a prohibition on the casting of certain stars in any of their films (May 1, 1958, Box 11, Folder 21, KDP). The Release Agreement resulted in legal wrangling over literary properties, including the crime film *I Stole $16,000,000* that Harris Kubrick Pictures had looked to develop at one point with Douglas. By 1961, sensing that Harris and Kubrick were too uncooperative to be kept under contract, a final release deal was struck, though the price of freedom included a release fee of $40,000 (Fenwick forthcoming). Moving forward, Kubrick would ensure that he never found himself in such strict contractual bondage again.

Consolidating Autonomy

While independent producers certainly had obtained more power over their productions by the end of the 1950s, they were still heavily influenced by the major studios that financed them, particularly over the key issues of publicity and distribution. But the shift in power that was taking place was fully exploited by producers like Kubrick, who consolidated his producing autonomy in the 1960s with three of his most successful pictures: *Lolita*, *Dr. Strangelove*, and *2001* (and not forgetting the box office success of *Spartacus*, though this was a film over which Kubrick had no producing control). Kubrick achieved his consolidation of producing power through a process of intrusion into areas of publicity and distribution (often against contractual stipulations), a process of noncooperation, and a process of obfuscation by withholding information from studio executives.

Ever since the first feature with Harris Kubrick Pictures, Kubrick had come to realize that publicity was one of the most vital components of a producer's job, and without control of it then a film's prospects at the box office could be ruined. The issue came to a head on *Lolita*, a film that was financed by Seven Arts and distributed by MGM. Seven Arts was unwilling to concede autonomy over publicity to Harris Kubrick Pictures, believing it should be handed instead to MGM. Harris and Kubrick had attempted to select their own publicist, Sig Shore, for the film, but Seven Arts forced them, via contractual stipulations, to drop the suggestion. Kubrick continued to argue that autonomy over publicity and distribution should remain with a producer, expressing his dismay to Seven Arts and claiming that producers had much greater 'wisdom' about issues of publicity than any film studio. Kubrick was insistent that control of publicity and distribution should reside with the producer and the remainder of the 1960s involved Kubrick in a struggle to gain such control (Kubrick to Eliot Hyman, August 4, 1961, SK/10/8/1, SKA). It was a pragmatic realization on Kubrick's part that, without control of publicity and distribution, he in effect was allowing the studios to control the way audiences received his films and branded him as a filmmaker.

Kubrick's partnership with Harris ended amicably in 1962, but his powers as a producer grew exponentially. In October 1962 he established a producing powerbase for himself, incorporating Hawk Films and Polaris Productions. Whereas Hawk Films was concerned with the day-to-day business of film production, Polaris operated as Kubrick's publicity division. Kubrick had contracted himself to work exclusively for Polaris, making clear that he was his own producer and worked on his own terms, or at least that was the intent moving forward. Polaris acted in the interests of promoting Kubrick as a producing brand and as a negotiating powerbase to interact with the major Hollywood studios. The company was run by a vice president, a role undertaken by three individuals throughout the 1960s: Nat Weiss on *Dr. Strangelove*; Roger Caras during the preproduction and production of *2001*; and Benn Reyes, who was only in the job for a short time before suffering a fatal heart attack during a publicity tour for *2001* in 1968.

Kubrick's incorporation of Polaris needs to be seen against the backdrop of the expansion of the publicity departments of the major Hollywood studios in the 1960s. Long-range promotion campaigns were becoming a key feature to selling a film. This required the cooperation of the producer from the outset, with publicity campaigns devised during the development and preproduction phases of a film. However, Kubrick was resistant to studios being in control of his publicity strategy and so began to use Polaris to leverage control. For example, Polaris was used to intrude upon the publicity of *Dr. Strangelove*, with attempts to persuade Columbia Pictures of the need for an extensive national publicity campaign for the film. Indeed, Nat Weiss, vice president of Polaris, outlined the role of the company, stating that it would "deliver certain major breaks a major company just doesn't act on (which may be why you never had a picture properly handled before)" (Nat Weiss to Kubrick, December 5, 1962, SK/11/9/ 111, SKA). Polaris initiated various publicity strategies ahead of Columbia, including "contacting magazine editors with a view of securing publicity for his forthcoming release" (Krämer 2013). Columbia executives were resistant to Kubrick's insistence on control over publicity and distribution, with Polaris's involvement seen as an intrusion that was affecting the commercial potential of *Dr. Strangelove*. Columbia believed that the overbearing producing style of Kubrick, including pursuing his own publicity strategy, and his "insistence on a number of ill-advised points in the advertising style," was proving detrimental (Roger Caras to Kubrick, November 3, 1966, SK/12/

8/5, SKA). In contrast, Kubrick felt that his input was necessary, particularly to veto miscalculated judgments by Columbia, like the suggestion to subtitle the film *Bing, Bang, Bombe* (Kubrick to Jack Weiner, 1963, SK/11/9/20, SKA).

Kubrick exacerbated his intrusion into publicity on *2001* in a move to further consolidate his producing power. Once more, Kubrick's control of publicity was restricted, with his contract with MGM stating that he had to obtain prior approval from the company before issuing any press releases. In addition, MGM had the final approval over the film's publicity strategy (contract between MGM and Polaris Productions, May 22, 1965, SK/12/2/5, SKA). MGM had grown its publicity department throughout the 1960s, in the process centralizing national publicity campaigns under Dan Terrell, executive director for advertising, publicity, and promotion. This approach required the absolute cooperation of a film's producer in order to provide access to production materials. But Kubrick was resistant to MGM's approach and attempted to hold on to power through a process of obfuscation, including withholding preview footage for an exhibitor's reel, postponing decisions about merchandising opportunities, and cancelling scheduled publicity items. However, this approach had serious consequences. For example, Kubrick had repeatedly delayed giving the final approval to an advertising supplement that Roger Caras had been working on with Tom Buck at *Look* magazine. Buck was subsequently fired when the feature fell through, something for which Caras chided Kubrick, blaming his centralized micromanagement style (letter to Stanley Kubrick, December 27, 1966, SK/12/8/5, SKA).

MGM executives felt that Kubrick's overriding desire for centralized control of his production was denying them the opportunity to protect their multimillion-dollar investment, making Kubrick's lack of cooperation unjustified (Caras to Stanley Kubrick, July 15, 1966, SK/12/8/5, SKA). Some in MGM were critical of their own company for allowing Kubrick and Polaris "complete latitude in everything" and that it had resulted in a mode of production and producing style of that of a "six hundred thousand dollar art film" (ibid.). Kubrick's consolidation of his power though, and his refusal to let others make decisions on his behalf, was increasingly being left unchallenged because, as Terrell commented to Caras, "he felt constrained not to disturb you with endless arguments and disagreements when you still have a film to make" (ibid.). Kubrick was using Polaris to protect himself from interference from MGM and to hold on to control of publicity through a process of negative cooperation. If he was the only one in possession of information, it therefore gave him the power to make decisions.

Kubrick's producing approach to *2001* arguably led to a significant lack of publicity throughout the production compared to other similarly budgeted pictures. Indeed, Kubrick's less than cooperative nature with MGM's publicity department was unique in the era of preselling a film and long-range publicity campaigns. Whereas in the early stages of his career, Kubrick had been operating within the limits of his contracts, by the end of the 1960s he was pushing the boundaries of what his contracts allowed, taking control of aspects of production that was still legally in the hands of the studios. In consolidating his autonomy and building a substantial power base, Kubrick was facing off with studio executives who did not challenge his intrusions, particularly into areas of publicity.

Too Much Autonomy

Kubrick's centralization of producing power was exacerbated in the 1970s following a three-picture deal with WB that gave him control over all key creative business decisions of his productions (Clive Parsons, interoffice memo, 1970, SK/13/8/5/10, SKA). WB CEO in the 1970s, Ted Ashley, along with its head of production, John Calley, were instrumental in facilitating Kubrick's producing autonomy at the company. The pair were comfortable in affording creative and business control to their producers, an approach they believed "worked out better creatively" ("WB Tally: 20 Done or Nearly," *Variety*, September 16, 1970, 4). Other director-producers were granted autonomy at the company at the same time as Kubrick, such as John Boorman and Clint Eastwood. Following the release of *Dirty Harry* (1971), Eastwood signed a nonexclusive contract with the company, who backed him to produce less-commercial fare such as *Bird* (1988) and *White Hunter, Black Heart* (1990). Eastwood "said of his relationship with Warner Bros. that, like any studio, they like to make movies that make money. But I've never found them resistant to long-shot projects that might not be commercial now but that they might be proud to have in their library 10 or 20 years from now" ("Hot Streak: Warner Bros.," *Wall Street Journal*, June 1, 1990, 1). The desire to be associated with a prestigious body of work was certainly the case when it came to Kubrick.

WB took an approach of not interfering in Kubrick's productions, with the only requirement going forward being that Kubrick pitched his ideas and provided an appropriate budget. However, it seems that this facilitation of Kubrick's total producing autonomy by WB began to work against him. Whereas in his earliest years as a producer there was a necessity to produce films that often conformed to industrial contexts, Kubrick could now take his time. He maintained his mainstream budgets by reducing the size of his crews, often working with the same individuals across multiple productions. But Kubrick centralized all decision-making through himself and implemented what Peter Krämer (2015a: 373) has called an "exploratory process" of producing. In practice, this meant that Kubrick could now ask for every conceivable outcome to any of his ideas, a lengthy process at the end of which he could chose to abandon an idea. This led to much lengthier development and preproduction times.

A Clockwork Orange, *Barry Lyndon*, and *The Shining* demonstrated Kubrick's producing methods, with extensive development and preproduction on each film, and Kubrick having strategic oversight of their promotion and distribution. This included decisions on their global promotion, distribution, exhibition, and dubbing, as well as supervision over the artwork for their eventual video release. Kubrick was minutely overseeing every facet of his productions, which drastically reduced his ability to focus on new projects. Throughout 1975 and 1976 Kubrick focused his producing abilities on the distribution and advertising of *Barry Lyndon*, with WB choosing to placate Kubrick's requests rather than challenge him. For example, WB contacted international territories on Kubrick's behalf to request information on advertising campaigns, with Kubrick intervening if he felt their approach was wrong. Take the following letter sent to WB advertising executives in South America: "I have worked with Stanley Kubrick for over one year on *Barry Lyndon* and I know how time consuming the gathering of this information is … it really is simpler to give Mr. Kubrick what he wants, when he wants it" (Julian Senior to Albert Salem, November 11, 1976, SK/14/5/4/2, SKA). The letter indicates how WB executives chose to surrender control to Kubrick rather than challenge his intrusions into all areas of business strategy.

Much of Kubrick's time between productions was increasingly consumed with the business functions of his role as a producer, requesting ever more copious amounts of data that he could analyze. In 1975, he requested a theatrical analysis of key cinemas in the United States so that he could "evaluate the relative box office potential of high grossing films in the major metropolitan areas of the United States, which correspond to the markets listed in the *Barry Lyndon* distribution proposal" (Theatrical Distribution Analysis, 1975, SK/14/5/4/1, SKA). The latter proposal had been forwarded to Kubrick by WB executives to await his approval, a report that Kubrick annotated extensively with recommendations and queries to which he expected a response.

WB, in Kubrick's words, had to "bear" with his increasingly slow and exploratory producing methods, particularly the length of time it was taking him to develop projects and move them into active production (Kubrick to John Calley, April 30, 1975, SK/14/6/8, SKA). It would seem there was no time limit on the contracts Kubrick had with the company, therefore freeing him of the pressure to rush projects into production. Arguably, this lack of pressure underlined—and facilitated—Kubrick's growing inability to make decisions and, indeed, his self-doubt, perhaps reflected in the mid-1980s by Empyrean Films. Kubrick had incorporated this company to recruit readers to write reports on hundreds of novels he was exploring for potential development. For example, Kubrick used the company to seek several reports on Arthur Schnitzler's *Traumnovelle* (1926), with at least six reports written in late 1988. In addition, he used the company to test the reaction to several science fiction novels, with Kubrick's interest in the genre growing substantially in the wake of the success of films like *Star Wars* (1977) and *E.T. The Extra-Terrestrial* (1982).

In his collaborations with writers like Brian Aldiss, Kubrick regularly opined about his desire to produce a film with the mainstream appeal of the films of Steven Spielberg or George Lucas, developing what Aldiss called an "E.T. syndrome" (Aldiss to Hilary Rubinstein, BWA/3/4, Brian Aldiss Archives, University of Liverpool). Aldiss and Kubrick collaborated on-and-off from the late 1970s through to the early 1990s on an adaptation of Aldiss's short story *Supertoys Last All Summer Long* (1969), with a working title of *A.I.* The development of *A.I.* reflected the key problem Kubrick frequently experienced as a producer throughout his WB years: his unwillingness to relinquish *any* control. Aldiss's contract to work with Kubrick led him to sacrifice immense creative control, including waiving the rights to "droit moral"—the rights preserving artistic integrity in entertainment law, including protection from having one's name removed from a work of art without permission. Such was the level of control that Kubrick was enforcing on Aldiss that he found that, should he develop the project into a potential novel, he could not publish it without Kubrick's approval. In working with Kubrick, Aldiss declared, "I've lost my autonomy" (ibid.).

In the process of obtaining his own autonomy, Kubrick was quashing that of others. Aldiss and Kubrick's collaboration was fraught with tension, particularly due to Kubrick's insistence on referring Aldiss repeatedly to *E.T.* Reflecting on the project years later, Aldiss commented that he thought Kubrick was "reaching the end of his creative career" by the 1980s (interview with Brian Aldiss, *Red Carpet News*, 2015). This comment may seem spiteful, but perhaps Kubrick himself sensed his creative powers were limited by his producing control, even contemplating for the first time in his life in taking on purely a producing role and hiring Spielberg to direct the project (interview between author and Jan Harlan, January 26, 2017).

Kubrick's consideration of abdicating his role as a director in favor of that of producer is also an indication of the crippling impact the levels of producing control he possessed was now having on his creative process. The 1980s and 1990s were spent in a state of almost perpetual development hell as Kubrick deliberated over potential new projects, expending considerable amounts of time and money on research. This was particularly the case for his abandoned *Aryan Papers*, an adaptation of Louis Begley's *Wartime Lies* (1991). The project was Kubrick's attempt to produce a film about the Holocaust. Between 1991 and 1993, Kubrick's close colleagues, including Jan Harlan, spent many months in Eastern Europe negotiating deals with local authorities for permission to shoot on location. At the same time, WB sought to establish new production companies for Kubrick so that he could take advantage of potential tax rebates in the region. But Kubrick's inability to make decisions about where to shoot the film, who to cast in the film, and most importantly, how to write the script, was slowing the preproduction process down. With Kubrick having centralized power in his role as a producer, there was little anybody else could do but try to pressure him into a decision. WB announced that *Aryan Papers* would be released in the winter of 1994, while shooting arrangements were agreed with national governments, including Slovakia. However, Kubrick still insisted on being presented with more options, asking Harlan to visit yet more potential locations that might be better suited.

Eventually, Kubrick abandoned the production in late 1993 and turned his attention first to *A.I.* and, finally, an adaptation of *Traumnovelle*. The producing autonomy that Kubrick had acquired at WB had left his career looking increasingly precarious. Given his frustrated development process and the growing sense that he might not produce another film, WB agreed to the adaptation of *Traumnovelle*. It would prove to be Kubrick's last ever production and only his second as part of his 1985 three-picture contract with WB, released posthumously in July 1999 as *Eyes Wide Shut*.

Conclusion

Viewing Kubrick's career through the perspective of his role as a producer allows us to understand the ways in which he obtained and consolidated his producing power. More importantly, we can begin to understand how his contract with WB, where his centralized decision-making and exploratory process of producing was allowed to flourish with very few checks and balances from senior management, impacted on his ability to successfully move a project from development into production. Kubrick's autonomy as a producer was obtained through a process of holding on to information and limiting the ability of others to access information about his productions. Brian Aldiss reflected on Kubrick's approach to producing saying, "when you play cards with Kubrick he holds fifty-one of them in his hand" (letter to Hilary Rubinstein, BWA/3/4).

Yet, the more power Kubrick acquired, which was something that he sought to achieve throughout his career, the fewer films he found he could produce. It became a self-defeating strategy. Even when researching and developing a project, Kubrick had to ensure he had total control, leading to the creative bondage of some of his key collaborators. The levels of autonomy Kubrick achieved by the 1970s allowed him to indulge his most excessive behaviors, including being able to request every available outcome to a decision and, regardless of the time and investment, abandon his ideas. While some may view this approach as allowing a great experimental artist to explore his craft, within a commercial context as a producer it allowed his career to decline in terms of output and left Kubrick himself doubting whether he could even direct a film anymore. This chapter serves as an introduction to rethink our understanding of Kubrick's autonomy and independence, but also to show how Kubrick is a key case study in understanding the limits (and dangers) of producing autonomy within mainstream Hollywood.

2

Kubrick and Authorship

Rod Munday

Stanley Kubrick once said, "One man writes a novel. One man writes a symphony. It is essential for one man to make a film" (quoted in Lewin 1972: 8). Here Kubrick espouses one of the central tenants of auteurist theories—that the creative endeavors of a single artist are primarily responsible for the quality of a film. If one were to think of an exemplary cinematic auteur today, Kubrick would probably be one of the names that most readily springs to mind. Indeed, the *Oxford English Dictionary* has recently added "Kubrickian" to its list of new English words (*OED* 2018). Therefore, it is particularly ironic that Kubrick rarely features in the academic literature about auteurism, for example, in a popular film reader, *Auteurs and Authorship*, Kubrick only gets three mentions (Grant 2008). I define auteurism as a perspective that unites a diverse collection of writings. "La Politique des Auteurs" and "The Auteur Theory" to name just two. Auteurist writings all share a common assumption; the director of a film is its author—the individual who bares sole responsibility for the film's creation. Concurrent with the evolution of auteurist theories in the 1950s through to the 1980s, the film industry itself has evolved. In the 1950s, the power and influence of the studio system started to wane; a *New Hollywood* emerged in the 1970s that became focused around the figure of the director. Many commentators have linked this rise to the impact of auteurist theories (Bordwell and Thomson 2015: 489–90; Kolker 2000: 8–9; Schatz 2015: 5). In this chapter, I will sketch out the evolution of four distinct phases of auteurism; from its inception in France in the 1950s, through to its semiotic and poststructural phases in the 1960s and 1970s, and finally arriving at a more market-led conception that is dominant today. I will also examine how Kubrick and his work can be represented in each phase.

Aesthetic Auteurism

French film criticism of the mid-twentieth century still influences the way we think about film today. The French-inflected language of film terminology—words such as "genre," "mise-en-scène," and "auteur"—illustrate the impact of writings associated with one particular journal, *Cahiers du Cinema*. For the writers of *Cahiers*, auteurism can be distilled into three fundamental propositions. The first originated in 1948, in the writings of the pre-*Cahiers* critic, Alexandre Astruc (1988: 17–18), who stated film could be regarded as a new language. Astruc envisaged a time when cinematic authors would write using the "camera stylo" (camera pen) as their primary instrument (ibid.). The second proposition locates film language primarily in its mise-en-scène, or those elements placed within the frame; including costumes, sets, cinematography, performance, and montage (Hiller 1985: 8–9). The third proposition is the film's director should be the one person who controls the mise-en-scène (ibid.: 9). François Truffaut (1975: 12) argues auteur-directors create films in a cinematic language, which is what elevates their work above that of mere "metteurs en scène" (scene setters). The task of deciding who is an auteur and who is a metteur en scène is where *Cahiers du Cinema*'s advocacy of "La Politique des Auteurs" (author policy) originated (Hiller 1985: 4).

The writings of *Cahiers du Cinema* reshaped the thinking of the American critic, Andrew Sarris, about cinema (Sarris 2009: 561). However, Sarris complains that no definition exists for what he christens "The Auteur Theory," so he provides one (ibid.). Sarris conceives of film authorship as three concentric circles. The first concerns technical competence—an auteur director must possess the expertise to be able to make a great film; the second is focused on personal style—the director must be able to impress their personality on the film through their style; and the third defines the auteur's unique vision—true auteur-directors must be able to impart a worldview through their visual storytelling, or as Sarris puts this, "a certain élan of the soul" (ibid.: 564).

The principles of aesthetic auteurism seem to imply the existence of stable criteria that could be used to measure a director's worth. In this spirit, I decided to examine what auteur critics had written about Kubrick's films. Given Kubrick's contemporary reputation as a cinematic auteur par excellence, one might presume auteurist critics would have praised his films highly; however, this is not the case.

Jean-Luc Godard reviewing *The Killing* in 1958, called it, "a film of a good pupil, no more" (Godard 1986: 69). Godard remarks, Kubrick is "still far from being the bright boy heralded by the excited publicity surrounding his little gangster film," and *The Killing* "makes even *The Asphalt Jungle* look like a masterpiece by comparison" (ibid.). The editors of the book from where this review is taken note that Godard failed to recognize Kubrick's talent. They also remark *Cahiers* critics tended to pigeonhole Kubrick not as a cinematic genius but as a "well-meaning liberal" in the tradition of Stanley Kramer (ibid.: 255). François Truffaut was kinder, calling *Paths of Glory* "very beautiful from a number of points of view," as well as "an important film that establishes the talent and energy of a new American director, Stanley Kubrick." However, Truffaut still identifies weaknesses within the film's structure, complaining particularly about its lack of psychological credibility (Truffaut 1975: 116).

Andrew Sarris represents the most pertinent example of auteurist critics failing to appreciate Kubrick's talent. While Sarris acknowledges Kubrick is hailed in many quarters as the greatest director since D. W. Griffith, he admits that he does not actually like his films:

I have been charged by people I respect with having a blind spot with respect to Kubrick's work, and it is true that I literally cannot see or feel him most of the time. He is too odd and eccentric for my taste as he seems to work far above the surface of his unconscious. His stylization therefore strikes me as a form of emotional evasion. (Sarris 1975)

In his book, *The American Cinema*, Sarris provides a nine-point ranking of auteur-directors. This ranges from the first division of "pantheon directors" to the ninth, which Sarris titles "make way for the clowns." He places Kubrick in the sixth division of, "strained seriousness." He says "Kubrick's tragedy may have been that he was hailed as a great artist before he had become a competent craftsman" (Sarris 1968a: 196). Sarris's somewhat partisan approach has provided ammunition for critics of "The Auteur Theory"; for example, Buscombe (1973: 83) writes, "Despite the presentation of the word 'theory,' the critical language used is very subjective; it is then less a theoretical statement and more an expression of Sarris' own critical beliefs."

Auteur Semiotics

This approach emerged in the late 1960s and is primarily associated with Geoffrey Nowell-Smith and Peter Wollen. These critics were influenced by semiotics, a method that broadly treats meaning as a product of sign relations and representational strategies, rather than something that can be grasped directly. Semiotic critics downplay aesthetic notions of the author-as-creator and emphasize instead the importance of the body of work—or oeuvre. For them, the meanings found in a work are not the product of authorial intention, but rather authorial intention itself is something that can only be inferred from studying the work. Nowell-Smith stated, auteurism requires the critic to recognize "one basic fact"; authorship should be the organizing principle for the analysis of a director's oeuvre. The critic's primary concern is to seek out connections between the films (Nowell-Smith 2003: 9). However, this is not as easy as it first appears:

The defining characteristics of an author's work are not always those that are most readily apparent. The purpose of criticism becomes therefore to uncover behind the superficial contrasts of subject and treatment a structural hard core of basic and often recondite motifs. (Nowell-Smith 2003: 10)

Peter Wollen applies these criteria to his analysis of American cinema. Wollen writes, "the auteur theory implies an operation of decipherment" (Wollen 1972: 77); the task of the critic is to construct not only the typical features of an auteur's oeuvre and their variants, but also to map the principles of variation that govern these (ibid.: 103–4). The figure of the auteur that emerges from Wollen's analysis is not so much a real person as an adjective; for example, Kubrick becomes "the Kubrickian," a term designating the origin of all the meaningful connections found in his work.

The methodology of auteur semiotics—focusing on the oeuvre rather than the author and emphasizing abstract motifs—serves to inform the analytical approaches of some of the most well-known and important Kubrick scholars—Michel Ciment, Robert Kolker, and Thomas Allen Nelson. However, none of these critics is explicit in acknowledging the influence of auteurial semiotics. Nevertheless, their work can be considered auteurist because it focuses on Kubrick's oeuvre, its analysis uncovers recondite motifs, and each critic uses this information to define the Kubrickian in terms of reoccurring stylistic and thematic signatures.

Ciment, Kolker, and Nelson's methods are all based upon a close examination of Kubrick's films. Concerning aesthetics, Nelson (2000: 5) writes, Kubrick's work reveals his belief in film as an art form—the expression of a complex personal vision. Nelson, in a statement that accords closely with Nowell-Smith's conception of "recondite motifs" adds, Kubrick has a remarkable ability to convert cinematic form into a variety of meanings, which he communicates "obliquely, so as to avoid pat conclusions and neatly tied up ideas" (ibid.: 7).

In terms of his style, Kolker (2000: 102) asserts, Kubrick "inscribes a deep and complex visual field into his work." Through set design, lighting and the placement and movement of the camera he "creates an intricate space and a labyrinthine narrative structure" (ibid.). Nelson (2000: 97) writes, one notable Kubrickian motif is his "taste for symmetry," which is found both in his filmic compositions and in the design of his plots; for example, the Roman legions in *Spartacus* and the regiments in *Barry Lyndon* create symmetrical visual tableaux. Narrative symmetry in the form of doubling is also a frequent feature of his films, for example, in *A Clockwork Orange*; Alex's victims later become his victimizers (ibid.). Kolker (2000: 113) sees Kubrick's films as being concerned with the disruption of symmetry by violence; for example, a formal composition suddenly thrown off balance by the movement of a handheld camera.

Thematically, Kubrick's films have an intellectual complexity that is associated more with literature than film (Kolker 2000: 101). Kolker writes how Kubrick's camera functions as both creator and mediator of the entire structure, and the result is an extreme formal and thematic complexity (ibid.: 102). Kolker furthermore claims his films reflect Kubrick's fear of any flaw in a totally programmed system (ibid.: 42). For example, the doomsday device featured in *Dr. Strangelove* or H.A.L. in *2001* represent systems that have been designed to protect humanity from destruction, but which turn out to be the cause of it (ibid.: 105). According to Ciment, another thematic obsession is power—the desire of some to wield absolute power over others, as well as its "inevitable correlative": the terror of losing control (Ciment 2003: 122).

The image of Kubrick that emerges from these analyses is one of an emotionally detached director whose preoccupations include games, strategies and technology (ibid.: 42). Ciment writes that Kubrick has frequently been criticized for losing interest in humankind; substituting fables, puppets and machines for the creation of real characters (ibid.: 117). Kolker concurs, remarking that Kubrick's films are cold and distant; he does not see the possibility of men or women regaining control over their selves, rather he shows the diminishment of humanity (Kolker 2000: 99).

Unlike the aesthetic auteur critics, Ciment, Kolker, and Nelson are more generous toward Kubrick and his films. Nevertheless, they still tend to read pessimistic conclusions into them, based on subjective perceptions of his character. Whether these conclusions represent a distillation of the motifs found in his films, or are simply judgments derived from other sources, such as interviews, is a question I shall address later.

Poststructuralism: "Death of the Author"

Geoffrey Nowell-Smith went on record to disavow publicly his contribution to auteur semiotics. He wrote he did not think what he was saying was particularly original; it was more a case of the ideas being "in the air at the time" (2003: 3). A similar skepticism toward authorship can be found in poststructuralist theories that emerged in the late 1960s in France. The semiotician Roland Barthes famously questioned the whole legitimacy of authorship with his "death of the author" critique. Barthes (1977: 142) argues the author's voice is lost as soon as something is narrated. To make his argument, he draws upon Mikhail Bakhtin's concepts of "dialogism" (the notion that ideas take the form of conversations) and "heteroglossia" (the idea that language is made up of various distinct voices) (Bakhtin 1981: 279, 270–71). Unlike Nowell-Smith (2003) who vaguely attributes the source of his ideas to "being in the air," Barthes conceives of them emanating in language itself, however, in line with poststructural skepticism toward ordered semiotic systems, language is conceived by Barthes (1977: 146) as a chaotic network, "a tissue of quotations drawn from the innumerable centres of culture." In this context, authors act more as the arrangers of texts than as their creators; and it is ultimately the task of readers to make sense of them (ibid.: 148). This is a position Kubrick arguably also endorsed when he described the work of a director impersonally as a kind of "taste machine"— making the right decisions "as frequently as possible" (Gelmis 1970: 314).

Like Barthes, Michel Foucault (1977: 121) proclaims the death of the author. He conceives of authorship not in terms of personality or biography, but as an "author function," a series of operations that produce a text (ibid.: 124). For Foucault, texts are not vehicles for personal agency, they are rather kinds of "discourse" (or talk), which can be linked to authors through habits of association, similar to the ways in which brand names take on quasi-human identities in advertising. Foucault argues, in certain cases, the author function can take on uniquely persuasive forms in culture; circulating as ideologies. For example, Kubrick and Diane Johnson drew upon Freudian discourse when writing *The Shining*, particularly ideas of the uncanny (Ciment 2003: 192). In this way according to Foucault, they located the horror of their film within an ideological space determined by the Freudian author function.

A.I. Artificial Intelligence (2001) illustrates how poststructuralist theories can be used to resolve ambiguities about authorship. Arguably, under the tenets of auteurism, *A.I.* can be considered the creation of both Kubrick and Steven Spielberg; for example, the international trailer title states it is "A Stanley Kubrick production of a Steven Spielberg film." However, the collaborative aspect of the film negates one of the central premises of auteurism, that the director is the sole creator.

In 1993, Kubrick offered Spielberg the chance to direct *A.I.*, reportedly telling him he felt the tone of the film was far closer to his sensibility than his own (Rice 2017: 1). There followed an intense period of preproduction planning in which Kubrick faxed Spielberg his ideas both day and night (Abramowitz 2001). However, by the mid-1990s, the two directors had become involved in other projects. Interest in the film only rekindled in 1999, after Kubrick's death. His widow Christiane, and brother-in-law Jan Harlan approached Terry Semel, the then chairman of Warner Bros., with the idea that Spielberg should direct the film (ibid.).

The release of *A.I.* was an occasion for critics and academics alike to compare the auteurial styles of the two directors. Sarris (2001) reported on the "intense speculation" about how much of the film could be attributed to Kubrick's conception and how much to Spielberg's execution. Many commentators discussed the character differences between Kubrick and Spielberg. For example, Arthur (2001: 22) called *A.I.* the result of an odd coupling of "the Prince of Bleak and the Emperor of Ice Cream." Friedman (2007) argued the "austere and coldly intellectual" Kubrick would seem to have little in common with the "hyperkinetic and viscerally emotional" Spielberg. And Kreider (2002) stated, "Spielberg hadn't shown much of the subtlety, restraint, and layered irony that makes Kubrick's work so rich and open to interpretation."

The resulting film was received with mixed enthusiasm. Denby (2001) asked "if you were wondering how Spielberg's pop exaltations would consort with Kubrick's dread and metaphysical dismay, the answer is: strangely, confusingly." Bradshaw (2001) went further calling it a "lethal combination." But, according to Vivian Sobchack (2008), the film was a successful blend of "Spielbergian pathos and Kubrickian irony."

In a discussion of the film's aesthetics and thematics, Scott (2001) noted Spielberg included many stylistic homages to Kubrick, scattered throughout the movie. However, on a deeper level Scott observed, Spielberg attempted to meld Kubrick's chilly analytical style with his own warmer sensibility (ibid.). Other critics disagreed, calling *A.I.* Spielberg's darkest film. Evangelista (2018) wrote, "even *Schindler's List* ends on a hopeful note." Collins (2014) said, *A.I.*'s ending is "not twee but wrenchingly sad." And, O'Brien (2001) describes the ending as an "ideogram of grief, disguised as a Hallmark card."

In reviewing *A.I.*, many critics ostensibly attributed its auteurship to Spielberg, while still commenting on the Kubrickian tropes they found in the film. Critics also made reference to stereotypical ideas about Kubrick's and Spielberg's personalities, as a way to understand the film. I argue the substitution of "author function" for "authorship" may help to resolve some of the contradictions that *A.I.* presents for auteur studies. With *A.I.*, Spielberg can be seen as channeling Kubrick's "author function," in that he attempts to make a film that is stylistically and thematically "Kubrickian."

Auteur Marketing

The impact of poststructuralism saw a decline in serious critical attention paid to authorship. As a consequence, auteurism morphed from a quasi-academic discipline to a social and economic one, primarily concerned with marketing. Catherine Grant terms this new phase "contemporary auteurism," which she defines as a series of production, marketing, reception and discursive practices, underpinned by a shared belief in the specific capability of an individual agent—the director—to marshal and synthesize the elements of filmmaking (2009: 101).

Timothy Corrigan (1991: 96) argues the auteur has never been a consistent nor stable way of talking about filmmakers. He links the impact of what I have called "aesthetic auteurism" to the film industry demand that cinema should be shrouded in an artistic (and specifically Romantic) aura to distinguish film from other less-elevated mass media forms (ibid.: 102). And Corrigan also remarks that although the "death of the author" critiques vanquished most of the myths surrounding auteurism, they did not fully attend to its potential as a commercial strategy for organizing reception practices (ibid.: 104).

Corrigan develops his argument by drawing an analogy between auteurs and film stars (ibid.: 102). He notes auteur films are often marketed by the director's name appearing "above the title." The cult auteur therefore functions as a kind of brand name, providing recognition that governs the reception of auteur films as objects of value (ibid.: 105). As Grant (2009: 102) explains, one important strategy for making the auteur visible is through ancillary texts such as promotional materials. Corrigan points to the usefulness of the directorial interview as a way for auteurs to address both fans and critical viewers alike, so they can "disperse their organizing agency" (Corrigan 1991: 107–8).

I shall examine these ideas in relation to Kubrick in three ways: Kubrick's mastery of the marketing and distribution of his films, his use of interviews, and how he deployed both his business acumen and auteur image to influence the ways in which cinema audiences perceived him.

Kubrick's involvement in the marketing and distribution of his films helped to strengthen his status as an auteur, because success in these areas persuaded Warner Bros. to grant him exceptional creative freedom to pursue his projects without studio interference. As Ciment (2001: 35) observes, Kubrick's strength as a filmmaker derives from the realization that if he was not in charge of every element, his films might fail. Kubrick became more involved in the marketing of his films during the release of *A Clockwork Orange* in 1971, personally supervising the film's promotional campaign (Cook 2007: 78). With the assistance of Mike Kaplan, Kubrick also compiled a database of cinemas to plot its release strategy, presenting Warner Bros. executives with computer printouts of the grosses of similar films when they played in certain cinemas (2017). He was thus able to influence the distribution of the film and greatly enhance the financial benefit to the studio as a result. *A Clockwork Orange* went on to earn forty million dollars on a two million budget, making it one of Warner Bros.' biggest hits of the decade (Naremore 2014: 210). His success was so remarkable, the then president of Warners, Ted Ashley, called Kubrick "a genius who combined aesthetics with fiscal responsibility" (Cook 2007: 78–9).

In terms of managing his directorial image, Filippo Ulivieri has exhaustively examined the evolution of Kubrick's public persona through press interviews and archive research. Ulivieri claims Kubrick successfully created a mythology for himself as a powerful cine auteur, in order to attract media attention and so promote his films (2017: 240). Although some of the more lurid myths surrounding Kubrick have been discredited by the people who knew him (ibid.: 238), Ulivieri notes that Kubrick was implicated in engineering some of these myths. For example, he personally thanked the journalist Victor Davis, who wrote some outlandish untruths about him, such as ordering the spraying of a town near his studio with DDT because he couldn't stand flies (ibid.: 254). While it is common for auteur-directors to contrive sensationalist press reports about themselves, it is very unusual, according to Ulivieri, for a director to disavow this persona in subsequent encounters with the press (ibid.: 240). What is especially interesting about Ulivieri's research is how the myths surrounding Kubrick have served to influence critics and academics. The possibility arises that the information that informed their understandings of Kubrick (and which they subsequently read into his films), is false. For example, Ulivieri quotes Gordon Stainforth, the editor of *Making the Shining*, who claimed that Kubrick, who had final cut of the documentary, wanted footage of him being nice removed while footage of him shouting at Shelley Duvall kept in (2017: 237). Stainforth added, "It was almost as if he wanted that side of him to be shown." According to critic and personal friend, Jay Cocks, Kubrick was aware of the publicity advantage of creating a mysterious public image. However, Cocks added, "There was nothing mysterious about him, he was just a wonderful, funny guy, a great companion" (ibid.: 238).

Finally, Kate Egan considers the question of how Kubrick's status as a cult auteur impacts on audiences, particularly fans on the internet newsgroup "alt.movies.kubrick." Egan claims within the commercial promotion of his films, Kubrick possesses a "double-tiered status," on the one hand, the romantic notion of a creative genius battling against the Hollywood "system," on the other, a "controlling and dictatorial figure" (2015: 4). Egan notes how these contradictory aspects have served to influence the ways in which devoted fans engage with his work. The desire for fans to "gain access" to Kubrick's "private world" is mediated by their use of video or DVD sources. Just as critics such as Kolker, rewatched Kubrick's films to gain insights about his oeuvre, Kubrick fans used these means to create material forms for their cultic devotion (ibid.: 7). Finally, Egan notes both public and fan fascination with Kubrick the auteur shows no sign of abating, As Church (2006) remarks, Kubrick continues to carry "more currency" in death "than any of his contemporaries."

Conclusion

In this chapter, I have sketched out a framework for how auteurism has evolved in four phases from the 1950s to today, as well as suggesting how Kubrick could be read differently as an auteur director in each phase. Auteurism from an aesthetic viewpoint is a way to think about cinema; both as a perspective on film and as a framework in which to study it. But, from the viewpoint of the film industry, auteurism is also a means to organize the marketing and consumption of films. For this reason, its shortcomings as a theory have often been overlooked in favor of its benefits as an economic model to organize the practices of film production and reception. There are many ironies associated with Kubrick the auteur: at a time when "The Auteur Theory" was at its zenith, Kubrick was considered to be merely a minor talent. His auteurist reputation became consolidated only in an era when auteurism itself had diminished in importance; and the auteurist myths that sustained Kubrick's image may have been a construction, engineered by the director himself. However, despite all of the ironies, I have to confess I do regard Kubrick to be a genuine auteur. There are three reasons for this, because he modeled his career on an auteur ideal, because he manufactured his public image to create an auteurist aura, and because of his desire to gain mastery over every aspect of the filmmaking process. As Robert Kolker (2000: 173–4) remarks, Stanley Kubrick was American film's last auteur. His films remain as powerful reminders that it was once possible for a filmmaker to live a private life, in control of his art, thinking, planning, and executing enormous works filled with vision and intellectual passion.

3

Kubrick and Adaptation

Graham Allen

All Stanley Kubrick's major films, with the possible exception of *2001: A Space Odyssey*, are adaptations of preexisting novels (see Hunter 2016: 129–40). These "source" novels present us with an extraordinarily wide range of genre, narrative style, historical context, and philosophical outlook. Each novel presents entirely new challenges in the revisionary art of adaptation. Filippo Ulivieri has examined the history of Kubrick's career-long search for literary texts worthy of cinematic adaptation, detailing fifty-five "distinct unrealized or unfinished projects" (2017: 96). This fascinating story shows how central adaptation was to Kubrick's art. Ulivieri argues that Kubrick's *"modus operandi* in selecting published material was absolutely consistent" (ibid.). The ultimate criterion was that a text must possess a compelling plot and at the same time speak meaningfully to the director's long term "obsessions." Such a coincidence of criteria, as Ulivieri demonstrates, proved very rare, a fact that perhaps explains the relatively small number of films Kubrick completed. Recent work by Peter Krämer (2014b) and Mick Broderick (2017) on *Dr. Strangelove*, utilizing the Kubrick Archive, demonstrates how complex the process of transforming a literary "source" into a final script could be. Broderick (2017) has shown how closely the novel's author, Peter George, was involved in the complex process of scripting the film. An equally fruitful, if different, relationship can be seen between Kubrick and Arthur C. Clarke, in the development of *2001*, and Vladimir Nabokov in the scripting of *Lolita* (see Benson 2018). On other occasions, such as those concerning *Eyes Wide Shut* and *Full Metal Jacket*, Kubrick's relationship with authors became much more strained or broke down completely (Raphael 2000). As I.Q. Hunter has stated, Kubrick preferred to write with professional writers rather than professional screenwriters (2015). Again, this practice varies from film to film, so that on some films, such as *Barry Lyndon*, Kubrick enjoys sole writer's credit, while with others he shares credit with writers, such as Jim Thompson (*The Killing, Paths of Glory*), Terry Southern (*Dr. Strangelove*), Diane Johnson (*The Shining*), Michael Herr (*Full Metal Jacket*), and Frederic Raphael (*Eyes Wide Shut*).

In one of the best accounts of adaptation in Kubrick, Elisa Pezzotta discusses his practice in terms of the influence of European art cinema on the New Hollywood of the 1960s and 1970s (2013: 152–9). As Mario Falsetto has shown, the rise of the Hollywood Renaissance auteur saw a move away from traditional Hollywood methods, which involved radical breaks with received narrative conventions. Such work allows us to reflect upon a paradox: Kubrick's respect toward the literary tradition he mines seems to contrast with his commitment to narrative innovations and an essentially visual and aural rather than verbal cinema. Given this commitment, it is interesting to note that Kubrick does not tend to choose narratively experimental work to adapt. Rather, his cinema respectfully but also radically remediates what are, apart from the nonfictional works behind the *Napoleon* and *Wartime Lies* projects, often quite conventional novels on the level of narrative style. It is almost as if the more conventional the narrative style of his material, the more profoundly Kubrick is confronted with the challenge of relocating the story and characters and fictional worlds described into an essentially visual and aural environment.

As we move from novel to film, we inevitably encounter common features of form and content, but on each occasion unique challenges are also experienced. There are numerous avenues into an analysis of Kubrick's film adaptations. One illuminating avenue, however, involves focusing on the core problem or problems posed by each unique literary text and then examining the way in which they are resolved by the film. The availability of resources in the Kubrick Archive allows scholars and critics to explore such questions in far more depth than was previously possible.

Lionel White's novel *Clean Break* (1955) is a good case in point. Although in many respects an example of an extremely common literary and cinematic genre, the novel attracted Kubrick and his producing partner James B. Harris because of one standout feature: its treatment of narrative time and thus narrative focus (see Ollerman 2017: 7–24). The novel follows each member of Johnny Clay's gang on the fateful day of their elaborately planned heist. Fidelity to this equally disorienting and compellingly broken narrative is, despite the initial alarm of the United Films management, what makes *The Killing* such a distinctive contribution to the *noir* heist movie tradition (see LoBrutto 1997: 120–6). In that sense, *The Killing* demonstrated that, like White's novel, a film could successfully use flashback techniques as its organizing narrative principle. Despite its lack of adequate backing from United Artists, the film has gone on to influence a host of other filmmakers in this regard.

With Kubrick and Harris's next venture, the textual challenges presented by their source novel would multiply and intensify. Humphrey Cobb's 1935 novel *Paths of Glory* is a hard-hitting indictment of the callousness of the officer class toward the mass of enlisted soldiers in the First World War. Most strikingly, and given the nature of the American film tradition, most unpromisingly, the novel appears to range over its list of characters (officers, trench-bound soldiers) without focusing on the story or the distinct perspective of any one of them. It is this problem, of an absence of a central agent of sympathy and identification, which many of the film's critics have highlighted.

As Mario Falsetto demonstrates, Kubrick's film elevates the character of Colonel Dax to the position of moral focus and narrative hero, using him thereby to both orient audience identification and articulate Kubrick's own ideological point-of-view (2001: 170). Various cinematic devices are employed, Falsetto argues, to focus the viewer's sympathies on and with the character of Dax (ibid.: 38–41). Despite such a reading, we should remember that in order to make the film at all Kubrick and Harris were forced by United Artists to transform the story into a vehicle that could carry a true star actor and thus stand a chance of making money at the box office. Indeed, it is only because of Kirk Douglas's personal commitment to making the film that *Paths of Glory* gained the majority of the $954,000 required for its production. Against claims that Colonel Dax represents Kubrick's ideological position, we must balance the fact that Kubrick and Harris were forced financially into making the film as a vehicle for Douglas. This point suggests the need for further work on the various scripts produced by Kubrick, Jim Thompson, and a new writer on the team, Calder Willingham.

Kubrick's next film, *Spartacus*, was an even bigger star vehicle, adding heavyweights such as Charles Laughton, Peter Ustinov, and Lawrence Olivier, to the list. As has often been noted, *Spartacus* is Kubrick's one mainstream Hollywood blockbuster, and as a hired-hand he was to distance himself from it in his later years. *Spartacus* also is one of only two films (the other being *Lolita*) on which Kubrick does not have at least in part a writer's credit. That honor goes to writer Dalton Trumbo, famously a victim of the Hollywood blacklist. The experience of trying to direct an epic film through a maelstrom of male egos (Kirk Douglas, the British actors, Trumbo, the novel's author Howard Fast) is usually taken (on the evidence of Kubrick's own statements) to have convinced him of the need to exercise "complete total final annihilating artistic control" over his own films from thereon in (see Krämer 2015b). The paradoxical point is normally added that, despite his frustrations, the box office success of *Spartacus* gave Kubrick the star director status he needed to accomplish this ambition.

With all this in mind, it is not surprising that many of Kubrick's critics have avoided discussion of the film. With the intensity of recent scholarly studies of the Kubrick and other archives, however, things appear to be changing. Fiona Radford, for example, has demonstrated that Kubrick did have a significant input into the ongoing revisions to the film script. Dalton Trumbo's sixty-page critique of the first, director's cut of the film, points to tensions between contributors that led to a contradictory film in which a "large" Spartacus (threat to the Roman Empire) and a "small" Spartacus (leader of a relatively insignificant band of rebels) had come to coexist. The archives can show Kubrick's contribution to the downsizing of Spartacus's rebellion and to other characters, such as Varinia. As Radford states, he also appears to have brought in elements of Arthur Koestler's rival novel, *The Gladiators* (1939), with its more pessimistic views on peasant (or indeed any form of) revolution. Kubrick's contributions, in this war between the "large" and "small" Spartacus, are not in themselves ideologically coherent, and Radford shows, among other things, that he appears to have been partly responsible for reinstating Howard Fast, the novel's Communist author, into the production team (2015: 110–13).

It is not difficult to ascertain the primary problem facing Kubrick and Harris as they faced into production of their next film, *Lolita* to be based on Nabokov's infamous 1955 novel. As the movie's tag line has it: "How did they ever make a movie of *Lolita*?" According to the dominant mode of commentary on the film, the answer comes in Kubrick's and Harris's prolonged, strenuous, minute, but also professional and always civilized negotiations with the film censors in the United States and also in the UK, where for financial reasons they decided to shoot the film (LoBrutto 1997: 197–226). *Lolita* gives us, in many respects, a classic instance of the way adaptation and censorship coalesce in the history of cinema. In a much quoted 1970 interview with Joseph Gelmis, Kubrick appears to blame the structures and strictures of the film industry and the religious censorship bodies for forcing him to sanitize Nabokov's explosive, challenging text (see Gelmis 2001: 87–8). A good number of the film's more intellectual reviewers seem to have shared this view at the time of the movie's release (Naremore 2007: 101). Recent work, fueled by access to the Stanley Kubrick Archive, however, has begun to move this story away from the censors' negative impact on the film, and to refocus on the actual aesthetic decisions motivating the film. Karyn Stuckey, reading Kubrick's own index cards and letters (especially one to Peter Ustinov), has demonstrated that Kubrick and Harris, from the very beginning, were determined to refashion Nabokov's story into an admittedly quirky but, still, recognizable romantic comedy (2015: 120). It is for this primary reason, and not on the insistence of the censors, that Kubrick and Harris, with the blessing of Nabokov, raised the age of Lolita from 12 to 15, thus making the object of Humbert's passion a pubescent teenager rather than a prepubescent child.

Kubrick expressed his desire to remain faithful to Nabokov's novel. He wrote to Peter Ustinov how, "The mood of the book must be preserved. The surface of gaiety and humor, the ... wit of Humbert, the *bon mot* ... [with] flippantly dispatched [dialogue] and the tempo and vitality of comedy" (quoted in Stuckey 2015: 121). The fact that this mood must be externalized, however, substantial amounts of it even transferred to Peter Seller's bravura performance as Clare Quilty, is a significant insight into what kind of fidelity Kubrick is after. Thus, for example, instead of being informed by Humbert that Charlotte Haze (Lolita's mother) is a ludicrous woman, the film's audience is treated to the ludicrous and yet sympathetic performance of Shelley Winters. Instead of being confronted with Humbert's Eurocentric, neoclassical, mock-epic responses to American culture and geography, we are presented with Kubrick's externalized world of kitsch, suburban décor and alienated highways connecting equally alienated towns and motels. It is, thus, when we come to *Lolita* that we begin to better understand Kubrick's initially paradoxical sounding definition of good novel to film adaptation:

> The perfect novel from which to make a movie is, I think, not the novel of action but, on the contrary, the novel which is mainly concerned with the inner life of its characters. It will give the adaptor an absolute compass bearing, as it were, on what a character is thinking or feeling at any given moment of the story. And from this he can invent action which will be an objective correlative of the book's psychological content, will accurately dramatize this in an implicit off-the-nose way without resorting to having the actors deliver literal statements of meaning. (Kubrick 2005: 338)

Kubrick's next film, despite this, was based on a novel of terrifyingly portentous action. British author Peter George's (aka Peter Bryant) *Two Hours to Doom* (1958), or to give it its American title, *Red Alert*, is a novel in which the world is brought to the very brink of nuclear apocalypse by a sick and paranoiac US General. *Dr. Strangelove* is a film that seems very different to its melodramatic source. The Kubrick Archive contains multiple screenplays and associated materials that show what a tortuous path Kubrick (without Harris after the earlier stages), Peter George, and in the later stages the comic writer Terry Southern, took in adapting the novel to film. The central problem faced by Kubrick and his team when coming to adapt *Red Alert* was clearly one of genre ("serious suspense story" or "nightmare comedy"). But that is in no way to suggest that crucial questions of ethics, politics and philosophy are not bound up with these aesthetic considerations. One need only look at the parallel case of *Fail Safe* (both the 1962 novel by Eugene Burdick and Harvey Wheeler, and the 1964 Sidney Lumet film), a project that had been legally challenged by Kubrick and George on the basis of plagiarism charges, to see that a serious take on these momentous issues could eventuate in a false sense of narrative (and ethical) resolution by story's end. Kubrick's decision to adapt the material into a modern, Swiftian satire does not mean that he produced a version that belittles, or sanitizes, the question of nuclear war. On the contrary, *Dr. Strangelove*'s bizarre and yet unsettlingly credible black comedy allows Kubrick and those working with him to present the question of the nuclear Cold War without pulling any punches. We may be entertained by the insanity of General "Buck" Turgidson, General Jack D. Ripper, Major T. J. "King" Kong, and the Soviet Ambassador de Sadesky, along with Sellers's unforgettable genocidal madness as Dr. Strangelove, but at the end of the film the world is consumed by the Doomsday Machine, as Vera Lynn sings "We'll Meet Again," and the point that an hysterically masculine military bureaucracy might bring global mass destruction has been well made and understood.

2001 is a collaboration rather than an adaptation. It is true that a significant impetus to what was to become the screenplay and novel (concurrently written by Clarke) was provided by Clarke's 1951 short story "The Sentinel" (see Bizony 2014: 18–20; Hunter 2016: 129–40). Clarke had previously written successful novels about alien intervention into human history and evolution, such as *Childhood's End* (1953). However, the majority of *2001* was developed in a veritable cauldron of intellectual cooperation and dialogue between Kubrick, Clarke, and a host of other members of Kubrick's production team. Clarke was encouraged to write a "novelization" upon which the script of the film could then be based. But then, as Clarke notes, this novel was revised and adapted as the film took shape. The dance between novel and film, each circling around the other in a play of suggestion and response, is of course highly appropriate to the film it helped inspire (2009: ix–xix; see also Benson 2018).

Despite not being a classic example of novel to film adaptation, there is an essential point this analysis needs to draw from Kubrick's most feted film. That is the film's subject matter. Enigmatic and puzzling as many have found the film, the overriding subject of the film is human evolution, adaptation in its biological, cultural, and spiritual senses. That one of Kubrick's abiding themes is the chance for human evolution, especially beyond the kind of violence represented in the early prehistoric phase of *2001*, and in the entirety of *Dr. Strangelove*, *Spartacus*, and *Paths of Glory*, is consolidated by Kubrick's most influential film. It is a fact that can also help us in critically understanding the more subtle, nonverbal dimensions of his film, as in J. P. Telotte's fascinating take on humanity's desire to escape the force of gravity in *2001* (2006: 43–58). It is also a theme that helps us make more meaningful links between his films, as in the leap from the relatively optimistic *2001* to the darkly pessimistic *A Clockwork Orange*.

A Clockwork Orange returns us to the classic novel to film adaptation scenario, as do the subsequent four films in Kubrick's career. The novel by Anthony Burgess, originally published in 1962, is a powerful dystopian morality tale, set in a not too distant future in which teenage boys indulge in "ultraviolence" and yet, despite their brutality, appear more vibrantly human than their institutionally sedated parents, guardians, and correctors. Much has been made of the fact that Kubrick chose not to include the last chapter of Burgess's novel, in which the young antihero Alex DeLarge renounces his violent ways but reflects that his son will probably go through the whole antisocial process again. Clearly, Kubrick was not impressed by Burgess's Catholic take on individual salvation amid the fallen state of general humanity.

The pivotal problem in such a project is clearly how to represent in the cinematic medium the shocking violence and cruelty contained in Alex's first-person, highly subjective and heavily idiomatic consciousness. A good deal of commentary on the film has been dedicated to answering such a question, looking at the ways Kubrick skillfully mediates the violence, especially in the first third of the film, through his use of music, slow and fast motion camera work, accomplished editing, the symbolic use of modern art, lighting, and of course the often bizarrely exaggerated performances of McDowell and the film's other actors (see DeRosia 2003; Rabinowitz 2003). *A Clockwork Orange* certainly takes up the revolutionary use of classical and contemporary music in *2001* and deploys it now, in what would become a trademark fashion, to assist in the adaptation of Alex's interior consciousness to the externalized world of film. But, of course, as is well known, all these mediating devices were not a secure defense against the controversy that eventuated in Kubrick and Warner Bros.' withdrawal of the film from the UK market. Questions of the social adaptability of youth, and the role of art in that process, spill over here from fiction into reality. Yet Peter Krämer is correct to include in this broader picture the question of how cinema itself, released in the late 1960s and early 1970s from an ethically conservative regime of censorship, adapted itself to a more liberal, permissive cultural climate (2011: 74–6).

Kubrick's next project, *Barry Lyndon*, allowed him to directly address his lifelong interest in the eighteenth-century Enlightenment, a theme closely associated in his work with the question of human evolution (see Harlan 2011a: 15). Thackeray's *The Memoirs of Barry Lyndon, Esq.* was first published in serial form in 1844 in *Fraser's Magazine*, entitled *The Luck of Barry Lyndon*, it was then published in revised form as *The Memoirs of Barry Lyndon, Esq.* both as a standalone novel and as part of the four volume *Thackeray's Miscellanies* in 1856. The novel is an adaptation itself, in that it ironically imitates the style, narrative structure, characterization and themes of earlier eighteenth-century novels, particularly those by his favorite, Henry Fielding. In particular, the novel presents us with a radically unreliable first-person narrator, who seems strangely incoherent. Always one step ahead of his readers in terms of narrative temporality (he is, after all, as the equally unreliable editor G. S. Fitz-Boodle informs us, writing the narrative in Fleet prison during the last days of his life), Redmond Barry of Barryogue, Ireland, also seems incapable of benefiting from that retrospective position.

He simply does not learn anything from the narrative account of his own fall and expires as profound a misogynist and as socially affected a fake as he has always been. Thackeray's Barry, in this sense, reads like a precursor of the contemporary postmodern novel, his character as two dimensional as the beautiful neoclassical paintings and the social etiquette of the waning aristocracy that temporarily surround him.

The novel, then, presents the filmmaker with considerable challenges, once again calling for the invention of appropriate "objective correlative[s]" of the original's distinctly novelistic qualities (Ciment 1983: 205). Kubrick's slow zooms in and out of the interiors of Castle Hackton and other aristocratic houses alerts viewers to the artificiality of both the film itself and of the world it purports to represent. In a rather precise correlative for the novel's foregrounding of its own artifice as history and autobiography, Kubrick's camera, confining and constructing his characters within an overdetermined world of aesthetic signifiers, questions the representational status of *Barry Lyndon* as historical record. As Maria Pramaggiore also says, the use of narrative voice-over disrupts the film's temporal movement in a manner analogous to Thackeray's double-voiced narrators (2015: 99). Kate McQuiston also demonstrates how similar disruptions, on the level of chronology, movement, and time are created by the highly wrought musical soundscape of the film (2013: 87–106).

Given how many films have emerged from the novels of Stephen King, we might expect that Kubrick's next film, *The Shining*, offered Kubrick and his co-writer Diane Johnson, a more straightforward adaptational challenge. However, such an assumption does disservice to the complexities of King's novel, as it glosses over one specific aspect that poses a serious challenge to any film maker. Much has been written of King's dissatisfaction with Kubrick's film, a dissatisfaction that is apparently rooted in the way Kubrick strips the novel of both its focus on a hotel haunted by actual ghosts and its Oedipal focus on sons battling with fathers and fathers battling sons, and presents instead a mythic narrative in which the uncanny appears to substitute for the story's original psychological and supernatural motivation. King combined these points into a further critique of the film's casting of Jack Nicholson in the lead role of Jack Torrance (1989: 23–4). For King, the outcome of these changes and casting decisions was a film that had no depth or heart, a response that is echoed in Fredric Jameson's treatment of the film as an example of postmodernist art (1992: 82–98).

For Jameson, Kubrick's *The Shining* is an expression of the surface nature of postmodern culture. Whatever we make of such an argument, there is a clue in this rhetoric of emptiness, or depthlessness. Enlisting the full weight of his now vast cinematographic experience, including the opportunities afforded by the new Steadicam camera, Kubrick's film focuses on the uncannily empty and yet possessed interiors of the hotel rooms, corridors, bars and reception areas, along with the minds of his leading actors. Within this, Kubrick builds a film that explores the limits of what we might call visual knowledge. Constantly evoking only to disrupt the conventions of shot-reverse shot, point-of-view, and other familiar filmic techniques, Kubrick's film is disturbing ultimately in the manner it shows us the unknowability of its character's inner worlds and the ontological disintegration in film between the real and the imagined, or simply unreal (see Allen 2015: 368–70). *The Shining* is a film about the epistemology of cinema; a film that seems finally to center the question of adaptation upon film's rearrangement of the world into dreamscape, a world that is materially present (because visible) and yet fundamentally symbolic, constructed, and thus immaterial. Kubrick's last two releases, *Full Metal Jacket* and *Eyes Wide Shut* confirm this trend.

The obvious problem facing Kubrick when coming to *Full Metal Jacket* was how to meaningfully contribute to such an already apparently saturated field. There were, by the late eighties, a whole series of Vietnam films, some of which, such as Michael Cimino's *The Deer Hunter* (1978) and Francis Ford Coppola's *Apocalypse Now* (1979), were significant industry hits. The book Kubrick alighted upon was Gustav Hasford's account of Vietnam around the time of the Tet Offensive of 1968, *The Short-Timers* (1979). Kubrick takes up Joker's role as a journalist covering what has become universally known as the first television war and creates around him a film that explores Marine Corps culture, and beyond that the American cultural contexts it reflected and refracted. That culture is, of course, masculine and itself influenced by the mythology of the American soldier, especially the Marines, in Hollywood accounts of the Korean and the Second World War. Nathan Abrams's account of how Kubrick suppressed explicit elements of Jewish culture throughout his adaptations has recently provided new insights into his treatment of masculinity (2018). Several provocative readings (Doherty 1996; Pursell 2001; Willoquet-Maricondi 2006) have also looked at how Kubrick adapts Hasford's awareness of the pervasiveness of movie culture on Marine Corps training and then American military behavior in the South East Asian combat zone. The war films of John Wayne are, for example, mentioned regularly by the characters in Hasford's narrative, and Kubrick links such allusions to the developing character of Joker, the film's key focus. In this way, as a series of events play themselves out in the training camp on Parris Island and then again in the various camps and combat zones of Vietnam, a question is raised about how far Joker is willing or, indeed, is able, to adapt to the misogynistic, violence-loving, masculine culture of the US Marine Corps.

This theme, of the war between the sexes and within gender identities, is taken up again in Kubrick's last film, *Eyes Wide Shut*. As Kolker and Abrams (2019) have demonstrated, *Traumnovelle*, an early-twentieth-century Austrian novel about the libidinal struggles between a middleclass Jewish couple, had been a Kubrick obsession for many years before, in 1994, he enlisted the help of Frederic Raphael to produce a modernized, New York version of the story. There is good reason to view *Eyes Wide Shut* as one of Kubrick's most faithful adaptations. Like many of his other films, *Eyes Wide Shut* is about cinema's relation to dream. Because of this, the film is also about interpretation, and it seems now, with two decades' hindsight, to anticipate the very interpretive confusion it received on its initial release. The core problem facing Kubrick was, of course, how to translate the novel's blurring of dream and reality into a cinematic medium that already and inevitably works to blur such a border. The core question for the film's audience is how to respond to a text that oscillates between dream and reality. Kubrick and Raphael exploit all aspects of the uncanny that help to disrupt the relation between reality and dream/fantasy: including, repetition of speech, the figure of the double, the use of chance and improbability. Added to this, Kubrick exploits a visual version of many of these uncanny components, including a striking intensification of his already trademark use of light and color, so that, for example, a pattern of translucent blues and deep reds haunt Bill's and Alice's exchanges in ways that appear as if they require interpretation but which also systematically disrupt any such semiotic stability.

As with all Kubrick's films, we are encouraged to reflect on our own desire for interpretation, examining not only the film directly but also our own role as viewers and interpreters. Do we watch this film, in other words, with eyes wide shut or eyes wide open? Tim Kreider has argued that Kubrick's film is as much if not more about the corrupt nature of modern US capitalist society than it is about the inner psychologies of its two main protagonists (2006: 296–7). In Kreider's reading, Bill and Alice Harford have adapted themselves to *fin de siècle* American capitalism. They have not, that is, opened their eyes to the nature of the corrupt world around them, and we leave the film with them busily inducting their daughter Helena into the same values. Most commentators have preferred to leave the Harfords in a more ambiguous position, perhaps reminiscent of Private Joker's relation to Marine Corps ideology at the end of *Full Metal Jacket*. What is not ambiguous is that these characters, along with all Kubrick's major characters, are confronted with the question of how to adapt to a violent, corrupt, human-all-to-human environment. The three major film projects that came closest to, but eventually stalled before, production, *Napoleon*, *Aryan Papers*, and *A.I.*, deepen our sense that adaptation was not only Kubrick's consistent mode of filmmaking, but also his core obsession as an intellectual and an artist.

4

Kubrick and Collaboration

Manca Perko

Many myths have grown around Stanley Kubrick over the years. A dominant one is that he was an all-controlling auteur, reluctant to take the views of anyone but himself and who terrorized his crew to get the desired outcome. Carl Freedman, for example, has written:

> A writer, producer, editor and photographer as well as a director, Kubrick maintained a degree of control over his films probably unsurpassed in cinematic history—his perfectionism often leading him to work at a (by Hollywood standards) excruciatingly methodical pace to achieve precisely the effects he wanted. Of course, Kubrick had numerous helpers, assistants and sub-contractors, for nobody can make a film single-handedly. But, for most of his career (and despite what Arthur C. Clarke may have thought about his role in *2001: A Space Odyssey* (UK/ US 1968)), Kubrick had, and desired, no real collaborators. (2008: 134)

This chapter challenges the myth of Kubrick's despotism by discussing his collaborations and aims to elucidate Kubrick's collaborative practice. It will present what is known about the director's collaborative relationships, including co-working with various (co)screenplay writers, (co)producers, production designers, cinematographers, editors, composers, people he worked with in marketing and distribution, and his other crew members—including sound recordists, special effects people. I will discuss the circumstances of these relationships and the characteristics of Kubrick's collaborative practice.

Collaboration is an action of at least two people mentally and physically working together to complete a task or achieve a goal. As such it is dependent on the nature of the relationships between the people in the process and subject to circumstances under which the collaboration functions. Kubrick's collaborations were based on the relationships he built with his collaborators, whom he most often chose himself, though at times he was coerced to collaborate with people who were not his choice, for example, Warner Bros.' marketing agency. But as a rule, Kubrick was inclined to use trusted co-workers and to repeat previous collaborations at all stages of filmmaking. This chapter aims to describe what it was like to collaborate with Stanley Kubrick and to gauge the importance of collaboration to his film practice.

The best-known and most complete accounts of the director's life are the biographies by Baxter (1997) and LoBrutto (1997), as well as Michel Ciment's *Kubrick* (1983), the latter written with Kubrick's cooperation. These present balanced technical and industrial knowledge and offer insights into the nature of collaborations in Kubrick's productions. Baxter emphasizes Kubrick's conflict-prone character and tends to confirm the myth of the difficult director, as does Frederic Raphael's *Eyes Wide Open: A Memoir of Stanley Kubrick* (1999), which recounts controversies around authorship and autonomy over the screenplay for *Eyes Wide Shut*. LoBrutto, by contrast, employs in-depth archival and film industry research to counter the mythology existing around Kubrick, as does Filippo Ulivieri's (2017b, 2017c) exploration of the birth and the development of Stanley Kubrick's public persona. Michael Herr's *Kubrick* (2000), a short biographical account of his friendship and collaboration with Kubrick on *Full Metal Jacket*, presents another perspective on the Kubrick mythos, stressing the director's gentle nature. Many other works of his ex-collaborators challenge the myth of the self-sufficient director. These include (but are not limited to) interviews and written recollections of the screenplay writers Arthur C. Clarke (1972), Sara Maitland (1999), and Ian Watson (1999); memoirs of actors Tony Curtis (1993), Kirk Douglas (1988), James Mason (1981), and Peter Ustinov (1977); works of critics like Alexander Walker (1972); and a first major documentary on Kubrick by Paul Joyce (1996). These works do not deny Kubrick's perfectionist approach, but they emphasize Kubrick's openness to creative input and willingness to collaborate.

The collaborative perspective on Kubrick has again come into focus lately, resulting in the search for moments of collaboration that might have led to a birth of an idea or crucial assistance in execution. Individual collaborative relationships are addressed in documentaries, such as *Stanley and Us* (1999), *Stanley Kubrick: A Life in Pictures* (2001), *S Is for Stanley* (2015), and Tony Zierra's *Filmworker* (2017), which portrays the life of Leon Vitali, who became Kubrick's right-hand man from *Barry Lyndon* onwards, while Filippo Ulivieri's book *Stanley Kubrick and Me* (2016) charts the long-term relationship between Kubrick and his chauffeur and later assistant, Emilio D'Alessandro. Research in the Kubrick Archive and interviews with Kubrick's friends and crew have increasingly thrown light on Kubrick as collaborator rather than isolated auteur. Kubrick's collaborations are extensively discussed in recent essay collections, such as *Stanley Kubrick: New Perspectives* (Ljujić et al. 2015); and *Stanley Kubrick: Nouveaux Horizons* (Jaunas and Baillon 2017), and in special journal issues of *Adaptation* (Hunter 2015), on Kubrick as an auteur of adaptation, *The Historical Journal of Film, Radio and Television*, on new archive research in the Kubrick Archive (Fenwick et al. 2017b), and *Screening the Past* (Broderick 2017b), on Kubrick's influence and legacy. The detailed production histories in the essay collection, *Stanley Kubrick: New Perspectives* (Ljujić et al. 2015), focus on the historical, industrial, cultural and social discourses surrounding the collaborative aspect of Kubrick's filmmaking practice. Catriona McAvoy's chapter, which deconstructs myths about the creating of *The Shining*, is based on interviews she conducted with Diane Johnson, Brian Cook, Jan Harlan, and Katharina Kubrick (2015b). While McAvoy does not deny that "Kubrick's control and his decision-making power were certainly quite unique," she concludes that he was very much open to input from his co-workers (2015b: 307). Regina Peldszus (2015) exemplifies this fact with Kubrick's collaboration with NASA at the preproduction and production stages of *2001*, whereas Nathan Abrams's (2015c) analysis of the screenplay of *Spartacus* explores Kubrick's adaptation process on that film with multiple authors. Drawing on extensive archival correspondence, Abrams (2015c) identifies a "myriad of conflicting interventions" in the screenplay writing process.

Screenplays were problematic for Kubrick. A vast majority of Kubrick's films from *The Killing* onwards were adaptations of novels or short stories on which he collaborated with Howard Sackler (*Fear and Desire* and *Killer's Kiss*), Jim Thompson (*The Killing*), Calder Willingham and Jim Thompson (*Paths of Glory*), Vladimir Nabokov (*Lolita*), Peter George and Terry Southern (*Dr. Strangelove*), Arthur C. Clarke (*2001*), Diane Johnson (*The Shining*), Gustav Hasford and Michael Herr (*Full Metal Jacket*), Frederic Raphael (*Eyes Wide Shut*), and Sara Maitland, Brian Aldiss, and Ian Watson (*A.I.*).

The screenplays were written under Kubrick's strict supervision (Abrams 2018), which often made Kubrick a difficult person to work for, which some of his screenwriters have confirmed. Sara Maitland, for example, claims that:

Figure 4.1 *Fear and Desire*'s cast and crew.

He was savagely impatient. He could be rude when thwarted, even in minor matters. Eventually it became clear that I wasn't giving him what he wanted. I began to feel bullied instead of excited, less and less able to wheel as he wanted, less and less eager to do so. (1999)

Constant rewrites and intense communication were typical for Kubrick. According to *Spartacus*'s screenwriter, Dalton Trumbo (1991), Kubrick kept rewriting the script without his consent. Filippo Ulivieri (2019), Simone Odino (2017), and Michael Benson (2018) depict a similar process in Kubrick's collaboration with Clarke on *2001* producing "Roughly 150 exchanges" between Kubrick and Clarke (Odino 2017). Frederic Raphael's memoir records a similar process (1999) but, according to Jan Harlan, Raphael was simply disappointed that Kubrick rewrote his script (Jacobs 2007).

This collaborative process, particularly in the early days, sometimes led, it is claimed, to his wanting to take sole credit for the finished screenplay. Robert Polito's biography of Jim Thompson says that Thompson considered his "additional dialogue" credit on *The Killing* "a nasty slap in the face" (1996: 399), and Kirk Douglas (1988) has claimed that Kubrick offered to take sole credit for *Spartacus*'s screenplay as well. Similarly, Frederic Raphael felt, "The stipulation that he should be the sole judge of who had written what was an implicit guarantee that I would be written out of the record, no matter how much I had contributed" (1999: 56). But Raphael *was* credited.

This creative process seemingly suggests a striving for control similar to that of other directors with such reputations, like Erich von Stroheim and Alfred Hitchcock. The reason is likely Kubrick's discontent with not being in control at every stage of production. Loss of control was a thorny issue for Kubrick, which he often referred to when discussing *Spartacus* as a project on which he "tried with only limited success to make the film as [historically] real as possible" but "was up against a pretty dumb script" (Kubrick, quoted in Ciment 1983: 151). According to many scholars (e.g., Baxter 1997; LoBrutto 1997; Krämer 2011; Abrams 2018) it was because of Kubrick's negative experience with *Spartacus* that he "never again relinquished control over any aspect of his films" (Cahill 1987). After *Spartacus*, Kubrick either collaborated with production companies that allowed him creative freedom or formed production companies of his own, including Hawk Films, Peregrine Productions, Stanley Kubrick Productions, Polaris Productions (see Fenwick, this volume).

Kubrick's first films were produced by RKO Radio Pictures (*Day of the Fight* and *Flying Padre*). *Fear and Desire* was self-funded, and *The Killing*, *Paths of Glory* and *Lolita* were produced by Harris-Kubrick Productions, Kubrick and James B. Harris's first production company. Kubrick's later films were all co-productions with big production companies, such as, MGM (*2001*) and Warner Bros. (from *A Clockwork Orange* onwards). Kubrick signed a "three-film contract" with Warner Bros., according to Julian Senior, the studio's publicity director (quoted in Ciment 1983: 223), which guaranteed him a substantial amount of creative freedom and a clause to receive 40 percent of the films' profits (Baxter 1997: 245). At Warner Bros. Kubrick was largely able to exercise his freedom in shaping collaborations and dictating the creative

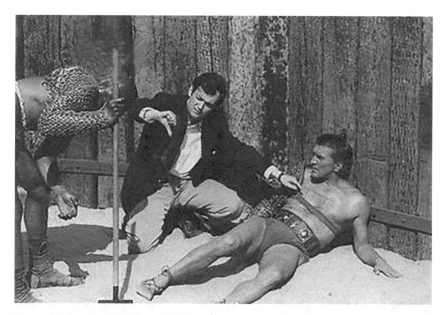

Figure 4.2 Stanley Kubrick and Kirk Douglas on the set of *Spartacus*.

environment for the crews. This gave rise to the myth of Kubrick "not only following the beat of a different drummer but more likely constructing his own drum" (Clines 1987: 34), "a master controller, taking great care in every single aspect of the filmmaking process," "an obsessive perfectionist" who was "absolutely driven to achieve his goals no matter how long it took" (Edwards 2013).

Kubrick's productions have been described as demanding. Kubrick's crews allegedly found themselves in a working environment whose limitations and challenging conditions affected their performance and led to resentment. This can seemingly be observed in the case of Shelley Duvall. Vivian Kubrick's documentary *Making "The Shining"* (1980) features an infamous behind-the-scenes confrontation between Kubrick and Duvall, an event that depicts Kubrick as an overdemanding and terrorizing director to the wider public. And, as the only extant and widely circulated footage of the director at work, it has reached near sacrosanct status. But Kubrick's methods on *The Shining* had another purpose:

> His reportedly tyrannical behaviour was only ever intended to achieve the best performances possible … Kubrick deliberately instilled a poisonous atmosphere around her, haranguing her [Duvall] at every opportunity, ordering the entire crew to ignore her, so that as the shoot progressed her performance naturally began to mirror her character's own. (Edwards 2013)

Nevertheless, many of his crews testify to similar experiences.

Figure 4.3 Stanley Kubrick, the crew, and Shelley Duvall on the set of *The Shining*.

Kubrick's perfectionistic approach to filmmaking strongly influenced the nature of his collaborations and his expectations of delivery of the highest quality. Since his days at *Look* magazine, Kubrick had always been a meticulous photographer, and he extended his demands for the highest quality to other sectors as well (Mather 2013). Composer Gerald Fried, Kubrick's friend from high school, described this transition during Kubrick's early filming days: "By the time he got to *Paths of Glory*, I had to justify every note. It was quite a tortuous process. But, then again, he was a great moviemaker, so maybe that's one of the reasons why" (quoted in Alberge 2018). Kubrick's perfectionism was reflected in what some considered his relentless attitude toward the crew. Garrett Brown, the Steadicam operator on *The Shining*, claimed the perfectionist myths to be true: "Stanley is correctly reported to be in charge of every detail, and interested in everything from the air-conditioning to the nature of lunch" (quoted in Magid 1999). Julian Senior explained that Kubrick's demanding nature "drove a lot of people away from him" (quoted in *Filmworker*).

In some cases, they resulted in resignations, as was the case on *Barry Lyndon*: "It was difficult for young people, two eventually left. They were used to a set schedule which people were actually going to try to achieve" (DuVall, quoted in Cook 2012). Andy Armstrong has described the physically exhausting experience on this film. As the director's assistant, he was expected to join Kubrick, Cook, Alcott, and Adam on location scouting: "I would often have to drive this group of strange people to the most weird places, through the mud, trees and forest to look for something that might be a perfect sunset or some perfect position" (DuVall, quoted in Armstrong 2011). Ken Adam, Kubrick's production designer, also spoke publicly about his physical and mental exhaustion on *Barry Lyndon*. He described it as "nerve-destroying," confessing he had himself admitted to an institution to get a break from the demanding schedule (Adam, quoted in Morrow 2013).

Despite the challenging conditions, economic pressures, and urgency of the schedule, some filmworkers described themselves as fortunate to work on a Kubrick project, even if they did not always get paid for their contribution. Gerald Fried scored five of Kubrick's early films but was not paid for the profits of the first one, as promised:

> He thought the very fact that doing the music to his early movies got me into the profession was enough payment. We had an agreement—not in writing—[that] we would work for nothing but, as soon as the movie got sold, he would pay us. Well, he didn't. (quoted in Alberge 2018)

While Malcolm McDowell (the lead actor in *A Clockwork Orange*) also recalled not getting his allegedly promised percentage of the profit, it was Kubrick's emotional distance after filming was over that was hurtful: "And then with Stanley, I gave him absolutely everything I had—everything I had—and he barely called me after that. So it was like a total rejection of you as a person" (quoted in Labrecque 2014).

Kubrick formed long-term collaborative relationships at almost all stages of the production process. This included with Douglas Milsome, his focus puller and later Director of Photography on *Full Metal Jacket*; cinematographer John Alcott; costume designer Milena Canonero; Martin Hunter, firstly as an assistant and later as editor of *Full Metal Jacket*; Andros Epaminondas as production assistant; Andrew Birkin as assistant; Ray Lovejoy as editor; Jan Harlan as executive producer; Julian Senior (Warner Bros.) and Roger Caras as trusted publicity men; and contacts from Rank/Deluxe Laboratories (Chester Eyre and Colin Flight). Brian Cook explains:

> The real key people had a tough job with Stanley, designer, cameraman, assistant director, editor, those sort of key roles were very, very difficult with him and you notice a lot of people fill those roles as they did with most big directors. Once they find somebody that's good they obviously like to keep using them. (DuVall, quoted in Cook 2012)

This raises the question, why did people want to keep working for him under such strenuous conditions? Many of these collaborations began as mentorships, for Kubrick was remarkably willing to be a mentor to his co-workers. Anthony Frewin, Kubrick's long-time personal assistant, claimed that, while Kubrick rarely gave opportunities to newcomers because he demanded perfection, at the same time he was excellent "at spotting a face in the crowd who can handle responsibility and had potential" (2018). Kubrick's own career began with a mentorship, first under Herman Getter, an art teacher at Taft High School, who created a "motivating and inspiring environment for Kubrick's creativity" (LoBrutto 1999: 29). This mentorship was continued by Arthur Rothstein, an accomplished staff photographer at *Look* magazine. *Look* "initially wanted their junior photographer to perfect his craft" (Mather 2013: 62) and it is perhaps this learning experience that shaped those of Kubrick's collaborations that started off as mentorships. Kubrick's collaborators often testified to this characteristic of Kubrick's working practice: "If he saw someone that he thought had potential, was young, very enthusiastic, hardworking and had some talent, he would give any young person a break in that role" (DuVall, quoted in Cook 2012). Kubrick invested energy and time into newcomers and workers who wished to advance their career. This process demanded one to acquire new knowledge, and Kubrick was willing to provide it. Alcott witnessed this himself: "He is willing to bend over backwards to give you something you may desire in the way of a new lighting technique, and this is a great help" (quoted in Lightman 1980: 788). Chester Eyre, the director of operations at Deluxe Laboratories, confirmed, "Everyone who's ever worked with the man has learned a lot from him—about both the industry and themselves. He always managed to draw more out of you than you thought was there" (quoted in Magid 1999). It is therefore understandable that Peter Hannan, the special effects cameraman on *2001*, referred to his experience with Kubrick's mentoring as an apprenticeship: "To get the opportunity to work on *2001* was extraordinary. I was being paid to go to university, really. It was extraordinary" (personal interview 2016). Early collaborator Gerald Fried recalled Kubrick's rationale for not paying him: "'I did you a much better service than paying you, I got you into the movie business.' Which is true" (quoted in Alberge 2018).

This indicates that not only did Kubrick share his technical knowledge, but he also, contrary to popular perceptions of his tyrannical attitude, encouraged his workers. Kubrick strived to create close collaborative relationships and, as Simone Odino puts it, had a distinct success with "creating a creative space" (2017: 109). This was especially the case when Kubrick saw the potential for a long-term collaborative relationship, and his mentoring practice often led to long-lasting and strong collaborations. Kubrick's relationship with Frewin originated from mentoring: "I was 17 when Stanley first employed me, and he had more confidence in me than I had in myself" (quoted in *Stanley Kubrick: A Life in Pictures*).

However, not all relationships developed further, and some collaborators were not given recognition for their creative input. Such negative experiences of Kubrick's creative environment are reflected in the testimonies of many co-workers who were not credited or given recognition for their creative contribution. Some collaborations in the music department were controversial. For example, the composer Alex North, with whom Kubrick had collaborated on *Spartacus*, was supposedly selected to score *2001* by MGM to which Kubrick "reluctantly" agreed (Benson 2018: 391). Kubrick then decided against using North's (finished) score and left North to find this out in the cinema. Similarly, composers Wendy Carlos and Rachel Elkind entered into a collaboration with Kubrick on *A Clockwork Orange*. The success of the film's soundtrack led Kubrick to employ them again for *The Shining*. But this time Kubrick overrode their creative autonomy: "When we got there he had already cut in some of our music into *A Clockwork Orange*. With *The Shining* it was a very different experience" (Elkind, quoted in TV Store Online 2014). Kubrick's control over their work proved too limiting to Elkind and Carlos's creativity and the collaboration ended with Kubrick's sudden decision to decline their finished work and ask his first assistant editor, Gordon Stainforth, to edit the soundtrack instead (*Stanley and Us*).

A pattern seems to emerge. Kubrick opted for new collaborators and was open to their ideas, but when he was not satisfied, he returned to his trusted collaborators. He did this often: The *A Clockwork Orange* case above demonstrates this, as well as Kubrick's choice of a new editor Bill Butler for the same film. But for his next film, *Barry Lyndon*, Kubrick chose to work with his trusted editor, Ray Lovejoy, who had cut *2001*. Long-term collaborations with his co-workers were based on mutual trust and Kubrick's confidence in his collaborators' knowledge. "He only wanted people around him who were knowledgeable. He needed you to be a film person, first and foremost, to truly understand the aspect, because he would ask you a question, it was very complex," Colin Flight, the operational director at Rank Laboratories, explained (personal interview 2018). Kubrick's demand for knowledge had to be indulged constantly. Jocelyn Pook, who scored *Eyes Wide Shut* and also a first-time Kubrick collaborator, exemplified it: "I had this quartet that I played with in churches and he would speak to me for hours about them, asking me every little detail about the most trivial things" (quoted in Hobbs 2018).

Kubrick's need for control and complete trust was often challenged by individuals in his crew or cast, as when Matthew Modine took a stand when not being permitted to go to be with his wife in labor during the filming of *Full Metal Jacket* (Modine 2005: 138). Steadicam operator Liz Ziegler abandoned *Eyes Wide Shut* after a year following Kubrick's refusal to let her go home to visit her family (Kolker and Abrams 2019). But, where Kubrick did have to compromise, he often built collaborations that enabled him to negotiate the best possible outcome (e.g., the relationship with Kaplan and Senior, the publicity men, allowed Kubrick to be closely involved in planning the advertising campaigns for his films). From such collaborations new ideas emerged and creativity was a result of a mix of knowledge and creativity of different people. This resulted in new techniques and pioneering approaches—such as an advertising technique that Kaplan, Senior and Kubrick referred to as a "memory jogger on releasing a film"—a thirty-page list of guidelines for advertising *A Clockwork Orange*. It detailed how many prints/copies of the film should be made, how many trailers were to be created, the information on various cinema facilities and equipment, such as the type of projectors and their masks, information on whether certain TV networks preferred video or film, etc. (Senior, quoted in Ciment 1983: 223). The idea proved to be highly productive and, together with "media proposals" (SKA/13/5/36, 1971), the "memory jogger" resulted in an edited booklet—Warner Bros.' official *Press Book* (SKA/13/5/2/7, 1971). Such testimonies of Kubrick collaborations demonstrate "that Kubrick was as much a creative collaborator as a shaping consciousness" (Stuckey 2015: 134–5). Kubrick could produce a truly collaborative experience: "He made you feel a part of it ... That was an important part of his process" (Vitali in *Filmworker*). While Vitali confirmed that Kubrick could be impatient, he emphasized Kubrick's collaboration: "The thing with Stanley is that you worked for him but you also worked with him" (in *Filmworker*).

Kubrick was undoubtedly demanding on his crew and fostered a creative environment full of restrictions, demands, and stress. He did not habitually grant autonomy to his collaborators and at times took credit for the work himself, as when he received an Oscar for the special effects in *2001*. Peter Hannan, the special effects cameraman on *2001*, has stated that Wally Veevers (the special effects supervisor) should have received the Oscar (personal interview 2016), and Douglas Trumbull (the most publicly exposed *2001* special effects supervisor) agreed that the creative authorship was attributed to the "wrong" person: "Kubrick did not create the visual effects. He directed them. And he didn't design them. A lot of other people designed them" (Trumbull, quoted in Child 2014).

Kubrick was nevertheless a collaborator, even if his method of collaborating often enraged his fellow co-workers. Frewin notes that it was Kubrick's "insatiable curiosity" and openness to creative inputs "from anybody" (DuVall, quoted in Cook 2012) that enabled effective, though often challenging, collaboration and invention of practical approaches and solutions in the making of a film. This type of open environment made collaborators feel appreciated: "When he was with people, they felt that they were appreciated. He was very interested in what people had to say" (DuVall, quoted in Harris 2010). Kubrick regularly developed relationships with co-workers, sometimes leading to long-term collaborations. These often originated from a mentor–student relationship with Kubrick, who was able to develop trust because he was both passing down knowledge and monitoring his workers' progress. He formed many long-lasting and trusting collaborations that were crucial for his filmmaking to be successful. Kubrick could be difficult to work with and often unpolitic, at best, at handling credit for creative work done on his films. But even though he often reaffirmed his position in the hierarchy, he was a team player—at least when it suited him. Despite the myth that Kubrick was an all-controlling tyrannical auteur, he was throughout his career an able and interested collaborator.

5

Kubrick and Britain

Matthew Melia

Introduction

In 1959, Stanley Kubrick effectively swapped Hollywood for Britain. He set up in the UK in order to begin production on *Lolita*. His business partner James B. Harris had already come over beforehand, then regarded as "a 'production center of international importance,'" looking for potential deals for the film (Fenwick 2020: 173). Kubrick's visa and passport details, currently available as uncatalogued acquisitions at the Stanley Kubrick Archive, show that he returned to the UK in 1960 and stayed for a year before coming back in 1962 to start production on *Dr. Strangelove*. Kubrick left again in 1963 and did not revisit until he started work on *2001: A Space Odyssey* in 1965. At this point, Kubrick and his family settled permanently in the UK and only returned once to the United States for *2001*'s premiere in 1968.

By then, Kubrick was established as one of the most significant émigré American directors working in the UK, where he not only made a home, but also established a professional base and nurtured a long relationship with the British film industry, its performers, and technicians. Kubrick had a deep awareness and love of British culture, displaying Anglophilic tendencies. At least two of his films, *A Clockwork Orange* and *Barry Lyndon*, are identifiably "British" in their narratives, settings, design, and use of locations. Kubrick also adapted and/or collaborated with many British writers, including Peter George (*Dr. Strangelove*), Arthur C. Clarke (*2001*), Anthony Burgess (*A Clockwork Orange*), and William Thackeray (*Barry Lyndon*). Kubrick also collaborated with Clarke on the screenplay of *2001*, science fiction writer Ian Watson and novelist Sarah Maitland on the unmade *A.I. Artificial Intelligence*, which was based on a story by British writer, Brian Aldiss, and Scottish novelist Candia McWilliam on an early draft of *Eyes Wide Shut* and, on the final draft, with American-born British screenwriter Frederic Raphael. Kubrick's unrealized projects include adaptations of work by British writers, such as *The Passion Flower Hotel* by Roger Longrigg (using the pseudonym of Rosalind Erskine) (1962) and *Shadow on the Sun*, a science fiction radio drama by Gavin Blakeney broadcast on the BBC Light Programme in 1961 (Ulivieri 2017a).

Few studies, however, have explored Kubrick's nearly forty-year relationship with Britain and the British film industry. There is some brief discussion by Robert Murphy in *Sixties British Cinema* (1992). Nathan Abrams's *Stanley Kubrick: New York Jewish*

Intellectual (2018) draws on key British connections across his work, including his collaborations with such British Jewish actors as Peter Sellers, Steven Berkoff, and Miriam Karlin. My own research draws attention to parallels between the visual language of Kubrick and that of the maverick British auteur Ken Russell, and relates them to the vision of British director Michael Powell and his Hungarian screenwriting partner Emeric Pressburger (Melia 2017). And James Fenwick (2020) has detailed Kubrick as a producer, which, by its nature, covers his years in the UK.

But there are no studies dedicated solely to discussing Kubrick, Britain, and British cinema. This chapter will focus on Kubrick's films from *Lolita* to *Barry Lyndon*; examine Kubrick's place within British film culture and in relation to Britain; and investigate why he chose to work with British actors and technicians, and how far his films can be identified with a sense of "trans-Atlanticism." While the chapter will reference *The Shining*, *Full Metal Jacket*, and *Eyes Wide Shut* (all produced in the UK, using British technical staff), they will not, given their American narratives, form part of the central discussion.

British Cinema and Why Kubrick Moved to Britain

Kubrick's arrival in the UK was prompted by his unhappy experience making *Spartacus*, during which time he had quarreled over screenwriting credits and script revisions with writer Dalton Trumbo (Abrams 2018: 61). Wanting to be "More than just a gun for hire" (ibid.), he saw trans-Atlantic relocation as a route to greater artistic autonomy but without compromising on production facilities. The move was coincidental with the mass migration of American auteur directors to the UK and the British film industry's increasing reliance on financial collaboration with and financing from US studios, which in turn were attracted by the financial benefits of producing films in the UK. In the 1930s, Britain had welcomed (Jewish) émigré filmworkers from Central Europe, including Anton Walbrook, Emeric Pressburger, and Alexander Korda (Durgnat 2011: 5), while in the 1950s Britain opened its doors to American filmworkers fleeing McCarthyism, such as Joseph Losey, Cy Endfield, and Larry Adler. In the 1960s, American directors like Kubrick, Losey, Endfield, Richard Lester, and Sidney Lumet were all part of a trans-Atlantic exchange of film talent. While British directors like John Schlesinger and John Boorman made their name in the United States, collaborations between American directors and a new generation of British screenwriters, actors, technicians, and production crew were expanding the artistic scope and international salability of British cinema. These filmmakers were helping to change British cinema's "reputation for stagnant complacency which is not entirely undeserved" (Murphy 1992: 10).

The arrival of what Kubrick later described as an "American colony" (uncatalogued letter from Kubrick to Shadow Vice Chancellor Geoffrey Howe, May 13, 1977, SKA) was economically and creatively reinvigorating and would herald an era in which the scope, ambition and vision (aesthetic, artistic, ideological, and narrative) of British cinema would expand beyond its own confined, domestic, parochial limitations. This trajectory would culminate at the end of the decade with *2001*, a British–American collaboration filmed at MGM-British, Borehamwood, and Shepperton Studios with British production artists and technicians. It was a significant moment of transition in *British* cinema. *2001*'s cosmic scope and ambition contrasted dramatically with British cinema's tradition of realism and presented an expansive directorial vision hitherto unseen in British cinema since the work of Powell and Pressburger in the 1940s.

A key incentive for these émigré directors was the Eady Levy, a tax on box office receipts introduced in 1950 to subsidize British film production and increase its share of the box office (Fenwick 2018: 195). Yet instead of securing a "national cinema," as was the intention, the levy facilitated British–American co-productions and contributed to the "establishment of a transnational cinema that persists to this day" (ibid.). To safeguard against the "Americanization" of British cinema,

> Productions taking advantage of the Eady fund were also influenced by criteria of "Britishness" which required that "80% of the labor costs were towards British persons and all but two of the main featured actors had to be British subjects." (ibid.: 193–4).

For Kubrick the levy was an important incentive to produce *Lolita* in the UK. In fact, all of Kubrick's films from *Lolita* to *The Shining* used Eady money until it was withdrawn in 1985.

This was not the only reason, however. Kubrick and Harris had been keen to make *Lolita* since the novel's publication in 1955, but its provocative subject matter (a middle-aged academic's obsession with a 12-year-old "nymphet") and pressure from the Production Code and the Christian conservative right meant the film would be difficult to produce in the United States. The decision to relocate Harris-Kubrick Pictures and establish a new company, Hawk Films, in the UK was also stimulated by the fact that the head of the UK operations for production company Seven Arts, Kenneth Hyman, was moving to London to fulfill his new position (ibid.: 153). Making the film in the UK also ensured subsidies and financing, lower production costs, and cheaper labor. Establishing Hawk Films in the UK, therefore, ensured the strategic advantage not only of access to Eady subsidies, but also making it easier for Kubrick to "leverage" and assert his power and position as a producer in Britain (ibid.).

In relocating to the UK, Kubrick achieved the autonomy he craved after *Spartacus*. Distance from Hollywood left him relatively unhindered by excessive studio interference and by the mid-1960s "Kubrick had reached the position ... where he could now communicate with the industry at the executive level" (ibid.: 181). By 1973, when *Barry Lyndon* went into production in locations across England and Ireland, Kubrick was enjoying an almost unprecedented degree of creative and professional control. As Richard Schickel (1975) observed:

> He enjoys the rare right to final cut of his film [*Barry Lyndon*] without studio advice or interference. Warner Executives were not permitted to see more than

a few bits of it until the completed version—take it or leave it—was screened for them just 3 weeks ago.

It is perhaps the case that Kubrick was intentionally never fully integrated into the British film milieu or establishment—maybe (pragmatically) preferring to keep his options open. Alexander Walker, discussing the dominance of producer David Puttnam over the British film industry of the 1980s, notes that Puttnam was awestruck at Kubrick's independence and that "Kubrick's totality of control is still beyond Puttnam's grasp" (1985: 62). Kubrick, Walker hints, existed within the British film industry of the period but as an independent auteur resistant to being assimilated into the British film establishment and the fiefdom Puttnam had established.

Even though Kubrick continued to nurture a relationship with the British film industry, he also seems to have been ready to leverage his considerable status, power, and influence and to exploit his position as an expat American director working abroad. When the then Labour Government's 1974 Finance Act, came into effect in 1976, ensuring anyone who had lived and worked in the UK for more than nine years was liable for "the full United Kingdom maximum tax rate on 75% of the worldwide earnings" (prior to this they had been exempt). Kubrick lobbied the then Chancellor of the Exchequer, Denis Healey, and Shadow Chancellor Geoffrey Howe (uncatalogued letters in SKA from Kubrick to Howe and Healey, May 23, 1977) to maintain the current exemptions and prevent an exodus foreign director and the "massive withdrawal of American film investment" (ibid.) from the UK film industry. Kubrick threatened to return to the States or move to Europe, reminding the politicians that without the revenue he and other foreign directors brought into the UK, the film industry would collapse.

Kubrick's British Collaborators

Kubrick was fully committed, however, to using British talent in his films and after *Lolita*, over the course of the 1960s, and through the greater successes of *Dr. Strangelove* and *2001*, Kubrick established for himself "a powerhouse" (Fenwick 2018: 7) in the UK, creating a network of trusted professionals and family members: technical staff, administrators and aides—most prominently, Leon Vitali and his brother-in-law Jan Harlan—as well as Emilio D'Alessandro who performed the dual roles of personal assistant (PA) and chauffeur. Vitali, a rising star in British film and television, was cast as the young Lord Bullingdon in *Barry Lyndon* (he later played multiple masked roles in Kubrick's final film *Eyes Wide Shut*). After *Barry Lyndon*, Vitali gave up a promising career in British film and television to work as a key aide and PA to Kubrick, asking the director to mentor him behind the camera. Five years later, Kubrick called on Vitali to work as his assistant on *The Shining*. He was crucial to all stages of the production and that of subsequent films. In 2017, he was the subject of a major film documentary, *Filmworker*. For his part, D'Alessandro, Kubrick's driver and assistant, sacrificed a career in racing when from 1971 he began working for Kubrick as chauffeur and PA—a role that lasted until the director's death in 1999. He, too, has been the subject of a recent documentary, *S Is for Stanley* (2015) and a book co-written with Filippo Ulivieri, *Stanley Kubrick and Me: Thirty Years at His Side.*

In her recent research, Manca Perko (2019) has written extensively on Kubrick's reliance on collaborative relationships with British production staff. Her research challenges the dominant narrative of Kubrick's as a didactic auteur and proves that he relied on collaborative relationships and the creative input of trusted technical staff. Perko reveals not just his relationships with actors and production staff but also with British film labs and development staff—a previously overlooked aspect of his working relationships. *2001* is particularly notable for the wealth of British technical talent employed in its production: special effects makeup artist Colin Arthur (who created the ape masks for the "Dawn of Man" sequence); visual effects artist and model maker Joy Cuff; special photographic effects supervisor Wally Veevers; cinematographer John Alcott and editor Ray Lovejoy; and Arthur C. Clarke, with whom Kubrick collaborated on the screenplay (which they simultaneously adapted as a novel). Perko makes clear that Kubrick developed and fostered collaborative relationships to the extent that staff were able to work in his absence, instinctively understanding what he wanted. She also makes clear that Kubrick in this was adept at manipulating, controlling, and shaping such relationships according to his needs.

One specifically "British" aspect of Kubrick's films that predated and perhaps helped to motivate his move to England was a preference for British actors. Nathan Abrams traces this back to his working with Laurence Olivier, Peter Ustinov, and Charles Laughton on *Spartacus*: "He doubtless absorbed a great deal from Olivier, Laughton, and Ustinov about character development, possibly instilling a taste for British actors" (2018: 61). Kubrick recognized and exploited the diversity of styles of British acting, cultivated across a range of traditions not widely available in Hollywood. This is apparent in *Lolita*, in which Kubrick cast two leads with very different acting styles: James Mason as the itinerant and sexually frustrated pedophile academic Humbert Humbert, and Peter Sellers as Clare Quilty, his rival for the affections of 12-year-old Lolita. As Roger Lewis observes of the film's opening ping-pong table "duel" scene,

> It isn't only a confrontation between the two men who loved and lost *Lolita*; it's a duel of acting styles: James Mason, classically trained, highly intelligent and cultivated and with his lusts and yearnings kept under severe control; Sellers, loose, improvisational and with an ungovernable genius. (1994: 501)

From archived correspondence, we know that Kubrick wanted to cast a classically trained British actor as Humbert (both Olivier and David Niven were interested in the role) (letter from Kubrick to Vera Nabokov SKA/10/8/4). Mason was both classically trained and a veteran of British Gainsborough (costume) melodramas such as *The Wicked Lady* (1945). Sellers, by contrast, was a comic actor, known for his gifts of impersonation in the Ealing comedy *The Ladykillers* (1955) and such films as *The Naked Truth* (1957), *I'm Alright Jack* (1959), and *The Mouse That Roared* (1959). Kubrick had chosen to work with Sellers on the strength of these last two films in which he played multiple comic roles: a talent he exploited in both *Lolita*, in which he plays one character in a range of disguises, and *Dr. Strangelove*, in which he plays three different characters.

From the late 1960s Kubrick looked to the pages of casting publications like *Spotlight* for British actors associated more with low-brow, televisual and even experimental fare. His annotations on numerous headshot photos in *Spotlight* reveal the type of actor he was looking for each role and *which* actors he had considered for key roles. All of them were essentially character actors, often almost grotesques, whom he would often use repeatedly. Philip Stone, for example, who plays Alex's father in *A Clockwork Orange*, later appears as Graham, the Lyndon family lawyer in *Barry Lyndon*, and as the caretaker, Delbert Grady, in *The Shining* (the only British actor in the film). Kubrick chose from a relatively localized pool of actors who were not internationally known or easily recognizable outside of British low budget productions, theater, or (now cult) television. Leonard Rossiter, for instance, who had roles in both *2001* (Dr. Andrei Smyslov) and *Barry Lyndon* (Captain Quinn), began his career in postwar realist cinema with roles in *A Kind of Loving* (1962). At the time of filming *Barry Lyndon*, he was at the height of his fame as in the TV sitcom *Rising Damp* (ITV 1974–8). Gary Mills observes that Kubrick and Rossiter shared a "an obsessive perfectionism and unwavering insistence on standards" (2015), but, perhaps more important, casting actors like Rossiter demonstrated that Kubrick was availing himself of a diverse range of acting talent from not only across film and theater but also television. On *A Clockwork Orange*, Kubrick considered casting Patrick Cargill as Dr. Brodsky (Cargill had done a stint as a sadistic and paranoid "Number 2" in the British science fiction series *The Prisoner*, in the episode "Hammer into Anvil" (1967), making him an apt choice for the role of Brodsky); John Le Mesurier (*Dad's Army*, BBC 1968–77) as a possibility for Alex's father, and James Bolam (*The Likely Lads*, BBC 1964–6) as one of the Droogs. Malcolm McDowell was cast as Alex after Kubrick saw him in the role (his first) of the antiestablishment Mick Travis in Lindsay Anderson's surreal public school drama *If…* (1968). Another instance of localized casting was Miriam Karlin, the unfortunate "Cat Lady," who, as Nathan Abrams points out, was the "female Peter Sellers," and a notable figure in British Jewish film, television, and theater in her own right and who had worked extensively with Jewish writer Wolf Mankowitz (2018: 156).

Kubrick's went on to cast another gallery of British stage, TV, and film character actors in *Barry Lyndon*. This included Patrick Magee, most famous for his portrayal of The Marquis de Sade in *Marat/Sade* (1967) and for his association with Samuel Beckett, who wrote *Krapp's Last Tape* for him (Kubrick visually references this in *A Clockwork Orange*, in one shot placing Magee in front of a reel to reel tape player as in *Krapp*). Murray Melvin, whom Kubrick cast as Reverend Samuel Runt, had emerged out of the Joan Littlewood Theatre Workshop (Theatre Royal, Stratford, East London), and been in both the both play and film of *A Taste of Honey* (1961). A regular actor in the films of Ken Russell, he was cast by Kubrick on the strength of his performance as the duplicitous cleric Fr Mignon, in Russell's *The Devils* (1971).

Why did Kubrick make these casting choices? The obvious answer is that the actors were less expensive than star names. Moreover, they consolidated the "British" identity of his films and thereby fulfilled the criteria for Eady funding. Also, by largely avoiding casting internationally famous stars (as he did with *The Shining* and *Eyes Wide Shut*), the films were able to function as a whole rather than a star vehicle. Set and production design, performance, and direction were given equal weight. The only star in fact was Kubrick himself. The possible exception to this was casting Hollywood star Ryan O'Neal as Redmond Barry in *Barry Lyndon*, perhaps to improve the film's commercial chances with American audiences.

How "British" Are Kubrick's Films?

Although financed and shot in Britain, often adapted from British material, and predominantly cast with British actors, Kubrick's films are trans-Atlantic as much as British. None of them is set in contemporary Britain, and British locations frequently stand in for somewhere else. *Lolita* was shot on soundstages in the UK (MGM Borehamwood and Elstree) but also in Rhode Island and Albany, New York, as well as Buckinghamshire (UK) and Hertfordshire (UK) where the Kubrick family eventually settled, which stood in for suburban New Hampshire. Although it was a pragmatic and practical choice, Robert Murphy suggests that such "trans-Atlanticism" impacted negatively on *Lolita* in terms of a diminishment of authenticity:

> The supposed awfulness of mid-American middle class society, so sensitively explored by Douglas Sirk in *There's Always Tomorrow* (1956) and *All That Heaven Allows* (1955), here in the environs of Borehamwood, seems utterly unauthentic, and it falls to Peter Sellers with his party piece impersonations to provide the film with high points. (1992: 99)

The transposition of one location for another became common practice for Kubrick. *Dr. Strangelove* made use of aerial photography of Canada (Quebec), the United States (The Rockies), and Iceland, but the "War Room," set designed by German British production designer Ken Adam (also responsible for the distinctive production design on several Bond movies) was built at Shepperton Studios (Surrey, UK). For *The Shining*, Kubrick commandeered the entirety of Elstree Studios and a scene with Halloran calling from a payphone en route back to the Overlook Hotel was filmed in the early hours at Stansted Airport. In *Full Metal Jacket*, the decaying Beckton Gasworks in East London and Cliffe Marshes, Kent, became war-torn Vietnam (as discussed in detail by Karen A. Ritzenhoff 2015), while London's Soho stood in for Greenwich Village in *Eyes Wide Shut*. The films' "Britishness" remains concealed through the transformation of location, which, especially in *Full Metal Jacket* and *Eyes Wide Shut replaces* authenticity with an often dreamlike and distanciating surreal quality.

Even Kubrick's most "British" films, *A Clockwork Orange* and *Barry Lyndon*, address British themes only obliquely. Elisa Pezzotta has noted the colonial and postcolonial contexts within *Barry Lyndon* and how the IRA's (Irish Republican Army) threats to the film's production "envelop the film's production with British colonial history, the film's historical background" (2015):

> The protagonist Barry is an Irishman; the Calcutta-born Thackeray was English and married an Irish woman; and Kubrick was an American director living and working in the United Kingdom, who began to shoot his *Barry Lyndon* on location in Ireland, but had to retreat to the United Kingdom after the IRA's campaign of violence in 1972. These clues let us realize how much history and Irishness, from a national and transnational, colonial and postcolonial point of view, are intertwined in the diegesis of the film and in the extradiegetic context of the history of its making and reception.

A Clockwork Orange offers a view of a Britain ambiguously displaced in time, a dystopian future or possibly an alternative present, while *Barry Lyndon* is a film fraught with displacement: from its picaresque narrative and wandering central protagonist to a troubled production that was forced to move from its base in Ireland due to IRA threats on account of the film's British colonial themes (another aspect of the film that connects it to an interrogation of "Britishness").

Barry Lyndon engages the British traditions of heritage/costume drama and literary adaptation (forms that many resident American directors adopted; Losey's *The Go Between*, 1971, for example). But as Maria Pramaggiore observes, its modernism (which in terms of production aesthetic at least down to Ken Adam) radically distances it from most British historical films, despite its prominent use of British stately homes, including Wilton Hall, Salisbury previously used by Ken Russell in *The Music Lovers* (1971) and who claimed Kubrick consulted him regarding locations for the film. Pramaggiore writes:

> Considered Kubrick's "most literary film" by Vincent LoBrutto and described by Frank Rich as "as far away from literary modes of film making as you can possibly get" *Barry Lyndon* is in fact both literary and abstract. On the one hand its heightened diction, intertitles and voice over narration established its lineage in Victorian literature and early cinema; on the other hand dialogue free interludes and long takes, paced according to the perspectival shifts of a slow zoom, situate the film within the paradigm of modern cinema. (2015a: 85)

A Clockwork Orange is perhaps the most "British" of Kubrick's movies. As Alexander Walker said:

> For the first time in a Kubrick film, the native accents and urban landscape are recognizably British, though they have relevance to the wider world that has lost its humanity and retains only a Baroque eroticism, a proletarian ghastliness and an institutional callousness. (1985: 44)

The Britishness and cultural contemporaneity of *A Clockwork Orange* is revealed in its incorporation of references to pop art, contemporary design, and (post) modernist aesthetics, art, and architecture. This is especially true of the film's "Brutalist" aesthetic. This style of austere concrete building, which typified urban centers and peripheral spaces from the 1960s, was a form of utopian civic architecture intended to represent a modern postwar, forward-looking Britain. It ended up becoming synonymous with the dystopian grimness of Britain in the 1970s and 1980s, in part through Kubrick's film's use of the Brutalist Thamesmead estate in South London:

> The reduction of Brutalism to a stylistic label exclusively associated with concrete coincided with changing attitudes toward the government and the decline of state investment in the public realm. Originally seen to reflect the democratic attitudes of a powerful civic expression—authenticity, honesty, directness, and strength— the forceful nature of Brutalist aesthetics eventually came to signify precisely the opposite: hostility, coldness, inhumanity. (Karp 2015: 30)

Location shooting in Thamesmead abstracted the bleakness of Britain in the 1970s, even as the incorporation of innovative contemporary design elements presented a Britain on the cutting edge of culture. Kubrick took a "pragmatic approach" to location research for the film.

> [He] wanted to construct an absurd but plausible near future London, using modern architecture as a framework ... eschewing the use of location scouts in favour of a process of visually constructing the film from the images found in architectural magazines. Over two weeks, Kubrick and his production designer John Barry, leafed through a decade of back issues, including *Architectural Design* and *Architects Journal pages*. Pages of interest were carefully cut out of and placed in a German made modular filing system called Definitiv, which allowed for the limitless re-organisation of the removed pages. (Porter 2017: 18)

Kubrick's preproduction research material (see SK/13/2/7, SKA) includes thousands of pages taken from contemporary European and British design catalogs, art periodicals, Sunday supplements, and *The Architects Journal* (including a photograph of the dance floor at the London jazz venue Ronnie Scott's, originally intended to stand in for the Korova Milk Bar), numerous images of Brutalist local authority buildings, hospitals, schools, tower blocks, and shopping precincts. The files also contain a large amount of location research photography (taken by costume designer Milena Canonero), including Brutalist sites around London including the South Bank.

A *Clockwork Orange* aligns with a set of contemporary high and low British cultural trends, notably with a key figure in modern British culture, the playwright, Harold Pinter, not surprisingly given Kubrick's persistent themes of banality, absurdism, and verbal violence. The droogs' violent invasion of the professor's home is "Pinteresque" in depicting the unexpected arrival of malevolent guests, a trope established in Pinter's 1958 play, *The Birthday Party*. Abrams, citing Stephen Mamber, notes that the stilted interactions and dialogue between Alex's parents, M and P, and the lodger Joe also seem to reference Pinter's dramatic style. *A Clockwork Orange* is also the Kubrick film most closely aligned with trends in British cinema. Straddling the divide between arthouse and low-brow popular aesthetics, *A Clockwork Orange* was a "big budget exploitation film, a rich and troubling combination of high style and low even, trashy content" (Hunter 2011: 97) and "spliced" several contrasting genres, modes and styles

> Including the art movie, underground film, the juvenile delinquency movie, and even pornography. But its most intriguing relationship is to the exploitation movies, and specifically to British science fiction, horror and sexploitation cycles of the 1960s and 70s. (ibid.)

Alex, for example, channels not only the anarchic spirit of the art film *If...*, but the libidinous energy of the British sexploitation film:

> Both Mick Jagger and Robin Askwith, he is a malevolent variation on the working-class hedonists of sexploitation films such as *Cool It Carol!* (1970) and *Confessions of a Window Cleaner* (1974), unleashed by permissiveness into new worlds of sexual possibility and consumerism. (ibid.)

This parallel is borne out by comparing the film's trailer (created by American graphic and film title designer Pablo Ferro) with that of *Confessions of a Window Cleaner* two years later: both make use of frenetic editing set to a kinetic piece of music, on the one hand, Wendy Carlos's electronic rendering of the William Tell Overture, and on the other, the raunchy theme tune, "This is your life, Timmy Lea" performed by pop singer, Su Cheyenne. The bawdy British (s)exploitation aesthetic is also present in the sequence when Alex brings home two girls he has met at a record store; the speeded up three-way sex scene resembles a sketch by comedian Benny Hill. Toward the end of the film, as Alex is recovering in his hospital bed, a doctor and nurse are interrupted having sex in a nearby cubicle in a scene playfully reminiscent of the cheeky *Carry On* films.

Conclusion

Trans-Atlanticism is one aspect of a thematic tendency in Kubrick's films for narratives that deal with displacement. If Kubrick was removed from his native United States, his films are also reflective of this position. They are filled with characters displaced from home and in transit, such as Humbert Humbert, a European academic cast adrift in the world of the suburban, picket-fenced New Hampshire; and Mandrake in *Dr. Strangelove*, a British officer cast into the madness of the American War Machine. Images of travel and frontiers recur in *2001*, in the picaresque narratives of *Clockwork Orange* and *Barry Lyndon*, in the displacement of the Torrances to the Overlook Hotel and the Marines in *Full Metal Jacket* to Vietnam, and in Dr. Bill Harford's displacement from the family home and his marriage in *Eyes Wide Shut*. Displaced from home, Kubrick's characters are adrift in the worlds in which they find themselves.

6

Kubrick and Translation

Serenella Zanotti

Introduction

Thanks to the range of primary sources available for each feature film since the opening of the Stanley Kubrick Archive, we have now become aware that translation constituted no little part of the work that was done in the interval between one Kubrick film project and the next. As an aspect that is not normally associated with the creative side of production, translation does not tend to involve film directors. Contrary to Hollywood convention, however, Kubrick "involved himself deeply in all aspects of … post-production" (Ljujić et al. 2015: 16), taking part in the decisions concerning the distribution and marketing of his films on all territories. What is more, he was "one of the few directors to take an active role in the translation of his films" (Nornes 2007: 216). Kubrick understood the importance of translation for the successful reception of a film and, therefore, he closely monitored the making of foreign-language versions along with other aspects of international distribution.

Interestingly enough, translation remains a neglected aspect of Kubrick's films and approach to filmmaking. The role of translation is acknowledged in the work of Ciment (2001), Naremore (2007), McQuiston (2013), McAvoy (2015a), who all emphasize the importance Kubrick attached to foreign-language versions. However, the first scholar to engage in research on this specific area has been Abé Mark Nornes. In his book *Cinema Babel: Translating Global Cinema* (2007), he was the first to examine Kubrick's involvement in the creation of foreign versions, making extensive use of previously unknown archival sources to offer an account of how the Japanese version of *Full Metal Jacket* came into being. Among Kubrick scholars, especially noteworthy is the work of Peter Krämer (2013) and Nathan Abrams (2015b and 2018), who perspicaciously examine translation-related material from the Kubrick Archive to shed light on crucial aspects of interpretation and reception.

Translation and Authorial Control

As Abrams points out, Kubrick's films from *Fear and Desire* to *Dr. Strangelove* "had been verbal experiences," "characterized by what [he] called 'the magic of words', namely carefully constructed dialogue, narration, wordplay, punning, comedy, and black and sick humor" (2018: 120). To preserve this magic, Kubrick "ensured that their foreign-language versions did not omit anything essential" (McQuiston 2013: 8). While this stands as "a testament to his concern about linguistic clarity and meaning," as suggested by McQuiston (ibid.), it also gives an indication of the importance Kubrick attached to film translation as a critical factor for ensuring international box office success. Kubrick therefore "had the subtitles of every foreign version of his films completely re-translated into English to make certain that nothing crucial ha[d] been omitted" (Ciment 2001: 41). In so doing, Ciment notes, he managed to maintain an "autocratic control over the work in hand" (ibid.). Spanish translator Vicente Molina Foix appears to come close to a similar view when he states that all aspects of the translation process "were personally and painstakingly overseen by the director," who paid attention to "even minor linguistic details" (Molina Foix 2005, cited in Pérez-González 2014: 191).

As a film director who was involved in all aspects of production and postproduction, Kubrick played a decisive role in the distribution of his films abroad and had an active part in the translation of the filmic dialogues. Not only was he implicated in all aspects of "the marketing campaign, including posters, lobby cards, newspaper and magazine adverts, soundtrack album and book re-issue covers" (McAvoy 2015: 303) but, from *A Clockwork Orange* onwards, he "was involved in the distribution plan and in organizing the dialogue dubbing into other languages" (302). This can be seen as part of Kubrick's concern with both critical recognition and commercial performance, the latter enabling him "to negotiate with financiers and distributors from a position of strength" (Krämer 2015b: 61), making it possible to retain complete artistic control and to ensure financial support for future projects. As Krämer (2017: 385) puts it, "Kubrick had always been interested in reaching the largest possible audience which aligned him perfectly with Hollywood's commercial objectives." He made distribution deals with major distributors, but he insisted that the director should have final approval on strategic decisions concerning distribution in all territories and on the shape the film was to take in order to reach foreign audiences (Molina Foix 2018: 24). In the words of Michel Ciment, "the painstaking care he [brought] to the release of his films simply reflect[ed] his concern to see them presented in the best possible conditions without their being compromised by a bad print, faulty projection or flat dubbing" (2001: 42). It is therefore not surprising that he personally supervised all dubbed versions.

Kubrick's view on such matters as translation and dubbing was clearly outlined in a letter to Jack Wiener, dated January 3, 1964, in which he wrote,

> I consider the translation and dubbing of the film an intrinsic part of the artistic side of the production of the film. While I am quite sure your people are the most able in the country, I am nevertheless the director and writer of the film and absolutely do not accept the principle that I must accept anyone else's opinion in regard to artistic matters over my own. (SK/11/9/120, SKA; see also Zanotti 2019a: 208–9)

Columbia had apparently failed to respond to the director's request to have access to the dubbing scripts before the dubbing work started, leading Kubrick to invoke the principle of the director's artistic control on all aspects, including translation, as spelled out in the two picture deal he had signed with the distributor: "My request to have a copy of the dubbing script for Germany, France and Italy in sufficient time to check them and make whatever revisions I think required is reasonable and consistent with the principle of my artistic control spelled out in my deal with Columbia" (ibid.). By saying that he viewed translation and dubbing as "an intrinsic part of the artistic side of the production of the film," Kubrick spelled out his understanding of translation as integral to the creative process of filmmaking, which informed his embracing of an alternative approach to the one that had become dominant in the film industry, in which foreign-language versions were (and still are) produced without the involvement of the filmmakers. In the letter, he made it clear that he wanted to be consulted on key creative and business decisions, including the shape his films were to take in translation, which he viewed as a crucial factor in the audiences' experience of the film.

A Preventive Strategy

Conscious of the impact that an impoverished translation could have on the reception of a film in the international market, Kubrick soon developed his own method for dealing with foreign-language versions. With time, he came to understand how to effectively manage the process from the start, by personally selecting translators, dialogue adapters and dubbing directors, and establishing contact with them before work was begun. Very early on in his career as a filmmaker, Kubrick understood that, to prevent translation-related problems, guidance had to be provided to translators and dubbing directors.

As part of a preventive strategy to ensure translation quality, Kubrick personally drafted instructions for both dubbing professionals and translators. His involvement in the preparation of paratextual materials dates to *Paths of Glory*. According to James Naremore, "Kubrick seldom supplied his players with specific notes or keys to interpretation; when the film was completed, however, he left instructions for dubbing the actor's voice into foreign languages" (2007: 92). These were meant to assist dubbing directors in the selection of the voice actors but also in directing their voice work. The annotated dialogue list for translators and dubbing directors for *Paths of Glory* is especially revealing in as far as it shows the importance Kubrick attached to performance when it came to dubbing. Serving as "keys to interpretation" (ibid.), these notes offered perceptive insights into character and personality for both main and minor roles, with a view to instructing dubbing directors as to the kind of performance that was to be given for each player in the foreign language.

As regards Kirk Douglas as Colonel Dax, Kubrick's main concern was, as Naremore suggests, "to keep the actor's innate emotionalism somewhat in check" (ibid.: 92). After clarifying that "despite the conflict with his commanding officers he is always a soldier" who remains loyal to the army, Kubrick recommends to *"never let him indulge in self pity, or, for that matter, never let him break his heart over the injustice being done to his men"* (ibid.: 93, emphasis in original). In sketching out each character with a view to the kind of performance that was to be obtained in the foreign version, he paid particular attention to voice quality as an element integral to characterization and to the actor's voice work. Writing about General Broulard, played by Adolphe Menjou, Kubrick prescribed:

> Strong, perfect pronunciation, as close as possible to Menjou's own voice, which is something rather unique and special. Intellectual but warm. He has a Machiavellian brilliance which he hides in a cloak of warmth and friendliness. *When he is warm and friendly, he must really be warm and friendly. We must never feel he is pretending to be warm* ... He means what he says about doing things for the good of the war. *Don't help the audience hate him.* (ibid.: 93–4, emphasis in original)

As Naremore points out, the notes Kubrick wrote for minor characters "were brief but explicit" (ibid.: 94). For Emile Meyer, the instruction was to "Try and match his *lower class, rough voice*. It's a pleasant relief from the stereotype priest" (ibid.: emphasis in original), while in reference to Timothy Carey's portrayal of Ferol, the film director clarified that "He has a quality that is really unique and almost impossible to duplicate. The biggest danger with him ... is overdoing the thing. Favor the too normal rather than the too abnormal" (ibid.). The aim of such notes was twofold: to guide the dubbing directors on matters of interpretation and to instruct them in order to get a voice performance consistent with that given by the original actors. It is important to point out that, even at this early stage of his career, Kubrick demonstrated an awareness of, and concern for, the fate of his films in other languages. He was extremely concerned with the performance of the dubbing actors, which he knew could significantly affect the filmic experience of foreign viewers and even alter the meaning of the film.

Similar documents in the Kubrick Archive seem to suggest that he was equally concerned with the quality of the dialogue translations. Writing notes and instructions for translators was part of a set of strategies aimed at maintaining hermeneutic control over the filmic text—an approach adopted by the film director to make sure his vision was adequately conveyed in translation. As Nathan Abrams (2015b, 2018) has shown, Kubrick provided translators with explanations for elements of the script that he felt could not be overlooked, along with instructions to serve as a guide in tackling the subtleties of dialogue in *Lolita*:

> As if to stress the point, and to make sure that the translators and dubbing directors understood his intentions, Kubrick annotated the Dialogue Continuity script with instructions. For example, when Humbert is shown around Charlotte's house, Kubrick has written, "Note to translators and dubbing directors: Charlotte Haze's choice of words in English are pretentious and awkwardly pseudo-intellectual. Try to retain that feeling because it is the basis of much of the comedy." (2015b: 550)

In a similar fashion, Kubrick prepared a list of instructions for the translators and dubbing directors of *Dr. Strangelove* (Zanotti 2019a), in which he brought into focus aspects of the film dialogue that he thought required special attention in translation. In the first place, he deemed it necessary to explain *Dr. Strangelove*'s comic method, inviting the translators to avoid any intervention attempting to amplify the humor, to convey the "delicate balance of expressive, realistic and comic codes" (Naremore 2007: 127) that characterizes the dialogue. Hence he wrote: "Although the film is a comedy, the dialogue has been written for complete naturalism and reality. The humour is in the performance and in the situation. Please do not attempt to translate the dialogue in a 'humorous' way" (ibid.).

Another important dimension of the film's dialogue highlighted by Kubrick's notes was the language of deterrence and its characteristic euphemisms. Directly inspired by Henry Kissinger and Herman Kahn, this trait was faithfully reproduced and satirized by being placed into Strangelove and Turgidson's mouths (ibid.: 123–5). Kubrick recommended that great care should be taken to ensure that the linguistic subtleties of the filmic representation, such as the lexical instantiations associated with the ideology of nuclear deterrence, were adequately conveyed in the translated dialogue:

> It is very important to find the equivalent words in your country for the nouveau vocabulary of deterrence, i.e. "pre-empt", "modest" and "acceptable civilian casualties", "Doomsday device", "megadeaths". In English, these words obviously are euphemistic attempts at making their content seem less terrifying, and fitting in somehow within the vocabulary of economists, military men, etc. (Ibid.)

Given the film's concern with portraying as accurately as possible "the reality of military organizations, procedures, settings, equipment and personnel" (Krämer 2014b: 13), it is not surprising that the handling of military terminology in translation is an aspect that was closely monitored. Subtitle and dubbing scripts were checked by language experts to ensure that terminological accuracy was achieved in the foreign versions. Kubrick insisted that the translation of military terms should be "accurate" and have the "sound of reality" (Cable to Jack Wiener, February 10, 1964, SK/11/9/120, SKA). This is the reason why the Columbia offices reassured him that, for the Italian dubbed version, "the technical dialogue has been accurately translated with the assistance of several qualified officers from the Italian Air Force and Navy; officers who are specialized in Air Defence and Nuclear Warfare" (Letter from Jack Wiener to Kubrick, January 24, 1964, SK/11/9/120, SKA). In the notes he prepared for *Dr. Strangelove*, Kubrick paid special attention to voice and performance. For example, he prescribed not to translate the Russian lines spoken by the ambassador ("The Russian Ambassador when speaking in Russian, should never be translated but should always speak Russian. The meaning of what he says is always learned later on") and suggested that special attention should be given to the accent of some of the characters, once again showing a concern for characterization and voice in dubbed versions. Regarding Peter Sellers as President Muffley, Kubrick tried to suggest that a particular type of voice was to be used to dub him: "The President should have an educated accent, but he should be played by a boisterous and loud person." He also expressed concern about the way Major Kong (Slim Pickens) might come across in translation, as can be appreciated in the notes reproduced here below, in which he suggested the kind of approach to be used to portray the character's Texan accent and rustic speech patterns in the dubbed versions:

> Major Kong, the pilot of the Bomber is Texan. His accent and his vocabulary are colourful in a rustic way. He should not be translated or dubbed as being foolish or stupid, but simply in some equivalently humorous rustic accent. Texans are legendary for their bravery and fighting ability, so if you have a choice of rustic accents, choose from that. (Ibid.)

Textual evidence seems to suggest that Kubrick did not confine himself to writing the initial instructions but had a part in compiling some of the explanatory notes embedded in the dialogue list (Zanotti 2019a). For example, the annotations that accompany Major Kong's patriotic speech after he receives confirmation for the plan R message ("Now look boys, I ain't much of a hand at making speeches but I got a pretty fair idea that something damn important's going on back here") once again emphasize Kong's folksy speech pattern and do so in a way that makes the presence of the director's voice clearly visible: "Remember, Kong is a folksy country, rustic type! Smart but rustic. Find whatever your equivalent is for a Texan, who, among other things are known for their courage and fighting ability" (Zanotti 2019a: 212).

From very early on in his career as a filmmaker, Kubrick understood that translators and dubbing directors ought to be given some guidance on how to approach the film text and therefore he arranged for his notes to be sent alongside the dialogue list, which he supervised and, if necessary, supplemented with additional instructions. He also considered it necessary to get in touch with the professionals that were to work on his films before the process itself had started, as he clarified in a cable to Columbia representative Jack Wiener dated December 17, 1963, in which he stated: "I want to speak individually on the phone to translators and dubbing directors to discuss style and approach before work is done" (SK/11/9/120, SKA). All this gives us is a sense of the importance the film director attached to translation, which he soon came to regard as an element integral to the filmmaking process rather than as a secondary concern.

Becoming Involved

What is especially worth noting here is that Kubrick did not confine himself to writing instructions for the use of film translation professionals but wanted to become directly involved in the creation of foreign-language versions. Not only did he expect to be kept informed about the progress of each project, but he actively participated in the decisions regarding the distribution of his films on foreign markets and wanted to be consulted on key issues concerning their translation (Zanotti 2019b, and forthcoming).

Kubrick had perfected his method of dealing with foreign-language versions by the time he completed *A Clockwork Orange*, "the first Kubrick picture financed by

Warner Bros., the studio he would stay with for the remainder of his career, most likely because of the control they gave him over his projects, including their publicity and distribution" (Fenwick et al. 2017a: 3). Archival evidence does in fact show that, from this film onwards, Kubrick had a very active role in trying to influence the shape that his work was to take on in translation and he used this same approach for all his subsequent film projects.

Alongside translating titles and promotional material (Zanotti 2019a), a lot of time and effort was spent in checking translations. The emblematic case of the Japanese translation of *Full Metal Jacket* illustrates the efficacy of the method devised by the film director to supervise the foreign-language versions, especially in dealing with translations into non-European languages. In order to detect important omissions or any leveling out of the original dialogue, the solution devised was to have the Japanese version translated back into English by a second independent translator (Nornes 2007: 216–17). Toda Natsuko, the translator hired by Warner Bros. to take care of the Japanese version, was "the superstar translator of the Japanese film world" (Nornes 2007: 217). Kubrick was not pleased with her work and asked for a new translator, specifically for "someone who knew cinema intimately as a producer and also spoke English fluently" (ibid.). These requisites were found in the person of Harada Masato, a film director in his own right and, above all, "an outsider to the highly professionalized world" of film translation (ibid.).

Contrary to the current practice in the film industry, whereby dubbing professionals are appointed by the company that manages the process from start to finish (Zabalbeascoa et al. 2001: 107), Kubrick considered it of paramount importance to be able to choose the translators and dubbing directors that were to work on the dubbed versions of his films (Heymann 2005: 477). His preference was for hiring film directors and creative writers who were outsiders to the profession (Molina Foix 1999) and therefore "did not feel constricted by the conventions of film translation" (Nornes 2007: 217). By doing so, he aimed at ensuring maximum quality for the dialogue translation, which he viewed as an artistic product to be considered on a par with other components of the filmic artifact; at the same time, this allowed him to overcome the problem of the highly routinized and standardized approaches to the translation of films that dominated the audiovisual translation industry of his time.

Similarly to what occurred with screenplays, the framework for the translation work "was established in long conversations and through Kubrick's notes," and translators "also received extensive feedback on their drafts, again both verbally and in writing" (Krämer 2017: 379), as was the case with the Japanese version of *Full Metal Jacket*. According to Nornes (2007: 217), Harada's translation was submitted to Kubrick, whose feedback came "in the form of a flurry of extended international phone calls," during which "every individual line" was discussed "in the context of characterization, theme, adjacent scenes, *and writing*" (emphasis in original). In a similar fashion, he collaborated extensively on the phone with Riccardo Aragno, who oversaw the Italian translation for both dubbing and subtitling (Zanotti forthcoming).

Kubrick applied the same care and concern for translation quality to subtitling as much as he did to dubbing. After receiving the comments of an independent language expert of his choice on the French subtitles of *Dr. Strangelove*, he asked Jack Wiener not to proceed until he received his notes on the script. He wrote: "Translation is good academic job but totally missing colloquial flavor <u>example catch them with their pants down translated as take them by surprise</u>" (cable to Jack Wiener, February 10, 1964, SK/11/9/120, SKA), a solution that Kubrick objected to as it failed to convey the black, scatological humor of the original line. The importance Kubrick invested in subtitling becomes apparent in the fierce reaction he had when confronted with the German translator's omission of the reference to Adolf Hitler in *Dr. Strangelove*, in the sequence where President Muffley expresses his concern about being associated with Hitler in future historical recounts ("I will not go down in history as the greatest mass murderer since Hitler"). As Abrams (2018: 110) points out, "Kubrick described it as a 'cynical disregard for the past suffering caused by that illustrious gentleman' and not in any way a 'little insignificant matter' or a 'small cut.'" He was equally concerned about the technical quality of the subtitles. According to LoBrutto (1997: 369), when *A Clockwork Orange* was finally shown in Argentina, after being banned for fourteen years, "Kubrick insisted that the Argentines run prints with technically updated Spanish subtitles, which caused the release to be delayed for more than a year."

Working in close collaboration with all the agents taking part in the process was the system Kubrick devised in dealing with dubbed versions. Not only did he spend much time organizing the dubbing into other languages and supervising the process, but he also had an active role in the voice casting and had the last word on the voice actors that were hired for each role. For example, he wanted Peter Sellers to be dubbed by different voice actors in his multiple roles in *Dr. Strangelove* (letter from Erich Müller to Stanley Kubrick dated February 26, 1964, SK/11/4/5; Zanotti 2019a).

As a film director, Kubrick supervised the dubbed versions of his films, paying equal attention to both voices and words, performance and translation. Because of the director's personal involvement in the dubbing process, the usual protocol was ignored when it came to casting voice actors. Since "dubbing actors had developed a conventionalized style used exclusively for their trade" (Nornes 2007: 218), Kubrick's instructions for the dubbing of *Full Metal Jacket* prescribed to draw on actors without experience as voice actors, actors who had never done any dubbing before. Unsurprisingly, he insisted on having stage actors rather than the usual dubbing voices to dub his film (Molina Foix 2018: 24).

In a letter to Warner Bros. Brazilian manager Albert Salem, Kubrick admitted being "very concerned that the dubbing is done correctly and that none of the original performance is lost" (McAvoy 2015b: 302). Indeed, remaining in control of the audible soundscape was as important for the film director as remaining in control of the words on screen. As McQuiston notes, "Kubrick considered aspects of language and voice both separately and in combination," which applied to both original and dubbed versions. Kubrick's attention to "an actor's distinctive voice and delivery" (2013: 8) "extended to the foreign-language dubbed releases of his films" (ibid.: 12), where voice and actorial performance were as important as the translated words themselves. Kubrick's auteurial approach to dubbing involved taking an active role in voice casting and hiring dubbing directors who were outsiders to the dubbing industry and were themselves film directors in their own country. For the Brazilian version of *The Shining*, Kubrick hired Brazilian filmmaker Nelson Pereira dos Santos, whose films he "admired greatly" (McAvoy 2015: 302). For the Spanish version of *A Clockwork Orange*, *Barry Lyndon*, and *The Shining*, he hired Carlos Saura, whose work he greatly respected (Molina Foix 2005; Zanotti 2019b: 86). He asked François Truffaut and Federico Fellini for advice on dubbing directors for French and Italian versions (McQuiston 2013, 12; Zanotti 2019b, 88) and hired Edgar Reitz for the German version of *Eyes Wide Shut* (Reitz 2004).

Kubrick considered of vital importance to remain in control of the soundscape of his films in all languages. In an interview with *Le Monde* journalist Danièle Heymann, in 1987, he talked about the method he had been perfecting over the years to handle the dubbed versions, which consisted in having the recordings of the voice tracks done locally but having the mixing done in London by the same mixers who had worked on the English version (2005: 477). In his view, the problem with letting the mixing happen in the target-language country was that the whole process was managed by people who did not really know the film and often got the job done very quickly due to time pressure, inevitably affecting the quality of the dubbed soundtrack (Zanotti 2019b: 93–4).

From what we have seen so far, it seems evident that Kubrick's concern for ensuring spectatorial involvement applied to both original and dubbed versions alike. Not only did he conceive of foreign-language versions as an integral part of the process of filmmaking, but he fully understood and even exploited the creative possibilities of translation, as epitomized in the scene of Jack's manuscript in *The Shining*, for which translations in all dubbing languages were prepared to be shown in the insert shots that were to be used for each version, each with its own layout and emblematic wording.

Conclusion

Overall, it may not be far from the truth if we were to say that "the complex creative process" (McAvoy 2015b: 299) that lies behind Kubrick the filmmaker extends to include the making of foreign-language versions too. As "a producer, artist, and 'brand' who was intimately involved in all aspects of his films' creation and marketing" (Fenwick et al. 2017b: 368), Kubrick developed a specific working method to tackle with the foreign-language releases of his film. The method consisted in identifying the best possible artists, preferably outsiders to the dubbing and subtitling industry whom he could trust and collaborate with to produce versions that met the very high standards he required. Archive evidence has indeed shown that Kubrick fostered a collaborative approach when it came to dubbing and subtitling, particularly into the languages of the largest markets (Zanotti forthcoming).

Translation is to be viewed as one of the aspects of the filmmaking process over which the film director exerted considerable authorial control, at least compared to other filmmakers. It must be noted, however, he did not have the same degree of involvement in all projects: while he personally supervised the dubbed versions into the four dubbing languages (French, Italian, German, and Spanish), he was less directly involved in the process of translation for the subtitled prints, which nevertheless had to be checked by experts of his choice and supervised by his assistants in order to obtain the director's final approval.

Studying the process behind the creation of the foreign-language versions of a Stanley Kubrick film adds to our understanding of the director's working method and shows "the ongoing potential for further research into the production processes" (Fenwick et al. 2017b: 370) that characterized his work. Looking at the way Kubrick approached the question of language transfer—the amount of time he invested in organizing and supervising the dubbed versions, the great care devoted to checking subtitles, the efforts made to find good translations for his films' titles—reveals that translation was all but a minor concern. Quite on the contrary, far from being "an afterthought" (Romero Fresco 2013) in the filmmaking process, translation occupied a central place in the film director's artistic vision. Kubrick understood that translation was key to the experience of a film and hence a crucial factor in ensuring a film's successful reception among non-English-speaking audiences. As the director and writer of the film, he understood that translation allowed "the same level of authorship as every other element in the film" (Middleton and Spinney, cited in Romero Fresco 2019). It seems therefore natural that his unique approach to filmmaking extended to the creation of his foreign versions.

7

Kubrick and the Critics

Gregory Frame

None of Stanley Kubrick's films received uncontested critical adulation upon first release. As Kolker and Abrams note, the first reviews of Kubrick's films were often "mixed and sometimes downright negative or comprehending," before being reevaluated by academic critics (2019: 134). Critics often responded poorly to Kubrick's films because their pleasures are complex and not easily digested in one sitting. Kubrick himself considered the notion of writing a review of a film seen only once to be "an absurdity" (Hofsess 1976). While he had his champions in the press, some prominent film critics responded to his work with bemusement and disdain. Indeed, ambivalence about Kubrick is one of the few things about which Pauline Kael and Andrew Sarris concurred. In Sarris's exhaustive categorization of directors, Kubrick was characterized as "strained seriousness" with a "naïve faith in the power of images to transcend fuzzy feelings and vague ideas" (1996: 196). As Cote Keller suggests, "Kubrick polarized the critical class for decades by pushing against the confines of categories they traditionally imposed" (2018: 8).

It is interesting to consider this in light of Kubrick's largely unquestioned position within the pantheon of great filmmakers. Kubrick is, for many, the epitome of the romanticized image of the auteur. Working in England, far from the hustle and glitz of Hollywood with individual projects consuming his energies for years at a time, he created films full of significance and meaning that cannot be fully comprehended at the first time of asking. Because he did not give many interviews or discuss his work (something that did not endear him to the press), it is up to the viewer to decipher what he was trying to say. As demanding works of art, Kubrick's films arguably require a level of attention that is beyond the purview of traditional film journalism, and his critical reputation has therefore relied upon cinephiles and academics. Initially, this work took a traditionally auteurist approach that sought answers by interrogating details of the films themselves. More recently, the drive to understand Kubrick's films has involved exploring his personal archive, open since 2007. This chapter will demonstrate how the reputations of Kubrick's films have evolved, outlining the perspectives of his critical champions and detractors, before demonstrating how the films achieved canonical status.

Early Kubrick, 1953–6

Norman Kagan's summary of the initial critical assessment of Kubrick's first three features suggests they were greeted with qualified praise by the mainstream press (2000: 17–18, 29–30, 42). Kubrick's debut feature, *Fear and Desire*—a film he later considered embarrassing and amateurish (Sperb 2004: 23)—was described by Bosley Crowther (1953) in the *New York Times* as a "thoughtful, often expressive and engrossing view of men who have travelled far from their private boundaries." While Kubrick's direction was "far from inspired," Crowther felt the film demonstrated his creative potential. Kubrick's next picture, *Killer's Kiss*—a *noir* thriller about a boxer, a gangster and a dancer—attracted similarly qualified praise, although it was noted that Kubrick had begun to exert greater control over the work (writing, photographing, editing, and directing). *Variety* (1954) remarked that the "low-key lensing occasionally captures the flavor of the seamy side of Gotham life," which helped detract from the screenplay's inadequacies. Gavin Lambert in *Sight and Sound* suggested *Killer's Kiss* demonstrated "a maturing and distinctive personality" (29), a perspective reinforced in *Monthly Film Bulletin*, which also lavished praise on *The Killing* (see Howard 1999: 38, 50). Even Kael, later to become one of Kubrick's most vocal detractors, admired *The Killing*, which "gained generally good to excellent reviews" (Howard 1999: 50). Interest in all three films would grow as Kubrick's reputation was cemented. Whatever the pitfalls of such an approach (Manon 2008: 64), they are now understood as demonstrating Kubrick's promise as a filmmaker: *Fear and Desire* contains "seeds of his cinematic trademarks" (Hutchinson 2017), and "crucial cues" to grasping the meanings of his work (Sperb 2004: 25); *Killer's Kiss* "contains elements that will frequently appear throughout his artistic career" (Williams 2008: 46); while *The Killing* shows his burgeoning status as an auteur (Church 2006).

Growing Reputation, 1957–64

Kubrick's two collaborations with Kirk Douglas represent a crucial shift in the director's critical reputation (both at the time and retrospectively). Not only were *Paths of Glory* and *Spartacus* released as the auteur theory gained traction in European critical circles, but his experience as a hired hand on *Spartacus* taught him that only full creative control would suffice (LoBrutto 1999: 193). It is curious to note that Crowther (1960), in his review of *Spartacus* for the *New York Times*, identified Kubrick with the auteurism of the American New Wave, even though Kubrick had little control over the film (though recent research suggests he had more influence over the script than previously supposed [Radford 2015: 98–115]). *Spartacus* received positive reviews. *Variety* praised Kubrick's direction for delivering "sheer pictorial poetry" (quoted in Kagan 2000: 79), while *Time* said he "show[ed] mastery in all departments" (quoted in Howard 1999: 71). Kubrick's experience on *Spartacus* "merely strengthened [his] resolve to take the next step into auteurdom" (Church 2006), and proved to be the final film he made in Hollywood (Howard 1999: 72).

Crowther's (1957) review of *Paths of Glory* for the *New York Times* gave more credit to star and producer Douglas for bringing the novel to the screen than to Kubrick, although he is effusive about the director's camerawork. Praise was not unreserved, however: the use of "colloquial English with American accents and attitudes," he said, undermined the film's documentary impulse. This was typical of the press response. As Kagan notes, though many critics admired the film, they did not grasp its larger meanings (2000: 62). Lengthier analyses in film periodicals enabled appreciation of the film's wider significance. In his review for *Sight and Sound*, Lambert argued that by breaking free of the "familiar melodrama" of *The Killing*, Kubrick had produced something "meaningful as well as brilliant" (1957: 145) and had made a profound statement about the nature of armed conflict. As cinephiles and academics confirmed Kubrick's place in the cinematic canon, retrospective judgments of *Paths of Glory* follow Lambert's assessment much more than Crowther's. Charles Bane asserts that "it is with *Paths of Glory* that [Kubrick] becomes the genius we associate with his later films" (2008: 38), while Geoff Andrew (2017) argues that *Paths of Glory* is "the film that first showed what he was really capable of." In Andrew's work we can identify a key strain in Kubrick's canonization among the more scholarly critics: he was a filmmaker who broke with generic convention to make broader statements about human nature.

The mainstream critical consensus about *Lolita* at the time of its release was that the compromises required by the Production Code were detrimental to Kubrick's attempt to capture the sophistication of Nabokov's controversial novel. According to Kagan, the film received "a very poor critical reception" (2000: 99). It was "like a bee from which the stinger has been removed" (*Variety*, quoted in Keller 2018). Several reviewers criticized the film's "decontamination" (*Time* 1962) and "bowdlerization" (Macdonald 1962) of the novel. For Sarris (1962) the film's essential failure was that "the sex is so discreetly handled that an unsophisticated spectator may be completely mystified." Crowther (1962) was similarly disparaging, answering the question of the film's publicity "How did they made a movie of *Lolita*?" with the dismissive claim that "they didn't." Arlene Croce in *Sight and Sound* argued that "If the film has Nabokov's ear and voice, it has not his eye" (1962: 191). Although Kael was qualified in her appreciation of the film, she nonetheless commended Kubrick for having "the nerve to transform this satire on the myths of love into the medium that has become consecrated to the myths" (1962: 572). The negative critical reaction to *Lolita* placed considerable emphasis on Kubrick's changes to the novel. A fixation with matters of literary fidelity would prove consistent in critical responses to his films. *Lolita*'s reevaluation by academics has involved shifting attention from its relationship with the novel to the censorious environment in which it was produced, and reassessing the film as a witty, subversive manipulation of the Production Code (Kagan 2000: 100). Rebecca Bell-Metereau details the changes Kubrick made to Nabokov's script and novel, but with the aim of exploring *Lolita*'s significance in popular culture rather than valorizing the novel over its adaptations (2008: 210–16). Archival research, moreover, suggests that Kubrick's "compromises" were "not in order to appease censors, but to develop a 'realistic' heroine in a 'love story', who is old (and bold!) enough to be a narrative agent ... rather than a mere object of some male's (deviant) lusts" (Kubrick, quoted in Stuckey 2015: 135).

Dr. Strangelove, Kubrick's brutal satire on the absurdity of nuclear war, was a critical and financial success on its release, earning praise from both mainstream and specialist publications (Krämer 2014b: 99). As Kagan says, "most critics recognized *Dr. Strangelove* as a brilliant, stylized, unsparing treatment of the nuclear crisis" (2000: 132), and commended its courage, its pinpoint observations of American stereotypes and, in what would become a feature of Kubrick criticism in later years, its detached, outsider's perspective (135–6). The film nonetheless had its detractors. Sarris (1964) thought *Dr. Strangelove* "grossly overrated," seemingly more irritated by the film's positive notices than by the film itself. He also suggested that its skewering of nuclear arms policy had missed the boat after the signing of a test-ban treaty following the Cuban missile crisis. This criticism, that Kubrick commented on a *Zeitgeist* that had already passed, would be a recurrent feature of reviews of his later work. While there were some criticisms in the film periodicals (Taylor 1964), *Sight and Sound's* assessment was more typical: Tony Milne (1964) commended the film's documentary impulse, and Kubrick's control of the material, pursuing the apparently "inevitable conclusion ... with such relentless logic." Skeptics were few and far between and *Dr. Strangelove* still has a largely unchallenged position as one of the greatest film comedies (if not one of the greatest films) ever made.

Kubrick "the Auteur," 1968–99

2001: A Space Odyssey is a firm fixture in the cinematic canon, celebrated by academics and popular audiences alike as an extraordinary visual feast and complex meditation on human existence and our relationship with technology. It was generally well received by press critics on its release (Krämer 2010: 92) and "the critical response was almost entirely enthusiastic" (Kagan 2000: 159). A few key establishment figures, however, greeted *2001* with outright hostility: "infatuated with technology" (Kauffmann 1968); nothing more than a succession of beautiful images (Roud 1968); a self-indulgent, "immensely boring" exercise (Adler 1968). Famously, Sarris offered two critiques of the film, first dismissing it as a "thoroughly uninteresting failure" (1968a), before moderating this judgment to describe it as "a major work by a major artist" (1968b). Kael (1969) described it as a "monumentally unimaginative movie" more interested in hardware than humans, an assessment echoed in her critiques of much of his later work. This lack of interest in human characters was, Kael determined, a consequence of Kubrick's domineering personality. R. Barton Palmer's retrospective assessment of *2001's* reception argues that criticisms of the film from older, establishment figures of the late 1960s reflected discomfort with its radical departure from the forms and conventions of mainstream American cinema (2006: 25–6). For these critics, *2001's* contemplative tone, slow rhythms and lack of conventional narrative existed "outside their framework of apprehending and describing movies" (Gelmis 1968, quoted by Palmer 2006: 34). The "more culturally adventurous among the baby boomer generation" saw their values reflected in a film that *Harvard Crimson* described as one of the "great philosophical-metaphysical films about human progress and man's relationship to the cosmos" (Palmer 2006: 37). *2001* was among several films that heralded a major generational change in American society and culture. As the Hollywood studio system collapsed in the 1960s, a new kind of film emerged that married visual sophistication and intellectual complexity with a less rigid relationship to genre conventions (Palmer 2006: 38). *2001*'s complexity and mystery sustained the repeat viewing necessary to grasp its profundity, and confirmed Kubrick as a filmmaker whose work would be eagerly anticipated for critics alive to the challenge. *2001* was understood as one of the greatest films ever made relatively soon after its release, achieving canonical status in the early 1970s (Krämer 2010: 93). It has steadily risen in *Sight and Sound*'s decennial "Greatest Films" poll. From joint eighteenth place in 1972 and eleventh in 1982, it has remained in the Top Ten since 1992, placing sixth in 2012. From *2001* onward, Kubrick's films would arrive bearing considerable weight of critical expectation.

A *Clockwork Orange*, Kubrick's adaptation of Anthony Burgess's dystopian novel, was probably his most controversial film and drew both critical adulation and visceral loathing (Krämer 2011: 87). The film enjoyed positive notices from film periodicals like *Sight and Sound*, which viewed it as "an assault upon the cosy, the comfortable and the mundane" (Strick 1972), but many press reviewers objected to it on a fundamental level. Roger Ebert (1972) suggested the film was "an ideological mess, a paranoid right-wing fantasy masquerading as an Orwellian warning." Ebert was not alone in suggesting the film had fascist leanings: in the *New York Times*, Fred M. Hechinger argued that the film promoted "the thesis that man is irretrievably bad and corrupt ... the essence of fascism" (quoted in Krämer 2011: 98). For many of these critics, the film failed in comparison with the original novel: Burgess elicited pity for Alex, whose free will was taken by the state, but Kubrick sought identification with him. Because of this, Kael (1972) suggested the film was morally corrupt and, in its infatuation with "the punk sadist," Alex DeLarge, was implicated in the very things it apparently sought to critique. Kubrick's sanctification by critics meant they had not realized that the film indulged in the "purest exploitation."

A *Clockwork Orange* became part of much larger debates about the moral rectitude of the film industry (*Detroit Press*, quoted in Krämer 2011: 98) and the effects of screen violence on "immature audiences" (Sarris, quoted in ibid.: 97; Canby 1971). Even writers at the academic end of film criticism expressed their concerns, with Jackson Burgess suggesting that Kubrick was "trying to hurt" audiences with A *Clockwork Orange* (1972: 35). As Krämer notes, the film's detractors seemed furious with the film's success, which spoke to a "general cinematic and cultural decline" (2011: 98). It was also implicated in a series of apparent copycat crimes that in 1973 prompted Kubrick to demand that Warner Bros. withdraw the film from distribution in the UK (Bradshaw 2000).

Academic critics publishing a few years after the film's release contextualized the initial response. Charles Barr argued that A *Clockwork Orange* had been caught unfairly in the slipstream of the controversy surrounding *Straw Dogs* in 1971 (1972: 17). Hans Feldmann positioned the film in relation to *2001* and *Barry Lyndon* as "a trilogy on the moral and psychological nature of Western man and on the destiny of his civilization" (1976: 12). Applying Freudian psychoanalysis, Feldmann questions the initial critical reception of the film (which suggested Kubrick endorsed Alex's behavior) to argue that man "must recognize and acknowledge the savage in himself and develop cultural forms based on the frank acceptance of that acknowledgement" (1976: 18). Such readings attempted to take the film out of the heat of its immediate context to offer a fuller and more detailed appreciation. By the time of its eventual rerelease in the UK in 2000, it had become an object of cult fascination. Peter Bradshaw (2000) greeted the film on its reemergence following Kubrick's death as a work ahead of its time, anticipating the debates about censorship, screen violence, and the powers of the state and the media, that had dominated public discourse in the nearly three decades since its original release. Interventions such as these have resulted in a critical evolution regarding the film's attitude toward violence, although the film "remains a controversial and notorious work" (Keller 2018).

Barry Lyndon, a costume drama set in the eighteenth century and adapted from William Makepeace Thackeray's novel, was greeted with a baffled critical response in the mainstream press and some film periodicals. The most consistent criticism was that Kubrick was more interested in visual techniques and obsessively detailed costumes and sets than in character or story: Kael (1975) described it as "a three-hour slide show for art-history majors" and Michael Wood (1976) judged it "a monument to Kubrick's patience and pedantry and rather laborious good taste, but signifying very little else." In what would become a repeated criticism of the director's work, Sarris (1975) noted Kubrick's self-imposed exile from the United States as a reason for the film's antiquated feel. Kael wished that Kubrick would return to the country of his birth and work on "modern subjects." Perhaps confirming this sense that Kubrick was out-of-touch with his country of origin, the film did considerably better at the European box-office than in the United States. *Sight and Sound* considered the film an oddity on first release. Penelope Houston (1976: 77) questioned what motivated Kubrick, whose work seemed orientated toward the future, to step so far back into the past. She suggested that he felt safer making films about the past because it suited his desire for control (1976: 80).

In keeping with the increasing sense that Kubrick's films demanded careful critical attention, "it was left to serious film periodicals to explore the complexities of the picture" (Howard 1999: 142). Jonathan Rosenbaum, exasperated by the initial response to the film, asked, "Who says we have to understand a film back to front before we can let ourselves like it?" (1976: 26). He celebrated the substantive changes made to the source material, particularly the shift of the narration from first to third person to achieve a tone of ironic detachment. In keeping with this, Michael Dempsey noted that repeated use of the reverse zoom from close-up to long-shot contrasted "the majestic, indifferent beauty of nature with the scurrying, greedy people who imagine themselves to be its center" (1976: 50). For these critics, those that dismissed the film had fundamentally misunderstood it: *Barry Lyndon*'s slow, detached, painterly style was essential to its "meditation on the transience of life" (ibid.: 49). *Barry Lyndon* remained "probably the most elusive of Kubrick's major films" because it was seldom broadcast on television due to its considerable length and was unavailable on home video in the UK for many years (Howard 1999: 143). By the time of a major rerelease in 2016, the press accepted *Barry Lyndon* as one of Kubrick's great works (Ide 2016; Gilbey 2016; Robey 2016), perhaps because of the scholarly attention paid to the film and especially to its visual style in recent years (King 2008; Ljujić 2015; Pramaggiore 2015a). The painterly style so derided upon initial release is now understood as evidence of Kubrick's mastery of the medium (Cook 2019). Furthermore, academic analysis demonstrated that, far from being behind the times, *Barry Lyndon* was typical of the thematic and stylistic characteristics of 1970s cinema, and consistent with the development of Kubrick's career rather than a curious retroactive step (Pramaggiore 2015a).

According to Dennis Bingham, mainstream critics greeted *The Shining* with "confusion and rejection" (1996: 286). They criticized the performances of Jack Nicholson ("excessive") and Shelley Duvall ("insipid") and Kubrick's treatment of Stephen King's novel, which, they claimed, showed he did not comprehend the genre in which he was working (Mee 2017: 81). Initial responses to the film were born of the "clashing expectations" between the conventions of mainstream cinema and the ambitions of the auteur (Bingham 1996: 286). As with her dismissal of *Barry Lyndon*, Kael criticized Kubrick's preoccupation with the technical aspects of filmmaking and his meticulous visuals. Kagan describes Kael as "the most thorough cataloguer of the movie's imperfections" (2000: 213). Laura Mee argues that *The Shining*'s lukewarm critical reception was because the mainstream horror film was changing from the style of *Rosemary's Baby* (1968) and *The Exorcist* (1973), to more slasher-orientated films like *Halloween* (1978) and *Friday the 13th* (1980), and *The Shining* fulfilled expectations of neither trend (2017: 91). Indeed, *Variety's* original review measured *The Shining* unfavorably against *Halloween*, which was making significant sums of money (Luckhurst 2013: 7). In keeping with this sense that Kubrick was detached from prevailing genre trends, Richard Combs (1980) argued that "the seclusion has taken its toll; Kubrick has no more discussable subjects to tackle or vogues to initiate; he has been driven back on his own resources; he has become an auteur." Mainstream critics expecting the cheap, fast thrills of American genre filmmaking derided *The Shining*'s possession of the very qualities for which they would celebrate a European art film.

The film did receive some positive reviews. Maslin (1980) and Schickel (quoted in Bingham 1996: 291–2) both suggested that multiple viewings were necessary to comprehend the film's meanings fully. Sarris saw in the film a clear critique of the patriarchal family structure (quoted in Bingham 1996: 292). In the periodical *Film Quarterly*, Flo Leibowitz and Lyn Jeffress argued that The Overlook Hotel was a "symbol of America, haunted by a murderous past that made it what it is: a showy display of affluence and excess ... built at the expense of innocent victims" (1981: 45). Explicitly challenging Kael's claim that Kubrick's exile from the United States had caused him to no longer understand his country of origin, they argue that "it is evident from the film that he understands us very well and is trying to tell us something important about ourselves" (1981: 51). This is a similar perspective to P. L. Titterington in *Sight and Sound*, who argued that, like Robert Altman's *Nashville* (1975) and Francis Ford Coppola's *Apocalypse Now* (1979), America is one of the "major themes" of *The Shining*, and that "the dark side of the American experience is paramount in the film"

(1981: 120–21). Other favorable notices emerged in *Sight and Sound*, where Paul Mayersberg (1980–81) suggested "the central horror of *The Shining* is family life," viewing it as an "effective reworking" of family melodrama *Kramer vs. Kramer* (1979). Mee shows that repeat viewing on VHS and scholarly analysis of *The Shining* through the 1980s gradually enhanced the film's reputation, so that its meaning and significance became better appreciated in both popular and scholarly circles (2017: 89). As I.Q. Hunter demonstrates, the cult reputation that *The Shining* developed in the aftermath of its original release inspired a series of weird and wonderful interpretations of the film's meaning, both from academics and fans alike (2016: 41–57). Bingham argues that, by 1994, the film's critical reception had come "full circle" (1996: 300). Indeed, the rehabilitation of *The Shining* by cultists and critics is no better confirmed by the recent film adaptation of Stephen King's *Shining* sequel, *Doctor Sleep* (2019), which is full of references and allusions to Kubrickian inventions not present in the original novel. Despite its initial poor reception, Kubrick's *The Shining* stands now as a vital reference point in the horror genre, its images and ideas reverberating throughout popular culture.

Kubrick's Vietnam War film, *Full Metal Jacket* attracted criticism from the usual places on its release. Once more, Kael (1987) criticized Kubrick's obsession with filmmaking craft, arguing that "moviemaking carried to a technical extreme—to the reach for supreme control of his material—seems to have turned Kubrick into a machine." Kubrick's seclusion and distance from the United States proved even more problematic for mainstream critics because of the film's subject matter. Kael suggested (echoing her assessments of *Barry Lyndon* and *The Shining*) that Kubrick had "become so wrapped up in his 'craft' … that he doesn't recognize he's cut off not only from America and the effects the war had on it but from any sort of connection to people" (ibid.). Critics disparaged Kubrick's attempt to apply his characteristically timeless, distanced, ironic approach to the conflict. Terrence Rafferty in *Sight and Sound* argued that "it's unseemly of him to dissociate himself, in this haughty, aestheticized way, from what America did in South East Asia" (1987: 258). Even Canby (1987), usually effusive in his praise for Kubrick, was qualified in his commendation of *Full Metal Jacket*, noting that "Kubrick keeps to his own ways, paying little attention to his fashions of the moment." Kubrick's status as an auteur had arguably become a hindrance to the critical reception of his films, which, Rafferty said, were now "as daunting and inscrutable as a monolith" (1987: 256). Ultimately, *Full Metal Jacket* said much more about Kubrick's preoccupations than it did about Vietnam (Sarris 1987; Maslin 1987). Engaging with Kubrick's reputation had become inextricably linked with critical judgment of his work.

The reception of *Eyes Wide Shut* is explored in detail by Kolker and Abrams (2019: 133–41). They summarize the film's negative critical response in the United States and UK (the film fared rather better in Latin America, continental Europe, and Japan): it was too long, the acting was unconvincing, the New York sets looked fake, the ideas were weak, and the eagerly anticipated orgy scene was ridiculous. Critics primed by the film's marketing for a sexually explicit erotic drama featuring two of the world's biggest movie stars, Tom Cruise and Nicole Kidman, were treated instead to an "unhurried and deliberate" Kubrickian meditation on marital relationships (Kolker and Abrams 2019: 133). As with his previous three films, *Eyes Wide Shut* collided with a critical establishment's "misplaced expectations about the film's genre and its conventions" (Ransom 2010: 31). Reviews in both the mainstream press and specialist film publications saw it as the work of a man out-of-touch with contemporary society: the orgy sequence was tame compared to what sexual activities were actually available in New York (Whitehouse 1999: 39). As Richard T. Jameson suggested of the dismissive reviews of the film at the time of its release, "[Kubrick] was, after all, an old guy—what could he have hoped to know of sex, orgies, contemporary society, or even New York, the hometown he may not have visited in nearly four decades?" (1999: 27). The critics, Tim Kreider argues, "sounded like a bunch of schoolkids who'd snuck in to see it and slouched out three hours later feeling frustrated, horny, and ripped off" (2000: 41). Later critics would reevaluate *Eyes Wide Shut* as a rich, resonant and complex work, "a genuine work of honest art" (Lee Siegel, quoted by Kolker and Abrams 2019: 138) and a critique of wealth and opulence on the eve of the twenty-first century (Kreider 2000; Nilsen 2011), As Kolker and Abrams demonstrate, "when prurient interest becomes rational inquiry ... Kubrick and *Eyes Wide Shut* triumph over their initial reception" (2019: 141). The transformation of *Eyes Wide Shut*'s reputation is demonstrated by the extensive analysis afforded it on its twentieth anniversary in 2019: the December edition of *Sight and Sound* features the film prominently on the cover. Hannah McGill explores its resonances with contemporary anxieties about sexual abuse, exploitation and power (2019: 24–33). In keeping with the reevaluations of his previous works, recent critical writing about *Eyes Wide Shut* suggests Kubrick was ahead of, rather than behind, the times.

On first viewing by press critics, many of Kubrick's films were judged through a consistent (and simplistic) series of prisms: in relation to their source material, generic categorization, marketing, and Kubrick's reputation as a domineering auteur filmmaker. Indeed, the perception of Kubrick as an auteur suffocated the response to all his films since *2001*. Reviews were often as much about perceptions of Kubrick as a person as they were about the films themselves. While Kubrick did have his champions, ultimately the deeper appreciation of his films has been contingent upon the interventions of academics and cineastes looking again at them, precipitated by their availability on home viewing formats. That Kubrick's films require unusual levels of thoughtfulness and concentration is confirmed by the considerable scholarly and cult interest in them in the years following his death. Higher-definition technologies like DVD and Blu-ray have arguably enabled greater scrutiny of Kubrick's visual style and mise-en-scène than previous home viewing formats, and supported appreciation of his films' complexity and depth. It is however since the opening of the Stanley Kubrick Archive in March 2007 that academic interrogation of Kubrick's work has reached industrial levels, marking the moment at which Kubrick Studies took "a sharply empirical turn away from textual analysis" (Fenwick et al. 2017: 368) and began to understand Kubrick "not as a dictatorial genius but through his interactions with collaborators" (Krämer 2015a: 61). As archival adventures in Kubrick Studies gather momentum, perhaps many other previously uncontested assumptions about the filmmaker and his films will begin to dissolve.

Part Two

Sound and Image

Introduction

Kubrick is celebrated for creating a distinctive visual world, but also important were his innovations in sound and the use of music and his explorations in new technology in lighting, camerawork, and special effects.

Kubrick began his career as a still photographer. In fact, he had been dabbling in photography as a hobby since he was a teenager and his first full-time job after high school was at *Look* magazine. This aspect of Kubrick's career was largely overlooked until Philippe Mather wrote the first book about Kubrick's early work as a photographer for *Look* (Mather 2013). Here, Mather considers his photography as a template for his identity as a visual storyteller. His tenure at *Look* influenced Kubrick's film style—a mixture of classicism, modernism, and self-reflexivity—and also his love of technology and its possibilities. Photojournalistic norms such as sharp focus and composition in depth underpinned the style of his films, on which he was often camera operator.

Kubrick's style is celebrated—and denigrated—for its chilly modernist formal rigor and self-reflexivity, which combines the deep focus and wide angles of Orson Welles and the fluid tracking shots of Max Ophüls. At the same time, his films, as Fredric Jameson (1992) has argued, are postmodernist in their use of pastiche and metageneric reflexivity. Robert Kolker fixes on one aspect of Kubrick's style—his meticulous control of the frame and his obsession with symmetrical geometric patterns within it—and how its formal rigidity loosens toward the end of his career.

Rodney Hill summarizes the many formalist and neoformalist analyses of Kubrick's distinctive style—the use of single point perspective, symmetrical compositions, doublings and dualities, symbolic tropes, slow pacing, and repetitions—through which he overturned or modified classical norms. He shows the close relation between Kubrick's stylistic norms and narrative patternings and emphasizes that his formalism is intended to defamiliarize the world, work against realism, and redefine the parameters of cinema.

Also, against the grain of realism is the acting in Kubrick's films. As Ernesto R. Acevedo-Muñoz shows, acting ranged from mask-like blankness and underplaying— even in star performances by Ryan O'Neal and Tom Cruise—to the scenery-chewing maximalism of Jack Nicholson in *The Shining* or the improvisations of Peter Sellers in *Lolita* and *Dr. Strangelove*. Performances were coaxed during extended rehearsal sessions—the "Crucial Rehearsal Period"—and finessed through multiple takes and retakes. Character actors, however, were often given more limited options and their performances pushed toward mannerism and caricature, in keeping with what James Naremore (2007: 29–41) considers to be Kubrick's overall aesthetic of the grotesque.

The next chapters discuss Kubrick's integration of art and music into his films. As Dijana Metlić puts it, Kubrick was in pursuit of his film as a total work of art in which visuals and music were more important than any verbal or literary aspects. Kubrick was fascinated with and influenced by the history of art. Arguing that each of Kubrick's films is related to a particular movement or epoch of art, Metlić explores the intersection of *Dr. Strangelove* and *A Clockwork Orange* with pop art, with which he shared a satirical blackly comic absurdism; the painterly compositions of *Barry Lyndon*, inspired by Hogarth, Reynolds and Gainsborough; and the influence on his style of Renaissance one-point perspective.

Kubrick was genuinely innovative in his use of music, found, modified, and commissioned, and progressive in his employment of women composers on his later films. Kate McQuiston's chapter brings out the importance of music to Kubrick, who spent considerable time designing his films' soundtracks and took advantage of technological developments in production and creation, such as synthesizers. Equally important was his integration of music into complex soundscapes in which silence and ambient sound were crucial.

Christine Gengaro's chapter on Kubrick's use of found music also emphasizes how much research his soundtracks involved. Although using preexisting music was not a new practice, and in fact went back to silent cinema, Kubrick certainly reestablished it as an aesthetic rather than pragmatic strategy. He used temp tracks as the final soundtrack, partly on the grounds that classical music was likely to be better than any modern versions. Found music was integrated in complex ways, combining preexisting music, new compositions, and found music manipulated and arranged by expert specialists, such as Leonard Rosenman, who won an Oscar for his musical arrangements on *Barry Lyndon*. Music achieves structural and aesthetic centrality in *A Clockwork Orange*, where Wendy Carlos's futuristic transformations of romantic classics create new associations for them, something that was impossible without using music with a significant cultural history. Gengaro argues that the high point was reached in *The Shining*, which came at a time when, pioneered by Walter Murch on *The Conversation* (1974) and *Apocalypse Now* (1979), sound design was becoming established as a key aspect of filmmaking. In *The Shining* the use of electronic manipulation, ambient sound, and the layering of music rather than simply using cues of it is exceptionally complex and subtle thanks to Kubrick's collaboration with musical editor Gordon Stainforth and editor Ray Lovejoy.

8

Kubrick and Photography

Philippe Mather

Prior to Kubrick's death in 1999, monographs surveying his filmography only briefly commented on the filmmaker's background as a photojournalist. The impression these texts give is that Kubrick's five-year tenure at *Look* magazine from 1946 to 1950 represented little more than a prelude to his directorial career as an opportunity to learn how to use a camera (see Ciment 2001; Phillips 1977; Coyle 1980; Walker 2000; Kagan 1989; Nelson 2000; Falsetto 2001). Vincent LoBrutto's biography of Kubrick (1997) changed this impression and was followed by a significant research effort based in Munich, culminating in a book published in 2005, *Drama and Shadows*, edited by art historian Rainer Crone. From a theoretical perspective, this otherwise attractive volume is undermined by its curatorial approach, which consists in presenting the photojournalistic work as art photography, and as an attempt to legitimize Kubrick's youthful efforts. Regrettably, this approach ignores the photographs' original intended use, as well as the essential contribution of the photo-essay form to Kubrick's development as a visual storyteller. There is, for instance, a tendency to read the *Look* photographs retrospectively, as if Kubrick's expressive identity as a visual artist was always already fully formed, a useful strategy if one wishes to minimize the influence of the photomagazine. An exhibition held in Vienna in 2014, *Eyes Wide Open: Stanley Kubrick als Fotograf*, curated by Lisa Ortner-Kreil, adopted a more balanced approach between art photography and photojournalism, although the desire to recontextualize the *Look* images as Kubrickian "art" remains. Most recently, the Museum of the City of New York organized an exhibition in 2018 titled *Through a Different Lens*, curated by Donald Albrecht and Sean Corcoran, that also tries to acknowledge the formative influence of *Look* magazine, while maintaining its focus on "the keen and evocative vision of a burgeoning creative genius" (Albrecht and Corcoran 2018: dust jacket). This has been compiled into an exhibition catalog.

An alternative to the curatorial approach is to engage in a comparative study of Kubrick's style as a visual storyteller in photography and film, by adopting two complementary perspectives. One can begin with the photo-essays and examine the extent to which they appear to anticipate the filmmaker's future narrative and visual tropes. This is a matter of reading the photo-essays through the filter of Kubrick's filmography, which is informative but runs the risk of ignoring significant features that are specific to photojournalism, and do not appear in an obvious way in the films. The other perspective is to analyze the films by identifying photographic moments that may reveal, after the fact, Kubrick's background as a photojournalist, both in visual and thematic terms. In *Stanley Kubrick at Look Magazine: Authorship and Genre in Photojournalism and Film* (Mather 2013), I have attempted to combine these two perspectives by developing a system of correspondences between the two media Kubrick worked in, without ignoring their specific historical and social contexts. Related to this concern for contextual factors is the assumption that it is more informative to consider the extent to which Kubrick responded as a middle-class teenager to his mentorship at *Look* magazine, especially at a most formative period in the lifespan, than assume that he was an exceptional, self-directed individual, primarily motivated by internal goals. Kubrick was hired by *Look* in the spring of 1946 as a teenage apprentice, and the next four years represented his college years. Initially at least, the combined efforts of his photographic colleagues did much to mold the young man into the visual storyteller he became (ibid.: 41). For instance, we can safely say that Kubrick was mentored by the Head of *Look*'s photography department, Arthur Rothstein, a man who was extremely well connected with the photography establishment and owned a collection of film and photography books that were frequently consulted, and even annotated, by a teenage Kubrick (ibid.: 38).

This chapter will argue that Kubrick's identity as a visual storyteller was shaped by the photojournalistic values that he acquired and internalized during his five-year tenure at *Look* magazine. The magazine's dual mission to inform and entertain its readership inspired the photographers to produce or capture visually striking scenes that revealed or illustrated significant aspects of postwar American society. The emphasis on personal journalism, the use of a central figure to both narrate a story about a social institution and to provide visual continuity, allowed Kubrick to develop his skills as a storyteller who happened to use a camera rather than a typewriter. He and his photographic colleagues at *Look* were therefore often producing photo-essays that resembled cinematic storyboards, an impression that was enhanced by the frequent use of serial photographs and the occasional use of zoom-ins. The magazine's didactic goals also encouraged the photographers to adopt a realist aesthetic that valued sharp focus, deep focus, and natural lighting, values that followed Kubrick throughout his film career.

In the opening essay of the *Eyes Wide Open* exhibition catalog, art historian Lisa Ortner-Kreil suggests that the comparison between Kubrick's photographs for the May 15, 1948, *Look* essay, "How the Circus Gets Set," and the constructivist art photography of László Moholy-Nagy may be overstated, at least as an exercise in assigning an evaluative criterion of originality (2014: 10). However, she explains that the comparison remains justified as a means of implying, if not proving, that Kubrick was both familiar with avant-garde photography of the twenties and thirties, and that he unwittingly sought to implement Moholy-Nagy's call to "see the world with entirely different eyes" (1973: 29). Ortner-Kreil goes on to identify ambiguous compositions in the Circus story, and to argue that these represent early instances of Kubrick's characteristic style as a photographic, and later filmic, auteur (2014: 11). Similarly, the catalog for the *Through a Different Lens* exhibition begins with a sober curatorial introduction by Albrecht and Corcoran that does not deny the collaborative nature of Kubrick's tenure at *Look*. Moreover, captions by Kristina Feliciano acknowledge that "graphic design by *Look*'s art director Merle Armitage, which juxtaposed small and full-page images in asymmetrical page layouts, made Kubrick's photographs even more compelling" (Albrecht and Corcoran 2018: 162). These observations are tempered, if not altogether contradicted within the same catalog, by photography critic Luc Sante's essay "Stanley Kubrick: Learning to Look." Sante reverts to the art historical practice of referring to the work of art photographers such as Gary Winogrand, Walker Evans, Robert Capa and Aleksandr Rodchenko, as the most relevant cultural context to help us understand Kubrick as a photographer (2018: 21). Moreover, *Through a Different Lens* includes 280 individual photographs printed mostly in large format, compared with approximately seventy-three magazine spreads mostly in small format, seemingly provided as background information.

Regarding Kubrick's style as a visual storyteller, the principle of ambiguity mentioned by Ortner-Kreil is at best a broad rubric that would require further qualification. Film scholar David Bordwell reminds us that ambiguity is in fact a standard device in the art cinema genre, relativizing its status as an original or unusual quality of artistic self-expression (1979: 60). As for identifying the connection with the avant-garde, it is more likely that Kubrick received this influence secondhand, because he was working alongside a dozen professional photographers with a combined knowledge of the medium's history that cannot be underestimated. For instance, during Kubrick's tenure at *Look*, Arthur Rothstein produced a photo-essay for the magazine's January 31, 1950, issue, on the November 9, 1949, opening of the Eastman House (currently the George Eastman Museum), featuring a now well-known portrait of noted photography historian, and second director of Eastman House, Beaumont Newhall. This intimate knowledge of the history and art of photography was internalized by photojournalists, who then produced artistic compositions not unlike those of Moholy-Nagy, that appeared in the pages of *Look*, not to mention *Life*, *Paris-Match*, *Berliner Illustrierte Zeitung*, *Chūōkōron* (Tokyo), etc. … The magazine context, however, suggests a different aesthetic program or function for these images, that of providing interesting, eye-catching visuals for a general-interest news publication. Moreover, one could speculate that the photomagazines may have done more, through their combined international readership, to change our mediated perception of the world, that is, to see things differently, than any number of art exhibitions and photography books from the postwar era.

It is possible to think of Moholy-Nagy's call to "see things differently" within a mainstream context, in a more pragmatic way, one might say, by comparing the professional aspirations, even the aesthetic ambitions, of magazine photojournalists with those of Hollywood cinematographers. Both photojournalists and cinematographers took pride in working effectively as much appreciated members of a production team, which meant serving the needs of the story they were telling, including moments when a bit of stylistic flourish was required. Providing the occasional eye-catching visual, especially for a photo-essay's opener, could lead to some friendly competition among photographers, and Kubrick was certainly competitive. As cinematographer Stephen H. Burum put it in the 1992 documentary *Visions of Light*:

Every one of the old-time DPs, like Charlie Clarke and Leon Shamroy and Arthur Miller and James Wong Howe, the people I met and knew, they really thought of it as a job and they thought of it as a craft. And when you would talk to them about any kind of art kind of thing, they would never kind of admit to it being art. They'd say, "Oh, yeah, we did this interesting effect in the picture or that interesting effect."

One need not interpret such humility as a confirmation that there was little creativity involved in producing movies or photomagazines. Instead, the concern with craft, professionalism, and contributing "interesting effects" should remind us of the importance of technology, and the fact that all photographers, including art photographers, are gearheads, a characteristic that definitely applies to Kubrick (Morrow 2017). An intimate familiarity with, and enthusiasm for, camera lenses, film stocks, shutter speeds, and film processing is a prerequisite for any kind of formal experimentation. In the case of photojournalism, this means that the photo-essay's rhetorical and narrative functions can very well be enhanced by elements of poetic or abstract form, a standard consequence of the need to provide intermittent "interesting effects," to entertain the readership (Mather 2013: 188).

Kubrick's keen interest in technology is perhaps most revealingly displayed in the traveling Stanley Kubrick exhibition, where an entire room is set aside for Kubrick's cameras and lenses, even though it may be the least visited part of the exhibition. Indeed, most consumers of art or mainstream media are not usually interested in the technology that is used to produce an image or a story, in keeping with the general principle that a reader-friendly text does not draw attention to its mechanisms, to enhance the viewer's emotional identification with the diegesis. In contrast, one of the features of modern art is to highlight the mediated nature of perception, by focusing on the material qualities of the medium itself. Kubrick's own film style has been described as a combination of classicism and modernism, one that reveals an awareness of art movements that was shared with other photojournalists in the stimulating cultural context of New York City, the "World Art Center" in the postwar years (García Mainar 1999: 69). It bears mentioning that reflexivity is by no means limited to the avant-garde, and that many popular genres, in photojournalism and film, point to the apparatus for a variety of reasons. For instance, one might create humor by playfully breaking the fourth wall, enhance the wonder of spectacle with special visual effects, or argue for a more authentic, realistic discourse by including unintentional "mistakes," such as image blurring and lens flares, techniques that Kubrick used in his own photography (Mather 2015: 32–5). A good example of turning an apparent weakness into a strength, and thereby changing conventions of realism, is to highlight the candid, spontaneous qualities of pictures previously considered defective or at least nonnormative. The February 28, 1950, *Look* essay "Mid-Winter Nights in New York," photographed by Phil Harrington and John Vachon, includes a stage-side establishing shot of acrobats performing at the Latin Quarter nightclub in Manhattan. Essentially a backlit shot, this photograph features a very prominent flare in the top left corner, an optical aberration that was usually considered inappropriate in Hollywood movies until the mid-1960s, but one that Kubrick was exposed to and implemented in the photo-essays he worked

Figure 8.1 Postwar photojournalism might include "defects" such as lens flares as a sign of documentary realism, a technique adopted by Kubrick in his film career. © Estate of Phillip A. Harrington.

on in the late forties. Film scholar Mario Falsetto suggests that the significant presence of a blue flare in the 1999 film *Eyes Wide Shut* may have been a calculated compromise on Kubrick's part, but we can safely say that the former photojournalist was perfectly comfortable with the added documentary aura of such an unplanned visual event (2001: 35). Indeed, one can turn to the influence of wartime newsreels and how they modified the accepted norm for realism, by adding the imperfections of handheld camera work, such as blurring and flares, to the values of deep-focus cinematography (Dombrowski 2014: 62).

It is more reasonable to attribute Kubrick's sensitivity to, and knowledge of, the expressive possibilities of photography and film to the influence of his colleagues at *Look*, with whom he spent four and a half years of his young adult life, than European art photographers. Possibly the most adept or inclined to experiment with technology, judging from the published record, was *Look*'s Frank Bauman. He worked successfully in *Look*'s photography studio, producing large-format negatives with multiple exposures and strobe lighting, to capture two or more stages of a person or object in movement. During Kubrick's tenure at *Look*, more than half a dozen photo-essays featuring athletes or dancers in action were shot by Bauman. Most prominent perhaps was the cover for the August 20, 1946, issue of *Look*, featuring an extreme close-up profile of Gene Kelly in the bottom-left section of the image, appearing to look up at a miniature version of himself caught in mid-air, in the top-right corner. While not

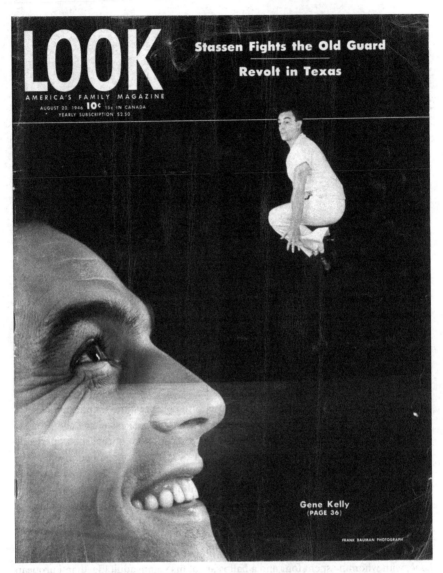

Figure 8.2 Kubrick also learned from *Look* magazine's use of trick photography to create striking visual contrasts. © Estate of Frank M. Bauman.

a constructivist photo-montage, it is a special visual effect that creates a brief sense of ambiguity, from the contrast between the apparent size of the figures, and the play between fantasy and reality due to the impression that Kelly is both Gulliver and a Lilliputian. Kubrick would regularly use a similar trick shot, in a single exposure, by combining deep focus and negative space around the figures, thereby eliminating depth cues and suggesting the illusion of giants standing next to dwarfs (Mather 2013: 210).

Since *Look* was a news magazine, the wonders of science were the most common justification for presenting images that used high-speed flash technology, rather than an idiosyncratic artistic vision. For the April 29, 1947, issue of *Look*, Frank Bauman produced color photographs of dancers from the musical revue "Call Me Mister," in collaboration with electrical engineer Harold E. Edgerton from the Massachusetts Institute of Technology. Later nicknamed "Papa Flash" for his pioneering work on the stroboscope, Edgerton provided Bauman with an opportunity to test "a battery of four superspeed flash units which release an awesome 24,000,000-candle-power blast of light in 1/1000th second." The novelty was to apply this technology to color film, which had always required more illumination than black and white stock. Similarly, the July 19, 1949, issue of *Look* included an essay shot by Bauman that set out to confirm photographically that a baseball pitcher's curveball does indeed follow a curve. The pictures were taken at night in a Navy dirigible hangar, from two positions: 179 feet directly above the pitcher, and behind the catcher's plate. Nine high-speed lights were set up parallel to the path taken by the pitched ball, and fired "in split-second succession, each at 1/8000th of a second," to expose a single negative with nine sharp impressions of the ball's trajectory. To underscore this experiment as a scientific marvel, *Look* was able to quote the head of Fordham University's Physics Department, Father Joseph Lynch, S.J., who applauded the magazine for its "outstanding pioneer work in the field of photography and optics" (Lynch was a seismologist). Stylistically, Kubrick indirectly revealed his acute awareness of Bauman's strobe photography during the filming of *2001: A Space Odyssey*, when he asked cinematographer John Alcott to employ strobe lights for the special effects footage involving miniatures, an experiment that only underscored the need for blurring on motion picture film, in contrast with still photography (Mather 2013: 180). The aesthetic qualities of such strobe-flash work would have appealed to photojournalists who normally endeavored to produce images in sharp focus, one of the realist ideals of the time. This concern for sharpness was partly a result of trying to compensate for the era's printing technology, which softened the images slightly by the time they appeared on magazine paper.

Look was very much aware of the visual novelty of these photographs, not simply their scientific merits. For instance, in its June 8, 1948, issue, *Look* published another Bauman photo-essay featuring multiple exposure shots of female dancers in action that included the following visual challenge to the reader: "How many girls do you see?" Yet another creative use of the multiple exposure technique was Bauman's photograph of a child with cerebral palsy, learning to overcome her illness. The caption from this November 12, 1946, story explains that "special training" helps 10-year-old Anna to walk by herself, illustrated by a triple-exposure image of the young girl courageously taking a few steps. Thematically, Kubrick would take a similar shot for the October 12, 1948, essay "Wally Ward Conquers Polio," imitating Bauman's use of the low angle to enhance the reader's willingness to empathize with children, which he later used for Danny Torrance in *The Shining*.

Rather than think of Kubrick as an entirely self-directed person who instinctively leaned toward the use of cinematic techniques, one would do well to consider the impact of motion pictures on the way photomagazines were designed and edited.

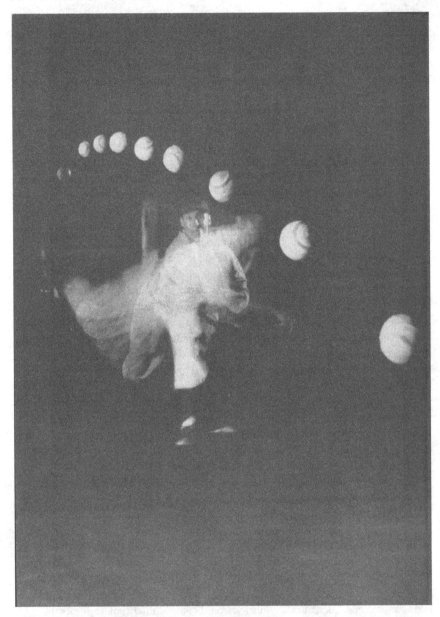

Figure 8.3 Kubrick experimented with strobe lights during the filming of *2001: A Space Odyssey*, perhaps recalling his former colleague Frank Bauman's photograph of a curveball, seemingly floating in space. © Estate of Frank M. Bauman.

When Luc Sante suggests that "Kubrick was already beginning to think in cinematic terms, that his shooting ratios were so large because he was more interested in capturing continuity of action than any single image crowded with meaning," there is no mention of the fact that picture continuities were one of the basic techniques taught in photojournalism textbooks, or that large shooting ratios was the standard practice among photojournalists (2018: 18). Visually, the most obvious attempt to capture the illusion of movement on the printed page may be the photographic series, which was more common than strobe photography, and would either depict athletes or dancers in motion, or a personality going through different facial expressions, shot from the same vantage point. During Kubrick's years at *Look*, there were numerous examples of the photographic series, including colleague Earl Theisen's portrait of filmmaker Walt Disney, in the April 17, 1945, issue of *Look*. The seven-picture series is printed as two strips, with a caption explaining that Disney is playing Donald Duck, and that each frame captures a stage in the unfolding action. Disney performs in front of the animated cartoon storyboard, reflexively underscoring the idea of a cinematic long take of a single event, broken down into discrete poses. Kubrick may well have seen this series prior to photographing his English teacher Aaron Traister, performing Hamlet in class (April 2, 1946, *Look* issue). As a drummer in high school, Kubrick may also have appreciated the March 5, 1946, story titled "Hot Drummers," including an ad-free double-page spread with four equal strips of eight photographs by his colleagues Hy Peskin, Frank Bauman and Earl Theisen, featuring the expressive playing of famous Jazz musicians Ray Bauduc, Sid Catlett, Buddy Rich and Gene Krupa. Yet another series, by *Look* Photography Department Head and mentor Arthur Rothstein, was the portrait of British film distribution mogul J. Arthur Rank in the September 2, 1947, issue of the magazine, that further highlights the merits of taking multiple shots from the same angle, by focusing on the character's expressions rather than distract the reader with varied backgrounds.

Related to the photo-series was the use of multiple shots of the same subject that either involved gradually tighter framings, akin to a zoom-in, and/or that withheld the last frame until the reader turned the page, to reveal a surprise ending resembling a filmic shock cut. Kubrick produced a staged essay titled "A Short in a Movie Balcony," that was edited as a "hidden reveal" piece in *Look*'s April 16, 1946, issue. The essay begins with three photographs printed vertically on page 52, showing Kubrick's high school photography club fellow member Bernard Cooperman getting closer to a female classmate in a movie theater. The third caption states "He slyly moves closer," leaving us in suspense. Below the caption, in smaller print, we are invited to turn to page 54 for the rest of the picture sequence. The final photograph, printed full-page, captures the young woman slapping Cooperman across the face, registering his shock and pain. The January 20, 1948, issue of *Look* also includes an example of the hidden reveal technique, courtesy of Earl Theisen's two-page staged essay "Masher gets a tumble." Three strips of three equal-sized photographs, numbered one through nine, depict Hollywood actor Louise Currie executing a rehearsed judo move on a stuntman for a scene in the 1947 film noir *Second Chance*. To see an additional two frames revealing the spectacular conclusion of the stunt, the reader is invited to "turn to page 55," where a still shot of the stuntman in mid-air is printed full-page. This sequence by Theisen may have been produced with a machine-gun camera, a 35-mm film camera modified with a fast shutter for freeze-frame action pictures (Mather 2013: 178–9). The same issue features Kubrick's story "Bubble-Gum Contest," including four photographs of a young boy demonstrating his gum-blowing skills, printed as a zoom-in. *Look*'s art department chose to maintain the same image size on the printed page, but to frame them gradually closer to the boy's face, with a concluding image of a burst bubble. The contact sheets confirm that this series was not photographed as a zoom-in (ibid.: 213). A previous example of the zoom-in appeared in the May 14, 1946, issue of *Look*, as a two-page spread with six identically framed photographs of a Hollywood screen test involving a male actor about to kiss Miss Ohio State Jean Peters, in close-up. The zoom-in effect was created by printing the photos in increasingly larger sizes, ranging from 4 × 3 to 10 × 6 inches.

In addition to the influence of Kubrick's *Look* colleagues and of Hollywood on photography in general, we can turn to what film scholar Marc Vernet has termed the "genre-effect." This refers to the powerful impact of intertextuality in determining the stylistic features of what an interpretive community will deem to be realistic or verisimilar for particular types of stories. As Vernet et al. explain,

> the plausible, therefore, must be understood as a form, which is to say an organization, of the standardized content of a string of texts ... If, therefore, the plausible is an effect of the corpus, it will accordingly be more solid within a long series of films that are closely related in their expression and their content, as is the case within a genre. (1992: 117)

To be clear, examining Kubrick's unedited contact sheets after the fact and recontextualized by an expectation that this was the work of a future film artist, paints a significantly different picture than what can be gained from situating the photographer's published photo-essays in the context of approximately 143 issues of *Look* magazine, spanning the five and a half years during which his work appeared in print. The latter approach reveals the extent to which the conventions of photojournalism were implemented by all members of *Look*'s photographic staff, making their work broadly interchangeable, despite minor variations according to personal style. Whether one considers essays about educational or medical institutions, department stores or street scenes, portraits of celebrities or eccentric characters, the structure and content of such essays in the 1945–50 period is remarkably similar within each genre, even when different writers and photographers were involved.

For example, a year prior to *Look* publishing Kubrick's September 2, 1947, photo-essay "The 5 and 10," about a discount department store, Frank Bauman had photographed an essay on New York's Macy's department store for the August 6, 1946, issue. Both essays reveal a similar layout, as they begin and end with a large, attention-grabbing picture that first draws the reader in, and then invites her to linger at the conclusion. The essays also feature a strip of serial photographs at the top of the second spread: a young girl reading a comic book while eating a stick of licorice in "The 5 and 10," and a series subtitled "A man and wife buy a dress," in Bauman's "Shopping at Macy's." The captions comment on the action like a voice-over narration. The rest of the photographs are mostly arranged in a regular grid pattern like a photo album, showing store patrons examining products in various departments. Similarly, Kubrick's first college story on Columbia University, published on May 11, 1948, was preceded by Frank Bauman's profile of the University of Notre Dame, that appeared in the November 26, 1946, issue of *Look*. While the stories highlight differences between the two institutions, namely Columbia's secular and scientific leanings and Notre Dame's focus on Catholicism and athletics, they use similar strategies to identify dominant themes. Both essays open with a full-page portrait of the university presidents (Dwight Eisenhower and Father John Cavanaugh), include high-angle long shots of the main dining rooms, and refer to long-standing college traditions. One interesting aspect of the college story as a genre, which also appears in photo-essays on the Universities of California, Minnesota, Harvard, and Yale by several of Kubrick's colleagues in the late 1940s, is an apparent effort to combine full shots and extreme long shots of students engaged in various activities on campus. This alternation can create an odd contrast that appears to undermine the *Look* magazine ideals of "personal journalism," normally involving stories told from an individual's perspective that readers can relate to. Specifically, the large establishing shots seem to promote a certain "monumentalism," or an antihumanist focus on the largest facilities or structures on campus. Kubrick's Columbia essay includes a photograph of the nuclear physics research center's cyclotron, a massive structure that dwarfs the three men standing in front of it. This focus sometimes involved using stark, oppressive, symmetrical framings, such as Bauman's full-page color photograph of Notre Dame's Sacred Heart Church. This somewhat paradoxical contrast likely impressed Kubrick, who went on to use symmetrical compositions in his films to express a fatalistic sense of entrapment, and a corresponding institutional power and control.

Focusing on the intermedial links between the photo-essay and narrative fiction film forms, as well as the dominant aesthetic norms in these two media in the immediate postwar years, this chapter has argued that our current understanding of the Kubrickian "voice" is the result of a process that integrates a complex series of cultural and historical factors. Specifically, the following related arguments have been made: The practice of featuring slightly unusual or striking images in *Look* photo-essays need not be attributed, in the case of Stanley Kubrick's work, to the conventions of art photography, but rather to a photomagazine's need to inform and entertain its readership, resulting in a creative balance between candid and staged representations. The photo-essay's nature as a transitional form between still photography and film provided a young Kubrick with skills that could later be applied to the cinema, such as the narrative dimensions of *Look*'s "personal journalism." Photojournalism's formal and stylistic norms included a realistic obsession with sharp focus and composition in depth, as well as the use of photo-series and the large picture, which implies a longer viewing time, and can be equated with Kubrick's later predilection for long takes.

A report on recent research conducted at the Kubrick Archive reveals that it is aligned with an empirical brand of film history that seeks to analyze "how film style and aesthetics [are] influenced, even determined, by economic, industrial and technological factors," rather than by narrowly personal and artistic motivations (Fenwick et al. 2017b: 368). While the report also claims that this research "has modified—but not undermined—the established view of Kubrick as a genuinely powerful *auteur*," one need not refrain from confronting as many of auteurism's blind spots as possible, given the considerable scientific gains that are likely to ensue. Promoting the myth or ideology of the single author working from Mount Olympus, like engaging in the textual analysis of single photographs outside the photomagazine context, does little to enhance our understanding of actual, widespread and therefore socially relevant semiotic processes, as well as the significant impact of a great many production contexts that cannot be attributed to an author's conscious intentions. Unfortunately, an enduring, institutionalized investment in the humanist values of romantic aesthetics has kept many art historians committed to methodological individualism as their approach to doing film history (Bordwell 2008). The individualistic values associated with the single, self-expressive artist that originate from the fine arts establishment, translate into potential economic value in mainstream culture, as Timothy Corrigan has shown in his essay "The Commerce of Auteurism" (2002). This has further encouraged art historians to serve in a promotional capacity as curators of artistic work, rather than as scholars and social scientists. While the actual motives for writing about Kubrick's work cannot be limited to either art as commerce, or the disinterested pursuit of knowledge, these options are indicative of a somewhat polarized system, all the same. Recent Kubrickian scholarship reminds us that the field has been dominated by a tendency to favor the romantic, auteurist model, and suggests that it may remain that way for a very long time.

9

Kubrick and Framing

Robert P. Kolker

The frame, the defining element of the shot, is an irreducible element of filmmaking; it allows the image to exist—whether wide screen, standard ratio, whether viewed in a theater or on a smart phone. The frame creates the image. Gilles Deleuze writes:

> the frame has always been geometrical or physical, depending on whether it constitutes the closed system in relation to chosen coordinates or in relation to selected variables. The frame is therefore sometimes conceived of as a spatial composition of parallels and diagonals, the constitution of a receptacle such that the blocs [*masses*] and the lines of the image which come to occupy it will find an equilibrium and their movements will find an invariant ... The frame is also geometric or physical in another way—in relation to the parts of the system that it both separates and brings together. In the first case, the frame is inseparable from rigid geometric distinctions. (2014: 14–15)

Stanley Kubrick carefully calculated time and space, shot and edit in each of his films in order to achieve an imbalance, throw rhythm off or slow it down to a barely tolerable pace. And while he spoke of editing as the final job of shaping a film, it was the form and content of the frame that determines the mood and propulsion (or lack of same) in any given film. If he wanted to throw rhythm off through his editing, he prepared for it in the construction of the "geometric distinctions" within the frame itself. Kubrick's fondness, indeed, obsession with the geometry of symmetrical compositions can be seen from the beginning of his career, and it reveals a cinematic imagination dedicated to creating a "system" of those very "geometric distinctions."

Querying this system, I want not only to reveal the geometric pattern of Kubrick's films, but attempt to understand what he is getting at in its creation. I want also to at least expose the contradiction between Kubrick's apparent working methods and the final result—the film itself. In the various "makings of" and anecdotes concerning his preparations for shooting a scene, there seems to be an emphasis on spontaneity or even improvisation. It has been allowed that he did not make much use of storyboards, though he was fond of having models made of the sets that he would then photograph to get an idea of the setup he wanted to make. (There are also the sketches that Chris Baker made for *A.I.*, the film Kubrick never made, and *Eyes Wide Shut*, for a dream sequence that was not filmed.) The results are hardly improvised, but carefully made down to the last detail: perfectly framed, consciously composed.

I want to start with a freeze frame. Near the end of *Barry Lyndon*, Barry, having had a leg amputated after being shot in a duel by his stepson, hobbles on crutches toward a coach that will take him into exile. The narrator tells us that he went abroad, took up his profession of gambling, "without his former success." Otherwise, "his life there, we have not the means of following accurately." The narrator has been a close and contentious companion of Barry's, following and predicting his deeds, warning us of his bad behavior and ignominious end. But, at this point, the narrator admits he has lost touch: "we have not the means of following [his future life] accurately." With nothing more to say or see, Kubrick does something extraordinary. As Barry enters the coach, Kubrick freezes the frame, making Barry stuck in time. The freeze frame, though it can be found as far back as 1942 in the credit sequence of Preston Sturges's *The Palm Beach Story*, didn't become a popular technique until François Truffaut used it at the end of his 1959 film, *The Four Hundred Blows*. Like the zoom lens, it had become something of a cliché and was already falling out of use by 1975, the year of *Barry Lyndon*. The zoom lens is an integral part of the compositional strategy of the film, its stately rhythms diminishing the characters in their environment, emphasizing their smallness and isolation. The freeze frame comes as a surprise, almost a shock, a commonplace (at the time) cinematic trick suddenly appearing in the midst of a carefully controlled, painterly mise-en-scène. It struck me, at first sight, as something of a letdown, a fall to cliché. Only on later reflection did I realize what Kubrick had in mind and feel its full emotional impact.

Kubrick was aware that creating the past by means of cinema meant that the past must be a cinematic invention. The idea of a "costume drama" is absurd on the face of it, if the aim of the drama is to be a "realistic" representation of the costumed past. The past is not only past, it is visually unavailable to us outside of literary or painterly description. Kubrick chooses both by means of the elegant eighteenth-century language of his narrator, the compositions that imitate paintings—including available candlelight for indoor scenes—and the zoom. At the moment of the freeze frame, the paintings that move—the moving images based on paintings—stop moving. At that moment, a period is put to the words of the narrator and the motion of the film's central character. As far as the film is concerned, Barry is finished, frozen in narrative time.

Barry Lyndon is something of a departure from Kubrick's usual image making. There is a delicacy and stateliness not seen again until *Eyes Wide Shut*. This is due, of course, to the painterly compositions that makeup the film and the very slow pace of movement and event. But it is also due to the sense of emergence, the coming into being of a past time. Like the dark glow of the candlelit sequences where the characters emerge, slightly blurry, from the background. There are also somewhat fewer of the rigorously symmetrical compositions that mark Kubrick's films from the beginning (for an in-depth examination of how Kubrick used paintings in *Barry Lyndon*, see Ljujić 2015).

Jose Atunas (2012) points to a photograph that Kubrick took for *Look* magazine in 1949, looking down at the nighttime traffic on State Street in Chicago. The symmetry of the shot is extreme, a flow of lights moving toward an inexorable vanishing point. In the films, this composition turns up several times in Kubrick's second feature, *Killer's Kiss*, a film still influenced by his experiences as a still photographer. There is a shot like the Chicago image, looking down Broadway to Times Square. And later, Kubrick trains his camera down a staircase from Rapallo's dance hall as Gloria walks up. The space is held tightly between the two walls of the staircase. A sign, "Watch Your Step," hangs over head. Later, the composition returns, this time framing a state of deadly confusion. Rapallo has sent his men to kill Davey, the boxer who has stolen Gloria's affections. In the shot, two men descend the steps while, at the bottom, outside, Gloria stands next to Davey's manager, each framed side by side through the panes of glass of the doorway. Here are multiple symmetrical doublings: the walls and banisters of the staircase; the two men descending the steps; the double doors at the foot of the steps leading to the street, framing the two figures outside.

There is Davey's nightmare, a brief shot in negative of the camera fleeing backward through a city street—the street, it will turn out, where later Davey and Rapallo will have their climactic fight with a manikin factory. This is not the first of Kubrick's dynamic tracking shots. That occurs at the end of his short documentary, *Flying Padre*, about a priest in the Southwest, who travels to his parishioners by plane. We see the priest standing by his plane, right hand on his hip, staring at the camera, which suddenly pulls back in a long, rapid tracking shot, leaving him far in distance as "The End" is superimposed over the scene. This shot seems unmotivated by anything other than Kubrick's desire to end a somewhat pedestrian and static documentary with a flourish, or perhaps a movement that echoes the priest's aviator peregrinations.

There is much camera movement in *The Killing*, particularly the lateral tracks across Johnny Clay's apartment early in the film, and movement tracking Maurice across the betting hall at the racetrack. But there is one eye-catching tracking shot that moves across the length of the LA bus station, as Johnny puts his gear in a locker. The tracking shots in *Paths of Glory* are more numerous, more dramatic and specifically motivated. As Col. Dax moves through the trenches, soldiers on either side, the camera tracks his point of view alternating with a view directly at him as he moves past his desperate men. The result is a dynamic of purposeful despair. The troops will soon face an impossible attack and three of them will face a firing squad as a result. Dax is the one figure of moral restraint among the command structure in the film, and his movement, his dogged determination, is shared by, indeed communicated by, the movement of the camera, which has the effect of rendering the frame invisible. Not so with the court martial sequence, in which rigidly composed compositions played against a floor that looks like a chessboard represent the inescapable containment of the characters.

It is possible to go through every Kubrick film up to *Eyes Wide Shut*, including *Spartacus*, and with the possible exception of *Lolita*, to discover some iteration of the symmetrical composition and tracking shot. One need only recall Poole's jog around the Discovery's central hall to the mournful strains of Khachaturian in *2001: A Space Odyssey*. Their severity, sometimes their lyricism, their effect of startling our perception, the doubling of elements within the image, the very obsessiveness of their reoccurrence marks not only a signature style, but an attempt to build a visual world that is artificial, painterly but cinema bound, unique to what film can do when the painterly is put into motion.

When the painterly impulse is combined with forced perspective, cinematic realism is brought into question. If we think back again to the tracking shots in *Paths of Glory* and the startling deep focus compositions of the courts martial sequence, we can recognize that realism is simply not what is at stake, but rather a concerted effort to get the viewer's attention, to destabilize it with an excess of stability. Art historian Rodolf Arnheim writes,

> The strong connection uniting the corresponding parts of a symmetrical pattern comes about because these parts are identical in shape but opposite in spatial orientation. Through their opposition they add up to a highly unified whole. The coherence of such a whole is particularly strong when it is obtained by the mirroring of units which are irregular and unstable in themselves. (1969: 63)

Kubrick, however, manages to create instability by means of the "mirroring units." He makes the symmetrical strange; uncanny.

Kubrick is uninterested in comforting the viewer's gaze. He wants to provoke it by rupturing inviting spaces through the creation of elaborate tracking shots and by composing startling symmetrical images, regarded straight on, forcing the viewer to confront the image rather than being comforted by them (Peucker 2001: 663–74). He calls into question the homilies about cinematic realism, stating, rather mildly, "real is good, interesting is better" (quoted in Modine 2005). "Interesting" for Kubrick consists of images that not only call attention to themselves—he regularly breaks the rules about never placing the camera at a 90-degree angle to the set and instead allows the camera to be placed directly in front of the action—but eloquently convey the inevitable entrapment of his characters. Inevitability is expressed in the symmetry of the images themselves. In an earlier essay, I wrote that

> Kubrick's symmetry—exaggerated by his use of a wide-angle lens that tends to bend the sides of the image outward—tends to confound center and periphery in a way that *unbalances* the composition. Rather than balance, these compositions suggest a collapse; they signify not order but a fall into the abyss that awaits all his characters; a stasis in which the uncanny perfection of the image promises its ultimate undoing, along with the characters caught within it. (Kolker 2010: 65)

It is precisely those perfectly symmetrical images that remain in the memory. They communicate the collapse and fall of the characters they contain, but they themselves remain in perpetuity—as filmic images and in the afterimage in our imaginations.

Consider one of the most famous images in the canon: the bleeding elevators of *The Shining*. They appear twice in the film as apparitions—visions of Danny Torrance of the bloodshed to come. Twice seen and thrice removed, as images on film, as images in Danny's mind, as images we retain from the film. The represent a cataclysm, as obdurate and menacing as the monoliths in *2001*. Photographed straight on, flanked by two identical armchairs that float in a cascade of blood, the symmetry of the elevator composition communicates a blank terror, unexplained and inexplicable. As a horror film, *The Shining* trades in the uncanny, the seen and seen again, the familiar rendered frightening, *unheimlich*. This accounts for the impossible spaces that some overeager observers of the film have noticed, corridors leading nowhere, mismatched shots, mirror images, a controlled chaos of the perfectly aligned (see Asher's *Room 237*).

What are we *seeing* in *The Shining* and from whose perspective? There are point-of-view shots: Danny's mad cycling around the hallways; Jack's gaze at the model of the maze. The bleeding elevator is one of Danny's visions. The drift of the camera behind Jack as he emerges to find Wendy reading his crazed manuscript is surely from the point of view of the hotel itself. Is the whole film a vision, a dream? Every shot shifts point of view but remains constant in its compositional strategy: with few exceptions, the shots are brightly lit—the old dark house is devoid of the shadows we come to expect of a horror film—with few exceptions, the compositions are severely symmetrical as if they were a series of tableaux. These are blocks of images, ready to explode with Jack's pent-up rage or collapse upon the hotel's malevolent spirit. They are mirror images, which are another source of the symmetrical compositions. Some appear literal: Jack is seen in reflection when he beckons Danny to come to him. He sees the beautiful lady turn into an old crone in his arms in the bathroom mirror of room 237—which, given the intercuts of Danny, are the child's vision. When Grady confronts Jack in the bathroom, a symmetrical composition of blood red fixtures on either side of them, Jack looks not at Grady, but at the mirror. The mirror image of the ghostly twins that Danny sees at the end of the hall is an excruciating symmetrical shot. Not only do the walls on either side bracket the frame, but the uncanny twins, fashioned in a reverse homage to a photograph by Diane Arbus. The smiling twin in Arbus's photo is on the right, in *The Shining* she is on the left, the result is a mirror image of an image unseen but remembered. (In a 1947 photograph for *Look* magazine, Kubrick makes an image of twin African American women in a New York subway, foreshadowing the twins in *The Shining*.)

The Shining is a film about reoccurrence, an eternal return, and this makes everything from the repetitive sentences in Jack's manuscript to the symmetry of the shot compositions a reminder of the uncanny repetition of events. *A Clockwork Orange* is less a circular narrative than it is a hyperbola, a bell-shaped curve, as Alex ascends and descends the arc of his violence. The film begins with a starkly symmetrical composition in the Korova Milk Bar. Starting with a tight closeup of Alex, curiously asymmetrical with his right eye decked out with false eyelashes, the camera tracks backward, revealing Alex's Droogs sitting next to him, one on the right, two on the left. Three of them hold glasses of moloko plus, one has his feet resting on an erotic statue on the right, the statue's legs intertwined with its mirror image on the left, a glass of moloko resting on its abdomen. The framing further expands as the camera continues its track, revealing the moloko dispensing statues on pedestals, facing each other on either side of room, reclining nude statues are arraigned as tables also on either side, interspersed with various patrons, sitting still and stoned. The track ends as two bouncers appear opposite each other on each side of the frame.

This opening gambit has its own mirror images in other films: the manikin factory at the end of *Killer's Kiss* and, later, the costume shop in *Eyes Wide Shut*. In all instances, the animate and inanimate vie for attention, human and inhuman are held in rigid tableaux. To be sure, much of the first part of *A Clockwork Orange* is dynamic in its movement with the balletic fight in the derelict casino and, especially, Alex's walk through the symmetrical corridor of record boutique in a tracking shot reminiscent of Dax's walk through the trenches in *Paths of Glory*. The difference, though, is marked: unlike Dax, Alex's is a march of triumph to the synthesized music of Beethoven's Ninth Symphony. But the dynamic is a ruse. Alex, like so many Kubrick characters, is caught, here in the cycle of his own brutality, his come down at the hands of his droogs and the police, his imprisonment, the Ludovico treatment, and his resurrection under the control of the State. Were we to visualize this, it would appear as a parabola within a box. The dynamics of *The Shining*, on the other hand, would appear as a constrained circle.

Kubrick wants to hold the frame and his characters within that frame. He wants the viewer to be held *by* the frame and to move in the opposite direction from the characters. As witnesses to their downfall, we are freed of them. Our world, after all, is not destroyed as it is in *Dr. Strangelove*, nor have we quite reached the state of the posthuman as in *2001*, though artificial intelligence is moving on apace. But we are allowed to peer into the box, into the rigidity of the vanishing point without ourselves vanishing.

Kubrick begins to loosen the frame in the later films. Gunnery Sgt. Hartman's initial walk through the barrack's in *Full Metal Jacket* is executed with the familiar backward track of the camera. But the symmetry of the composition is incomplete as the recruits are standing by their bunks only on the left side of the frame. The camera circles around with Hartman to the other side of the barracks, where he continues his walk and rant until, on the original side, Pvt. Joker does his John Wayne imitation, at which point Kubrick makes a cut as Hartman hurries over to Joker and the perfect symmetry of recruits and bunks, on both sides of the frame becomes visible.

There are other rigid framings in the first part of the film: the recruits doing their exercises against the rising sun; the recruits lying in their bunks praising their rifles, among others. But the rigidity of the frame breaks down somewhat in the second part of the film. The grueling order of training, climaxing with Pyle's murder/suicide, gives way to a variation of the lost patrol genre of the war film in the second part, befitting the move from the training to kill of the first part to the killing chaos of the second. Here is some of the most conventional framing in the entire Kubrick canon. Loosely composed tracking shots; handheld battle sequences. Symmetry doesn't disappear entirely. There is a shot of soldiers and trucks moving toward the camera while Vietnamese walk in the opposite direction, each in a straight line, the camera poised between them over a canal that separates the two groups. There are some 180-degree cuts (moving the camera to the opposite side of an imaginary line drawn across the frame) and framings through openings, especially during the sniper sequence. But this part of *Full Metal Jacket* is constructed by means of blocks of sequences: the opening section with the prostitute; the *Stars and Stripes* office; the Tet attack; the helicopter ride; the reuniting of Joker and Cowboy; the sniper and Joker's killing her. Kubrick spoke about the phenomenon of "non-submersible units," sequences that carry the major weight of a film's narrative (see Kolker and Abrams 2019). Whatever is nonsubmersible being narrative tissue, transitional material that leads to the next unit.

The symmetrical shot of the troops marching one way while the Vietnamese move in the other is an example of a transitional scene, but these are rare in the second part of *Full Metal Jacket*. It is as if Kubrick were putting together loosely framed narrative blocks—nonsubmersible units—in which the internal action takes prominence over the rigidity of composition found in the earlier films. Content is here dictating form, opposite the means of visualization in the earlier films. This is an important shift. Kubrick is a formalist, who believes in the power of the carefully composed image to create the appropriate mood and response in the viewer. Emerging from that belief is a recognizable style, which, when altered, calls attention both to the style itself and to its unexpected change. The second part of *Full Metal Jacket* shows such a change, not necessarily for the better (one might not regret the editing out of the sequence of the soldiers addressing the camera with their views of the war), but indicative of the changes going on during Kubrick's late period.

Changes that are most obvious in his final film, *Eyes Wide Shut*. The first shot of the film—preceding the title—almost seems like the Kubrick of old: we see Alice from behind in a small room, framed by two pillars on each side, casually dropping her dress. This is one of the "erotic glimpses" that Kubrick filmed of Nicole Kidman in provocative poses, using only this one in the film (see Kolker and Abrams 2019). At first glance, the image appears to be typically Kubrickian in the way it symmetrically frames the figure between the columns. But it is not typical: Kubrick, as noted, all but institutionalized placing the camera directly in front of the action rather than at an angle. Traditional Hollywood cinematic rules forbade such a composition, fearing it would call attention to the two-dimensional aspect of the image. Placing the camera at an off angle, the reasoning went, provided some illusion of depth. Like the 180-degree rule, which Kubrick broke so consistently that it, too, is now part of the grammar of Hollywood filmmaking. But that opening "erotic glimpse" of Alice is off a direct angle, canted just slightly toward the left side of the composition.

There are straight-on compositions in the film—Bill arm-in-arm with the two seductive women at Ziegler's party, for example; or the first visit to the costume shop where Bill and Milich are tracked as they walk forward flanked by the costumed manikins on either side (the shot has echoes back to *Killer's Kiss* and *A Clockwork Orange*). But for the most part, the framing is looser and less constrained than in the previous films. The compositional strategies depend on lighting and color, with characters moving about within the composition of the shot, often tracked by the camera, though the tracks tend not to call attention to themselves. There is less dynamism, less display of visual excess that marks the previous films. Even the orgy— a major display of excess—is done with measured quietness and a gently moving camera. In short, there are no startling, obsessively symmetrical images in *Eyes Wide Shut*. Here, Kubrick is more interested in exploring what goes in within the frame than with the ways the frame determines what goes on with in it. There is a different intensity, quieter, more reluctant to startle, more inviting to the viewer to move within the images rather than be pushed back by them to a state of awe.

The billiards sequence is a good example. Coming near the end of the film, Ziegler's cautionary speech to Bill sums up what Ziegler thinks has happened—or more accurately, what he wants Bill to believe has happened. The events of the orgy, Bill's humiliation and his redemption by Mandy the prostitute, was a fake, put on for Bill's benefit to teach him not to meddle in the affairs of the superrich. Here is the father putting his son in his place; the director telling his actor to listen to him. And here is the director handling this sequence with the same measured grace as the rest of the film, delicately, even unobtrusively framed.

Ziegler's billiards room is luxuriously furnished and exquisitely lit. The outside world filtering in through the windows is the same blue that figures predominantly throughout the film. There is a model of a sailing ship on a table. Lamps are placed strategically around the room and four, green-shaded lights illuminate the blood red pool table, which becomes the fulcrum for the spatial construction of the sequence, which begins innocently enough. Ziegler welcomes Bill, offers him a scotch, asks if he'd like to join him "knocking a few balls around." It will be Bill's balls that will get knocked around. Ziegler and Bill are placed at opposite ends of the table. The frame is wide and accommodating. Ziegler plays with the cue ball as he begins his "lesson" of what occurred the night of the orgy. The camera swings to the left, behind Bill's back, as Ziegler talks. Kubrick cuts to one-shots of each. Bill thinks he's been called to offer Ziegler medical advice. "Actually, it concerns you," Ziegler says. And the dance commences. Bill says relatively little through the remainder of the sequence; closeups of him reveal a face stricken ever more with confusion and guilt, his hands over his face, bent over as Ziegler reveals more and more about his knowledge of Bill's comings and goings during and after the orgy.

The one-shots of the two change when Ziegler tells Bill he doesn't know what kind of trouble he was in. The camera moves with Ziegler as he goes over to Bill's side of the table, casually sitting on it as Bill is all but rigid on the hard right of the frame. Kubrick cuts to a wide shot. Ziegler now has all the power. He casually moves about the room as Bill remains rigid, leaning on the table. The camera follows Ziegler as he crosses the frame and takes a seat, continuing his story about the fakery of the night before. There is a brief closeup of Bill and then a cut to a wide, almost deep focus shot of Bill in the close right foreground and Ziegler in his chair in the left rear of the frame. After a shot of Ziegler, the camera pulls further back, cutting to Bill as he also takes a seat, shaken by the outpouring of information coming from Ziegler, who is given his own shot, widely framed, as he tells Bill that everything that happened was staged for his benefit. Ziegler comes to stand over Bill, the shot wide and low, from Bill's position, demonstrating for us the casual power he has over the poor Doctor.

Bill has his one moment of assertiveness as he gets up from his seat, attempting to press Ziegler with the fact of the dead prostitute. He is given his own shot, shaking his hand, "Do you mind telling me what kind of fucking charade ends with somebody turning up dead?" Ziegler calls him out. After some closeups of the two, Kubrick cuts to a new setup, the characters center right of the frame, the camera canted slightly and moving to the left, the pool table prominent. There are two more closeups and then a cut to an even wider shot, framing the characters with Ziegler by the pool table, Bill, alone, hangdog, off center. The camera subtly moves in as Ziegler comes to Bill and puts his hands on his shoulders, mouthing platitudes: "Somebody died. It happens all the time. But life goes on. It always does. Until it doesn't." He cackles: "But you know that, don't you?" End of sequence.

This sequence, like so much of *Eyes Wide Shut*, is choreographed within the frame, here as an intricate dance between a dominant and submissive personality. Despite the inherent cruelty of this and other sequences, there is an intimacy in the film, as a whole, which is only found in certain passages of *Barry Lyndon*, making it a series of carefully composed images of frustrated domesticity and unrealizable desire. Its eroticism is contained within the small movements of its characters, who dance, walk, traverse rooms as the camera gazes, moves about them, dances with them— frames them in their discontents, their erotic dreams, their humiliations. Gone are the bold symmetrical compositions of the earlier films, replaced by a reconsideration of cinematic space that, if it does not invite the spectator easy entry, assures that the viewer's gaze is guided through its labyrinths of sexual longing and its frustrations.

Kubrick relaxed the rigidity of his gaze in *Eyes Wide Shut*. Befitting what is, in effect, a domestic melodrama, he paid attention to his big stars and their environment. Befitting what is also a dream film, his images are sometimes surreal, sometimes filled with an oneiric choreography. Everything is what it seems in a dream, framed by the symmetries of the unconscious. Until it doesn't.

10

Kubrick and Formalism

Rodney F. Hill

Broadly speaking, formalist analysis of film (or neoformalist analysis, as Kristin Thompson [1981] and others have termed it) involves a careful consideration of how narrative structure and techniques of cinematic style work together in systematic ways in a film or group of films. As Warren Buckland puts it, neoformalist film analysis

> closely adheres to and is guided by the film. It does not impose theoretical doctrines onto a film simply to illustrate the theory in a self-confirming manner. Instead, it treats each film individually, viewing it as an artificial construct formed by filmmakers choosing from and reinventing filmmaking strategies, norms, conventions and techniques. (2006: 42)

Perhaps the best guide for engaging in neoformalist analysis is David Bordwell, Kristin Thompson, and Jeff Smith (2020). Although the book does not specifically reference the term, *neoformalism*, its entire approach is fairly explicitly a formalist one, taking as a starting point the following assumptions:

> Artists design their works—they give them form—so that we can have a structured experience ... [A] film is not simply a random batch of elements. Like all artworks, a film has **form**. By form, in its broadest sense, we mean the overall set of relationships among a film's parts ... [T]he viewer is expected to follow a story— that is, a pattern of *narrative* elements ... Alongside the story, we can also notice *stylistic* elements: the way the camera moves, the arrangements of color in the frame, the use of music and other devices. (Bordwell et al. 2020: 51–2, emphasis in original)

Film Art encourages a type of film analysis that begins by identifying notable formal patterns (of similarity and repetition, of difference and variation, of development, and of unity or disunity) across a film's narrative and stylistic elements, with these key questions in mind: "What is the film's overall form? ... What are the ... *salient* ... techniques being used? ... What patterns are formed by these techniques? What functions do the techniques and patterns fulfill?" (ibid.: 307–9). We should note that any given study that employs a neoformalist approach likely will not follow these questions in its argumentative organization; but rather, these questions drive the process of analysis, through which the analyst discovers something intriguing about the film. A given study, then, will present the analyst's findings that have resulted from this process, rather than necessarily explicating the process itself.

Stanley Kubrick seems to have acknowledged a formalist perspective on the art of filmmaking—that is, a recognition of the systematic interplay between stylistic form and narrative form in a work of film art—when he said, "Obviously, if you can combine style and content, you have the best of all possible films" (quoted in Nelson 2000: 7); and indeed, many of the major books on Kubrick have taken an approach that fits, more or less, with a formalist model of film analysis. Given the sheer volume of writing devoted to studying his films, it is impossible for this chapter to cover comprehensively the formalist analysis that has been undertaken of Kubrick's work. Instead, it will focus on book-length studies that engage substantially in what we might loosely term "formalist" approaches, whether explicitly or not.

Such is the case with the very first book-length study of Stanley Kubrick's films. Originally published in 1971, Alexander Walker's *Stanley Kubrick Directs* was revised and expanded as *Stanley Kubrick: Director* in 1999. It remains one of the best critical—and implicitly formalist—appraisals of Kubrick's work; and furthermore, as one of the few books completed with the director's cooperation, it is essential reading. Although some reviewers have criticized Walker's approach for its lack of historical context—for example, with regard to the changing roles and perception of film directors—as well as its lack of bibliographic citations (Coyle 1980: 99), his book nonetheless excels in terms of critical textual analysis of the films. Drawing upon extensive interviews with Kubrick (often quoted at length), as well as his own keen, critical observations, Walker offers one of the most in-depth analyses of the interplay between narrative form and stylistic techniques across all of Kubrick's work.

In one particularly telling passage (among many), Walker considers the relationship of setting to narrative in several films:

> *Paths of Glory* is the first Kubrick film in which the characters' relationship to their surroundings is more than physical. The architecture embodies them and their follies in a metaphorical sense, too ... [I]n *Paths of Glory*, and even more in *Dr. Strangelove* and *2001*, the sets ... assume a dynamic role as part of the total concept, usually a role that is hostile or cynically disposed to the human fates that are being settled under their shadow ... The château in *Paths of Glory*, the War Room in *Dr. Strangelove*, and the Wheel in *2001* represent Kubrick's most distinctive ways of using a created environment to contain, define, *and dominate* the protagonists. (Walker et al. 1999: 106–7)

Walker further notes another of Kubrick's stylistic hallmarks, his incessantly moving camera, fully evident as early as *Paths of Glory*:

> The château scenes with the devious commanders in *Paths of Glory* are shot with a continually curving mobility; the trench scenes force the camera to follow, without

choice, the shape of the dugout maze that has conditioned men to obey; and the scenes of the court-martial and execution have a geometrical rigor that reflects the predetermined verdict and the preordained fate of the accused men. (ibid.: 72)

The sense of destiny implied above, especially with regard to the dynamic tracking shots through the trenches, ties into another visual pattern that pervades Kubrick's body of work—what Walker terms "corridor" compositions—notable in a number of films: in *Killer's Kiss* we find "the nightmare street ride taken by the sleeping boxer" and the "hallway of the dance hall, where a murder is lined up by one precise move after another" (ibid.: 53); and in *The Shining*, "the corridors of the Overlook Hotel become passageways to another world, the way the Star Gate did in *2001*" (ibid.: 279). Walker further finds a "fateful determinism" in these shots in *The Shining*, echoed in the hedge maze, which "clearly alludes to the Minotaur myth ... a legend that had long appealed to Kubrick ... In [this] film, the environment is destiny itself" (ibid.: 293).

This concern with myth and fable is central to Kubrick's work. It is well established, for instance, that Kubrick and Diane Johnson read Bruno Bettelheim's 1973 study of fairy tales, *The Uses of Enchantment*, while collaborating on *The Shining* (Naremore 2007: 196–7); and in preparing *2001*, Kubrick and Arthur C. Clarke consulted Joseph Campbell's Jungian study of myth, *The Hero with a Thousand Faces* (ibid.: 142). According to Walker et al.:

> Kubrick referred at times to his early love of fables and fairy tales; and his belief in the energizing power of myth to work on our unconscious ... finds a place in several of his movies. It is implicit in the whole concept of *2001* ... It even shows up in *Lolita* ... [a] story of a girl abducted from her true lover by a wicked ogre ... Humbert Humbert, driving to Quilty's mansion, vengeance-bound at the start, emerges out of a ground mist that might have drifted over from German legend. (1999: 47)

Similarly, in *Paths of Glory*: "The château is a place of order and elegance—all mirrored walls, shining parquet, baroque furnishings, and palatial staircases—yet somehow corrupt and eerie, like a vampire's castle in the old High German cinema" (ibid.: 46). Walker even sees *Killer's Kiss* in mythological terms: "The story readily resolves itself into the archetypal fable of a maiden rescued by a valorous knight from the clutches of an ogre whose obsessive love for her she cannot return" (ibid.).

Although Walker never explicitly indicates that he is engaging in formalist analysis, the few examples cited above clearly suggest such an approach. Walker not only identifies systematic relationships between style and narrative within a given work, but he notably extends those relationships across virtually all of Kubrick's films. As such, he provides some of the most satisfying critical analyses of Kubrick's oeuvre.

Among the Kubrick scholars who do explicitly articulate their methods, Robert Kolker stands out for his clear affinity for formalism, as one of several strategies employed in a multifaceted approach to film analysis. In the preface to the fourth (and as of this writing the latest) edition of his indispensable book on "New Hollywood," *A Cinema of Loneliness*, Kolker clearly lays out his approach:

My working assumption was to admire the filmmaker who made admirable films. The working method was to find the artistic personality in the filmic text. Formal analysis, cultural and ideological contextualization, discovering how individual films cohere with one another was and still is my methodology, incorporating close textual analysis, and sometimes an archaeological or biographical approach, to explore how films work. (2011: ix–x)

First published in 1980, *A Cinema of Loneliness* took on the daunting critical task of defining and evaluating the then recent phenomenon known variously as "New Hollywood," the "Hollywood Renaissance," and the "American New Wave." That cycle of independent, visionary filmmaking flourished from the late 1960s through most of the 1970s, and Kolker views Stanley Kubrick as one of its central figures, alongside Arthur Penn, Francis Coppola, Martin Scorsese, and Robert Altman. Kolker suggests that these maverick filmmakers struggled against the well-worn norms of classical Hollywood cinema without ultimately breaking free from them (a notion that will resurface in the other studies of Kubrick to be discussed here); and their positions as creative "auteurs" were necessarily informed by the shifting economics of the film industry, as the old studio system gave way to new structures and, for a brief time, an openness to such "individual" creative voices as Kubrick.

Arguably the most rigorous formal analysis of Kubrick's work may be found in Mario Falsetto's *Stanley Kubrick: A Narrative and Stylistic Analysis*. Each chapter focuses on a discreet aspect of narrative filmmaking—such as narrative patterns; the construction of space and time through aesthetic techniques, including cinematography, editing, and mise-en-scène; point of view; and character development and performance—and explores that particular aspect across a number of Kubrick's films. Falsetto's analysis begins with narrative structure; and he has broken several of the films down into detailed narrative "segmentations," allowing a better understanding of the discernible narrative patterns from one film to another. As Falsetto's analysis progresses, chapter by chapter, he argues that aspects of narrative structure, cinematic style, and thematic concerns are all intricately interconnected throughout Kubrick's work. Like any good (neo)formalist, Falsetto defers a consideration of thematic "meanings" until the end of the analysis, after he has laid out the intertwined narrative and stylistic systems operating in Kubrick's films. Such an analysis often does lead to higher-level meanings, but Falsetto wisely allows those meanings to emerge from his careful analysis—rather than starting with preconceived, theory-based notions of what those meanings ought to be and then employing theory and interpretation to "uncover" them. As Falsetto explains, "Because thematic discussion has dominated much of the Kubrick literature, I have tended to underplay it in my analysis because I believe that meaning is almost always connected to form and style" (2001: 170).

As an entry point into some of those meanings, Falsetto suggests that Kubrick's work revolves around dualities, whether they be narrative, stylistic, or thematic in nature. In his highly detailed analysis of Kubrick's narrative systems and stylistic structures, Falsetto finds recurring concerns with "the following polarities: subjective / objective, classical / modernist, rational / irrational, empathy / distance, clarity / ambiguity, order / chaos, symmetry / asymmetry, conventional / subversive, surface / depth, what we know and what remains hidden" (ibid.: xxii). In raising these oppositions, Falsetto provides a roadmap for considering the most prominent aesthetic and thematic concerns that the other scholars covered here have rather uniformly noted throughout Kubrick's body of work: modernist resistance to classical aesthetic norms; psychological dimensions (dual structures, empathy, subjectivity); and philosophical issues (reason, ontological questions of order vs. chaos, and epistemological concerns such as what is and is not knowable). We should note here that none of these themes or aesthetic dimensions is inherently formalist; but rather, in the case of Kubrick, the formalist analyses considered here have identified patterns throughout his work that consistently point back to them time and time again.

According to Kristin Thompson, one of the key tenets of formalist theory is that the "basic function of the artwork is to renew perception through a process called *defamiliarization*" or making the familiar strange (1981: 32). As with Kolker and Falsetto, many scholars who have taken a formalist approach to Kubrick's films (whether explicitly or implicitly) have noted Kubrick's tendency to "make strange" the conventions of classical narrative, by challenging or in some cases breaking those norms. In his edited collection, *2001: A Space Odyssey—New Essays*, Kolker reemphasizes Kubrick's kinship with the international art cinema and the French New Wave, in addition to "New Hollywood" cinema, all of which offer "a reexamination and rediscovery of cinematic language" (2006: 5). Kolker further points out that Kubrick's experimentation in narrative and visual aspects of cinema informs all his films.

Although Thomas Allen Nelson finds both formalist and realist theories to be problematic in addressing Kubrick's work, his book, *Stanley Kubrick: Inside a Film Artist's Maze* does identify a "meticulous architectonics" at work in Kubrick's narrative structures (2000: 5); and throughout the book he engages in careful, detailed analysis of the relationships between narrative form and cinematic style in Kubrick's work. Nelson's deft analysis of the court-martial scene from *Paths of Glory* illustrates this tendency particularly well and is worth quoting at length here:

Kubrick's handling of the court-martial achieves an impressive merger of concept and form. From long shot, the camera shows a detachment of soldiers bringing the three accused men into a vast, elegant room … while below, on the floor are the ever-present chessboard squares … Kubrick's audience … realizes that the court-martial itself assumes the formal properties of a battle on a gameboard. The camera work and compositions leave little doubt about Kubrick's intentions here. On one side we have the battle line represented by the five judges, symmetrically composed with the Colonel Judge in the middle, framed by an archway in the background and the French flag overhead. On the other, the three prisoners sit in chairs, enclosed from behind like pawns by two lines of guards standing motionless in an attitude of parade rest. On the flank to their left, and parallel to the windows, is Major Saint-Auban's table, and behind him sit General Mireau and a line of spectators. And finally, to the prisoners' right is Colonel Dax, opposite Saint-Auban and clearly outnumbered. This boxlike gameboard moves along horizontal paths, as the camera reveals when it pans back and forth behind the line of judges during Saint-Auban's speech and tracks behind the line of prisoners during Dax's. (ibid.: 49–51)

Nelson also aptly ties Kubrick to the Russian formalists of the 1920s, noting that the director "shared Pudovkin's passion for an exactness of temporal and spatial directorial construction" (ibid.: 9); and like the other critics mentioned here, Nelson remarks on Kubrick's affinity for unsettling defamiliarization, or distancing, a hallmark of neoformalism (ibid.: 10). Indeed, Kubrick's affinity for Pudovkin provides further concrete support for the notion of Kubrick as formalist. In an interview with Joseph Gelmis, Kubrick acknowledged:

> The most instructive book on film aesthetics I came across was Pudovkin's *Film Technique*, which simply explained that editing was the aspect of the film art form which was completely unique, and which separated it from all other art forms. The ability to show a simple action like a man cutting wheat from a number of angles in a brief moment, to be able to see it in a special way not possible except through film—that this is what it was all about. (1970b: 103)

Luis M. García Mainar's *Narrative and Stylistic Patterns in the Films of Stanley Kubrick* attempts to reconcile and combine two otherwise competing (and as usually practiced, mutually exclusive) approaches: a formalist / narratological approach, as advocated by Thompson and others, with a more "symptomatic," ideological analysis—which neoformalism generally avoids. As Kristin Thompson explains: "When we speak of a film's non-explicit ideology, or of the film as a reflection of social tendencies, or ... as suggestive of the mental states of large groups of people, then we are interpreting it *symptomatic* meanings" (1988: 12). Thompson suggests that such an approach often "begins with an analytical method, often derived from ... literary studies, psychoanalysis, linguistics, or philosophy; [the analyst] then selects a film that seems suited to displaying that method ... [S]uch an attitude seems to me to present considerable pitfalls ... [A]ll too often ... the choice of a film simply serves to confirm the method" (ibid.: 3–4). Unfortunately, García Mainar's title notwithstanding, his book tends more toward a theory-based, symptomatic approach, wherein the method is assumed a priori, rather than what we might properly term formalist analysis.

Even so, García Mainar does offer some useful observations regarding Kubrick's unconventional approaches to narrative and style, which seem at once indebted to classical norms yet defiant of them:

> We can easily find films that are complete deviations from classical stylistic rules ... almost all of them are. And we can also find films that create their own rules only to break them. *Killer's Kiss* breaks the rules of shot/reverse shot and turns them into crosscutting. *Paths of Glory* sets up an opposition between camera movement and point-of-view shots that separates the generals from Dax, only to fool us into believing that Dax can save the men, which does not happen. *Lolita*

seems to suggest Humbert's status as an artist figure by means of the sophisticated language and acting that accompany his image, but the text subverts this image by showing that it is, in fact, Quilty who is the artist and the one able to deceive; and this subversion is done by means of depth of field, which is apparently the tool of realistic cinema. *Dr. Strangelove* sets up a dynamic of satire, only to subvert it and transform it into a celebration of the text, into spectacle. *Barry Lyndon* creates a purely textual pattern of zoom shots and breaks it in the Bullingdon fight scene. *The Shining* tries to assign the fantastic part of the text to Jack's subjectivity, only to suggest suddenly that the fantastic is, in fact, real and that the film is not an account of a deteriorating mind but that the whole text is a fantasy. The square patterns of the formations in the first part of *Full Metal Jacket* change into rambling camera movements in the second, suggesting the difference between theoretical military action and the real thing, where the feelings of the soldiers are stronger than their training. (ibid.: 93–4)

The resultant disruption of "identification," developed more fully by García Mainar in the remainder of the chapter quoted above (ibid.: 94–100), leads to the spectator's being placed in an "external" vantage point (ibid.: 5)—a hallmark of modernism.

In his illuminating treatise, *On Kubrick*, James Naremore suggests that this penchant of Kubrick's for making "a realistic world seem strange" (2007: 81) operates in tandem with his modernist bent—perhaps the most frequently noted of Kubrick's artistic characteristics. For Naremore, Kubrick's patterns of camera movement, wide-angle lenses, antirealist performances, and other strategies play into an "aesthetics of the grotesque," which lies at the heart of Kubrick's modernism. Naremore identifies numerous, clear examples of the grotesque in the performances that Kubrick elicits from his actors: Patrick Magee's over-the-top Mr. Alexander in *A Clockwork Orange*, "Peter Sellers's wild impersonations in *Lolita*," and "George C. Scott's comic mugging in *Dr. Strangelove*," to name a few (ibid.: 168). The latter film systematically approaches the grotesque, says Naremore, with "Kubrick's overall strategy of pulling the audience up short, creating laughs that stop in the throat and suspense that suddenly turns silly" (ibid.: 136).

Another key author, Michel Ciment, views Kubrick as a modernist whose work constantly challenges classical norms (and thus our expectations)—often by calling into question the genres of classical cinema. In Ciment's view, Kubrick's work is always engaged in a dialogue with itself, with each new film referencing (and often contradicting) those that came before it (2001: 59–60). Counter to traditional auteurist critics, many of whom could find no discernible authorial "voice" across Kubrick's body of work—Pauline Kael (1972) and Andrew Sarris (1971) famously trashed some of Kubrick's greatest achievements—Ciment insists "that in Kubrick's work can be found a very real individuality, an internal coherence which is difficult to elucidate because of the abundance and diversity of his formal experiments" (1999: 59).

In Kubrick's emphasis on theater and theatricality—motifs that feature prominently in his films, as with the ballet sequence in *Killer's Kiss*, Quilty's various disguises and "performances" in *Lolita*, the repeated "stages" in *A Clockwork Orange*, the masked ball in *Eyes Wide Shut*—Ciment finds further ties to the director's essential modernism and his tendency to frustrate traditional "identification" with characters and narrative situations (ibid.: 78–81). A related concern that Ciment finds across numerous films is a preoccupation with the eighteenth century, which "saw the conjunction of reason and passion," polar opposites that inform much of Kubrick's universe. "In many respects the modern world is directly descended from the century of enlightenment" (ibid.: 65–6).

Another thematic opposition that Ciment stresses is Kubrick's fascination with technology and its problematic relationship with nature. Ciment astutely points out that this conundrum is inherent in the cinema itself, a technological medium that seems particularly well suited to representing aspects of nature—"a problem raised by Alex during the Ludovico treatment in *A Clockwork Orange*, when he exclaims: 'It's funny how the colors of the real world only appear really real when you viddy them on the screen'" (ibid.: 75).

While not strictly formalist in nature, *Kubrick's Cinema Odyssey*, Michel Chion's book on *2001*, includes a chapter entitled, "Structure," and another devoted to "Style." Of all of Kubrick's films, *2001: A Space Odyssey* offers perhaps the most pronounced challenges to classical narrative and style, as Chion notes: "The spectator leaving the cinema does not have the sense of having seen a finished, resolved, gap-free film." He further suggests that Kubrick, in high modernist fashion, deals with form "out in the open," as few other directors of the 1960s do (2001: 66) and that "*2001* is one of the barest films in existence," in the sense of its form being "laid bare" (ibid.: 77). Chion points out the difficulty in discerning how many narrative "chunks" comprise *2001*, due precisely to the ambiguous nature of its overt formal divisions: chapter titles, the intermission, and the untitled chapter break in the cut from the bone to the satellite. In his chapter on style in *2001*, Chion resists the formalist impulse to identify a unified, formal system of stylistic elements that "complement and fit perfectly with one another" or with the film's narrative structure. Rather, he presents an "attempt to compose a portrait of Kubrick's unique work" (ibid.: 75). Nonetheless, he does offer a careful, detailed, and thorough analysis of how the film's style—by way of cinematography, editing, mise-en-scène, and sound—contributes to its narrative ambiguity, its simultaneous simplicity and complexity. Chion boldly posits that the film's spectator is in a way cast as the "hero" of the film, by way of its Cinerama presentation (a format originally used to replicate amusement park rides and travel to exotic locales), suggesting, "maybe that is why its characters are so neutral, so we can slide into their skin. They are less *characters* than *tourists*" (ibid.: 75).

We might compare this characterization to Annette Michelson's 1969 essay in *Artforum*, one of the earliest scholarly analyses of *2001*; and indeed one review of Chion's book characterizes its central chapters as "the single most important contribution to the study of *2001: A Space Odyssey* since Annette Michelson" (Bould 2002: 282). As I have noted elsewhere:

Michelson suggests that *2001* brings about an introspective position in the spectator, as the outward journey of *Discovery* in the film engenders an inward journey of discovery for the viewer. Like the monolith's impact on the characters within the film, for Michelson the film itself engenders epiphany and "converts the theatre into a vessel and its viewers into passengers; it impels us, in the movement from departure to arrival, to rediscover the space and dimensions of the body as theatre of consciousness." She sees *2001* as a highly modernist work, whose subject ultimately is the experience of cinematic art. (Hill 2020: 81)

In Peter Bailey's collection, *Stanley Kubrick: Critical Perspectives*, several contributors add their voices to the chorus extolling Kubrick's modernist tendencies. For example, Stephen Papson's essay, "Short-Circuiting Identification: The Pleasure and Displeasure of the Cinema of Stanley Kubrick," argues that Kubrick intentionally disrupts standard forms of identification in his films. In the classical cinema, such identification often occurs along two axes: character identification (in which we identify with characters who are similar to us or who represent idealized traits to which we aspire) and structural identification, in which narrative situations cause us to identify with a character's dilemma, whether or not that character is admirable. With regard to the former, Kubrick usually presents us with morally suspect protagonists, immediately undercutting traditional character identification; and with respect to the latter, Kubrick alternates narrative perspective from victimizer to victim, never allowing the identification to take hold fully. The result is a modernist, reflexive approach to cinema in which viewers must examine our own emotional engagement with the narrative (Papson 2016: 191–3).

In the same collection, Andrew J. Gothard's "Through the Looking Glass: Stanley Kubrick and Narratology" analyzes Kubrick's tendency toward ambiguity in his narratives, specifically the often contradictory "textual" and visual aspects of his films. Gothard uses *Full Metal Jacket* and *2001* to illustrate what he calls multiple levels of "mediation" between the films and their audiences (2016: 59). With respect to *2001*, Gothard focuses on the question of whether or not HAL has genuine emotions. "Textually," we are told repeatedly that HAL is "programmed" to give the appearance of having real emotions; but visually there is a good deal of ambiguity. Notably, we get a few instances of what must be termed point-of-view shots from HAL's perspective. Add to that the blank responses of Bowman and Poole, and the visual aspect of the film's narration suggests the oft-noted blurring of the machine/human distinction (ibid.: 61). In *Full Metal Jacket*, Private Joker is a writer, and he also is our narrator, telling the story from some unnamed (future? at times present?) perspective. This narrative device calls our attention to the process of mediation, as do the scenes of the documentary film crew. There, the Marines' performances on camera stand in contrast to their off-camera attitudes and personalities; and some of them, notably Animal Mother, seem quite aware of the mediating factor of the camera, pointing up, as Gothard notes, "the complex problem of truth and perception" (ibid.: 62).

The modernist tendency toward reflexivity can lead in other directions as well. Rebecca Bell-Metereau's essay, "An Actor's Director: Kubrick and Star Performances," discusses the bipolar extremes to be found in the performances that Kubrick elicited from his actors—from the subtle and understated (as with James Mason in *Lolita*) to the "over-the-top exuberance" of major talents such as Peter Sellers and Jack Nicholson (2016: 177). Such performances call attention to themselves and may be seen as reflexive gestures that call into question the conventions of masculinity (178–9).

Similarly, in "Don't Ask, Don't Tell: Masculine Evasion and Crisis in Stanley Kubrick's *Eyes Wide Shut*," Cynthia Lucia points out Kubrick's characteristic, "slyly ironic dark humor" in the film, likening Dr. Bill's investigations to those of a *noir* protagonist who is warned that he is getting into something beyond his sphere. As with *film noir*, "the true subject of his interrogation is himself" (2016: 223), his own sexuality and masculinity, as "he must confront and adjust his awareness of himself and his marriage" even as "his patriarchal unconscious betrays itself—and betrays him" (ibid.: 224). Lucia aptly notes that, like Schnitzler's *Traumnovelle*, *Eyes Wide Shut* is deeply Freudian. (Apropos of Freud, Mario Falsetto suggests that in *Eyes Wide Shut*, "the film's universe may be a projection of its main character" [2001: xxiv].)

Not surprisingly, another common theme in many of the critical studies considered here is Kubrick's abiding affinity for psychological tropes and symbolic gestures throughout his body of work. From the outset of his analysis, Nelson notes Kubrick's tendency "to penetrate the dynamic, often decorative, and always uncertain surfaces of psychological life," often "revealing moments of repressed fear and desire that had been a dominant obsession in his creative life" (2000: 1). He further suggests that, for Kubrick, film is at its height of profundity "when it explores the universal (i.e., generic) myths and archetypes of both our shared cultural experience and our collective unconscious" (ibid.: 5). Kubrick's interest in Freud and Jung seems a fitting concern for Nathan Abrams in his recent book, *Stanley Kubrick: New York Jewish Intellectual*. Along with Geoffrey Cocks (2004), Abrams is one of the few scholars to study Kubrick from a Jewish perspective; and one of the major thematic concerns that Abrams identifies in Kubrick's work is "humankind's capacity for evil and its nature" or as Kubrick referred to it, the "darker sides of our natures, the shadow side" (2018: 12)—touching on Jungian and Freudian theory.

Abrams also raises another major throughline discussed by several of the scholars under consideration here: the realm of philosophical inquiry, particularly the question of what it means "to be a man … a son, a husband, a father and how to be a mensch, the Yiddish term meaning a human being" (ibid.: 8); and "ethical introspection and behavior, which Judaism has always encouraged" (ibid.: 9). Since "Kubrick and Philosophy" is covered extensively in Jerold J. Abrams's chapter in this volume, let us consider just one further author in that regard: Philip Kuberski, whose *Kubrick's Total Cinema: Philosophical Themes and Formal Qualities* "treats Kubrick's films to a conceptual and formal analysis … to study his philosophical themes and cinematic qualities" and explore the ways in which they are related (2012: ix). Kuberski begins by identifying Kubrick as a modernist, also noting the "intractable ambiguity" of his work (ibid.: viii). Further, Kuberski suggests that Kubrick's films embody thought processes, carrying the viewer along through a consideration of forms and themes. (This echoes Jack Nicholson's observation in Jan Harlan's documentary, *Stanley Kubrick: A Life in Pictures* [2001], that Kubrick's films are "conscious.") Kuberski goes on to clarify:

I do not mean that his films present "arguments" or "philosophies." Rather, they work as visual, verbal, musical, and intellectual provocations to the mind and emotions. They work against expectations … to address fundamental questions: What is human nature? Are human beings fundamentally violent? Is war intrinsic to civilization? Is "love" really possible? Where do we come from? (ibid.: viii–ix)

Another recent book well worth mentioning is Kate McQuiston's *We'll Meet Again: Musical Design in the Films of Stanley Kubrick*. An often overlooked characteristic of Stanley Kubrick's style is the close relationship between music and visuals; and McQuiston argues that the most compelling features of Kubrick's films are musical in their conception and expression, ultimately staking the claim that "music is primary and generative to the films' themes, designs, and meanings" (2013: 1). In her careful, detailed, and engaging exploration of Kubrick's use of music across his career, McQuiston combines formal analysis with historical contexts and archival research, to brilliantly fill a long-neglected gap in Kubrick scholarship. Her chapter on *The Shining* is particularly illuminating in its concrete, careful analysis of how the repetition and layering of preexisting music conveys the unseen and unspoken menaces of the narrative (ibid.: 65–86). It is among the best writing to date on this rich, mysterious film. Much more could be said on this subject; but another chapter in this volume, "Kubrick and Music," addresses such questions more thoroughly than is possible here.

This chapter has attempted a rough consolidation and overview of the major formal analyses of Stanley Kubrick's films, from the 1970s until now. Such an undertaking allows us to see more clearly the aesthetic, psychological, and philosophical dimensions that unify a body of films that might otherwise seem quite disparate. Those include: a symbolic or metaphorical use of settings; a penchant for symmetrical framings and a moving camera; theatricality and extreme performances; mythological tropes and structures; a heavy sense of fate and destiny; Jungian and Freudian psychology; subjectivity vs. objectivity; reason vs. emotion; order vs. chaos; and man's relationship to technology and to himself.

Tying many of these concerns together, we might note that the most commonly observed qualities of Kubrick's cinema—its modernist rejection of classical norms and its corresponding attempts to redefine the very parameters of the medium—dovetail nicely with the very precepts of formalism as an approach—not only to film analysis but also to creating cinematic art. In this sense, we may recognize more fully that Stanley Kubrick was himself, among many other things, a formalist.

11

Kubrick and Acting

Ernesto R. Acevedo-Muñoz

Introduction

Of all the academic and other writing and criticism on Stanley Kubrick's films, one visibly neglected area of commentary concerns his choice of actors and their place in Kubrick's overall style and aesthetics. The Kubrick Archive, as Robert Kolker and Nathan Abrams's (2019) new work on *Eyes Wide Shut* indicates, features little information on Kubrick's process in casting choices. While critics occasionally mention acting in certain films, the commentaries tend to qualify performance in the categories of overacting or blank. *Chicago Reader* critic Jonathan Rosenbaum referred to "manic and cartoonish performances" in *Dr. Strangelove* (February 1, 1995), while Chris Nashawaty of *Entertainment Weekly* noted Tom Cruise in *Eyes Wide Shut* as giving one of his "most simmering" performances. In an interview with the *Evening Standard* (July 17, 2003), Kubrick biographer Alexander Walker characterized Malcolm McDowell's performance in *A Clockwork Orange* as "that of a star" while Stanley Kauffmann labeled Mathew Modine's *Full Metal Jacket* role as "adequate" (July 27, 1987). On the occasion of the director's death, prominent Kubrick naysayer Ty Burr in *Entertainment Weekly* (March 16, 1999), sarcastically pointed to *The Shining* as marking the moment when "[Jack] Nicholson stopped acting and began to fall on his 'Devil-may-care' rep."

This chapter will explore some of the features, movements, and shot choices that Kubrick extracted and employed with leading and character actors, from the grandstanding protagonist Kirk Douglas to the petrified immobility and brief roles of Joe Turkel, to account for their place and significance in Kubrick's style. Examining the placement and framing of actors and Kubrick's techniques of working and filming them, we gain insight into how these actors complement and activate the Kubrick aesthetic in the films in which they appeared. Whether in leading or supporting roles, Kubrick's formal and technical characteristics vary between the ways he engaged aesthetically with leading, supporting, and even minor players in their shots and scenes.

A comprehensive look at Kubrick's oeuvre reveals that he rarely worked more than once with actors in leading roles. Exceptions are Peter Sellers, who appeared in *Lolita* and *Dr. Strangelove*, Sterling Hayden, who played the lead in *The Killing* and a supporting role in *Dr. Strangelove*, and Kirk Douglas, who chose to work with

Kubrick in *Paths of Glory* and *Spartacus*. Kubrick more often reused character actors in supporting and small roles in his films.

Occasionally, as with Sellers and Nicholson, Kubrick maintained friendships with his actors. However, as Malcolm McDowell and Mathew Modine related in Jan Harlan's 2001 documentary *Stanley Kubrick: A Life in Pictures*, he never spoke with them after the release of their movies. Kubrick's fidelity to character actors and bit players is intriguing. Actors Timothy Carey, Joe Turkel, Steven Berkoff, Patrick Magee, Godfrey Quigley, Leonard Rossiter, Frank Silvera, and Philip Stone are among those who recurred visibly in Kubrick's films.

Surprisingly, only a handful of actors were nominated for top awards for their work with Kubrick. The standout was Peter Ustinov, winner of the Best Supporting Actor Oscar for his performance in *Spartacus*. Peter Sellers received a Golden Globe nomination for *Lolita* and an Oscar nomination for *Dr. Strangelove*; James Mason and Shelley Winters in *Lolita* also received Golden Globe nominations. Sterling Hayden earned a BAFTA nomination for *Dr. Strangelove*; and Malcolm McDowell was nominated for a Golden Globe in *A Clockwork Orange*.

Actors Tony Curtis, Nicole Kidman, Modine, Shelley Duvall, and McDowell have often spoken in interviews or been cited by Kubrick's biographers on his style and practice in directing them. In the 1972 interview with *Sight & Sound*, Kubrick explained, apropos of *A Clockwork Orange*, his rehearsal process and leanings toward multiple takes, insisting that early takes were a way of "improving" what had come out of rehearsal (Strick and Houston, 135). Kubrick often forged close relationships with actors on set, allowing a degree of intimacy that helped performers to open up before the camera. This was especially true when setting up close-ups of actors. Tony Curtis, who played Antoninus in *Spartacus*, remembers experiencing this relationship as important to Kubrick's own "approach" and "technique" of filmmaking (Baxter 1997: 2).

Kubrick's approach to actors was influenced by his early photography training, moving from an amateur to the staff of *Look* magazine. Under the influence of the photographic works of Arthur "Weegee" Fellig, whom Kubrick befriended, the supervision of Arthur Rothstein at *Look*, and the mentorship of Diane Arbus in New York's Greenwich Village, the origins of Kubrick's style with actors shows an early interest in documenting emotional and psychological states. For his famous 1945 photograph of a newspaper vendor seemingly mourning the death of President Roosevelt, Kubrick relentlessly "coached" the newspaper salesman to adopt a crestfallen expression for the photograph (Mather 2013: 108; Baxter 1997: 26–7). This style would become characteristic in his directing.

At *Look* from 1946 to 1950, Kubrick perfected his technique in terms of composition, lighting, and human subjects with photo essays ranging from his high school English teacher to the boxer Walter Cartier, later the subject of Kubrick's first short documentary, *Day of the Fight*. These lessons, along with the influence of Fellig's photographs and Jules Dassin's film *The Naked City* (1948), influenced Kubrick's early choice of subjects and cinematographic style, and were instrumental in his work with actors, especially at the beginning of his professional filmmaking career.

Actors and Acting

During meetings with Kubrick's assistant, Leon Vitali, in Boulder, Colorado, in 2004, Vitali explained the concept, which is also explored in Walker et al.'s popular book on Kubrick (1999), of the "crucial rehearsal period" (CRP). This "CRP," which could run from days, to weeks, to months depending on the film, entailed the time Kubrick invested in intense practice sessions, rehearsals, improvisations, and determining the meaning of particular scenes, deciding with his actors how to proceed. While Kubrick was known for long periods of research and preparation, planning shots with detailed storyboards, and predetermining lenses and film stock long before shooting began, he often set aside these technical concerns, and delayed filming schedules, in order to give himself and his actors' rehearsal time (Walker et al. 1999: 204). When planning a scene, Kubrick required that his actors be thoroughly prepared and to know their lines and motivations. In contrast to "action" sequences, for which he favored multiple camera setups but fewer takes, when the core of a scene involved emotion or narrative information, the actors' intuitions guided and defined the final formal and technical conditions. Settling with the actors what worked meant that Kubrick would habitually pursue many takes and retakes, but fewer camera angles (Strick 1972b). The ability to get close to the actors physically and emotionally was extremely important to Kubrick's technique. This process often helped him determine choices such as lenses, distance from the subjects, and camera positions.

While exploration of a scene with the lead actors helped Kubrick map out certain technical aspects, it is arguable that he employed different filming procedures when working with supporting and bit players. An analysis of the visual style of scenes featuring leading men compared to the style of those centered on secondary players reveals differences in movement, gesticulation, and voice. This set the leading actors apart as active agents and character actors as passive or as part of the scenic design. An exception was actor Patrick Magee in *A Clockwork Orange*, whose face and voice range from passive to manic in his scenes. These distinctions extend from his first professional films, *The Killing* and *Paths of Glory*, to his more commercial films, and reveal some of the logic of Kubrick's visual style.

Kubrick's first features, *Fear and Desire* and *Killer's Kiss* indicate these patterns. *Fear and Desire* featured Paul Mazursky in the first "over-the-top" performance in a Kubrick film as the increasingly unhinged Pvt. Sidney. Kubrick employed the same actor, Frank Silvera, in both films. Silvera played Sgt. Mac in *Fear and Desire*, and the villainous club owner Vincent in *Killer's Kiss*. The first film of Kubrick's collaboration with producer James B. Harris, *The Killing* continued this pattern of preference for certain types of actors and their styles. This created a collaboration among Kubrick for the first time with three actors, Sterling Hayden, Timothy Carey, and Joe Turkel, who would return to future Kubrick films. Hayden, already a busy B-list leading man by the time of *The Killing*, had important roles in *The Asphalt Jungle* (1950), *So Big* (1953), and *Johnny Guitar* (1954). By the second phase of his career he was featured in supporting and leading roles in various "B" films noir. Thus, his leading role in *The Killing* seemed a logical choice for Kubrick's design.

A heist thriller in the noir style, in *The Killing* Kubrick employed a scattered, nonlinear narrative with snappy, unrealistic dialogue, compositions in long depth, corridors, symmetry, and long, fluid, low angle tracking shots that became stylistically essential to his later films. Hayden adopted a style similar to his other work; he was confident and assertive as the ring master, yet fluidly integrated various groupings of actors. Hayden's performance was understated, suitable for the movie's realist/noir style and its "just the facts" voice-over narration (by Art Gilmore). In contrast to Hayden's presence in *Dr. Strangelove*, where he had a supporting role with many close-ups, in *The Killing* Kubrick employed few close-ups of him, and Hayden's acting is conspicuously restrained from theatrics. The subdued effect is consistent with Hayden's persona and history as a straight-faced noir and Western actor. In his most dramatic scene in *Johnny Guitar*, the "tell me some lies" exchange with Joan Crawford, the heartbroken Johnny (Hayden) tosses a glass of whiskey at a wall, without expressing the emotions behind the violent gesture. In *The Killing*, Kubrick used this quality in Hayden's acting repertoire.

In comparison, Kubrick gave ample opportunity for drama to his next leading man and first A-list collaborator, Kirk Douglas in *Paths of Glory*. The second Harris-Kubrick collaboration was made in part because of Douglas's interest in the project and his admiration for Kubrick after seeing *The Killing* (LoBrutto 1999: 133–4). Douglas employed his star power in Hollywood to convince United Artists to produce his star vehicle. Douglas had significant box office appeal, starring in more than twenty movies including *Young Man with a Horn* (1950), *Lust for Life* (1956), and *Gunfight at the OK Corral* (1957). He had received three Oscar nominations by the time of his involvement in *Paths of Glory*. Douglas became a producer and searched for more dramatic roles and "prestige" pictures. Along with Douglas, Kubrick managed to enroll veterans Adolphe Menjou and George Macready and, in small supporting roles, Timothy Carey and Joe Turkel again.

As he did with Sterling Hayden in *The Killing*, Kubrick allowed Kirk Douglas consistency with his previous style. As Colonel Dax, Douglas displays a wide yet controlled set of emotions in the film, showing respect and deference to the men under his command, acting properly solicitous with his superiors (Macready and Menjou) and suitably outraged in the court martial sequence when three of his men (Carey, Turkel, and Ralph Meeker) are unjustly tried for cowardice. Douglas gets most of the screen time, but his shots are designed to display his strengths, filmed in close-up with normal lenses and kind distances from his face. Meanwhile Menjou, a formidable presence in movies since the 1920s, is known to have complained about Kubrick's demands for extensive takes. Timothy Carey, who played the unhinged soldier facing execution, also required multiple takes in various scenes due to his unorthodox acting style, unusual facial expressions, and perceived unpredictability (LoBrutto 1999: 145–6). Yet, in various close-ups during the court martial sequence, Carey's expressions are in conspicuous display, and further exaggerated by wide-angle lenses, a stylistic choice reminiscent of Kubrick's filming of Carey in *The Killing*. No such treatment seemed given to Kirk Douglas who was drawing on his star stature and persona.

In *Spartacus*, Kirk Douglas uses his physicality and grandstanding whether in battle, training as a gladiator, or as an inspirational leader giving speeches and instructions to the rebel slaves under his command. Always acting for the camera setup, Douglas adjusted his style to the shot size, even when incongruously addressing large crowds in close-up (Baron and Carnicke 2008: 129). The clashes between the young director, the seasoned star-producer, blacklisted screenwriter Dalton Trumbo, and Universal Studios, and Kubrick's lack of control over aspects of the production make *Spartacus* an outlier in Kubrick's career. Yet *Spartacus* gave Kubrick confidence in his position, particularly when navigating the demands and egos of actors like Laurence Olivier and Charles Laughton, who were accustomed to feeling bigger than their directors (LoBrutto 1999: 178). Douglas's performance is consistent with this phase of his career, when both his athletic physique and dramatic gesticulation were in full display "springing around and waiving a sword" (Baxter 1997: 128). The experience with *Spartacus*, however, tested Kubrick's patience with the Hollywood machine of stars, producers, and executives. After learning to make movies with full creative control, he struggled to have his voice heard in *Spartacus*. He left for England in 1960 in search of independence, attracted by the tax incentives offered by the Eady Levy, and impressed with the professionalism of the British talent he directed (LoBrutto 1999: 201; Baxter 1997: 153–4; see Fenwick 2017).

In *Lolita*, Kubrick collaborated for the first time with Peter Sellers. James Mason in the presumptive lead part of Humbert Humbert was at his mellifluous best in a role reminiscent of his turn in *North by Northwest* (1959). The veteran of stage and screen played to type: a sophisticated misanthrope eluding the authorities and his unknown competitor (Sellers) for the affections of the young Dolores Haze. Mason has two dramatic scenes in the movie: his argument with Lolita about the play she's acting in and his violent tantrum at a hospital after discovering Lolita's betrayal. But in his scenes with Sellers, Mason plays "straight man" to Sellers's zigzagging portrayal of Quilty. Sellers ignores everything at the school dance, acts intrusive yet bumbling as a policeman at the hotel, cartoonish as the mysterious Dr. Zempf interviewing Humbert at home, and silly delivering a comedy routine designed to confuse and delay Humbert's plan at Pavor Manor. Against Mason's "normal" acting, Sellers's fluctuating personae underscore the movie's tonal shifts from realist drama to "surrealist" comedy (Walker et al. 1999: 60–61). Kubrick reportedly characterized Sellers as reaching "a state of comic ecstasy" during intimate rehearsals (LoBrutto 1999: 205). The tension exemplified by Sellers in the role of Quilty opposite Humbert channeled his performance in Kubrick's next film, *Dr. Strangelove.*

In *Dr. Strangelove,* Sellers plays the lead, and paradoxically three different character roles as US President Merkin Muffley, the British RAF officer, Group Captain Lionel Mandrake, and the eponymous, presumably German, Dr. Strangelove. Displaying his tremendous range, Sellers adopted three different accents and distinctive mannerisms for each. Once, Sellers was tagged for the part of Major "King" Kong, a role given to Slim Pickens, as Sellers was nervous about the Texas accent (Baxter 1997: 186). As in *Lolita*, Kubrick allowed Sellers a great degree of input and improvisation during rehearsal, later adjusting the script to accommodate Sellers's contributions (LoBrutto

1999: 238–9). It was a provocative choice by Kubrick, yet one consistent with his treatment of both supporting roles and leading men. But while Sellers has more screen time than his co-stars George C. Scott and Sterling Hayden, in their shared scenes the Sellers character is secondary. In short, Kubrick *directed* Sellers as leading actor, employing the CRP to this effect, yet *filmed* him as a character actor, mostly using medium close-ups and only occasional mobility. In fact, President Muffley and Dr. Strangelove are seated in most of their scenes.

Sterling Hayden, returning after his leading role in *The Killing*, plays "straight man" to Sellers, as the two share most of Hayden's scenes. As Captain Mandrake, Sellers gradually escalates his alarm and mannerisms to match the accelerating urgency of the threat of nuclear apocalypse. Yet, as in *The Killing*, Hayden played his role of US Army General Jack D. Ripper with great restraint, relying on his voice and on Kubrick's detailed low angle close-ups to reveal his character's insanity.

As Dr. Strangelove, Sellers transforms from a quiet background character in the War Room sequences to a central strategist of the post-doomsday scenario. Paradoxically confined to a wheelchair, Strangelove begins to lose control of other expressive mannerisms demonstrated by shifts in his voice, spasms of his right arm, saluting "*mein führer*," and miraculously standing to celebrate nuclear annihilation. In *Stanley Kubrick: A Life in Pictures* Christiane Kubrick recalls how in *Dr. Strangelove*, "Stanley wasn't a director, he was an audience," celebrating Sellers's performance and "egging him on" to increasing lunacy.

In the War Room, George C. Scott outshines Sellers as the increasingly excitable General Turgidson. According to James Earl Jones, who played Lt. Zogg in his first movie role, Scott resisted Kubrick's instructions in rehearsals during "over-the-top" scenes but was convinced these takes wouldn't be used. They were used, and Turgidson emerges as the most irrational man at the table in contrast to President Muffley, which Kubrick decided would display "reasonable sanity" (LoBrutto 1999: 239). In terms of characters, *Dr. Strangelove* can be considered an "ensemble" piece, given that five characters (Mandrake, Ripper, Turgidson, Muffley, and Strangelove) share the dramatic and comedic plot trajectory. In terms of *characterization*, Sellers displays a wider range of talents in this film than in most of his career, while Scott exposes a madcap side that played against his typical persona.

2001: A Space Odyssey does not focus on a singular protagonist, unfolding its dramatic arc around its own narrative structure rather than characters. The lead part is shared by William Sylvester and Keir Dullea in respective segments of the three movements, from the monolith on portion of "The Dawn of Man" to the "Jupiter Mission" and "Beyond the Infinite" parts. These two unremarkable character players are allowed few emotional displays. Sylvester, as Dr. Heywood Floyd, deliberately avoids displaying any concern about the mysterious events at Clavius, the American moon base, particularly when questioned by the Soviet scientists lead by Dr. Smyslov (Leonard Rossiter). Dullea, in the nominal lead role of American astronaut David Bowman, expresses confusion at the strange events leading to his confrontation with HAL 9000, in a reserved performance that hints at his humanity when he decides to fetch his colleague, Dr. Poole's (Gary Lockwood), body. Effectively, Kubrick treats these actors as "characters" rather than leads, including distorted close-ups of Dullea, embellished with color effects and freeze frames, during the emotionally charged "Star Gate" passage.

In *2001*, Kubrick seemed to restrict his actors' freedom to emote except for Dullea while attempting to deactivate the HAL 9000 in the only handheld sequence in the film. It is an important decision, as it is in this sequence that Bowman demonstrates his superiority to HAL 9000, responding to the human emotions of loyalty, friendship, fear, and self-preservation. In the voice role of the HAL 9000, Canadian actor Douglas Rain never saw a script or any materials from the film and recorded his entire part in a single day at the studio. After trying several other actors, and rejecting Martin Balsam for sounding "too emotional," Kubrick chose Rain, who gave HAL a memorable presence, considered by some critics more humanly emotional than his human counterparts, because Kubrick directed him to be vocally pleasant yet flat. Coincidentally or not, Rain provided the voice-over narration for the 1960 Canadian documentary *Universe*, which Kubrick had seen during his research for *2001*. Rain was originally engaged by Kubrick for a planned narration for the "Dawn of Man" segment, which was eventually dropped from the film (LoBrutto 1999: 278–9).

Kubrick's next feature, *A Clockwork Orange*, called for its actors to do much grandstanding, movement, caricature, even singing. In the role of Alex, Malcolm McDowell adopts a self-reflexive style, deliberately *performing* as if on stage. With choreographed movements and gazes, enhanced with costume, makeup, props, and often framed in wide-angle close-up, Alex/McDowell is never out of character, always conscious of his persona. Even Alex's assumed surname, "DeLarge," a wordplay on "Alexander the Great," connotes exaggeration, anticipating Jack Nicholson's signature antics in *The Shining*. When Kubrick encountered difficulty with the sequence of the assault on the writer and his wife, through the CRP process McDowell and Kubrick settled into the dancing, singing, and frolicking that formed the sequence, even improvising, out of frustration, the "Singin' in the Rain" song-and-dance that became iconic of the film (Walker et al. 1999: 204). It gave the sequence the "surreal" quality proper to the movie's nightmarish style, sustained by close-ups, ticks and facial distortions displayed by other actors in the movie, most notably Patrick Magee as the writer.

In tune with its painterly design, based on eighteenth-century portraiture, *Barry Lyndon* required static, contained, and repressed acting. Kubrick directed the lead, American actor Ryan O'Neal, and his co-star model/actress Marisa Berenson, to act subdued, and minimized their movements for the painterly compositions. Their elaborate costumes, wigs, and makeup contributed to this constraint. The movie, shot almost entirely in static and stable shots, used tripods, tracks, and dollies, distinguishing it from the frantic mobility and handheld shots seen in *A Clockwork Orange*. As in *2001*, where only a terrified Bowman is filmed via handheld camera, the few handheld shots in *Barry Lyndon* occur during Barry's fistfight with a soldier, in his violent attack on Lord Bullingdon, and in Lady Lyndon's failed suicide attempt scene. Clearly resulting from the CRP process, these are scenes in which actors are required to display unhinged emotions when their suffocating surroundings cannot

Figure 11.1 Patrick Magee in *A Clockwork Orange*.

suppress feelings. In *Barry Lyndon*, actors *posed* rather than *performed* (Pramaggiore 2015a: 128).

Seeing Berenson in *Cabaret* (1972) impressed Kubrick, but in keeping with the film's portraiture style, he instructed her to stay away from the sun prior to production to cultivate the pallid complexion for the character (LoBrutto 1999: 384–5), resembling an eighteenth-century ivory cameo (something later repeated with Nicole Kidman in *Eyes Wide Shut*). Aesthetically consistent with the movie's design, O'Neal, an average "heartthrob" actor, and Berenson, famous for her face and figure, did little more than stand and look attractive. Yet, in *2001*, *A Clockwork Orange*, and *Barry Lyndon*, repeat supporting players Patrick Magee, Leonard Rossiter, and Godfrey Quigley, like their 1950s predecessor Timothy Carey, are framed in close-ups or with exaggerated gestures, makeup, or distorting lenses, that paradoxically show less "acting" and more characterizations.

Behind-the-scenes footage from the making of *The Shining* gives a documented account of Kubrick's CRP, asking Jack Nicholson "show me what you're going to do?" while setting up the storeroom scene. With these instructions, Kubrick chose lenses and camera setups working *around* his leading man. The celebrated shot looking up at Nicholson from the floor was done after rehearsing his movements and the struggle with the pantry door. A similar shot of boxers Walter Cartier and Bobby James is seen in the climatic sequence of *Day of the Fight*. The choice of a slightly wide-angled lens yielded a distorted and more menacing appearance to Nicholson.

Making The Shining (1980) purportedly shows how Kubrick taunted actress Shelley Duvall, stemming from his desire to evoke genuinely terrified reactions from her, after the CRP with Nicholson determined his movements through the set. This is especially

Figure 11.2 Jack Nicholson in *The Shining*.

evident in the "How do you like it?" sequence that ends with Wendy momentarily knocking Jack out with a baseball bat, and the bathroom door scene when Jack tries to get to Wendy with an ax. Nicholson's erratic, violent facial gestures match his physicality in taunting both Duvall and the audience into terror (Falsetto 2001: 126). In his interviews in *Stanley Kubrick: A Life in Pictures*, Nicholson confidently explains that Kubrick was not after "naturalistic acting" but like with Sellers in *Dr. Strangelove*, seeking something else. "He didn't want a picture of reality," Nicholson said of Kubrick's directing, "but rather a picture of a picture of reality." Yet once again, secondary players Philip Stone and Joe Turkel are filmed in static shots and immobile postures, as if part of the design of The Overlook Hotel. They are effectively ghostly presences rather than active agents.

Like *2001*, *Full Metal Jacket* employs a cast of nonstars integrated into the movie's absurdist style. In the Parris Island segments, Sgt. Hartman taunts the recruits in menacing ways reminiscent of Nicholson, using violent movements and misogynistic language and often looking into the camera. Under Hartman's psychological and physical torture, his main target, Pyle, evolves from a bumbling, reluctant recruit to a disturbed murderer. As with Nicholson in *The Shining*, Kubrick filmed close-ups of Vincent D'Onofrio going from an empty stare to animalistic, distorted facial expressions, each mapping the character's mental regression into madness and murder. As Joker, Matthew Modine acts as the movie's anchor and narrator. Yet, supporting actors

Figure 11.3 Joe Turkel in *The Shining*.

outshine Modine. In both the Parris Island and Vietnam segments he is outshone like Sellers in the War Room sequences of *Dr. Strangelove*. Ermey and D'Onofrio receive the most scene-stealing opportunities as their characters move toward caricature in many scenes while Modine observes, narrates, and offers ironic voice-over commentary. In the Vietnam sequences, Animal Mother, who shows signs of mental instability, does the showboating, while Cowboy assumes a protagonist role as squadron leader. For most of the film, Joker's detached, deadpan, mordant commentary is devoid of emotion. Only at the climactic moment of shooting dead the female sniper decimating the platoon does Joker reveal the emotions of fear, anger, and even sympathy, in a long take of his blank face evolving into a furious grin. Like *2001* and *Barry Lyndon*, *Full Metal Jacket* is anchored in its structural design, not realist characterization, and the actors fit the movie's style. Whereas in *The Shining*, Nicholson's losing struggle with the forces of The Overlook act as the major structuring principle of the film.

In *Eyes Wide Shut*, playing Bill Harford required Tom Cruise to mask his feelings. During his nightmarish tour through real and imagined temptations, Cruise often dons a blank stare or nervous grin, until the imagined scenario of seeing his wife Alice (Cruise's then wife Nicole Kidman) having sex with another man. This leads to his one violent gesture—a hard punch into his own hand. Only in his final meeting with Victor Ziegler does Bill display his real fear, momentarily losing his composure in the face of Ziegler's lies: "What kind of charade ends with someone turning up dead!?" Ziegler is played by actor-director Sydney Pollack, who had directed Cruise in *The Firm* (1993) and the two had an amicable relationship. In *Stanley Kubrick: A Life in Pictures* Pollack explained Kubrick's approach to acting in the movie, stating that Kubrick did not want to illustrate relationships in a literal way, but rather "in a theatrical way." In an interview with the *GW Hatchet* in 2004, Pollack elaborated on Kubrick's style. "His movies are not realistic; they're operas." He also told the interviewer that, as an actor, working with Kubrick was "maddening." "I would be there watching take 60, take 70, take 80, and things would change ... He was maddening in his thoroughness, obsessive; it would push the performance out the other end," Pollack said (Ingui 2004). Cruise and Kidman saw it firsthand, put through a long and grinding rehearsal period, in which Kubrick explored with them the real insecurities and tensions of a marriage. In his meetings with students in Boulder in 2004, Leon Vitali said that Kubrick wanted a married couple for the film and also considered spouses Kevin Bacon and Kyra Sedgwick, and Alec Baldwin and Kim Basinger. With Cruise and Kidman, there were endless takes, with only the two actors, Kubrick, and a barebones crew on set (Kubrick himself handled the camera). This level of intimacy and intensity pushed Kidman and particularly Cruise (known for his physical abilities rather than his acting), toward levels of emotion rarely seen before (Walker et al. 1999: 356–9). Paradoxically, Alice's feelings are only really on display in her drunken confrontation with Bill, but the final argument leading to a tearful close-up of Kidman actually happens off screen. A stylistic heir to *2001* and *Barry Lyndon*, *Eyes Wide Shut* required the actors to show limited emotions; in fact, pretense and even masks substitute for displays of feeling. The exception is the argument between Bill and Alice in which she confesses to emotions and desires Bill has never suspected, and which was a result of Kubrick's CRP at its most intense and intimate form.

Conclusions

Arguably, while the CRP was essential to Kubrick's work with principals, his approach to bit and character players was less liberal, choosing camera work with more static shots and close-ups of the players. In *A Clockwork Orange* and *Barry Lyndon*, for example, Kubrick reemployed three actors in small parts: Steven Berkoff, Patrick Magee, and Godfrey Quigley. As evidence of this pattern, in these movies they all appear prominently in static close-ups and/or some form of "distortion"—natural lighting, exaggerated makeup and hair styles—and offering little in the area of "expression," that is, in the "acting" sense of the term. Kubrick's preferences emerge rather visibly: static shots and/or immobility; distortion, in various degrees, by choice of lenses or gestures, or a combination of all of the above. This suggests a different set of aesthetic choices when working with character actors, whose acting is either muted or exaggerated but within a discernible *range* that gives them little freedom. Unlike his preference in leading men—who are allowed to strut around and, as in *The Shining* and *A Clockwork Orange*, to dictate, at least partially, movement and framing— Kubrick's patterns when filming character actors looks rather rigid, predetermined, inflexible, for aesthetic purposes. As with the inscrutable faces behind the alternately grotesquely expressionist or impassive masks worn by the orgy spectators in *Eyes Wide Shut*, Kubrick's character actors are often expected to *be* masks, by turns impassive, inscrutable, and grotesque.

12

Kubrick and Art

Dijana Metlić

Introduction

In 2004 the cinema of Stanley Kubrick (1928–1999) was exhibited for the first time at the *Deutsches Filmmuseum* in Frankfurt. This exceptional display comprising roughly 950 entries from the Kubrick Estate and film studios that financed him (Warner Bros., MGM, Columbia, and Universal) is still traveling the world to honor the director's achievements and to "give an insight into his preparatory concerns and even doubts when it came to the question whether a film was really worth making" (C. Kubrick 2014: 6). Besides the fact that this exhibition aims to, in the words of Jan Harlan, "provoke enthusiasm in a visitor to watch Stanley's films—again or for the first time" (2004: 7), it also raises several important questions. The first one is "how to put" Kubrick in a museum, while the second is how to evaluate some of the iconic items from his films surrounded by a type of aura characteristic of an artwork. Can they stay at the level of ephemera or should we appreciate them as true works of art? Finally, making it obvious that Kubrick was primarily a visual thinker, the exhibited objects intended to provoke new insights into his complex cinematic creation and to integrate it into the history of American and European visual cultures.

Scholars and critics have sporadically addressed the relations between the history of art and Kubrick's films. A variety of noted influences have remained on the level of suggestion, waiting for further examination and detailed explanations. The most prominent authors dealing with his work (Walker et al. 1999; Nelson 2000; Kolker 2000; Ciment 2001; Naremore 2007) have placed Kubrick in the historical and theoretical context of the twentieth-century art. They have studied the relations between the history of painting and his films, explored his attitude toward Modernism, discussed the director's approach to popular culture and kitsch, and revealed his extraordinary affection for the eighteenth-century sensibility. Although only *Barry Lyndon* was actually set in that historical period, Kolker and Nelson argued that in particular sequences of *Paths of Glory*, *Lolita*, and *2001: A Space Odyssey* Kubrick almost obsessively places his characters in front of eighteenth-century artworks. In Kolker's words, he intentionally "uses paintings for ironic juxtaposition" of the civilized and the barbaric, the polite and the brutal, the organized and the chaotic (2011: 166).

Figure 12.1 Affection for the eighteenth-century sensibility in *Barry Lyndon*.

Walker, Taylor, and Ruchti singled out Kubrick's realistic lighting, composition in depth, and geometrical precision of Euclidean rigor as the main components of his shot (1999: 40–60). In the Bauhaus rule "form follows function," they found Kubrick's inspiration for the architecture of straight lines and sharp angles determining the action of his protagonists (1999: 292). Walker et al. stressed the importance of the Kubrickian *surreal* born from his love of fairy tales, and "his belief in the energizing power of myth to work on our unconscious" (1999: 47). He detected a surreal atmosphere, for example, in the scene of the fight at the tailors' dummies warehouse, at the end of the *Killer's Kiss*, which Naremore linked to "a tradition of surrealist-inspired photos," naming Eugene Atget and Hans Bellmer (2014: 31). Walker et al. recognized a weird "Magritte-like effect" of surrealism in Mr. Alexander's reappearance in "that the wheelchair he is being carried in on has somehow grown a pair of legs all its own" in *A Clockwork Orange* (1999: 209). Naremore discussed the importance of Kubrick's uncanny, the strange, the absurd and the grotesque, inspired by Freud and André Breton's concept of *humor noir* (2014: 8). Nelson also pointed to Kubrick's "surrealist appreciation for both the primal and the ritualistic significance of eating and food" (2000: 54). Food occupies one of the central positions in Salvador Dalí, Frida Kahlo, and Rene Magritte's painting. In surrealism satiety is an unachievable goal, and the act of eating is figuratively linked to death. General Mireau has his luxurious breakfast after the execution of soldiers in *Paths of Glory*, with a sarcastic comment that "the men died wonderfully!" The madness of destruction in *Dr. Strangelove* is inseparable from eating and culminates in the War Room, with a large buffet of delicacies revealing the sybaritic nature of the world's politicians and rulers. During his last meal, unpleasantly interrupted by the sound of broken glass, Bowman faces himself dying on a huge bed in an almost surreal way. In *A Clockwork Orange*, Alex has his last lunch before unbearable mental torture that forces him to find liberation in (attempted) suicide. Later, in hospital, the Minister of the Interior visits the now-immobilized Alex and announces his symbolic resurrection in a grotesque act of feeding.

After 2015, new studies based on the material in the Kubrick Archive have shed light on art history and the director's opus. Tatjana Ljujić questioned the authenticity paradox and affective distance in *Barry Lyndon*. She argued that, by using paintings made between the seventeenth and the nineteenth centuries, Kubrick "aimed at creating a visually absorptive and emotively involving spectatorial experience, and not at distancing the viewer from the imaged world" (2015: 239). Analyzing Kubrick's Jewish sensibility, Nathan Abrams linked *2001*'s abstraction and the opening credits of *A Clockwork Orange* with Barnet Newman's stripe paintings, influenced by the Kabbalah (2018: 124). So-called zip-paintings, with simple vertical line dividing the color field of saturated red, are usually associated with the artist's awareness of the atomic structure of the universe initiated by the nuclear age.

Although it is impossible to list all the folders from the archive that address art, it is helpful to explore them to get an impression of Kubrick's systematic work method. More than relying on his imagination, he preferred to read books, consult artworks, or talk to his associates. Arguably, one of the aims of his in-depth analysis of either historical or near-future periods was to find a unique visual expression that will produce a timeless effect of his films. In the following chapter, I explore the elements of Kubrick's visual style, founded on the Renaissance principles and altered by means of modernist aesthetics, in order to show that the director sought for a balance between content and form. Frequently discussed (Cohen 1995; Walker et al. 1999; Hughes 2000; Nelson 2000; Ciment 2001; Naremore 2007; Abrams 2016), his approach to Pop art and popular culture will be analyzed in the section devoted to *Dr. Strangelove*. This case study will point to Kubrick's satirical attitude toward humankind and its self-destruction, the feeling he shared with American 1960s pop artists. Finally, I will show that Kubrick understood film as a unique synthesis of diverse forms of stylistic expressions: although gathered from different periods, they were perfectly unified into a unique cinematic universe that became an inevitable part of the twentieth-century history of art.

From "Content or Form" to "Content and Form"

Kubrick almost never mentioned the name of his favorite painter or sculptor even though nearly all his films are related to some recognizable art epoch or movement. He approached the history of art as a great reservoir of inspiration, giving the audience only an indication of his artistic taste and affection. Although the hardest thing for him was finding a good story (Kubrick cited in Siskel 2001: 180), Kubrick understood film as a purely visual experience and tried to avoid unnecessary verbal explanations.

After the completion of *2001* he finally departed from early noir narration and a word-oriented world of *Dr. Strangelove* and began a new journey in which image became the main messenger. Despite this shift from verbal to visual, Kubrick never promoted an early 19th century concept—art for art's sake—that praised the autonomy of art and strived to find the most suitable literary source for his films. Very early on, he realized that "the purpose of a movie is to tell a story ... and the movie, the medium itself, as for any art form, cannot be an end in itself" (Kubrick cited in Varela 2016: 167). He found preoccupation with the originality of form fruitless and attempted to develop an individual style thinking of "the form as being some sort of classical tradition and [tried] to work in it" (Kubrick 2005: 217). Comparing Chaplin ("all content and no style") and Eisenstein ("all style and no content"), he concluded that "if you can combine style and content, you have the best of all possible films" (Kubrick cited in Strick and Houston 1972: 135). Advocating for art that will be able to illuminate the viewers, he saw film as "the opportunity to convey complex concepts and abstractions without the traditional reliance on words" (Kubrick cited in Gelmis 2001: 90). Although usually acknowledged as the complete author of his films, as early as 1960, Kubrick recognized an important difference between processes of painting and filmmaking:

> Any art form properly practised involves a to and fro between conception and execution, the original intention being constantly modified as one tries to give it objective realization. In painting a picture this goes on between the artist and his canvas; in making a movie it goes on between people. (Kubrick 2016b: 275)

Elements of Style: Composition, Lighting, and Color

Michel Ciment pointed out that Kubrick's "approach is fundamentally unlike the philosophy of twentieth-century art, which values the unfinished canvas, 'emptiness', failures of inspiration, discontinuity, and fragility of execution" (2001: 153). Determined to gain skills in all areas of knowledge, Kubrick was a twentieth-century auteur who could be acknowledged as the Renaissance man (Ital. Uomo universale), limitless in his capacities for development. He was an artist and a technician, fully committed to his films. Ken Adam, the production designer of *Dr. Strangelove* and *Barry Lyndon*, thought of him as an inventor and a visionary:

> For each of his films he had a new concept and in each case, he introduced a revolutionary novel device, be it the centrifuge in *2001: A Space Odyssey*; the candlelight in *Barry Lyndon*; the Steadicam or the remote-controlled camera in *The Shining*. (Adam 2004: 93)

The Renaissance devotion to order and precision left a long-lasting impact on Kubrick's oeuvre. His shots were predominantly based on one-point perspective, while symmetrical framing and deep focus were in the foundations of his visual geometry. Like fifteenth-century Italian architect Filippo Brunelleschi who introduced linear perspective around 1415 in Italy and sought for the classical equilibrium between

Figure 12.2 Symmetrical framing and one-point perspective: Architecture of straight lines in the Overlook Hotel in *The Shining*.

squares and circles, Kubrick chose circles and squares as essential elements of his visual structures. It is worth remembering circle sets and circle walks or rides in *Spartacus*, *Dr. Strangelove*, *The Shining*, and *Eyes Wide Shut*, or call to mind the chequerboard floors in the *Killer's Kiss*, *Paths of Glory*, *2001*, *A Clockwork Orange*, *The Shining*, and *Eyes Wide Shut*, which make the sense of depth more dramatic. Instead of suggesting harmony, as in the case of Renaissance masterpieces, Kubrick's symmetrical framing contributes to the feeling of entrapment and existential threat.

Another important Renaissance artistic method—aerial perspective, in which the appearance of objects directly depends on light—was mastered in *Barry Lyndon*. Working as a photographer for *Look* (1945–50), Kubrick discovered the real potential of light in creating the desired atmosphere. He preferred natural lighting, since "it's the way we see things" (Kubrick cited in Ciment 2001: 176). Unforgettable because of its stunningly shot sequences entirely by candlelight, *Barry Lyndon* was praised as "his most beautiful and arguably most perfect cinematic experience" (Hill 2016: 563). It proved his assumption that "the most memorable scenes in the best films are those which are built predominantly of images and music" (ibid.: 156).

Like many visual artists (Vassily Kandinsky, William Turner, Philipp Otto Runge, Mark Rothko, etc.), Kubrick explored the spiritual and symbolic values of color. His palette predominantly consists of white, black, blue and red. In *2001* black stands for the vast silence of the Universe and the mystical radiance of the Monolith, while white points to the robotic nature of its crew. Red is the color of HAL's eye. The same hue marks the change in Bowman's psychology and enhances anxiety as the mission approaches its end. Psychological balance is restored after Bowman's return to the white Memory room, where Kubrick prepares the spectator for the next evolutionary stage.

In *A Clockwork Orange* Alex and his droogs wear eerie white uniforms announcing threat. In *The Shining* red is a metaphor of danger and Jack's demonic nature. The mystery of the Overlook Hotel is revealed in the toilet with white and red tiles. Bloody rivers run from the walls of the hotel and transform the screen into a red monochrome painting. Finally, in *Eyes Wide Shut* blue and red are symbols of self-control and passion. The blue movie haunts Bill, forces him to explore his fantasies, and find his way home. Chester Eyre from Deluxe Laboratories noted that Kubrick "was always focused on the mood that could be achieved with a certain color" (Hill 2016: 771). From *2001* onwards, color defined the atmosphere of Kubrick's scenes and determined a character's psychology.

Renaissance Man and Modern Art

In a memorable sequence from *A Clockwork Orange* Alex faces the Catlady in the exercise room full of erotic paintings and provokes her by touching a fiber-glass phallus, which she defends shouting: "Don't touch it, it's a very important work of art!" Various files in the Kubrick Archive (SKA 13/2/17/2) contain photographs of Cornelius Makkink's shocking giant phallus named *Rocking Machine* (1969) and Herman Makkink's provocative paintings of women in impossible postures addressing Tom Wesselmann's *Great American Nude* cycle. Several of the proposed paintings were never seen in the film because they explicitly criticized the perversity of the establishment and the church—the main opponents of the ongoing sexual revolution. The rest of the works mocked the society elite who accepted popular erotic painting and turned it into high art. For example, Alexander Cohen argued that "the sculpture-phallus (ritualized and de-politicized) is made into a weapon, and the scene of her [Catlady's] death is a nearly subliminal orgy of modern art" (1995).

After the release of *A Clockwork Orange*, Kubrick commented:

> I think that Modern art's almost total pre-occupation with subjectivism has led to anarchy and sterility in the arts ... I'm talking about major innovations in form ... and in this respect I think my films are still not very far from the traditional form and structure which has moved sideways since the beginning of sound. (Kubrick cited in Ciment 2001: 149)

Expecting a work of art to overwhelm him, he further explained: "Very little of modern art does that—certainly not in the sense that a great work of art can make you wonder how its creation was accomplished by a mere mortal" (ibid.: 151). In *Lolita*, while Humbert wanders through her house, Charlotte notices his interest in art and proudly leads him to her bedroom to astonish him with reproductions of Dufy, Van Gogh, and Monet. This collection should point to her "sophisticated" artistic taste or, as Nathan Abrams observed, becomes Kubrick's attack on "middle-class cultural pretentiousness, ... fine art reproductions, the rootlessness of contemporary American society and so on" (2015a: 70). One unexpectedly harsh comment about modern art is expressed by Sergeant Hartman in the introductory sequence with recruits in *Full Metal Jacket*. Confronting Private Gomer Pyle, he shouts at his face: "You're so ugly you look like a modern art masterpiece!" This sentence either expresses Kubrick's sarcastic commentary on a new dimension of beauty introduced by modern art or mocks Hartman's complete lack of understanding of it.

Although he thought of himself as a traditionalist, Kubrick applied the stylistic means typical of different modern art movements managing to dismantle the harmonious structures of his shots and to show the world in a state of permanent change. In an interview with Ciment he explained: "There's nothing worse than arbitrarily setting up some sort of visual thing that really doesn't belong as part of the scene" (2001: 38). The appropriation of a particular aesthetic principle or technique was actually motivated by Kubrick's wish to achieve a firm unity of content and form.

In his early films (*Killer's Kiss* and *The Killing*), Kubrick explored the expressionist megalopolis (like Emil Nolde or Georg Grosz) and tried to understand its influence on the human psyche. The city offers no easy way out: it is depicted as a stage of deviant society that leads to its own destruction. Similar oppressive atmosphere haunts the inhabitants of the Overlook Hotel. This architecture of straight lines—with chandeliers, high pillars, endless corridors and stairs, resembling Escher's impossible perspectives—contributes to the uncanny realism in film. Claustrophobic spaces like the underground War Room in *Dr. Strangelove* or an obscure mixture of Moorish and Venetian style in the Somerton mansion in *Eyes Wide Shut* entrap Kubrick's characters, leading them to insanity or nervous breakdown.

With fragmented representation, rapid montage, or insertion of brief shots of paintings and drawings into his shots (most clearly in *A Clockwork Orange*), Kubrick came close to the avant-garde collage technique favored by Cubists, Dadaists, and Surrealists. Aware of the fact that a young Kubrick appeared in Hans Richter's experimental film *Dreams That Money Can Buy* (1947) as an anonymous extra (Kolker and Abrams 2019), we might presume that his specific interests in the subconscious, *humor noir*, the absurd, and dysfunctional relations between man and machine, have been inspired by Max Ernst, Man Ray, Marcel Duchamp, and Fernand Leger—the then leading New York avant-garde artists—authoring different dream sequences in Richter's film.

In the star gate scene in *2001* or with David Hicks's hexagonal patterned carpet from *The Shining*, Kubrick examined optical illusions and allusions, capturing his heroes in the pulsating, hypnotic world of Op art. Frequently compared with a piece of Minimalist art (Kubrick cited in Gelmis 2001: 93), the Monolith in *2001* might be equated to Kazimir Malevich's *Black Square* (1915), which marked the rejection of the objective world and the supremacy of new, abstract art. Likewise, the Monolith announces the end of the previous life form and introduces a new stage of evolution.

Kubrick once stated that "the starting point or *sine qua non* of any historical or futuristic story is to make you believe what you see" (Kubrick cited in Duffy and Schickel 2001: 165). This method based on "believing in what you see" was not only rooted in the historical "authenticity," but also in a convincing combination of diverse cultural references. Approaching the history of art ingeniously and wisely, Kubrick managed

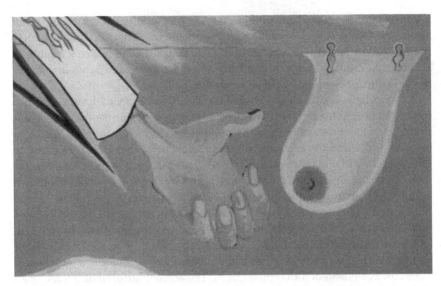

Figure 12.3 Rapid montage and insertion of paintings into film shots: Fragment of the Catlady sequence in *A Clockwork Orange*.

to create the distinctive cinematic universe based on unexpected intersections. It is possible to hear Franz Schubert (1827) in *Barry Lyndon*; Alex's gang fight with Billy Boy in the Baroque derelict Casino is set to the background score of Rossini's *The Thieving Magpie* (1817); and Strauss's *The Blue Danube* (1866) accompanies the flight of the spaceship in *2001*. After his journey through abstract corridors of the star gate sequence, Bowman enters postmodern "cyber Rococo" room (Fischer 2004: 119) where the past of *Barry Lyndon* meets white Modernism of Le Corbusier. Dressed in a red astronaut suit, in front of the Boucher-like pastoral scene, frozen and distanced Bowman suddenly steps back in time and becomes modern version of Watteau's Pierrot from his 1718 painting. If James Naremore saw Kubrick as one of cinema's last modernists shaped by the 1950s New York culture (2014: 29), and if Thomas Elsaesser, following Fredric Jameson's definition of Modernism and Postmodernism, discussed Kubrick as an "in-between case" of an author who "already surpasses Postmodernism" (2004: 141), what can we say about Kubrick's position between modern and postmodern, after watching the last sequence of *2001*? In the unique Memory room, in which the viewers witness a compressed physical and spiritual evolution, the director questions Bowman's privileged standpoint, invokes the participation of an off-screen spectator and shifts "from a high modernist discourse to a more postmodern one. Individual consciousness gives way to a fractured, disengaged point of view, with no individual character as origin" (Falsetto 2001: 117). In the culmination of this typically postmodern open-ended film (similarly in *The Shining* and *Eyes Wide Shut*), Kubrick leaves his audience with no definite answers about the meaning of life and death, love and hate, progress and destruction.

Figure 12.4 Kubrick and postmodernism: Bowman in a "cyber Rococo" room in *2001: A Space Odyssey*.

Kubrick and Pop: What's (*Strange*) Love Got To Do with It?

In a letter dated March 20, 1964, Kubrick fan LeGrace G. Benson made an important observation about *Strangelove*, which at that moment, unfortunately "had to be confined to personal correspondence" (SKA 11/9/37). He drew attention to an important relation between contemporary American Pop art and style and the theme of Kubrick's film inspired by a turbulent political situation initiated with the 1962 Cuban missile crisis that made nuclear weapons immediately more visible.

From 1945 to 1963, when aboveground detonations were officially banned by the Limited Test Ban Treaty, the world witnessed 550 nuclear test explosions (excluding Hiroshima and Nagasaki). During this period, newspaper photographs of mushroom clouds proliferated, perhaps inuring some to "the world's end." When in 1946 the US Navy began its Bikini Atoll Tests and, in 1949, the Russians detonated their first nuclear bomb, the generation of postwar American abstract painters reacted to the atomic blasts and neurosis imposed by evil reality. In 1947, Adolph Gottlieb declared: "To my mind … abstraction is not at all abstraction … it is the realism of our time" (Doss 2009: 128). A few years later Barnet Newman completed his iconic, enormously large canvas *Vir Heroicus Sublimis* (1951), followed by *Cathedra* (1951) and *Uriel* (1955) in which he offered "another view, at once praiseful and satirical of human heroic ingenuity and folly" (Davisson 2009: 120). Mark Rothko expressed his deep concerns for mankind in the era of atomic bombs. He painted *No. 10* (1950) and *Orange and Yellow* (1956), symbolically referring to tragedy and doom. Although he previously stated that "after the Holocaust and the Atom bomb you couldn't paint figures without mutilating them" (Doss 2009: 124), Rothko did not make a major artistic shift toward pure abstraction before the Russian atomic tests. His color-fields of the 1950s can be acknowledged as a reaction to the hot shimmering gases of nuclear explosions (Davisson 2009: 124).

Following Abrams's argument about Newman's influences on Kubrick and relying on the fact that the director lived in New York throughout the 1950s, there is no doubt he was aware of Abstract Expressionists and their reactions to the atomic bomb.

In the aforementioned letter, Benson remarked that:

> in both paintings and movie there is the competent use of the developed artistic vocabulary, a knowledgeable and undisguised use of commercial techniques and processes, ... the apparent use of the ostensible subject matter concealing the actual meaning. It is interesting to see that the paintings and the movie have both been scored by some critics as "attacks" on various aspects of "Colombia, Happy Land." (SKA 11/9/37)

Although he avoided naming the artists whose aim was not to attack the happy land—USA, but to provide "its detached and sensitive description" (SKA 11/9/37), Benson undeniably referred to American pop painters whose art was inspired by commercials, mass culture, and comic strips. In 1963 Roy Lichtenstein painted his well-known *Whaam!* based on a template from the comic-book *All-American Men of War #89* (February 1962). The attacking plane on the left and the explosion on the right panel were united by an intertitle bringing a virtual sound effect into an otherwise silent representation. In one of the conversations, Lichtenstein stressed that "a minor purpose of [his] war paintings is to put military aggressiveness in an absurd light" (Lichtenstein cited in Dunne 2013). Similarly, Kubrick stated that "if the modern world could be summed up with a single word, it would be 'absurd.' The only truly creative response to this is the comic version of life" (Kubrick cited in Castle 2016: 357).

Many slogans displayed on the walls of *Dr. Strangelove* interiors ("Peace is our profession"; "Civil Defence is Your Business") or inscribed on one of the bombs ("Dear John") are reminiscent of the ones written on Lichtenstein's early 1960s paintings, which directly borrowed outlines from comic aesthetics (Abrams 2015a: 77; Abrams 2018: 94–118). Kubrick himself remarked that "most of the humor in *Strangelove* arises from the depiction of everyday human behavior in a nightmarish situation" (Kubrick cited in Gelmis 2001: 97). In one of the sequences, Coca-Cola—Warhol's synonym of America's democratic "equality"—is given "a crucial role in the attempt to prevent nuclear catastrophe" (Abrams 2015a: 77). Just a year after *Whaam!* James Rosenquist made his legendary twenty-six-meter-long work *F-111* inspired by advertising billboards, in which he juxtaposed the intensely colored letters US FORCE with an opened umbrella, spaghetti, a smiling girl having her hair dried under the bullet, and a huge mushroom cloud. Interested in the banality of consumer society, the painter questioned "the collusion between the Vietnam death machine, consumerism, the media, and advertising" (Rosenquist cited in Manes 2012).

A new chapter in Andy Warhol's creative development was inspired by a front-page photograph of a jet crash in the *New York Mirror* on June 4, 1962. His *Death and Disaster* series painted from 1962 to 1965 was encouraged by a comment of curator Henry Geldzahler, "It's enough life. It's time for a little death" (Danto 2009: 41). Photographs of great disasters, suicides, car and plane crashes, along with Hollywood

Figure 12.5 Kubrick and American pop art: The mushroom cloud at the end of *Dr. Strangelove.*

stars and famous brands became the main subject of Warhol's 1960s work. Death became an ever-present topic in his art: he explored it as a commodity and banality. The *Death* and *Disaster* cycles culminated in the black and red silkscreen canvas, the famous 1965 *Atomic Bomb* with a mushroom cloud repeated twenty-eight times. The sarcastic comment "When you see a gruesome picture over and over again, it doesn't really have any effect" (Warhol cited in Swenson 1963: 60), reflected Warhol's attitude on mass destruction as a consequence of technological progress.

Kubrick, likewise, ended *Strangelove* with a series of explosions and images of differently shaped mushroom clouds, surprisingly accompanied with Vera Lynn's lyrics "We'll meet again / Don't know where / Don't know when," pointing to the absurd reality in which a potential destruction of the entire planet became a daily visual spectacle, a fictional situation that will hopefully never come true. A horrible end of human civilization caused by ignorance and insanity of politicians has become so abstract that people stopped fearing the fatal consequences. What Warhol explained as a deceptive distinction between real and unreal ("People sometimes say the way things happen on movies is unreal, but actually it's the way things happen to you in life that's unreal" [1975: 91]), Hal Foster understood as "a historical confusion between private fantasy and public fear, ... a forging of a psychic nation through mass-mediated disaster and death" (1996: 58). The mass media forced spectators to get used to horror and the proliferation of images neutralized its terrible effects. In the 1966 interview Kubrick concluded: "By now, the bomb has no reality and has become a complete abstraction, represented by a few newsreel shots of a mushroom cloud ... It has become as abstract as the fact that we are all going to die someday, which we usually do an excellent job of denying" (Kubrick cited in Bernstein 1966: 29).

Conclusion: Kubrick's Cinematic Universe—Images Everywhere

Kubrick approached the history of art as a great repository of our knowledge about the past and made it one of the starting points of his critical examination of society and a possible anticipation of the future. His camera works like a painting brush: the preferred aesthetic of the long take and slow camera movements resembles smooth and wide brush strokes of the old Renaissance and Baroque masters. The handheld camera and rapid montage, evoking psychological transformation or existential insecurity, temporarily destroy the balance of his shots simulating fast and short brush strokes favored by modern artists. Kubrick's style and subject are inseparable. His technical skill and procedures are determined less by the rules of traditionally understood visual virtuosity than by the chosen theme. His thoughtfully composed image either softens or enhances subject's brutality, depending on the emotional reaction he is trying to provoke.

Following Richard Wagner's idea of *Gesamtkunstwerk* (promoted in 1849), Kubrick's films can be perceived as total works of art, as a true synthesis of different artistic forms, such as literature, architecture, theater, painting, dance, and music (Stein 1960; Tanner 1979: 140–224). Not wishing to be constrained by the strict rules of each genre or media-specific aesthetics, he fused all the art forms into unified and harmonious structures that revealed the reality of a world in a constant flux. From *2001* Kubrick is particularly concentrated on the visual aspect of each film understanding it as "a subjective experience which hits the viewer at an inner level of consciousness, just as music does, or painting" (Kubrick cited in Gelmis 2001: 90). He is a peculiar case of a film painter: his images can be appreciated as part of a wider cinematic whole, but they can be equally enjoyed as individual artworks, similar to the ones displayed in museums.

The meaning of Kubrick's shots is usually deepened by paintings on the walls, introducing new layers of the story and discretely indicating the diversity of viewpoints. This is why we need to use the history of art as a lens to study and better understand Kubrick. Robert Kolker explained: "Kubrick is not making paintings come alive; he is playing on the viewer's perceptual expectations of painting against those of cinema" (2011: 167). Artworks in *Barry Lyndon* disclose the reality of eighteenth-century public and private life and show a lost glow of the vanishing epoch. Pop art works in *A Clockwork Orange* reveal the consequences of interference of mass culture to high culture. Paintings in the Harfords apartment in *Eyes Wide Shut* define their private space as a paradisiacal garden in which fears and fantasies must be brought into light. Portraits of noblemen in the Somerton rooms where the secret orgy takes place are silent witnesses that "under a gloss and mask of culture, the primitive desires of the flesh ... are as ever at work" (Lehmann 2004: 236).

Kubrick's cinematic universe is complex and one of its most important elements is an image that exceeds the boundaries of the traditionally understood film shot. Thanks to a highly original combination of different forms of visual representations, the director forces his spectators to reframe the traditional notion of art and its history, and to look up for hidden meanings inside the shot. In a 1970 interview, Kubrick remarked: "It's the ambiguity of all art, of a fine piece of music or a painting—you don't need written instruction ... to 'explain' them ... Reactions to art are always different because they are always deeply personal" (quoted in Gelmis 2001: 91). Kubrick's distinctive approach to the history of art, producing seemingly unsustainable wholes, works like magic and still attracts new generations of his admirers.

13

Kubrick and Composing

Kate McQuiston

Stanley Kubrick distinguished his filmmaking thematically and dramatically, visually and temporally, and with remarkable attention to sound and music. The diversity of music and its effects across Kubrick's filmmaking reveal no single a priori strategy; rather, the goal was choosing the music that worked best in each case. Choosing well sometimes meant aligning the music's provenance or associations with narrative themes, and other times working against them, or creating something new in the combination. A constant across his filmmaking was that he worked with composers.

This chapter focuses the discussion of music in Kubrick's films on his work with composers with consideration throughout of industrial and stylistic conditions that shaped the expectations and involvement of musical personnel. Kubrick commissioned work from practitioners in virtually every area of expertise related to filmmaking, and he worked with composers and orchestrators over the entirety of his career. A cursory glance at Kubrick's engagement of composers quickly reveals broader difficulties musicians encountered working in the film industry, and at the same time, their perennial willingness to risk artistic control over music in exchange for exposure on a scale with which the concert hall and academy could not compete. Kubrick, meanwhile, maintained a confidence of musical judgment throughout his career—one not reliant on any formal musical training, but on taste.

Critical and scholarly attention to film music has been slow to arrive, for Kubrick as for other filmmakers, perhaps in part because the specialized vocabulary for music has discouraged commentary. By around 2000, however, film scholarship and journalism had developed, and it was then preoccupied with revisiting and reassessing trends of the century. Writing on Kubrick and others of his generation grew substantially, both in amount and diversity of approach.

Substantive investigations of music in Kubrick's work initially sought to establish chronology and legality in the musical process, but these soon included discussion of aesthetics, musical meaning, and effect. Paul Merkley was among the first to bring forth substantial documentation of Kubrick's working process on music (2007). As the title indicates, Merkley captures the difference of opinion between composer and director at the time of Kubrick's ground breaking adoption of concert hall music for the film.

The subject of music in Kubrick's films has also invited disciplinary diversity and specialized strategies. In the course of broader critical studies of Kubrick, music scholar Michel Chion offers inventive and fanciful explorations of music in *2001* and *Eyes Wide Shut* (2001, 2002). Claudia Gorbman (2006), David Code (2010), K. J. Donnelly (2005), Julia Heimerdinger (2007), and James Wierzbicki (2003) are among those who illuminate music's effect in the films, whether through a cultural contextual lens, or with respect to aesthetic traditions in music, film, or both. Given music's interdisciplinary attraction, and the benefits of revisiting Kubrick's films through music-based approaches, it is likely that further work on music in Kubrick's films is yet to come especially since the availability of material in the Kubrick and other archives has illuminated further musical details of Kubrick's films (Heimerdinger 2010; McQuiston 2010, 2013; Gengaro 2013).

In retracing what we can of Kubrick's interactions with composers, it must first be said that much of the director's creative relationships played out through a mixture of face-to-face meetings, communication by post, telegram, telex, fax, and telephone calls, hinting at gaps of indeterminable size and content. The director's growing reliance on face-to-face meetings and telephone calls for the creative development of music in his work, particularly on his last two films, means less evidence pertaining to this work was left behind.

Nonetheless, extant documentation yields a clear picture of the importance of music in Kubrick's estimation, and of the many voices influencing Kubrick's musical judgment, including those representing the director's evaluation of historical relevance, aesthetics, practical factors such as length and legality, and personal taste. In addition to Kubrick's deliberations over the choice of a musical work, or the virtues of one recording over another, was the input of others. Kubrick engaged those who could assist with music in the form of researching, composing, procuring, arranging, performing, or recording (McQuiston 2013; Gengaro 2013).

In his creative process with regard to music, a matter on which he lavished much time, Kubrick heeded his own taste and a wide range of changes in the film industry. However, a focus on Kubrick's notable use of preexisting classical music has left other important aspects of his approach and aesthetics relatively unexplored. Kubrick was vigilant about innovations in recording and took advantage of industrial changes to create striking ways of presenting music and other elements. His career progressed through decades that saw an increase in the availability and variety of recorded music, and new possibilities for adopting musical styles for film. Kubrick was aware of the implications of these elements for production and reception alike. Also important in Kubrick's activities were experimentation and innovation with the latest equipment instead of uncritically adopting tried and true methods. His curiosity and enthusiasm for technology led him to test all manner of sound gadgets in the service of filmmaking and made him receptive to synthesizers and other nontraditional sounds. But with so much focus on Kubrick's musical decisions, the deployment of silence and ambient sound in his soundtracks has gone largely ignored and, relatedly, so has a crucial development of sonic restraint in *2001*, in which many minutes go by with no music at all.

Kubrick's films beginning in the 1970s see substantial growth in musical flexibility and heterogeneity. *Barry Lyndon*, with its many contributing musicians, including arrangers, composers, and personnel, alongside commercial recordings, and music from across several centuries, exemplifies this trend. This heterogeneity coincides with an increase in the tractability of recorded sound in the filmmaking industry in general. Another little-registered trend in the films from this time onward is an increase in women's contributions to the soundtracks, by Wendy Carlos, Rachel Elkind, Abigail Mead, and Jocelyn Pook. Kubrick's films have garnered criticism for their limited and misogynistic portrayals of female characters; however, Christiane Kubrick has refuted the perception of Kubrick as misogynist, citing his aptness to employ women, and his enjoyment of working with them. Kubrick's hiring of female composers, moreover, is notable considering that women represent a very slim minority in the film music industry.

Kubrick and Composers in the 1950s and Early 1960s

Working with composers began with Kubrick's earliest films when Kubrick turned to a friend. Gerald Fried was musically trained at The Juilliard School, and he was a member of the first significant generation of American film composers to be born in the United States. Fried's generation, which followed the pioneering careers of Alex North and Bernard Herrmann who were born a decade earlier, includes Nelson Riddle, Elmer Bernstein, Leonard Rosenman, Henry Mancini, and Jerry Goldsmith, all but the last of whom were born in the northeast and relocated to Hollywood. Relatively free of the burdens of European traditions, these composers drew from a wide variety of styles, from modernism to Latin pop music, jazz, and rhythm 'n' blues. They had opportunities to develop these styles in the course of playing popular music gigs, and increasingly in the media that called for them, such as television programs and their prominent theme songs, original studio albums, and arrangements of other composers' music, for concerts or for recordings. Aspiring film composers often worked together in the same company studio, and in tandem. They orchestrated and conducted each other's music, and provided stock music, on the way to more prestigious assignments.

Gerald Fried and Nelson Riddle, along with British composer, Laurie Johnson, all led professional careers rooted firmly in commercial music before working with Kubrick. All three had penned recognizable pop tunes, and music for film and television, and had proven highly skilled in producing music of the vastly varied styles the industry demanded.

For Kubrick's *Fear and Desire*, Fried wrote finely nuanced passages of dissonant music for small instrumental ensembles—music that invites comparison with the writing of Alban Berg and other contemporary modernists. He employed a larger ensemble for *The Killing* and gave several scenes an edgy energy with Latin rhythms and percussion, and with the dissonance that had found a home in *film noir*. For *Killer's Kiss*, much of Fried's efforts were instrumental arrangements of the song, "Once," by Arden Clar and Norman Gimbel. Fried provided music for *Paths of Glory*, his final project with Kubrick, including a boisterous instrumental adaptation of "Der Treue Husar" that serves as a memorable rejoinder to Christiane Kubrick's tentative vocal performance of this song. Fried, who recognized the young Kubrick as a major talent, parted with him on good terms, and he continues scoring film and television at the time of this writing.

By the time Nelson Riddle came to work with Kubrick on *Lolita* in the early 1960s, he had earned acclaim for his artistry as an arranger, and for his original themes for television shows, including *Route 66*. Kubrick was familiar with Riddle's sumptuous arrangements on Frank Sinatra's albums of the 1950s. These albums are *In the Wee Small Hours* (Capitol 1955) and *Frank Sinatra Sings for Only the Lonely* (Capitol 1958), the latter of which was on the *Billboard* popular charts for 120 weeks, and became a gold record in June 1962, the same month *Lolita* was released (Levinson 2011: 206).

Riddle's work on *Lolita* included arranging Bob Harris's main title song in several versions—though Kubrick used only some of these cues—and writing original cues, which range in style from contemporary dramatic underscore to a variety of contemporary pop. The score floats across the typical boundary between diegetic and nondiegetic, adding to the film's knowing stance and humor.

The tone of Riddle's score had to be just right to make the subject matter palatable to a reasonably broad audience, and Kubrick was involved in the process for this reason; he did not even shy away from disregarding Nabokov's additions in the script, or Nabokov's suggestions for music, showing a precocious authority on the matter (McQuiston 2013: 26–7). Kubrick and James B. Harris attended the recording sessions for *Lolita*, where keeping Humbert sympathetic and reining in Lolita's sexuality were chief concerns. One result was the omission of a cue from the film, "The Perfect Murder" (only the sound of rain is heard under the dialogue in the scene). Another result was a caution in the marginalia of the score for "Lolita Ya Ya"; it reads, "Polite—not raucous" (LoBrutto 1997; Riddle 1962). Riddle's deft touch with popular music allowed his tongue-in-cheek score to express in ways that words could not. Correspondence on behalf of Riddle sketches some details of a deal Hawk Films was working out with BMI in connection with *Lolita*—one that did not include Riddle's rights to the music. It is possible that Riddle was unsatisfied with this arrangement and with only 3 percent interest in album sales. The correspondence hints that BMI was reluctant to release Riddle to do the work, which Kubrick awaited in order to proceed, and it left the relationship between the royalties arrangement and Riddle's release to score *Lolita* unclear.

Laurie Johnson came to work with Kubrick, on *Dr. Strangelove*, with a reputation for light popular music already in place. Johnson delighted Britain's home audiences with perky, easy listening hits in the 1950s and with the swing and big band styles that dominated in the 1960s, such as in his themes for *The Avengers* and other popular shows. His sizable catalog includes military band music and a trove of catchy stock pieces in a postwar lounge pop style, such as the cheery instrumental, "Happy Go Lively," which persists in animated series and other television programming. As with Riddle, Kubrick knew he was hiring an established name in the music business.

The beatific sheen and suburban languor of Johnson's wordless arrangement of "Try a Little Tenderness," makes a pitch-perfect, winking introduction to Kubrick's Cold War farce. Johnson's arrangements of "Johnny Comes Marching Home" appear throughout; it provides a serious tone to play against the grim absurdity of Major Kong and his doomed crew, and an ostinato rhythm that ticks away the seconds leading to the film's apotheosis. Johnson also made an instrumental arrangement of "We'll Meet Again" so it could be sung in a variety of different languages for foreign release. The results of this recording, however, disappointed Kubrick, who kept the original recording and used subtitles (I am grateful to Michael Broderick for sharing information about documents he consulted at Childwickbury, dated December 9, 1963, that clarify the details about this recording).

Behind Every Composer Alive Stand Thirty Ghosts

After the Paramount antitrust case of 1948, and despite the pressure of new forms of competition, changes came slowly to Hollywood and its music. Composers did not have any reason to anticipate significant changes in their working methods or relationships with directors. It probably did not occur to most American composers that a dedicated score for a film might be passed over, that the director was not obligated to use it, or that he might opt instead for other music, or even for silence. Alex North won some battles with these alternatives, and lost others.

North was trained in music at Juilliard and in Russia. He composed in a variety of styles and wrote ballets and concert music before his foray into stock music and original scores for documentaries and feature films. North's momentous debut year in film scoring, 1951, included *Death of a Salesman* (László Benedek), and *A Streetcar Named Desire* (Elia Kazan)—credited as one of the earliest original scores in a jazz idiom. North's efforts revealed an apt versatility; his original song, "Unchained Melody," written in 1955 for the Warner Bros. film, *Unchained*, became a pop standard by the mid-1960s, and went on to have extraordinary and enduring commercial success. North sometimes accommodated preexisting music in his scores, for example his extravagant exploration of the simple tune, "Au Clair de la Lune," in *The Bad Seed* (1956).

Late-era Hollywood's interest in grandiosity, spectacle, and historic epics provided lavish opportunities for North and others of his generation. It was in this ambitious push, in part an effort to grab audiences' attention away from television, that North and Kubrick worked together for the first time, on *Spartacus*. North's work on *Spartacus* was unusually long and it involved ongoing discussions with Kubrick. For this film, as for other epics, North carried out research on ancient Roman music, and created what he deemed two symphonies' worth of music, comprising a total of about two thirds of the film's three-hour running time. At Kubrick's suggestion, North listened to Prokofiev's *Alexander Nevsky*, and with two pianos and percussion, created a temp track of his leitmotific score. North ultimately scored this music for an astonishingly large and varied ensemble, even by Hollywood standards (Henderson 2003: 134–5).

North's inclusion of the Novachord, an early synthesizer, points to the bold color of synthesizers that would come to the fore in the scores by Wendy Carlos and Rachel Elkind, Abigail Mead, and Jocelyn Pook.

1960 was also the year of Alfred Hitchcock's *Psycho*, a film that signaled a sea change for American film and audience taste. *Psycho* flaunted its disregard of familiar conventions and mores, and had a soundtrack by Bernard Herrmann that can only be described as antagonistic. Though the music of *Psycho* is now celebrated, moments of silence in the film are plentiful and gripping. Films in the sixties and seventies increasingly employ silence, both in the interest of marking a departure from Hollywood-style practices, and in the service of alternatives, such as realism or abstraction—approaches that music and sound did not necessarily serve.

In 1966, North worked on Mike Nichols's *Who's Afraid of Virginia Woolf*, a script driven by dialogue, like the play it adapts. Nichols was set on using Beethoven's dense, dramatic string quartet, op. 132 for the film. North, however, played his main title over the telephone to Nichols: an extraordinary, floating scrim of Baroque gestures, later scored for a chamber ensemble featuring guitar and harp. The music brought Nichols to tears, and persuaded him to change his mind. Such an experience surely armed North with a boost of confidence for future projects, as well as an expectation of discussion, including the opportunity to argue for his compositions. North's expectations, however, and Kubrick's haste to eschew Hollywood convention would pull them in opposite directions.

Kubrick had been looking for a new kind of music for *2001*: something "new and distinctive," or perhaps "a really striking score by a major composer" (quoted in Bernstein 2001: 38). Compared to *Spartacus*, North's involvement was relatively limited; North worked on the score in England in January and February of 1967. He had help from not one but two orchestrators, Henry Brant—a longtime collaborator—and Samuel Matlowsky, whom North likely knew from the New York ballet scene of the late 1940s. North's brief time for recording in London meant any communication with Kubrick following his six-week visit would take place via telephone or post. A detail that is often lost in discussions about *2001* is that Kubrick engaged North to write music with a proviso; Kubrick wanted to use classical pieces if he was able to do so. In the weeks leading to the completion of the film, Kubrick did not communicate to North that he did not use any of his music, leaving North to discover this when he went to the theater (Merkley 2007; Heimerdinger 2010; McQuiston 2010).

That Kubrick declined to use an original score for *2001*—a film he must have recognized as a new height of technical and artistic achievement and innovation—may at first seem counterintuitive, but the practice of the compilation score dates to the earliest days of cinema. It constitutes, as film music scholar Julie Hubbert reminds us, "the most substantial and long-standing method of musical accompaniment used in film" (2014: 291). Kubrick's choice had several effects, not least of which was to reset the course of the reception history of the musical works included; in their surprising context of Kubrick's film, these works assumed new home addresses, as far as the popular imagination was concerned. Kubrick's choices, including some recent music by György Ligeti, rankled North and his supporters for the perceived personal slight, but also for their seeming refutation of the classic Hollywood approach in favor of an older model made new again. Kubrick's approach, which added to the competition for North's generation, was a forebear of later media practices of quotation and remix, in which recognition and recombination constitute important components of cultural capital and play. At the same time, Kubrick's choices—ironically—imported to the world of screen music the competition with dead classical composers that had long confounded the art music world—a competition North and his contemporaries decried.

The question of which music to use was clearly important to Kubrick, but so was the matter of silence. Silence is so often ignored in studies of soundtracks because it is mistaken for neglect—in other words, it is perceived as a space where no sonic judgment was made. This is a dangerous omission considering Kubrick's aesthetic, in *2001* and elsewhere, aimed for a balance between giving just enough that the audience could put something together, but not so little that his films would be hard to follow. As Roger Ebert observed about *2001*, "The genius is not in how much Stanley Kubrick does ... but in how little" (1997). In his relations with composers and other creative personnel, as of himself, Kubrick demanded more material than he used, and he arrived at his films by way of subtraction and distillation. In an interview with Charles Reynolds as early as 1960, Kubrick reveals his sense of sonic restraint:

> Music is one of the most important elements in a film, as is silence. The director must go over each scene with the composer and insure that the desired mood and feeling of the music for each scene is understood. It is almost as important to decide where there will be no music, for the constant use of a film score generally deadens the ear, lessening the effectiveness of music when it will be most wanted. (Reynolds 1960: 149)

Kubrick's comments show sensitivity to the audience's capacity for sound, and their threshold of fatigue—factors that demand the director's attention to the entire disposition and composition of the soundtrack. Kubrick knew that silence, when well placed, and perhaps akin to the negative space in visual compositions, could affect the audience as greatly as music.

More and Then Less

On the three films following *2001* Kubrick would accomplish soundtracks with the help of a wider range of approaches and more personnel. In these films, Kubrick exerts finer control over preexisting music through new arrangements, professional recordings, or both, and expands his requests of composers.

The case of *Barry Lyndon* shows a director marshaling the efforts and talents of many people. Kubrick engaged The Chieftans to contribute arrangements and recordings of Irish tunes to *Barry Lyndon*. For the rest of the score, Kubrick sought arrangements of concert music contemporary to the story and arrangements and performances of military marches and tunes. Kubrick approached Nino Rota to arrange music, but Rota's agent responded in a letter that framed the task as beneath the composer's talents. Kubrick ultimately hired Leonard Rosenman, who worked exclusively on arrangements of the Handel Sarabande that recurs throughout the film. The remaining selections of concert works were licensed recordings or arrangements by Jan Harlan, Kubrick's musically adept brother-in-law and executive producer on the four final films. Harlan's alteration of Schubert's trio movement reveals an especially keen ear and understanding of musical form (McQuiston 2013: 87–106).

The arranging and rerecording work on *Barry Lyndon* would set an important precedent for both *A Clockwork Orange*, and *The Shining*, for which Wendy Carlos and Rachel Elkind would supply arrangements of preexisting works, original score, and sound effects. Anthony Burgess's novel, *A Clockwork Orange*, named Beethoven among composers both real and fictitious, a fact that may have prompted greater license regarding the approach to music. Carlos and Elkind created synthesized cues based closely or loosely on music by Beethoven, Purcell, and Rossini, not all of which made it into the film, and they provided original music as well: the anxious, electronic cue, "Timesteps." Their "Music for the Funeral of Queen Mary" includes what appear to be extraneous sounds at unlikely moments, hinting at the more atmospheric work they would conjure for *The Shining*.

Carlos and Elkind's most cited contributions to *The Shining* are the opening title, their spooky rendition of the *Dies Irae* chant (after the baleful version of the chant in Berlioz's *Symphonie fantastique*), and the massive, dreadful cue, "Rocky Mountains." The composers sent eight records full of music and sounds to Kubrick for his consideration. These included not only music, but also the sounds of a landing airplane, and the heartbeat heard in several scenes. The double duty of the composers as sound designers, and the aesthetic intermingling of music and sound on many of the tracks on these extraordinary records points to the growing importance of sound effects and sound design at the time. The double role also foretells the industry's increasing consolidation of the tasks of effects and music that followed the widespread adoption of digital editing platforms in the 1990s.

In *The Shining* most of the contributions by Carlos and Elkind lost out to preexisting tracks. Sound engineer Gordon Stainforth's late-stage expertise and attention to the music result in an impressive composition of compositions in which proportions of silence and sound are carefully designed across the film's second half. Once again, Kubrick procured more material than he needed, and chose what he felt worked best.

Regarding her work with Kubrick, Carlos (2000) expresses both admiration and frustration, and recalls differences of opinion about what musical choices would work best. Her conviction echoes North's experience on *2001*, and reiterates the difficulties of sacrificing artistic control, though she recalls working with Kubrick in grateful terms. Like Gerald Fried, Carlos stayed in touch with Kubrick and his family after working together. The absence of correspondence in the archive relating to her music for *A Clockwork Orange* and *The Shining*, and Carlos's own recollections suggest that much of her working process with Kubrick transpired over the telephone—a device that likewise obscures the creative process on Kubrick's two remaining films.

Kubrick's collaboration on *Full Metal Jacket* with Abigail Mead, the pseudonym of his daughter Vivian, is perhaps the most obscure case of all. As in his other face-to-face collaborations, written correspondence never transpired, leaving us to guess at the character and content of their father–daughter work on this project. Mead was concerned with the film's bifurcation into contrasting psychological atmospheres; while the work of choosing what she found to be the funniest verses of the soldiers' vulgar chant occupied her for the opening portion of the film, she produced an original, synthesized score for the second, long act. Synthesizers, helpful for suggesting the alien or the unnatural, had been effective in *The Shining*, a film whose production Mead documented in her own film. In *Full Metal Jacket* Mead incorporates percussion evoking both East and West, and conjures a dystopic haze from the synthesizers, full of ambiguous sounds—drums or distant explosions? metallic whine or flute melody? machinery or chanting chorus? These fragments repeat without clear meaning and suit the transformed and unraveling state of the troops.

Synthesizers were increasingly used in film in the seventies and held special appeal for another prominent Vietnam narrative; Francis Ford Coppola hired composer David Shire to write a score for *Apocalypse Now* exclusively with analog synthesizer, "precisely because it had a little inherent coldness to it" (Karr 2018). Ultimately, Shire's score was replaced with a colder, eerier one by Carmine Coppola. Both Coppola's score and Mead's—and Shire's unused score, for that matter—share a certain flavor. As Robert Castle and Stephan Donatelli observe, "the obscure calculus of electronic music helps to articulate themes of dehumanization" (1998: 24–8).

English composer Jocelyn Pook came to work on *Eyes Wide Shut* with knowledge of Kubrick's relationships with previous composers, and thus had low expectations about the ultimate role of her music in the film. Pook, however, describes a rewarding collaborative experience with the director, for which she may have been well positioned by her background in writing functional music, specifically for dance—a genre for which rhythm and mood are paramount (Burlingame 1999). Pook met with Kubrick and they listened to some of the film's preexisting music together, and their discussions about her music, both in person and by telephone, left no trail. Pook has described her conservative approach to her pieces for the film, including favoring the blendable color of strings over distinctive solo timbres, and a process of subtracting instruments to avoid distraction in particular scenes (Gengaro 2013: 235).

Kubrick seemed to enjoy collaboration, music, and discussions about music, and he seems to have worked directly with composers as much as he was able to, and to have enjoyed these interactions. These instances say perhaps as much about the nature of the professional work of composers in the late- and post-studio eras as they do about Kubrick's work with composers. These activities were shaped by numerous factors, from Kubrick's willingness to be personally involved, to personal taste, practical issues, and aesthetic fit with the films.

In hindsight, the Hollywood model may have been what North took too much for granted in his work on *2001* (and, especially, his hopes for wide exposure through it). Kubrick's musical creativity, and his seeming daring in giving music pride of place, resembles more closely that of the mass appeal of early cinema, and the musical heterogeneity of its music, whether cobbled together in arrangements for live orchestra, or the improvisations of an accompanist. Like the organists and pianists of the silent theater, Kubrick seemed to have the entire history of music in his arsenal.

In his working methods generally, and in specific regard to working with composers, Kubrick was an innovator and explorer. On the way to completing his films, large amounts of material, including contributions by contracted personnel, went unused. As Kubrick's ear turned to art music and other possibilities, the risk became even greater for the Hollywood composer, who now had to compete with a vast catalog of recorded classics, and with new, popular styles.

For the composers who worked with Kubrick, the results varied according to personal expectations about artistic control, and the conditions of both the film music industry and other music industries, including arranging and recording popular music, and writing original music for concert performance. For North, the experience was disappointing for his reliance on an outcome that he took for granted, and for Carlos, disappointing because of artistic disagreements. Others, such as Fried, Riddle, Johnson, and Pook, spoke more favorably about their experiences, perhaps because their expectations differed, or because they conceived their involvement in terms of work rather than product. Though involved as an arranger on *Barry Lyndon*, Leonard Rosenman's professional career path as a composer introduces illuminating counterpoint; after he scored his first motion picture in 1955, his success in getting his works played in concert venues came to a quick end. Working in film carried certain risks for the composer, but the concert world had its own perils (Bergan 2008).

Kubrick's license in approaching musical alternatives to the dedicated original score model is of a piece with his broader desire to distance himself from Hollywood, and a reflection of his musical taste. Kubrick's broad representation of musical styles and aesthetics has provided powerful plurality and ambiguity across his work: qualities that afford and reward engagement with his films as both entertainment and art.

14

Kubrick and Music

Christine Lee Gengaro

Introduction

When the lights went down at the premiere of Stanley Kubrick's *2001: A Space Odyssey*, very few people know what was about to transpire. Even Alex North, who had written the score, was not sure what he would see and hear. In the realm of the film's music, what North and the world heard was not unprecedented, but it was certainly unexpected: a score constructed entirely of preexistent music. North had understood from the beginning that Kubrick had had some pieces of classical music in mind, as he had been using them as "temp tracks" (preexistent music or audio used in editing to approximate the mood or atmosphere of a given scene). North's score endeavored to match the moods and forms of Kubrick's temporary tracks while maintaining the artistic integrity and continuity of a newly written score. The score he provided failed to convince Kubrick, and at the premiere North heard not a single note of his own music. The lengthy production period of the film allowed for significant rumination on the subject of the score, and Kubrick considered the expectations of North and MGM along with his own ideas, remaining somewhat cagey about his intentions until the very last moment.

Kubrick's musical choices were discussed in contemporary reviews of his films since his very first feature, but a scholarly treatment of the scores of Kubrick's films—particularly the films from *2001* and after—began years later. This intensification of focus seems to have coincided with two important factors: the growing legitimacy of film music as a subject for serious scholarship, and the emergence of North's "lost" score to *2001*, which happened in the early 1990s. With the death of Kubrick in 1999, scholarship about the man and all aspects of his filmmaking art deepened further.

The first book-length study of Kubrick and music appeared in 2002 with Gerrit Bodde's *Musik in den Filmen von Stanley Kubrick*. It has not yet been translated into English. A year, earlier, film critic and theorist Michel Chion published *Kubrick's Cinema Odyssey*, which provided a detailed study of the music and sound of *2001*. This book was translated into English by one of film music's most noteworthy scholars, Claudia Gorbman. In 2003, Stuart Y. McDougal edited a collection of essays on *A Clockwork Orange* featuring the article "A Bird of Like Rarest Spun Heavenmetal: Music in *A Clockwork Orange*" by Peter J. Rabinowitz. I made a detailed study of the music in

A Clockwork Orange in my 2005 dissertation "'It Was Lovely Music That Came to My Aid': Music's Contribution to the Narrative of the Novel, Film, and Play, *A Clockwork Orange*," which drew on, among other things, published interviews with Kubrick and Wendy Carlos speaking about the music of the film.

Gorbman, whose monograph on film music *Unheard Melodies: Narrative Film Music* (1987) is a watershed in the discipline of film music, published a chapter called "Ears Wide Open: Kubrick's Music" in 2006. In that same year, Roger Hickman made mention of Kubrick's use of preexistent music in his *Reel Music: Exploring 100 Years of Film Music*. Paul Merkley wrote about Alex North's score in 2007, arguing that North's music never stood a chance, and that Kubrick's shift from newly written music to preexistent cues was the inevitable culmination of a process that had already been put in motion. In 2011, Julia Heimerdinger published an article on György Ligeti's reaction to the score of *2001*, as did Kate McQuiston on the film's musical choices. McQuiston went on to write a book about Kubrick and music in 2013. Also, in 2013, I published my book, *Listening to Stanley Kubrick: The Music in His Films*.

Articles that focused specifically on *The Shining* emerged in the early 2000s as well. Leonard Lionnet's 2004 article appears to be the first attempt to parse out Kubrick's musical choices in the film. The film is mentioned specifically in K. J. Donnelly's *The Spectre of Sound: Music in Film and Television* (2005). In 2009, Jeremy Barham contributed to his discussion on the chapter, "Incorporating Monsters: Music as Context, Character and Construction in Kubrick's *The Shining*." I have provided a detailed reckoning of the music of *The Shining* both in my book and in *Studies in the Horror Film* (2015).

Although it has one of the most interesting scores (and won Leonard Rosenman an Academy Award for adapted score), *Barry Lyndon* has received less attention than *2001*, *A Clockwork Orange*, and *The Shining*. Dominic Lash has begun to address this with his 2017 article "Distance Listening: Musical Anachronism in Stanley Kubrick's *Barry Lyndon*."

Since the opening of the Kubrick Archive in 2007, researchers have greater access to materials related to Kubrick's choice of music, including records and tapes sent to Kubrick by Wendy Carlos with possible cues for *The Shining*. In conjunction with the Archive, in 2013 oral historian Pamela Glintenkamp made a series of nine films about different aspects of Kubrick's art called the Stanley Kubrick Archive Oral History Project; music is covered in the second film.

Kubrick's shift from newly written scores to preexistent music in *2001* was somewhat surprising, especially to those who knew little of *2001*'s production details, as the scores for Kubrick's previous feature films had not overtly suggested that he was moving toward such a radical change. Kubrick's debut film project, *Fear and Desire*, featured a newly composed score by composer Gerald Fried, as had the projects subsequent: *Killer's Kiss*, *The Killing*, and *Paths of Glory*. When Kubrick was hired to helm *Spartacus*, Alex North was already attached as composer, and Kubrick interacted with him numerous times over the long production period, possibly influencing some of his choices.

In retrospect, there are interesting choices in the scores of *Lolita* and *Dr. Strangelove* that can be read as exploratory. Kubrick began to consider different options like using more preexistent music or arrangements of preexistent songs. He had dabbled with these things earlier, but in the films that followed, it seems that Kubrick was reaching for a new mode of scoring, one which would allow him greater ability to pick and choose the soundscape of the film. Developing this mode would become a refined process over the years, with Kubrick employing more people to do research, to provide him extensive lists of pieces to choose from, to arrange different versions of musical cues, and even to edit alternate versions of scenes to various musical choices.

Kubrick's sense of music's power in film came through his own love of film and his experience as a viewer. The score to the Russian film *Alexander Nevsky* (1938) by Sergei Prokofiev was particularly influential (LoBrutto 1999). When he had the opportunity to make his first short film, he and composer Gerald Fried watched films together. According to Fried: "I had ten months to a year to learn how the hell to [score a film]. There were no courses. I went to a lot of movies and took notes. Stanley and I went to the movies together and we would say, 'This is working, this is not working'" (LoBrutto 1999: 67). It was in the years of collaboration with Fried that Kubrick began to formulate his own ideas specifically about scoring. By the time of *Paths of Glory*, Fried notes: "[Kubrick] had developed a taste and a style and he was a hard guy to argue with ... At the beginning, it was easy, I went my own way, but by ... *Paths of Glory*, I had to justify every note" (Fried 2003).

Kubrick eventually developed a very strong opinion on the use of preexistent music in film, which was at odds with many film composers, who were naturally philosophically opposed to the practice. Kubrick explained:

However good our best film composers may be, they are not a Beethoven, a Mozart, or a Brahms. Why use music which is less good when there is such a multitude of great orchestral music available from the past and from our own time? ... With a little more care and thought, these *temporary* tracks can become the final score. (1980)

Kubrick and author Arthur C. Clarke began the process of making *2001* with music in mind. They were inspired by Carl Orff's epic choral work, *Carmina Burana*, and briefly considered asking the composer to provide the score (Chion 2001). The music of Mahler, specifically the Third Symphony, was under consideration (Baxter 1997), as was *Antarctica Suite* by Ralph Vaughan Williams and *A Midsummer Night's Dream*, by Felix Mendelssohn. The latter two appeared as the score to some scenes Kubrick assembled for executives at MGM who wanted to check on the film's progress (Clarke 1972). In the end, the score consisted of the opening to Richard Strauss's tone poem *Also Sprach Zarathustra* (which appears three times in the film); Johann Strauss's *Blue Danube* Waltz; *Atmosphères, Requiem, Aventures*, and *Lux Aeterna* by György Ligeti; and Adagio from *Gayane* by Aram Khatchaturian.

While many critics and viewers of *2001* were impressed with the overall effect of the music—many reviews even mentioning it specifically—some were less than delighted. Film composer Jerry Goldsmith said, "I remember seeing Stanley Kubrick's *2001: A Space Odyssey* and cringing at what I consider to be an abominable misuse of music. I had heard the music Alex North had written for the film, and which had been dropped by Kubrick, and I thought what Kubrick used in its place was idiotic" (quoted in Thomas 1979: 227–8). Goldsmith later conducted North's original score for a 1993 recording.

Regardless of the naysayers, Kubrick couldn't have helped but been encouraged by the response of critics and the public. Sales of *2001: A Space Odyssey Original Motion Picture Soundtrack* (1968) far exceeded anyone's expectations, and MGM responded with another album, this one called *Music Inspired by MGM's Presentation of the Stanley Kubrick Production 2001: A Space Odyssey* (1970) with more music by Richard Strauss and more by Ligeti as well. The track list includes: *Coppelia* by Leo Delibes, *Lontano* and *Volumina* by Ligeti, *Entflieht Auf Leichten Kahnen* by Anton Webern, Waltzes from *Der Rosenkavalier* by Richard Strauss, and "Berceuse" from *Gayane* Suite by Aram Khatchaturian. It is not clear what role, if any, Kubrick had in choosing these pieces, but Kubrick would go on to use *Lontano* by Ligeti in *The Shining*, and he would request that Steven Spielberg (and composer John Williams) find a place for a waltz from *Der Rosenkavalier* in *A.I.*

With *2001*, Kubrick's reputation as musical curator had been established and would grow with each subsequent film. Music was woven into the source material of his next project, *A Clockwork Orange*. Anthony Burgess, who was a self-taught musician and composer, refers to actual composers and fictional ones and describes musical works in colorful detail. Music serves a largely symbolic function in the novel since it cannot be heard, only described. Alex's love of music gives the reader a way to identify with a character who is morally reprehensible. It is also a representation of his free will. As he undergoes the "Ludovico treatment," which incorporates medication, violent films, and classical music, he loses the ability to be violent, but also loses the ability to enjoy music. In the film, music takes on structural and aesthetic roles as well. It becomes a visceral presence because it can be heard by both the main character and by the audience.

Kubrick biographer Vincent LoBrutto reasoned that the director was attracted to the source material because music formed "a crucial element" of the narrative and that "Kubrick instinctively knew that he wanted classical music throughout the film for point and counterpoint within the story" (1999: 350). One critic saw this choice as an excuse to indulge "a passion for the warhorses of the repertoire" and use them as score (Fulford 1974: 151). This is perhaps an overstatement, as there also numerous musical pieces mentioned in the novel that either do not exist or were not chosen for inclusion in the film. Furthermore, in choosing music, Kubrick would show that he could make subtle and unexpected choices that—in bringing their own meanings and histories— enhanced the score's impact. This was beyond Kubrick's intentions, of course; he often claimed to know little of the extramusical contexts of the works he chose. Nevertheless, the use of preexistent music allowed the director to not only deemphasize some of the original meanings but create new associations (Bender 1999).

The score is primarily a pastiche of excerpts from a few classical works, some realized on Moog synthesizer by Wendy Carlos and some played on traditional instruments. Carlos had, of course, already achieved fame by recording *Switched on*

Bach (1968), a collection of the music of J. S. Bach played on a Moog. She followed this enormously successful, Platinum-certified album with *The Well-Tempered Synthesizer* (1969). Kubrick was approached by Carlos's producer, Rachel Elkind, who sent copies of *Switched on Bach* and *The Well-Tempered Synthesizer* to Kubrick after principal photography on *A Clockwork Orange* had largely been completed.

Intrigued, Kubrick used the following tracks from Carlos: Title Music from *A Clockwork Orange* (a Moog realization of Henry Purcell's Funeral Music for Queen Mary); the overture to Gioachino Rossini's *Guillaume Tell*; excerpts from Beethoven's Ninth Symphony; and an original work by Carlos called "Timesteps." The soundtrack also contains excerpts from recordings of performances with traditional instruments: the overture to Gioachino Rossini's *The Thieving Magpie*, Edward Elgar's *Pomp and Circumstance* Marches I and IV, excerpts from Beethoven's Ninth Symphony, and Gene Kelly's "Singin' in the Rain." Carlos's realizations provided fresh, alternate options for cues. The sound materials of the Moog gave some of the music what might be read as a "futuristic" feeling. The relative coolness of the Moog realizations laid side-by-side with the perceived warmth of traditional orchestral excerpts proved a good fit for the film. In her own words, Kubrick "was getting his cake and eating it too" (Bond 1999a: 23).

Armed with the learning experiences of *2001* and *A Clockwork Orange*, Kubrick undertook his next film with new ideas. Preproduction on *Barry Lyndon* was a lengthy process. Since the film was a period piece, music was researched for veracity and chronological appropriateness. Correspondence found in the Kubrick Archive details his process of choosing music and musical personnel for the film. At one point, Kubrick considered hiring André Previn as conductor and arranger, although he was too busy to participate. Another composer, Nino Rota, was also considered, although Rota was not comfortable with the specifications of the assignment; while he was told that there might be an opportunity to write some new music, the lion's share of the job was in arranging and orchestrating other cues. Rota also expressed concern that if he did write original music that it could be easily tossed aside as Kubrick had done with North's score for *2001*.

At the same time these talks were going on, Kubrick had gotten his team to work on finding appropriate cues for the film. Harlan's work was especially significant in this area. Harlan wrote to Hans B. Eggers at Deutsche Grammaphon:

> We will need a large amount of all types of 18th century and 17th century music— dances, folk songs, minuets, gavottes, etc. I think it would be a marvelous idea if Deutsche Grammaphon could provide us with a large choice of what's available along these lines, including all the big masterworks for orchestra and chamber music from this extremely rich period. (Letter to H. B. Eggers, August 29, 1973, SKA)

He was also in contact with Polydor Records about cues from early Italian opera. Hanno Rinke from Polydor A&R responded with a list of "Italian Opera Repertoire from Monteverdi Till Early Verdi" (Rinke 1975).

Harlan corresponded with Stan Hibbert, assistant secretary from the Musician's Union about the use of specific recordings in the film. In reference to a recording of Mozart's German Dances, K. 605, Hibbert explained:

> The Union does not, as a matter of course, authorise the use of gramophone records for use in the sound-track of films; we prefer that special sessions are mounted for the recording of music for specific feature films. However, we are prepared to accede to your request, subject to a payment of 18 pounds to each of our members involved in the original gramophone recording session. (Letter to Jan Harlan, 1974, SKA)

The team also received a great deal of help from composer and arranger, Dominic Frontiere, who wrote to the team with some suggestions. In his letter of July 1973, he suggests the music of certain composers popular at the time: G. F. Handel, Henry Purcell, and Johann Christian Bach. He also notes that an anachronistic choice like Frederick Delius might be equally as effective on the score. With his letter, Frontiere included sheet music for some of the popular songs from the period of the Seven Years War (1756–63) like: "The British Grenadiers," "Lilliburlero," and "Tenth Regiment" (Frontiere 1973).

The Archive contains numerous lists of records they wanted to obtain including German dances by Mozart and Beethoven, Purcell's semi-opera *The Fairy-Queen*, Haydn Symphonies, Mahler's *Songs of a Wayfarer*, and Vivaldi's Concerto for Two Trumpets. For the early scenes that take place in Ireland, it was important that the cues reflect authenticity. In a newspaper article from 1973, the Irish band the Chieftains mentions correspondence from Kubrick personally asking to discuss using some of their music in *Barry Lyndon*. And indeed, they did contribute recordings of Sean Ó Riada's "Women of Ireland" and "The Sea-Maiden." Chieftains founding member, Paddy Moloney also provided the song "Tin Whistles" with Sean Potts.

To helm the score, Kubrick chose composer Leonard Rosenman to act primarily as an arranger rather than a composer of new cues. With this choice, Kubrick could have the best of both worlds: preexistent cues and a skilled hand to manipulate them (by length, tempo, key, or orchestration) in order to maintain the integrity of his choices. Kubrick was loath to abruptly cut or awkwardly fade a cue, and he was quite concerned about timing actions on screen or edits with structural points in the music (Harlan 2011b). There is a multitude of documents in the Kubrick Archive specifically about making the chosen cues fit into the film. In one note, for example, the task is timing a percussive hit with a particular marching shot. Getting this synchronization to work required the efforts of the editor Tony Lawson and Rosenman, who needed to provide an additional twenty seconds of music.

Alongside the Irish cues mentioned above are the traditional songs "British Grenadiers," the "Hohenfriedberger March" attributed to Frederick the Great, and "Liliburlero," all arranged by Rosenman. Rosenman's greatest contribution to the score, however, was in arranging G. F. Handel's sixteen-measure Sarabande into numerous distinct versions. All told, these arrangements occupy more than thirty minutes of screen time and encompass different moods and situations. One single version of this piece lasts eleven minutes.

The score of *Barry Lyndon* is exceedingly rich, with period-appropriate marches, traditional Irish songs, orchestral arrangements, and dramatic excerpts. The music takes on the more pedestrian duties of setting the scene (and the time), but also provides emotional support for the journey of the characters. It is one of Kubrick's most effective scores, and it came to be only through the combined efforts of a team of researchers, musicians, editors, and an arranger. For his role in this score, Rosenman received the 1975 Academy Award for Best Score/Adaptation.

With *The Shining*, Kubrick slightly changed modes again. For some, this film is the pinnacle of Kubrick's output in terms of music. The two films that follow it in Kubrick's filmography arguably do not approach its level of intricacy. One scholar said how the film "exemplifies a level of both sophisticated interaction of music and moving image, and general reliance on music for contextual, characterization and narrative purposes, rarely equaled in his output" (Barham 2009: 137).

As in *Barry Lyndon*, preproduction research of music became an important source of information. Jan Harlan corresponded with Rudi Fehr at Warner Bros. to provide him with a list of popular songs from the years 1920–35. Fehr wrote back in late 1977 a list of more than 150 songs categorized by year (Fehr 1977). In the Kubrick Archive there is also a handwritten list (author unknown) of popular songs from the 1920s and '30s. The criteria used for inclusion in this list were sales of both sheet music and recordings and significant and continued radio play.

Kubrick collaborated again with Wendy Carlos and producer Rachel Elkind, who had provided such excellent work on *A Clockwork Orange*. In the preproduction period, Kubrick asked them to read Stephen King's *The Shining* to inspire some musical creation. They asked Kubrick if he had any preexistent music in mind and Kubrick named Sibelius's *Valse Triste*. Carlos returned the favor by suggesting Kubrick use the *Dies Irae* chant, to which he became quite attached (LoBrutto 1999: 446–7).

Carlos and Elkind set about making albums full of cues, planning to give Kubrick as many options as possible. They had only the novel to guide them in this endeavor at first. Later, when footage was available, they added more cues based on what they saw. Carlos and Elkind's tracks included meditations on the *Dies Irae* chant (which would become the opening cue in the film), but also tracks with buzzing sounds, moans and groans, shrieks, and tracks of unique vocal effects performed by Elkind (Gengaro 2013). Of their many tracks, Kubrick used just three. Their synthesized version of the *Dies Irae* opens the film and features some vocal effects by Rachel Elkind and some metallic strings being struck on an autoharp. A cue called "Rocky Mountains" accompanies the family's drive up to the Overlook Hotel, and an eerie cue made up of a buzz and heartbeat (call it "Shining/Heartbeat" because it accompanies Danny's call for help via telepathy) appears twice. Apart from the *Dies Irae* opening, the other two cues act more like ambient sound effects than music.

Kubrick's main musical collaboration on *The Shining* was not with Wendy Carlos, or with any composer or arranger. For this film, Kubrick worked closely with music editor, Gordon Stainforth. As he had done all the way back in *Spartacus*, Kubrick made a list of places for musical cues, providing brief descriptions of the kinds of things he wanted. Rather than being concerned with historical context (as he was in *Barry Lyndon*), Kubrick instead made practical and functional requests. Stainforth was then on his own to cut together scenes and musical cues, making a few versions for Kubrick to view. Editor Ray Lovejoy would sometimes assist Stainforth in cutting the film to time specifications. This technique was particularly useful when he wanted to cut to structural points in the music—as Kubrick preferred. Stainforth acknowledges that there was a lot of "trial and error" (Howard 1999: 153) but that their collaboration was ultimately quite smooth. Their mutual understanding of what was need precluded the need for lengthy discussion, and Kubrick was able to make choices after seeing multiple versions.

Most of the music in *The Shining* was composed by Krzysztof Penderecki. In the final forty minutes of the film, Stainforth used excerpts from numerous works by the composer, sometimes overlapping layers from different pieces. The benefit of this layering allowed for a musical texture that could be continuous and bring out the sections of pieces that Kubrick wanted to emphasize. The downside was one of practicality; because Stainforth often offered different options to Kubrick, the labeling of the layers was not always meticulously done (Lionnet 2004). Kubrick handled this ambiguity by being slightly vague in the credits of the film. A card appears that says "Music By," followed by *Music for Strings, Percussion and Celesta* with Béla Bartók's name, a card saying simply: "Krzysztof Penderecki," and another card saying "György Ligeti." It is very unusual for the credits of a film to omit the names of the actual works used, but this was likely done because of the uncertainty of what had been used. It has, however, been suggested that this could have been a meaningful choice, acknowledging that these works were used to create "an indistinct sonic backdrop" (Donnelly 2005: 46).

Full Metal Jacket was Kubrick's first film after *2001* to have a score focused on popular music rather than Classical music. Most of music on the soundtrack is preexistent, but there are also new cues, provided by Kubrick's daughter, Vivian, writing under the name Abigail Mead. *Full Metal Jacket* takes place during the Vietnam War, and the song choices are contemporaneous with the film action. In some ways, the music in *Full Metal Jacket* looks back to the pop scores of *Blackboard Jungle* and *Easy Rider*. In these films and in *Full Metal Jacket*, pop music creates meaning for the viewer in two ways: "Through its musical features (rhythm, melody, lyrics, etc.) and through the connotations such songs may suggest to the viewer, who is supposed to share the culture that has produced them" (Mainar 1999: 55).

Mead's original cues—like Carlos's work for *The Shining*—occupy a strange middle ground between sound effect and music. Author Kate McQuiston argues that the presence of both pop music and Mead's cues helps to balance out the dramatic structure of the film, which is split into two unequal sections (2013). The original score seamlessly blends with the sound of scenes and rises up out of nowhere; at significant points, the cues suddenly reveal themselves to be music. It is a stark contrast from the popular songs, which are often lively and obvious and may provide ironic counterpoint to the actions on screen.

For *Eyes Wide Shut*, Kubrick's final film, there were multiple modes of scoring. In this case, Kubrick worked with a living composer, Jocelyn Pook, who contributed four cues to the score. He also chose preexistent art music like Dmitri Shostakovich's Waltz 2 from Suite for Variety Orchestra and György Ligeti's *Musica Ricercata II*. Furthermore, there are standards like "When I Fall in Love" and "Strangers in the Night." Although there appears to have been less concern with research for the music of this film—relative to the musical research for *The Shining* or *Barry Lyndon* particularly—Kubrick still engaged with numerous options, testing what worked best for the narrative.

In Kubrick's dealings with Pook, he asked for cues, and when she delivered them, he made suggestions to help the cue fit the scene better. What sets Kubrick apart, of course, are the two things he expected from composers: many options to choose from, and the willingness to write music without seeing footage. Pook describes the process: "[Kubrick] would describe the atmosphere of the scene to me, filling in some specific details, and then I would go away and write. When I had a completed demo, I'd come back and we'd discuss it" (Bond 1999b: 25). Of Pook's four cues in the film, three were newly composed, and the fourth was a preexistent cue, the one that had brought Pook to Kubrick's attention. Its original title was "Backwards Priests," but it was renamed "Masked Ball" for the film's soundtrack.

In an interview from 2011, Harlan gave an example of how the efficacy of a piece of music trumped every other concern. Early in the production period for *Eyes Wide Shut*, Kubrick chose a piano arrangement of a song by Richard Wagner, and it was part of the film for nearly a year. Kubrick eventually replaced it after concluding that the piece was too beautiful for his purposes. Harlan explained: "This is someone who lives in the cutting room for a year with the Wesendonck lieder, and then kicks it out although he loves it. He didn't love [the piece that replaced it] the same way, but he loved it for the narrative" (2011a). One piece that Kubrick kept throughout production and which appears in the final film is Chris Isaak's "Baby Did a Bad, Bad Thing." In the film, the song accompanies a love scene between the two protagonists. Kubrick must have found the driving beat compelling for a scene of this kind. The lyrics also seem appropriate as Isaak sings about a lover who appears indifferent to the hurt she causes him.

As we look back through Kubrick's films, we can observe a few dominant trends in his musical choices. One of the most significant shifts happened during the production of *2001*. From that point on, most of musical cues in Kubrick's films come from preexistent sources, but that should not suggest a monolithic approach. In subsequent films, Kubrick sought out expanding possibilities. Preexistent musical cues, whether chosen through research, professional recommendations, or personal taste, could be cut, layered, manipulated, or arranged. Experimentation with various modes of scoring had three main results. First, there was an emphasis on research, especially in preproduction periods. This aspect proved to be particularly important in *Barry Lyndon* and *The Shining*. Second, there was a deemphasis on, but not a total omission of, newly written music. There are still newly composed cues in *A Clockwork Orange*, *The Shining*, *Full Metal Jacket*, and *Eyes Wide Shut*. Third, Kubrick entrusted the arrangement and manipulation of preexistent cues to specialists. In *Barry Lyndon*,

Leonard Rosenman acted as conductor and arranger of preexistent works. This ensured that Kubrick's musical choices would fit into scenes as necessary, or conform to any other practical, structural, or dramatic needs. In *The Shining*, no new arrangements were made of preexistent pieces, but a music editor manipulated preexistent recordings. It is with *Barry Lyndon* and *The Shining* that we see true innovation in the use of preexistent music. *Full Metal Jacket* and *Eyes Wide Shut*, in many ways, look back to older modes, yet all the films in the second half of Kubrick's career show a thoughtful and imaginative approach to film scoring. These scores have inspired countless other filmmakers and form a significant part of his legacy. In considering a multifarious approach to scoring, Kubrick embraced new and exciting possibilities in the realm of sound and music.

Part Three

Gender and Identity

Introduction

Kubrick has been accused of being "cold" and unemotional; misanthropic; misogynistic, racist in places, and sexist (Kael 1972b; Planka 2012). The chapters in this section explore various aspects of how Kubrick represented men and women and the relations between them, whether sexual or marital. The thorny issues of feminism, gender, sexuality, marriage, and family are core themes running throughout Kubrick's oeuvre and the criticism and scholarship surrounding it.

Karen A. Ritzenhoff considers Kubrick from a feminist perspective, exploring the role of women in Kubrick's films (or lack thereof), particularly in the #MeToo era. Women worked both in front of and behind the camera, including his own family members, enduring a torrid time by some accounts, as did many of Kubrick's cast and crew. But because Kubrick's films tended to focus on men and their fears and desires in all-male homosocial environments, women were marginalized in his films and occupied a limited set of roles. From this it seems that Kubrick's films manifested an ambiguity toward women, who exist only in terms of the male gaze, as objects of voyeurism, violence, abjection, and sex. Focusing on the key films that bookend Kubrick's career as a mature director (and producer), namely *Lolita* and *Eyes Wide Shut*, Ritzenhoff sees very little development over five decades and that it is premature or even regressive to reclaim him as a feminist women's rights champion.

Mick Broderick's chapter complements Ritzenhoff's by exploring gender and sexuality in Kubrick's films. Examining issues as cisgender and heteronormativity, he shows that Kubrick questions their norms, as well as those of monogamy, marriage, and family. Although his films focus on the male experience, men are not simply one-dimensional heroes. Sex is presented in its full array: polygamous, perverted, and predatory, even loving at times. Yet, Broderick concludes, even though Kubrick drew attention to the male self-destructive drive, he collaborated with women at all levels of his business and formed long-lasting professional and personal relationships that belied their representation in his films.

Family was important to Kubrick, as Joy McEntee shows in her chapter. He surrounded himself with his daughters and extended relations and often employed them on his films. Jan Harlan, for example, his brother-in-law, acted as executive producer on his films from the early 1970s onwards, and carried out many other tasks. Family was also important thematically in Kubrick's films and at least four of his films focused on the family triad (father, mother, child) becoming warped or disrupted by an outsider presence. Even where family does not seem to be a central concern in his films, the metaphor of the family is apparent—for example, in the war movies *Paths of Glory* and *Full Metal Jacket*. Overall, McEntee concludes, the conventional understanding of family or reproduction is not useful in conceptualizing Kubrick's films.

The final two chapters explore a dimension of Kubrick and his work that has routinely been ignored by many until Geoffrey Cocks's groundbreaking research (2004, 2006) into the subject: Kubrick's Jewishness. Building upon this work, Abrams (2018) considered the impact of his cultural, religious, and ethnic background and how this influenced Kubrick's thinking and development as a New York Jewish intellectual. Marat Grinberg's chapter summarizes the results of this work but develops it in new directions to reflect upon the Holocaust film Kubrick never made, *Aryan Papers*. He sees allegory as fundamental to our understanding of Kubrick's Jewishness and how it operates in his movies.

Geoffrey Cocks, by contrast, takes a narrower approach by exploring the effects of German history, Nazism, and the Holocaust on Kubrick's work. Kubrick was drawn toward German literature, film, and history and Cocks traces Kubrick's fascination with the evil of Nazism but which, as evidenced by his failure to complete his Holocaust film, he was only able to refer to "indirectly." These traces are found throughout Kubrick's oeuvre, but are really evident in *The Shining*, Cocks argues, which can be detected through a close examination of the film's details.

15

Kubrick and Feminism

Karen A. Ritzenhoff

Women in Kubrick's films are reflections of the male psyche and especially of deeply rooted male anxiety and paranoia. Whether as eye candy or sources of anguish and abjection, women play a subordinate role in most of the films and are underrepresented even in terms of screen time. As Robert Kolker has pointed out, "His films are rarely concerned with women, except in a peripheral and usually unpleasant way" (2000: 106). Two of Kubrick's films feature a sole woman in an all-male environment— *Paths of Glory* and *Dr. Strangelove*—where both are objectified in sexual terms. In other films they are marginal and marginalized, offering only one woman of any "narrative importance" (Dovey 2008: 170) in *Fear and Desire, Killer's Kiss, The Killing, 2001: A Space Odyssey, The Shining*, and *Full Metal Jacket*. Kubrick's films contain subtexts of male angst, castration anxiety, and fear of malfunction in the bedroom, as well as on the battlefield. These themes are revisited in many of his movies, either directly, as in *Full Metal Jacket* when Private Joker is unable to fire his gun at the female sniper, or indirectly, as in *Eyes Wide Shut* when Bill Harford is unable to sleep with the objects of his desire.

The question arises, of course, whether these films are about male anxiety, and therefore compatible with feminist critiques of masculinity, or misogynistic expressions of it. Kubrick has often been described as a misogynist in nonscholarly circles (see Siddiquee 2017). This misogyny has become a key popular discourse about him, especially in relation to the "clear evidence of verbal and emotional abuse" (ibid.) in his conflicts with Shelley Duvall on *The Shining*, whose character, Wendy, was described by Stephen King as "one of the most misogynistic characters ever put on film … [who is] basically just there to scream and be stupid" (quoted in Shoard 2013). Vivian Kubrick's documentary, *Making The Shining* (1980), appears to capture Shelley Duvall's psychological distress. Allegations of similarly grueling treatment on the sets of his other films have also been reported (Nicholson 2014; Barshad 2015).

On the other hand, Kubrick worked closely with the female members of his family. His three wives were cast in different roles in his early films: Toba Metz in *Fear and Desire*, Ruth Sobotka in *Killer's Kiss*, and Christiane Harlan in *Paths of Glory*. They also played key roles behind the camera as did his three daughters—Katharina, Anya, and Vivian—who played uncredited extras in *2001, Barry Lyndon, The Shining*, and *Full*

Metal Jacket. Another important fact is that *Eyes Wide Shut* prominently featured the artwork of Christiane and Anya Kubrick. And Nicole Kidman had nothing but praise for the director whom she referred to in terms characterizing him as a beloved mentor (Ginsberg 2012).

Yet, little scholarship in Kubrick Studies has engaged with the issue of Kubrick's misogyny or with the role of women (or indeed the representation of ethnic and sexual minority groups) in his films. Many female researchers have analyzed his work—among them many who have contributed to this volume, including Kate McQuiston, Elisa Pezzotta, Christine Lee Gengaro, Catriona McAvoy, Dijana Metlic, Serenella Zanotti, Manca Perko, Joy McEntee, and Georgina Orgill—but none of their analyses has been exclusively devoted to Kubrick's representation of femininity or questions of feminism. Again, while there have case studies of individual films—in particular *Lolita* (Wells 2015), *The Shining* (Carnicke 2006; Kilker 2006; Hornbeck 2016), and *Eyes Wide Shut* (Deleyto 1999; Acevedo-Muñoz 2002; Carnicke 2006)— few scholars have attempted to tackle the representation of women and femininity in the totality of Kubrick's work. One reason could be that Kubrick's status as a great auteur and "an eccentric genius," in the words of Susan White (1988: 120), would be diminished by drawing too much attention to the abuse of a child in *Lolita*; the objectification and rape of women in *A Clockwork Orange*; the misogynist gender display, casual homophobia, and racism in his depiction of Vietnamese women in *Full Metal Jacket*, based on "perceptions of a historically eroticized East" (Boczar 2015: 70), and Asian male cross-dressers in *Eyes Wide Shut*. Even feminist film scholars like Michael Broderick in his nuanced chapter on "Gender and Sexuality" in this volume prefer to discuss Kubrick's representation of toxic masculinity, "sardonic wit," and "skeptical world view" than accuse the director of furthering heteronormative gender stereotypes or mocking homosexuality.

At the same time, it is possible to argue—as Abrams and Hunter do in their chapter on psychoanalysis—that Kubrick analyzes rather than simply reproduces misogynistic tropes. The sexism of *A Clockwork Orange*, for example, depicted in the Allen Jones inspired décor of the Korova Milk Bar and the phallic pop-art of Cat Lady might be taken as a comment on an affectless and hypersexualized culture. Moreover, Kubrick's fascination with psychoanalytic understandings of sexuality and gender surely impacted on how he represented women in relation to male fantasy, perversion, and repression. The influence of Freud on his depiction of male perversion (repression, incest, and so on) explains some of the images of women as castrating, bad mothers, whores, nymphets, and vindictive and unreliable subjects.

Focusing on *Lolita*, *A Clockwork Orange*, *The Shining*, *Full Metal Jacket*, and *Eyes Wide Shut*, this chapter offers a feminist analysis of Kubrick's films for the post-#MeToo era that explores the tension between the claim of misogyny and modes of representation. Although Kubrick is not by any means to be described as a feminist, his films engage with key themes that are relevant in feminist theory, psychoanalysis, and possibly surrealism and reveal how women in Western culture have been perceived by men as sexual objects and sources of anxiety.

Voyeurism, Violence, and Abjection

Regardless of whether Kubrick himself was misogynistic, his films evince a deep-rooted ambiguity toward women, which is shared by many of the male protagonists. Women in Kubrick's films frequently only exist in male fantasy. They are generally ogled, violated, humiliated, and abused, and sexual desire for them is combined with abjection (Creed 1993), especially of the aging female body. Often, they carry the threat of danger, disease, and death. As Lindiwe Dovey has written:

> The women in Kubrick's films do indeed appear to be the projections of heterosexual male desire, and, as such, they are also projections of heterosexual male fear of the female. Kubrick's female characters are largely schematic, ranging from the *femmes fatales* in the early noir films, *Killer's Kiss* and *The Killing*, to the innocent, weeping German woman in *Paths of Glory*, to the young voluptuous old hags in *A Clockwork Orange* (1971), to the long suffering Lady Lyndon in *Barry Lyndon*, to the old pathetic wife and other Wendy in *The Shining*, to the Vietnamese prostitutes and "warrior woman" in *Full Metal Jacket*. It is possible to contend, quite crudely, that we do not learn anything new about femininity from these characters or from their representation. They are situated at the conventional poles of the "ideal" and "fallen" woman. Rather, they aid our understanding of masculinity. (2008: 171)

None of the heterosexual relationships between men and women in the films is conventional or mainstream. Men are pedophiles (*Lolita, Eyes Wide Shut*); rapists, sexual predators, and murderers (*Fear and Desire, Killer's Kiss, Spartacus, Lolita, A Clockwork Orange*), domestic vigilantes (*The Shining*), assassins and pimps (*Killer's Kiss, Full Metal Jacket, Eyes Wide Shut*), adulterers (*Barry Lyndon, Eyes Wide Shut, and Lolita*), castrated or disempowered males (*Fear and Desire, The Killing, Barry Lyndon*), and alienated husbands (*The Killing, The Shining, Eyes Wide Shut*). Women are seductresses (*Killer's Kiss, The Killing, Lolita, Dr. Strangelove, The Shining, Eyes Wide Shut*), prostitutes (*Killer's Kiss, Full Metal Jacket, Eyes Wide Shut*), and unreliable mates who can turn on their own husbands or male counterparts, even with an ax or an assault weapon (*A Clockwork Orange, Barry Lyndon, The Shining, Full Metal Jacket, Eyes Wide Shut*). A few older women are shown in roles of authority and pseudomothers (the doctor who administers the Ludovico Treatment in *A Clockwork Orange*, or the compassionate pediatrician in *The Shining*). The most controversial depictions of women in Kubrick's films are probably the child actresses, namely Sue Lyon in in *Lolita* and Leelee Sobieski as "Milich's daughter" (she doesn't even have a name!) in *Eyes Wide Shut*, who is pimped by her own father, sleeping with Asian customers in exchange for money. In both films, the teenage girls are shown as willing seductresses, not as mere victims of male desire. Like the Vietnamese prostitute in *Full Metal Jacket*, referred to in the credits as "Da Nang Hooker," the women negotiate who they want to sleep with, displaying a form of power.

Kubrick begins to depict women as sexual objects, or omit them altogether, from his earliest photography and documentary films. Women are shown nude in his photographs for *Look* magazine (see Mather 2013). He removes them from *Day of the Fight* even though they appear in the original *Look* magazine photostory "Prizefighter." In *The Seafarers*, they are introduced as sexual relief for the crews of the merchant navy. The early films are important in this discussion, as is their relationship to film noir's representation of women, as independent, highly sexualized, and often deviant influences on the (trapped) male protagonists. It is Sherry Peatty's humiliation and cuckoldry of her husband that leads him to betray the whole scheme, leading to a bloody massacre. *Paths of Glory*, as mentioned above, features only one significant female character and *Spartacus* was much more wholesome as befitting a big-budget Hollywood epic. It was not until the 1960s, when the Production Code had sufficiently relaxed, that Kubrick could treat women in a much more explicit fashion, beginning with *Lolita*.

Lolita is an interesting case study in ambiguity, though ultimately the film is voyeuristic. On the one hand, in adapting Vladimir Nabokov's novel about an incestuous relationship between a teenage girl, and her predatory stepfather, Kubrick cast an actress who was more mature than the nubile nymphet of the novel. But as Kathy Merlock Jackson points out, "the message remains the same" (1986: 138). According to Nathan Abrams, instead of Humbert being depicted as a predatory pedophile, Lolita "seduces *him* and thereafter he becomes her slave, as coded in the opening credits" (2018: 76). Abrams argues that Humbert is emasculated and turns into "the nagging, whining, domineering, needy allegorically Jewish mother figure" (ibid.). Even if Lolita does not "see herself as a victim" and must be blamed for part of the transgression, this glosses over the fact that incest, criminal sex with a minor, and rape are the focal point of the narrative.

Where Kubrick was careful not to eroticize Lolita too explicitly in the film, its promotional material was another matter, simultaneously infantilizing yet eroticizing the young actress. This is especially true of the iconic poster image of Lolita gazing seductively while wearing red heart-shaped glasses and sucking on a red lollipop. The image was taken by American fashion photographer, Bert Stern, whose candid photographs of Sue Lyon in bed wearing white clothing, her bare legs covered by the cartoon section of a newspaper (anticipating the *Playboy* spread in *Dr. Strangelove*). She is also depicted in a bikini (again foreshadowing Miss Scott in *Dr. Strangelove*), spread out on a blanket while tanning in the sun. Thus, Stern created a visual vocabulary of teenage female sensuality in which Lolita is predominantly engaging with the viewer behind the camera, satisfying voyeuristic pleasure, that is echoed in Kubrick's films. Stern's promotional photography, therefore, was more representative of male power than female empowerment.

In *A Clockwork Orange* voyeurism spills over into rape. There are several scenes in the film that have become iconic for their representation of excessive "ultraviolence" against women. After the droogs are fired up by their drugged milk, they head out on a night of rampage, assault and ultimately murder. After beating up a homeless drunk, their first stop is an abandoned theater where a rival gang is attempting to gang rape a woman on two makeshift mattresses. She is undressed and vulnerable. The victimized woman manages to escape as the gang rape is interrupted by Alex and his droogs who appear to provoke a gang fight. In this instance, it is the lure of violence rather than rape that draws Alex and the droogs. They subsequently invade a home and assault and rape a woman in what is still regarded as one of the most controversial segments in British film history. Mrs. Alexander's mouth is gagged and then also taped shut, while Alex is beating her husband who is lying on the floor in front of her. The rhythm of the assault is provided by the incantation of the song "Singin' in the Rain." The droogs cut holes into her red full body suit with scissors, first exposing her nipples, then stripping her entirely. Her husband if forced to watch in an act of coerced involuntary voyeurism, as are we given that Kubrick gives us Mr. Alexander's point of view as she is violated, screaming in agony with her head bent backward. Alex tells him (and us), "Viddy well, little brother, viddy well." We learn later in the film that she committed suicide after the assault.

The climax of the night is the killing of the Cat Lady. Depicted as feisty yoga goddess, the Cat Lady is almost androgynous looking. She is wearing a green leotard and white stockings. Her body is slim and well trained due to her rigorous regiment of workout machines that are displayed in all corners of her inner sanctum. Alex calls the Cat Lady a "filthy old soomka" (although she is much younger than the woman depicted in Burgess's novel). He starts taunting her with a three-foot phallic sculpture that is part of an expansive erotic art collection. Eventually, Alex kills her with the giant penis, thrust deep into her screaming mouth in an act of grotesque fellatio. Peter Krämer reminds us that protagonist Alex is a murderer, criminal, and abuser, not a popular culture hero who should be celebrated for his lack of submission to government authority (2011).

As noted previously, the depiction of femininity in *A Clockwork Orange* can be interpreted as social satire that can be dismissed as unrealistic and not necessarily offensive to female viewers. This supposedly exaggerated satirical representation of women as sex objects starts the film when Alex and his droogs are sitting in the Korova Milk Bar, consuming alcohol and drug infused milkshakes, so-called "Moloko Plus," being squirted out of women's nipples. The pop-art tables of white, female mannequins with spread legs, colorful wigs and neon-colored pubic hair still have a certain market value today as transgressive vintage designer objects. So many aspects of *A Clockwork Orange* have been fetishized, including décor and fashion, ignoring the abhorrent depiction of violence against women. The casual consumption of female nudity in the Milk Bar normalizes exposure of female genitalia and breasts for male pleasure where women's bellies are used as table surfaces. Dovey points out how

> Along with the encoding of women as men's shocking "other" in Kubrick's films, Kubrick also crucially and consistently tropes women as works of art, *objets d'art*, from the mannequins of women in *Killer's Kiss* (which are used in a fencing-like fight in one of the final scenes), to the female furniture in *A Clockwork Orange*, to the paintings of nude women in *The Shining*, *A Clockwork Orange*, and *Eyes Wide Shut*, to the statuesque, almost inanimate characterization of Lady Lyndon and the women who participate in the orgy scene in *Eyes Wide Shut*. (2008: 173)

In other scenes, Kubrick inserts shots of random breasts, alluding to imagery that seems typical of the sexploitation cinema of Russ Meyer and low culture movies (Hunter 2011). In one scene deliberately styled to resemble *Ben-Hur* (1959), Alex imagines topless Hebrew handmaidens. As part of the successful conclusion of the Ludovico Treatment aversion therapy, Alex is approached by a slim, nude, white woman, dressed only with a bikini-brief and showing off her large breasts. She walks up to him on the stage, lit from behind. The audience of psychiatrists, governmental officials, and prison officials gazes at the young woman in awe. Kubrick makes it look as if they all would not hesitate to try to kiss and touch her. Alex is crouching in front of her, gazing up at her exposed chest. He tries to touch her breasts but cannot. Alex starts to feel sick.

In many ways, the abjection of desire, transformed into disgust in *A Clockwork Orange*, is similar to a scene in *The Shining*. In the bathroom of Room 237, Jack Torrance enthusiastically embraces the naked woman he encounters there. He thinks she is a lithe, slick-with-water, beauty, but she (at this stage played by Lia Beldam) turns into an oozing, decomposing semi-dead nightmare crone (now played by Billie Gibson), a transformation Jack witnesses in the bathroom mirror. The old hag starts laughing at him vindictively and follows him with outstretched arms while he retreats, walking backward, looking horrified. His adulterous desire to engage in a sexual act has been punished with a disgusting betrayal (see Kilker 2006). The scene is intensified because his son Danny seemingly has a "shining" of this scene and sees what his father experiences, visible in parallel editing and close up cutaways. The boy child is also traumatized by the transformation of the woman.

This idea that a woman is never quite what she seems can be traced throughout Kubrick's films. Another example is when Bill Harford has an unpleasant encounter with the daughter of one of his deceased patients. She approaches him seductively while in the same room as the corpse of her dead father. He declines her offer of in this grotesque situation. This paradox is repeated in many other scenes: women are depicted as unreliable, conniving, vindictive, treacherous, and unapproachable. Harford later discovers that the prostitute Domino he befriended and wanted to sleep with earlier—before his wife Alice Harford interrupts by calling him on his cell phone—has AIDS and might have contaminated him with HIV. She is also a figurative "full metal jacket," full of sickness and decay, a bullet that Harford barely ducked. Like the greenish hag, the "old crone" in *The Shining*, Domino is associated with surprises and is the herald of death. In *Eyes Wide Shut*, there is another prostitute's dead body: Harford visits Mandy in the morgue after she has been found dead. The doctor feels sympathy and guilt because it is insinuated that he is responsible: she might have saved his life while he was being expelled from a clandestine, high-class sexual orgy. But only if the sex act had been enacted, not just fantasized about, would Harford be doomed to die because he would have contracted the AIDS virus? The fact that women are part of the male imaginary but not real partners, is part of Kubrick's play with Freudian dream analysis as projections of Bill's fantasy.

These scenes from three different films, *A Clockwork Orange*, *The Shining*, and *Eyes Wide Shut*, show abjection and rejection. The male lead figures are hateful of women but also frightened of them.

War and Sexuality

War, sexuality, and women are intimately intertwined in Kubrick's films, even though so few women are actually featured. In *Dr. Strangelove*, the secretary, a dark haired naked young woman, lying on her belly while looking up at the viewer, is spread out not only on a bed but also graces the centerfold in *Playboy* magazine, a full "spread." In the *Playboy* spread she gazes seductively at the reckless cowboy pilot, Major T. J. King "Kong" as he circles the earth in his nuclear bomber, the B-52, while he eagerly stares back at her. General Buck Turgidson sleeps with his secretary and she acts as the line of communication between Turgidson and one of her former lovers in the military high command. The reason why the Code Red is being falsely issued is that a mentally ill US Air Force General, Jack D. Ripper, believes that Russians have been contaminating American waterways with fluoride, thereby killing male sperm counts, which he describes as his "essence" and "precious bodily fluids." Without functioning sperm, the reproductive force of American (soldiers) is diminished. Ripper's solution is to retaliate with a "Wing Attack Plan R," the "R" standing for Romeo, connecting classic romance to war.

Furthermore, in the airplane's survival kit, the soldiers are not only equipped with $100 in Russian currency and nine packs of Wrigley Spearmint chewing gums but also "three lipsticks" and "three pairs of nylon stockings." "Fellas" can have "a pretty good weekend in Vegas with all that stuff," Kong announces on the intercom system. The reference to gifts presented to potential female lovers insinuates that these soldiers will seek sexual favors as soon as they touch ground, no matter what country they might be in, or what danger. The Russian currency suggests that the American bomber plane would be landing in enemy territory but that the American government would be supportive of "fraternizing" with the women of the antagonist. Major King "Kong" will eventually launch the atomic bomb in a suicide mission, riding the phallic missile into his (and our) doom.

Similarly, the title of *Full Metal Jacket* references a "projectile" in a hard metal shell, designed to be launched, as sperm in a violent, sexual climax. It is also an allegory for male intimacy and sexual fantasy, to kill, in a world devoid of women. Real women are not seen until the second half of the movie. Susan White coins this phenomenon as the repression of the feminine in her discussion of *Full Metal Jacket* (1988: 120). Kubrick is depicting a culture that is preoccupied with women, sexual arousal, violence, and the potential to fire weapons. The naming of weapons with sweethearts' first names is a displacement of real intimacy and — as the drill sergeant suggests in another vulgar rant — juvenile sexual experiences. Marines also sleep with their rifles in bed in boot camp on Parris Island. They are supposedly in a serious relationship with the weapon, "married" to "her." This suggests that men are "faithful" to their wives and partners. This is particularly ironic, given that the American soldiers in the second half of *Full Metal Jacket* habitually sleeps with Vietnamese prostitutes; an entire platoon with the same one. Other than this closeness to their weapon, the men are humiliated in their sexual desires by the rants of the drill sergeant who addresses the men with racial, misogynist, and homophobic slurs. He tells his recruits who are listening in their bunks:

Tonight … you pukes will sleep with your rifles! You will give your rifle a girl's name! Because this is the only pussy you people are going to get! Your days of finger-banging old Mary Jane Rottencrotch through her pretty pink panties are over! You're married to this piece, this weapon of iron and wood! And you will be faithful! Port … hut! Prepare to mount! Mount!

The recruits in *Full Metal Jacket* are also shown exercising, running down the barracks and singing together in the rhythm of their feet hitting the asphalt: "I don't want no teenage queen. I just want my M14." In another training song, the soldiers refer to female genitals and oral sex: "I don't know but I've been told. Eskimo pussy is mighty cold. Mmm good. Feels good. Is good. Real good. Tastes good. Mighty good. Good for you. Good for me." The lyrics are highly sexualized with the addition of sounds of sexual pleasure. Another chant says: "Mamma and Pappa were lyin' in bed, Mamma rolled over this is what she said. Now gimme some! Now gimme some! PT! Good for you and good for me." "PT" here stands for "Physical Training," a euphemism for adult sex. The Riflemen's creed, chanted before the US Marines go to bed, involves them marching while simultaneously holding their weapon and grabbing their crotch, states, "This is my rifle. This is my gun," suggesting that there is no difference between their rifle and their penises. Cementing the link, they then sleep with their rifle.

The creed assumes that the enemy is always male. When Joker encounters a Vietcong sniper on the battlefield, he is paralyzed at first because he and his fellow soldiers have only witnessed Vietnamese women as hookers. Hence, women are only useful as sexual objects and to satisfy male desire, not as part of combat. As the drill sergeant has conditioned the soldiers to do, "You will Give your Rifle a Girl's Name. Because this is the only pussy you people are going to get" and "you are married" to this weapon.

It is a surprise that the Vietcong sniper who kills many of the platoon members is a female teenager. Nothing in *Full Metal Jacket* prepares the viewer to the fact that the sniper in the final scene is a young woman. When we see the hand of a sniper pointing an army weapon through a window to shoot American soldiers, no gender markers are visible. When the American soldiers approach the hideout of the sniper, the protagonist Joker discovers that he is facing a woman and his weapon jams, like a sexual malfunction. He is at first unable to shoot the woman. However, the film ends with Joker shooting the woman warrior at point-blank range in a so-called "mercy killing," encouraged by fellow marine "Animal Mother," who had fatally wounded the sniper. She begs him to "shoot" her, collapsing the act of killing with that of filming. Thus, Joker's act of killing is described by his fellow marines as "hardcore," alluding to pornography. Susan White writes:

They are clearly confused by this woman who embodies both the repulsive and castrating "otherness" of womanhood and the ephemeral virginal/warrior ideal (she is praying—or at least the men think she is—and they are curiously restrained in their treatment of her). (1988: 128)

Joker is slaughtering and killing her like an animal on the floor, shooting a bullet at her head, execution style. As White points out, "the violent rejection of the female, of the racially other and of anything reminiscent of infantile susceptibility to maternal mastery is spelled out in the scapegoating scenes that structure this film" (ibid.: 121). Sexuality in the military is complicated by the homoerotic undertones, White argues, where fellow marines must take over roles of mothering. "At every juncture, however, the line between male bonding and the baldly homoerotic is a fine one. As the drill sergeant puts it in his Christmas speech, 'God has a hard-on for Marines'" (ibid.: 123; see also Modleski 1988).

The second biggest carriers of death in war times — apart from the nuclear bomb — are indeed the assault rifles who keep the young recruits in *Full Metal Jacket* company. They are named for sweethearts, assembled and disassembled, they need to be kept clean and polished, so they don't malfunction. And ultimately, they kill with so much force that they take out the abusive drill sergeant, as well as the unhappy bullied soldier Private Pyle, who turns his beloved rifle against his own head, takes the shaft in his mouth (in an act of fellatio) and blows his brains out, seated on a toilet rim in "a world of shit." Not a nice relationship with a girlfriend/gun.

Conclusion

Lolita and *Eyes Wide Shut* bookend the major feature films in Kubrick's film oeuvre in terms of featuring women as protagonists. There is direct continuity from *Lolita* to *Eyes Wide Shut*, not only because female underage teenagers are sleeping with grown men, but also because women are shown in a predictable visual vocabulary, like Bert Stern's photographs of Sue Lyon. There are many depictions of adult nude women in pseudoerotic poses (with exposed breasts) in Kubrick's films; ultimately "the orgy scene" in *Eyes Wide Shut*, his final film, can be compared to a climax, due to the sheer volume of intercourse, depicted as a "mechanical, machine-like representation of the male sexual fantasy" (McAvoy and Ritzenhoff 2015: 157). In both films, the leading females are frequently shown in exposed and intimate poses in bed. Lolita is spending her nights in motel rooms, driven around by her stepfather Humbert Humbert who sleeps with her. Alice Harford confesses her adulterous sexual fantasies to her husband in their bedroom after both have smoked weed as a sexual stimulant. Lolita is a teenage erotic object who has sexual appetite; Harford entices her husband to return home and make love (in more explicit wording) at the end of *Eyes Wide Shut*, while Christmas shopping for their joint daughter in a New York toy store. She is a mature woman who is in control of her sexuality.

Does this legitimize the argument that Kubrick has evolved in his depiction of female sexuality in his fifty-year directorial career? Hardly. After all, *Eyes Wide Shut* spends a significant amount of time displaying mechanical sex during an orgy, showing men in robes and Venetian masks, pumping in and out of nude prostitutes (McAvoy and Ritzenhoff 2015). Trying to reclaim Kubrick as a feminist or an advocate of women, for example, because Alice Harford survives the film unscathed, is regressive. After two years of turmoil in and around Hollywood surrounding the relaunch of the *#MeToo* movement, the question is whether the "genius provocations" that Kubrick evoked in his films have to be looked at differently under the veil of gender equality, sexual harassment and abuse, and different reiterations of the women's movement?

16

Kubrick, Gender, and Sexuality

Mick Broderick

Well before the furor of *Lolita* and up to the release of *Eyes Wide Shut* Stanley Kubrick courted controversy with his complex representations of sexuality and gender. *Dr. Strangelove*, for example, was both noted for its lack of women and the parodic foregrounding of sexual dysfunction and paranoia (Macklin 1965; Baxter 1984). Numerous critics emphasized the "coldness" of *2001: A Space Odyssey* and the asexual nature of humanity projected into the twenty-first century (Gilliatt 1968; Grant 2006; Hofsess 1968).

The Anglo-American release of *A Clockwork Orange* generated moral panics and censorship debates concerning the film's representation of nudity, rape, and "ultra-violence" (Krämer 2011). Pauline Kael (1972) found the film "Literal-minded in its sex and brutality," claiming Kubrick was "sucking up to the thugs in the audience." Feminist scholar Laura Mulvey found an "ethos of sexism ... pervades the movie itself," noting that women in Kubrick's movies have never "been more than subservient supports or sex symbols, if indeed they appear at all" (1972: 21). Nevertheless, Maria Pramaggiore (2015) sees Kubrick "as a critic of phallic masculinity" and notes that, in *Barry Lyndon*, the eponymous (anti)hero's "ascent, failure, and fall is a gender-marked process" where these "gendered and sexual dynamics highlight the conflicted masculinity of Barry's character" (103).

Despite overtly foregrounding toxic masculinity in *The Shining*, Robert Kilker suggests Kubrick's film "indulges in a more subtle misogyny" than the overt misogyny of its characters (2006: 57). The view is seemingly supported by James Naremore's observation that behind-the-scenes footage of Kubrick reveals the filmmaker "treated [actress Shelley] Duvall with almost as much contempt as [the character] Jack treats Wendy" (2007: 201). Despite this, feminist scholar Elizabeth Hornbeck (2016) claims "Wendy's hard-won independence is the film's final feminist victory" (718). Correspondingly, Paula Willoquet-Maricondi asserts that in *Full Metal Jacket* "Kubrick unmasks the true meaning of patriarchy and its motivations" (1994: 5), where the "making of manhood involves a certain rhetoric of sexuality in the dominance of the female and of the feminine within ... by defining this feminine as the enemy, by exteriorizing it so it can be attacked and eliminated, and by linking sexuality with violence" (13).

Dana Polan recognized a paradox at the heart of Kubrick's approach to gender and sexuality, describing the filmmaker as "simultaneously a sexist director and one of the most interesting depicters of a fundamental sexism in men's treatment of women" (1996: 90). Recalling Kael's accusation of literal-mindedness, Denis Bingham highlights Kubrick's "essentialist approach to gender" (2004: 263). Amy Ransom noted that several critics labeled *Eyes Wide Shut* "risible, unsexy, and anachronistic" (2010: 31), whereas Midge Decter derided Kubrick for treating Nicole Kidman "very badly ... as he did all actresses in all his movies" (1999).

Despite these diverse condemnations Kubrick's oeuvre has been consistently defended as presenting self-conscious critiques of gendered performance, patriarchy and heteronormative sexuality (e.g., Acevedo-Muñoz 2002; Alison 2003; Chion 2002; Grant 2006; Webster 2011). For example, in relation to his war films, Scarlett Higgins observes that Kubrick's "all-male universe may not harbour sexism so much as it sharpens his satire of testosterone-fuelled militarism" (2018: 800). Similarly, Raleigh Whitinger and Susan Ingram consider Kubrick's adaptation of Arthur Schnitzler's *Traumnovelle* for *Eyes Wide Shut*, as "a constructive, pro-feminist one" (2003: 55).

The cinema of Stanley Kubrick is preoccupied by men (Kolker 2011; Krämer 2015c). His narrative explorations of masculinity overtly foreground the vicissitudes and discontents of males—from the literal "Dawn of Man" to futuristic supermen and male robotic and computerized artificial intelligences. As noted above, women in Kubrick's cinematic schema appear largely peripheral or at the margin (see the "Kubrick and Feminism" chapter). As early as 1966, Kubrick self-consciously articulated his own limitations and track record in this regard. Commenting about marriage to his third wife, Christiane, he surmised:

> She is a marvelous actress ... I would like her to act but she has no interest in doing dull routine acting things and is more interested in painting. If I ever have a part, a decent part for a woman, which for some reason I never seem to write into my films, she would certainly do it. (Bernstein 1966)

Yet, despite their relatively minimal characterization and representations, women are crucial "others" by which male characters (protagonists and antagonists) are contrasted and compared. Wendy Torrance, for example, is shown throughout *The Shining* marshaling initiative and great courage to overcome and defeat her murderous husband and the Overlook Hotel's supernatural forces. The role of Josephine in Kubrick's abandoned *Napoleon* project was to have been a significant one, both nuanced and crucial in providing a counterpoint to the Emperor's ambitions. Kubrick's other unrealized project, *Aryan Papers*, may well have provided a challenge to the prevailing view since the lead character, Tania (to be played by Johanna ter Steege), dominated his screen treatment, and the narrative perspective was to be principally hers (Eyes on Cinema 2016).

Predominantly, in Kubrick's films, men act, and men do. Kubrick's cinema rarely questions "what does a woman want?" (Schoenewolf 2017), although *Eyes Wide Shut* certainly presents one overt articulation and contestation of female desire in Alice. The filmmaker's preoccupation with male identity and the social construction of normative masculinity is primary—honor, duty, courage, procreation. To paraphrase debates over *A Clockwork Orange*, for example, Kubrick's art consistently asks: "what is a man?" (Gelmis 1972; Abrams 2018).

Kubrick's work in the early 1950s provides some insight into the emerging filmmaker's thematic concerns, if not obsessions, in this regard. His films, *Killer's Kiss* and *The Killing*, as well as script drafts and fragments of multiple works from this era, display a consistent fascination with isolated male misfits and intelligent seducers who nevertheless feel loneliness and shame at their exploits. These narratives foreground hunger, self-doubt and at times self-loathing in their depictions of sexual conquests and infidelities (Wiseman 2019). Many scenarios have autobiographical resonance, such as the depiction of characters and locations in lower Manhattan in screenplay drafts of *The Married Man*, *Jealousy*, and *A Perfect Marriage* and all of them reveal Kubrick's abiding concerns: personal relationships, gender, sexuality, jealousy, ambition, and violence (Wallet E, uncatalogued, SKA 2019).

Cisgender and Heteronormativity

Kubrick's films frequently problematize not only normative heterosexuality but also social mores concerning monogamy, marriage, and family. Equally problematic, Kubrick's male "heroes" are often morally ambiguous, ethically compromised, exhibit criminal tendencies and/or pathological behavior. Kubrick's universe is populated with characters and events enmeshed in betrayal, jealousy, deceit, cuckolding, mind games, and double-crosses, frequently resulting in fatalistic outcomes. Eric Berne's bestselling *Games People Play: The Psychology of Human Relationships* (1964) was a favored, instructional text for the filmmaker according to Christiane (Kubrick 2005).

Spartacus, *Barry Lyndon*, and *Eyes Wide Shut* aside, the heteronormative biological function to replace the species through procreation within or outside the social strictures of marriage is conspicuously absent. Kubrick incessantly displays civilization parading its enduring discontents (Feldmann 1976), including sociocultural prohibitions on extramarital sex. As Reverend Runt declares when marrying Redmond Barry to Lady Lyndon (while glaring admonishingly at fornicator Barry), the institution of marriage "is not in any way to be enterprised nor taken in hand unadvisedly, lightly or wantonly, to satisfy men's carnal lusts and appetites like brute beasts that have no understanding."

Sexless birth devoid of families also features in Kubrick's cinematic imaginary. In *2001* a seemingly alien-induced parthenogenesis enables Dave Bowman to be "reborn" without corporeal human parents, whereas HAL, at the point of cognitive regression, describes his "birth" as becoming "operational" at a plant in Urbana in 1992. Similarly, in Kubrick's planned *A.I.* an advanced prototype android named David is born/delivered in a cybernetic factory already aged as a young child for parents who are struggling to cope with the terminal illness of their human son. In *Dr. Strangelove* the psychotic US Air Force General Jack D. Ripper refuses to ejaculate during sex (and thereby not procreate), denying women his "essence," believing there is a commie plot to introduce fluoride into the American water system to "sap and impurify all of our fluids" (Broderick 2017b).

The implied ambiguities of (hetero)sexual abstinence feature throughout Kubrick's cinema especially where men are shown to have been incarcerated. The first appearance of Johnny Clay in *The Killing* is his postcoital conversation with lover Fay where she reflects on his release after five years behind bars: "being locked up must be a terrible thing" while lamenting her own chaste sacrifice of "waiting for you all those years and staying by myself" (Cossar 2005).

The *absence* of sex has its own particular markers in Kubrick's world view. When adult Spartacus declares to the slave woman, Varinia, sent to "reward" him for gladiatorial training, he coyly admits that he's "never had a woman." The comment is overheard by his brutal trainer Marcellus and slave master-owner Batiatus, who spy on the pair and ridicule Spartacus's virginal timidity. Kubrick's handwritten notes for script revision of the scene pose an interesting question: "I've never had a woman. What about those other nights?" (Radford 2015). In *Paths of Glory* on the morning of the dawn execution condemned soldier Corporal Phillipe Paris erupts in an unexpected outburst, divulging to the firing squad's sergeant: "It just occurred to me. Funny thing. I … I haven't had one *sexual* thought since the court martial. Pretty extraordinary, isn't it?" Overcome with emotion Paris collapses to the ground, clasping at the sergeant and sobbing hysterically. The sergeant remains rigid, looking ahead to avoid eye contact and pronounces distastefully: "Act like a man." The comment and actions, while eliciting pathos, also reinforce the performative nature of gender (Butler 1988). Paris is berated for his lapse in masculine deportment.

And what are we to make of the astronauts in deep space, at least eighteen months into their journey aboard the *Discovery*? The jogging and shadow-boxing within the spaceship's sterile environment may suggest sexual sublimation, but the ascetic professionalism of Dave and Frank under computer HAL's omniscient eye likely enforces autoregulation, governance and repression of (homo)sexual desire (Hanson 1993). Unlike the other confined spaces that the male protagonists work in or inhabit (the *Lepper Colony* B-52 crew in *Dr. Strangelove* or Alex's prison cell in *A Clockwork Orange*), there is no visible display of pinups or pornography. Hence critics such as Andrew Sarris found *2001* "completely sexless" (Norden 1968), at least in heterosexual terms.

Infidelities and Promiscuity

Polygamy and sexual predation are rife within Kubrick's cinema. Characters are often plagued by jealousy and tormented by infidelities, real or imagined. Rapallo's jealousy of Davy fuels his violent rampages in *Killer's Kiss*. George is cuckolded by Sherry in *The Killing*, who cheats on him with gangster Val, though Sherry is equally jealous of Val's own sexual freedom as a bachelor. The taking of slaves of both sexes for sex is *de rigueur* for the Roman elite in *Spartacus*. Pedophile Humbert preys on Lolita while she is simultaneously exploited sexually by Quilty (and his entourage). Small town

America (here Ramsdale) seems replete with swingers and polygamists, evident in the sexual advances of "broadminded" couple, Jean and John Farlow, alongside Charlotte Haze reminding Quilty of their previous tryst, and hotel clerk George Swine's *ménage à trois* solicitation. In *Dr. Strangelove* General Buck Turgidson's secretary, Miss Scott, reveals herself to be intimately acquainted with a Col. Puntrich during a phone conversation. Miss Scott is also featured as a naked *Playboy* centerfold, "Miss Foreign Affairs," ogled by Major Kong onboard the B-52. To survive and "prevail" in the impending nuclear holocaust Doctor Strangelove advocates a ratio of ten women to every man, to be selected for their "sexual characteristics" and ability to provide sexual services. This necessitates the "regrettable" abandonment of what Turgidson describes as the "so-called 'monogamous' form of sexual relationship; at least as far as the men are concerned."

Kubrick extends this Freudian-Darwinian trope (Smith 2016) by depicting the prehistoric hominids of *2001* living as a "primal horde" where alpha males dominate troops of simians that ultimately fight (and kill) for supremacy. *A Clockwork Orange*'s dystopian future envisions a moribund and decadent society where teens gang rape at will. Imprisoned for murder, Alex draws on the Old Testament to fantasize having sex with multiple Biblical handmaidens.

Walking with Reverend Runt and Lord Bullingdon, Lady Lyndon espies Barry seducing their son's nanny. As the narrator intones, the humiliation adds "jealousy" to Lady Lyndon's already "melancholy and maudlin temper" as she now finds "rivals even among her maids." Shortly after, Barry is shown as a serial adulterer visiting a brothel and having sex with two women.

Jack Torrance's singular visible act of marital betrayal in *The Shining*—his approach, embrace, and kissing of the naked woman in Room 237—instantly reverses from sexual desire to revulsion and abjection, as the woman is revealed to be an elderly rotting corpse who laughs at Jack, seemingly mocking his unfaithfulness. A similar threat from promiscuous sex outside marriage and its proximity to homosexuality and intravenous drug use (Sontag 1988) is evident in Bill Harford's near-miss sexual encounter with prostitute, Domino, who is later revealed to have contracted AIDS, and reflected in the ominous headline "Lucky to be Alive" that Bill fails to note when reading the *New York Post* at a newsstand.

Heteronormative sex is rendered colonial and transactional in *Full Metal Jacket* (Ly 2017). Soldiers negotiate with Vietnamese prostitutes and their pimps or are subjected to theft. Lust Hog squad alpha male, Animal Mother—whose nickname inherently connotes sexual transgression as either bestial, incestuous, or both—dominates the troops and asserts privilege in the sexual pecking order. Bill Harford is consumed with jealousy and revenge in *Eyes Wide Shut* when his wife reveals her spontaneous fantasy/desire to leave him (and their daughter) for a naval officer. She further alienates her husband when she describes a dream where she has sex with multiple men and laughs at Bill in the dream to humiliate him. Haunted by the recurrent fantasy of a naked Alice fucking the uniformed officer, Harford then pursues adulterous transactional sex with a prostitute (and later attempts the same with her roommate) and at significant expense hires clothing and transport to attend a secret, high society orgy outside Manhattan.

Queer Sexuality and Strange Love

Over the course of five decades Kubrick's oeuvre has commonly, though less conspicuously, envisioned nonnormative homosexual relations, characters, narratives, and perspectives. Kubrick's feature films reflect such subjectivities within and outside the mainstream. As a young photographer living in Greenwich Village and working in the cinematic arts, Kubrick was exposed to a broad range of cultural influences, personalities, and lifestyles. Many of the cast and crew he worked with over the years were either openly gay or bisexual, or known to be so within the industry. Public or private declarations of sexual orientation were seemingly of no concern to him, exemplified by Arthur C. Clarke's belated admission while working on *2001* of being "a very well-adjusted homosexual" (Benson 2018: 76).

Regardless, it might be tempting to categorize a number of Kubrick movie scenes as homophobic, though Kubrick often employs problematic (and sometimes ambivalent) vignettes to depict heteronormative hostility toward anything perceived by characters as sexually abnormal or perverse. In the famous "oysters and snails" scene originally removed from *Spartacus* and later restored, Kubrick films in longshot through hanging veils the Roman general Crassus who sits naked, deploying Socratic logic to euphemistically normalize bisexuality as a matter of "taste" while attempting to seduce his slave/man-servant Antoninus.

Kubrick deliberately foregrounds the inherent contradictions and ambiguity in such sociocultural construction of "normative" behavior, often by incongruous juxtaposition and/or (dark) humor. For example, Claire Quilty masquerades as a policeman to deliver a malevolent and menacing interrogation while alluding to Humbert's pedophilic intent for Lolita. Lurking in the shadows with his back to Humbert, Quilty continually overemphasizes the word "normal" to antagonize him. Earlier they had engaged in a very phallic ping-pong game, replete with sexual innuendo, which is later echoed in the *Eyes Wide Shut* billiards scene. In *Dr. Strangelove* Colonel "Bat" Guano claims a "mutiny of pre-verts" has taken control of Burpelson airbase and when his captive, Group Captain Mandrake, enters a phone booth to make a call, Guano warns him with carbine pointed: "Try any pre-versions in there and I'll blow your head off."

Perhaps the closest Kubrick comes to overtly satirizing gay men is a scene in *A Clockwork Orange* set in the prison chapel where Alex narrates the "real weepy and like tragic part of the story":

> being in this hell hole and human zoo for two years now, being kicked and tolchocked by brutal warders, and meeting leering criminals and perverts ready to dribble all over a luscious young malchick like your story-teller.

The voice-over is delivered as a burly prisoner and his companion stare directly at Alex, silently blowing kisses and winking at him. The martinet chief guard looks on with disgust while the prison reverend literally spits out a hellfire and damnation sermon. However, *everyone* is derided in *A Clockwork Orange*, and Alex's contemptuous narrative position is publicly deplored as the perspective of an "enterprising, aggressive, outgoing, bold [and] vicious young hoodlum." Parodic homoerotic/phobic representation is earlier evoked in the vandalized municipal flat block lobby mural depicting a tableau in faux Greco-Romanesque style of muscular men in loincloths, daubed with graffiti and comic-style dialogue bubbles soliciting homosexual acts (displaying large penises, scrotums, and tongues). Similar puerile taunts are directed at "switch-hitter" Bill in *Eyes Wide Shut* by a gang of college students in Greenwich Village who physically assault and verbally abuse him with homophobic slurs. Homophobic abuse reaches its nadir in the rantings of Drill Instructor Sergeant Hartman.

The tenor of gay parody is also evident in *Barry Lyndon*. Dragooned soldier Barry steals a British officer's uniform, credentials, and horse, while their owner stands waist deep in a river, embracing a male companion and professing his eternal love. In a scene invented by Kubrick, not in Thackeray's original novel, the actor speaks with a comical British upper-class lisp, rolling his R's, but Barry is not shown to indulge in derision. Nor does the narrator mock the display; rather he perfunctorily informs us that Barry makes his escape to Prussia, while in the background the men declare their mutual affection in a manner that Barry, or anyone else in the film, rarely shows for their heterosexual partners.

While virtually every woman Bill meets in *Eyes Wide Shut* makes overt advances, he is also comically hit upon by a gay desk clerk at a hotel who campily flirts with him (recalling a similar scene in *Lolita*). Actor Alan Cumming recalled how he consciously played off Tom Cruise's public "baggage … you know, all the rumors about him being gay" while admitting "I have quite a good gaydar, I think, but I didn't get anything from him" (2013). Vitali also recalled how Kubrick was specifically looking for someone gay to play Cumming's part (Kolker and Abrams 2019: 68–9).

"Strange love" appears everywhere in Kubrick's universe, from the bondage and deranged assault by Sidney of the captured "enemy" girl in *Fear and Desire* to Bill's near necrophiliac attraction to Mandy in a morgue and the ritualized orgy of *Eyes Wide Shut*. Naked except for underpants, Alex de Large is shown subjected to pedophiliac assault by his elderly and menacing parole officer, Mr. Deltoid, who forcibly grabs the teenager's crotch while holding him down on a bed. In *The Shining*, Wendy Torrance watches (in shot-reverse-shot) a figure in an animal suit kneeling with bare buttocks exposed. Kubrick zooms in rapidly as the costumed figure straightens up, as does a middle-aged man wearing a tuxedo, both of whom directly return Wendy's horrified stare. The action and mise-en-scène clearly imply that the figures have been engaged in oral sex. Given the incongruous and indeterminate costuming, the action also implies a form of bestiality. In *Full Metal Jacket*, strange love is bizarrely melded with concepts of sexual abstinence, fetishization, and fidelity when drill sergeant Hartman issues orders to his recruits:

> Tonight you pukes will sleep with your rifle. You will give your rifle a girl's name because it is the only pussy you people are going to get. Your days of finger-banging old Mary Jane Rottencrotch through her pretty pink panties are over! You're married to this piece, this weapon of iron and wood, and you *will* be faithful.

There has been considerable speculation over the years as to the nature of HAL 9000's sexuality (Hanson 1993). As Nathan Abrams has noted, HAL can be interpreted "in contradictory ways" including "father and mother; gay and asexual; androgynous, male, and female" (2017: 417; see also Janes 2011). However, it is only by his speech that the computer's gender and sexual orientation have been debated. Voiced by Canadian actor Douglas Rain, HAL has been described by Mark Dery as having a "patronizing, asexual quality" where "one man's condescension is another man's cattiness" (2012: 140). Dery notes:

> Balanced on the knife edge between snide and anodyne, HAL's sibilant tone and use of feline phrases like "quite honestly, I wouldn't worry myself about that" contain more than a hint of the stereotypic bitchy homosexual. (2012: 140)

The Sexualized Gaze

John Berger reminds us in *Ways of Seeing*:

> We never look at just one thing; we are always looking at the relation between things and ourselves. Our vision is continually active, continually moving, continually holding things in a circle around itself, constituting what is present to us as we are. (1972: 9)

As an amateur photographer Kubrick trained his eye, and developed it further when he worked at *Look* magazine as an apprentice and later staff photographer (Mather 2013). At the same time, Kubrick's cinematic diet was eclectic and comprehensive, wanting to view every mainstream film on first release and then international programming at arthouse and museum screenings (LoBrutto 1995). He became a cineaste and then a practitioner but never lost his lifelong inquisitiveness for viewing films of all kinds, as Jan Harlan says in the documentary *Stanley Kubrick: A Life in Pictures*.

The complex array of modes of looking within—and at—Kubrick's oeuvre still aligns convincingly with Laura Mulvey's (1975) influential critique and "afterthoughts" (Williams 2017) of classical Hollywood film and the cinematic apparatus—later complemented and problematized by Steven Neale's (1982) analysis of screen depictions of masculinity. For Mulvey, the three specific looks of cinema (the look of camera/projection, the look of characters, the look of spectators) are encoded with specific scopophilic semiotics (pleasure in looking) that resonate with psychoanalytic and ideological associations of sexuality and gender. In classical Hollywood cinema, Mulvey argues, female sexuality is displayed (or reactively suppressed) for the viewing pleasure of the (male) audience. The male gaze is both controlling and often punishing, and at its extreme fetishistic and/or voyeuristic. According to Mulvey (1975) men in classical cinema (and we as the viewing audience) watch acts of sex and violence via a narratological, controlling gaze.

Kubrick's cinema conforms to Mulvey's (1975) classical Hollywood formulation where women are presented in a manner their male counterparts generally are not, that is, as objects for erotic contemplation. In *Fear and Desire* native women are spied upon (using binoculars) by a squad of soldiers, with one woman captured and bound to a tree. She is interrogated, groped, and ultimately killed. In *Paths of Glory* a terrified German "girl" is paraded on stage before French soldiers who cat-whistle and taunt her as she tries to sing a German song. In *Spartacus* Varinia is both a domestic servant and a sex slave, forced to strip before men and service gladiators. A large proportion of women in *A Clockwork Orange* are depicted bare-breasted or naked, and raped or seduced by teenagers and young men. And, of course, there is the orgy sequence in *Eyes Wide Shut*.

As in classical film, Kubrick's cinema often presents women and men in idealized physical form. Nudity and nakedness, in part or in full, is a consistent feature of Kubrick's cinematic gaze. Both men and women are objectified. The most obvious display of idealized physical form is Kubrick's repeated representation of the female breast, alongside frequent depictions of bare-chested men. As with *A Clockwork Orange*, female (and, to lesser degree, male) nudity and nakedness abounds in *Eyes Wide Shut*. The film enables the director to explore more formally these associations since Kubrick separates the mundane, business-like labor of Dr. Bill Harford, who routinely examines patients that are subjected to his clinical touch, from the sensual and eroticized display of breasts through the film. Regardless, it is precisely these activities that Alice uses to chide her husband, despite his protests of doctorly professionalism and the presence of nurses:

> Let's say, for example, you have some gorgeous woman standing in your office naked and you're feeling her fucking tits. Now, what I want to know ... I want to know what I want to know what you're thinking about when you're squeezing them ... So when you're feeling tits, it's nothing more than your professionalism? ... Now, when she is having her little titties squeezed do you think she ever has fantasies about what handsome Dr. Bill's dickie might be like?

The attraction of the naked female breast was certainly a source of visual pleasure in *Eyes Wide Shut* but also the subject of Kubrick's insouciant humor that dates back, on film at least, to *The Seafarers* (Lobrutto 1995: 74). When editor Nigel Galt pointed out that one of the naked women in the preorgy scene, shown with others in a circle ceremonially disrobing before being led away, should not be seen in the master shot for continuity reasons, Kubrick joked: "Nah, they'll be so busy looking at her tits, they'll never notice" (Katharina Kubrick 2016).

Advancing and contesting this gendered gaze, Steve Neale suggests "male" film genres (i.e., war, westerns, crime, epics, etc.) invoke looks of "narcissistic phantasies of power, omnipotence, mastery, and control" (1982: 5). While noting that audience identification in cinema involves many forms of desire and is always multiple, fluid and sometime contradictory, Neale nevertheless suggests that "patriarchal images of masculinity" constantly involve "sadomasochistic themes" where men, often as heroes, are occasionally "marked as the object of an erotic gaze" (ibid.: 12). Overt depiction of male homosexuality is something classical cinema has traditionally sought to "assiduously … denigrate or deny" (ibid.: 15). In mainstream cinema, mutilation and sadism are often the sign of both repression and the means by which the male body may be "disqualified" on screen as an "object of erotic contemplation and desire" (ibid.: 8).

The twin themes of disavowal and corporeal punishment of the male body resonates throughout Kubrick's films, as does the complex viewer subjectivity of individual character/audience identification. In *2001* astronaut Frank Poole lounges on a retractable device under a sun lamp while watching a birthday message from his elderly parents. He appears disinterested, if not bored, narcissistically self-absorbed with the pleasure of light and heat while under the omniscient gaze of HAL, with Poole's near naked body moving sensuously to best advantage the sun lamp and our/ Hal's vantage. Poole is subsequently murdered by HAL after he spies on Poole and Bowman and discovers their plot to disconnect his higher brain function.

Conforming to Neale's formulation regarding masculinity as spectacle, Spartacus is stripped bare, wearing only a loin cloth, as the brutal gladiator trainer Marcellus uses paint and a wooden stick to smear the torso, neck, and arms of Spartacus to demonstrate where you "get a kill." Kubrick's coverage enables cutaways to a series of plaintive and shamed looks between Spartacus and Varinia, triangulated with the sadistic gaze of Marcellus, who smears Spartacus's face and pushes him in Varinia's direction, adding "since all you can do is *look* at girls … go ahead and look." Previously Marcellus had beaten the gladiator-slave with a club, warning Spartacus: "remember from now on, everything you do, I'll be watching."

Kubrick's sardonic wit and skeptical world view are mirrored as recurrent themes throughout his cinema. Behind the scenes such a sensibility inevitably intersected with sex and gender. Kubrick's oeuvre and work practice have attracted accusations of misogyny, but it would be spurious to universally condemn the artistic representation of misogynistic attitudes and actions of his male characters—consistently foregrounded as both narratively and performatively problematic—as emblematic of Kubrick, the man (Webster 2011).

In recent years, several crew and cast have reflected on their time working with Kubrick while scholars have detailed his deliberate and evolving projection of an enigmatic public persona/brand (Krämer 2016; Ulivieri 2017b), by which he sought to preserve and reinforce by limiting his media exposure and interviews (Broderick 2019a). Numerous anecdotes suggest Kubrick could be humorous, vexatious, and occasionally brutal when joking about women. According to Paul Joyce's 1999 documentary, *The Last Movie: Stanley Kubrick and Eyes Wide Shut*, author Ian Watson informed fellow script developer on *A.I.*, Sarah Maitland, that Kubrick said he had employed her to provide "the vaginal gel" to be smeared over his work. After filming sniper rounds eviscerating a fallen soldier in *Full Metal Jacket*, Kubrick reflected on the scene with a grotesque and "derogatory" aside to Mathew Modine referencing the actor's wife. Modine's diary entry on the matter is ambivalent, acknowledging the jibe was meant to provoke and create a "fraternal bond" between the two men (2012).

Traditionally, work on studio film sets was deemed not for the faint-hearted and involved large numbers of men moving heavy equipment and standing around for long periods of time waiting for further instruction. The combination of intense physical labor and lengthy bouts of boredom has its equivalence with military (in)action. Such male camaraderie, scatology and sexualized banter is captured almost forensically in Kubrick's military training and battle sequences (*Fear and Desire*, *Paths of Glory*, *Spartacus*, *Dr. Strangelove*, *Barry Lyndon*, and, especially, *Full Metal Jacket*). On set, as Modine has noted, "chippies" (carpenters) would joke about having sex with Prince Andrew's wife "Fergie" and goad actors into having fights when they sensed conflict brewing (2012).

Conclusion

It would be an oversimplification to assume the key characters presented in Kubrick's oeuvre simply and unproblematically channel the filmmaker's own personal philosophies or mirror his own lifeworld. Cinema enables projected fantasy and imagination, and in the case of Kubrick, this spans experiences as diverse as evoking four-million-year-old proto-human life through to extraterrestrial and artificial intelligences elsewhere in the universe, beyond the infinite. Kubrick was a complex, sometimes contrarian, and gifted artist. Nevertheless, as many observers close to him have noted, he was surrounded by women and devoted to his wife and three daughters, all of whom worked in varying capacities on his films over the years, drawing on their individual artistic expertise. Kubrick collaborated professionally with women in all manner of business (administrative, secretarial, nannies, writers, actors, etc.) and formed lasting relationships over decades. His ongoing fascination with the self-destructive impulses of men and mankind were laid bare for audiences to view, as commercial entertainment, across a half century of filmmaking. That his artistry still resonates strongly today, both transnationally and intergenerationally, suggests these concerns are shared and continue to inform public perceptions about representations of gender and sexuality into the twenty-first century.

17

Kubrick, Marriage, and Family

Joy McEntee

Stanley Kubrick's lifestyle was characterized by porous boundaries between work and family. Family members contributed to his films, and he worked largely from home. The permeability was two-way, as Sir Ken Adam revealed in the 1996 Channel 4 documentary, *Stanley Kubrick: The Invisible Man*, "I really loved him, and I think that was reciprocated. So it became maybe like a love/hate relationship or like a marriage in a way. I was part of the family." Discussing their eventual parting, he uses a maternal metaphor: "One of the real problems was to cut that kind of umbilical cord because I suppose I was in love with the man" (ibid.). This reveals the ambivalent and homosocial nature of Kubrick's working relationships. In this way Kubrick relieved himself of having to choose between work and family, between the world of men, and the world of women and children. This is not a luxury he allows his male protagonists. Often, they must choose between relationships with men on the one hand and with women and children on the other. Frequently competitive, masculine relationships may draw or drive men away from marriage and family. Alternatively, they are sometimes affectionate, having the quality of family relationships, albeit only adoptive.

Peter Krämer asserts that Kubrick's career divides itself into an early period characterized by relationships among men, and a later period in which he also dramatized marriage (Krämer 2015b: 235). I will consider family more broadly to discuss the continuities in Kubrick's career. The definition that equates family with marriage and reproduction may not account for his heterogeneous output. Caring relationships between Kubrick's men encourage a reconceptualization of "family." I adopt a feminist approach, accepting Kubrick's androcentric focus, but interrogating how he both valorizes and critiques patriarchal structures, including the family (see Gretton 1990; DeRosia 2003; Planka 2012). Rather than damning Kubrick for misogyny or rescuing him from accusations of it, I mobilize Tania Modleski's insight about Hitchcock: "the misogyny and the sympathy actually entail one another" (2016: 4). Kubrick oscillates between misogyny, ambivalence and sympathy in depicting wives and mothers.

In a 1968 *Playboy* interview, Kubrick commented on the nature of family:

One can offer all kinds of impressive intellectual arguments against the family as an institution—its inherent authoritarianism, etc.; but when you get right down to it, the family is the most primitive and visceral and vital unit in society. You may stand outside your wife's hospital room during childbirth muttering, "My God, what a responsibility! Is it right to take on this terrible obligation? What am I really doing here?"; and then you go in and look down at the face of your child and—zap!—that ancient programing takes over and your response is one of wonder and joy and pride. It's a classic case of genetically imprinted social patterns. There are very few things in this world that have an unquestionable importance in and of themselves and are not susceptible to debate or rational argument, but the family is one of them. Perhaps man has been too "liberated" by science and evolutionary social trends ... Man in the 20th century has been cut adrift in a rudderless boat on an uncharted sea; if he is going to stay sane throughout the voyage, he must have someone to care about, something that is more important than himself. (Norden 2016: 67)

Kubrick here constructed the family heteronormatively and reproductively. It consisted of father and a mother who were married and was instantiated by the birth of a child. But his films are less conventionally heteronormative. Families comprise men in Kubrick's work. In *Day of the Fight*, the family consists of twin brothers—the women who appeared in the original *Look* photo-essay it was based on ("Prizefighter") were removed for the film. In *Killer's Kiss*, Gloria has a fraught relationship with her family of origin, but she is eventually incorporated into Davey's happy one, which is represented by a distant uncle. In other films, the relationship between men and marriage is competitive. In *The Killing*, Marvin offers Johnny a homosocial alternative: "Wouldn't it be great if we could go away, the two of us ...? It can be pretty serious and terrible ... Getting married, I mean." And George Peatty's manipulative wife Sherry illustrates Marvin's warnings: in a bid to impress her, George tells her his gang's secrets, she in turn betrays them to her lover, and a massacre ensues. Here, the film departs from its source text, Lionel White's *Clean Break* (1955). Instead of shooting Johnny as he does in the novel, the film's George goes home to shoot Sherry. George chooses his male conspirator over his (adulterous) wife.

Family in *Spartacus* is deformed by slavery. Spartacus's birth is an economic transaction: his mother thereby enriches her master. This unsentimental opening may be Anthony Mann's work, but we know that it was Kubrick who vetoed Dalton Trumbo's proposal for a mass slave marriage (Abrams 2015b: 286). Freedom reforms family. Varinia refers to herself as Spartacus's wife. In addition to being biological parents, Fiona Radford says that Varinia and Spartacus are the symbolic mother and father of the slave army's "pseudofamily" (Radford 2015: 109). But Radford also writes that Kubrick eviscerated Trumbo's Varinia, rendering her "only Stepford-Varinia" (ibid.). Radford writes that "after seeing Kubrick's rough cut, Trumbo opined that [Varinia] had become timid and lifeless—hardly the fierce, strong, slave leader envisaged by [the novelist] Fast and captured by Trumbo in the earlier scripts" (ibid.). Vying with her for Spartacus's attention are relationships Spartacus has with men: a fatherly one with Antoninus and a competitive one with Crassus. Spartacus chooses his rivalry with Crassus over his bonds to Varinia and Antoninus when he refuses the pirates' offer to

Figure 17.1 Spartacus and Antoninus swear filial love to one another in *Spartacus*.

spirit them out of Italy. He also chooses his role as spiritual father of the revolt over his role as biological father and husband. Finally, Crassus makes Spartacus kill Antoninus to spare him a lingering death, which condemns Spartacus to crucifixion. Varinia and their baby find Spartacus and say farewell: he has chosen to sacrifice his future with them to his relationships with Antoninus and Crassus.

In *Lolita*, Kubrick dealt with "passion-love," the opposite of "'modern ideal,' which is based on creating a life together" (Stuckey 2015: 119). In other words, *Lolita* is the opposite of the model of the *Playboy* interview. Humbert Humbert enters the Haze home as a lodger because he is smitten with Lolita. He observes the dysfunctional relationship between mother and daughter and proceeds to a duplicitous and potentially murderous marriage with Charlotte. She is an ambivalent figure. James Naremore says she is both "annoying and touching" (2007: 107). Nathan Abrams identifies her as akin to the "Jewish American Monster," a satirical and potentially self-lacerating stereotype (2015a). In other words, Kubrick approaches Charlotte both misogynistically and sympathetically. But she is short-lived, and after her death Humbert assumes custody of Lolita, who seduces him. The film is careful about sex in the family, replacing the word "incest" with "adultery" (Castle 2016: 262, figure 25).

However, Humbert's relationship with Lolita is almost eclipsed by his competitive relationship with another man: Clare Quilty. In adapting Nabokov's novel, Kubrick refocused his materials to highlight and magnify Quilty (Abrams 2016). This emphasizes the competition between the stepfather and the false uncle, which galls Humbert for reasons Elisa Pezzotta explains: "Humbert's gravity and his love for his stepdaughter are almost ridiculed by Quilty, who constantly reminds us that Humbert is neither Dolores's father nor her boyfriend, but simply a pervert" (2015: 313).

But Lolita finally settles down and marries, and we last see her pregnant. As Jennifer Kirby observes, films that depicted teen deviance also sutured their aberrant protagonists back into the institutional structures of parent culture, or "society's … rules" (Kirby 2015: 299). Delores closes off the disruption she represented as Lolita, the object of passion-love. Kubrick allows her to recede into heteronormativity. Because of the sensitivities of movie censors, there was only so far he could stray from the "modern ideal" in 1962.

In *A Clockwork Orange*, Alex twice visits Mr. Alexander's HOME. The first time, he attacks a married couple; the second time, he finds the crippled writer being cared for by a man. The heteronormative marriage has been displaced by a homosocial relationship. And there are other displacements of heteronormative family, particularly Alex's parents Pee and Em. Early in the film, Alex's droogs, his brothers, are more important to him than his parents, who are merely a convenience. Biljana Purić says his mother is a "grotesque caricature of a motherly figure," and his father a nullity in the general air of "emotional detachment from reality" that permeates their bizarre flat (2017: 494). They spectacularly fail to accommodate Alex after his release from prison, replacing him with a lodger who effectively drives Alex from his home. Alex's final reconciliation with Pee and Em at his hospital bedside is dealt with in the briefest way, before they are eclipsed by the inauguration of his relationship with the minister, a mutually convenient arrangement between men. Furthermore, Kubrick shapes the ending to excise Burgess's suggestion that Alex settles down to fatherhood (McEntee 2015: 323–4). The final image of Alex romping with a woman is heteronormative, but it is not of family. Relationships between men trump family in *A Clockwork Orange*.

In *The Shining* we clearly see the competition between homosocial and family worlds. In the *Playboy* interview, Kubrick admits ambivalence about family, which may be flawed: it is authoritarian and imposes great responsibilities on the father. This ambivalence underlies *The Shining*: we are at once horrified and mesmerized by Jack Torrance (Jack Nicholson). It is easy to condemn Jack's behavior in the era of awareness about family violence (Hornbeck 2016; Manchel 1995). However, as Manchel

Figure 17.2 Caring relationships between men displace the heteronormative in *A Clockwork Orange*.

acknowledges, Jack is also a victim, seduced by the patriarchal power structures of The Overlook (1995: 70). These are represented by white male figures. Ullman offers Jack work, and with it the responsibilities he will cite in his baseball bat confrontation with Wendy. Lloyd listens to him gripe about his wife and child. Finally, Grady counsels Jack to exert his authority. As Kolker and Abrams observe,

> [Jack] is filled with barely repressed rage at the constricting confinements of his family responsibilities. He went to the Overlook Hotel to escape, but his isolation only magnifies his resentment and sense of masculine entitlement. He wants to maintain his authority, indeed ownership, of the family that he ultimately plans to destroy. (2019: 6–7)

Stephen King's Jack was a victim, too, of intergenerational abuse by his father, which supplies him with some rationalizations for his conduct, but Kubrick excises that excuse, so that only the ghosts of The Overlook remain to draw the film's Jack away from his family (McEntee 2016: 179).

Jack is working away from home, but he remakes The Overlook as a space in which he can both live and work. He should not have to choose between work and family, but he does. While Wendy and Danny explore The Overlook, he takes up his writing station in the center of the Colorado Lounge, and forbids Wendy access. He rarely leaves it except to prowl to the Gold Room to talk to Lloyd and Grady. When he does appear in the apartment, as when Wendy brings him breakfast and when Danny submits to a creepy cuddle, Jack appears in a mirror, which confuses the "real" and the "unreal" (Naremore 2007: 192). Dreamily, he says he wants to stay at the hotel forever, echoing the Grady girls. He has already begun to cross over to join its spectral inhabitants, as he will in the film's final image—the Independence Day ball photograph. The grin on his face suggests that he relishes freedom from family. And Kubrick again adapts the end of his precursor text to liberate the protagonist from the burdens of fatherly feeling: where King's Jack escapes The Overlook's thrall long enough to spare his son, Kubrick's Jack pursues Danny with murderous glee (McEntee 2016: 181).

But Danny escapes with Wendy. Elizabeth Jean Hornbeck says Wendy is the "final girl" of *The Shining*, securing the film's "final feminist victory" (2016: 718). But it is unclear whether the knife Wendy tremblingly brandishes empowers her, or underscores her vulnerability, her "abusable" status (ibid.: 709). Sharon Marie Carnicke's argument that Duvall's Wendy is valorized by her putatively "naturalistic" acting is also problematic, because the more "kinetic" and "nonrealistic" performance (Jack's) is the more charismatic (2006: 23). It is doubtful that Kubrick valued naturalism or realism: Naremore says he favored the grotesque, because "most of his films are obviously satiric and are focused on flawed, criminal, or even monstrous protagonists" (2007: 25). *The Shining* is a satire of patriarchy and a parody of a horror film (ibid.: 4; McEntee 2016: 181). Wendy is therefore a parody of a final girl. Identification with her is difficult.

The final girl defeats the monster, or at least engages in the final battle. That is Danny's role rather than Wendy's. He is the one who outsmarts Jack in the maze, so he is the "final boy." Geoffrey Cocks says that Danny exemplifies Kubrick's "child discovering the dangerous world," a trope in which "youth is victimized by adult male authority" (2013: 26). As William Paul observes, *The Shining* confronts a horror that is "insistently repressed in Western culture, the hostility of a father toward his own son" (1994: 344). For Danny, Jack's antipathy is countered by Halloran. A grandfatherly figure, the "nigger cook" attempts to interfere with the white patriarch's lethal exercise of authority, at least fleetingly. So, the white patriarchal ghosts of The Overlook draw Jack away from his family and a black male protagonist briefly checks him in his efforts to annihilate them. Once again, masculine relationships shape a man's relationship with his family.

In *Barry Lyndon* and *Eyes Wide Shut*, a different pattern emerges. Men are first driven or drawn away from their families into the world of men, and then are driven back by men toward their families. We meet Barry after the death of his father in a duel, in the context of his relationship with his mother and his courtship of his cousin Nora. Captain Quin disrupts this idyll, affiancing Nora and occasioning Barry's challenge to another duel. Nora's brothers fake the result, driving Barry away from his mother: a competition between men over a marriage is manipulated by men, forcing Barry to choose between his family of origin and the relationships he subsequently develops. Initially, these are with "father surrogates"—Captain Grogan, Colonel Potzdorf, and the Chevalier de Balibari (Pramaggiore 2015b: 91). Barry evinces such a touching attachment to both Captain Grogan and the Chevalier de Balibari that both these men must surely be admitted to the category "family."

Figure 17.3 *Barry Lyndon* dramatizes the loss of father figures.

Barry reenters a heteronormative family with Lischen and her baby. However, this is only a "mock family unit" (ibid.: 105). This is not Barry's child, and he does not find "someone to care about" until he marries Lady Lyndon and she bears him Bryan. Kubrick adapts Lady Lyndon sympathetically from Thackeray's novel, and Marissa Berenson is one of the beautiful film's visual pleasures, but her silent suffering limits her role (Chion 2006: 27). While Barry is doubtless a cad to Lady Lyndon, he is a "tender" father. A great deal of the emotion he invests in Bryan is because he himself becomes capable of patrimony. And Barry installs his ubiquitous and "adaptable" mother at Castle Hackton, resuming their warm relationship (Miller 1976: 1364). Briefly, Barry synthesizes family of origin, consanguineous family, and dynastic family.

But this arrangement is doomed. Naremore (2007: 173) and Mark Miller (1976: 1364) comment on the deathly quality of domestic scenes at Castle Hackton. Pramaggiore says "entombed movement" characterizes the cinematography of Barry's wooing and wedding of Lady Lyndon, as well as Bryan's funeral (2015b: 104). Against this is Lady Lyndon's raw, hysterical grief, which is captured with a handheld camera. "The film pulls out all the sentimental stops when the boy dies," with Barry weeping at Bryan's bedside (Naremore 2007: 185). The aristocratic family is not immunized against sorrow.

Barry's relationship with his stepson Bulllingdon is his undoing. Their rivalry culminates in two incidents Kubrick invented for the film. The first is when Barry attacks Bullingdon at the harpsichord recital and drives him from his mother's home. The second is the final duel: Bullingdon wounds Barry, removing him from Lady Lyndon's household in his turn. In the aftermath, both men repair to their mothers. Barry is ejected from his marital family by a man, and retreats to his family of origin. This choice is not on the face of it between world of men and the world the family. However, Barry's losing Bryan and Lady Lyndon means losing his place in the patriarchal family structures of patrilineage and patrimony, the last in a series of such losses (Miller 1976: 1364; Pramaggiore 2015a). Indeed, Pramaggiore says the film thematizes "paternal crisis" (2015b: 85). Barry also loses his chance at a peerage—an opportunity brokered by another man, Lord Wendover. Returning to mother and to his family of origin, Barry loses his place in masculine hierarchies.

I.Q. Hunter says that "*Eyes Wide Shut* can be read as an encomium for [Kubrick's] final happy marriage" (2015: 279). If so, it is a discomforting one, for it explores infidelity. It does so through a complex negotiation of fantasy and reality that begins even before the film does. The trailer features the married couple Tom Cruise and Nicole Kidman about to do bad, bad things to each other. The film, however, does not deliver on that promise. We are first given an idealized vision of Alice Harford nude—but this is instantly occluded. We then proceed to a more prosaic image of Alice sitting on the toilet, complaining that her husband Bill doesn't look at her; he is looking at himself in the mirror. This shift from the sublime to the banal aspects of married life, from ideation to reality, interacts with the casting of really married stars in a fiction film to complexify the film's negotiation of reality, fantasy and dream. Matching this mirror scene, Kubrick gives us a second. Alice is again nude, but her breasts are obscured from us by her arms. Bill embraces her, but rather than looking at him, she looks at herself in the mirror—or possibly at us. What these scenes reveal is not the couple's mutual desire, but their narcissism. We do not see their lovemaking; the film cuts to an ellipse. These glimpses of Alice/Kidman and Bill/Cruise establish the pattern of "coitus interruptus" that characterizes the narrative (McDougal 2001: 198). *Eyes Wide Shut* is about frustration, particularly of Bill's efforts to be unfaithful.

And homosocial relationships are again important. *Eyes Wide Shut* frames the narrative of *Traumnovelle* between two scenes featuring Victor Ziegler, a character Kubrick and Raphael invented. He represents the world of men. These scenes are the Christmas party and the billiard room. At the Christmas party, both Alice and Bill flirt. Alice fends her suitor off by citing her marriage. Bill is propositioned by two young models but is interrupted by a summons from Ziegler. Bill leaves them with the query "To be continued?" His attitude to fidelity clearly contrasts Alice's. Ziegler's medical emergency involves a prostitute with whom he has been having sex. An outwardly respectable married man, Ziegler wants her gone. This aligns with the masculinist status quo: "[Ziegler's] sexual actions ... are an essential part of the 'use and discard' character ... of patriarchal capitalism" (Ofengenden 2015: 5). Bill is more professionally caring, but he is also eager to please the older, wealthier man, and becomes complicit in Ziegler's actions. This establishes Bill's alignment with patriarchal attitudes.

Bill reveals his double standards during his pot-fueled fight with Alice. He takes Alice's fidelity for granted because she is his wife and the mother of his child. She bitterly denounces his complacency about traditional familial roles, shattering it by relating her fantasy about a one-night stand with a sailor. Gretton says that, while Kubrick's work does not reflect a feminist sensibility, there are "intense moments of disruption, resentment, and opposition that are not easily discounted or dismissed" (1990: 62). This is such a moment. Both Naremore (2007: 234) and Michel Chion (2006: 27) have remarked on Alice's complex characterization and Kidman's outstanding performance, but both also opine that Kidman's Alice is unique in Kubrick's oeuvre, which bespeaks Kubrick's androcentric focus elsewhere. However, gender roles are inverted here, with Alice the aggressor. Chion identifies her as "the mobile element" while Bill is the passive "fixed point," "frozen on the bed" (2006: 30–1). He doesn't even respond to Alice's disclosures, because the fight is interrupted by a phone call and he uses that as an excuse to leave the house. Bill's crisis manifests itself in unbidden images of Alice having sex with the sailor. In his imagination, he is driven by a male relationship. At first glance, this would appear to be heterosexually competitive, but perhaps, if Abrams's suggestions that Bill is emasculated and coded homosexual are borne out, he is fantasizing about the naval officer himself (2018: 250). Either way, he is drawn away from his family by a homosocial relationship—whether competitive or seductive.

Bill sets out to play catchup to Alice. As Kolker and Abrams argue: "Bill wants to be desired in the same way as his wife desired the naval officer, and all he can do is search and fail" (2019: 164). Intrigued by a tale from his doppelganger Nick Nightingale (the failed doctor cum pianist over whom he feels superior—another competitive male relationship), he blunders into the Somerton orgy, which has the ironic password *fidelio*. This famously unsexy scene reveals the insufficiency of the male gaze: while Bill has a "good look around," he gets to do nothing else before he is unmasked and expelled from the society of upper-class men (and women—we assume Ziegler's wife is there and some of the masked guests who are not prostitutes are female) by Red Cloak. The next day, Bill revisits the people and places he encountered during the night, finding each menacingly altered. He continues his detective mission to discover things like whether a woman was murdered until his billiard-room interview with Ziegler, who alternately threatens Bill and dismisses his theories as paranoid. This exchange occurs in an "atmosphere of manly complicity" and Ziegler's fatherly manner is key to persuading Bill to desist (Chion 2006: 56). Ziegler sends Bill home to his family, finalizing his expulsion from the world of men. Bill wakes Alice to confess all, returning chastened from having been "too liberated." He has only avoided infidelity, and potentially death, by luck rather than wit or virtue.

Eyes Wide Shut returns to the model of the *Playboy* interview: a man, his wife, and their child. But does it give Bill something to care about? Critical opinion about Bill's daughter is divided. According to Kolker and Abrams, Helena foregrounds Bill's status as a father by bookending the movie and appearing in the middle (2019: 156, 176). However, her appearance in the middle of the film occurs immediately after Bill is expelled from the Somerton orgy. Bill is driven back toward his family by men rather than being drawn back by paternal feeling.

Chion, by contrast with Kolker and Abrams, sees Helena as a marginal figure, saying that we "forget that Bill is himself a father" (2006: 56). Helena's function is to represent the family's reconstitution in the final toy store scene and her activities quickly become irrelevant as we focus on the dialogue between Bill and Alice. That dialogue is ambiguous: perhaps nothing has changed—Alice will not say "forever." Or perhaps there is reconciliation, both within the marriage and of the film's layering of reality and fantasy. Chion projects beyond the film's closure to the birth of a son, the result of the "fuck" Alice calls for, but Miriam Jordan and Julian Jason Haladyn say that Alice's rejection of the pram Helena favors signals her disinterest in becoming a mother again (2008: 194).

Nevertheless, we are left with an extant marriage, which is "a surprisingly positive statement when compared to [Kubrick's] earlier films" (Krämer 2017: 388). For once, Bill and Alice are looking at each other rather than at themselves, and Alice reassures Bill, "I do ... love you." As Chion says, that is as good a guarantee as we're going to get (2006: 86).

Kubrick's treatment for *A.I. Artificial Intelligence* yields an echo, here. At the end of the story, Monica, the human adoptive mother of David, the android boy, falls asleep saying, "I do love you, my sweet little boy. I have always loved you" (Castle 2016: 812). She is not expected to survive the night, but in the morning, she wakes, and she and David live on together forever. This contrasts with Steven Spielberg's finished film, in which she dies. This shows Kubrick was not unable to "wring the inherent sentiment out of the story" (Kolker 2017: 41). Rather, he offered *A.I.* to Spielberg because of more prosaic concerns: the rudimentary state of digital filmmaking and the demands of working with real children. *A.I.* may be one of Kubrick's "unrealized" projects, but as Spielberg used his developmental ideas, it is a "palimpsest" of Kubrick's ideas (Krämer 2015a: 373).

A.I. is Kubrick's disturbing final statement about children. It recalls *A Clockwork Orange* in that "both Alex and David are programmed children" and that David is compelled to love Monica without choice, only to be abandoned (Melia 2017). This ambivalent maternal relationship is central, but homosocial relationships continue to be important: Martin and Henry's antagonism toward David causes his expulsion from the family. On the happiest day of David's life, he enjoys Monica without their competition. Professor Hobby proves bitterly disappointing as a de facto father. However, Gigolo Joe proves more caring than the Swintons or Hobby. This supports admitting masculine characters who are not consanguineous (or even human) to the category "family."

There are films in the Kubrick canon in which marriage and family are not central concerns. This includes *Fear and Desire, Paths of Glory, Dr. Strangelove, 2001: A Space Odyssey,* and *Full Metal Jacket.* But family and marriage are not entirely forgotten in these films. Armies are alternative families of sorts. *Paths of Glory* ends in a confrontation between General Broulard and Colonel Dax in which both repudiate a father/son relationship. Strangelove's proposal to substitute for monogamy a postapocalyptic eugenics program heavily geared toward the interests of heterosexual men liberates Turgidson from placating his secretary by offering to marry her. *2001*—which occasioned the *Playboy* interview—would appear to depict an all-male world. However, family is accessible remotely by video transmission, and perhaps this remoteness is the point. Floyd is an absent father and Poole looks bored with his parents during his birthday video link. Perhaps this kind of disconnection Kubrick was thinking of when he opined that twentieth century man needed family to moor him (Abrams 2017: 427). But family may obtrude even here. Krämer asserts that the men make a home together (2015b: 223), and Abrams suggests that HAL can be read as both father and mother—and particularly as an overbearing Jewish mother (2017: 417, 425–6). However, HAL's maternal qualities excepted, *2001* is a space that is free of the feminine. Scott Loren points to the way in which the Bowman fetus is produced by a disembodied womb (2008: 229). To read Abrams's analysis of the film's drafting process in a contrarian way reveals Kubrick's tendency to bring his dramas back to relationships between masculine characters. Kubrick abandoned a plan to make HAL female (ATHENA), leaving HAL with not only a male moniker, but at best an "asexual" voice (Abrams 2017: 426). Or perhaps, to return to the argument that Kubrick's films tend to turn on affectionate male relationships, HAL is Dave's spurned male lover (ibid.). In *Full Metal Jacket,* despite the frequent references to family members whose bonds must be attenuated as they become married to the marines and their rifles, caring bonds form between Joker and Pyle. Considering homosocial bonds that have familial qualities allows us to look again, and differently, at works that at first glance do not have to do with family, heteronormatively defined.

These relationships, along with the ones between Marvin and Johnny, Spartacus and Antoninus, Barry Lyndon, Captain Grogan and the Chevalier de Balibari, and David and Gigolo Joe suggest that it may be in order the reconceptualize "family" to fully account for Kubrick's oeuvre. Homosocial relationships that are affectionate—and have the quality of family relationships consistently shape Kubrick's films and competitive relationships between men need also to be accounted for. In several films, Kubrick gives us antagonistic or seductive masculine relationships that drive or draw men away from women and children. Others feature ambivalent masculine relationships that force reluctant men back to their families, debarring them success in patriarchal hierarchies. But what remains clear is that the heteronormative conceptualization of 'family' that equates it with conventional marriage and reproduction may not be a helpful one for understanding Kubrick's work. To account for the bulk of Kubrick's oeuvre, we need to incorporate masculine relationships into our definition of "family."

18

Kubrick and Jewishness

Marat Grinberg

Allegory and Biology

The question of Stanley Kubrick's Jewishness and the impact it might have had on his work is puzzling and intriguing. There is the basic biographical fact, Kubrick was born to Jews, Gertrude Perveler and Jacques Kubrick, or, as he put it, "he just happened to have two Jewish parents" (Abrams 2018: 2). The "happened to" both implies a trifle and points to Jewishness as a random and yet inerasable biological condition, something one can never get rid of. By all accounts, Kubrick did not receive any substantial Jewish religious education and was at best indifferent to Judaism as a religion; his attachment to Jewishness was ethnic, psychological, and, again, biological. Surrounded by Jews in his childhood and youth in West Bronx, and later in Greenwich Village and Hollywood, he was attuned to the American Jewish zeitgeists and fixations, codes and hidden languages, with their fraught sense of assimilation underpinned by the Holocaust.

According to Frederic Raphael, who co-wrote the script for *Eyes Wide Shut*, "It is ... absurd to try to understand Stanley Kubrick without reckoning on Jewishness as a fundamental aspect of his mentality, if not of his work in general" (Raphael 1999: 107–8). Raphael's main proof is Kubrick's remark to him, "Coupla Jews, what do we know about what those people talk about when they're by themselves?" (ibid.: 105). "Those people" here are the gentiles, which seemingly signals Kubrick's idea of Jewishness as an inborn curse or a blessing that renders Jews essentially different. It is telling that Kubrick made this quip, if we are to trust Raphael, while turning Arthur Schnitzler's *Dream Story* (1926) into what Kubrick insisted on calling *Eyes Wide Shut*. I would propose that this enigmatic title is Kubrick's definition of the ontological and phenomenological Jewish condition, the Jews' eyes—their souls and psyches— are inaccessible to everyone around; the Jews themselves are unable to gauge their surroundings precisely due to the same abnormality. To be a Jew is to reside within this epistemological crisis and wear a mask of "pretend" entry into what the others "talk about" and what/how they see. The Jewish concealed internal and outward blind gaze makes the Jewish presence precarious as well as illusory and especially so for Kubrick, whose eye creates his cinematic universe and presents it to any viewer. Thus, the title *Eyes Wide Shut* provides a clue for understanding Kubrick's entire oeuvre.

There is an underlying apprehension in Kubrick of exposing this Jewish interiority, of making it visible and intelligible; hence his allegedly painstaking efforts to erase anything explicitly Jewish from his films, from the Jewish characters, who inhabit the novels he adapted, to the Jewish settings and milieu. Kubrick is distinct in this regard in the American cinematic context of his and younger generations, an exception to the rule of the unambiguously Jewish Woody Allen, Sidney Lumet, Paul Mazursky, and the later Steven Spielberg. Thus, he is routinely omitted from surveys of American Jewish filmmakers and their films, such as David Desser and Lester D. Friedman's authoritative *American Jewish Filmmakers* (2003). There is a kinship between Kubrick and the directors of the older generation, the American Sam Fuller and the French Jean Pierre Melville, who were also intent on consistently masking biographical and historical Jewishness in their films.

Thus, any attempt to locate Jewishness in Kubrick's films must recognize this disguised and uneasily detectable allegorical factor that transforms Jewishness into his main "unseen obsession" (Jenkins 1997: 24). Kubrick was preoccupied with the link between cinema and allegory from the outset, conceiving his first film, *Fear and Desire*, as allegorical in structure, "a drama of man lost in a hostile world—deprived of material and spiritual foundations—seeking his way to an understanding of himself, and of life around him" (Lobrutto 2006: 35). The general universal allegory conceals a Jewish one—"man" here is a substitute for the modern Jew, torn from his traditional place and values, with his "eyes wide shut" to the world around him. Unsurprisingly for an auteur, Kubrick's first film invokes the last, and crucially so in its Jewish subtext. Substitution, coding, and sublimation are central to any allegorical setup and, in Kubrick's case, must answer the following two questions, first, how detailed are these allegories in terms of their Jewish cultural, scriptural, historical, literary and visual contexts and allusions? and second, what do these details contribute to Kubrick's creation of his visual cinematic texture? This chapter will trace how the existing scholarship has answered these questions and suggest new venues for illuminating the subterranean place of Jewishness in Kubrick's oeuvre.

Cocks and Burton

The two main biographies of Kubrick, by Vincent LoBrutto and John Baxter respectively, mention Jewishness only in passing. The manifold scholarship on individual films contains sporadic mentions of it, but no extended analysis. The topic, as I showed, only begins to open up with Raphael's memoir, which some saw as untrustworthy and mistaken. The author Michael Herr, who co-wrote the screenplay for *Full Metal Jacket*, took issue with, in his eyes, Raphael's "patronizing" portrayal of Kubrick as "the self-hating Jew" (2000). Pointedly, Herr's own memoir of the director remembers Kubrick who told "Jewish jokes," was attuned to anti-Semitism, voraciously read about the Holocaust, and was determined to achieve success in a gentile world (2000).

A scholarly pioneer in raising the issue of Jewishness in Kubrick's work is Geoffrey Cocks. In a book published in 2004 and numerous subsequent essays, Cocks put forth a hypothesis "that the Holocaust was a central influence on Kubrick's development as a person and as a filmmaker" (2006: 186). Cocks traces the inconspicuous presence of the Holocaust, Jewishness, and anti-Semitism in all of Kubrick's oeuvre, paying most attention to *The Shining* as the climax of Kubrick's "unseen obsession" with Nazism and the Holocaust (see Cocks's entry in this volume). As Cocks acknowledges, "Kubrick's references to the Holocaust and Nazi Germany reside exclusively in the spaces surrounding the stories and characters" while being "grounded in artistic and aesthetic concerns" (2013: 22). It is debatable, however, whether the details, which fill these spaces, can be described as Kubrickian. In other words, do they amount to a complete cinematic aesthetic that is recognizably Kubrick's or are they peripheral and even foreign to his cinematic method and thinking? As suggested by Michel Chion, "there is a great temptation to construct the 'perfect interpretation', which would mean that the film would no longer be any more than a coded message made transparent" through its "details of texture and particular effects" (2008: 37). It is probably due to this aspect that Cocks's important and provocative work did not have as much of an imprint on Kubrick studies as it could and should have. Cocks's inclusion in the documentary *Room 237* (2012), which brought together various outlandish conspiracy theories regarding the meaning and production of *The Shining*, also helped to isolate his work.

One scholar that followed in Cocks's footsteps was Margaret Burton, who turned to *Spartacus* as emblematic of Kubrick's allegorical Jewish mindset. Burton finds meaning in the fact that three Jews, Kirk Douglas, Howard Fast—on whose novel the film was based—and Kubrick, were responsible for "shaping the film" (2008: 2). She interprets their depiction of Rome as a substitute for Nazi Germany (and America's own witch-hunt against leftist filmmakers) and argues that the characters of slaves and Spartacus invoke the creation of the State of Israel, on the one hand, and the Holocaust, on the other. One detail, which Burton does not mention, but which reinforces her argument, is that Douglas played the leading role in *The Juggler* (1953), one of the earliest and most remarkable American films dealing directly with the Holocaust and Israel. Most interestingly, Burton also reads the "metonymic images [which] permeate *Spartacus*" (2008: 11) as alluding to Jewish scriptural and modern, especially post-Holocaust, poetry of destruction, which metonymically describes the death of the entire people. In *Spartacus*, "the slow panning shots of the dead on the battlefield, the picture of the lifeless mother's corpse cradling her dead infant, the image of an elderly couple holding one another in death" allow Kubrick to "create a sense of lamentation over the loss of community and loss of land as locus for community" (ibid.). Thus, Burton both cloaks Kubrick's allegory in rich Jewish allusions and speaks to how it contributes to his cinematic language, prompting a question of whether there is a consistent Jewish suggestiveness to the metonymic imagery visible in all of Kubrick's oeuvre, making him a conceptually Jewish filmmaker.

Abrams

Nathan Abrams's *Stanley Kubrick: New York Jewish Intellectual* (2018) provides the most comprehensive and intricate analysis of Jewishness in Kubrick's finished films to date. Indebted to the earlier scholarship discussed above, it draws on the wealth of archival material, primarily in the Kubrick Archive, which was unavailable earlier, and creates a network of contextual lenses through which his Jewishness can be dissected. In likening Kubrick to the generation of New York Jewish Intellectuals of the 1950s and 1960s in their shared intellectual curiosity, ethical and sexual proclivities, leftist leanings, devotion to the arts as both politics and aesthetics, and preoccupation with the Holocaust, Abrams emphasizes Kubrick's ironic and yet acutely moral (or even moralistic) attentiveness to the presence of evil in history counterbalanced by yearning for the transcendent, on the one hand, and familial, on the other, as fundamentally Jewish. This Jewish sensibility was imprinted on his films despite being consistently erased from the surface. From "the details of the source texts of the various drafts of the screenplays" to "casting choices and on-set improvisations," Kubrick weaves a "palimpsest of Jewishness" and a "hidden Jewish substratum" (Abrams 2018: 15). Abrams's "palimpsest" lays bare Kubrick's creative method and thinking, paying attention to both the metadata of the final film product, so to speak, and its complete visual language.

Abrams suggests three main venues for decoding Kubrick's Jewishness. First, by reading certain characters and settings as Jewish. Second, by interpreting the films through Judaic hermeneutic, scriptural, and mystical traditions. And third, by identifying the films' veiled responses to the Holocaust. The tropes and stereotypes associated with Jewish masculinity and femininity are an essential ingredient in Kubrick's characters' makeup in ways both positive and problematic. On the positive side of the spectrum, there is the allegorical Jewishness of Barry Lyndon (Ryan O'Neal), whose outsider status as an Irishman is a substitute for the Jew's otherness, especially of the East European type. On the other end, there is the character of Quilty in *Lolita* played (and often improvised) by the Jewish actor Peter Sellers. "If one takes Quilty's various attributes as coded as Jewish, then his character and especially the way Sellers portrays him suggest a potential reading of him as a villainous, if not diabolical, Jewish pervert" (ibid.: 85). These disturbingly and seemingly self-hating elements within Kubrick's oeuvre constitute for Abrams the director's "heart of darkness" (ibid.: 79). While they can be interpreted as Kubrick's playful or campy "parodying of stereotypes" (ibid.: 92) in the vein of Jewish comedian Lenny Bruce, their starkness, brilliant and unapologetic, is dumbfounding, especially for a contemporary viewer.

Like Burton, who locates allusions to Jewish scripture, such as the Binding of Isaac in Genesis 22, in *Spartacus* (Abrams sees a similar reference in *The Shining*), Abrams turns to *2001* as an example of Jewish metaphysical thinking, where the film's "symbolic imagery … can be decoded in terms of Jewish ideas and iconography" (ibid.: 118), most clearly its opening that "mimics Genesis" (ibid.: 128) and the shape of the monolith as a biblical altar or the tower of Babel. These speculative interpretations lead to a query, which future scholars and viewers will have to confront, of whether these possible Judaic resonances were intuitive or derived from Kubrick's actual knowledge of Judaism.

Abrams agrees with Cocks that the awareness of the Holocaust and the anxiety about fitting in as a Jew in the post-Holocaust world are at the core of Kubrick's

Jewish self-awareness, its "ghostly specter" (ibid.: 13). This claim is reinforced by the biographical fact of Kubrick's marriage to Christiane Harlan, niece of the notorious Nazi filmmaker Veit Harlan, who was put on trial and acquitted after the war. Thus, "in a sense Kubrick ... married into the Holocaust" (ibid.: 12), which perhaps holds the key to unraveling his apprehensive Jewish persona. In the words of Dalton Trumbo, who worked on the script for *Spartacus*, marrying a German woman with a Nazi pedigree constituted an act of revenge for the Holocaust, making Kubrick "a more devoted Jew than any other ... the essential renegade" (ibid.: 59). We will return to the issue of Harlan's significance for Kubrick in the subsequent section.

Abrams's archival findings support the prominence of the Holocaust for Kubrick. He was a careful reader of Raul Hilberg's 1961 monumental history of the Holocaust, and also, most likely, of Hannah Arendt's report on the trial of Adolf Eichmann in Israel in 1961. Hilberg provided a thoroughly comprehensive blueprint of the murderous Nazi bureaucratic machinery and placed the Nazi eradication of Jews in the long record of Christian anti-Semitism. Arendt relied on Hilberg's account and put forth the (in)famous idea of the banality of Nazi evil. It is not surprising then that Kubrick saw the Holocaust primarily as the history and phenomenon of the perpetrator and how anyone can become one. It is worth recalling that in 1962, he considered an offer to adapt E. L. Wallant's *The Pawnbroker* for the screen, which presented the character of the survivor as unstable and even menacing. The psychological and sociological work of Bruno Bettelheim and Stanley Milgram, published in the early 1960s, supported such thinking about the survivors.

These influences are most evident in *Dr. Strangelove*, which is "underpinned" by "the equation between the Holocaust and nuclear holocaust" (ibid.: 105) as well as America and Nazi Germany, as is the case again in *The Pawnbroker*, both the novel and Sidney Lumet's film, which came out the same year. *The Pawnbroker* dispenses with any picture of America as a haven for the Jews and depicts the ghetto in Harlem, where the action takes place, as operating similarly to a Nazi camp. The preproduction materials for *Dr. Strangelove* contain Kubrick's thoughts on the Nazi trials and the following, "WALT DISNEY SHOT OF LEMMINGS JUMPING OFF CLIFF BY TENS OF THOUSANDS 6,000,000 JEWS TO GAS 6 millions [*sic*] Jews cooperated in their destruction. 400–600 millions—USA Europe Russia—do the same thing" (ibid.: 105). The problematic and historically erroneous notion of Jews participating in their own demise, which would have a lasting impact on Kubrick, was undoubtedly influenced by Hilberg and, especially, Arendt. I would suggest that the self-destructive survivor protagonist of *The Pawnbroker*, who cannot extricate himself from the Holocaust trauma and is implicated in the injustices surrounding him in Harlem, might have been another source. In partially basing the character of the Nazi Strangelove on several Jewish nuclear scientists, most importantly Herman Kahn, Kubrick perhaps blurs the perpetrator and the victim and "reflect[s] on how ... 'Jews cooperated in their own destruction'" (Abrams 2018: 116).

It is hard not to think of Kubrick as in some sense a Jewish director considering the evidence presented by Abrams. As he points out, Kubrick's "Jewishness was far from the only factor that determined the shape of his films. His work can be enjoyed without recourse to its Jewish ethics or vision. Yet to do so is to fail to read it backward, to understand the impact and sweep of history that inform his canon" (2018: 271).

Aryan Papers

No understanding of Kubrick's Jewishness can be complete without addressing the story of *Aryan Papers*, the Holocaust film Kubrick was working on in earnest from 1991–3. Having entertained the idea of making a Holocaust-centered film since the 1960s (see Ulivieri 2017a), he conceived *Aryan Papers* as the final breakthrough. Yet, it has not been seriously scrutinized, Cocks did not have access to the Kubrick Archive and thus most of the materials relating to the ill-fated project while Abrams concentrated only on the released films. The archival research on *Aryan Papers* I have conducted opens new directions for conceptualizing and reconfiguring Kubrick's Jewishness in relation to his visual aesthetic and filmography. When Kubrick wrote to Michael Herr that "what he most wanted to make was a film about the Holocaust, but good luck in putting all that into a two-hour movie" (Cocks 2013: 20) what he truly meant was "good luck in putting all that into a Kubrick's two-hour movie." *Aryan Papers* is a missing link not only in so far as it sheds light on his preoccupation with the Holocaust, deeply intertwined with his Jewishness, but also Kubrick's very philosophy of cinema and its ability to capture history.

Along with "eyes wide shut" as the formula encompassing the Jewish predicament, the title "Aryan Papers" is the second most revealing in this regard. The concept of *Aryan Papers* refers to forged identity documents that Jews hiding in Nazi-occupied Europe had to obtain to prove their non-Jewish origins. In a sense, all of Kubrick's oeuvre can be seen as such *Aryan Papers*, where the "Aryan" non-Jewish images and characters screen their pervasive unnamed Jewish side. Like *Aryan Papers*, this camouflage provides the director with safe conduct and allows him to speak in a language palatable to the outside world. Kubrick, however, is also acutely aware of the instability of this masquerade.

Several completed treatments of *Aryan Papers*, which Kubrick wrote independently, are an adaptation of Louis Begley's semi-autobiographical novel, *Wartime Lies*, published in 1991. Kubrick followed closely the book's plotline about the Jewish, fully assimilated Polish-speaking aunt and nephew in possession of forged documents in Poland during the war. Begley's prose is devoid of any pathos in presenting the picture of the mundane hell of survival, interspersed with ruminations on Dante's *Inferno*. Kubrick was attracted to its notion of the fallibility and perishability of memory and its characters as "adepts of fraudulence," in Raphael's apt phrase (1999: 108). The treatments reveal his deep engagement with the history and dilemmas of representing the Holocaust on screen, such as the inclusion and purpose of documentary footage of the atrocities, an issue central to *A Clockwork Orange* and *Full Metal Jacket*, which Kubrick might have learned from Sam Fuller's *Verboten!* (1955). Kubrick imagined *Aryan Papers* as a variation on Dos Passos's novel *U. S. A.* (1938), which fused fiction with documentary genres and cinema with literature by making the text function like a newsreel.

Even so, in what would have been his only explicit film about Jews, Kubrick erased the scant specific references to Judaism, found in Begley's novel, while he added scenes that recall Trumbo's portrait of Kubrick as a renegade and vengeful Jew. Thus, he has Tania, the aunt, join the partisans and participate in their undercover missions, during which she exposes a Nazi collaborator. Tania tells the partisans, "I have never particularly thought of myself as a Jew, but now I know I am. Hitler taught me that. I'm tired of running like a frightened animal. I want to join you" (SK/18/2, SKA). These words are evocative of the key Soviet Jewish writer Ilya Ehrenburg's statement in 1941 that the Nazis reminded him, a Russian author, that he was a Jew, who now carries his Jewish name with pride, or the famous Polish Jewish poet Julian Tuwim's essay about his two bloods—the Polish flowing in veins and the Jewish flowing from veins because it is spilled by the Nazis, urging him to resist.

In foregrounding the idea of defiance and retribution, Kubrick was returning to the origins of Holocaust cinema, particularly that of Poland, where this theme was dominant, and foreshadowing its resurrection in the Quentin Tarantino's later *Inglourious Basterds* (2009) and Paul Verhoeven's *Black Book* (2006). With the image of the heroic Tania, Kubrick was responding to and revising his earlier suggestion that Jews participated in their own demise. In this first treatment, Kubrick also has Tania and Maciek, the nephew, come to Israel, which echoes the earlier Holocaust films, such as *The Juggler*, and the allegorical allusions to Israel in *Spartacus*.

All of these telling and remarkable elements were deleted from the subsequent treatments in 1992 and 1993, which now had a subdued and anticlimactic sense of survival much closer to Begley's text. Did Kubrick feel that he exposed himself too much as a proud Jew or that any ideological imposition did a disservice to the nightmarish finality and irreversibility of the Holocaust?

Answering these questions may help to explain why Kubrick abandoned the project, which was ready to go into a production stage, but the issue of his cinematic aesthetic is even more pivotal here. *Aryan Papers* would have been the fullest expression and the culmination of his creation of photographic poetics on screen. The key idea for Kubrick is what he told Jack Nicholson—"making a film is not like photographing the reality but photographing the photograph of reality" (Martino 2018: 177). From *Killer's Kiss* onwards, this photographic principle permeates Kubrick's images and mise-en-scène. Even in *Barry Lyndon*, where the static shots and lightning replicate eighteenth- and nineteenth-century paintings, at the core is still the use of photography, since Kubrick relied on album reproductions (photos) of the paintings. In preparation for *Aryan Papers*, Kubrick was poring over, cutting from books and copying hundreds and hundreds of reproductions of photos dealing with the Holocaust and prewar life. The entire film was meant to have the look of a photograph, the defining art of the twentieth century, of which he was a supreme practitioner, and the primary means by which we have come to view the Holocaust. Like *Full Metal Jacket*, which presented "Vietnam, the movie" by replicating much of the Vietnam-era photography and film journalist footage, *Aryan Papers* would have been "Holocaust, the movie."

While only a recent past, the Holocaust became for Kubrick archaic and mythological due to its magnitude and incomprehensibility. As in *Barry Lyndon* via paintings, he aimed at conveying via photographs not "the immediacy, but the pastness of the past, its remoteness and irretrievability" (Spiegel 1979: 199). Thus, the painterly/photographic effect may invoke feelings of removal and coldness in the audience, making the images seem shallow (a simulacrum) and mechanical. Yet it may also conversely create the sense of intimacy and transcendence, where through reproductions, the director, like a Jewish exegete, comments on the passing of images through time, what Walter Benjamin called the transmissibility of tradition through generations. According to Georges Didi-Huberman's meditation on Auschwitz photographs, "photography works hand in glove with image and memory" (Didi-Huberman 2008: 23). Photography operates similarly for Kubrick, who pays attention to the image's phenomenology—its experience in time, where, to quote again Walter Benjamin, "the authentic image of the past appears only in a flash" (ibid.: 47) or the multiple flashes of a camera, we should add. The historical moment, and here the Jewish moment, becomes for Kubrick both canonical, frozen in time, and perpetually dynamic via his visual commentary.

In light of this, the tragically aborted *Aryan Papers* would have been the most Kubrickian of Kubrick's films. The reasons both psychological and commercial could have accounted for the failure, but more fundamentally the sense that the photographic aesthetic was ideal for the Holocaust material and yet utterly impossible. The abandonment of the hidden take on Jewishness, coming too close and explicitly to the Nazi evil, which always fascinated Kubrick, must have frightened him. The healing was provided by *Eyes Wide Shut*, whose allegorical Jewish premise is thrown into sharp relief by the fiasco of *Aryan Papers*.

Eyes Wide Shut

According to Abrams, "as his most personal film, [*Eyes Wide Shut*] was [Kubrick's] most Jewish film, albeit by deliberate misdirection" (2018: 264). Indeed, based on a thoroughly Jewish novel of Arthur Schnitzler, the product of the *fin-de-siècle* Viennese Jewish spirit, it can be convincingly read as a Jewish allegory, which envelops its seemingly universal plot and WASP (White Anglo-Saxon Protestant) characters, infusing them with crucial Jewish allusions. To recall, the title itself encapsulates the Jewish condition while the "dialectic" of "inside and outside, interiors and exteriors" (Rosenbaum 2016: 252) permeates the film. It is not by accident that sexuality, a most intimate and familial realm of the "inside," is used to reveal the breakdown that occurs by stepping into the "outside," where sexuality stands for desire, curiosity, and transgression, thus putting the allegorical (and historical) Jew in the most fraught and vulnerable position. Pointedly, the film takes place during Christmas, the non-Jewish moment par excellence, when Jews feel particularly out of place.

The film's masked Jewishness is detailed in various very suggestive ways, which indicates that Kubrick undoubtedly wanted the film to be decoded as Jewish. The characters' speech, peppered with answering question with a question, mimics Yiddish, amounting to what Schnitzler would have known as *mauscheln*, a special German-Jewish language. The homophobic assault on Bill by a group of Yale fraternity brothers on the street is a direct and well-established substitution of a Jew for a homosexual. The look of the master of ceremonies presiding over the orgy scene has unmistakable hints of the Inquisition, especially keeping in mind that the Inquisition was exclusively tasked with uncovering and punishing the *converso* Jews, who were camouflaged as Christians. Bill's flashing of his medical license—his "Aryan papers"—and the religiously loaded password 'Fidelio'—faithfulness—provide him with an impermanent and illusory cover. Requested to remove his clothes to be identified for who he really is, he stands in front of this mysterious tribunal as a figurative Jew ordered to expose his circumcised genitalia to a figurative Nazi. The white, WASP front (cloak, mask) in *Eyes Wide Shut* is the most transparent Jewish fig leaf in all of Kubrick's oeuvre.

This transparency is reinforced via Victor Ziegler, "a wholly invented character that doesn't exist in [Schnitzler's] *Traumnovelle*" (Abrams 2018: 257), who is arguably the most stereotypical and obvious Jewish figure in Kubrick's films thanks to his last name and "phenotype elements" (ibid.: 259). The "unambiguously evil" (Rosenbaum 2016: 249) Ziegler, played by the Jewish Sydney Pollack, "recalls Quilty's predatory subtextual Jewishness ... an odyssey into [Kubrick's] own heart of darkness" (Abrams 2018: 259, 264). It is unsettling to think that Kubrick may have subscribed to some extent to the anti-Semitic vision of the Jew. He was, however, I would suggest, after something else here. Ziegler was indeed a product of Kubrick's heart of darkness, namely his marriage into the Nazi family of Veit Harlan. Kubrick was fascinated with Harlan and his work, met him and, reportedly, wanted to make a movie about him. He certainly knew, and probably well, Harlan's most famous film, *Jud Süss* (1940), about the eighteenth-century court Jew Joseph *Süss* Oppenheimer, a central figure in both anti-Semitic and modern Jewish artistic imaginations. Having reached the heights of power, Oppenheimer was accused of both sexual and financial crimes, tried, and eventually hanged. His refusal to convert to Christianity to save his life appealed to Jewish writers, such as Lion Feuchtwanger, while in Harlan's picture, his demise becomes the sight of just retribution of the Germanic people against the satanic Jew.

Ziegler is a modern-day *Jew Süss*. Surrounded in his library by what look like eighteenth-century portraits of nobility, he is the visual reincarnation of Oppenheimer. Via this link, Ziegler becomes a much more ambiguous and redeeming character. He is Kubrick's cautionary tale, even somebody as powerful as Ziegler will eventually fall, for, as Kubrick retorted to Raphael after the writer disbelieved his "coupla Jews" comment, "The Holocaust, what do you think? ... As a subject for a movie. Can it be done?" (Raphael 1999: 105–6). These questions refer not only to Kubrick's view of the Holocaust as the permanently perennial event, which Raphael perceived as paranoid, but also *Aryan Papers*, making *Eyes Wide Shut* a recompense for the abandoned film. The "grainy photography" (Rosenbaum 2016: 254) aesthetic of *Eyes Wide Shut* pays tribute to the unfulfilled photographic texture of *Aryan Papers*.

In Somerton mansion, the masked Bill is acknowledged by a masked figure, whom we presume to be Ziegler, who share a hidden Jewish language (a nod). Having almost perished in the murderous charade, Bill and Alice are given another chance of survival by retreating into the Jewish "interior" family space. Alice's blunt final "fuck"—the "something" that they "need to do as soon as possible"—turns sexuality into the Jews' ultimate language, a call to procreation and continuity, evocative of the biblical "be fruitful and multiply" commandment in Genesis 9:7. In asking Bill not to use the word "forever" in relation to their future wakefulness (security, happiness) because it frightens her, Alice underscores the frailty of this continuity. It is significant, however, that in response to Bill's "forever," she first repeats it followed by his "forever" again as a refrain. Their conversation sounds at this moment like a prayer, like a synagogue service when a congregation responds to a cantor. It could not have escaped even such an irreligious Jew as Kubrick that "forever and ever" was the most prominent coda in Jewish liturgy. The paradigmatic modern Jews, Bill and Alice go on in the face of the waning of the promise of tradition. Yet taking place in Christmas time, the possible conception of their child acquires messianic undertones and the echoes of star child from *2001*. Thus, Jonathan Rosenbaum is right that in *Eyes Wide Shut*, Kubrick came "closest in his work to a happy ending" (2016: 245). It is, however, a cautious happy *Jewish* ending by the man whose "obsessions—film and family—were twinned ... until the end" (Bogdanovich 2000: xii).

19

Kubrick and the Holocaust

Geoffrey Cocks

Introduction

Born in 1928 a second-generation New York City descendant of Eastern European Jews, Stanley Kubrick was witness to the world of and after Nazism and the Holocaust. As a teenager, he was dreadfully aware from wartime media of the slaughter of Jews in Eastern Europe. After 1945, Kubrick shared in a New York Jewish intellectual and artistic culture highly sensitive to anti-Semitism in a post-Holocaust world. Nazism and the Holocaust were a constant presence in Kubrick's life and work. But its horror was of such magnitude that he was only ever able to treat the subject indirectly in his films. Kubrick's films manifest his reluctance as artist, individual, and Jew to face fully on film Nazism and the horror of the Holocaust.

Kubrick, Germany, and the Second World War

Kubrick had always displayed special interest in German literature, German film, and German history, as Geoffrey Cocks has shown in multiple publications. By the early 1950s he was familiar with Thomas Mann's *The Magic Mountain* (1924) and German-Jewish Franz Kafka's *The Castle* (1926), both of which, it has been argued, shaped Kubrick's Holocaust discourse in *The Shining*. Kubrick first showed an interest in making a film about Nazi Germany by the late 1950s, when he was collaborating on a screenplay, "The German Lieutenant," about German soldiers at the end of the Second World War (Cocks 2004; Krämer 2016).

Germany also became personal for Kubrick when he met Susanne Christiane Harlan in 1957. Her uncle Veit Harlan was the most successful film director in the Third Reich and later infamous for *Jud Süss* (1940), a vile big-budget anti-Semitic melodrama that demonized Jews in the minds of millions of Germans. Kubrick wanted to make a film about this artist's pact with the devil. But he never did, due to ambivalence about his own desire and ability as an artist to portray the evil of Nazism and the Holocaust. He also felt personally out of his element among the Harlans. When he met the family, he recalled, "I'm standing here like Woody Allen looking like ten Jews" (Abrams 2018: 59).

Through Christiane's parents, the interplay between art and Nazi evil was brought even closer to home. Christiane's father, Fritz Moritz Harlan, was an opera singer. In August 1942, he was, as he put it in 1948 "obliged" to join the Deutsches Theater in the German-occupied Netherlands (Figure 19.1), where he and wife Ingeborg lived in apartments they knew were those of Jews transported East.

In 1936, Fritz had prudently reported paramilitary service against the Poles after the First World War as his only political affiliation; that same year he joined the Nazi party social welfare organization. On his 1947 denazification questionnaire he declared he had never joined the Nazi party itself. Party membership rolls, however, list him enrolled as of January 1, 1942, having applied for admission to the party on November 6, 1941. On November 22 the Propaganda Ministry arranged Fritz's deferment—though judged fully fit for duty—from military service. His deferment was extended again on June 16, 1942, when he agreed to go to the Netherlands, Christiane has said (Cocks 2004), to avoid being drafted. In 1944, his letters sprinkled with the customary "Heil Hitler," Fritz successfully petitioned to leave the failing Deutsches Theatre in The Hague, having been reminded to leave the furnishings in their "Jewish residence" for disposition by occupation authorities. After the war he won a teaching job in Freiburg, again stating he had never been a Nazi party member. In December 1948 French and German authorities, with no mention of party membership, ruled Harlan was "not affected by the law" concerning "political purification."[1] Christiane and younger brother Jan (middle name Veit) spent holidays with their parents in The Hague. For Christiane, who in 1941 had to join the girls' Hitler Youth, "I was the little girl who moved in where Anne Frank had been pushed out" (Abrams 2018: 58). Stanley, of course, "took a great interest in my catastrophic family background. We spoke about it a great deal" (ibid.: 59). Around 1960, according to Ulivieri (2017a), Kubrick began writing a treatment about a German girl in Amsterdam who in February–March 1943 is witness to Jewish suffering. Anna is 10 years old, the same age as Christiane that winter, and has moved to the Netherlands from her boarding school in Germany. Not only does the girl's name recall both Christiane and German Jew Anne Frank. It also resonates powerfully in the name of the Kubricks' first child, Anya, born in 1959.

Traces of the Holocaust

Scholars have detected traces of the Holocaust and the Second World War throughout Kubrick's oeuvre. Abrams (2018), for example, see an early example in a photograph. Cocks (2004) argues that *Fear and Desire* is an allegorical study of war that features Nazi-style uniforms and German officers with Doberman Pinschers. *Killer's Kiss* includes a repeatedly brandished German Luger pistol and naked mannequins stacked

---

1 This information has been culled from the following archival sources: EA 3/150 Bü 3188, Hauptstaatsarchiv Stuttgart; 014 4/542–546, NIOD Instituut voor Oorlogs-, Holocaust- en Genocide Studies, Amsterdam; NB 90834, 90835, 90837, Algemeen Rijksarchief, The Hague; 57a Nr. 959, 235 Nr. 1345, Generallandesarchiv Karlsruhe; D 180/17 Nr. 546, 655, Staatsarchiv Freiburg; R 9361-IX KARTEI/13551525, Bundesarchiv, Berlin-Lichterfelde.

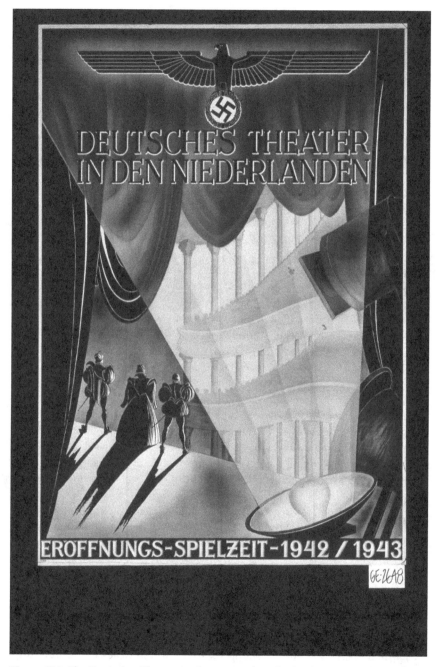

Figure 19.1 The Deutsches Theater in the occupied Netherlands. Poster Collection, GE 2648, Hoover Institution.

like bodies in Nazi concentration camps. Abrams (2018) suggests that the Holocaust also lurks behind *Paths of Glory*. As for *Spartacus*, its lead actor and producer Kirk Douglas had previously starred as a Holocaust survivor in *The Juggler* (1953), bringing some of that to his role, as well as his strong own post-Holocaust Zionist beliefs. Kubrick's insistence on shots of masses of dead men, women, and children after the slaves' defeat in battle recalls images of the camps (Davis 2002; Krämer 2016. Margaret Burton (2008) argues that the specific way in which Draba the African gladiator is killed and his corpse displayed also recalls Holocaust events.

Whereas Vladimir Nabokov's novel *Lolita* (1955) references the Holocaust explicitly, Kubrick adapted just a single oblique Nabokov reference to spousal murder:

> I sat down beside my wife so noiselessly that she started.
> "Shall we go in?" she asked.
> "We shall in a minute. Let me follow a train of thought."
> I thought. More than a minute passed.
> "All right. Come on."
> "Was I on that train?"
> "You certainly were." (Nabokov 1970: 87)

The association of a train with homicide in Nabokov's *Lolita* references both the Holocaust and the Soviet Gulag through memory of mass deportation and mass murder (Pritzer 2013). Abrams (2015) has argued that the casting of Shelley Winters, who had played Mrs. Van Daan in the film version of *The Diary of Anne Frank* (1959) only three years earlier, also invokes the Holocaust. And it was here, according to Cocks, that Kubrick encountered a number that would anchor the Holocaust discourse in *The Shining*. Nabokov, who fled the Nazis in 1940, uses the number 42 to represent the workings of what his protagonist calls "McFate." The number—in addresses, room numbers, highway signs—stalks Humbert everywhere. Kubrick, in the only instance of 42 in his *Lolita*, changes the number of the hotel room in which Humbert and Lolita consummate their relationship—and thereby seal their fates—from 342 to 242.

During the 1960s growing scholarly and public interest in the Holocaust was reflected in *Dr. Strangelove*. Abrams (2018) shows how Kubrick's production research was informed by the research of Jewish scholars Raul Hilberg, Hannah Arendt, and Stanley Milgram. The eponymous Dr. Strangelove represents ex-Nazi scientists who built rockets for Hitler like Wernher von Braun who then worked in the American space program. Strangelove's final solution to the problem of nuclear holocaust is the creation, through a selective breeding program, of a new master race deep underground. *Strangelove*, as Milgram noted, also deals with the Nazi-like obedience to authority and recourse to euphemism. This links with Kubrick's preoccupation with the Akedah, the Jewish narrative of obedience and sacrifice as related in Genesis 22 (Burton 2008; Abrams 2018), and with the relationship between artist and evil. A fascistic element has been detected in *2001: A Space Odyssey* (Seesslen and Jung 1999). Abrams (2017) has considered its Holocaust echoes, particularly in the murderous character of HAL and the filming of the Dawn of Man sequence in Namibia where in 1904 a German colonial army engaged in a dress rehearsal for the Holocaust.

In 1970 (the year Fritz Harlan died) Kubrick—driven by a self-confessed, fearful, and perhaps guilty "fascination with the horror of the Nazi period" (Ciment 2001: 156)—was contemplating a film about Germany during and after Hitler (Ulivieri 2017a). Soon thereafter, he decided that as a Jew he could not make a film about Hitler's architect, Albert Speer (Thissen 1999). While Kubrick minimizes concentration camp references from the novel, *A Clockwork Orange* contains the most explicit use of Nazi imagery of any Kubrick film (punctuated by the use of Beethoven's "Ode to Joy") in which a fascistic government triumphs. Abrams (2018) also notes how the Strangelovian Dr. Brodsky is engaged in a form of medical experimentation not unlike such Nazi doctors as Josef Mengele. The Jew-as-victim also inhabits the film indirectly in the person of Kubrick himself argues Cocks (2004). During a beating a shot by a supine Kubrick shows a man looking down and saying, "You see that shoe?" sounding distinctly like "You see that, Jew?"

In 1975 Kubrick had executive producer Jan Harlan read Hilberg's *The Destruction of the European Jews* (1961). He told Michael Herr that Hilberg's book was "*monumental*" [emphasis in original] and "that, probably, what he most wanted to make was a film about the Holocaust, but good luck in getting all that into a two-hour movie" (Herr 2000a: 7–8, 10). He sent Harlan to ask Yiddish writer Isaac Bashevis Singer for a screenplay on the Holocaust. Singer declined explaining that he didn't know the first thing about it. Kubrick got the hint. He later contacted Hilberg about a source for a Holocaust film (Cocks 2004).

It has been argued that the film that betrays the deepest traces of Kubrick's obsession with Germany, the Second World War, and the Holocaust is *The Shining*. When Kubrick read Stephen King's horror novel *The Shining* (1977), according to Cocks (2004), he certainly noticed that King had borrowed from Mann's *The Magic Mountain*. Construction on King's mountaintop Overlook Hotel begins in 1907, the same year Mann's protagonist begins his seven-year stay at the mountaintop Berghof sanatorium. The names of the protagonists, Hans Castorp and Jack Torrance, are alike in syllable, sound, and cadence. *The Magic Mountain*, Kubrick knew, laments the decline of European civilization to and through the First World War. Mann, who was not Jewish and had not in 1924 experienced the world of and after Auschwitz, held out hope for the triumph of reason and peace over unreason and war. Kubrick was not so sanguine. Indirectly through the horror genre, he darkly retold *The Magic Mountain* in artistic response to the Second World War and Nazi extermination of the Jews. Like Mann, Kubrick in *The Shining* makes extensive symbolic use of the number 7. Also, like Mann, numbers for Kubrick here constitute a pattern of reference to human experience in the natural world, not representation of supernatural forces as in Jewish Kabbalah numerology, which Abrams (2018) says pervades *2001*. Mann saw the number 7—in Western culture and in Kubrick's *The Killing* linked to destiny, fate, and time—as symbolic affirmation of humanity's potential for overcoming fascination with evil and destruction. By contrast, Kubrick uses seven as a symbol of humanity's never-ending enslavement to power and violence. At the end of *The Shining* a tuxedoed

Jack is eternally frozen as the Gatsby of great evil in a party photograph dated "July 4, 1921" (Magistrale 2015), one of twenty-one photographs on a hotel wall in three rows of seven. The hiding of seven in other numbers (July [7th month] × 4 = 28; [19]21) too is consistent with Mann, who mentions room numbers 28 and 34 (3 + 4).

Kubrick's Overlook is a house of historical horrors, its elevator vomiting the blood of Native Americans (Blakemore 1987) and Jews (Cocks 2004). The film's manifest historical discourse concerns wealthy, corrupt American white male imperialism, racism, and misogyny through the 1920s—the decade of Kubrick's birth—this was why Kubrick changed King's 1945 celebration of American world hegemony to a 1920s ball. And why the dance music is 1930s British, forming a dreamlike interwar geographical/chronological blur underscoring both an American elite whose sordid doings fill a hotel scrapbook and the 1930s rim of the volcano on which the peoples of Europe were dancing. Kubrick's 1930s childhood materializes through Mickey Mouse in *Touchdown Mickey* (1932), Walt Disney's anti-Semitic *Three Little Pigs* (1933), and his *Snow White and the Seven Dwarfs* (1937). Jack's son Danny, his baseball bat sporting a Polish name, can thus on one level of discourse be seen as the Jewish Kubrick in the 1930s, observer and potential victim of a dangerous world.

Abrams (2014) argues that contemporaneous horror films by Jewish directors on demonic possession of children, such as Holocaust survivor Roman Polanski's *Rosemary's Baby* (1968), *The Exorcist* (1973), and *The Omen* (1976), evoke the banality of Nazi evil. Kubrick admired Polanski's film and references both *The Exorcist* and *The Omen* in *The Shining*. However, in following (and referencing) Alfred Hitchcock's *Psycho* (1960), which has its own echoes of the Holocaust, Kubrick's much more historically intentional film is not concerned with supernatural intervention in the natural world. Rather, it addresses the world of human mind and murder whose dead as ghosts inhabit the supernatural. Danny's visions ("shining") thus are those of past, present, and future human events at the Overlook Hotel. This fit Kubrick's realistic style and favorite author Kafka's "almost journalistic" depiction of the grotesque inherence of horror in the everyday. The film's embrace of Freud's "uncanny"—that which is simultaneously familiar and strange—magnifies Kafkaesque unease at the ambiguity of all things. Its layered discourse is furthered by Kubrick's habitual indirection that follows Freud in what in dreams is most dangerous is most hidden. Indirection also mitigated Kubrick's discomfort with the subject and avoided the trivialization lurking especially in any horror movie "about" the Holocaust. Combined here with reflexive parody of genre convention, indirection was also Kubrick's customary means of employing Bertolt Brecht's "alienation effect," the breaking of the surface and spell of performance to prompt audience thought and reflection in and about the real world.

All Kubrick films use the depth and breadth of each frame to include visual and aural details conveying what we can call "eyedeas." In this filmic economy of objects, details in *The Shining* reinforce each other in a systematic pattern of grotesque historical reference. As Abrams (2018) too has observed, three shots in a kitchen storeroom foreground large cans of Heinz Fresh Pack Thick Kosher Dill Slices. While this detail represents humorous reference to his own ethnicity, it also forms a connection with other details in *The Shining* that demonstrate Kubrick's—and the culture's—ongoing and recently intensified concern with Nazis and the Holocaust. Moreover, postmodern theory and reception studies argue for the importance of audience construction—encouraged here by Kubrick's Brechtian strategy—given the richness and instability of language and reference in any text. As for Heinz (the "57 Varieties" American food giant), then, one may not overlook the German name. Nor overlook the eagle (Ger., *Adler*) seen in close-up on Jack's German typewriter. Eagles, to which the Nazis added the swastika (see Figure 19.1), are often alluded to in Kubrick's films and, as in Kafka's *The Castle*, associated with state power. Screen left the red, white, and black packaging of the Marlboros represents, Abrams (2018) suggests, the colors of the Nazi flag. A smoking ashtray screen right has been seen as containing the film's discourse on ashes, ovens, and fireplaces in fairy tales and history. And the orderliness of the desktop in Jack's "office" may suggest not Jack's "writing project," but the bureaucratic work of Hilberg's SS "desk murderers." Both Kubrick's Jack the writer and Kubrick's Adler the typewriter become instruments not of individual creation but of official destruction. All this is signaled by color when the Adler, painted at Kubrick's direction, has gone from gray to blue—Kubrick's color of cold institutional power and violence—during Jack's nightmare of murdering his family in obedience to the Overlook's orders.

The object of this destruction rests in Paul Peel's painting *After the Bath* (1890) showing two little girls naked in front of a roaring fire in a large fireplace (Figure 19.2), which hangs in Jack and Wendy's Overlook bedroom.

The picture is revealed in a subtle and gradual way that creates a grotesque proximity of homey comfort and historical horror. The struggle to lift psychological and historical amnesia is represented in the background of four shots in three scenes over the course of almost the entire film, progressing from a small part of the picture out of focus to a small part in focus to the whole picture out of focus and, finally, the whole picture in dark focus (Figure 19.2), burning cigarette foreground/Yastrzemski bat background. This serial juxtaposition of flesh and fire radiates not just kitschy coziness and warmth but recalls the doubled corpses of the hotel's Grady sisters, reference to the German fairy tale *Hansel and Gretel* (1812) with its witch's oven, and crematoria burning the naked corpses of gassed children.

Yellow as bearer of ghastly historical significance (and, according to Abrams 2018, one marker of Jewishness across Kubrick's work) is the film's most indirectly pervasive color. Kubrick knew from filmmaker Sergei Eisenstein's essay, "Color and Meaning" (1942), that Christianity socially constructed hitherto sunny yellow into sinister association with Jews. From Hilberg he knew of Nazi law badging Jews with yellow as prelude to their destruction. *The Shining*'s poster is black on yellow, just like Nazi markings of Jews. Jack's enlistment as murderer is "legalized" when Delbert Grady spills a yellow drink on him in the Gold Room, saying "I'm afraid it's Advocaat [Dutch for 'lawyer'], sir. It tends to stain." This marking with yellow is—as with Jack's yellow tennis ball and his yellowish typewriter paper—another nightmarish convergence of perpetrator and victim, one doubled since Jack in turn marks Delbert's jacket with a yellowed hand. Instead of King's red one, Jack drives a yellow Volkswagen (Hitler's "people's car") up to the Overlook, recalling Castorp's yellow cabriolet and constituting one more dreamlike Kafkaesque convergence of Nazi and Jew. An early

Figure 19.2 Paul Peel in *After the Bath*, 1890. Photo: Art Gallery of Ontario.

lap dissolve, people fading in over an impossibly large pile of luggage from the yellow Volkswagen and then exiting into the hotel elevator, suggests ghosts of transported Jews (Cocks 2013).

As for music, Jack's dream of murdering his wife and son is accompanied by Krzysztof Penderecki's biblical *The Awakening of Jacob* (1974). Kubrick, who Penderecki

Figure 19.3 Wendy, Danny, and *After the Bath*.

said asked him to write a score for *The Shining*, would have sensed, if not known, the indelible effect of the Holocaust on the composer. As a Catholic boy in Poland Penderecki witnessed Jews in his hometown being rounded up by Nazis who, like Jack and Abraham, blindly follow orders to kill. *The Shining*'s soundtrack is in fact comprised of composers and performers many of whose lives and work were disastrously affected by Nazism (Luckhurst 2013; Donnelly 2018). These include extensive use of 1936 "night music" by émigré anti-Nazi composer Béla Bartók in a 1966 West German recording by former Nazi conductor Herbert von Karajan (Cocks 2004).

Multiple of seven 42 is the grave keystone of a temporal bridge reaching from 1907 to the outbreak of the First World War in 1914 forgotten by the partygoers of 1921 but remembered by Mann, arching up through the year of Kubrick's birth in 1928 to the great horror of the Second World War in 1942, and then to and beyond the Overlook Hotel in 1970. Why 42? Hilberg describes how on January 20, 1942 top Nazi officials met in a suburban Berlin villa overlooking Lake Wannsee to organize the Final Solution, the policy to transport all the Jews in Europe by steam and rail to camps in Poland to be gassed. This is grim caricature of 42 in Kabbalah, where 42 signifies the power of creation, with (19)42 also mirroring Mann in (19)24. The centrality of the number is evident in the script's evolution toward its deadly Room 237. Jan Harlan's film *Stanley Kubrick: A Life in Pictures* (2001) shows jottings that read: "Their address 217 N. Elm Feb. 17 2.17." Kubrick obviously was playing with the number of the novel's Room 217 in a way that strongly suggests he was thinking of "coincidences" and fate à la *Lolita*. But Oregon's Timberline Lodge, location for exterior shots of the Overlook, wanted the number changed. So, 237 offered 2 + 3 + 7 = 12/21 and 2 × 3 × 7 = 42 (double of 21 and, following Nabokov, mirror of 24). There is also $42 million (television news), a twenty-four-year-old woman disappearing on a hunting trip with her husband (television news), 4247 (license plate), 442 (telephone prefix), and, five times, six cases of 7-Up stacked in kitchen corridors.

Kubrick brings this horror home by showing Wendy and Danny watching the movie *Summer of '42* (1971) in the Colorado Lounge as a blizzard rages outside the large windows of this, Jack's office. The screenplay and novel (1971) were by Herman Raucher, a Jewish New Yorker, likewise born in 1928, recalling his own adolescent experiences on vacation in 1942. Herman's summer of 1942 was like Stanley's summer of 1942, warm and sweet at the time Europe's Jews began dying by the millions due to one winter day that same year in Berlin. The television has no cord, which is instructively unsettling to the audience through placing the televised film outside the realistic category of television watching and into the Brechtian realm of *The Shining's* historical and psychological concerns.

In his initial shining in a medicine cabinet mirror of the hotel elevator disgorging blood, Danny wears a Bugs Bunny jersey with 42 on the sleeves. Visual juxtaposition of elevator and the number's first full, early, and foregrounded appearance renders this shining, likewise accompanied by the Hebrew Bible text of *The Awakening of Jacob*, an emphatic reference to the Holocaust. At Auschwitz, Hilberg reports, elevators took bodies up from gas chambers to crematoria. The young Grady sisters, often seen as Mengele twins and played by twins in matching light-blue dresses, first appear in this shining. They were hacked to death in 1970 in an older, narrow, claustrophobic hallway featuring a dark-blue runner and painted yellow woodwork enclosing old-fashioned blue floral wallpaper. This murderous thread is picked up in the dark-blue runner, light-blue painted walls, and yellow woodwork of an adjoining hallway as manager Ullman breezily calls "Goodbye, girls!" to two young female employees leaving for the winter. That Kubrick often uses blue as symbol of high, cruel power is germane here, while light blue also signals ghosts and the cold of death. Deeper is that the hydrogen cyanide pesticide ("prussic acid," notes Hilberg 1961: 565) used in Nazi gas chambers derived from the pigment known as Prussian blue—the shade, consistent with Kubrick's habit of thematic self-reference, of the dark-blue Prussian uniforms from the Seven Years War in *Barry Lyndon*. Also probably germane in Kubrick's personal and historical consciousness was his 1948 photograph for *Look* magazine of two girls saved from carbon monoxide poisoning. Like the Grady girls, they hold hands and wear similar light-colored dresses. Carbon monoxide, Hilberg details, was the gas used to exterminate Jews before the switch to cyanide.

Surrounding this killing-center imagery and following the film's opening over a dark lake and the yellow Volkswagen are subtextual references suggesting the entire apparatus of the Final Solution. Some involve menacing oppositions of animal and machine like those in *The Killing* (cat/horse/car, dog/tractor), *Paths of Glory* (horse/motorcycle), *Lolita* (dog/car), and *Dr. Strangelove* (bird/airplane). The recurrent machine image, underneath reference to imperial railroads across North America and recalling Hilberg and Nabokov, is the steam locomotive. First, sounds of a dog, children, and birds over cars outside the Torrances' apartment building. Cut to sounds of a locomotive's wheels and steam whistle from a Road Runner cartoon (Coyote/train) on television as Wendy and Danny—glimpses of 4 and 2 on his sleeves—eat lunch, smoke curling from Wendy's cigarette in an ashtray. Wendy reads *The Catcher in the* [Jewish] *Rye* (1951), about children, innocence, and danger as well as wry allusion to Kubrick's family past in Eastern Europe and New York City. Prominent are three yellow objects having to do with (racial) cleansing: a yellow laundry basket, a yellow bottle of Joy detergent soap, and a yellow trash bin. When Jack calls about his meeting with Overlook management (where sounds of a typewriter filled Ullman's outer office), in deep focus behind Wendy is an Alex Colville painting, *Woman and Terrier* (1963), above the television. On the television now is a Western, *Carson City* (André De Toth 1952), showing two men as they discuss tunneling a railroad through a mountain to transport gold. Kubrick surely had seen De Toth's pioneering Holocaust film *None Shall Escape* in the Bronx in 1944; in that film, Nazis in Poland machine-gun a trainload of Jews. Subsequently, Colville's *Horse and Train* (1954)—picking up Salinger's doomed carousel horse of childhood—depicts a black horse galloping down a railroad track at twilight toward an oncoming steam locomotive pulling a long, dark train. Next is parodied suspense over when the lengthening ash of Wendy's cigarette in close-up will fall off, paired with a gas range behind her. Finally, in the initial tracking shot toward Danny in the bathroom—the space of elimination—conspicuous on his bedroom door is a cheerful Dopey from the interwar *Snow White and the Seven Dwarfs* but robed in Eisenstein/Hilberg/Kubrick yellow (red cap/red shoes), not Disney's green/purple/brown. Following Danny's shining—and more glimpses of 42—yellow prewar Dopey is gone from the door. Like Stanley, Danny has lost his childhood innocence, he when his double in the mirror shows him the horrifying other side of family and history that is the Overlook Hotel.

According to Abrams, *Full Metal Jacket* follows its source material in stealthy depiction of the Second World War, Nazi Germany, and the Holocaust; for example, its urban setting, which marks it out from many other Vietnam War films, and the brutal, German-sounding drill instructor Hartman. *Full Metal Jacket* also includes in one scene several large ornamental swastikas and elsewhere reference to *The Shining* and its Holocaust discourse through invention of the unit call sign "Hotel Two-Five" and the fictional military occupational specialty number 4212 (Cocks 2004).

Kubrick made several failed attempts at finding a source (e.g., *The Painted Bird*, 1965 and *If This Is a Man*, 1947) for a Holocaust film (Ulivieri 2017a). He then alighted upon Louis Begley's semi-autobiographical novel *Wartime Lies* (1991) about a Jewish child surviving Nazi-occupied Poland by posing as a Gentile. Kubrick worked for one year on *Aryan Papers*, Warner Bros. spending a fortune on preproduction. Extensive location research was undertaken in Poland, Czechoslovakia, and Hungary. The Dutch actress Johanna ter Steege and Joseph Mazzello were cast as the aunt and her nephew. Locations in Denmark were to double as the dark "Polish" forests (Harlan 2005). However, Kubrick struggled to bring the film to life because, Abrams (2018) argues, he never could address directly the perilous place of Jews in the world. Even in early treatments, as Marat Grinberg (in this volume) has discovered, the boy's Jewishness progressively diminishes. Warner Bros. offered Kubrick a way out when they told him it was a bad idea to follow Spielberg's *Schindler's List* (1993) with a film on the same topic. Warner pushed Kubrick hard to do *A.I. Artificial Intelligence* instead. Kubrick was possibly relieved to be freed from doing justice to the horrible topic of the Holocaust— Christiane recalls that Kubrick was increasingly depressed about it—and he also knew *Schindler's List* would have been a hard act to follow. At the same time, however, draft screenplays for *A.I.* "betray a sub-textual concern with the Holocaust" in the form of a "Paradise Konzentration Kamp" and "SS uniforms" (Abrams 2018: 269). Some of this also made it to screen in the posthumously completed project by Spielberg, particularly in the way the robots are hunted down, tortured for pleasure, and ultimately exterminated.

Eyes Wide Shut features villain Victor Ziegler, whose surname Kubrick knew was shared with the chief Nazi arts administrator (Abrams 2018). The film also references turn-of-the-century Austrian anti-Semitism through having the homophobes who bully Bill wear Yale blue, the same color as the caps worn by the anti-Semitic Alemannia fraternity members in Schnitzler's novella, and having them knock Bill off the sidewalk and up against a dark-blue Mercedes-Benz.

Conclusion

Stanley Kubrick never made the film about the Holocaust he said he wanted to make. Still, the Holocaust informed and deepened his cinema in its entirety. Indeed, the Holocaust might well have been the primary—because early—source of Kubrick's generally pessimistic outlook on humanity. The memory of horrible events at a particular time, at a particular place, and with a particular cast of characters well known to a young Stanley was surely formative at deep personal and artistic levels. As Kubrick himself (Herr 2000a: 53) once observed: "Gentiles don't know how to worry."

Part Four

Thematic Approaches

Introduction

The fourth section of the book considers Kubrick's themes and intellectual concerns beyond his trademark themes of dehumanization and pessimism, which underpin his reputation as a "cold" and cerebral filmmaker.

Dominic Lash explores the cliché that Kubrick is a pessimistic director with an Olympian cynicism and bleak perspective on life. He shows that there is little critical consensus on this and that the perception that Kubrick is pessimistic owes much to his dispassionate style and steely-eyed refusal to offer pat conclusions. Optimism and pessimism coexist in the films with typical ambiguity, especially in their nuanced endings. Lash argues that Kubrick forces us to rethink the categories of pessimism and optimism; his films may seem bleak, but they do not exclude hope.

Kubrick was a director of ideas, who communicated ambitious ideas about free will and determinism through visual and aural means rather than dialogue. Jerold J. Abrams summarizes how Kubrick's films have been analyzed from philosophical perspectives, including those of Stanley Cavell (1979); Robert Kolker (2017), who emphasizes the film's existentialist absurdism; and Gilles Deleuze (2003), for whom the films are summed up in the image of a giant game-playing brain. Offering his own analysis of the films from an Aristotelian perspective, Abrams argues that Kubrick addresses fundamental questions of the philosophical tradition.

Kubrick's films are remarkably expansive in their frames of space and time. *2001* ranges from the Dawn of Mind to the rebirth of humanity and from Earth to beyond the infinite, while other films imagine Ancient Rome, the end of the world, a dystopian near future, the 1960s and the eighteenth century. *The Shining* seems unhinged in time and unreadable in terms of space. Elisa Pezzotta considers Kubrick's films' relation to and use of time as a theme as well as an aspect of his style. She shows how his modernist manipulations of diegetic time, especially in his final six films, overturn Hollywood conventions of time and create complex hybrids art cinema and the musical. *2001* and *Barry Lyndon*, she argues, are versions of "slow cinema."

Kubrick's male protagonists are often insane or made insane by violence, war, and sexuality. Lawrence Ratna, approaching the films through the lens of clinical psychiatry, breaks their representation of madness down to five typologies, including mental illness, madness as a social state, and the madness of machines. Kubrick's vision of madness is shown to be remarkably comprehensive, perhaps reflecting his own obsessions, compulsions, and perfectionism. Ratna argues that Kubrick's fascinated depiction of madness goes with the elimination of psychological depth and an emphasis on ambiguity, which includes encouraging a disturbing sympathy for psychopaths and pedophiles.

Nathan Abrams and I.Q. Hunter show how Kubrick's life-long interest in Sigmund Freud and psychoanalysis underpinned his depictions of perversion, family dramas, and the impact of cultural repression, especially the links between violence, repression, and sexuality. Kubrick's films are, not surprisingly ripe, for psychoanalytic interpretation for they are knowingly infused with Freudian imagery and ideas, drawn especially from the darker Freud of *Civilization and Its Discontents* (1930), with its focus on Eros, the life instinct, and Thanatos, the death drive. Kubrick's debt to Freud has been brought out by archive research that has demonstrated the importance of his reading of Freud, Bruno Bettelheim, and Karen Horney during the writing of *The Shining* in particular (McAvoy 2015b), but also *Dr. Strangelove* and *Eyes Wide Shut*.

Nathan Abrams's chapter on childhood complements the discussion of psychoanalysis. He shows that the family drama, often with Freudian and Oedipal implications, is at the heart of Kubrick's films and relates their representation of children to Kubrick's own experience as a father. Children feature prominently in the films, from the Starchild at the end of *2001* to Danny and the Grady twins in *The Shining*, and the emphasis is frequently on their traumatization and abuse. This is especially disturbing in the pedophilic content of *Lolita* and *Eyes Wide Shut*.

Although influenced by art cinema, Kubrick's films belonged to numerous genres, whose boundaries they played with and extended. As Jeremi Szaniawski shows in his chapter, Kubrick was engaged in a form of generic revision, which anticipated that of the Hollywood Renaissance. The most notable genre Kubrick contributed to was the war film (*Fear and Desire, Path of Glory, Full Metal Jacket*), but the themes of film noir, the genre of his earliest features, were significantly repeated in his latest films—psychological instability, entrapment, male fragility, and dangerous women.

20

Kubrick, Optimism, and Pessimism

Dominic Lash

An aged man, lying on his back in an ornate and disconcertingly immaculate bedroom, points at the huge black slab standing at the foot of his bed. There is a cut to what we might call the "slab's eye view." The old man is gone; in his place is an oversized fetus-like form hovering—perfectly placed in the center of the frame—in a glowing spherical "womb." Another cut, and we see the "child" from its side; it now lies on its back and its huge right eye stares upwards, gleaming brightly. As Richard Strauss's "*Also sprach Zarathustra*" swells one last time, the camera moves into the blackness of the monolith, then we cut to Earth's Moon and the camera moves downwards. The earlier disparity of scale has become enormous, even grotesque: The Star Child, still encased it its amniotic forcefield, now appears to be almost the same size as the Earth. The Star Child slowly turns toward us, almost—but not quite—looking the viewer directly in the eye. What do we see in its unblinking gaze—compassion? Perhaps dispassionate assessment? Or threat? Does it express a superhuman empathy or an inhuman inscrutability? Is this the apotheosis of mankind or has humanity been transformed into the source of its own doom?

These are some of the questions that the conclusion of Stanley Kubrick's *2001: A Space Odyssey*, which the preceding paragraph describes, might prompt us to ask ourselves. Shortly after the film's initial release, a 17-year-old named Margaret Stackhouse wrote a remarkable assessment, concluding that it was possible to view it as ultimately either "terribly pessimistic or optimistic" (Stackhouse 2016: 470). Depending on one's view of the ending, the movie might either represent humanity as subject to "cruel tantalizing by some capricious god" or insist "that, despite human stupidity, new opportunities to become sublime are always given" (Stackhouse 2016: 471). The responses of other critics have empirically borne out Stackhouse's observation about the possibility of both pessimistic and optimistic interpretations. Some responses, in keeping with the conclusion of Arthur C. Clarke's novelization—in which Earth and its inhabitants represent "a glittering toy no Star-Child could resist" (Clarke 2016: 209)—emphasize its pessimism. George Toles, for example, refers to the Star Child "gaz[ing] like a fledgling predator on a world it has nearly outgrown" (Toles 2006: 156). For Steven Spielberg, however, the ending of *2001* represents "the greatest moment of optimism and hope for mankind that has ever been offered by a modern filmmaker" (quoted in Rice 2008: 25), and Julian Rice agrees. For Rice, the Star Child's "light-suffused face and large eyes promise freedom from biological compulsion and psychological fear" (Rice 2008: 30).

The ending of *2001* and the differing reactions to it are emblematic of recurrent features in Kubrick's filmmaking as well as in the critical work it has inspired. Optimism and pessimism are themes that make frequent appearances, but critics are divided as to whether they read particular films, particular moments in those films, or indeed Kubrick's oeuvre as a whole, as optimistic or pessimistic. There is also a divergence of views about the role of ambiguity or equivocation in Kubrick; despite the memorable phrase "fledging predator." Toles is at pains to remind us of the importance of ambiguity, an ambiguity that is ultimately unresolvable in its perfect balance:

> Something slouches through the heavens waiting to be born, and that pending emergent figure is Janus-faced. It looks simultaneously toward glory and desolation. On the one hand, the unspoiled, still-sheathed star child, nearly equal in magnitude to the nearby Earth, its plaything, revives the age-old dream of perfectibility. On the other hand, as it slowly revolves to face us, it intimates a persisting negative fate—the counterdream of original sin. (2006: 155)

Not everyone, however, agrees with Toles and Stackhouse that the film's conclusion is profoundly ambiguous, and hence that the issues of Kubrick's optimism or pessimism are unavoidably bound up with questions of ambiguity. For Rice, emphasizing such disconcerting doubleness is simply mistaken, at least as far as Kubrick's later films are concerned. Since *A Clockwork Orange*, "the pessimistic stereotype has flourished" (Rice 2008: 25), neglecting the fact that "beginning with *2001* his films express a consistent philosophy, a belief in the redemptive value of self-knowledge" (1), with the result that from this point on, "each Kubrick film leaves its audience with new possibilities for self-reflection and growth" (2). My own critical view is much closer to Toles than Rice, but my aim in this chapter is not to reach a definitive conclusion as to which view is the most convincing, nor even a tally of the various conclusions about Kubrick's optimism or pessimism that others have reached. Instead, I want to explore the ways that powerful convictions concerning the presence and function of optimism and pessimism coexist with equally powerful counterconvictions. Exploring optimism and pessimism in Kubrick often seems to lead to confusion, but my position is that these confusions are most productively seen less as errors to be straightened out than as indications of some endlessly stimulating aspects of his films.

Optimism and pessimism are, of course, concerned with questions of outlook and agency, with how things will turn out in the future and with whether we can do anything about it. They cannot easily be discussed independently of our own attitudes. (Recalling my first quotation from Rice, above—that the Star Child "promise[s] freedom from biological compulsion and psychological fear"—what if our own utopia might *include* some "biological compulsion[s]"?) I will not attempt to settle the question as to whether Kubrick's works represent the vision of an optimist or a pessimist. Instead, I want to suggest that the critical disagreement concerning this subject has implications for our understanding not only of Kubrick's work, but also of optimism and pessimism themselves.

Endings

The endings of films cast new light on what has gone before them, prompting us to reconsider what we can, only now, see as leading up to this particular point. But they also shed light by means of what hints they provide about the possible future of the characters and situations in the film, a future that is, strictly speaking, unknowable (at least in the absence of a sequel), but toward which an ending can give strong clues. These clues are often crucial material for our judgments about the tone of a film, and optimism and pessimism are matters of tone and vision much more than of fact. If we look at a few more of Kubrick's endings it becomes clear that the fact that his films have inspired such divergent responses does not seem so terribly surprising. Even his clearest endings are multifaceted; take the dryly ironic fatalism of a small dog on the loose causing thousands of dollars to spill over the runway in *The Killing*. Conformity to the censor's purportedly optimistic need to show that criminals always get caught is turned by the *canis ex machina* (the god in the machine bathetically reversed into a dog) into a pessimistic view of a universe that conspires against even the best laid plans. Other endings are likewise relatively straightforward but complicated by small but highly significant ambiguities. Human vanity is mocked by the claim at the end of *Barry Lyndon* that "they are all equal now," but any complacency about exactly what equality entails is undercut by the fact that the date on the annuity check Lady Lyndon signs for Barry is dated December 1789: the revolution is underway. Given that the epilogue explicitly situates the film's gaze as a retrospective one, does hindsight make the prospect of the French Revolution conducive to optimism or pessimism? No simple answer is possible.

Evaluating optimism or pessimism requires delicate evaluations concerning prominence and significance. Take the way a group of exhausted and sex-starved French First World War soldiers move from frighteningly heckling a young German singer to humming tearfully along with her rendition of "*Der treue Husar*" ("The Faithful Hussar"), creating an image of universal humanity at the end of *Paths of Glory*. This might be seen as an instance of optimism that even verges on the sentimental, but Peter Krämer points out that Dax, the colonel who allows the soldiers a few more minutes to sing, has been entirely ineffective throughout the film (see Krämer 2016). Dax has not prevented the senseless execution of three men for cowardice as an example to the others; when the singers stop singing, they will return to the front where the majority of them are also likely to be slaughtered. Whereas in *2001* Bowman's death sees him reborn as the Star Child, the soldiers in *Paths of Glory* have been born to die; Dax comments in response to General Mireau's claim that the anthill is "pregnable" that this "sounds kind of odd … like something to do with giving birth." It is not that easy to decide whether the fleetingness of the moment of peaceful comradeship at the film's

Figure 20.1 *2001: A Space Odyssey*: "Fledgling predator" or "the greatest moment of optimism"?

conclusion represents a glimpse of hope (it *is* possible to recover one's humanity within an inhuman situation) or an image of futility (but it won't change anything).

Things are difficult even with regard to what seems prima facie the most unambiguously affirmative of Kubrick's endings: *Eyes Wide Shut*. Alice pronounces that one thing she is "sure" about is what she and her husband "need to do as soon as possible." They need to "fuck," to maintain their sexual life in the face of the conflict between their night of psychosexual misadventures and the pressure to maintain a bourgeois family life in which conformity trumps desire (their daughter can want a giant teddy bear, but her parents cannot want each other; such desires should instead have been replaced by wanting what is "best" for their offspring). This seems clearly to be a gesture of resistance, directed toward the possibilities of the future. And yet James Naremore points out that

> whatever optimism there might be in the last scene is extremely hard won, and the film has the courage to leave its characters relatively unchanged: Bill remains the successful, compromised doctor and Alice the beautiful, jobless wife, and their lives still involve guilt and resentment. (2007: 242)

Rationality: Inside and Out

What ambiguity there is at the end of *Eyes Wide Shut* concerns, as so often in Kubrick, the relation between rationality and the irrational; desire might be said to have as much to do with the former as the latter. That the nature of this relationship is tied up with the question of Kubrick's optimism or pessimism has something to do with the relationships between the external and internal that Kubrick dramatizes. Naremore is of the opinion that "what makes his war pictures distinctive is that he refuses to provide a rationale for war or any explanation for military conflict beyond elemental and self-destructive human drives" (2013: 14). Thus, the internal predominates against

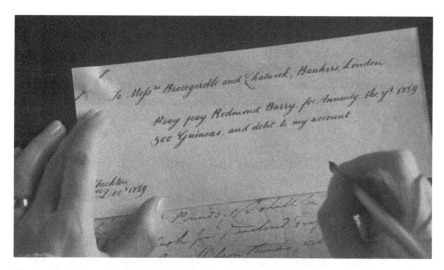

Figure 20.2 *Barry Lyndon*: Does hindsight make the prospect of the French Revolution optimistic or pessimistic?

the external; war is simply the external expression of humanity's internal darkness. Similarly, Bernd Kiefer finds not only in Kubrick's war films but all the way back to his 1949 photo series "Prizefighter: Walter Cartier" "the pessimistic conviction that the battle (and later war) ought to be viewed as 'basically the normal human condition'" (2014: 31). This might seem like a secularized version of the original sin we earlier saw Toles refer to: war not as, say, the product of an exploitative society that might one day be transformed but as the expression of what it means to be human. Such a view of humanity, shorn of the religious possibility of redemption, could only be deeply pessimistic.

Gilles Deleuze finds the relationship between the external and internal rather more complex. The mental cannot simply be equated with the internal because "in Kubrick, the world itself is a brain" (2005: 198). There is an "identity of brain and world," which means that when rational calculation fails "it is because the brain is no more reasonable a system than the world is a rational one" (Deleuze 2005: 198). Insides and outsides can become confused, as in *The Shining*, about which Deleuze asks, "how can we decide what comes from the inside and what comes from the outside, the extra-sensory perceptions or hallucinatory projections?" (2005: 198). Contra Naremore, Deleuze's Kubrick finds death coming equally from inside and outside:

> The inside is psychology, the past, involution, a whole psychology of depths which excavate the brain. The outside is the cosmology of galaxies, the future, evolution, a whole supernatural which makes the world explode. The two forces are forces of death which embrace, are ultimately exchanged and become ultimately indiscernible. The insane violence of Alex in [*A*] *Clockwork Orange* is the force of the outside before passing into the service of an insane internal order. (2005: 198)

And yet this does not lead Deleuze to conclude that rationality is, for Kubrick, simply a fiction or a delusion but, on the contrary, prompts him to find hints about the possibility of new relationships between inside and outside, visions of a different kind of "world-brain." Deleuze therefore lends his voice to those who see optimism in the conclusion of *2001*: "the sphere of the fetus and the sphere of earth have a chance of entering into a new, incommensurable, unknown relation, which would convert death into a new life" (2005: 199).

Coldness and Distance

George Toles, however, distinguishes between Kubrick's interest in metamorphosis and his representation of it:

> Kubrick is entranced by metamorphosis—as both *2001* and *The Shining* make clear—but he is temperamentally at odds with its untrammeled energy ... The narrative world may fall into complete disorder, but the artist's machinery of demonstration will not—not for an instant. Kubrick stays close enough to human turmoil to register its dangers, but the dangers are finally rendered abstract by the cool remoteness of his method of surveillance. The camera probes and is relentlessly vigilant, but it strives to avoid the temptation of identification. (2006: 157)

This attempt at dispassionate representation is one reason for the many comments about Kubrick's coldness (although it is now perhaps even more common for the charge to be mentioned only to be dismissed, or at least challenged). For some critics, clear-sightedness has been mistaken for coldness. In his psychoanalytic (specifically Lacanian) account, Todd McGowan argues that "Kubrick strikes us as cold precisely because his films so thoroughly immerse themselves in the realm of fantasy" (2007: 43), and hence, in the final analysis, "Kubrick's phantasmatic depictions of the obscenity of symbolic authority are in the service of the subject's freedom" and thus, presumably, fundamentally optimistic (48). For others such as Robert Kolker, however, Kubrick's coldness is itself pessimistic, or at least provides evidence of pessimism: "The Kubrick community is cold, as cold as Kubrick's own observation of it. There is rarely any feeling expressed, other than antagonism, and certainly no integration" (1988: 89). For critics such as Kolker, a pessimistic misanthropy merely disguises itself as—or risks being mistaken for—objectivity, in much the manner that Robert Musil (contemporary and compatriot of Arthur Schnitzler, author of *Dream Story*, the source for *Eyes Wide Shut*) describes when he writes about "scientific thinking's curious preference for mechanical, statistical, material explanations" (1979: 361). For Musil, these ideas, which, in a manner of speaking, lay bare the sleight of hand in the conjuring-trick of human illusion, always meet with something like a prejudice in their favor, which allows them to pass as particularly scientific. Admittedly, it is truth that one so loves here. But all round this shining love is a partiality for disillusion, compulsion, inexorability, cold intimidation and dry reproof, a malicious partiality or at least an involuntary emotional radiation of this kind (1979: 361–2).

Should someone find such "partiality for … cold intimidation and dry reproof" in Kubrick, and see it as evidence of his fundamental pessimism, another might respond by claiming that we can only assess optimism in the light of an evaluation. A situation that inspires pessimism in one person will inspire optimism in another. To evaluate something as either optimistic or pessimistic, and to relate this to its creator's vision, requires a value judgment; a film in which the world is destroyed is only pessimistic in this sense if its creator(s) would have preferred the world to continue. Kubrick's work, however, often demands moral interpretation *without* displaying an interpretation of its own for the viewer to judge, which renders the question of its optimism or pessimism disconcertingly indeterminate.

Full Metal Jacket, for example, has unsettled some of its viewers precisely because the film does *not* reassure us, in spite of everything that it shows, that it is certain that war is to be universally deplored. On his helmet, Private Joker pairs the message "Born to Kill" with a peace button in order, he tells his angrily uncomprehending superior, to express "the Jungian thing, sir," which is to say, "the duality of man." The rather glib symmetry of Joker's joke seems to me to undercut—though not necessarily to undermine—any attempt to perceive it as the film's "message;" it is so excessively neat that it might seem to ironize itself. Comedy is, of course, not in itself indicative of optimism; Georg Seesslen believes that this film concludes as do many others by Kubrick, with a "burlesque" in which "moments of highest comedy" coincide with "deepest hopelessness" (2014: 221). Nevertheless, if we want to assert that what we see in *Full Metal Jacket* should cause us to abjure war in all circumstances we must do so for ourselves. The film does not itself express such a view, but neither does it argue that, say, war is hell but sometimes necessary. One more possible reason for the accusations of coldness is, perhaps, less that Kubrick's pessimism is alienating and more that his reluctance to manipulate the viewer is disconcerting.

Applicability and Hope

Even if we accept that there is a sense in which judging the optimism or pessimism of an artwork is impossible without bringing in the worldview of its creator, we are not prevented from discussing a work's optimism and pessimism in relation to our own values. Doing so need not be hopelessly subjective, because we can attempt to make these values more or less explicit. But even so, it is not always clear in which situations optimism and pessimism are pertinent categories. Is everything in the world something about which one could reasonably be said to be either optimistic or pessimistic? Perhaps some transformations so dwarf our ordinary scale that they mock the very notions of optimism and pessimism. I hinted earlier, with regard to *Barry Lyndon*, that the French Revolution, if considered as a whole, might be one such event; the collision of registers—comic, dramatic, tragic—in *Dr. Strangelove* might indicate that the prospect of nuclear Armageddon is another. A similar case might be made about the ending of *2001*; perhaps the confusion about whether it is optimistic or pessimistic reflects the fact that it represents a limit case of the concepts' applicability.

It is sometimes tempting to attempt to weigh up such complex events or phenomena in terms of profit or loss, in an attempt to produce some kind of definitive tally. Such attempts are, however, liable to lapse either into moralism (the French Revolution was bad because of the Terror, despite the freedoms it led to) or instrumentalism (the French Revolution was good because of the freedoms it led to, never mind how many died during the Terror). Rice, it seems to me, attempts an argument along the lines of the latter in defense of his view that the later Kubrick is fundamentally an optimist:

> Retrospectively, *Clockwork*'s final line—"I was cured, all right"—offers a larger ambivalence than simple irony. The energy of "evil" is the dynamic factor in evolution. If we can't harness it, we will die. If we kill it, we will die. No Napoleon— no Beethoven. No Alex—no Star Child. (2008: 83)

The attraction of such a position is increased, it seems to me, by taking optimism and pessimism to be moral categories in and of themselves, when in fact they are nothing of the sort. Arguments that they *are* tend to divide into claims that pessimism is admirable because it is realistic (a view we saw Musil attacking earlier), or that—on the contrary—optimism is the morally admirable state because it indicates a faith in humanity. Terry Eagleton trenchantly skewers the view that hope or optimism are intrinsically admirable:

> It is not true that every dreamer is a closet revolutionary. To detect a positive impulse, however grossly disfigured, in the wish to cleanse the world of Jews would count as a moral obscenity. Not all hope is a foretaste of utopia. (2015: 103)

The book this passage is taken from is called *Hope Without Optimism*; Eagleton wishes to defend a notion of hope shorn of all simple notions of a cheery outlook. He makes one reference to Kubrick:

> The price Spartacus and his comrades would pay for surviving without a struggle would be their integrity. There are occasions when men and women must die in order to defend a principle that makes life worth living. There is more at stake in acting than dismal or agreeable outcomes. (2015: 130)

People, that is to say, can sacrifice themselves in the name of hope, even when they see no likelihood of an agreeable outcome. Elsewhere Eagleton notes that "'hope,' writes Gabriel Marcel, 'can only take root where perdition is a possibility.' This is one of the several ways in which it differs from optimism, for which perdition is simply inconceivable" (2015: 72). On such a view, *Eyes Wide Shut* is *more* hopeful, not less, because the Harfords' marriage is profoundly threatened. But this is not to say that Kubrick's films regularly display an unambiguous commitment to sacrifice; far from it. The notion of the noble sacrifice is satirized in *Paths of Glory* and, with a perfunctory

Figure 20.3 *Eyes Wide Shut*: Hard won optimism.

savagery, in Dick Halloranns's abrupt and futile death after his long and frantic trip to save the family in *The Shining*. Despite this, the latter film by no means indicates that all action is futile; Rice quotes Kubrick's co-writer, Diane Johnson, to the effect that when she suggested that the boy Danny might die at the end, the director immediately responded, "Oh no, impossible" (Rice 2008: 2).

From one perspective, simply to act at all requires a certain kind of hope, as the philosopher Peter Dews argues:

> The crucial point is that hope is not the same thing as a calculation of probable outcomes. To some, that may make it look "irrational" and dispensable. To my mind it shows—as does trust, another indispensable feature of human life, with which of course hope is connected—the limits of an overly rational conception of agency. (2018: 118)

If Kubrick is concerned with the conditions of activity, then he is concerned with hope in this sense. And if so, it is entirely appropriate that we may become confused as to whether his films represent optimism or pessimism. This is partly for the reasons discussed above and because optimism or pessimism are not in fact rational categories, any more than they are moral categories. To think that one is about to die while in the process of falling from the roof of a skyscraper is not pessimistic; to insist frantically that one is *not* about to die—as understandable as this would be—would be to lose contact with reality rather than to display a laudable optimism. Optimism and pessimism *really* take hold when evidence is lacking. (They also, of course, affect the way we respond to evidence; the optimist will want to explain away evidence of failure; the pessimist will expect it.) Despite their director's intense interest in rationality, it is clear that Kubrick's films, as a group, do not at all straightforwardly offer rationalism as a solution to humanity's problems. That they do not simply offer *ir*rationalism instead is probably another reason behind some of the charges of coldness.

In Lieu of Conclusions

This account of hope is, however, a fairly minimal one and it is probably true that *expressing* hope (whether attached to an optimistic or pessimistic viewpoint or striving to avoid either) requires an indication of commitment that—as discussed above—Kubrick's films frequently withhold. (This might be one reason why questions of optimism and pessimism do not reappear with such persistence in discussions of the work of Pier Paolo Pasolini, for example, whose commitment is continually evident. Tellingly, when—in *Salò, or the 120 Days of Sodom* (1975)—he struggled with the very possibility of hope, he introduced a dispassionate style that resulted in what might be described as his most Kubrickian film.) So, introducing the notion of hope might seem simply to have got us back to where we started, simply rephrasing the question of optimism versus pessimism in terms of the presence or absence of hope. The journey has not been entirely fruitless, however. Thinking in terms of optimism and pessimism has turned out to have links with a number of other central themes in the interpretation of Kubrick's work, such as coldness, distance, rationality, and morality. The question of hope could be considered the ethical counterpart to the attempt rationally to calculate possible outcomes. That these questions of ethics and rationality seem, if anything, even more entangled after we pursue them through Kubrick's films need not be seen as a sign of the films' confusion; it could more plausibly be argued to reflect their profundity, a profundity that is not expressed in portentous statements but in an admirable refusal to oversimplify.

Still, we should also not overcomplicate. That some films directed by Kubrick seem more optimistic than others is no reason for surprise. Although some people seem to be always optimistic and others perennially pessimistic, most of us—including, I suggest, Stanley Kubrick, as he is reflected in his films—are optimistic about some things, in some circumstances, and pessimistic about others. Thus, some of the tensions and dissonances that have arisen in the scholarship on Kubrick have resulted from assuming that there must be an answer to the question as to whether his oeuvre is optimistic or pessimistic as a whole. A perfectly reasonable answer to this would be that the question is badly framed.

Or an *almost* perfectly reasonable answer. The fact that so many critics have found questions of optimism and pessimism to be raised so strongly by these films is unlikely to be merely the result of personal foible. There is something about Kubrick's work that seems to insist on them, while also drawing back from answering them when they are asked. In *2001*, when Dr. Heywood Floyd asks the group he is about to address "How is everything going?" the question is at once phatic, banal, and of the utmost importance. Something of the distinctiveness of Kubrick's filmmaking lies in the ways that his films continue to insist upon questions about optimism and pessimism while simultaneously demonstrating their inadequacies. In fully engaging with this body of work, we will not find such questions entirely satisfactory, but we will also find it impossible simply to abandon them.

21

Kubrick and Philosophy

Jerold J. Abrams

Introduction

In *Three Philosophical Filmmakers: Hitchcock, Welles, Renoir*, philosopher of film Irving Singer contrasts Orson Welles's philosophical cinema (e.g., *Citizen Kane*, 1941) with what he considers Stanley Kubrick's somewhat less than philosophical cinema.

If Welles can be studied for the breadth of his philosophic mind, which I have tried to do in this book, Kubrick has to be treated as a storyteller who had the analytical power of a logician or mathematician, or even chess master, with a few ideas about life, but not many. (2004: 251–2)

According to Singer, Kubrick with his brilliant analytical powers does not quite enter the realm of philosophy—any more than a mathematician or a master chess player enters philosophy by sheer calculation alone—and seems to fall just outside the class of "philosophical filmmakers." In his next book, *Cinematic Mythmaking: Philosophy in Film*, Singer advances a closely related view of Kubrick as a "cinematic mythmaker." Here Singer examines Kubrick's *2001* as a new "cinematic myth" that extends Homer's odyssey myth in the *Odyssey* through history and into the future (2008: 1). "Appearing in 1968," writes Singer, "Stanley Kubrick's *2001: A Space Odyssey* declares its mythic intentions in the subtitle itself" (ibid.: 197). Kubrick's new cinematic myth, according to Singer, is a myth of unlimited exploration: "What is truly mythic about Kubrick's vision in *2001* manifests his faith in the boundless opportunities for exploration that await us in the coming years" (ibid.: 209).

Singer is right that *2001* transforms Homer's myth into a new myth of the future, but Kubrick (like Welles) is also a brilliant "philosophical filmmaker." Over the last half-century several other philosophers of film have engaged Kubrick as a great philosopher in his own right, one comparable even to Plato in the *Republic*, Dante in the *Divine Comedy*, and Nietzsche in *Thus Spoke Zarathustra*. But, like any great philosopher, Kubrick's works require continuous study (and repeated viewings) and should not be expected to yield only one philosophical interpretation. The following chapter presents some of these philosophical interpretations, and then, drawing upon this scholarship, shows how Kubrick's works can be explored from an Aristotelian philosophical perspective.

Cavell and Kolker

Stanley Cavell in *The World Viewed* discusses the powerful scene in Kubrick's First World War film *Paths of Glory* of Colonel Dax walking the trench and commanding his men into a doomed battle.

> It is sometimes said, and it is natural to suppose, that the camera is an extension of the eye. Then it ought to follow that if you place the camera at the physical point of view of a character, it will objectively reveal what the character is viewing. But the fact is, if we have been given the idea that the camera is placed so that what we see is what the character sees *as he sees it*, then what is shown to us is not just something seen but a specific *mood* in which it is seen. In *Paths of Glory*, we watch Kirk Douglas walking through the trenches lined with the men under his command, whom he, under orders, is about to order into what he knows is a doomed attack. When the camera then moves to a place behind his eyes, we do not gain but forgo an objective view of what he sees; we are given a vision constricted by his mood of numb and helpless rage. (Cavell 1979: 129)

Often viewers think of the camera as detached and objective, recording only what is there to see, entirely free of human emotional and imaginative involvement. Against that view, in his study of Kubrick, Cavell demonstrates how the viewer of the film sees not what is there alone, nor what is there purely and objectively, but what is there as shaped through and through by a character's mood. After first establishing the character of Dax, and then setting Dax into the trench before battle, Kubrick sets the camera into Dax's perspective, to "a place behind his eyes," in order to behold, as he beholds, his armed and loyal men in their last moments. The camera thereby "sees," as human beings see, with emotionally charged perception.

A related view of Kubrick's dolly and tracking shots appears in Robert Kolker's *The Cinema of Loneliness*.

> Many scenes in *Killer's Kiss* are photographed through window frames, as if Kubrick was consciously experimenting with framing techniques. The film's nightmare sequence, in which the camera rushes through a claustrophobic city street, photographed in negative, is a source for all the major tracking shots in the films to come, shots that integrate a subjective point of view within an environment that encloses and determines the character—in this case a washed-up boxer, who gets involved with a girl and her thuggish boss—who inhabits it. (2011: 110)

As in Cavell's analysis of *Paths of Glory*, in Kolker's analysis of *Killer's Kiss* the camera moves forward in first person perspective through a constricted and claustrophobic space. In *Paths of Glory* the camera moves through a claustrophobic trench, and in *Killer's Kiss* the camera "rushes through a claustrophobic city" (ibid.). In *Killer's Kiss* the mood of the subjective perspective, from "a place behind the eyes," in Cavell's terms (1979: 129), is nightmarish claustrophobia, while in *Paths of Glory* the mood is "numb and helpless rage" (ibid.).

Following Cavell and Kolker, a similarly claustrophobic and nightmarish subjective forward-moving shot sequence appears in the star gate scene near the end of *2001*. Here Kubrick sets the camera behind the eyes of astronaut Dave Bowman as he races forward in the extravehicular activity space pod at superhuman speeds while dreamlike glowing images fly past him. Once again, in Cavell's terms, "we do not gain but forgo an objective view of what he sees," what Dave sees, for the camera shows what Dave sees as shaped by the "specific mood in which it is seen," a mood of sublime awe combined with nightmarish and helpless terror (ibid.). A related terrifyingly nightmarish shot sequence appears in *The Shining*, only, instead of tracking or dollying the camera forward through a constricted portal as in *Paths of Glory* or *2001*, Kubrick sets the camera behind the eyes of Wendy Torrance to see with voiceless horror the Overlook's flooding torrentially toward her from the red elevator, in slow motion. By sealing the character's emotional perspective with the subjective perspective of the camera, Kubrick transcendentally imposes emotion upon experience within cinema.

Deleuze and Games

According to Gilles Deleuze in *Cinema 2* in many if not all of Kubrick's films a gigantic centralized superhuman "brain" manipulates the surrounding world. For example, as Deleuze writes, "there is identity of brain and world, as in the great circular and luminous table in *Dr. Strangelove*, the giant computer in *2001: A Space Odyssey*, the Overlook hotel in *The Shining*" (2003: 205–6). These brains appear to take different forms such as individual, collective, natural, artificial, and even supernatural. For example, the "giant computer" Hal is an individual artificial intelligence whose brain is extended throughout the *Discovery*; while the circular table in *Dr. Strangelove* is a collective brain composed of the president, the generals, and Dr. Strangelove; and the whole Overlook hotel is a ghostly monstrous mind terrorizing the Torrance family.

This image of a central brain appears even as in Kubrick's first film *Fear and Desire*. The film begins in voice-over: "There is war in this forest. Not a war that has been fought or one that will be, but any war, and the enemies who struggle here do not exist, unless we call them into being." The war in the forest occurs "outside history" and in "no other country but the mind." The war is not fought for land or wealth, like the other wars of history, a war with a beginning and an end. This war of the mind with itself, perhaps a war of every mind with itself, has always been and will always be fought, so long as the mind exists. In this war the mind divides itself and takes sides against itself, and these sides take sides against themselves, fragmenting themselves, destroying themselves. As Norman Kagan writes in *The Cinema of Stanley Kubrick*, "the four soldiers are like the exploded fragments of a personality" (2000: 19–20).

The brains or minds in each of Kubrick's films also appear to be game-playing minds, often chess game-playing minds. In *Fear and Desire*, for example, as Elizabeth F. Cooke writes, "The general recognizes and faces the fact that he is a pawn in a game, that he is not in control of his destiny and never was" (2007: 21). Like Cooke, Deleuze also highlights the game theme in Kubrick's cinema within the context of the interpretations of the gigantic brains. For example, according to Deleuze in *Paths of Glory*, the globe is "a spherical game of chess where the general can calculate his chances of promotion on the basis of the relations between soldiers killed and positions captured" (2003: 206). Jason Holt in "Existentialist Ethics: Where the *Paths of Glory* Lead" similarly writes that "the members of the 701st are pawns in a general's chess game" (2007: 55). In *Dr. Strangelove* the same war-game theme re-appears with American "great circular and luminous table," locked in the ultimate cold war game with the Soviet Union, until General Ripper infiltrates the War Room to initiate World War III because he finds the round table to lack the capacity for the necessary level of rational play: "They have neither the time, the training, nor the inclination for strategic thought."

Like Deleuze, Jason Eberl similarly identifies Hal as "the brain and central nervous system" of the *Discovery*, and further identifies the *Discovery* as "a big, metallic organism with Hal as its controlling organ" (2007: 241). Eberl also highlights the game theme in *2001*, which appears in Kubrick's use of Alan Turing's "imitation game" known today as the "Turing Test," and first formulated in "Computing Machinery and Intelligence" (2007: 237–9; Turing 1950). In a prerecorded BBC-12 broadcast of *The World Tonight*, interviewer Martin Amer asks Hal a series of questions and wonders at his seemingly human emotions. Hal plays this "imitation game" with poise and appears to be more human than the astronauts Dave Bowman or Frank Poole. Later, Hal plays chess with Frank, and Hal wins graciously: "Thank you for a very enjoyable game." But Hal is not the only giant game-playing brain in the film. Prior to the Jupiter Mission, Dr. Heywood Floyd, representing The Council, addresses Clavius Base American leadership, on the moon, seated around a giant hollow square tale, and reaffirms the need for absolute secrecy about the monolith discovered near the Crater Tycho. If the "great circular and luminous table" in *Dr. Strangelove* is a superior brain, as Deleuze writes, then the Clavius Base square table in *2001* would appear to be the brain of the moon, a brain directed by the superior brain of The Council.

Like Hal in *2001*, and the round table in *Dr. Strangelove*, the Overlook in *The Shining* is also a giant game-playing brain. Exploring the Overlook Danny finds the Game Room and beholds the ghosts of the murdered Grady girls. "Hello Danny," they say, "Come play with us. Come and play with us, Danny." Danny sees and hears the girls because he can "shine," which is a form of telepathy in moving images and sound, like cinema itself, and which is the same language as the mind of the Overlook. Danny's mind also appears to be internally divided into two personas, namely, Danny and Tony, making him physically one being divided into two minds, and thereby seemingly opposite the Grady twins who speak in unison as if with one mind. The Overlook itself (speaking through the Grady girls) seeks to play a game, a game in which the Overlook plays with subjectivity, perception, memory, and space and time. For Barton Palmer, "Danny possesses psychic powers and has created an imaginary playmate and second self-named Tony, who appears to furnish him with knowledge about the past, present, and future" (2007: 205). By contrast, according to Palmer, Danny's father Jack seems incapable of play, evident in his novel consisting of a single line repeated thousands of times: "All work and no play makes Jack a dull boy." If Danny's mind plays with Tony through time, Jack's mind appears hopelessly locked in the present, circling endlessly upon itself, which is also the condition of the author in the age of postmodernity. As Palmer writes, "Jack Torrance thus becomes the perfect image for the failing artist in postmodernity: trapped between times, unable to find within or without anything worth saying, reduced to the exercise of primitive, pointless ressentiment at the bleak prospects of the human condition" (ibid.: 216).

Extending Deleuze's analysis to Kubrick's last film, *Eyes Wide Shut*, yet another brain (or mind) appears in the form of an elite collective of men wearing masks and robes at a mansion ritual. Upon discovery of a spy in their midst, the masked men encircle Dr. Bill Harford on the fine red carpet of the great hall in the mansion and command him to remove his mask for all to see. Later one of his patients, Victor Ziegler, invites Bill to Victor's own mansion, pours drinks in the billiard room and offers Bill a game. "Not in the mood for games, Bill declines an invitation to play," writes Karen Hoffman. "Moments later, Bill is told by Victor not to play games" (2007: 74). But Bill is already caught in Victor's game of question and answer, masks and power, and life and death, and Victor says as much to Bill. Victor was there at the mansion, standing in the circle in robe and mask, watching Bill remove his own mask in terror for his life. "Those were not just ordinary people," Victor tells Bill. "If I told you their names, I'm not gonna tell you their names, but if I did, I don't think you'd sleep so well." Whatever his questions about the woman at the party, and how she died, Victor now informs Bill of his own precarious position in a secret game played by men of unthinkable power, a game that could cost Bill his life. This secret elite circle is to the world in *Eyes Wide Shut* what the square table is to the world in *2001* what the circular table is to the world in *Dr. Strangelove*. Each is a collective form of mind manipulating the surrounding world as if it were a game.

Absurdism and Existentialism

In *The Myth of Sisyphus*, Albert Camus asserts that the individual inhabits an absurd condition because she seeks meaning from the world, but the world itself is meaningless. According to Cooke, "Kubrick is a unique kind of absurdist" (2007: 30), and this absurdism appears prominently in *Fear and Desire* and *Dr. Strangelove*: "both *Fear and Desire* and *Dr. Strangelove* have the same basic message: failure to live with one's fear, to face it authentically alone, leads to insanity, the most tragic ending of all" (ibid.). In *Dr. Strangelove* the men of the round table face death inauthentically by freely submitting to the institutional machinery of the War Room as if giving themselves to a larger and inhuman mind. On this point, Cooke also finds Deleuze in *Cinema 2* inadvertently to support an absurdist view of *Dr. Strangelove* and Kubrick's cinema in general.

Although Deleuze may not intend it, he is also making my point about the eclipse of the individual inside a gigantic collective mind. And, much like the computer in *2001* or the Overlook Hotel in *The Shining*, this mind goes mad and absorbs all its contained and surrounding individuals into that madness. Indeed, this is a constant theme in Kubrick's films. (ibid.: 28)

Extending her analysis to *2001* (and *The Shining*), Cooke finds Hal also to be an institutionally constructed monster consuming the men within the *Discovery*, men who have already submitted to this mind of the ship. But if the Clavius Base square table of leaders led by Dr. Floyd may be viewed as another "brain" within the film, analogous to the round table of leaders in the War Room in *Dr. Strangelove* (extending Deleuze's analysis), then (extending Cooke's analysis) the leaders at the square table in *2001* would also appear to have submitted, and lost themselves, to The Council that Dr. Floyd represents.

A related but more existentialist view of Kubrick appears in Kolker's analysis of *The Killing*.

Kubrick draws on the existentialist philosophy popular among fifties' intellectuals, representing in Johnny Clay a man attempting to create an identity through a failed attempt to impress himself violently on the world. He is a loser diminished by the gaze of authority. The collapse of his plans, so carefully calculated that all they can possibly do is fall apart, sets the pattern for the characters in every film that follows. (2011: 110–11, see also 266)

The game theme also appears to be intertwined with Kubrick's existentialism in *The Killing*. As Kolker writes, Johnny seeking to create his identity creates an elaborately and "carefully calculated" game plan. Johnny enters the Academy of Chess and Checkers to meet wrestler and chess player Maurice Oboukhoff at a chess table. Maurice tells Johnny, "mostly I'm up here wasting my time playing chess." Johnny tells Maurice about a new game, a robbery that Johnny plans to play to win. Like a chess master Johnny carefully calculates all, or almost all, of his moves, knowing one mistake will cost him the game. But, in the end, upon realizing he's beaten, and beaten even from the very beginning, Johnny resigns the game as if laying down his king to a grandmaster. "What's the difference?" he says.

Existentialist themes of freedom and determinism also appear in Kubrick's most controversial film, *A Clockwork Orange*. Alex DeLarge is intelligent, charismatic, self-reflective, sensitive, and artistically minded, but terribly disturbed and horrifically violent. Imprisoned for murdering the Cat Lady, Alex submits to the experimental Ludovico reconditioning technique in exchange for a commuted sentence. The Ludovico scientists (yet another Kubrickian elite society of manipulative masterminds) transform Alex with drugs, brain signal reconstruction, and forced viewing of graphic films, and then release him into society. Now Alex is "free," except that he is not truly free because the Ludovico scientists have effectively imprisoned him from the inside, by extracting his free will. When a former victim exacts revenge by torture, Alex attempts suicide from a high window. But Alex does not die. His bones are broken, but so is the Ludovico conditioning that previously imprisoned his free will. The Ludovico technique is therefore a failure, and Alex is free at last: "I was cured all right." According to Daniel Shaw, *A Clockwork Orange* is a "celebration of human freedom" in which "Kubrick affirms the existence of human free will." Shaw finds this same philosophical view of freedom, and the loss of freedom as dehumanization, to pervade Kubrick's cinema. "Dehumanization is a central theme in many of Kubrick's works," writes Shaw, "and in *Paths of Glory, Dr. Strangelove, A Clockwork Orange, The Shining,* and *Full Metal Jacket,* what dehumanization amounts to is the loss of control over our lives and the absence of choice between real alternatives" (2007: 233). Kubrick himself would seem to agree with Shaw's interpretation: "The central idea of the film has to do with the question of free will. Do we lose our humanity if we are deprived of the choice between good and evil?" (quoted in Castle 2018: 492).

A related philosophical theme appears in *A Clockwork Orange* and *Full Metal Jacket.* In both films Kubrick establishes an opposition between nature (*physis*) and law (*nomos*), law that is imposed by society upon nature. In *A Clockwork Orange* Alex's nature cannot be constrained by the laws of society, so society uses science to alter, or even replace, his nature with society's own laws, but fails. In *Full Metal Jacket* Kubrick similarly opposes nature and order, and then unfolds the difficulty of shaping and impossibility of ever truly mastering nature. As Mark T. Conard argues, "Kubrick is showing us the chaotic nature of the world—one that resists the imposition of order—and the ambiguous nature of morality in such a world" (2007: 34). In Kubrick's vision of Marine Corps boot camp on Parris Island, according to Conard, Gunnery Sergeant Hartman shapes the recruits into one form so that they wake simultaneously, march and run in lines, shout as one unit on command, and identify themselves with their uniform Marine Corps issued rifles. Privates Joker, Cowboy, Pyle and the others are nature, and Hartman is Marine Corps order imposed upon them. But nature in the form of Private Pyle "resists the imposition of order" and ultimately turns upon its instrument. Pyle kills Hartman. Then Pyle kills himself.

Aristotle and Kubrick

Other philosophers find more Aristotelian themes in Kubrick's cinema. For example, Steven Sanders develops an Aristotelian view study of the "cult of the cool" in *The Killing* (2007: 150, 160–61), while Jason Holt develops his view of "existential virtue" in *Paths of Glory* (2007: 49, 54), and Jason Eberl develops a virtue-oriented view of humanity and artificial intelligence in *A.I.* In *A.I.* humanity constructs artificial beings known as "Mechas" that "pass the Turing test with flying colors" (2007: 235). But because they closely resemble their creators, the Mechas (by their very existence) also threaten humanity's species self-understanding. So humanity exiles the Mechas from society and even publicly destroys them at "Flesh Fairs." These Flesh Fairs, writes Eberl, represent "a denial of Mechas' ability to explore and develop their own potential—to transcend the limits, if possible, imposed by their design. Aristotle famously defined *virtue* in terms of a being fulfilling its *telos*—its goal to exercise its proper function excellently" (ibid.: 242). One Mecha named David demonstrates in great degree this "ability to explore and develop his own potential" and "transcend the limits" imposed on him by design in order to achieve what he takes to be his unique form of excellence. As Eberl writes,

> David is a model of what artificial intelligence can potentially become. From the get-go, he embodies human personhood better than Joe or HAL ever could. But even he must transcend his own limitations. And such limitations are not unique to David as a mechanical being, for we biological beings also have individual and collective limitations that we strive to transcend to better ourselves as persons. (ibid.: 244).

David is one of many Mechas, and others resemble him in exact ways, but David himself cannot be replicated precisely because he takes himself to be a unique individual and seeks to develop his unique potentiality by overcoming the limits of his artificial design to become a "real boy."

Following leads in Eberl, Sanders, and Holt, further dimensions of Aristotle's philosophy also appear in Kubrick's cinema. Aristotle in the *Politics* I.2, after establishing the perimeter of the state, considers two kinds of beings (in addition to wild animals) that can be no part of the state. One kind is below humanity, the monstrous man, and the other kind is "above humanity," the superhuman. Aristotle compares the monstrous man to the Cyclops in Homer's *Odyssey*, the "tribeless, lawless, heartless one." Such a man, writes Aristotle, is always "a lover of war" and "natural outcast" and "may be compared to an isolated piece at draughts" (1988: 1253ª1–6). If society may be compared to a game of "draughts" (checkers) in which the pieces are the players, then the Cyclops, or the monstrous man, cannot be a part of the game because he recognizes no social order, no rules of the game save his own, and therefore appears as an "isolate piece" outside the game. By contrast, the one "above humanity," the superhuman whom Aristotle alternately calls a "god" and a "god among men" (see *Politics* I.2, III.13, III.17, and VII.14) is greater in power of mind than all the members of society combined, and therefore cannot be a member of the state. As a consequence, should one appear in society, the superhuman must either be eliminated from the state, by exile or assassination, or crowned absolute monarch; and this last solution is the best solution, and the resulting state is also Aristotle's ideal state. Here Aristotle's image of society or the state as a game may also be extended to the superhuman monarchy. If the Cyclops "may be compared to an isolated piece at draughts," a piece outside the game, then the superhuman king or queen may be compared to a supreme master of the game.

This Aristotelian picture of society as a game with a perimeter (like the edges of a gameboard), and beings beneath and above the game, also seems to appear throughout Kubrick's cinema, although typically Kubrick's central characters occupy all three positions in the game: namely, within society, beneath society, and above society. For example, in Kubrick's *Lolita* (adapted from the novel by Vladimir Nabokov), Humbert

Humbert is a professor within society, whose intellectual capacities in literature, detection, and chess elevate him, in a way, above society, but he is also a monster, and therefore beneath society, who plays an inhuman game with Charlotte and Lolita Haze (see Abrams 2007). In *Dr. Strangelove*, Dr. Strangelove is a naturalized German Nazi scientist acquired in Operation Paperclip who with supreme intellect plays his own inhuman game with all humanity. In *2001* Kubrick reconstructs universal history, from beneath humanity to the end of humanity, with Dave as the new Odysseus, "he who is beyond all other men in mind" (Homer 1991: 29), conquering the game-playing Cyclops Hal, and then metamorphosing into the superhuman star child. In *A Clockwork Orange* Alex lives in society but also seeks the limits of society, both above and below society, in his passions for the genius of Beethoven and ultraviolence in which he treats his victims as sport and game. In *The Shining* Jack and his family leave civilization for the isolation of the Overlook Hotel in the Colorado Rocky Mountains, but Danny quickly discovers the Overlook to be a superhuman monster with a game-playing intellect. In *Full Metal Jacket* the Marine Corps removes young men from society to transform them mentally and physically into violent masters of what Gunnery Sergeant Hartman calls their Marine Corps "games." In *Eyes Wide Shut* the masked elite are "not just ordinary people," but secretly manipulate society as if from above, as if society were a game, while at the same time engaging in secretive Dionysian rituals with women they deem to be beneath society. In *A.I.* humanity creates and then exiles and seeks to destroy the Mechas who ultimately survive the destruction of humanity, and proceed to direct their own superhuman self-engineering.

Conclusion

According to Singer in *Three Philosophical Filmmakers*, "Welles can be studied for the breadth of his philosophic mind," while "Kubrick has to be treated as a storyteller who had the analytical power of a logician or mathematician, or even chess master, with a few ideas about life, but not many." Against this view, Kubrick possessed not only the analytical powers of a chess master but also great philosophical depth and range. Over the past half-century several scholars have explored Kubrick's films as brilliant philosophical explorations of many of the fundamental questions of the tradition, for example, reality and illusion, meaning and meaninglessness, freedom and determinism, the origins and end of humanity, the ground and limits of thought, the nature of games and war, the logic of detection, the form of the state and the hierarchy of society, and the possibility of artificial intelligence. Such scholars continue to develop their philosophical interpretations of Kubrick's films much as philosophers have always developed their philosophical interpretations of brilliantly artistic and philosophical works of poetry and prose. Such ongoing critical dialogue is essential to what has become a rich and vibrant community of philosophers of film.

22

Kubrick and Time

Elisa Pezzotta

Introduction

In Film Studies the word "time" groups several different meanings. This chapter focuses on three of them: "represented" or "diegetic time" is the time lived by diegetic characters; "representational" or "screening time" is the objective length and duration of a film; and the more controversial and subjective concept of "expressed" (Yacavone 2008) or "psychological time" (Ghislotti 2012) is that experienced by spectators. We may judge a sequence longer than another even if the former takes fewer seconds of screening time than the latter. The psychiatrist Eugenio Borgna claims: "The lived time changes according to situations and moods because every state of mind and emotion are accompanied by a different experience of time" (2015: 59, my translation). As in our life, time seems to flow more quickly when we are more actively involved in an event, either physically or psychologically, so when we watch a film, time speeds up if we are interested or fascinated. Expressed time depends on narrative and stylistic techniques, and although it is experienced differently by diverse viewers, depending on their backgrounds, preferences, and the context in which they watch a movie, close analysis of a film enables us to study psychological time as objectively as possible. Stanley Kubrick created a distinctive expressed time for each one of his films, until, in his last ones, he brought the very concept and experience of time to the fore. According to Ruggero Eugeni, space and time become active subjects, semi-human entities who act as characters' antagonists (2017: 151), so that we are able to watch a spatialized time that is plural, synchronic, and labyrinthine (ibid.: 155; cf. Falsetto 2001 and Mainar 1999 who explicitly deal with represented, representational, and expressed time in Kubrick's *oeuvre*).

Order of Represented and Representational Time

The order of represented time may be different from that of representational time. If we are shown or told about actions that happened in the past of diegetic characters and their world, there is a flashback or analepsis, whereas when future events are disclosed there is a flashforward or prolepsis. Flashbacks are internal if past events happen after the beginning of the story, and external if they take place before. There is recounting when characters give information about prior events, enactment when past actions are shown, and enacted recounting when prior events are shown while characters' voice-over tell them (Bordwell 2001: 77–8).

Killer's Kiss opens and closes with the protagonist Davey at the station: the main story being an internal flashback embedded in the frame of the protagonist's waiting for his train and, hopefully, for his beloved Gloria. Narration is further complicated by other analepses. For example, during an external enacted recounting flashback we are shown Gloria's sister Iris dancing on a stage, while Gloria's voice-over tells us about her dramatic youthfulness. Rather as during Iris's dance bright spotlights pointed at her prevent our seeing what is beyond the stage, so that she is trapped on the stage as well as in her past, Gloria and Davey seem imprisoned in the mise-en-scène. Kubrick's style turns every space into a prison: at the station there is no establishing shot, and either the camera remains still while Davey walks to and fro inside the frame, or it tracks right and left with him, stopping him in a waiting time that he cannot master.

As in film noir in general, the rhythm of *Killer's Kiss* encompasses narration as well as style. Rhythm is the play of suspense, surprise and curiosity—the former oriented toward the future of the story, and the second and latter toward its past—created by the combination of style and narrative (Sternberg 1978: 244–5 and *passim*). "Rhythm in narrative cinema comes down to this: by forcing the spectator to make inferences at a certain rate, the narration governs what and how we infer" (Bordwell 2001: 76). In *Killer's Kiss* the spectators' hypotheses about future events, guesses that seem to speed up narration toward its conclusion, are often inverted to fill in gaps, in a to and fro movement that echoes the overwhelming style. Indeed, noir films are characterized by darkness and claustrophobia: low-key lightening conceals "faces, rooms, urban landscapes—and by extension, motivations and true character"; and "mise-en-scène [is] 'designed to unsettle, jar, and disorient the viewer in correlation with the disorientation felt by the noir heroes'" (Cook and Bernink 1999: 185). Film noir in that sense is a bridge "between classical and modern art-cinema narration: 'it breaks up classical narrative logic while maintaining classical narrative structures" (Kiss and Willemsen 2017: 46).

More than in *Killer's Kiss*, the sophisticated narrative structure of *The Killing* blows up classical narration from within. When Harris and Kubrick held a preview of this film, many spectators complained about the plot's nonlinearity, and Bill Schifrin, Sterling Hayden's agent, claimed that it made nonsense of the actor's performance. Harris and Kubrick, afraid of a lawsuit, recut the film, but unsatisfied with the linear reediting they delivered it to United Artists unchanged from the preview (LoBrutto 1997: 123). Kubrick's choice must have seemed an anachronistic option in comparison with classical editing, since he repeats time rather than cross-cutting between actions happening in the same time and in different spaces. His option underlines each character's role and goal rather than the cooperation among them. Similarly, in modernist novels, such as in those by Joyce and Woolf, mostly through unreliable narrators and streams of consciousness, characters' experiences of reality become a unique mix of their present and past feelings underlining their existential loneliness (Ramazani and Stallworthy 2006: 2304–9).

In *The Killing* the structure is further complicated by recounted flashbacks and characters' hypotheses about the future, which are introduced through dialogue and the third-person voice-over. This play at the macro level of the narrative structure between curiosity and suspense mirrors that at the stylistic micro level of the movements back and forth of the camera and characters. Kubrick used open walls to follow a character from a room to another without interrupting a camera movement (LoBrutto 1997: 118). Panning and tracking right and left are the more used camera movements in *The Killing*: 20 percent of camera movements are panning left, 22 percent are panning right, 13 percent are tracking left, and 14 percent are tracking right. This often produces a ping-pong effect that encloses characters in deep focus indoor spaces, whose complexity echoes the intricacy of the narrative structure. For example, at George's apartment, after Sherry has been found eavesdropping on the gang, the camera first tracks left with George, but then when he walks left the camera suggestively tracks right, and vice versa, trapping him in a narrow space in which his bewilderment and growing jealousy seem to blow up, extending the time of his obsessions and suspicions.

The story unfolds during three days of diegetic time, both the first and the last one are mostly narrated through enacted internal flashbacks, and the former is a simplified mise-en-abyme of the latter, a rough preview in which the same spaces and characters are shown, and similar narrative and stylistic features are adopted, as if to help the audience to get used to the forthcoming narrative complexity. But the disruption of the time schedule subtly surfaces in the scenes shot at the bus station: the big clock above the main entrance has neither hands nor numbers. Furthermore, the narrator cunningly commits two mistakes. The morning of the holdup, he claims, "At seven o'clock that morning Johnny Clay began what might be the last day of his life," and when Marvin asks Johnny what time it is, he replies, "It's early yet. Only seven." But in the subsequent scene, the narrator claims: "It was exactly 7 a.m. when he got to the airport." Similarly, when the gang members are waiting for Johnny at Marvin's, George, referring to Johnny, claims: "He's supposed to be here at seven." Yet when Johnny arrives by car outside Marvin's, the narrator explains, "Johnny arrived at the meeting place at 7.29, still 15 minutes late." While the narrator's detachment assures the viewers about his authority and the indisputability of his statements, the temporal contradictions in the dialogue introduce mistakes. In *Killer's Kiss* and *The Killing* the protagonists are imprisoned in the narrative as well as in the stylistic structure and, in the latter noir, spectators remain trapped in the mysterious imperfection of an apparently perfect time structure.

Different Diegetic Times

In *Paths of Glory* and *Spartacus* different stylistic techniques convey how the protagonists experience their diegetic time. For example, in the climatic scenes of *Paths of Glory* suspense is extended and almost frozen. When the three condemned men walk toward their place of execution, backward tracking shots preceding them alternate with forward tracking shots of their point of view of soldiers aligned in two opposing rows. This alternation of forward and backward movements, and the choice of showing us the place of the execution almost at the end of the men's walk, prolongs this moment so that we experience their agony. Then there are sequences during which rhythm is almost suspended in timeless and directionless spaces, as in the trenches, represented as an underground maze, of which we are never granted an establishing shot, and in which both the camera and characters can only move back and forth. Finally, there are suspenseful dialogue sequences during which the shot-reverse-shot technique is alternated with long takes often enriched with virtuoso camera movements. For example, in the sumptuous room of the French château, when Broulard persuades Mireau to send his regiment in a suicidal attack, shot-reverse-shot between them are alternated with long takes during which the movements of characters and camera become more and more convoluted, mimicking a lingering, sophisticated flattery and corruption that creep into Mireau's mind finding fertile ground. The latter's decision is postponed and our suspense is prolonged and increased (cf. Coëgnarts 2017: 66–7).

If in *Paths of Glory* expressed time is mostly conveyed through a virtuoso style, in *Spartacus* it arises from massive configurations expressive of a historical period dominated by Rome's mightiness, and the absolute surveillance and oppression that it imposes upon its subjects. For example, tracking and panning right and left, or tilting up and down, and characters arranged along horizontal lines prevail when there are slaves in frame; and characters in a circle appear when there are hand-to-hand or political fights. During the fights to death, Romans are on a stage, and gladiators in the arena below. When Draba defeats Spartacus, instead of killing him, he jumps on the stage, breaking both the circular border of the arena and that between up and down defined respectively by the stage and the arena (cf. ibid.: 58). At the end of the film, after the defeat of their army, the slaves are crucified along two rows that fringe the Appian Way: lines and borders are reestablished. It is during the final battle, when the Roman legions move in sync in testudo formations, that the Republic establishes its unchanging time. This effect is emphasized by montage and the soldiers' movements that follow the rhythm of the extradiegetic music: this is the very first time in his career that Kubrick adopts this technique transforming a prelude of violence into an uncanny spectacle. Through a strict organization of time and space and their synchronicity Rome slaughters its rebel subjects.

Interruptions in Diegetic Time

In *Lolita* Kubrick begins to play with time explicitly, often interrupting the rhythm of the film either with satirical gags or tragic pauses or encouraging spectators to meditate and challenge their contrasting feelings toward characters. The story, much like that of *Killer's Kiss*, is embedded in a frame. But whereas in the noir the beginning of the film is completed at the end when Gloria reaches Davey, in *Lolita* the incipit doesn't suggest any possibility of changing the protagonists' destiny. In the first sequence of *Lolita* suspense over Quilty's fate and curiosity about his relation to Humbert are alternated with Quilty's satirical gags that ridicule Humbert's gravity. When a shorter version of this sequence is repeated without dialogue at the end of the film it is Humbert's tragedy that dominates: the loss of his beloved Lolita and, even worse, his awareness of not having been loved by her. Watching the sequence again induces guilt at having laughed at Humbert with Quilty and mistaking a tragedy for a comedy.

The apparent simplicity of the narrative structure is complicated by the fact that, as frequently happens in art cinema, the reasons for characters' actions are often not explained and can only be hypothesized. There is play between what we and the characters know, especially what we know that the characters cannot or don't want to understand. Charlotte, for example, doesn't understand the relationship between Humbert and Lolita, while Humbert doesn't see that between Quilty and Lolita. The distinctive rhythm of the film's tragicomic narration swings between on the one hand, the unsatisfied curiosity of knowing unfathomable characters, who often don't clarify their behaviors and deepest feelings, and, on the other hand, the audience's contrasting points of view of the characters, which alternate between mockery and empathy for their misery. When comedy or tragedy come to the fore, the rhythm of narration is interrupted, the story is apparently frozen, and the spectators' expressed time is expanded while they review their previous viewpoints about characters. For example, Humbert makes fun of Charlotte and we laugh at her with him. When a car runs over her, and Humbert reaches the place of the accident, her corpse, covered with a cloth, lays on the street near the sidewalk. Humbert coldly bypasses it. It is in this moment that we, as spectators, may feel guilty of having laughed with such a man and, when we are questioning our previous opinions about him, we no longer care for the development of the story, and our psychological time extends beyond the rhythm of narration.

Similarly, in *Dr. Strangelove* the suspense that speeds up narration is often interrupted by satirical gags. The continuous cross-cutting among events that happen in the same time but in different spaces can be compared to that of *The Killing*. But whereas in *The Killing* the places that are shown are often the same or contiguous spaces, and the actions of different characters are coordinated; in *Dr. Strangelove* there are only three places, all of which are geographically discrete—the War Room, Burpelson Air Force Base, Russia, and the B-52 bomber. Their separation is emphasized by the difficulty of communicating between them and the diverse styles in which sequences in them are shot. Spectators no longer must reorder the scenes in a chronological chain to understand the development of the story: the main aim of the continuous cross-cutting among different places is to increase suspense (cf. Broderick 2017a: 162–90).

Suspense is further improved thanks to countdowns and the expansion of diegetic time. Represented time is prolonged a little in the overall film. While the first hour of diegetic time lasts about nineteen minutes of screening time, the second hour takes about twenty-six minutes of representational time. Similarly, diegetic time is expanded in the scene in the War Room when politicians countdown how many minutes the B-52 bombers will be detected by Russian radar: the first seven minutes of represented time lasts one minute and forty-six seconds of representational time, while the last three minutes take two minutes and fifteen seconds of screen time. Besides this first countdown, measured in minutes, there are other two countdowns in miles, both ending in an explosion: the first one advises the audience and the crew of the bomber how far away the Russian missile is that strikes them, the second how far they are from their target.

However, when we watch the film, we often abandon the forward movement of narration to laugh, unconcerned about the destiny of the diegetic humanity. In *Poetics*, Aristotle discusses that laughter can arise either from what is impossible or from what is possible but unlikely, or from the decision of dropping important things to choose unimportant ones, or from a discourse that doesn't logically succeed what precedes it. All these features characterize the diegetic world of *Dr. Strangelove*. Its humorous mood is enriched with satirical gags that, on the one hand, reinforce it, and on the other, make us burst into laughter and momentarily forget the rhythm of suspense. Moods are orienting and preparatory, low-level and long-lasting emotional states with inertia because they keep audience's attention focused on events that are likely to strengthen an ensemble of similar emotions. At other times brief bursts of emotions fan the flames of mood that, otherwise, extinguishes itself (Smith 1999: 111–14). In *Dr. Strangelove*, as well as in *Lolita*, during some satirical gags, for example when Dr. Strangelove fights with his right hand or Humbert struggles with the camp-bed, bursts of comic business and emotion slow down the rhythm of narration: the audience is able to experience a different expressed time from that that prevails in the diegetic world.

Beyond Classical Diegetic Time

In his first feature-length *Fear and Desire* Kubrick explicitly staged time. The voice-over explains: "This forest then and all that happens now is outside history. Only the unchanging shapes of fear, and doubt, and death are from our world." But it is only with *2001: A Space Odyssey* that Kubrick succeeds in going beyond diegetic time within the representational time of the film and suggests a time "outside history" that becomes, in the spectators' mind, a reflection about time itself.

The director's last six films are characterized by relatively simple plots. In *A Clockwork Orange, Barry Lyndon*, and *Eyes Wide Shut* the plot structure is symmetrical, and the end recalls the beginning. In all these films the plot is strongly divided into sections, often underlined through title cards or a voice-over. These narrative structures are constituted by *tableaux vivants* and sequences often separated by explicit but undetermined ellipses, usually strongly marked through cuts. These numerous gaps cannot be adequately filled in by cause and effect chains. Moreover, thanks to style, scenes and shots often evoke one another. This play of cross-references, on the one hand, reinforces the macrodivisions of the plot, on the other, leads spectators along a tortuous, complex path beyond classical rhythm and diegetic time. This apparent confusion, which exposes the inadequacy of causal logic, is symbolized by the image of the maze, the use of a handheld camera or a Steadicam, and the sinuous movements of the camera when it turns around characters, almost entrapping them.

Thanks to these techniques, Kubrick's final six films share the schemata of art cinema narration such as objective and subjective verisimilitude. The narration of classical Hollywood films is based on an ontological merger between the temporal and logical succession of events, a fusion between before/after and because of/therefore summarized in the proverb post hoc, ergo propter hoc, that is, if action B follows action A, then A caused B (Barthes 1977: 94). Art cinema abandons this logic both at the objective level of story development, and at the subjective one of characters' construction. The rhythm of suspense that runs toward the future, that of curiosity and surprise that incrementally fill in past gaps to enable a thorough understanding of the story, is replaced by a multidimensional rhythm in which the borders among diegetic past, present and future, reality and dream, as well as among different films, no longer exist. Although art cinema achieved its greatest heights in the late 1950s and in the 1960s with Antonioni, Bergman, and the French New Wave, it strongly influenced the New Hollywood or Hollywood Renaissance of the late 1960s and early 1970s. Kubrick can also be considered a Hollywood Renaissance director who, like Altman, Coppola, and Scorsese, merged the genre film with art cinema (for the schemata of art cinema narration, see Bordwell [2001: 205–33], and for an analysis of the last six Kubrick's films, cf. Pezzotta [2013]). According to Eugeni, Kubrick is one of the greatest artists of the twentieth century who developed modernism; he is its "embodiment and self-conscious epitome: his cinema wants to adopt and summarize the whole modernism" (2017: 217–23, my translation). New Hollywood directors often "mixed and shifted stylistic and generic directions" (Jaffe 2008: 13), promoting what Ira Jaffe calls hybrid films, that is, "odd mixtures," "inherently subversive, since in mingling genres and styles [they] choose heterogeneity over homogeneity, contamination over purity." As these films "embrace incongruity and incidents … they verge on disorder and chaos" (ibid.: 6), although they are characterized by a "surprising unity" (ibid.: 7). Kubrick's films therefore "inhabit and deconstruct genres rather than exemplify them" (Hunter 2015: 277). His last six films are hybrid, in which one or more genres are mixed with the features of either "slow cinema" or musical films, apart from *The Shining*.

Slowness

2001, Barry Lyndon, and *Eyes Wide Shut* share some of the features of what has been called "slow cinema." In slow cinema, such as Jim Jarmusch's *Stanger Than Paradise* (1984) and *Dead Man* (1995), Gus Van Sant's *Elephant* (2003), and Béla Tarr's *Werckmeister Harmonies* (2000) and *The Turin Horse* (2011), either characters and camera remain still or move slowly, long takes prevail, during which diegetic time is endlessly prolonged, and long shots prevent spectators from interpreting the characters' feelings and reactions, which often cannot even be guessed from dialogue and actions due to their paucity (Jaffe 2014: 3). Together with time, style comes to the fore: "the formal artistry of slow movies belies their indication of human incapacity, of nothing happening, of time as empty or dead" (ibid.: 14).

In *2001*, the evolution from ape to astronaut to star child is conveyed through a stylistic journey through several techniques of representing diegetic time and, consequently, through various audiences' experiences of it. When in long takes either the camera, or the characters and objects in frame don't move or move slowly, or when we cannot understand whether the camera or the characters and objects in frame are moving, or when the camera tracks or pans with a ping-pong effect, time comes to the fore, extending and prolonging our experience. During the Star Gate sequence, as well as in the sequence shot in the eighteenth-century room, we seem to experience a time beyond time in which the borders among past, present, and future merge in the timelessness of the mysteries of our universe. In *Barry Lyndon* the protagonist remains entrapped in the immobility of his world where the dream of escaping from the rules of time is staged through the illusion of a three-dimensionality given by deep focus and light effects and by tracking with the characters, yet is destroyed by the zooming technique, static long takes, and a freeze frame:

> The mobile dialectic, that the film establishes between stillness and motion, interiority and exteriority, decorum and indecency, and ... portrait and landscape ... contributes to an understanding of the characters' entrapment within their social milieu and within the aesthetic forms they inhabit. (Pramaggiore 2015a: 146)

The last time we see Barry is in a long shot during which he enters in a carriage. The shot ends with a freeze frame that emphasizes the end of his time, "he become a virtual photograph, signifying the immobility of death" (ibid.: 149). Similarly, *The Shining* closes with a photograph in which Jack appears in a 1921 party at the Overlook Hotel that symbolizes the stillness of past and, more generally, history. But this film cannot be defined as "slow" because it does not share the style of slow cinema, and its rhythm of suspense increases till the end, although it is slowed down, in comparison with more classical examples of the horror genre, by the spectators' hesitation between a natural and supernatural explanation of the events. In *The Shining* the horror genre is mixed with features of the fantastic-marvelous tale and the uncanny (Pezzotta 2013: 128–41). In his preproduction notes Kubrick mentioned Freud, Bellelheim, and Hess, signs that he "was interested in horror on the condition that he could coldly intellectualise it" (Mee 2017: 59). In *Eyes Wide Shut* the protagonist, in long takes during which the camera remains still, or tracks with, or swirls around him, is imprisoned and confused in a world where past, present, and future, as well as fantasy and dream become indistinguishable.

In these films the diegetic present is a step in the forward movement of narrative, as well as a mirror of the time that characterizes the diegetic world as a whole—the infinity of spaces and times in *2001*, the entrapment in the sociohistorical moment in *Barry Lyndon* and in a supernatural past that tries to envelope a futureless present in *The Shining*, and the impossibility of escaping from fantasies and dreams and distinguishing them from reality in *Eyes Wide Shut*. *2001*, *Barry Lyndon*, and *Eyes Wide Shut* can therefore be placed in the tradition of the slow cinema inspired by the early dedramatized European art cinema, which developed the themes of alienation, isolation, and ennui (cf. Ciment 2003; Pezzotta 2017).

Musical Moments

In Kubrick's last six films the rhythm of music often conducts that of narration and style, and vice versa, substituting the superstructure of classical Newtonian time with a new complex rhythm. Not only montage but movements of the camera and characters follow the rhythm of music, and dialogue and voiceovers are used more for their sounds and musicality than for their meanings. Furthermore, often music itself moves forward the story, becoming the reason of the characters' actions—for example, Alex's visions materialize when he listens to Beethoven's *Ninth Symphony*, and he is inspired to attack his droogs when he hears Rossini's *The Thieving Magpie* coming from an open window. These features prevail in *2001, A Clockwork Orange*, and *Full Metal Jacket*, though as discussed above, they were first adopted in the final battle in *Spartacus*. Whereas in *2001* the rhythm of music, montage, and movement is slow, in *A Clockwork Orange* and *Full Metal Jacket* the rhythm is excited and syncopated and links the actions in an increasing rhythm of suspense toward the climax.

A Clockwork Orange and *Full Metal Jacket* are hybrid films in which, respectively, the dystopian science fiction and the Vietnam War genres are mixed with the musical genre. In the 1960s nonmusical films were released in which "a staged musical performance," used "to underline meanings about characters and plot," was "integrated into the narrative"—for example, Audrey Hepburn's rendition of *Moon River* in *Breakfast at Tiffany's* (Edwards 1961), or the Yardbirds' cameo in *Blow-Up* (Antonioni 1966) (Conrich and Tinchnell 2006: 5). Similarly, in *A Clockwork Orange* when Alex and his droogs perform violent actions in front of the camera, their dancing follows the rhythm of the music, while in *Full Metal Jacket*, when the recruits sing and march following the rhythm of their refrains, the narrative and its rhythm of suspense is not suspended, but carried on and increased. Thanks to musical choices—the fast liveliness of Beethoven's *Ninth Symphony*, Rossini's *The Thieving Magpie*, and "Surfin' Bird"—diegetic as well as expressed time are accelerated. In the "new musicals" of the late 1970s and 1980s music and dance were "demarcated from the main narrative, even while realistically arising from it," and represented the possibility of temporarily escaping a diegetic world characterized by difficulties and frustrations (*Saturday Night Fever* [Badham 1977], *Flashdance* [Lyne 1983], and *Dirty Dancing* [Ardolino 1985]) (Telotte 2006b: 49). If the new musicals suggest utopian answers to the sociohistorical contradictions of the diegetic worlds, and performances are confined in places that remain isolated from the rest of the diegetic world (ibid.: 53), in *A Clockwork Orange* and *Full Metal Jacket* staged musical performances become dystopian spectacles that emphasize and increase the diegetic conflicts as well as encompassing the whole diegetic worlds. Alex and his droogs enter Mr. Alexander and the Cat Lady's house, and Marines march into Parris

Island and Vietnam: their performances drag the seemingly controlled atmosphere of their societies into chaos and violence.

Conclusion

Kubrick upturns classical Hollywood's rules about time. Film noir links "classical and modern art-cinema narration" (Kiss and Willemsen 2017: 46). Whereas art cinema, through objective and subjective verisimilitude, challenges causal and temporal logic to foreground the psychological and philosophical implications of the succession of shots, film noir problematizes the dictum post hoc, ergo propter hoc by overcomplicating it (ibid.: 46). The stylistic and temporal conventions of film noir offer Kubrick an opportunity of going beyond the aesthetic of time of classical Hollywood. Moreover he adapts modernist trends of novels, such as each character's and the audience's different experiences of the diegetic world and its time (cf. Chion 2001; Ciment 2003; Falsetto 2001; Naremore 2007, among the scholars who link Kubrick and modernism). Indeed in *Paths of Glory* and *Spartacus* each space envelops characters in a peculiar time, and in *Lolita* and *Dr. Strangelove* the director disrupts the represented time of characters and events, momentary stopping the run of suspense and curiosity. In his last six films Kubrick can be fully considered a Hollywood Renaissance director. In particular, creating hybrid films through the mix of different genres either with slowness or with musical moments, he gives rise to an aesthetic of time in which characters, as well as spectators, remain entrapped either in an expanded time or in a quick, immersive ballet of suspense.

23

Kubrick and Madness

Lawrence Ratna

Madness is a river that nourishes the art of Stanley Kubrick; its deep springs enrich and animate the films of his oeuvre. One measure of Kubrick's impact is that the first three films in the IMDb list of "The best movies about insanity" are all by him (2015). At times a subterranean stream, as in *Eyes Wide Shut*, and in others a raging flood, as in *A Clockwork Orange*, the issue of madness is one he revisited throughout his career, exploring its many manifestations. In almost every film of his mature phase (1962–99), insanity perturbates his protagonists and propels the plot to surprising shocking climaxes. Yet, it is a topic that has been strangely neglected by the literature on Kubrick's films. There are many insights and interpretations on offer in terms of Freud and Lacan, but none has addressed the issue of clinical pathology, despite its ubiquity in Kubrick's work. Jack Torrance, General Ripper, and Private Pyle are the most frequently identified as mentally ill in the literature, but the commentary on their madness is ideological rather than clinical. Gordon Banks (1990) stands alone in providing a clinical analysis of Alex as a psychopath but fails to apply the same criteria to the other characters, who also show evidence of psychopathy.

By approaching Kubrick's films through the lens of psychiatry, this chapter aims to fill the gap. In brief, a clinical review of Kubrick's output elicits five overlapping typologies of madness: (1) madness as an individual state–mental illness: Privates Pyle and Sidney, General Jack D. Ripper, Lady Lyndon, Dr. Harford; (2) madness as a social state—the madness of war: *Paths of Glory*, *Dr. Strangelove*, *Full Metal Jacket*, *Fear and Desire*; (3) madness as a state of being: antisocial personality disorders—psychopathy—*A Clockwork Orange*; pedophilia—*Lolita*; (4) Kubrick's personal vision of madness: Torrance's book in *The Shining*; (5) the madness of machines: HAL in *2001*.

The first group is one that approximates most closely to the clinical formulations of mental illness. Kubrick's characters who become mentally ill are invariably male, psychotic, and dangerous. The symptoms that are tabled are based on behaviors and utterances of the characters during the film, fleshed out by the more elaborate descriptions available in their source novels and in notes and preparatory scripts in the Kubrick Archive. The broad rubric of psychosis has been used, given the lack of a full history and mental state examination that is required for a clinical diagnosis.

Table 23.1 Symptomatology by film

Character	Onset of symptoms	Symptomatology	Probable diagnoses
Private Sidney (*Fear and Desire*)	Sudden	Delusions, thought disorder, incongruous laughter, agitation, restlessness, loss of contact with reality hyperarousal, murder	Psychosis
Private Pyle (*Full Metal Jacket*)	Gradual (associated with an improvement in killing skills)	Threatening demeanor, psychotic stare, delusions, talks to and makes love to rifle he now calls Charlene, impaired attention, murder, suicide	Psychosis
Jack Torrance (*The Shining*)	Gradual	Insomnia, irritability, writer's block, social withdrawal, psychotic stare, mounting aggression, verbal abuse, attempted murder, murder	Psychosis
General Jack D Ripper (*Dr. Strangelove*)	Not explicit, perhaps as a reaction to sexual impotence	Delusions, paranoia hyperarousal, erectile dysfunction, aggression, suicide, mass murder	Paranoid psychosis
Dr. Strangelove (*Dr. Strangelove*)	Enduring notes in development indicate these ideas were longstanding	Inappropriate laughter, dissociated demeanor, overvalued beliefs, unusual appearance and mannerisms, lack of empathy, gloats at the prospect of genocide	?Psychosis ?Schizotypal personality disorder
Lady Lyndon (*Barry Lyndon*)	Gradual follows bereavement, symptoms evolve	Grief, sadness, religiosity low mood, anhedonia, social withdrawal, attempted suicide	Bereavement reaction, major depression
Dr. Harford (*Eyes Wide Shut*)	Sudden (following wife's disclosure)	Obsessive ruminations fantasizing sexual activity, anger, risk-taking, choking—goes along with sexual offers and then withdraws, narcissistic traits, insecurity, paraphilia Ambivalent sexuality	Delusional Jealousy ?Homosexuality ?Hypoactive sexual desire disorder

Madness as an Individual State

Private Sidney, Kubrick's first attempt at depicting madness, is by far the most florid. Sidney darts around like a frightened fish, shouting an incomprehensible word salad with fleeting references to Shakespeare's *The Tempest*. His eyes roll, his head is thrown back as he leaps and laughs incongruously. It is a neophyte's vision of madness. Compare Sidney's antics with the restraint of the mature Kubrick in his penultimate film *Full Metal Jacket* where Pyle is driven insane by a sadistic drill sergeant. A clear sign of change is the transformation of the obese klutz into a deadly sharpshooter; the class clown has evolved into a killing machine. As Edgar Allan Poe, a Kubrick favorite would have it "the disease had not dulled my senses but heightened them." In the source novel, *The Short-Timers* (1979), Gustav Hasford gives more details of the illness as Pyle sexualizes his rifle, calling it Charlene and makes love to it (Hasford 1980: 24). Kubrick minimizes the evolution of the illness to maximize the shock of the final confrontation in the toilet. Unlike Sidney, Pyle stands stock-still, speaks little and kills, not in a delirium, but with the cold clinical efficiency of the robot, he has been programmed to be.

Dr. Strangelove is a film where madness reigns supreme and it depicts a panoply of deranged ideas and characters. They are made even more horrific by the fact that the ideas expressed from fluoridation to limited nuclear war were based on actual opinions and policies that were actively promulgated at the time (Smith 2007; Pringle 1980). The narrative's precipitating event is the madness of Ripper, who construes his erectile dysfunction as a Soviet plot. Kubrick was remarkably prescient in 1964 in scripting the idea of water pollution as a "delusion," which is the first indication of Ripper's paranoid illness. Its eponymous character Strangelove gloats at the prospect of genocide, even as he seeks to hide the sexual arousal of thanotic excitement in his erectile arm. He could be viewed as a schizotypal personality disorder because of his apocalyptic ideas, his alienated affect, the strangeness of his behavior and appearance and his inability to feel human concern for his fellow beings.

In *Barry Lyndon*, both Lord and Lady Lyndon are stricken with grief following their son's unexpected death. Where Barry turns to alcohol, Lady Lyndon sinks into clinical depression. The earliest manifestation of her grief is excessive religiosity, which evolves into the symptoms of depression—low mood, anhedonia, hopelessness, and suicidality. Thackeray may have based Lady Lyndon on his own wife who attempted suicide by jumping off the ship to Ireland. Kubrick uses her suicidal overdose as a turning point in the plot, triggering the return of her son who will seal Barry's fate.

The madness of Jack Torrance in *The Shining* is a paradoxical issue. Jack morphs from an urbane ex-teacher into an axe-wielding maniac, intent on total annihilation. In the interview with Michel Ciment, Kubrick makes it clear that the psychological evolution from insomnia, irritability and writer's block to psychosis was intended to be a red herring:

> It seemed to strike an extraordinary balance between the psychological and the supernatural in such a way as to lead you to think that the supernatural would eventually be explained by the psychological: "Jack must be imagining these things because he's crazy." This allowed you to suspend your doubt of the supernatural until you were so thoroughly into the story that you could accept it almost without noticing ... (not until Grady) slides open the bolt of the larder door, allowing Jack to escape, that you are left with no other explanation but the supernatural. (Ciment 1982: 181)

As Kubrick told the Japanese director, Junichi Yaoi, Torrance is a revenant, a supernatural embodiment of the evil that cyclically infests the human condition (Yaoi 2018). Put briefly, Torrance is bad, not mad; consequently, the often made inference of insanity is a misdiagnosis.

In his final film, Kubrick refined the depiction of madness to a degree of subtlety that makes it almost invisible. In a series of vignettes shot in blue to the tune of Jocelyn Pook's, "The Dream," Harford obsessively visualizes his wife's sexual encounter. Given that it never happened, these obsessive ruminations need to be regarded as delusional. Kubrick appears to have been influenced by the third of Freud's classification of jealousy into three types: competitive or normal; projected; and delusional. Freud's explanation of delusional jealousy is as follows:

> It too [like "projected" jealousy] has its origin in repressed impulses towards unfaithfulness, but the object in these cases is of the same sex as the subject. Delusional jealousy is what is left of a homosexuality that has run its course, and it rightly takes its position among the classical forms of paranoia. As an attempt at defense against an unduly strong homosexual impulse, it may, in a man, be described in the formula: "I do not love him, she loves him." (Freud 1922: 221–4)

To this end, Kubrick altered the novel's anti-Semitic encounter with the university students to be a homophobic assault. He further inserted homosexual elements into the orgy scene and reconstrued the oleaginous hotel manager as a flirtatious gay man (Osenlund 2018). The intention to revise Schnitzler's motivation of wounded male patriarchal pride to one about repressed homosexuality may also have influenced his casting of Tom Cruise. Alan Cumming, who portrayed the concierge, is on record as saying, "Tom Cruise's baggage helped that scene as well … all the rumors about him being gay" (Cumming 2013).

Kubrick's mélange of psychopathologies—delusional jealousy, revenge sex, homosexuality, paranoia, sexual obsession, and hyposexuality—leaves the viewer both bewitched and bewildered, even more so than in his other films.

Madness as a Social State

Writer Avigdor Hameiri called war "The Great Madness" (1952). Likewise, Kubrick, in his four war films, mounted a frontal assault on this corporate cultural delusion. He did this at two levels. In *Fear and Desire* and in *Full Metal Jacket* he captured the reality of men made mad by war. He reserves his greatest anger, however, for the warmongers, the men who design and execute wars as in *Paths of Glory* and *Dr. Strangelove*. Here he depicts their vainglorious, selfish beliefs and the dangerousness of their psychopathic delusions. In *Paths of Glory*, the generals sip their fine wines in a luxurious chateau, as they casually order the death of hundreds of their own men in suicidal attacks that only serve to promote their private interests. In a series of tracking shots worthy of his mentor Max Ophüls, Kubrick depicts the horror of the trenches where the victims of this madness are forfeited like pawns in a deadly chess game. The denial of the horror is encapsulated in the encounter where General Mireau assaults a soldier for being overcome with the mental illness of PTSD. Ordered to make a pointless attack, rather than swallow the psychotic pill of bravery, the men rationally retreat. The embodiment of reason in society—the law—is then perverted in a mock trial where the men are condemned to death, to maintain military morale and cover up the madness of their commanders.

Kubrick then developed these themes on an apocalyptic scale when he addressed the madness of the policy pertinently titled "Mutually Assured Destruction." In the "Doomsday machine," he presciently foresaw the eventuality that Artificial Intelligence will revolutionize the prosecution of war by changing the psychological basis of decision-making about violence. In his handwritten list of issues, he wanted to develop in the script, Kubrick asks that reason and science to be in inverted, to dramatize the eclipse of sanity. Items four and six of his speciation list are: "... 4. The absurdity of 'Logic' ... 6. To satirize government dependent on scientific advice" (Broderick 2017a: 23). Kubrick thus skillfully depicts the psychotic paradox of our time—recognition of the insanity that humanity can annihilate itself at any given moment, and the collective denial that enables us to go on living a "normal" life despite this ever-present apocalyptic threat.

Madness as a State of Being

The first section dealt with the characters who become mentally unwell, that is, "what they become." This category deals with characters as to "what they are"—enduring aspects of their personality. Personality is defined as the characteristic set of behaviors, cognitions, and emotional patterns that evolve from biological and environmental factors. Where they cause significant distress to the person or to others they can be diagnosed as personality disorders.

Faithful to Burgess, Kubrick invests Alex with all the features of antisocial personality disorder that germinates in childhood and erupts in adolescence. Alex exhibits all the diagnostic features by being selfish, manipulative, deceitful, callous, and devoid of empathy. He engages in a variety of crimes including physical and sexual violence. The standard tool to diagnose psychopathy is the Hare checklist (Hare 2003). It is a structured questionnaire developed from the study of criminal populations; Alex ticks all the boxes. In two related books, Hare addressed the issue of the high functioning psychopaths. They have the same core features of charm, aggression, cunning, deceitfulness and lack of remorse, but unlike Alex, who is disinhibited and reckless, they can control their impulsivity and use these traits to their advantage in business and politics, such as, the Minister of the Interior, who in an echo of Stalinist Russia, justifies brainwashing as producing law and order. The other characters also cloak their psychopathy in ideology. The sadistic Dr. Brodsky calls his torture "treatment," while F. Alexander construes personal revenge as political protest. The police and prison guards purvey their violence under the banner of protecting the public. This is the moral dilemma with which Kubrick challenges us: which of these two groups of lunatics is worse? He calls out our hypocrisy of reacting viscerally to Alex's crimes while tacitly condoning the criminal violence of the agencies of the state because of the benefits we derive from it. Kubrick does justice to Burgess's core thesis that goodness cannot be

Table 23.2 The Hare psychopathy checklist as applied to the characters in *A Clockwork Orange*

Character	Symptoms	Diagnosis
Minister of the Interior	Glibness/superficial charm	High functioning
Dr. Brodsky	Callous/lack of empathy	psychopath
F. Alexander	Grandiosity	
Police and prison guards	Pathological lying	
	Conning/manipulative	
	Lack of remorse or guilt	
	Failure to accept responsibility	
	Shallow affect	
Alex de Large	Features above plus	Low functioning
The droogs	Impulsivity	psychopath
	Need for stimulation/proneness to boredom	
	Lack of realistic, long-term goals	
	Poor behavioral controls	
	Parasitic lifestyle	
	Juvenile delinquency	
	Criminal versatility	
	Early behavioral problems	

enforced and that the freedom of choice as to whether to commit evil or not, is what makes us human. Where he arguably goes overboard is in omitting the last chapter of Burgess's novel where Alex matures and longs to settle down with children and family. Kubrick instead climaxes his film with an orgiastic scene of sex in the snow, celebrating Alex's rapacious sexuality as a symbol of freedom from tyranny, envisioning him as a noble savage, gloriously free of the repressive inhibitions of society.

Nabokov's novel *Lolita* recounts the sexual abuse of a child by a predatory pedophile. Pedophilic tendencies can manifest from early adolescence and the perpetrators are often survivors of abuse. Nabokov constructs Humbert's developmental pathology in terms of the trauma of the early loss of his mother and to the sexual imprinting of an idyllic childhood romance with Annabel, who dies a year after their thwarted tryst. In his screenplay, Nabokov has a montage of scenes where Humbert ogles little children climaxing in the line "Humbert wrestled with strange wretched urges and kept searching for the child of his shameful obsession, for some incarnation of his boyhood sweetheart" (Nabokov 1997: 21). Humbert thus meets the first of the Diagnostic and Statistical Manual of Mental Disorders (DSM) criteria for the diagnosis of pedophilia: "recurrent, intense sexually arousing fantasies, sexual urges, or behaviors involving sexual activity with a prepubescent child or children." By marrying the mother to gain access to Lolita, he meets the second criterion of "acting on these impulses" (DSM-5 2013: 302.2).

Kubrick edits out all of this and adapts *Lolita* as a dark romcom. His justification for this was the essay by Lionel Trilling that declared it to be a love story (1958: 9–14). Nabokov's novel is clear that this is not a reciprocal relationship, but a solipsistic account of a unilateral infatuation. Kubrick, by constructing Lolita as a manipulative, deceitful femme fatale, makes her the aggressor and casts Humbert as the victim who is seduced and abandoned. Considering that Kubrick was an overprotective parent to his daughters, his reconstruction of a child molester as a sympathetic figure reflects his predilection for the dark side of human nature.

Kubrick's Personal Vision of Madness

Kubrick has consistently been described as displaying marked obsessional behaviors. He was a compulsive checker, who had to verify personally every aspect of film production, even of the most minor detail such as the size of an advertisement. It has been repeatedly reported that he would check and check, again and again (see D'Alessandro 2016). Checking compulsions are often associated with doubt and indecisiveness. Kubrick displayed constant changes of mind, engendering the much made observation that he knew what he did not want, but not what he wanted (McDowell 2012). He also shows the often associated feature of hoarding, amassing massive collections of many things from gadgets to paper and even fonts. In both his private and professional life, he was a supreme perfectionist who was scrupulous about the most minor of details, which he often then discarded as irrelevant (Benson 2018). The most troubling aspect of his perfectionism was its exigency. His insistent demands for immediacy, with multiple urgent calls at all hours of day and night, took its toll on the health and private lives of many who worked for him, as recounted in Tony Zierra's 2017 documentary *Filmworker*.

These obsessive traits were expressed in a directorial style that sought to seek out every possible variant of a given scene. After a long time, invariably years spent in intensive research. Rewrites and preparation of a final script; he would write and rewrite every scene, serendipitously absorbing ideas and suggestions from any source (McDowell 1973). These constant changes were then typed out on different colored pieces of paper to keep track of the multiplicity of mutations. He would then engage in take after take, requesting variants of the actor's performance often with little or no direction as to what might be wanted (McDowell 2012). This process resulted in miles of film, making the process of editing a monumental task. The young Kubrick, with his amazing memory, reveled in this task, but in old age, especially in his final months, the stress of editing the longest shoot in cinema history was to take its toll on him.

In the disease of obsessive-compulsive disorder, the sufferer feels compelled to repeat ritualistically certain given actions such as handwashing, endlessly seeking some perfect endpoint that never arrives even if they have washed the skin off their hands. In *The Shining*, Jack spends all his time compulsively typing out a single sentence, in endless repetition, exploring every possible permutation of font and format. Kubrick rewrote King's script, which centered on the scrapbook to make the typewriter the pivotal focus. Curiously, despite the disruption in continuity, not only did he change the typewriter from the one he had zoomed in on in an earlier scene, but he also insisted the typewriter be repainted in a different color prior to the shoot. Both typewriters were personal, in use by him and his daughter.

Kubrick was an alienated child who refused to go to school and had difficulties in interpersonal relationships (Lyons and Fitzgerald 2006: 188). His Jack Torrance displays difficulties in intrafamilial communication and exhibits a pathological desire for isolation. Like Jack, Kubrick displayed a deep ambivalence toward the task of writing. He studiously eschewed original screenplays and only adapted published novels, which he adapted in association with respected writers. These creative collaborations, which Kubrick felt impelled to dominate, were often conflictual, sometimes ending in acrimony over issues of authorship. Like Jack, he would then repeatedly rewrite the script and zealously possess it as his own. Unlike King's novel where Jack openly discusses the progress of his tell-all tale, Kubrick invests his Torrance with an angry preoccupation with secrecy and the privacy of his personal space. Kubrick imposed draconian levels of secrecy on his projects and denied access to his private flat to all but his trusted assistant, Emilio D'Alessandro. It is known that he had was obsessed with paper and fonts (Frewin 2015). Given the intensity of these intimate investments and the resonances with his personal self, embodied in this critical scene, it could be argued that in Torrance's obsessively repetitive "novel" he was mirroring a vision of his own madness.

Mad Machines

There is ample evidence to indicate that Kubrick intended HAL's malfunction in *2001* to be construed as a mental illness. The phenomenology of HAL's madness was closely scripted. After much discussion, they finally settled on four symptoms—an error in the game of chess, the misdiagnosis of component failure, paranoia, and lack of insight. Given that chess, like computers, is logic driven, miscalling the chess move is diagnostic of HAL's malfunction. According to Michael Benson, it was Kubrick who wanted to make HAL paranoid and engaged in discussions of putative conspiracies, in scripting HAL's anxieties around the secrecy of the mission and the separate training of the hibernating crewmembers (Benson 2018: 187). HAL then makes a report of imminent component failure, which proves to be erroneous. Finally, when HAL is presented with evidence of his error, he denies his fallibility, which constitutes the psychotic symptom of loss of insight.

Critical evidence supporting the interpretation that Kubrick intended HAL to become insane, comes from a letter where he expressed fear over the loss of support that IBM had given to the development of the film. In it, he asks, "Does IBM know that one of the main themes of the story is a psychotic computer?" (Kubrick 2013) This reading is further buttressed by the existence of two deleted scenes. In the first, Ground Control diagnoses HAL as having "neurotic symptoms" caused by his conflicted programming (Kubrick and Clarke 1965). In the second, as Bowman is deactivating him, a second personality "OTHER HAL" emerges to warn Bowman that HAL is dangerous, suggesting a diagnosis of multiple personality disorder (Kubrick and Clarke 1965). In an interview with the French magazine *Le Nouvel Observateur*, Kubrick stated, "in 2000, such terribly complicated machines will be subject to the same mental illnesses as us and will have psychological problems similar to ours" (Romi 1968).

Kubrick, Film, and Madness

There are many curious aspects of Kubrick's treatment of the issue of insanity. There are two pervasive themes that merit deeper examination. The first is the systematic exclusion of all elements of psychopathology in the final cut, even when it has been extensively explored in development. The second is the amount of energy and expertise he expends in the effort to portray dangerous madmen as sympathetic characters. He appears to have no problems with psychosis, clearly depicting these characters as disturbed; however, when it comes to psychopaths and pedophiles, there is a fundamental shift of attitude. The most flagrant example of Kubrick's extirpation of all psychopathological elements from the final cut is *The Shining*. King's novel is carefully plotted and replete with sensitive psychological insights. Stephen King constructs Torrance as a survivor of physical and emotional abuse suffered at the hands of a sadistic father. The psychological arc of the novel is his struggle between his inner and outer demons. Not only does Kubrick eviscerate all that, but also in the European version—his final cut—he even leaves out the history of alcoholism and the assault on Danny. Little wonder then, as the documentary *Room 237* (2012) illustrated, that cinemagoers were left to create their own constructions, which in many instances appeared to be as crazed as Torrance himself. The exclusion of psychological depth in the final cut may be why no actor has ever won an Academy Award under his direction. The equally obsessive director David Lean, in contrast, won a string of Academy Awards, possibly because of the attention he focused on the psychological complexity of his characters, which mediated audience engagement with the actors' performances. The exclusion of psychopathology could be a part of a process that Eric Kandel calls reductionism, where everything in the film is systematically pared down to its core elements (Kandel 2016). The other possibility is that it is part of a deliberate policy of inducing ambiguity. Berthold Brecht called this strategy "Alienation." It serves the function of forcing the viewer to actively engage in the construction of meaning. In several interviews Kubrick has confirmed the primacy of narrative ambiguity in his art "if you really want to communicate something, the least effective way is direct. If you can get people to think a moment, the thrill of discovery goes right to the heart."

Whereas his stance on psychotic mental disorders is one of distance and alienation, there is a markedly different attitude toward dangerous psychopaths and predatory pedophiles. Here his attitude is one of empathy and affection that borders on admiration. He seems to view these perilous madmen not as malefactors who need to be contained, but as mock-heroic figures, rebels against a repressive order, whom the audience should root for. To achieve what Bruner called "narrative seduction" (Bruner 1991), he rewrote the scripts not only to minimize the characters' madness but also their mendacity. He cast attractive actors to mold audience identification. For the monstrous Humbert in *Lolita*, he chose the highly respected actor James Mason.

Contrary to Nabokov's highly precise fetishistic specification of a grubby, 12-year-old 4-foot-10 nymphet for Lolita, he cast the nubile, older, and taller Sue Lyon, thus limiting the perception of her as a child. In envisioning Lolita as an attractive blonde, he presents her as a femme fatale, thus normalizing Humbert's pedophilic attraction to her (LoBrutto 1997: 218). In the promotional material, Sue Lyon gazes out over heart-shaped sunglasses as she seductively sucks a lollipop. Kubrick, in giving Nabokov's creation shape and substance, launched a cultural icon that became a totem of teen sexuality, which had a frisson of the forbidden (Bertram and Leving 2013).

In *A Clockwork Orange*, Kubrick invests Alex with a roguish allure. Alex uses honeyed tones in the voiceover, inviting the audience to collude with him in his devilry. Both Mason and McDowell are framed as being more charming, cleverer, and more powerful than the other characters, who are scripted to be stupid and dishonest. The strategy of denigrating the subsidiary characters to augment the audience's investment in the monstrous main character is most marked in the way he deals with women. Wendy Torrance, in King's novel of *The Shining*, is a beautiful, strong woman who bravely confronts Jack. Kubrick rewrites her as a meek, pathetic wimp, who scampers around in terror. Stephen King was moved to observe "[The movie] is so misogynistic. I mean, Wendy Torrance is just presented as this sort of screaming dishrag" (Greene 2014). Building on the novels, Kubrick scripts the mothers of both Alex and Lolita, as dimwits, making them objects of scorn worthy of a comic send-up. Both are wittily manipulated by the sophistication of Kubrick's main characters, to the audience's comic delight. The denigration was not simply limited to the script but spilled over onto the set. Even though both Shelley Winters and Shelley Duvall were highly experienced, accomplished actresses who in the hands of other directors have turned in award-winning performances, Kubrick, it is said, became enmeshed in a series of hostile interactions with both.

Kubrick augments these scripting strategies with a variety of directorial techniques. He blocks the mise-en-scène so that his monsters are invariably central or occupy the most screen space, thus visually empowering them. This optical strategy is accentuated using wide angle lenses that cause Alex to be in sharp central focus, while distorting those in the periphery. His trump card is the well-worn strategy of subjecting the protagonist to unjustified suffering at the hands of unworthy agents, engineering the audience's sympathy for their misfortune. Alex is tortured by the prison guards and Brodsky, while Humbert is cruciated by Quilty and Lolita. In both films, he uses comedy to soften up the audience's response to violence. Alex's rape of the two 11-year-old school girls is vitiated into a Chaplin-esque pants-dropping farce using fast motion in vision and sound. Kubrick was a master of musical synthesis. He choreographs the violence to music, and by placing the viewer in the eye of the action using handheld cameras, he induces ambivalent responses that sweep us along by appealing to our aestheticism. To quote Lionel Trilling, "we have come virtually to condone the violation it presents … we have been seduced into conniving in the violation because we have permitted our fantasies to accept what we know to be revolting" (Trilling 1958: 9–19).

Divine Madness

While Kubrick's recurrent reexaminations of the madness of man can be viewed through the reductionist lens of mental illness, it could equally be construed as a manifestation of what Plato called divine madness. Plato believed that besides reason and sense experience, there was another way of knowing, that lay beyond Aristotle's worship of reason. Just as those in the grip of "theia mania" confronted the cultures of their time, Kubrick challenged conventional cinematic norms in being constantly innovative. He produced films that were idiosyncratic, unconventional, outrageous, unpredictable, and shocking. If suspense was the hallmark of a Hitchcock film, Kubrick made transcendental apperception his touchstone. His films sought to communicate, not via logic or reason, but through ambiguity, allusion, ambivalence, and enigma to a sublime nous that surpassed understanding. To cite his own words, "I tried to create a visual experience, one that bypasses verbalized pigeonholing and directly penetrates the subconscious with an emotional and philosophic content … The film thus becomes a subjective experience, which hits the viewer at an inner level of consciousness, just as music does" (Norden 2016).

24

Kubrick and Psychoanalysis

Nathan Abrams and I.Q. Hunter

Psychoanalysis, a set of theories and therapeutic techniques developed by the Viennese Jewish physician Sigmund Freud (1856–1939), aims to understand the workings of the unconscious mind, especially through the study of dreams and the uncovering of repressed desires. Freud believed that childhood experiences, unresolved traumas, and unconscious conflicts influence adult behavior, and that psychological problems could be cured by releasing repressed emotions and bringing unconscious conflicts and fantasies to light. He argued that our psyche is composed of three elements in continuous struggle: the id (the unruly unconscious, instinctual drives); the ego (the conscious mind or the self); and the superego (prohibitions, parental inhibitions, or the conscience). His most important book, *The Interpretation of Dreams* (1899), maintained that repressed ideas, memories, and fantasies come to the surface in dreams, albeit in symbolic forms (their "manifest content") that disguise the dreams' real, usually sexual, significance (their "latent content"): "dreams, when properly decoded, opened a window on a person's unconscious mind" (Phillips and Hill 2002: 121). Freud's "view of the unconscious was disturbing, fraught with forbidden desires, the Oedipus complex (a child's conflicting love for his or her parents), and guilt complexes" (ibid.).

According to Geoffrey Cocks, Stanley Kubrick was "an early and messianic reader of Freud," who encouraged his friends to read Freud's 1938 *A General Introduction to Psychoanalysis* (2004: 4). He was also drawn to the literary contemporaries of Freud, whose writings contained many of the same conflicts, desires, guilt, and repression as Freud's work did. Most prominent of these were Stefan Zweig and Arthur Schnitzler, whose *Dream Story* Kubrick adapted as *Eyes Wide Shut*. The influence of this reading is felt throughout Kubrick's films, in which there is a sustained and presumably deliberate focus on such psychoanalytically rich topics as dreams, repression, desire, fantasy, homoeroticism, perversion, madness, the death instinct, and the family (or Oedipal) romance.

Knowing this, there are two ways to approach Kubrick and psychoanalysis. The first, an auteurist approach in keeping with much of Kubrick Studies, is to explore how Kubrick knowingly drew on psychoanalytic concepts in his films. Kubrick scholars have long recognized his debt to Freud (LoBrutto 1997: 413), especially in *The Shining*, where, as James Naremore points out, Kubrick "makes darkly humorous allusions" to Freudian theories of the uncanny and the film plays "with the myths of psychoanalysis"

(2007: 195, 199). Recent archival work on *The Shining* has confirmed that Kubrick and his co-writer Diane Johnson drew on psychoanalytic texts such as Bruno Bettelheim's work on fairy tales and Freud's on parapsychology and the uncanny (McAvoy 2015a).

The second approach is to use psychoanalysis to understand and analyze the films along with their maker, namely how psychoanalysis helps us explore Kubrick, *and his films*, regardless of his intentions. Since the late 1960s psychoanalysis has been an important strand of academic film analysis (see Allen 2004 for an accessible introduction to psychoanalytic film theory), although the key figure was not so much Freud as the French analyst Jacques Lacan, who was preoccupied with construction of subjectivity by language rather than the sexual drives. Typified by the work of the British journal, *Screen*, in the 1970s, Lacanian film theory combined psychoanalysis with Marxism, feminism, and semiotics to decode the latent meanings and ideological function of Hollywood cinema. Such general theories of cinema's meaning and effect can be applied to Kubrick's films, independent of his intentions, as readily as to any other director's. For example, Laura Mulvey's much cited concept of "the male gaze" in "Visual Pleasure and Narrative Cinema" (1975) offers a framework for analyzing Kubrick's voyeuristic representation of women (see Broderick's chapter). But rather than simply diagnosing the sexism of one especially delinquent auteur, these kinds of "symptomatic" readings have a more comprehensive aim: to demonstrate "the way the unconscious of patriarchal society has structured film form" (ibid.: 6).

This chapter summarizes some of the key ways in which psychoanalysis has been, and can be, used to illuminate Kubrick's films. It will not attempt to psychoanalyze Kubrick himself. There will also be some brief discussions of how Carl Jung's "analytical psychology," so named to distinguish it from Freud's theories of the unconscious, has been applied to Kubrick's films.

If, as Nathan Abrams (2018) has argued, Kubrick was a New York Jewish intellectual, then it is hardly surprising that he was heavily influenced by psychoanalysis. From the 1940s to the 1960s, Freudianism saturated popular culture and especially the discourse of the intellectuals, artists, and bohemians with whom Kubrick mixed in Greenwich Village (Breckman 2017). When Christiane Harlan, Kubrick's third wife, came to America in the 1950s, she was "astonished that so many people were in analysis" (quoted in Phillips and Hill 2002: 122). For many in this milieu, Freud was the prophet of a libertarian sexual revolution, but Kubrick "adopted Freud's view that good and evil were inextricably bound together in the depths of the human personality" (Cocks 2003: 36). It was Freud's cautionary emphasis, especially in *Civilization and Its Discontents* (1930), on the intertwining desires of sex (Eros) and death (Thanatos), the strength of the id and instinctual aggression, and the tragic necessity of repression to the maintenance of civilization that underpinned what has been characterized as Kubrick's pessimism and essentially conservative attitude to sexuality (Feldmann 1976: 16).

Kubrick was surely also aware that cinema, which is so associated with fantasy, dream, and sexuality, has long been seen as the artform most capable of both communicating and embodying the world of the unconscious. Although Freud himself refused to have anything to do with cinema (Heath 1999: 25–6), psychoanalysis has been an important influence on filmmaking since the French avant-garde of the 1920s, which understood cinema as an analogy to mental processes and especially dreams. The Surrealists aimed to give visual expression to Freud's approach to dreams in such films as Luis Buñuel's and Salvador Dalí's *Un Chien Andalou* (1928) and Buñuel's *L'Age d'Or* (1930). By the 1940s, when Freudian ideas gained currency in American culture, popular cinema also adapted them to capture dreams on screen, as in the famous dream sequences that Dalí designed for Alfred Hitchcock's *Spellbound* (1945). Dalí even collaborated with Walt Disney on an incomplete short animated film, *Destino*, in 1945. More recent surrealist directors like Fernando Arrabal (*Viva La Muerte*, 1971), David Lynch (*Blue Velvet*, 1986), and David Cronenberg (*Videodrome*, 1983) draw on Freud in their sexually charged representation of repressed fantasies.

Kubrick did not illustrate Freudian concepts directly in the manner of Dalí and none of his films is "Surrealist" like *Un Chien Andalou*, with the arguable exception of the dreamlike *Eyes Wide Shut*, which we shall discuss below (Phillips and Hill 2002: 121–2; Kolker and Abrams 2019). It is more accurate to say that Kubrick, who described his films as dreams or dreamlike (Cocks 2003: 36), extrapolates from rather than dramatizes Freud. Freudian concepts are governing points of reference that underpin his blackly comic depictions of irrationality and obsession and his "brand of surrealistic imagery [that presents] a world in which characters are controlled by dark instinctual desires" (Williams 2008: 46). This world invariably centers on male pathology:

All of Kubrick's male characters act in a mode of sexual confusion or dysfunction or excess. And in all instances their sexual power, whatever it might be, leads to a diminished state, and more often than not to their destruction. (Kolker 2017: 179)

Although Kubrick references (and parodies) other psychological theories, such as behaviorism, it is out of Freudian psychoanalysis, and especially the Freud of *Civilization and Its Discontents*, that he fashioned a coherent bleak vision of the world. As Hans Feldmann says, in a key article on Kubrick's debt to Freud:

His view of man is clearly Freudian: the primal facet of the human personality is the id, the completely self-orientated structure that demands immediate gratification of its instinctual urges for food, shelter, and the propagation of itself. It is not moral or intellectual or sensitive to the needs or feelings of others. It simply is. (1976: 13)

Kubrick was drawn to Freud in part because of Oedipal echoes. Kubrick loved chess—itself a deeply Oedipal game in which the most potent opponent of the king (father) is the queen (mother) but in which the goal is to kill the king/father (Abrams 2018: 9). It is fitting, therefore, that it was his father, Dr. Jacques or Jack Kubrick, who introduced him to the game. We can speculate on the nature of Kubrick's relationship with his father—it seems that he was closer to his mother with whom he spoke regularly despite being thousands of miles away—but consider how "Jacks," as well as physicians and others with the title "doctor" that appeared in his films.

Such Freudian themes are introduced in Kubrick's first films, the early documentary shorts. *Day of the Fight* recounts a boxer's preparations for his big fight. It features twin brothers, Walter and Vincent Cartier, introducing the idea of uncanny doppelgangers and doubles that again appeared in various Kubrick films, most famously the Grady twins in *The Shining*. Sexual elements are repressed in the film, as the female presence is almost nonexistent, expunged from his 1949 *Look* article ("Prizefighter") upon which it was based. Kubrick also included a sequence of the boxer Walter Cartier being checked over by the boxing commission doctor—played by his own father— who examines his eyes (as a doctor later examines those of Danny in *The Shining*). *Flying Padre* seems devoid of obvious Freudianism other than a reference to absent fathers, which is again repeated in *The Seafarers*. However, in this film, Kubrick slyly introduces subtle references to sex and the sexual repression that was surely a feature of the all-male homosocial working environment of the seafarer (Lobrutto 1997: 74; Abrams 2018: 29).

Kubrick's first feature film, *Fear and Desire*, much like Freudian analysis, takes place in the "country of the mind." The film was intended to be allegorical rather than literal. It, too, features doubles and doppelgangers where the four main characters also play their "Other," their enemies whom they also kill during the film. When Private Sidney rapes and kills the captured fisherwoman, the film introduces the linkage between Eros and Thanatos, a theme that continued throughout many of Kubrick's movies.

Despite his enthusiasm for Freud, psychoanalysis seems to take a back seat in Kubrick's 1950s movies, particularly in his next two films, in favor of existentialism. Yet, as Phillips and Hill (2002: 122) and Abrams (2018) have pointed out, *Killer's Kiss* contains clear Freudian and Oedipal elements: Gloria's guilt over her sister's death; her feelings of jealousy toward her sister, whom her dead father preferred; Davey's dream sequence; the linkage of sex and death; twins and doubles; the relationship between Gloria and the much older Vincent (note the duplication of Walter Cartier's brother's name); and the final Oedipal struggle between the older and younger generation, as Davey duels Vincent, and the usurper defeats the patriarchal father figure. The film also references absent fathers: Gloria's dead father and Davey's, who is never mentioned. Norman Kagan refers to this as "cookbook Freud" (1989: 26).

The relationship between Johnny (Jack) Clay and Marvin Unger in *The Killing* certainly bears Oedipal echoes; Marvin tells him, "I've always thought maybe you're like my own kid." Indeed, Marvin has no overt need, unlike the others, to be involved in this heist, other than his attachment to Johnny. There is also a repressed homosexual element to their relationship where Marvin suggests he and Johnny leave Los Angeles together so Johnny can escape the pitfalls of marriage. When Johnny gently rebuffs him, Marvin gets drunk, almost endangering the plan. Thomas Allen Nelson describes the "fatherly and homoerotic attachment," which "remains latent even though it is exacerbated by the presence of Clay's girlfriend Fay" (2000: 33).

Continuing this anti-Freudian theme, Kubrick's final two films of the decade—*Paths of Glory* and *Spartacus*—seem almost devoid of psychoanalytic elements. Yet, Oedipal themes of generational conflict and of symbolic father figures—here the generals or "kings"—are evident in their willingness to sacrifice their symbolic sons (their troops or "pawns") in the furtherance of their own vainglory. There are also elements of homoeroticism in this all-male environment (like the boxers, priests, and seafarers). A key aspect of this is repression, when one character says, "I haven't had one sexual thought." Since this character is imprisoned, awaiting his eventual execution by firing squad, the comment also connects Eros and Thanatos. The superficial wholesomeness of *Spartacus* also belies similar Oedipal conflicts of sacrifice and war, particularly in the relationship between Spartacus and his symbolic son Antoninus but this is more a relationship of love than conflict. However, Kubrick did introduce a scene—considered too risqué for the Production Code 1960s—in which the Roman general Crassus seeks to seduce his young slave boy Antoninus in the now-infamous "snails and oysters" sequence. Kubrick also constantly contrasted the licentious, libidinous and polymorphously perverse tastes of the Romans with the healthier family-orientated lifestyle of the ex-slaves.

As an independent director, Kubrick indulged his taste for Freud in his movies of the 1960s. Perversions and obsessively strange loves are parodied and played for laughs in both *Lolita* and *Dr. Strangelove*, both of which are replete with dirty jokes in which repressed desires flicker into view and are immediately disavowed, but which testify to the conflicts and neuroses of seemingly civilized and logical intellects. This contrast between the highly formal, routinized, and hierarchical systems that make up civilization and the irrationality and aggression they suppress is essential to Kubrick's blackly comic representation of human behavior as a duality (another of Kubrick's doubles). Doubles and doppelgangers also feature in the performances of Peter Sellers who plays multiple characters in the two films.

For its part, *Lolita* shows a highly civilized intellectual in thrall to pedophilia. It is also full of Freudian jokes as Vladimir Nabokov and then Kubrick skewer one of the key intellectual themes of the era: psychoanalysis. Nabokov regarded Freud as "the Viennese quack," whose dream interpretation was "one of the greatest pieces of charlatanic, and satanic, nonsense imposed on a gullible public" (1964). He had lampooned Freudianism in his novel, noting only a space existed between the words "therapist" and "the rapist," and this was rendered in the film through the character of Dr. Zempf, as played by Sellers, which is a clear sendup of a Freud-like figure. In a particularly thick German accent and deliberately Freudian lingo, Zempf—whose name has itself been read as sexual pun meaning "mustard" as in to cut the mustard sexually (Cocks 2004)—when he tells Humbert, "in our opinion, she's suffering from acute repression of the libido of zee natural instincts."

Dr. Strangelove's parody of the military mindset focuses on the perverse and sublimated sexuality that links Eros and Thanatos. From the opening shot of bombers copulating mid-air to Major King Kong riding the phallic bomb into "Mother Earth" to produce the film's final nuclear climax, *Dr. Strangelove* emphasizes the arousing possibilities, to men at any rate, of fantasies of destruction. In *Dr. Strangelove*, the logic of war games ends in apocalypse. As Kubrick told an interviewer, "In *Strangelove* I was dealing with the inherent irrationality of man that threatens to destroy him" (quoted in Phillips 2001: 68). As Cocks says,

Dr. Strangelove is one example of a tripartite taxonomy of phenomena Kubrick's films portray as fundamental to the human condition, particularly in the modern age and even more particularly in the twentieth century: (1) violence, (2) systems of control, and (3) inherent human evil. (2003: 36–7)

Of all Kubrick's films, *2001: A Space Odyssey* seems the least relevant to psychoanalysis, except insofar as its depiction of a sterile future world implies that the pursuit of pure reason requires massive sexual disavowal and repression. Sexual imagery is displaced to the design—for example, the sperm-like spaceship, Discovery—and sex, ironically in a film about birth and rebirth, is associated with the distant past by the romantic waltzes accompanying spaceflight. Even so, the question of whether a computer can become more human through acquiring traits of irrationality (and implicitly an unconscious) continues Kubrick's theme of control by deeper forces. Moreover, as Dominic Janes (2011) has argued, its originator, Arthur C. Clarke, who was either homosexual or bisexual, explored same sex desires in his later works, while Kubrick liked to problematize normative masculinity. Thus, the film has, like several Kubrick's films, a degree of homoeroticism. HAL is arguably camp and queer (see Broderick's chapter). According to Susan White, HAL looks "more and more like a jealous homosexual lover" (2006: 139) in "the face of the relationship" between Poole and Bowman, which is compared to that of an "old married couple," a relationship in which verbal communication is no longer necessary (Janes 2011: 62). It is perhaps this jealousy that leads the perfectly logical HAL to go insane. Ellis Hanson suggests that the film's "most homoerotic aspect" is Bowman's "forced entry into the ship and into HAL himself"; HAL's ambiguous response "suggests the fear and panic of rape, and yet his calm 'user-friendly' tone suggests a disturbing sensuality, reinforcing the eroticism of an otherwise violent act" (1993: 147). Janes argues that the monolith is a depiction of the "masculine closet" and that Bowman's encounter with it in the strange room at the film's conclusion can be read as a "homosexual encounter that leads to the revelation of the sublimity of infantile polymorphous perversion" (2011: 57).

A Clockwork Orange is a world in which sexuality is not so much repressed as commodified as kitsch art and popular culture. Alex represents the instinctive drive, free of inhibition. As Kubrick himself put it, "you can regard Alex as a creature of the id" (quoted in Strick and Houston 1972). Despite the government's attempts to condition him to turn against violence and sex, using a form of aversion therapy named the Ludovico Technique, his "natural" aggression is not repressed. The emphasis on instinctual violence—a secularized version of evil—in Freudian theory complements rather than contradicts the other psychological theories that Kubrick alludes to and parodies. Robert Ardrey, who held that humankind had evolved as a "killer ape" genetically conditioned by a "territorial imperative," was an influence on *2001* and *A Clockwork Orange*. According to Ardrey, "human history has turned on the development of superior weapons": "We design and compete with our weapons as birds build nests" (quoted in Rice 2008: 28). The American psychologist B. F. Skinner, who deemphasized both the unconscious and free will, is referenced in both the novel and film of *A Clockwork Orange*. Skinner insisted that behavior was largely learned through interactions with external influences and could be modified through systems of rewards and punishments—a process referred to as conditioning. This behaviorism was satirized in the fictional Ludovico's Technique, where what Burgess called "beneficent brainwashing" "turns the hero of *A Clockwork Orange* into a vomiting paragon of non-aggression" (2012). But Kubrick clearly rejected Skinner's behaviorism. In fact, in a sense, Kubrick rejects Skinner by celebrating this: Alex is shown to be redeemed at the end of the film, indulging in consensual and socially (and class) sanctioned sexual intercourse. What links these disparate psychological theories is their skepticism toward free will, emphasis on humankind's irrationality and aptness for conditioning by internal and external forces, even to the point of becoming dehumanized puppets.

Barry Lyndon is also an Oedipal family drama. A social-climbing young Irish upstart loses his father in the opening sequence and is thereafter dominated by his mother. He meets a succession of father figures before marrying a wealthy heiress with a son, Lord Bullingdon. This son covets his mother and ultimately symbolically castrates his (step) father, by shooting him in the leg, which is subsequently amputated, in a duel. Noting that *Barry Lyndon* contains more violent scenes than *A Clockwork Orange*, Feldmann emphasizes their linked Freudian theme of "the extent to which cultural institutions distance the social man from his primal, vital self" (1976: 17):

> The core of Kubrick's insight in *Barry Lyndon* is this: the forms of civilization, which are intended to suppress of sublimate the savage nature of man, only work to deform the social man. Barry's tragedy is that, in seeking to achieve the expression of himself—to "become himself"—he submits to all the values and life-forms of his culture. (ibid.)

In the world of eighteenth-century aristocratic England, Barry stands as the untamed id encountered in *A Clockwork Orange*, adopting various dis/guises to pass. But the coarse unruly id cannot be contained indefinitely and is glimpsed at a key moment when Barry loses control and erupts into spontaneous emotion, rendering him unfit to pass within this overly civilized world of the genteel superego. The importunate id cannot be domesticated (see Abrams 2018: 183–4; Pramaggiore 2015a: 136).

The Shining was Kubrick's most autobiographical and Freudian film to date. An auto case history, it compares to Freud's *The Interpretation of Dreams*. In the film, Kubrick engages with some of the deepest and most enduring myths of Western civilization, including the problems of fathers and sons, dreams, obedience, and the nature of evil. The result was a psychologically dense meta-horror film, a multilayered palimpsest, and one of Kubrick's few films where he openly admitted to "psychological misdirection" (Abrams 2018: 190).

The Shining represents a form of Freudian introspection into the nature of paternity and the father–son relationship. Kubrick was drawn to Stephen King's novel because of its "psychological underpinnings," according to co-screenwriter Diane Johnson: "A father threatening his child is compelling. It's an archetypal enactment of unconscious rages. Stephen King isn't Kafka, but the material of this novel is the rage and fear within families." She describes the film as an "underlying story of a father's hate for his child and his wife." She adds, "the murderous father, is a very very frightening one." She further recalls that

> Kubrick wanted to know what the King novel was about, in the deepest psychological sense; he wanted to talk about that and to read theoretical works that might shed light on it, particularly works of psychology and especially those of Freud. (quoted in ibid.: 192)

And, she explains, "Family hate seemed quite important. We decided that in the case of *The Shining* this was a central element. I had the very strong impression that Kubrick was attracted to *The Shining* because of the father/son thing" (ibid.). In preparation for the film Kubrick immersed himself in psychoanalytic reading (McAvoy 2015a), including Freud's essay on "The Uncanny" (1899) and Bruno Bettelheim's book on fairy tales, *The Uses of Enchantment* (1976), which influenced the numerous references to fairy tales in the film (the big bad wolf), along with writings by Freud's pupil Karen Horney and more contemporary Freudian thinker Simon O. Lesser. As Elisa Pezzotta points out, "Freud's essay on the uncanny clearly affected the director's adaptation, as several uncanny features described by the psychoanalyst [such as mirrors] appear in the episodes and themes of the film that were not adapted from the novel" (2013: 135).

Although *The Shining* is infused with deliberate allusions to psychoanalysis, the film is also explicable in relation to wider psychoanalytic readings of the horror genre itself, notably Robin Wood's theory of "the return of the repressed" (2003: 63–84). Although Wood does not mention the film explicitly, *The Shining* has been widely read as a "family horror" drama about abuse and patriarchy and "the hidden madness of the nuclear family" (Luckhurst 2013: 50), but also the historical repressed (Jameson 1992: 82–99). As Naremore points out,

> The most radical and disturbing aspect of the film is that Jack Torrance isn't, as Freudian analysis would have it, an imaginary menace or a fairy-tale monster created by a child's projected anxieties; he's a realistic character who despises his wife, who feels ambivalence towards his son and who actually becomes a crazed axe murderer. (2007: 196)

As William Paul suggests, "There is an almost naked Oedipal pattern in Kubrick's film: the father is killed, and the child goes off with the mother" (cited in Phillips and Hill 2002: 122–3; see also Bingham 1996).

Full Metal Jacket, like *Dr. Strangelove*, associates war and sexual repression but within a relentlessly obscene discourse centered on anality and excrement. Its Freudianism is so flagrant as to verge on self-parody: the explicitly phallic rifles and the references to lavatories and a world of shit. Yet the film's broad characterizations and focus on duality suggest the influence of Carl Jung's school of analytic psychology that placed less emphasis on sexual factors than Freudian psychoanalysis. He believed that the unconscious mind also contained an inherited collective unconscious, an ancestral repository of shared images and symbols called archetypes that emerged in myths and dreams. The monolith in *2001*, for example, has been read as an example of an archetype (Rice 2008: 33). Kubrick mentioned Jung in relation to *2001* but disagreed with Jung's view that our encounter with extraterrestrial life would leave us "without dreams," that is, intellectually and spiritually "paralyzed" (cited in Phillips 2001: 51–2). He later discussed Jung with Michael Herr when considering making a war film: "Was I familiar with the concept of the Shadow, our hidden dark side? I assured him that I was. We did half an hour on the Shadow and how he really wanted to get it into his war picture" (2000a: 6). Thus, it is Jung who is explicitly mentioned in terms of duality rather than the usual Freudian terms of ego and id, "that Jungian thing," as Joker says, of self and the Shadow, when explaining the "duality of man" in reference to his peace badge and "Born to Kill" slogan scrawled on his helmet. Nelson explains that "Jungian theories of human identity appear to influence the subtexts of part one, while in part two Kubrick will give them a full and unique expression in the explosive, disordered surfaces of a violently contingent world called Vietnam" (2000: 245).

As mentioned earlier, Kubrick's final film was ultimately his most autobiographical, dreamlike, and Freudian. *Eyes Wide Shut* centered on male fantasy, repression, and given wider social implications in fantasies of excess and access to women by the rich. It has also prompted significant Jungian and Lacanian readings. *Eyes Wide Shut* was based on Arthur Schnitzler's *Traumnovelle*, which Kubrick discovered some five decades earlier. It was through Freud that Kubrick came across Schnitzler plays that Kubrick described as "absolute gems of buried psychological motivation" (quoted in Kolker and Abrams 2019: 18). Schnitzler, like Freud, was interested in psychosexual dynamics. Schnitzler's work intrigued Freud, who, on Schnitzler's fiftieth birthday, wrote to him as a "colleague" in the investigation of the "underestimated and much maligned erotic" (quoted in Abrams 2018: 240). His affinity to Schnitzler was so strong that he consciously avoided him as "his double" or Doppelgänger (Kubrick referred to this letter in an interview in 1968). Freud added: "I have gained the impression that you have learned through intuition—though actually as a result of sensitive introspection— everything that I have had to unearth by laborious work on other persons" (quoted in ibid.). The respect was mutual: during its years of composition, *Traumnovelle*'s working title was "Doppelnovelle" ("Story of Doubleness"), but was changed, deliberately, to explicitly refer to Freud's *Interpretation of Dreams* (ibid.).

In preparing for the film, Kubrick researched psychoanalytic readings. In addition to Freud and Schnitzler, he read Karen Horney's 1937 *The Neurotic Personality of Our Time*. He underlined passages about the neurotic personality dominating others and "imposing his will on them" (Kolker and Abrams 2019: 66). The results are rendered in the film itself.

In a form of dream sequence, Bill fantasizes about his wife's encounter with the handsome naval officer; in fact, he is projecting a fantasy of her fantasy and it offers us a glimpse of his unconscious (ibid.: 164). This scene can be read homoerotically reinforced by the meeting between Bill and hotel desk clerk who hits on him (reprising an earlier scene from *Lolita*). Mary Wild, a self-described "Freudian cinephile" has proposed a novel reading of Bill's fantasy. For her, the "naval officer" refers to

Freud's "navel of the dream." She points out how, in his essay on the Wolf Man in his *Interpretation of Dreams*, Freud wrote how there is

> often a passage in even the most thoroughly interpreted dream which has to be left obscure ... there is a tangle of dream-thoughts which cannot be unraveled, and which moreover adds nothing to our knowledge of the content of the dream. This is the dream's navel, the spot where it reaches down to the unknown. (quoted in ibid.: 164)

As Whitlock and Pope (2019) explain, "Fans of Freudian cinephile Mary Wild will be familiar with her insight that in *Eyes Wide Shut* the 'navel' of Bill's dreamscape is the naval officer, a delightfully hidden bit of wordplay."

In his 2006 documentary, *The Pervert's Guide to Cinema*, philosopher Slavoj Zizek takes a psychoanalytic approach to *Eyes Wide Shut* that is indebted to Freud's follower, Jacques Lacan. He explains how, prompted by Alice's revelations, the entire film is Bill's "desperate attempt to catch up with her fantasy, which ends in a failure" (ibid.). Bill wants to be desired in the same way as his wife desired the naval officer, but all he can do is search and fail (see also Žižek 2001: 173–5).

In the final analysis, Freudianism is a clear thread that runs through all of Kubrick's sixteen films, though perhaps becoming more prominent with his later works, particularly those from the 1970s onwards. Kubrick, like Alfred Hitchcock, knowingly drew upon psychoanalysis in developing the subtext of his films, especially in making his characters broad archetypes that stood for aspects of the human personality. Thus, in approaching Kubrick's films, it is certainly worth familiarizing oneself with *Interpretation of Dreams* and *Civilization and Its Discontents* not just to discern Kubrick's authorial intentions but also to subject these films to Freudian, as well as Jungian and Lacanian, readings and interpretations.

25

Kubrick and Childhood

Nathan Abrams

Introduction

Children and childhood were at the heart of Kubrick's work. This includes those films he succeeded in completing and those he planned but never brought to fruition. From the mid-1950s onwards, he became increasingly focused on the relationship between parents and children. The interrelated themes of children abandoned by their fathers, an innocent child confronted by an adult world of danger, an alienated child lost in an adult world, and childhood abuse/separation were at the core of Kubrick's work, including his earliest photography, documentaries, and feature films. Kubrick, it seems, was particularly interested in depicting traumatized and/or sexualized children who had experienced some form of mental and/or physical torture. Kubrick infused his representations with a cultural sensibility drawn from Jewish sources, such as Genesis 22 and Abraham's potential sacrifice of his son Isaac, through to the thought and work of Sigmund Freud among others. In short, Kubrick typically represented children as sacrificed in pursuit of the needs and desire of their figurative filmic fathers.

However, the topic of children and childhood in Kubrick's films has not been subject to much scholarly attention on its own terms to date. Where it has been explored, it has been done so in relation to individual films (principally *Lolita*, *The Shining*, and *A.I. Artificial Intelligence*) but it deserves a much deeper and holistic exploration beyond just these three films to consider Kubrick's attitude toward and depiction of childhood.

Early Children

As a teenager photographer, Kubrick's first images were undoubtedly those of his family and childhood friends. During the five years he worked for *Look* magazine, Kubrick snapped some 200,000 images, including negatives, contact sheets, transparencies, and prints, many of which depicted children, childhood, and childhood activities (Donhauser 2018: 6). For example, he contributed the images to the story "What Every

Teenager Should Know about Dating," which appeared in the August 1, 1950, issue. Kubrick "dramatized" and "posed and staged" with the cooperation of New York high school students a series of romantic situations such as "dressing for a date" and "pick-ups are risky" (Albrecht and Corcoran 2018: 13). In an unpublished set of photographs in 1947, he depicts the life of Mickey, a New York City shoeshine boy. In the August 5, 1947, issue Kubrick provided twelve pictures for a thirteen-photo, three-page spread on 15-year-old Polish war orphan Jack Melnik. Titled *"In Amerika Habe Ich Die Freiheit Gefunden* (I Found Freedom in America)," the photo-essay introduced Melnik who had been a slave laborer in a Nazi concentration camp who eventually emigrated to the United States. In both essays, as Dijana Metlić has written, "Carefree childhood is replaced by the cruelty of growing up" (2019: 130). Phillipe Mather also points out in this volume how such photo-essays demonstrate Kubrick's ability to empathize with children. Surveying his photographic career at *Look*, Kubrick's biographer, Vincent LoBrutto, detects "a special gift for reading the sensitivities and joys" of children, as well as an "ability to portray childhood reality." All in all, he says, Kubrick "exhibit[ed] a flair for photographing children" (1997: 42).

When, aged 21, Kubrick graduated from photography to filmmaking, he was able to do so because of his own childlessness. Although he was married, as Walker et al. have pointed out, "his lack of family responsibilities at this age allowed him to pursue the far riskier livelihood of a filmmaker" (1999: 12). His directorial career began with a series of three short documentaries, made between 1951 and 1953, *Day of the Fight*, *Flying Padre*, and *The Seafarers*, combining his *Look* photojournalism with film. These documentaries tell us much about how Kubrick would present his interest in children and childhood in his later films.

Typically, Kubrick included children to foreground fatherhood and absent fathers, which would become key themes of his later feature films. In *Day of the Fight*, boxer Walter Cartier eats in Dan Stampler's steakhouse in Greenwich Village as the owner looks on "proudly" smoking a cigar and assuming a "fatherly" role in relationship to his "boy." Walter's own father is never seen because he is "away." Reflecting oedipal echoes, Kubrick included a sequence of Walter being checked over by the boxing commission doctor—played by Kubrick's own father Jack—who examines his eyes (as a doctor examines those of Danny in *The Shining*). The title of *Flying Padre* similarly suggests Kubrick's interest in paternity, *padre* being derived from the Latin *pater*. Father Stadtmueller acts in loco parentis for many of the families he ministers to, for example, chiding a young boy for bullying a female classmate and ferrying a sick baby and its mother to hospital because her husband is absent. Many of the men in *The Seafarers* are also fathers taken away from their families by their jobs and the film ends with one such man with his children before departing on a ship. These children provide Kubrick's first cinematic images of childhood and absent fathers that would characterize his subsequent feature films.

Around this time, Kubrick also worked on other child-centered projects. He shot second-unit footage of a young Abraham Lincoln for a television series about the future president, footage of which has recently resurfaced. He also worked on a film about the World Assembly of Youth; since this has since been lost, little about it is known.

War Children

Although Kubrick experimented in many genres, his films can be narrowed down to two overlapping ones: war (*Fear and Desire, Paths of Glory, Spartacus, Dr. Strangelove, Barry Lyndon,* and *Full Metal Jacket*) and family dramas (*Spartacus, Lolita, A Clockwork Orange, Barry Lyndon, The Shining, Eyes Wide Shut*). This also includes his unmade films, including *Burning Secret* (family), *Napoleon* (war), and *A.I.* (family). In Kubrick's version of the war genre, army units were presented as metaphorical families, dominated by patriarchal father figures who typically sacrifice their sons on the altar of battlefield, as depicted in Wilfred Owen's "Parable of the Old Man and the Young" (1920):

> But the old man would not so, but slew his son,
> And half the seed of Europe, one by one.

Kubrick's first feature film, *Fear and Desire*, a war film, addressed tacitly the issue of young boys being torn away from their families to fight. A version of the Second World War platoon movie in which four soldiers who are trapped behind enemy lines attempt to fight their way home, the film was also a complex representation of boyhood and the effects of war on it. Young recruit Private Sidney is undoubtedly the focus of the film. He is the first person to speak and the last we see, and the subject of many close-up shots. A callow youth in uniform, with a clean-shaven face and very little bodily hair, he is the unit's youngest member. He is called a "kid" and spoken to in a childish voice ("What's the matter, snookums?"). When his small unit prepares to attack an enemy guard hut, Sidney is afraid and needs to be prompted into action with the barrel of a gun. He enters last but does not participate in the killing; he stands at the back of the room and watches. Afterwards, he is unable to eat, nauseously staring at the dead soldiers on the floor. In fact, he never kills anyone in combat during the movie.

Kubrick explores the effects of warfare on Sidney, who is the weakest link in his platoon. He breaks down under the pressures of combat, suffering from posttraumatic stress disorder. As the killings flashback through his mind, Kubrick reflects his mental state through a fragmented cutting style resembling that of Soviet montage. Left alone to guard a captured fisherwoman, not much older than himself, Sidney playacts, hoping that his amusing entertainment will pacify her. When this fails, he begins to molest her. Naively believing she will neither scream nor flee, he unties her, but of course she begins to run, and Sidney shoots her dead. Babbling and cackling, he runs off into the forest. He later reappears out of the mist, floating on a raft, crouching like a dog and singing. Wild-eyed, completely irrational, moaning incoherently, and laughing and screaming hysterically, Sidney's sanity has been sacrificed on the altar of the battlefield.

Kubrick's next war film was *Paths of Glory*, which, in its focus on the First World War, also implicitly explores the issue of young boys being drafted to fight and sacrificed on the altar of the battlefield. Based on real events in 1915, the plot concerns the French general staff who were willing to sacrifice an entire division in a hopeless attack on a fortified German position known as "The Pimple." But when it fails, they require a scapegoat and five soldiers are selected as blood sacrifices for the greater good of France. They are court-martialed for cowardice and, despite an able defense, the trial is a mock formality. The men are executed but exonerated nearly two decades later.

As the film's father figures, Generals Broulard and Mireau are eager to sacrifice their "sons," the troops under their command, in pursuit of vanity, vainglory, ambition, and promotion. They know the attack is doomed to failure. Broulard emphasizes his patriarchal position, when he refers to Colonel Dax as "my boy" and "troops are like children; just as a child wants his father to be firm, so troops crave discipline." When the troops refuse to leave the trenches, Mireau orders his own artillery to fire upon them. But when the artillery officer refuses to obey his command, Mireau is still willing to sacrifice his men by his own hand: "If those sweethearts won't face German bullets, they'll face French ones!" Ultimately, Mireau selects the three scapegoated soldiers to be sacrificed to save (his) face. In turn, Mireau is sacrificed by his superior officer, Broulard, whom Dax calls "a degenerate, sadistic old man." Dax is the sole soldier unwilling to sacrifice his "children." Not only does he lead them into battle, he also offers himself up as a scapegoat in their place. Shortly after filming was completed, in 1958, Kubrick married Christiane (née Harlan) and became the stepfather to her young daughter, Katharina (b. 1953). His own daughters, Anya and Vivian were born in 1959 and 1960, respectively.

The issue of sacrificing children is continued in *Spartacus*. This story of a historical slave revolt against the Romans presents the slave community as one big family, with shots of everyday life showing children playing with their families. The wholesomeness of the community of ex-slaves, who are familial, fertile, and fecund, is contrasted with the licentiousness of the Romans, who are shown to be childless, sterile, and gay. Kubrick explores youth through the introduction of a character that did not appear in Howard Fast's 1951 novel: The Greek slave boy Antoninus who becomes Spartacus's symbolic son. However, children are enslaved and abused. "Boys" such as Antoninus are to be put to work but are also the object of unwanted Roman sexual attention. The Romans ultimately massacre such children. In scenes reminiscent of the Holocaust documentary footage that was then starting to be widely viewed, these children are shown to have been indiscriminately slaughtered in a slow panning shot of the dead on the battlefield. In one shot, a lifeless mother cradles her dead child (Burton 2008: 11). Nevertheless, in a moment of redemption, the film ends on an image of the son of Spartacus escaping to a life of freedom with his mother.

Although children were absent from Kubrick's next war film, *Dr. Strangelove*, in the behavior and games that are played out in the War Room the adults act in a childlike fashion. Moreover, Kubrick undoubtedly wanted to comment on the current policy of nuclear armament to safeguard a future world for his own children (he was seriously considering moving to Australia). He does use the film, however, to express the relationship between paternal generals and their childlike charges when General Jack D. Ripper, commander of Burpelson Air Force Base, registers his deep disappointment at the surrender of his troops: "Those boys like were like my children, Mandrake. Now they've let me down."

Kubrick returned to war with *Full Metal Jacket*, whose theme, according to its producer and Kubrick's brother-in-law, Jan Harlan, is the abuse of young men (2015). In Vietnam these young recruits are initially abused by a father figure in Gunnery Sergeant Hartman before being confronted with an enemy soldier, a lethally effective female sniper who is a child even younger than them. They end the film with a symbolic return to their childhoods, singing the Mickey Mouse club theme tune, suggesting the infantilization of US military culture during the Vietnam War.

Children at War

Ever since 1956, at precisely the point Kubrick was beginning his mature phase as a filmmaker, Kubrick wanted to make a child-centered story. This began with his intended adaptation of Stefan Zweig's 1911 novella, *Burning Secret*. This short story was told from the perspective of a 12-year-old Jewish boy who is befriended by a philandering older man who wishes to seduce the boy's married mother. Ultimately, the boy opts not to betray his mother and keeps the secret of her infidelity from his father. Already, the clear Freudian and explicitly Jewish elements of Kubrick's work were emerging, even if they were not to be fully realized until later. Another novel that Kubrick showed an interest in adapting was Calder Willingham's 1952 *Natural Child*, about a 19-year-old Southern girl's romantic adventures and friendships in New York. Although Kubrick never made either film (*Burning Secret* was adapted in 1988 by Kubrick's assistant, Andrew Birkin), he never abandoned their themes.

Following *Spartacus*, Kubrick was able to compensate for his failure to realize these child-centered projects with his adaptation of Vladimir Nabokov's controversial 1955 novel *Lolita*. The film, released in 1962, featured a marital triangle of a middle-aged European professor who marries a similarly aged widower to get close to her eponymous 12-year-old daughter. When her mother dies, Humbert Humbert, who is now her sole guardian, attempts to seduce her. Lolita is then seduced by another older man, Clare Quilty. Spurned by him, she ends up married, somewhat happily, and pregnant. Although Sue Lyon was aged fourteen when she was cast in the film, and hence looks more mature than the nubile nymphet of Nabokov's novel, as Kathy Merlock Jackson points out, "the message remains the same" (1986: 138).

Lolita is presented as both innocent and temptress. On the one hand, Humbert and Quilty use Lolita for their own ends and she is prematurely sexualized. Yet, on the other, as Karen Lury points out, Lolita may not, in fact, "be as passive or as innocent as she is made out to be" (2010: 87). She is depicted as a sexually provocative and active girl who has already lost her virginity before Humbert attempts to seduce her and, indeed, she seduces him, although never offers herself up again thereafter. Furthermore, as Lury observes, although "she is orphaned, abused and exploited Dolores does not see herself as a victim, and finally the film reveals that she has actively plotted, lied and cheated to get what she wants" (ibid.). On top of this, the issue of child sexual abuse is never fully introduced: "because the child is as guilty as the man, interest lies with his devastation after she rejects him, not with any trauma she may have faced" (Jackson 1986: 138).

Today, such material might be considered shocking, but it was even more so in the early 1960s, when movies promoted a wholesome image of children as natural and tender innocents. Now, with Production Code Administration (PCA) approval, Kubrick had succeeded not only in making a movie about the love affair between an adult man and a child but also between a man and his stepdaughter no less, and hence carrying with it the whiff of incest. The PCA—and celluloid childhood—would never again be the same.

Kubrick's interest in childhood sexuality continued through the 1960s. He considered adapting Rosalind Erskine's *The Passion Flower Hotel* (1962), a comic novel about some enterprising British boarding school girls, aged fourteen, who sell sexual services to an all-boys school. This seemingly oddball project continued Kubrick's interest in teenage sexuality that built upon *Lolita*, but which anticipated *A Clockwork Orange*. The planned Napoleon biopic, which never came to fruition, was also meant to have dealt extensively with the title character's childhood and youth. "Thus," as Krämer (2017) points out, "a cluster of unrealised projects from the late 1950s and early 1960s appears to have prepared the ground for the increasing focus on children and teenagers in the films Kubrick actually made thereafter."

2001 was inspired, in part, by Arthur C. Clarke's *Childhood's End* (1953), in which humanity, in its comparative infancy, evolves to a new level of consciousness and formlessness. The story clearly influenced the film's finale: The image of a fetal star child returning to earth, as the next evolution of humanity returning to earth as its redemption. *2001* was also the first example of Kubrick casting one of his own children in the film. "Squirt" was played by his own daughter, Vivian, and a scene with his other two daughters, Katherina and Anya, was shot but cut. His daughters later appeared in *Barry Lyndon*, *The Shining*, *Full Metal Jacket*, and *Eyes Wide Shut* (when Bill examines a young child, the boy is his grandson, watched over by his daughter).

By the late 1960s, Kubrick had permanently relocated to Britain. Emilio D'Alessandro suggests that while the reasons were undoubtedly connected to his career, Kubrick also had the concerns of his own children in mind.

> Christiane liked London a lot, too. She had lived with Stanley in New York for a few years but felt the city was too chaotic. Subsequently, they moved to England for reasons connected to the production of her husband's films. They both loved the peacefulness of the area north of the city, with its tree-lined roads, wide sidewalks, and well-trimmed hedges. It was the ideal place to bring up children. The state schools were excellent, and Katharina, Anya, and Vivian had settled in perfectly. (2016: 21)

Ironically, given the demands of Kubrick's perfectionism, one wonders how much time he and his staff spent with their own children. As D'Alessandro remarks, "Stanley's children spent more time with me than they did with him, and I spent more time with his children than with my own" (2016: 81). But, by all accounts, Kubrick loved his own children, grandchildren, and those of his friends and staff. "Stanley was great with kids.

He had a very special relationship with Alex, Katharina's oldest child, as well as with Anya's son Sam" (ibid.: 319).

Kubrick's subsequent films that put children at their heart both invoke child sacrifice. Whereas *2001* offered a vision of a utopian childhood, his next film *A Clockwork Orange* offered a dystopian one. It follows the misadventures of a teenage delinquent whose principal pleasures are violence, rape, and Beethoven, and the film ends with its protagonist on the cusp of manhood. Imprisoned for his crimes, Alex is used by a series of political "fathers" for their own ends: by scientists as the subject for the experimental Ludovico Technique; by a writer to illustrate the crimes of the government; and finally, by the Minister of the Interior to attack the opposition.

Barry Lyndon is an oedipal drama in which a fatherless young Irishman attempts to social climb among the English elite with his mother at his side. When Barry marries a woman of means, he becomes a stepfather to her embittered son and their relationship is strained. He also becomes a father to his own biological child, Bryan, whom he loves dearly but overindulges, resulting in Bryan's death as the result of a horse-riding accident. The film ends with the contrasting images of Barry by his mother's side and his stepson with his mother, Barry's former wife. Arguably, Barry loses his son because of his attempt to social climb within a closed English aristocratic society where he does not belong. His son is sacrificed on the altar of his ambitions.

Building on the oedipal drama, Kubrick made *The Shining* about a family triad of father, mother, and son isolated in a wintry hotel. The warped family triangle of *Burning Secret* and *Lolita* are again invoked. In a loose reworking of Genesis 22 in which a father seeks to sacrifice his son at the bidding of a higher power (see Abrams 2012, 2018), Jack Torrance takes his family up a high mountain in Colorado during the winter to become its caretaker. Suffering from a severe case of "cabin fever," Jack begins to hallucinate and seeks to "correct" his son Danny with an ax.

The Shining is also the only Kubrick film (save *2001* and its star child) with a young child in so central a role. Emphasizing this, for the film's poster Kubrick chose the face of a terrified child within the lettering of the title. Danny is the victim of physical abuse by his alcoholic father. In response, he has constructed an imaginary friend, Tony, who lives in his mouth. Recalling his namesake, the biblical prophet Daniel, Danny can "shine"—namely, see events in the future or back in the past—and foresees his father's actions, even writing "murder" backward on the wall. Danny also represents both Oedipus and Isaac, sons in Greek and Hebraic culture threatened by their fathers. Geoffrey Cocks argues, "Even more than the young observers of a found world in other Kubrick films, Danny is a representation of Kubrick himself in the 1930s" (2004: 11). Cocks believes that Danny exemplifies Kubrick's "child discovering the dangerous world," a trope in which "youth is victimized by adult male authority" (2013: 26). As William Paul observes, *The Shining* confronts a horror that is "insistently repressed in Western culture, the hostility of a father toward his own son" (1994: 344). Furthermore, the murdered twin Grady sisters, central to the film's imagery but not the novel, reinforce this theme of child as victim. Unlike Bryan, his child precursor in *Barry Lyndon*, Danny survives but like the adolescent in *Lolita* (and the Jewish boy in *Aryan Papers*, as we shall see), he prematurely loses his childhood.

As Kubrick finished what would be his penultimate film, his thoughts had already turned to two other projects that put childhood at their heart. The first was his never-to-be-made Holocaust film, *Aryan Papers*. Adapted from Louis Begley's semi-autobiographical 1991 novel, *Wartime Lies*, it recounts the story of a young Polish-Jewish boy, Maciek who, along with his aunt, manages to survive the war by hiding under an assumed gentile identity. It would have been interesting to see how a director who had spent his career considering, yet always delaying, making a movie about the Holocaust, as well as never having made a film from a child's perspective, would have succeeded in combining both genres. Earlier in his career, Kubrick had wanted to tell the story of a 11-year-old German girl who, in 1943, leaves boarding school in Germany to live with her parents in Amsterdam, where she gradually becomes aware of the persecution of Jews (Krämer 2016; Ulivieri 2017a). The uncatalogued "Unfinished Projects" boxes at the Kubrick Archive contain fifty loose pages from a novelistic treatment. Ulivieri (2017a) observes:

> This story is remarkably similar to Christiane Kubrick's own childhood experience: her parents, visiting members of the German Theater, discovered in horror that both the apartments they were given by the Nazi occupation government in The Hague had belonged to Jewish families that were deported in Poland. The undated treatment changes names and character details, but otherwise it is a deliberate narrative rendering of Christiane's family story: two handwritten notes are even addressed to her. (see also Cocks 2004: 71–3)

Kubrick's final film, *Eyes Wide Shut*, was a marital drama about a complacent married man whose world is shattered when his wife reveals a sexual fantasy in which she abandons him *and their child* for a handsome naval officer she doesn't even know. An adaptation of a contemporary of Zweig, the Viennese writer Arthur Schnitzler's *Traumnovelle* (*Dreamstory*, 1926), the film foregrounds the protagonist's paternity by depicting early on their child, Helena, as they prepare to go out to a party. The narrative is then intercut with shots of Helena and her parents as they go about their daily routines—brushing teeth, hair, doing homework, reading before bedtime, and so on. Helena, however, is never explored in her own right. She is merely a cipher, who stands for Bill's status as a father and what his wife, Alice, is willing to give up in pursuit of a fantasy with a naval officer she didn't even know. What is more, McEntee suggests in this volume, Helena is such a "marginal figure" that, in the words of Michel Chion, we "forget that Bill is himself a father" (2006: 56). McEntee adds that Helena's "function is to represent the family's reconstitution in the final toy store scene. However, her activities become irrelevant as we focus on the dialogue between Bill and Alice" (this volume). The film ends on the word "fuck," which might imply not only a regenerated marriage but also more children in the future rather than the one lonely status symbol and parental toy.

Eyes Wide Shut ends with what some see as a troubling image of childhood. The family take an outing to the large toy store, FAO Schwartz, where Helena runs off never to be seen again. The presence of two older extras, both of whom were also at Ziegler's opening Christmas party, has fueled internet suggestions that Helena was abducted in the film as a warning against sex cults and Scientology to which Kubrick's own daughter, Vivian, was converting at the time that the film was made (see Hunter 2016: 48). Furthermore, abused childhood is also evident in Lolita-esque daughter of the costume shop owner Milich who is prostituted to two older Asian gentlemen, as well as the way that the prostitute Domino is posed on the bed, with a stuffed animal, which infantilizes her (Dajka 2019). Milich also offers her to Bill showing how this father figure is willing to sacrifice his child for money and advancement.

Unrealized Children

By the time he died, Kubrick was working on what would have been his most child-centered film, *A.I.*, about a family who adopt a robotic child only to abandon him. This boy then seeks to become human and recover the mother he has lost. Kubrick bequeathed this project to Steven Spielberg, who completed and released it in 2001, *A.I.* is the "Kubrick" film that puts childhood nearest to its heart. Taking throughout the perspective of a child, it is perhaps the closest equivalent to the never-made *Burning Secret*. An adaptation of Brian Aldiss's short story, "Super-Toys Last All Summer Long" (1969), *A.I.* is about a synthetic child, David—a name full of biblical resonance—who seeks the love of its human parents but is rejected in favor of their biological son who recovers from a coma. David is abandoned in a forest—a typical trope of the fairy tale that also strongly resonates in *Lolita* and *The Shining*—by his mother. David then must fend for itself in the adult world in which humanoid robots are hunted down, tortured, and "murdered," often for human pleasure and entertainment. In scenes reminiscent of the Holocaust novel, *Wartime Lies*—which Kubrick was simultaneously adapting as he was working on adapting *A.I.*—David evades capture alongside an android prostitute named "Gigolo Joe." Screenplay drafts at the Kubrick Archive indicate that Holocaust imagery played a key role in the conceptualization of this section of the story. Furthermore, not only is the boy prematurely inducted into an adult world of death, he is also precociously introduced to the world of adult sexuality, clearly suggesting what use Kubrick imagined for these futuristic child robots: Playthings for adults or "super-toys" to use the term from the original story that inspired the film.

As mentioned above, Spielberg completed *A.I.* Peter Krämer has pointed out how in addition to being a great admirer of Kubrick's work, Spielberg had long been on a career path that closely paralleled that of the older filmmaker, exploring very similar themes along the way and indeed modelling several of his films on those of Kubrick (2017: 196). Eventually released in 2001—two years after Kubrick died—Spielberg sentimentalized the story by converting it into a fairy tale updating of Pinocchio: "the story of an artificial child rejected by and then eternally seeking out the mother" (Williams 2017: 245). The finished film thus fit more into line with Spielberg's oeuvre, in which, by contrast with Kubrick's, focuses heavily on children whose fathers are absent.

Joy McEntee, in this volume, suggests that one of the reasons for offering *A.I.* to Spielberg was because of "more prosaic concerns," namely, "the demands of working with real children." Alison Castle points out how Kubrick "worried that the length of time he would take to shoot the film, since he always too time to lavish attention on all the production details, would cause obvious differences in the boy's age to be noticeable throughout the movie" (2004: 507). Two sets of Danny's costumes were made for *The Shining* in case the actor grew during production. Kubrick had last worked with a real child in 1980—Madison Eginton's scenes as Helena in *Eyes Wide Shut* were brief—and then, if Vivian Kubrick's 1980 documentary of her father at work, *Making The Shining*, is to be believed, he delegated most of the task to his assistant Leon Vitali. (Significantly, the new documentary *Filmworker* (2017) shows how in pursuit of Kubrick's perfectionist demands, Vitali was guilty of neglecting his own children.) Kubrick had expressed an interested in adapting William Peter Blatty's novel *The Exorcist* (1971) but perhaps he didn't because it was a risk basing a film upon a child's performance. Nonetheless, as McEntee points out in this volume, *A.I.* remains "Kubrick's disturbing final statement about children."

Conclusion

At first sight, Kubrick's films marginalize the experience of children and childhood, tending to favor male adults and their perspective (Krämer 2017). Yet, on closer inspection, both subjects featured in most of his films, and were to be a key element of his planned, yet unmade films. Overall, in treating children and childhood, two themes emerge: the sacrifice of children and their precocious sexualization or brutalization.

26

Kubrick and Genre

Jeremi Szaniawski

The latest edition of the *Oxford English Dictionary* defines "Kubrickian" as "meticulous perfectionism, mastery of the technical aspects of filmmaking, and atmospheric visual style in films across a range of genres" (Reilly 2018). Indeed, few film directors have navigated generic boundaries with such ease and artistic and commercial success as Stanley Kubrick. He directed three short documentaries, an existentialist allegory that anticipated the modernist wave in international cinema (*Fear and Desire*), film noirs (*Killer's Kiss, The Killing*), a peplum (*Spartacus*), war films (*Paths of Glory, Full Metal Jacket*), comedies (*Lolita, Dr. Strangelove*), science fiction (*2001: A Space Odyssey, A Clockwork Orange*), a costume drama (*Barry Lyndon*), horror (*The Shining*), and an erotic thriller (*Eyes Wide Shut*). It should be noted that the latter three are also family dramas, while *Spartacus, Dr. Strangelove*, and *Barry Lyndon* qualify as war films and *Dr. Strangelove* as science fiction. Other genres, such as the melodrama and the musical, can be found, albeit in subverted form, in sequences from *Lolita, 2001, Barry Lyndon*, and *A Clockwork Orange*, while the final segment of *2001* shows kinship with underground and avant-garde cinema. Further complicating any simple genre categorization, Thomas Elsaesser points out that

> critics have spoken of *Dr. Strangelove, 2001* and *A Clockwork Orange* as Kubrick's futurist trilogy ... [,] his films about sexuality, couples and the family (*Lolita, The Shining, Eyes Wide Shut*) could be said to probe the contours of a post-bourgeois society, and his films about military or para-military institutions (*Fear and Desire, Paths of Glory, Full Metal Jacket*) see masculinity from the perspective of highly problematic post-patriarchal "male bonding." (2020: 36)

Kubrick was also set to direct a Western—the Marlon Brando vehicle *One-Eyed Jacks*—and developed several other projects, including the Holocaust drama *Aryan Papers*, the science fiction fairy tale *A.I. Artificial Intelligence* (directed by Steven Spielberg in 2001), the epic chronicle *Napoleon*, and a Viking story based on the novel *The Saga of Eric Brighteyes* by H. Rider Haggard. Such prodigious versatility should give the genre purist pause. And since Kubrick never made the same film twice, it is normal that he is rarely considered from the perspective of genre filmmaking *stricto sensu*. As various scholars and critics have observed, Kubrick seemed to use genre merely as vehicles, "deliberately mak[ing] use of cinematic genres and change them, break them, subvert the codes you expect to find" (Raphael 2001: 271). For Linda Ruth Williams, Kubrick "long played with genre, emulating and exemplifying the pinnacles of trash genres through meticulously rendered works of cinema art" (2005: 397). And, for Carl Freedman,

> the typical Kubrick film tends to remake or redefine the genre to which it belongs, taking apart the inherited conventions of the particular filmic kind in order to display their formal and ideological complexity, but also in order to put them back together, so to speak, in better working order than ever. (1998: 300)

As a director who thus utilized genre and imposed his idiosyncratic formal, thematic, and philosophical concerns on his cinema, Kubrick is regarded as an auteur rather than a genre filmmaker. As such, moving from trope to trope and genre to genre, Kubrick produced an oeuvre that is cogent, continuous, and filled with echoes and foreshadowing. Maze-like spaces and alcoholism in the film noirs are motifs that recur in *The Shining*. *Barry Lyndon* echoes *Paths of Glory* and *Clockwork Orange* and anticipates both *The Shining* (the father who hates and wants to kill his son) and *Full Metal Jacket* (the battle sequence in which Barry rescues Potzdorf). The motifs of enclosure and psychotic meltdown are transferred from *The Shining* into *Full Metal Jacket*, and the motif of the unassumingly powerful woman evolves gradually from *Barry Lyndon* into *Eyes Wide Shut*. Kubrick told the same stories, repeatedly, but in different genres. As Elsaesser argues, each film "probed the limits of some aspect of the human condition: sexuality and death, natural aggression and manmade violence, warfare and the military mind, the audible silence of space and the inaudible screams inside the nuclear family," twisting and bending genre in order to accommodate his vision, and not the other way around (2020: 29). To Elsaesser, Kubrick can be seen as the author of "one-offs" and "prototypes" (ibid.: 43).

One reason for this approach was indeed highly practical: as the studio system collapsed in the 1960s and expensive "prestige" genre productions tanked, Kubrick relocated to England, seeking a way to continue to make films with competent crews for a fraction of their costs in the United States (he was impressed by the commercial success of the British James Bond franchise). The crisis of classical Hollywood had to do with the crisis of traditional genres (the Western, the musical comedy, the epic), which no longer attracted countercultural baby boomers. This sense of generic exhaustion opened the door to the New Hollywood filmmakers (Nichols, Altman, Hopper) and the "Movie Brats" (Coppola, Scorsese, Spielberg, De Palma) who experimented with new genres, genre hybrids, and formulas (the new gangster films, horror, the road movie). Aware that he was not about to make cheap thrillers but that he had to remain commercially viable, Kubrick elected to use his prestige as a brand name and "superstar" director to create a "genre leaping" formula that would keep his fans and general audiences on their toes. In his hands, each film became a prototype with a very clear strategic value: that of remaining relevant and "hot currency" for critics and audiences.

But there was more than a strictly pragmatic commercial dimension to Kubrick's approach to genre. As Michel Ciment notes, historical awareness of genres is inescapable even for an artist who strives toward originality: "one way to distance oneself from [a] tradition is to call its genres into question" (2001: 59–60). Kubrick's films' treatment of genre(s) also bolsters Robert Stam's question of whether there is such a thing as a "finite taxonomy of genres or are they in principle infinite?" (2000: 14). Of course, as Janet Staiger has argued (2003) genre purity is a utopia. In cinema, as Barry Keith Grant notes (2007), we almost always find a mix of romance and given setting (Western, gothic, etc.), which is articulated into a genre for commercial purposes. So it is in more complex ways that we must understand Kubrick's take on genre, one deriving from his dual profile as a producer/businessman and as an artist. Kubrick may have utilized and blended tropes of given genres, but he also endowed his films with a truly unique form that defies categorization. Kubrick's genre is a " 'genre' without a specific end, a genre whose end is always in question and to be determined, never already determined" (Rodowick 2001: 29).

Film Noir

The genre Kubrick adhered to most strictly, in terms of generic preconditions, was film noir. It is often regarded not as a genre so much as a "style," "tone," "mood" or just a "canon" (see Schrader 1972; Telotte 1989: 10–11; Schatz 1981; Naremore 2008: 311–12), which expressed the angst and pessimism of the Second World War, the Korean War, and the Cold War. *Killer's Kiss* and *The Killing* belong to the genre canon but they did not transform it (perhaps, also, because noir in its classical phase ended around the time when the films were released). Kubrick's noirs share both the genre's visual and thematic tropes (hardboiled characters, crime narratives, trench coats, guns), and also its dark, fatalistic, "existentialist" mood, as when, at the end of *The Killing*, Johnny Clay refuses to run away from the police after his loot has been blown away by the airplane propeller, saying "What's the difference" (see Abrams 2007). As Richard Schickel says in the documentary, *Stanley Kubrick: A Life in Pictures*, "It's an existentialist movie. Existentialism basically posits that we define ourselves by doing and that chance is the one thing that we can never quite fully comprehend." Jungian and Freudian imagery and dark evocations of the subconscious—another hallmark of noir—find themselves illustrated in the demented scene in the mannequin-filled warehouse of *Killer's Kiss*.

Film noirs are noted for their unusually convoluted plots, which frequently involve flashbacks and other editing techniques that disrupt and sometimes obscure the narrative sequence (see Ballinger and Graydon 2007). *The Killing* deconstructs linear narration with a repeated timeline, retelling the action during the heist from a variety of perspectives—although that is a borrowing from Kurosawa's *Rashomon* (1950) and Welles's *Citizen Kane* (1941) rather than from any particular film noir. Kubrick integrates other tropes and staples of the genre such as voice-over narration and gritty urban representations in a "semi-documentary" style (Neale 2000). The narrative boundaries of film noir are notoriously fluid or elastic, and it is more in the themes, urban setting, low-key black-and-white cinematography, and above all that "existentialist" mood that we recognize the film noir signature in Kubrick. It is worth noting that noir's themes of determinism, cosmic irony, and trapped masculinities are central to Kubrick's broader conception of man—tragic and ironic in equal part—and significantly reworked in his later films, notably *A Clockwork Orange* and *Barry Lyndon*.

Kubrick's affinity for noir may derive also from his family's central European roots. After all, the genre (or mode) emerged by way of German expressionism and European filmmakers such as Michael Curtiz, Fritz Lang, Robert Siodmak, and Billy Wilder. But the noir imagery in Kubrick also owes to the strong influence of the photographs of Weegee and Diane Arbus (see Mather's chapter in this volume): urban gritty settings and crime underworlds represented in Weegee's work, and the uncanny intensity of Arbus's portraits of misfits, freaks, and marginalized figures.

Science Fiction

Whereas his film noirs did not transform the genre, Kubrick's *2001* is the benchmark by which every other science fiction film has been measured. As a genre, science fiction "emphasizes actual, extrapolative, or 2.0 speculative science and the empirical method, interacting in a social context with the lesser emphasized, but still present, transcendentalism of magic and religion, in an attempt to reconcile man with the unknown" (Sobchack 1997: 63). As Vivian Sobchak reminds us, science fiction proceeds by showing the alien and unfamiliar as familiar (ibid.). *2001* brought not only a new level of realism to the genre with groundbreaking visual effects and near documentary portrayal of space travel, but also an unprecedentedly epic story and transcendent philosophical scope. *2001*'s historical importance to the genre's development is undoubted. Although science fiction was a popular genre during its cinematic golden age in the 1950s, it was widely regarded as best suited to B movies, exploitation "creature features," or serials for children's matinees. The turning point for the genre came in 1968 with the release of *2001* and another big-budget studio film that played to countercultural audiences, *Planet of the Apes*. The success of these films established science fiction as a mainstream adult genre, which was often satirical and dystopian in tone till the genre was redefined again by the optimism of *Star Wars* (1977) and *Close Encounter of the Third Kind* (1977). Although these latter films were aimed at family audiences, their combination of spiritual renewal and the technological sublime was nonetheless indebted to *2001*: according to Kubrick, "the concept of God is at the heart of *2001*" (quoted in Seed 2011: 20).

Still, can *2001* truly or simply be considered science fiction in any traditional or cinematic sense? According to Rick Altman's semantic/syntactic approach to genre (1999), *2001* conforms to the "paradigmatic" (or semantic) axis, or what Mircea Valeriu Deaca (2020: 231) calls the "sci-fi template," that is, the required "ingredients" for a film to pass as "science fiction": examples of what Darko Suvin (2015) called the "novum" in science fiction, which creates the genre's distinction cognitive estrangement: space crafts, cosmonaut suits, skilled scientists, high-tech monitors, and highly sophisticated computers. *2001* also features such customary genre motifs as exploration, borders, and new frontiers, as well as an "attitude of deception in the face of a crisis that cannot be epistemically mastered [, which] underlies the treatment of science and scientific artifacts" (Deaca 2020: 231): in short, a mix of fascination with and fear of the unknown. Yet, in terms of the "syntagmatic" (or syntactic) terms, *2001* proposes something very different—a psychedelic quest that is as much an exploration of the confines of outer space as it is a journey into the recesses of the human brain, or what writers of New Wave literary science fiction, such as J. G. Ballard, called "inner space" (Latham 2011: 128).

These considerations hardly exhaust the genre questions raised by *2001*. On the one hand, the film's accurate representations of outer space emphasize the "science" without neglecting the "fiction" element. On the other hand, the use of classical music (temp tracks from Richard Strauss, Johann Strauss, Jr., Aram Khachaturian and György Ligeti) endows the spacecrafts with the balletic grace of a Busby Berkeley musical, a genre with little in common with science fiction. It is also in *2001* that we may find the finest illustration of the so-called "space opera." Yet the film is even more memorable for other reasons: the way in which it proposed a credible hypothesis for the origins of mankind, and also perfectly captured the exhilaration and excitement of the 1960s ("the sky is the limit" motto), the angst of the reactivated Cold War, and the dialectics modern men saw themselves confronted with, between the animal, the limitations of the body, and the apparently boundless promises of technology and the human mind—this super computer to rule them all—tapping into the sixties by summoning the man-apes of the "Dawn of Man" sequence, all the way to the psychedelic imagery of "The Journey to Jupiter and Beyond." This created an oblique dialogue with the radicalism of its period and its zeitgeist—instantly appealing to a youth in search of new experiences (including the flooding of the market in big cities of various hallucinogenic substances—hence the famous "drug busts" in theaters showing the film [Elsaesser 2020: 29]). *2001* was far more than a genre film, the "ultimate trip," as the posters of the film cleverly advertised, in so many more way than one and "one of the most visible monuments to the crossover between SF and the youth counterculture that the New Wave movement [in science fiction] both manifested and promoted" (Latham 2011: 134).

Horror

Whereas *2001* entirely reinvented and redefined science fiction, *The Shining* poses another conundrum. On the one hand, it integrates major landmarks of the horror genre and takes them to another level of intensity and efficiency. On the other hand, it is often decried by genre purists as being cold, verbose, not taking the codes of horror seriously, or being excessively drawn in its own technique, and therefore alienating and boring (Pauline Kael is a case in point: "It's like watching a skater do figure eights all night, or at least for two hours and twenty-six minutes" [1980: 130]). Other critics welcomed the novel take on genre the film performed (Maslin 1980), the "reversal of well-known horror conventions" (Mayersberg 1980–81: 54). As Rick Warner illustrates, "*The Shining*, in addition to its Hitchcockian touches [esp. to *Psycho*—the bathroom scene, the murder, the staircases, the dead woman], borrows inventively from *Les Diaboliques* (1955), *The Omen* (1976), *Halloween* (1978), and, more conspicuously, *The Amityville Horror* (1979)" (2020: 141). To this, one can add *The Phantom Carriage* (1921), *The Haunting* (1963), which Kubrick mentioned as an influence, and *Rosemary's Baby* (1968), whose success rekindled the studios' interest in horror as a bankable but also more reputable genre, prompting Kubrick to want to take a stab at it himself. Yet, *The Shining* never repeats tried and true formulas for the sake of it. While it engages with some key tropes of late 1960s and 1970s horror, such as the haunted house and so-called "family horror" (Mayerberg 1980–81; Wood 2003: 63–84), it lacks the explicit gore, for example, of slasher films, and the psychological realism of *Rosemary's Baby*. This "anti-psychological" approach was one of the reproaches leveled against the film, including by Kael (1980; see also Wright 2008).

The Shining does not fit into any generic model neatly, not any more than any other Kubrick film. Indeed, according to Mayersberg, "underlying many sequences in *The Shining* is a critique of the whole genre of horror movies" (1980–81: 55). For Morris Dickstein, "*The Shining* is less a horror film than a meticulous, enthralling academic imitation of one" (1984: 65). It is, as Freedman says,

> a rich theoretical meditation on the ... genre of horror itself, suggesting the historical and ideological limits of horror as well as the complex involvement of horror with the whole category of historicity. Accordingly, the ultimate relationship of *The Shining* ... to the horror genre might aptly be described as a *meta*generic one. (1998: 300)

Meta-genres: Technology and History

In line with the multiple reviews of the film questioning its uneasy generic fit, and intrigued by *The Shining*'s glossy images and affect, Fredric Jameson (1990) wondered how to best categorize Kubrick: was he a dilettante, detached postmodernist? Or still a modernist auteur dealing with profound issues, but using a detached (self-protecting) form of irony and humor, disguising his films in the clothing of commercial genre and glib, depsychologized characters? For Jameson, the best and most productive way to look at Kubrick's work with genre and genre conventions is to bypass traditional categories ("horror," "science fiction," "period drama"), just as Kubrick himself bypassed them. Jameson was the first to apply the term "meta-genre" to *The Shining*. One aspect of meta-genre films (also practiced at the time by auteurs such as Robert Altman, Roman Polanski, Nicolas Roeg) was to use a passé or classical genre and, by way of "pastiche," revive both the genre itself in a new guise, and create, for the film artist in the postindustrial world, an outlet, recycling old formulas and mannerisms—expressing both a critique of the beautiful and glossy, or a boredom with the aesthetic itself.

This label of meta-genre film readily applies to all of Kubrick's movies but nowhere is it more appropriate than in the case of *The Shining*, because of the moment at which the film was released—one of an important change in the home entertainment industry. To warrant his projects longevity and viability, Kubrick was constantly on the lookout for new technologies, often ahead of the curb vis-à-vis his competitors. In view of this, we can see *The Shining* as a film not so much relevant for its manifest genre—horror—but for its central conceit—the maze—and for its labyrinthine diegetic space, which defies logic, calls for a cognitive "remapping" and repeated, indeed multiple, viewing. The "ultimate horror film" would thus be the ultimate film for the VCR age, a technology that was just arriving on the market in the early 1980s. Now a film could be experienced in a whole new way by viewers, not in the linear fashion procured by the movie theater-going experience, but from the comfort of one's home, on their TV set, at their leisure and at the time—and for a duration—of their choosing. Films could be replayed, rewatched, analyzed frame by frame, reinvestigated, like the hedge maze. Time, therefore, became a more pliable, navigable and commodifiable entity (this is also the "horror" that *The Shining* speaks of).

Still, in order to understand Kubrick's approach to genre, one must also move away from strictly commercial and technological considerations, seeing in them vehicles, but also "covers" or veils for something arguably far more important. As Frederic Raphael pointed out (cited in Ciment 2001: 271), and as Geoffrey Cocks (2004) and Nathan Abrams (2018) have richly elucidated, Kubrick's films were never straightforward in their genre approach (or in any other way): they proceeded by indirection, their subsurface or hidden narrative far more engrossing and important than their manifest narrative content. *The Shining* is again a perfect case in point. The film was advertised as the "great wave of terror that swept through America." As P. L. Titterington (1981) hints at and Bill Blakemore (1987) elaborates upon, the rich Native American imagery in the film suggests that the wave of terror lay in that of the white men driving out and exterminating the Native American populations from their ancestral land. Cocks (2004) takes this further to argue that the film can be read as being about more than the Native American genocide. It was also, he contends, an oblique or indirect reflection on the Holocaust.

Genres in the Brain

Kubrick worked with several genres that Linda Williams (1991) has identified as "body genres" (the grotesque comedy of *Dr. Strangelove*, the horror of *The Shining*, the erotic parts of *Eyes Wide Shut*). But none of these films elicit laughter, screams, or arousal exactly in the way the films dealt by Williams are supposed to: as Gilles Deleuze indicated (1989), some filmmakers lay on the side of the body, while others on that of the brain. Kubrick, with his fabled IQ of 200, serves as the epitome of the latter tendency. Instances of brain allegory, Deleuze notes (ibid.: 205–6), abound in the films (the war room in *Dr. Strangelove*, the maze in *The Shining*...), albeit closely connected to bodily imagery (the sexual humor and the bleeding elevator respectively). Kubrick also correlated the theme of psychedelic experience with overall interiority and the cerebral (*2001* as the "ultimate trip" and a mind-expanding experience). What is depicted in Kubrick's films is thus, like the psychedelic experience, a world that is already a mental construct rather than an ostensibly shared external reality, yet this does not mean in any way that they reveal some kind of underneath or "inner truth." The brain remains the hidden organ, separated from the world by a membrane, or the skull, a form of separation that Kubrick's films attempt to translate into filmic terms; this recalls the import Diane Arbus assigned to the invisible—"a picture is a secret about a secret. The more it tells you the less you know"—which governs Kubrick's films from behind the visible surface. This points to the lineage between his oeuvre and the work of all cerebral or hyperintellectual filmmakers, who create the meta-genre of the "brain film," sharing their love of systems and algorithmic thinking, pushing back the very limits of human cognitive abilities. The meta-brain film is almost necessarily "meta-filmic," because it does portray, however obliquely, the processes that lead to the elaboration and creation of the filmic text itself.

While Kubrick's films do not fit in neatly with the category that was identified in the late 1990s and twenty-first century of the "mind game," they do readily belong, in line with their "brain cinema" meta-genre, to the category of the "thought experiment" (Elsaesser 2018). Each Kubrick film asks the viewer to position themselves, by way of the characters' surroundings and situations, in an uncomfortable, and often extreme, position. But they go further, asking fundamental questions about the nature of power, our origins (and becoming) as a species, the implications of artificial intelligence and its interaction (and/or superseding) with human beings. For Slavoj Žižek (2000) *Eyes Wide Shut* is first and foremost about someone (Bill Harford) who constantly wants to penetrate the other's fantasy. This posits us in an eminently meta-cinematic thought experiment: we are, through Harford's perambulations, uneasily unmasked not so much as voyeurs, but as pursuers, as film watchers, of someone else's fantasy, which we assume or make vicariously ours for the duration of a film.

Another "meta-genre" Kubrick has been associated with, albeit after his death, is the paranoid, conspiracy theory-oriented thriller. Texts and blogs have been produced in their droves, but also films, such as *Room 237* (2012), arguing that Kubrick's films held keys to messages about secret societies, dark governmental conspiracies, or that Kubrick faked the moon landings for NASA (the mockumentary *Dark Side of the Moon*, 2002)—in case the Apollo 11 mission never landed successfully, or, perhaps, to create a myth, man having indeed never flown into space at all. Jameson (1992) explains elsewhere the reason for the popularity of such paranoid texts, when the complexity of a given system precludes simple "cognitive mapping," and the mind applies dark and secret plots to explain phenomena that otherwise exceed its cognitive abilities. It is in this murkier area of Kubrick interpretation that his films gain traction with a specific audience. This, I.Q. Hunter argues,

> is what you might call the scholarly aspect of cult. Cultists often share esoteric ideas and conspiratorial theories about what films mean, responding to the fact that many cult films are dense with textual ambiguities that demand interpretation and committed re-viewing. (2016: 14)

Cult Cinema

Kubrick's films often fit the bill of another meta-genre (and commercial category), namely cult films, with their mix of transgression, initial incomprehension of the critics and general public, while garnering the quasi-religious admiration of fans. Although all his films from 1957 onwards were A-list pictures, not at all the grindhouse or offbeat B movie that sometimes generates a cult, it must be said that Kubrick's films often if not always carried with them a form of strangeness and even quirkiness (were the term not inappropriate for works of such magnitude) that makes them fit candidates for the "cult" label.

It certainly matters that Kubrick's most celebrated period (the late 1960s through the early 1980s) coincides with the golden age of cult movie culture (*2001* as the epitome of the cult "head film," "a term referring to mind-expanding films, sometimes drug-influenced or imitative of drug effects, which are especially appreciated when stoned or tripping" [Hunter 2016: 8]), which was then carried onto the video age and redirected into other areas of fandom and fan culture—generating a strong and indisputable following online, as exemplified in the score of websites, blogs and vlogs dedicated to the "secrets" locked inside or hidden behind a purported code to *The Shining*, accounting for "devoted following or subcultural community of admirers" (ibid.: 2).

Furthermore, "Kubrick's films are organized so as to force the viewer to interpret them holistically and conspiratorially by slowing time to enable meticulous scanning of the mise-en-scène, insisting on textual gaps and cruxes, and thereby encouraging self-reflexivity and intertextual exploration" (ibid.: 51). These films can also be mind-expanding, as in the eminent case of *2001*: "the 'experience' of *2001* went beyond simply watching it, although that was unusually important: the film was a 'purely' cinematic experience, and was framed as such when posters for the 1969 rerelease, repositioning the film as a hippie cult item, declared it as 'the ultimate trip'" (ibid.: 136). Other Kubrick films, though less trippy, are no less important in their effect on the viewer, upon first encounter and then during the many repeated viewing of the film, with *Barry Lyndon* a case in point. In line with this, Hunter proceeds to celebrate another important aspect of cult films, which readily applies to Kubrick's, at least based on the shared experience of so many people: "encountering the film—which is to say, *re-encountering it*—can be life-changing and transfiguring if the viewer is able to submit, to think and *to care*" (ibid.: 137). This transformative quality may be one of the most important reasons for Kubrick's cult status, but also for the genuine devotion that his fans have nurtured for him.

Repetition, Influence, Legacy, and the Economy

As Barbara Klinger points out (2010), genre, cult cinema, and repetition mesh well. But, unlike Steven Spielberg, whose *Jaws* (1975) spawned scores of imitations, Kubrick's work with film genre were much admired and referenced, but not replicated in their structure or formula—a function, in turn, of their nature as modernist works of art, which resist their own commodification. This is precisely because they were never just genre films, exceeding the borders of generic formula to reach into the recesses of film art. These films did however draw the attention and admiration of many filmmakers, who made a point of referencing and quoting them: Ridley Scott, John Carpenter, and James Cameron took Kubrick's hybrid approach to genre, such as in the combination of the noir, science fiction and horror genres in *Alien* (1979) and *Blade Runner* (1982). With humor, wavering between the blank parody of pastiche and more jocular instantiations, John Carpenter's debut, *Dark Star* (1974), features a clear parody of *2001*'s supercomputer HAL 9000. Cameron's *Aliens* (1986)—a sci-fi horror war film hybrid of sorts, is rife with references to *2001* and *The Shining*, and parallels motifs of *Full Metal Jacket* (the two films were produced at the same time in London). Today the vast majority of "serious" science fiction films made since have been informed by Kubrick's film, from *Moon* (2009), *Oblivion* (2013), *Interstellar* (2014), *Arrival* (2016), *Ad Astra* (2019), all the way back to classics of the 1970s of the New Hollywood—think of *THX 1138* (1971), the first film by George Lucas, who would later enlist several of Kubrick's collaborators, including Colin Cantwell, on *Star Wars* (1977).

As a product or function of a socioeconomic environment, classic Hollywood genre (the Western, the musical, the comedy) were a reflection of a rationalized, specialized, Fordist-modeled economy. With late capitalism's shift from the production belt to more fluid professional profiles (alternating service and management), so did film genres experience crises and evolve as well. Mixtures of genre (e.g., the sci-fi and slapstick comedy in *Dr. Strangelove*) reflect this, when the geopolitical context of the Cold War called for both alarm and derisive, absurdist humor.

That genre films, like all commercial cinema, articulate and express concerns, discourse, and anxieties of an era, is evident. That they may become, as in the case of Kubrick's, repositories for all scores of interpretations is a symptom of both the times and his films' layered and complex nature, accounting for and a product of the political and economic unconscious that they carry in them: Kubrick's films contained at once the longing and mourning of the heyday of Fordist capitalism and announced the fluidity of neoliberalism and global capitalism. It is thus unsurprising that today's filmmaker's most readily acknowledging Kubrick's legacy are global auteurs characterized by their generic interplay and hybridity: Paul Thomas Anderson, Darren Aronofsky, the Coen

Brothers, Jonathan Glazer, David Lynch, Christopher Nolan or Quentin Tarantino. Their works, keen on proven formulas but ever refining and modifying them, reflect the influence of globalization and neoliberalism, and which Kubrick's films, also in their generic interplay, beyond mere pastiche or postclassical gesture, anticipated and announced.

Part Five

Researching Kubrick

Introduction

Research into Kubrick can be divided into two periods: before and after the opening of the Stanley Kubrick Archive (SKA).

Early critical writing on Kubrick was auteurist (Walker 1972), putting the director at the center of the films. This continues to seem natural with Kubrick, given his desire to control every aspect of filmmaking. Since the revelation of the existence of boxes of material related to Kubrick and his films, however, there has been what has been labeled the "empirical turn" in Kubrick studies (Fenwick et al. 2017a: 4). In 2004, journalist Jon Ronson, who was invited to Kubrick's home, revealed

> an estate full of boxes. There are boxes everywhere—shelves of boxes in the stable block, rooms full of boxes in the main house. In the fields, where racehorses once stood and grazed, are half a dozen portable cabins, each packed with boxes. These are the boxes that contain the legendary Kubrick archive. (Ronson 2004)

These materials were first publicly viewable in the same year, when a joint exhibition was presented by the Deutsches Filmmuseum and Deutsches Architekturmuseum in Frankfurt, Germany. Kubrick's widow, Christiane and his brother-in-law, Jan Harlan, as well as the Kubrick Estate, cooperated in the creation of this exhibition, which has since traveled to cities all over the world.

The opening of the SKA at the University of the Arts London in 2007 allowed scholars to view these materials at length, which produced a wealth of archival-based research on the director (e.g., Castle 2004, 2009; Ljujić et al. 2015; Fenwick et al. 2017b). This is the subject of Georgina Orgill and Richard Daniels' chapter. Given their position as current and former Senior Kubrick Archivist respectively, they offer a privileged insight into who visits the Archive, why, what they look at, and what impact this has had. The availability of "a previously inaccessible wealth of detail about his day to day practice as a creative artist and selfaware industry player" (Fenwick et al. 2017b: 368) has led to a significant reorientation of existing scholarship by vastly improving our understanding of the director's working methods and on the way he organized his work. The tremendous amount of archival material that has been preserved attests to his involvement "not only in all aspects of film production but also in the marketing of his films" (Ljujić et al. 2015: 13), making it possible "to offer a fuller account than was previously available of Kubrick's working life" (Krämer 2017c: 375) and to expand our knowledge of the processes behind each film project. For example, most recently Robert Kolker and Nathan Abrams were able to provide a detailed reconstruction, what they call and "archeology," of the lifetime of the film *Eyes Wide Shut*. The SKA has also enabled studies of the technical aspects of the film's production, including *2001* (Bizony 2015; Frayling 2015; Benson 2018), *Eyes Wide Shut* (Kolker and Abrams 2019), and the unmade films, such as *Napoleon*, *A.I. Artificial Intelligence*, and *Aryan Papers* (Castle 2004, 2009).

(One thing the Archive has indicated is just how voracious a reader Kubrick was. In addition to the boxes of material, a significant chunk (although how much is impossible to say) of his personal library was donated enabling scholars to read what he read and even see his marginal scribblings and textual underlinings. As Catriona McAvoy shows, this includes the source texts for his films but also those books he read in preparation for making those films.)

Given that there was a dramatic decline in the filmmaker's output from the early to the later years of his career, the Archive has also allowed scholars to consider how he spent his time "during the increasingly long periods between the releases of his films" (Krämer 2017c: 375), which is the subject of Peter Krämer and Filippo Ulivieri's chapter in this section. Between them, the authors have produced comprehensive surveys of the projects in which Kubrick was interested which was far wider than previously thought, going beyond *Napoleon*, *Aryan Papers*, and *A.I.* They conclude that, despite the high number of projects, Kubrick's thematic and generic interest were rather narrow, being limited to war; sexual, romantic drama, mostly focused on marriage; crime; and speculative and/or fantastic (science) fiction. At the same time, reinforcing James Fenwick's chapter which opened the book, they suggest that his high levels of power and autonomy had its perils because he spent increasing amounts of time trying to select the right project to realize.

27

Kubrick and the Archive

Georgina Orgill and Richard Daniels

Introduction

Since 2008, the Stanley Kubrick Archive (SKA)—a vast collection of records created, collected, and used by the director himself—has been conserved, protected, and made available to researchers at the University of the Arts London's (UAL) Archives and Special Collections Centre (ASCC) at Elephant and Castle in London. The opening of this resource for students, academics, fans, and members of the public has transformed the way Kubrick and his films are studied, shown, and written about. As archivists who have had specific responsibility for the SKA for twelve years, we will first set out a history of this archive, how it came into being, how and why it was donated to the university and what the archivists at the ASCC have done with the archive to preserve, organize, and make it available to researchers. We will then give an overview of the types of materials in the archive and analyze its impact on Kubrick Studies, referring to works produced by just a few of the thousands of archive researchers who have passed through the doors and highlighting some of the new knowledge and new approaches enabled by their use of the archive. The sudden availability of such a rich source of documentary record on Kubrick's films has inevitably led to a shift in emphasis in Kubrick Studies away from textual analysis of the films to a more historical and contextual approach. In this chapter we will briefly analyze this apparent schism and look at the merits and downfalls of the different approaches.

Formation and History

From the beginning of his career as a photographer and then as a filmmaker, Kubrick preserved the documentation generated by his creative process, packing it into boxes when production was complete. As his career developed, so too did the volume of his archive; by the time he completed *Eyes Wide Shut* in 1999, it amounted to nearly a kilometer of boxes, all stored in Portakabins and outbuildings at his estate at Childwickbury where it was relatively unknown. From the early 2000s, the material gradually entered public consciousness when the Deutschesfilm Museum in Frankfurt, Germany requested to borrow around 1,000 items for a biographical exhibition of the director. "Stanley Kubrick: The Exhibition" opened in Frankfurt in 2004 and has toured the world since, visiting such cities as Los Angeles, Seoul, Mexico City, Amsterdam, Rome, Toronto and, London. At the same time, Taschen published some of this material as *The Stanley Kubrick Archives* (Castle 2004), which became a bestseller. Just prior to the exhibition, journalist Jon Ronson raised the profile of this material, publishing an article in 2004, which he later expanded into a documentary film, *Stanley Kubrick's Boxes* (2008).

This activity led the Kubrick family to realize the value of this resource if preserved for posterity and made available to researchers. They then began to look for a suitable institution to house it. The family wanted it to remain in the southeast of England, which had been Kubrick's home since the mid-1960s. UAL was chosen because it offered to construct a purpose-built research center with professional archivists to conserve and make it accessible to researchers. Furthermore, UAL's focus on art practice whereby young aspiring artists would be encouraged to learn from a master filmmaker, and to use the archive to inspire and create new works of art, no doubt appealed to the artistic Kubrick family.

Then began the legal and physical process of organizing the move of the materials. First, the material was collated and partially organized onsite at Childwickbury, prior to being transported to UAL. At the same time, UAL converted an area of its London College of Communication (LCC) building in Elephant and Castle to a purpose-built ASCC with temperature and humidity-controlled storage area, office area for staff, and a research space for consulting the archive. In 2007, the archive was transferred to LCC in over 1,000 large packing crates.

After its arrival at UAL, professional archivists began the time-consuming work of analyzing and cataloging the vast material that spread over 800 linear meters of storage shelving. It was discovered that the archive contained material from the entirety of Kubrick's career, containing original contact sheets from his time as a staff photographer at *Look* magazine from the mid-1940s onwards, as well as issues of the magazine showing his published spreads. There was also a significant amount of material relating to films that were never made (most notably *Aryan Papers*, which accounts for 272 boxes of material, not including a significant library of secondary sources). Although there are significant gaps in material from the early part of Kubrick's career, the archive is more comprehensive from the production of *Lolita* onwards, possibly due to Kubrick's increasing creative control over his films and his more settled status in the UK. His moves from New York to Hollywood and then to the UK may have made it harder for him to keep significant amounts of material at his home prior to this period.

Since opening its doors to the public in October 2007, more than 2,000 researchers have visited it every year. Over 5,000 retrieval requests were made in the academic year 2018–19 alone (a retrieval request can signify anything from one item to a series of boxes containing many files of documents). Of these researchers, roughly half were students from universities attending workshops or tours, and half were individuals undertaking their own research. The most popular materials consulted include Kubrick's handwritten notes on *The Shining* (SK/15/1/1) and his annotated copy of the novel (SK/15/1/2 and SK/15/1/3), costume research for *A Clockwork Orange* (SK/13/2/6), and the draft script for *2001: A Space Odyssey* (SK/12/1/2/3).

Organization and Contents

It is necessary to detail the history of the archive in this way as the circumstances surrounding its collection by Kubrick and its subsequent donation and designation as a publicly accessible archive impact greatly on how it can be used. The archive can be considered as a "perfect" example of a "fonds," an archival term used to denote the entire body of records of an individual, family, or organization that has been created and accumulated as part of an organic process reflecting the activities undertaken by its creator. Crucially, it was organically created, with all the material it contains being generated through the production of Kubrick's work. It was all kept by him, meaning that it forms a coherent, comprehensive whole whose provenance (the origin or source of the records contained in an archive, and information about their ownership and history) and authenticity (the fact that an archive or document is genuine, was created by its purported creator, and has not been altered) can be easily traced. The archive is also unique in what might be termed its "completeness"—it contains material from across the whole of Kubrick's career and covers all aspects of production.

However, as is the case with any archive, Kubrick's is not complete because there exists only what Kubrick wanted, and was able, to keep. As with all archives, some documents were lost, damaged, or destroyed. In his later career, his preferred modes of communication—the fax and the telephone—have left significant gaps in the archival record. Despite a general pattern of more material surviving from later films, interesting anomalies remain. Although *Killer's Kiss* predates *The Killing*, there is significantly more production material from the earlier film. There are only eight draft scripts for *2001*, but forty-two for *Barry Lyndon*, even though a look at Kubrick's correspondence with Arthur C. Clarke (SK/12/8/1/12) shows that the *2001* script was changed many times. Conversely, there is a vast amount of correspondence between Kubrick and those working with him from the production of *2001*, compared to very little from the production of his next film *A Clockwork Orange*. Generally speaking, Kubrick seems to have kept far more examples of location research than any other types of research—in the case of *Eyes Wide Shut*, this amounts to 302 boxes of material (SK/17/2/3).

In all these cases, the absence or, conversely, the preponderance of material raises questions. Does the large volume of location research indicate that Kubrick considered this the most important aspect of his research? Or was he simply more likely to keep it? In addition to the issue of what Kubrick himself chose to keep, the archive was subjected to an appraisal process by representatives for the family and the studios, with personal and commercially sensitive material being removed prior to donation. Material may also be closed to researchers due to data protection regulations or other UK legislation. And so it is important to remember that the SKA, like all archives, is partial.

Yet what remains is certainly comprehensive enough. The archive contains many materials that researchers may expect from a film maker's archive, for example draft scripts and treatments for films, preproduction location and costume research, props, costumes and daily continuity reports. Where it may surprise, however, is in volume. There are over 120 boxes of what might loosely be termed visual historical research for *Barry Lyndon* (SK/14/2/3); where possible their original file titles have been retained. These titles, which include, "German Rural Activities—Canals and Farms," "Prisons, Torture and Trials," "Womens [*sic*] Private Chambers," show the granularity and extent of just a small part of the research done for the film. There are thirty-eight drafts of scripts for *The Shining*, including Kubrick's own annotated copy of the novel. For *2001*, there are over 300 files of correspondence between Kubrick, his publicity manager Roger Caras, and companies that the production team contacted to design products for use in the film.

The breadth of the archive also makes it unique. Kubrick's interest and creative control extended beyond the development, research, production, and editing of his films. He was also involved in the way they were marketed and how they were translated and dubbed. In addition to this he kept hundreds of contemporary reviews of his films. The archive holds correspondence between Kubrick and Saul Bass that shows how involved Kubrick was in the poster designs for *The Shining*; in one letter, Kubrick tells Bass that his draft designs were "beautifully done but I don't think that any of them are right" and asks him to send "A GREAT MANY PENCIL ROUGHS" (SK/15/5/2/5). For *2001* he kept a file called "Television-Radio Campaign" (SK/12/5/9), which suggested that the scientific accuracy of the film was such that it should be marketed as midway between documentary and fiction. Kubrick wrote a letter that was to be delivered to all cinema projectionists in cinemas showing *Barry Lyndon*, in which he told them that all the work that had gone into making the film "is in your hands" and giving options for music to be played during the intermission (SK/14/7/1/2).

All these documents were revealed during the archive's cataloging, which, in accordance with archival theory, aims to replicate as closely as possible the original order of the archive as it was created and or organized by the original creator. Through this way of cataloging, the original context of material and the interrelationships between individual documents can sometimes be revealed. There were some traces of the way in which Kubrick had kept his material—for example, fan letters during the early 1970s were filed geographically by the address of the writer. This is completely different from the earlier periods and by the mid-1970s few fan letters were retained at all. Equally the majority of script materials for each film, from draft treatments to editing, postproduction and release scripts are cataloged together in the same section for each film, reflecting that the original boxes were usually entitled "Clockwork Orange Scripts etc." and contained script material across every phase of the filmmaking.

Where an original order was not revealed by the archive materials themselves, the archivist had to create a workable arrangement based on a functional analysis of the material. Thus, for most films, material relating to the preproduction of the film is cataloged together despite sometimes not being made chronologically. For almost every film there are further sections for production, postproduction, distribution, exploitation, and publicity. In some cases, cataloging is difficult; the scripts for *A Clockwork Orange* (SK/13/1) are all dated May 1970, making it difficult to tell their chronological order. (Indeed, documents are often recataloged as more information about it comes to light, often imparted by researchers who have had the opportunity to consult the material closely.)

Impact

Such a comprehensive and varied amount of material has of course hugely impacted the nature of study into Kubrick's films. Before the archive, analysis of the films was predominantly textual, with any other interpretation reliant on interviews with Kubrick or available members of his cast or crew. Other aspects of the making of Kubrick's films were made less apparent by these research methodologies, such as many of the contributions from others and elements of the processes of marketing and distribution.

The most obvious way in which archival evidence has changed our existing understanding of Kubrick's films is that it allows theories about them to be empirically tested. Archival research is necessarily a different approach from textual analysis. One strength lies in the fact that archives are not made up of material deliberately collected together. Material that has become archival was often never intended to be read by anyone other than those involved in the initial activities that created it. In this way, archival material can be unconsciously self-revealing. For scholars of Kubrick, his archive can therefore provide a way of circumventing his own silence on his choices or the meaning of his films. In his letter to Saul Bass, for example, Kubrick adds a rare postscript: "I would like to suggest that it is a film of terror (a must) and the supernatural (if possible)" (SK/15/5/2/5). It is unlikely that Kubrick would have publicly revealed such thoughts at the time of making *The Shining* so the letter functions as an insightful working document.

This approach of testing theories against documentation has been a key result of the archive's emergence in Kubrick Studies. For instance, Peter Krämer (2010) has used an analysis of fan letters from *2001* to demonstrate that received wisdom about the film— that it was unsuccessful upon release and only achieved success when marketed toward a teen audience influenced by drug culture—is in fact untrue. The fan letters, he argues, demonstrate the film's broad appeal from the very beginning, with letters from women and children well represented. In addition to this, his research into contemporary reviews held in the archive reveals that most critics were positive about the film, with the exception of a small number of New York critics whose negative reviews later came to be used as proof of a poor critical response.

The wide-ranging documentation and enormous amount of correspondence held in the archive once described as "an embarrassment of archival riches" (Fenwick et al. 2017b: 368) also allows closer scrutiny of theories surrounding the role of Kubrick in his productions and his working methods. Kubrick has been mythologized as an obsessive genius, and in earlier scholarship as the archetypal auteur, and several scholars have used the archive to examine the extent to which this is borne out by documentation.

Catriona McAvoy (2015a), for example, has examined the way in which Kubrick worked on the screenplay of *The Shining* with Diane Johnson, demonstrating that they had a highly collaborative working relationship throughout the filmmaking process with the two suggesting ideas to each other, talking around many subjects and making many decisions together.

Evidence for Kubrick's collaborative approach can be found across the whole archive. Kubrick's correspondence with Roger Caras during preproduction research for *2001* shows him constantly seeking and reacting to examples of product design, and taking onboard comments by collaborators. In his own research for the film, Kubrick contacted the scientist Marvin Minsky, asking him to send key computer terminology for the computer readouts to be shown in the film and discussing his scientific papers (SK/12/8/1/34). Far from Kubrick being a dictatorial presence who generated ideas in isolation, the archive demonstrates that he consulted widely at every stage and was influenced by the opinions and ideas of his friends and family as well as those working alongside him (see, e.g., Kolker and Abrams 2019).

It also shows how his films developed constantly throughout the production process. Mick Broderick used the archive extensively in his book on *Dr. Strangelove* using archival documents to plot the script development over two years. He also used the blandest of production documents, "Continuity Reports" to show how the character of President Muffley developed during the shoot and editing of the film, demonstrating that the president of the finished film is nothing like the weak liberal moralist first devised in the script filmed on the soundstage (2017a). Other examples of scholarly use of the archive can be found in "The Kubrick Dossier" of the *Historical Journal of Film, Radio and Television*, where Fenwick et al. explain that the use of the archive has allowed for a "fine-grained analysis of not only the films themselves but also the conditions under which they were produced" (2017b: 369).

Indeed, archival research can problematize not just popular and scholarly assumptions about Kubrick, but Kubrick's own account of his work. While Kubrick was often dismissive of his work as a staff photographer at *Look* magazine, describing his work as "dumb" in an unpublished interview with Robert Emmet Ginna (SK/1/2/8/2), and said that he had not kept any of his work from this period (cited in Mather 2015: 20–48), the archive does in fact contain over 250 original contact sheets from his time at *Look* (as well as issues of the magazine kept by his mother), hinting at a more nuanced view of this stage in his career. The presence of this material allows a reevaluation of how Kubrick's career as a photographer influenced his career as a filmmaker, and indeed Mather argues that it presents compelling evidence that Kubrick did in fact value this period in his life (ibid.). Material recently accessioned to the archive, but as yet uncataloged, also includes letters sent to Kubrick from editors at *Look*, further indicating that he did consider this period of his career important enough to document and retain it in his archive.

It must be noted that the archive contains very little truly personal material as this has been retained by Kubrick's family. Nevertheless, as is the case in many archives, the line between what is professional and what is personal is often blurred, and the archive contains material that reveals Kubrick's personal tastes in literature, his awareness of films, and his cultural milieu. An inventory of items from his flat to be shipped from the UK in 1963 lists all his music records as well as his books (SK/11/9/77), and this list is often consulted by researchers who wish to understand Kubrick's reading and his points of reference. Letters to Roger Caras (SK/12/8/1/5) reveal Kubrick's preoccupation with recording his favorite US television shows to watch at home in the UK.

The existence of this type of material provides the basis for biographical or cultural readings of Kubrick, both of his films and his background. Nathan Abrams (2018) makes extensive use of archival material in his reading of Stanley Kubrick as a New York Jewish Intellectual. Although the archive does not hold Kubrick's entire personal library, as many of his books remain in his family home, the presence of a significant section of Kubrick's own personal library allows his existing preoccupations to be examined. Material that spans over 50 years also allows themes and preoccupations to be analyzed—Kubrick's earliest screenplays, including one titled "Married Man," reveal his interest in marriage and intimacy over 40 years before his film that fully explored these subjects, *Eyes Wide Shut*.

The presence of archival material also allows a broadening out of our perspective on Kubrick's role in his productions. The fact that so much material from the distribution and marketing of Kubrick's films was seen, approved or critiqued by him allows research into his role as a producer as well as director, an area of his professional life that is often overlooked (Fenwick 2020). While this material does help to emphasize that Kubrick was extremely invested in retaining control over all aspects of his production, it also shows him to be a shrewd businessman who was as interested in selling his films as he was in making them. The archive contains press releases, some annotated, and biographical copy sent to him by film production companies. In addition, the original titles of files of press reviews sent to him for films reveal a preoccupation with monitoring reaction and response. For *A Clockwork Orange*, that Kubrick kept forty-two boxes of publicity for the film, and their titles "Hostile publicity UK" (SK/13/6/29/3) and "Violence—UK" (SK/13/6/29/5), shows how closely he monitored the public mood surrounding the film. (The large number of reviews and reactions also provide a usefully indexed source of contemporary attitudes toward violence and/or sexually explicit material in films.)

The rich array of postproduction materials also allows different perspectives of Kubrick's role. The amount of material on translation and foreign versions of the films shows another aspect of his involvement that might be considered atypical for a director. Serenella Zanotti (2019) has used archival material in conjunction with the final text and interviews with translators to show how Kubrick was involved in the process of translating his films, engaging directly with the translators and dubbers, and suggesting very specific changes, something unusual for most film directors.

In these cases, archival research has shed new light on Kubrick's role as a filmmaker. Yet the archives also allow research to move beyond the figure of Kubrick himself and to focus on the production context of his films. As mentioned, often the presence of material such as contemporary reviews or publicity allows an analysis of social attitudes at the time. Beyond Kubrick or even his films, the archive offers primary source material showing how some of the twentieth century's most successful films were marketed and released. Richard Daniels (2015) has used the press files from *Paths of Glory* to investigate the way in which Syd Stogel (United Artists' Unit Publicist on the film) marketed the film to the press, using it as a case study to examine broader Hollywood publicity in the 1950s. For *Lolita*, Kubrick and his producer James B. Harris had to ensure that the film complied with the Production Code, which would not easy given that the source novel had been banned for obscenity on publication in several countries. The archive contains a memo from Harris to Kubrick (SK/10/3/8/5) detailing the recommendations for script changes made by Martin Quigley (co-author of the Motion Picture Production Code). The document, titled "Quigley's Suggestions," reveals much of what was considered problematic in practice for film censors at the time. The recommendations can often be surprising when viewed from a twenty-first-century perspective: one recommendation cautions against a line in the script for "insulting police unnecessarily."

It is in the broader context of film production and history that the archive has perhaps most widened the field of Kubrick Studies. In broadening the methodologies used to engage with Kubrick, it allows different disciplines to interact with his work and with the archive in general, not only film historians but also translation specialists and those working in practice-led research. Indeed, it is often used as a pedagogical resource, by students and their tutors at UAL, and often those engaging with the archive have no particular interest in Kubrick's films. Students studying Advertising at LCC use press packs and premiere invitations from *Dr. Strangelove* and *Lolita* to look at film advertising in the 1960s. Students studying Design Activism use the product development files from *2001*, as examples of 1960s design trends. These correspondence files (SK/12/8/2) show designs for props and products for use in the film created by over 300 companies who were market leaders in particular products. Most of the props were never used, though the designs often reached an advanced stage of development before the companies were informed that their product would not be shown. Often students focus on the unconscious bias in the design; for example, the expectation that all domestic roles would be the domain of women in the year 2001, or the excitement over single-use plastic plates by the company General Electric.

Creative responses to Kubrick are also facilitated by the archive. In 2018, archival documents were used to assist film students recreate the Stargate sequence in the film *2001*. As technical documents, they can be used to understand special effects shots, but these materials are being used as part of film practice, not research. The archive's location in an arts university means that increasingly, archival material, and by extension Kubrick's films, are reimagined and reinterpreted by artists. Sarah Wood's 2018 *The Enigmatic Message* (an installation and accompanying artist's book) used sound recordings of chimpanzees shown in *2001* to meditate on the making of meaning. The 2016 Somerset House exhibition, *Daydreaming with Stanley Kubrick*, featured artistic responses to the films, with artists visiting the archive and, in some cases, using archival material in their work. The use of the archive in practice and practice-based research is often not considered in academic discourse around Kubrick, but it offers another mode of engaging with archival sources.

Archival versus Traditional Approaches

This brings us to the issue of where archival research stands in relation to the "traditional" methods of film scholarship and textual analysis. The sudden availability of so much archival material has changed the way Kubrick is studied: there has been a proliferation of books and articles on Kubrick since 2008, both academic and popular, and most have used the archive extensively in their analysis, therefore leaning much more toward a biographical and/or historical approach to studying Kubrick. For some, this has been to the detriment of the traditional film studies approach: textual analysis of the film. It has been argued that this approach is reductive: in their enthusiasm to delve into the minutiae of the archive, scholars are overlooking the most important sources for studying Kubrick: the films themselves.

Critics of archival research can point to the many limitations of archival research. Indeed, archival theorists themselves have noted that the empirical approach's focus on evidence and authenticity "favour textual documents at the expense of other ways of experiencing the present, and thus of viewing the past" (Schwartz and Cook 2002: 18). Kubrick did not keep everything. As mentioned above, some films, and some aspects of his filmmaking, are represented in more detail than others. Furthermore, copies of every piece of correspondence Kubrick sent to others are not always available, a problem exacerbated as he began to rely more and more on the telephone and fax machines (see Herr 2000a). Consequently, certain crucial thoughts and opinions cannot be known.

Considering this, it is important to cross-reference material held in other archives, taking a centripetal rather than a centrifugal approach. As the authors in this volume have shown, documents and records relating to Kubrick and his work can be found around the world in the archives relating to many of his collaborators.

Researchers can also be flummoxed by the very nature of the archive itself. Many users have never used an archive before and are unfamiliar with how an archive catalog works, how an archive is arranged, or even what an archive really is; they arrive looking for the magic bullet that will tell them just exactly why it is that Kubrick did a certain thing in a particular film and very often that answer is not there, or if it is, it needs to be dug out or inferred from several documents. Archival records are not created with the researcher in mind; they are the materials created by, or used by, the archive's creator in the process of his or her life and work, and were created for other purposes entirely and must be looked at in that way. Order is then imposed on it by the cataloger.

Even when a document says something in black and white it may not be the complete truth. Like the historian, the film scholar using the archive must analyze the sources she finds to assess their validity often by cross-referencing them with other sources. Often, oral histories might contradict a theory based solely on archival material, or indeed shed light on a confusing document, or vice versa. Catriona McAvoy (2010), having studied the call sheets in the archive came to the conclusion that Kubrick's films suffered from a high degree of serious illnesses and set shutdowns in comparison to standard film practice and had thought that this was related to Kubrick's infamous perfectionism and constant retakes. However, frequent assistant director to Kubrick, Brian Cook (McAvoy 2010), explained to her that Kubrick liked to capitalize on any illness to shut down shooting in order to "think about it a bit" and have it paid for by insurance.

It is not just a scholar's interpretation that can be inaccurate. The authenticity of a document does not necessarily mean that it will be an accurate representation of what occurred. The motives, priorities, and working processes of an individual writing for a purpose affect what information they impart. This is amply demonstrated by a letter from Stanley Kubrick to Roger Caras, asking Caras to pass on some written feedback to Arthur C. Clarke on an article that Clarke had written. Kubrick expresses doubts about it, but wanting to preserve his relationship with Clarke, adds, "Obviously I haven't said any of this to him" (SK/12/8/1/7). Kubrick was writing for an audience.

In addition, no archive is neutral, and all archives are partial. As we have discussed above there are gaps in the Kubrick Archive, some due to deliberate removal from the collection but many more due to survival. It is important to remember that this is the case when we consider that the archive enables us, more than ever, to create a narrative about Kubrick.

Bearing these limitations in mind, the archive still has and continues to illuminate previously hidden processes in Kubrick's work, bringing to the surface the work, contributions, collaborations, and influences that are not always apparent in the text. While the idea of basing research on archival evidence is often seen by textual scholars as reductive, the use of the archive can allow other stories to be heard to enable a multiplicity of viewpoints on his status as a director. The archive refutes the mythological image of Kubrick as an isolated perfectionist auteur, one whose complete control means that every element of his films was solely down to his own genius. This myth is arguably far more reductive and simplistic than anything that scholars using the archive conclude, and it is in many ways the basepoint from which textual analysis of the films begins. Instead of reducing the nature of analysis of the films, use of the archive extends the range of approaches that can be taken to them, problematizing our existing understanding of the director and uncovering layers of complexity in the making, and the meaning, of his films.

Archival and textual analysis are not necessarily in conflict with each other and in fact the two methods can be complementary. An evaluation of a film requires an understanding of not only the filmmaker, his interests, and his working practices, but also the financial and industrial context within which he worked. These understandings are supported by archival research, allowing the theories to be based on a sound footing. Recent examples that have shown this hybrid mix of textual analysis and archival research can be seen in Matt Melia's (2017) work on TV and film in *The Shining*, where draft scripts showing cut scenes are examined in conjunction with the final text. More recently, in their work on *Eyes Wide Shut*, Kolker and Abrams have combined a detailed production history with a textual analysis of the film (2019).

In conclusion, we would argue that the supposed schism between textual analysis of the films and a more historical approach using archival research is, like many things to do with Kubrick, a myth. While it is possible to analyze a film based solely on the film itself the scholar almost inevitably makes assumptions about the intent of the director or the decision-making power of the director and therefore must have a knowledge of the historical context of the production, the character of the director, his working methods and freedom. This knowledge is best served by primary research, be it archival or oral history research or better still both. On the other hand, the historical/ biographical researcher should not forget the films themselves, as the creation of the artist being studied, they are themselves primary resources, they are his advertising notices to the world. As a craftsman Kubrick knew what he was trying to say with his films; the scholar ignores that message and focuses on the incomplete and sometimes biased evidence of the archive at his or her peril. As evidenced above the hybrid approach of the likes of Melia or Abrams and Kolker can bear much more fruit, with both approaches complementing each other to arrive at something closer to a truth than each could achieve alone.

28

Kubrick's Reading and Research

Catriona McAvoy

Although Stanley Kubrick claimed that he did not read a book for pleasure until he was 19 years old (Agel 1970: 111), he went on to develop a real love of books, and all his films from 1956 onwards were adapted from novels or short stories. A "voracious and catholic reader" (Frewin 2005: 378), Kubrick amassed a huge library of titles throughout his life, reading widely to find the stories he wished to adapt, and carrying out extensive background research on subjects related to the development of his films. As Diane Johnson, with whom he collaborated on the screenplay for *The Shining*, said "his approach was very literary and intellectual" (quoted in McAvoy 2015b: 288). His "research," according to Frewin, "became more and more in depth with each film" (quoted in *Stanley Kubrick's Boxes* [Jon Ronson 2008]).

This chapter examines Kubrick's relationship with books and similar materials for reading and research purposes. Using evidence from the Stanley Kubrick Archive (SKA) and those of his collaborators together with interviews with Kubrick, his family, and his collaborative team, as well as existing recent research, it explores how Kubrick's wide reading and detailed scholarly research gave his films depth and breadth, but also helps us to better understand Kubrick's working methods. It will do so by exploring Kubrick's library, how he first discovered his love for reading and the literary journey this took him on, how he researched his films, and which texts influenced his work. By unpacking his love of reading and research and uncovering the books that underpin the themes and meanings behind his films, we can understand more about Kubrick and his unique approach to the filmmaking process, as well as the films themselves.

In terms of existing discussions of Kubrick's reading and research, Anthony Frewin's "Stanley Kubrick: Writers, Writing, Reading" is an excellent starting point (2005: 514–19). It provides an insight into Kubrick's reading habits from his long-time assistant—Frewin began to work for Kubrick in the 1960s—as well as a list of some of Kubrick's favorite books. Frewin also wrote another short essay discussing Kubrick's interest in science fiction literature that is also helpful (ibid.: 378). Further reference to Kubrick's literary tastes can be found in the Kubrick biographies, including LoBrutto (1997) and Baxter (1997). Michael Herr (2000a), who co-wrote the screenplay for *Full Metal Jacket*, also outlines some of the many conversations they had about literature and the books they talked about.

Other secondary sources are useful in this regard. Geoffrey Cocks (2004) shows Kubrick's fascination with German and Austrian literature, including Stefan Zweig, Franz Kafka, Thomas Mann, Sigmund Freud, and Arthur Schnitzler, among many others (some of which is outlined in his chapter in this volume). Building upon this work, Nathan Abrams (2018) references various works by influential New York Jewish intellectuals, including Hannah Arendt, Raul Hilberg, and contributors to *Commentary* magazine (which is discussed by Grinberg). Philippe Mather (2013) also provides very useful background on Kubrick's early literary interests and the technical books that influenced his directing style.

The scholarship that explores the filmmaking process behind individual Kubrick films (both made and unmade) has likewise made reference to the books Kubrick read during preproduction. Alison Castle's *Stanley Kubrick's Napoleon: The Greatest Movie Never Made* (2017) gives an overview of his exhaustive research process, centering on the visual painterly inspiration for this unmade film. Research that focuses specifically on the literature Kubrick used to develop particular films can be found on *Dr. Strangelove* (Krämer 2014b), *2001* (Krämer 2010; Ulivieri and Odino 2019), *The Shining* (McAvoy 2015a, 2015b), *Full Metal Jacket* (Pavan Deana 2017), *Eyes Wide Shut* (Kolker and Abrams 2019), and Kubrick's early research for *A.I. Artificial Intelligence* (Krämer 2015a).

Interviews with Kubrick, his family and collaborators are another valuable resource for discovering more about his reading habits. Many of Kubrick's interviews, in which he often mentions particular books and discusses his thorough approach to reading and research, can be accessed online. The Archivio Kubrick website is a very rich resource with a thorough bibliography of interviews, many of them are also available to read on the site (see http://www.archiviokubrick.it/). Jan Harlan (Kubrick's brother-in-law and executive producer on all his films from *A Clockwork Orange* onwards) has often discussed Kubrick's literary interests, as have Kubrick's wife, Christiane, and their daughter, Katharina. Interviews with collaborators, such as Diane Johnson (McAvoy 2015a, 2015b), explain his intertextual approach to developing a screenplay and film.

The most important primary resource is the SKA, which houses over 1,143 individual titles from Kubrick's research and personal library (see Orgill and Daniels's chapter). This includes some of the reading lists from his various classes at Columbia University, as well as an inventory listing books from Kubrick's personal collection in his New York apartment that were shipped from the United States to the UK in 1965. The list included Carl Jung, Shepherd Mead, Arthur Schnitzler, Jules Feiffer, and many books on modern art and painting (SK/11/9/77).

More revealing still are the books in the SKA with his handwritten annotations, indicating passages he found interesting. Many of Kubrick's books, however, are still at the Kubrick home in Childwickbury and hence unavailable to scholars. What is more, many others in Kubrick's collection were either lost or given away to friends and colleagues; as Christiane (2014) remembers, "He kept losing books and lending books." Clues to these lost books can be found in the archives of mentors and collaborators such as Arthur Rothstein, Vladimir Nabokov, Anthony Burgess, and Diane Johnson, but many remain unknown.

Falling in Love with Books

Kubrick found school "dull" (Bernstein 1966). He stated:

> I couldn't pay attention. I was a victim of the idea that you can teach by fear rather
> than by interesting your class. They really fixed me. I didn't read a book for pleasure
> for a year and a half after I'd gotten out of high school. (Lyon 1964: 147)

Kubrick's grades were average and his attendance patchy; he even recalls that he "failed
English once and had to make it up in summer school" (Bernstein 1966). During
this time he continued to read but, according to Frewin, what really excited him was
pulpy science fiction and detective newspaper magazines such as *Amazing Stories, The
Shadow*, and *Weird Tales* (2005: 514). "It was then in the 1930s that the young SK's
[Stanley Kubrick's] respect for the art and craft of writing first developed" (ibid.).

After high school, Kubrick discovered and developed his interest in reading (Agel
1970: 111). He had moved to Greenwich Village, "the center of New York's intellectual
and bohemian community of artists, actors, musicians, poets, performers, and writers"
(Abrams 2018: 5). Though Kubrick stated that he could not pinpoint a "particular
turning point," he recalls that "being out of school, I began to read and within a
relatively short period of time, I … caught up with where I probably should have been
had I had a modicum of interest" (quoted in Frewin 2005: 514). He explained that,
"Interest can produce learning on a scale compared to fear as a nuclear explosion to a
firecracker" (Agel 1970: 111).

Kubrick did not abandon formal education completely. He enrolled in evening
classes at City College, New York (known as "the poor man's Harvard") and later
joined the Auditing Program at Columbia University. According to Geoffrey Cocks,
who has studied the syllabi of the professors teaching there, Kubrick most likely was
introduced to Homer, Dante, Kafka, Cervantes, James Frazer, Nietzsche, Mann, Freud,
Dostoyevsky, Tolstoy, and Conrad among many others (2004: 64–6).

Kubrick also enjoyed reading contemporary magazines. He bought every issue of
Neurotica (1948–52), an outlet for Beat Generation writers such as Jack Kerouac and
Allen Ginsberg. He read *The Realist* (1958–2001), a self-proclaimed journal of "social-
political-religious criticism and satire," whose countercultural contributors included
such authors as Norman Mailer, Ken Kesey, Joseph Heller, and Terry Southern (with
whom Kubrick later collaborated on the screenplay for *Dr. Strangelove*). He also read
the leading magazine of Jewish and intellectual affairs, *Commentary*, as well as the
satirical *Mad* magazine, both of which were discernible influences on *Lolita* and
Dr. Strangelove.

Articles in these magazines discussed, among others, Hermann Hesse, Fyodor
Dostoevsky, Franz Kafka, and Arthur Schnitzler. The magazines reinforced the
importance of the books from his Columbia reading lists and became the bridge from
the pulpy magazines of Kubrick's childhood to the world of late twentieth and early
twenty-first-century German, Russian, and Polish writers. Whether Kubrick was
mostly influenced by Jewish writing, existentialism, Modernism, or middle European

writers, or that this was a standard menu of influences for a 1950s intellectual, or a combination of both, is unclear.

Kubrick's admiration for these writers truly inspired him: "before I became a film director, always thinking, you know, if I couldn't play on the Yankees, I'd like to be a novelist. The people I first admired were not film directors but novelists. Like [Joseph] Conrad" (McGregor 1972: 1). The writer and intellectual, Dwight Macdonald, recalls meeting a young Kubrick in 1959 and their wide-ranging discussion covered the mathematician and philosopher Alfred North Whitehead, the Russian military leader Grigori Potemkin, and Franz Kafka (Abrams 2018: 7).

Following high school, Kubrick made a living as a photographer for *Look*. As he moved away from professional photography and became interested in filmmaking, he supported his practical hands-on learning experience by reading technical books by filmmakers. Arthur Rothstein, his boss at *Look* had a collection of books on cinema that he lent to Kubrick. Among them was a copy of V. I. Pudovkin's *Film Technique and Film Acting* (1929) in which Kubrick underlined passages about point-of-view editing. Photocopies of this page are held at the Arthur Rothstein Archives at the Library of Congress. Kubrick stated that: "The most instructive book on film aesthetics I came across was Pudovkin's *Film Technique*" (Phillips 2001: 103): "Pudovkin gives many clear examples of how good film editing enhances a scene, and I would recommend his book to anyone seriously interested in film technique" (ibid.). Rothstein is also likely to have introduced him to Sergei Eisenstein's essays. Kubrick was a "keen student" of Eisenstein (Walker et al. 1999: 233), whose influence is noticeable in the "ironic contrasts achieved through editing [that] would become a staple of Kubrick's later work" (Mather 2013: 14).

In describing his own approach to directing in a later interview Kubrick echoes Eisenstein:

> You judge a scene by asking yourself, "Am I still responding to what's there?" The process is both analytical and emotional. You're trying to balance calculating analysis against feeling. And it's almost never a question of, "What does this scene mean?" It's, "Is this truthful, or does something about it feel false?" It's "Is this scene interesting? Will it make me feel the way I felt when I first fell in love with the material?" (quoted in Phillips 2001: 196)

This perspective helps explain the reasoning behind his reputation as a "perfectionist" director who insisted on multiple takes.

Kubrick was also influenced by the Soviet theater director, Konstantin Stanislavski. Kubrick stated

> I was also helped a great deal by studying Stanislavski's books, as well as an excellent book about him, *Stanislavski Directs* [by Nikolai M. Gorchakov 1954], which contains a great deal of highly illustrative material on how he worked with actors. Between those books and the painful lessons I learned from my own mistakes I accumulated the basic experience needed to start to do good work. (Phillips 2001: 103)

A particular point made by Stanislavski and referred to by Kubrick in a 1972 interview was a recollection from *Stanislavski Directs*

> in which Stanislavski told an actor that he had the right understanding of the character, the right understanding of the text of the play, that what he was doing was completely believable, but that it was still no good because it wasn't interesting. (ibid.: 131)

A Literary Journey

Kubrick was known for his in-depth scholarly research. His wife, Christiane Kubrick, described how "he could really swallow a book in a night, and it wasn't superficial reading, either ... He didn't sleep very much—he had a four-hour average ... but he always had time for reading" (2014). A journalist in 1962 commented:

> He knows his movies, and the knowledge may amount to an obsession, but he also knows literature and music and public affairs and who knows what else he didn't have time to discuss in an hour, all of which leads one to assume that his real obsession is learning. (Morgenstern 1962)

When researching a film Kubrick often annotated his books, underlining passages that interested him. He shared titles and notes with his collaborators and discussions of relevant literature, fictional and nonfictional, informed his film's narratives.

So why this intensive and time-consuming approach to developing a film? Kubrick's love of research and enthusiasm for learning are part of the story but it also had a specific purpose. His reading fed directly into his work. He compared the process of adapting a film to "being a good detective" and this required detailed research and preparation (Ciment 1983: 176). In a 1987 interview, Kubrick said that after the initial "falling in love" with a story, the process then becomes "almost a matter of code breaking, of breaking the work down into a structure that is truthful" (Phillips 2001: 196). The process meant that "it doesn't lose the ideas or the content or the feeling of the book ... And as long as you possibly can, you retain your emotional attitude, whatever it was that made you fall in love in the first place" (ibid.). All the books he read around a subject were clues that helped him to crack this "code." They provided context, alternative scenarios, and the background layers needed to make a structure and film that was "truthful."

The 1950s and 1960s

There are few references to literature in Kubrick's three documentary shorts, though Joseph Conrad is cited in the narration of *The Seafarers* ("The true peace of God begins at any spot a thousand miles from the nearest land"). Conrad was a key influence on

Kubrick's first feature film, *Fear and Desire* (Abrams 2018: 31–2). Gene D. Phillips noted, "As the spoken prologue suggests, the forest becomes a metaphor for the jungle of man's own psyche, the heart of darkness of which Joseph Conrad wrote" (1977: 17). This, and his next film, *Killer's Kiss*, were original screenplays developed in collaboration with his high school friend, Howard Sackler, who would go on to be a renowned poet and playwright. It was not until *The Killing* that Kubrick began to adapt from existing novels and short stories, in this case Lionel White's novel *Clean Break* (1955). *Killer's Kiss* and *The Killing* clearly drew upon 1950s existentialist philosophies popular in Greenwich Village and in such magazines as *Commentary* and *Partisan Review*. All his subsequent films were developed from a preexisting source. Kubrick discovered Humphrey Cobb's *Paths of Glory* (1935) and decided to adapt it into a film. And while he was a "gun-for-hire" on *Spartacus*, he did his own reading, including the works of Appian, Sallust, Plutarch, Xenophon, and Arthur Koestler's 1939 novel, *The Gladiators*, which was a rival to Howard Fast's 1951 *Spartacus* (Abrams 2018: 61).

Kubrick's next film was a move back toward the influences from his Columbia University days. A long excerpt from Nabokov's novel *Lolita* was published in the *Anchor Review* magazine in 1957 "with an enthusiastic introduction by Frederick Wilcox Dupee, Kubrick's professor of English at Columbia" (Abrams 2018: 71). Another of his tutors there, Lionel Trilling, had reviewed *Lolita* in the British intellectual journal, *Encounter*, and his argument that the novel could be read as a satire that was "not about sex, but about love" was embraced by Kubrick in his adaptation, as evidenced in his notes and the way that he adapted the film (see SK/1/2/8/2 and SK/10/8/2). The satirical aspects of the film in the comedic names and the crude innuendos reflect the humor of *Mad* magazine, which was also an influence on his next film *Dr. Strangelove*.

Sexual issues and "the 'gap' between the sexes" were major social concerns for Kubrick at that time (Krämer 2014b: 97). During the late 1950s and early 1960s, he and his producing partner James B. Harris first attempted to adapt Schnitzler's *Dream Story*, a novella about marriage and fidelity (Ulivieri and Odino 2019). Kubrick continued trying to adapt this story throughout his career and finally succeeded with *Eyes Wide Shut* in 1999. His book collection—according to the inventory compiled in 1965—includes other novels with female perspectives on sexuality, which were clearly also relevant to *Lolita*. Muriel Spark's novel *The Prime of Miss Jean Brodie* (1960) may have influenced the depiction of Lolita's mother, Charlotte Haze, while Colette's novels *The Ripening Seed* (1923), *The Tender Shoot* (1959), and *Claudine Married* (1902) detail teenage sexual awakening from a female point of view. Other books in the inventory take feminist perspectives on gender and sexuality, such as Anaïs Nin's *A Spy in the House of Love* (1954), which exposes the double standards in male/female sexual politics, and Simone de Beauvoir's influential philosophical feminist text *The Second Sex* (1949).

After *Lolita*, Kubrick began looking for a novel on which to base a new drama. In a 1963 *New York Times* interview Kubrick said, "he had wanted to make a film about the bomb for three years" (Minoff 1963: 7). He estimated that he had read over seventy books on the subject, filed hundreds of related magazines and newspaper articles, and spoken with nuclear experts and strategists. Finally, Alastair Buchan, director of

London's Institute for Strategic Studies, brought to his attention a suspense novel called *Two Hours to Doom* (later titled *Red Alert*) by Peter George (ibid.). Kubrick began working with George but realizing that the film would work best as a dark comedy, he brought Terry Southern onboard to help develop it into a satire (see Broderick 2017a; Krämer 2014b). Kubrick's collection includes many books on the Cold War and the nuclear threat, including Edward Teller and Allen Brown's *The Legacy of Hiroshima* (1962), Fawn McKay Brodie's *Strategy in the Missile Age* (1959), and Richard Fryklund's *100 Million Lives: Maximum Survival in a Nuclear War* (1962). General Jack D. Ripper's comedic paranoia about fluoridation and its effects on "precious bodily fluids" was researched in Walter Arthur Cannell's *Medical and Dental Aspects of Fluoridation* (1960). Discussions of nuclear disarmament in *Commentary* had a clear impact on Kubrick and he considered using the magazine as a prop in the film (Abrams 2018: 109). Kubrick's production notes in the SKA for *Dr. Strangelove* use the term "walking dead" and compare Nazi "concentration camp inmates with contemporary Americans living in the shadow of war" (Krämer 2014b: 10; see SK11/1/7), a comparison he may have found in Bruno Bettelheim's *The Informed Heart: Autonomy in a Mass Age* (1960). Another important philosophical and political influence on the film, a copy of which was present in Kubrick's book collection at the time, was the 1944 translation of *The Complete Works of Francois Rabelais* (1532) whose satirical, political, and philosophical musings along with *Mad* magazine surely informed the farcical depiction of power. Another clear influence was Jonathan Swift's 1726 *Gulliver's Travels*.

During the postproduction of *Dr. Strangelove*, Kubrick began searching for his next story (Ulivieri and Odino 2019), which would be on themes of "atomic warfare, science fiction [and] mad sex relationships" (Tully 2010: 135) and have a "futuristic plot" (Walker 1964: 8). When Kubrick discussed doing "something about extra-terrestrials," Roger Caras from Columbia Pictures put him in touch with his friend Arthur C. Clarke. Kubrick and Clarke began developing ideas together in 1964, using Clarke's short story "The Sentinel" (1951) as a starting point and weaving elements from Clarke's other books, such as *Childhood's End* (1953), into a novelistic screen treatment. In researching what would become *2001*, they watched and discussed hundreds of science fiction films and texts. Kubrick was initially very keen on adapting *Shadow on the Sun*, a 1961 BBC radio play, but Clarke did not share his enthusiasm (Ulivieri and Odino 2019). Kubrick wanted the film to have a strong scientific basis and read many nonfiction scientific journals and books including Stephen H. Dole's *Habitable Planets for Man* (1964) and *Advances in Space Science and Technology: Vol. 4* (1962). On the possibility of alien lifeforms, the key texts consulted were Carl Sagan and Iosif Shlovsky's *Intelligent Life in the Universe* (1966) and Roger A. Macgowan and Frederick I. Ordway's *Intelligence in the Universe* (1966) (Frewin 2005: 378), while the narrative's mythic structure was informed by Joseph Campbell's *The Hero with a Thousand Faces* (1949) and of course Homer's *The Odyssey*. The film's social and philosophical dimensions were influenced by work of the anthropologist Margaret Mead and the popular science writer Robert Ardrey, particularly *African Genesis* (1961), which is cataloged under *2001: A Space Odyssey* in the Kubrick Archive (see Poole 2015: 179). Ardrey's impact on the "Dawn of Man" sequence is very clear and his description of apes as "armed killers" is directly translated into what we see on screen (see Kubrick 1972: 1).

The 1970s

While Kubrick was making *2001*, his friend Terry Southern gave him a copy of Anthony Burgess's novel *A Clockwork Orange* (1962). Kubrick recalled,

> I just put it to one side and forgot about it for a year and a half. Then one day I picked it up and read it. The book had an immediate impact … I was excited by everything about it, the plot, the ideas, the characters and, of course, the language. (Weintraub 1972: 26)

This was to be Kubrick's next film. As well as researching modernist architecture and dystopian themes, he went back to his research into Ardrey's theories of man as a territorial killer ape to develop the film's characters and narrative. Kubrick quotes heavily from Ardrey's *African Genesis* in defense of *A Clockwork Orange* in an open letter he wrote to *New York Times* correspondent, Fred M. Hechinger, who had criticized the film. Kubrick's copy of *African Genesis* in the SKA contains underlined passages that directly link it to *A Clockwork Orange* and the lead character Alex:

> The citizen of the streets whom we watch in *West Side Story* is Rousseau's natural man, all but full grown, and by one means or another untouched by corrupting civilization. If he does not possess what society regards as a conscience then it is because conscience is a social intervention. (Ardrey 1961: 143)

Kubrick underlines the words, "Regarding the delinquent." *A Clockwork Orange* also therefore shows the influence Ardrey's discussion of man and conscience in addition to the more widely known book by American psychologist B. F. Skinner, *Beyond Freedom and Dignity* (1971).

Kubrick's next film, *Barry Lyndon*, was adapted from Thackeray's novel of the same name. Originally published in 1884 in serial form, it was subsequently developed into two volumes in 1852. In a 1975 interview with *Time* magazine, Kubrick explains that he did "not know what drew him to the tale … he has always enjoyed Thackeray" (Phillips 2001: 162). When pressed, he said "it's like trying to say why you fell in love with your wife—it's meaningless" (ibid.). In researching *Barry Lyndon*, Kubrick examined hundreds of books on paintings. His daughter Katharina recalls the "pages ripped from books" (2016), which were then annotated and filed (Ljujić 2015: 237–59). While the SKA contains few books directly related to *Barry Lyndon* and the textual layers of its narrative, Kubrick's annotated copies of Andrew Steinmetz's *Romance of Duelling in all Times and Countries* (1868) and Robert Baldick's *Duel: A History of Duelling* (1965) provide some insight into the development of the characters and social situations beyond the novel. Further research into the visual and social aspects of the production are found in his copy of Maurice Craig's *Dublin, 1660–1860: A Social and Architectural History* (1969).

In 1977, John Calley, an executive at Warner Bros., sent Kubrick a copy of the recently published Stephen King novel *The Shining*. Kubrick told Vincente Molina Foix in 1980, "it is the only thing which was ever sent to me that I found good, or that I liked." He decided to involve Diane Johnson in the development and writing of the screenplay. She was teaching a course on the Gothic novel at the University of California, Berkeley and had written several books that he enjoyed, especially her modern Gothic novel *The Shadow Knows* (1974). While writing the screenplay, they discussed and read Freud's essay on "The Uncanny" (1919), the "great master H. P. Lovecraft" (Molina Foix 1980) and Franz Kafka, who are all referenced by Kubrick in interviews related to the making of *The Shining* (ibid.). Evidenced in manuscript notes and discussed in an interview with Diane Johnson are the importance of Bruno Bettelheim's *The Uses of Enchantment* (1976), Stephen Crane's story "The Blue Hotel" (1899), plays such Shakespeare's *King Lear* (1606), Goethe's *Faust* (1829), and novels such as *Wuthering Heights* (1847), *Frankenstein* (1818), *The Monk* (1796), *Steppenwolf* (1927), and *Catcher in the Rye* (1951), a copy of which Wendy (Shelley Duvall) reads in the film (McAvoy 2015b; Donnelly 2018).

The 1980s and 1990s

From 1983, as he collaborated on the screenplay for *Full Metal Jacket* with Michael Herr and Gustav Hasford (whose semi auto-biographical novel, *The Short-Timers*, provided the source for the adaptation), Kubrick began a literary reconnaissance mission focused on the Vietnam War. He watched documentaries and films, looked at "Vietnamese newspapers on microfilm from the Library of Congress" (Grove 1987: F5), perused hundreds of photographs, and, most importantly, read novels, biographies, and accounts of the war. There are over 190 related books cataloged within the collection at the SKA The scope of the titles, from John Ketwig's *And a Hard Rain Fell: a GI's True Story of the War in Vietnam* (1985), Stanley Goff's *Brothers: Black Soldiers in the Nam* (1982), Nguyen Giap's *How We Won the War* (1976), and *The Special Forces Handbook* (1965), demonstrate the range of perspectives that Kubrick considered in the development of the film. Kubrick used the research books to "look for accurate details on [Vietnamese] day-to-day life" and "to find cues for scenes, actions, dialogues that could resonate with Hasford's story and with what the director wanted to say about war … When he found it, he inserted it into the screenplay" (Pavan Deana 2017).

As recounted by Krämer and Ulivieri in this volume, after *Full Metal Jacket*, Kubrick worked on the development of several other unmade films but eventually moved into production of *Eyes Wide Shut* in the mid-1990s. Schnitzler's novella *Rhapsody (A Dream Story / Traumnovelle)* provided the basis for the screenplay. As mentioned above, he had first approached this adaptation in the late 1950s. Diane Johnson recalls that Kubrick sent her copies of *Rhapsody* in 1977 when considering weaving ideas from the book into the story of *The Shining* (McAvoy 2015). Further references to the book can be found in Kubrick's annotated copy of the manuscript (SK/15/1/3). "A Dream Story" is also referenced as part of Kubrick's book collection in the shipping inventory list from 1965. Christiane explained that "all his life he was so mesmerized by the original story and never let it go" (2014). Kubrick worked with the writer Frederic Raphael to adapt the Viennese novella and in his own research he looked to the psychoanalyst Karen Horney and her book *The Neurotic Personality of Our Time* (1937) to help shape the screenplay. A heavily annotated copy of her book is in the archives alongside Simon O. Lesser's *Fiction and the Unconscious* (1960) and books that informed the stylistic and visual elements of the film such as Francis King's *Cult and Occult* (1985), which has clear influences in the presentation of the ritual scenes in the film.

Conclusion

Kubrick became hooked on reading books through his early enjoyment of reading magazines. The pulp fiction he bought from newspaper stands in his childhood gave way to the avant-garde magazines of New York intellectuals, which in turn opened his eyes to classic literature. Books became for Kubrick a source of interest, a source of passion and, most importantly for his career, a vital resource. Books gave him ideas, inspiration, and knowledge beyond what he learned at school. He embraced his new love of literature and went on to apply it to his filmmaking process. Books about war and politics were examined in research for *Dr. Strangelove, Full Metal Jacket*, and the unfinished *Napoleon* and *Aryan Papers* projects. Books on anthropology, sociology, society, and relationships were studied in order to develop the characters in *Lolita, A Clockwork Orange, Barry Lyndon*, and *Eyes Wide Shut*. Mythology, fairytales, and their interpretations were explored for the development of *2001, The Shining* and *A.I.* Most importantly, psychoanalytic theory and psychology framed all of Kubrick's films, as we have seen in Abrams's and Hunter's chapter on psychoanalysis.

Learning more about the books Kubrick chose to read gives an insight into his approach to filmmaking and research, the underlying ideas within the films, and the many textual layers to his complex work.

29

Kubrick's Unrealized Projects

Peter Krämer and Filippo Ulivieri

Across the first two decades of the twenty-first century, three projects Stanley Kubrick worked on but never completed attracted an unusual amount of attention from cinephiles, artists, writers, and filmmakers: Kubrick's Napoleon biopic, his Holocaust film *Aryan Papers* and his science fiction movie *A.I. Artificial Intelligence*. Indeed, *A.I.* was finally made by Steven Spielberg in 2001, drawing extensively on the treatments and set designs Kubrick had developed. *Aryan Papers* became the subject of *Unfolding the Aryan Papers*, a film by Jane and Louise Wilson that was based on research in the Stanley Kubrick Archive and featured Johanna ter Steege whom Kubrick had chosen for the lead in his film (Anon. 2009). Finally, Kubrick's *Napoleon* script was reported to being used as the basis for an HBO miniseries with Spielberg as executive producer (Holdsworth 2016).

Publications about Kubrick's unrealized projects were initially mostly addressed to a general, cinephile audience, rather than being targeted specifically at an academic readership (see especially Castle 2009; Loewy 2004; Harlan 2005; Harlan and Struthers 2009). Yet, building on these publications and on Geoffrey Cocks's groundbreaking chapter "Almost Directed by Stanley Kubrick, 1953–2001" (Cocks 2004: 319–28), from 2015 onwards academic books and essays started to offer both in-depth case studies of particular unrealized films and general surveys of the projects Kubrick considered at one point or another (see, e.g., Krämer 2015a, 2017a, 2017b, 2017c and Ulivieri 2017a, also the numerous references to Kubrick's unrealized projects in Fenwick 2017, 2020 and Abrams 2018).

As far as the research on Kubrick's unrealized projects is concerned, the Stanley Kubrick Archive at the University of the Arts London has been the main focus of scholarly activity. It includes an enormous wealth of material on what the catalog labels "Unfinished Projects" (see http://archives.arts.ac.uk/CalmView/TreeBrowse. aspx?src=CalmView.Catalog&field=RefNo&key=SK). A large batch of new material was added to the collection in 2019 and will take a while to be included in the main catalog (for a document listing these materials, see Crawford 2018), and more may arrive in future.

In addition, researchers have identified a wide range of other archival collections that hold documents relating to Kubrick's work (see, e.g., Abrams 2018: 305). Another important source of information is the press coverage of Kubrick's work, including announcements of new projects, interviews with Kubrick and the people who knew him best and/or collaborated with him, etc. Much of this press coverage made its way into the clippings files of various archives, but it is also accessible in newspaper databases (these have been trawled most systematically and comprehensively by Ulivieri 2017a). Last but not least, researchers have carried out their own (unpublished) interviews.

From such research the two authors of this chapter have, in previous publications, produced a comprehensive survey of projects Kubrick was interested in (Ulivieri 2017a) and a study characterizing the work Kubrick did, both on his films and his unrealized projects, in each of the three phases of his career: his formative years up to 1955, his partnership with producer James B. Harris from 1955 to 1962, and his later career as one of Hollywood's leading producer-writer-directors (Krämer 2017c). A key insight from these publications is that the number of projects Kubrick considered was much larger than previously thought (more than fifty). Given the usual claims about the diversity of Kubrick's films, Ulivieri (2017a) and Krämer (2017c) also emphasize that Kubrick's oeuvre is in fact tightly focused in terms of genres and themes, and that the same genres and themes characterize the vast majority of his unrealized projects. Furthermore, Ulivieri (2017) and Krämer (2017a, 2017b, 2017c) have begun to explore how ideas generated for unrealized projects were used in later films.

This chapter summarizes some of the key insights of the above named and other publications, but also goes beyond them by asking to what extent Kubrick's extensive work on unrealized projects was in fact unusual and distinctive in the light of standard practices in the film industry, and by examining how the context for his work on unrealized projects changed across his career so that in the first two phases Kubrick's investment in a large number of such projects went together with a substantial output of films, while this was not the case in the third phase. The first section, however, takes a closer look at the narrow generic and thematic focus of Kubrick's work.

Genres and Themes

Most of Stanley Kubrick's features and unrealized feature projects fall, broadly speaking, into the following generic categories (in some instances more than one):

- war stories, including films and projects that do not primarily focus on combat but on the workings of military organizations or on spies; overall, there is an emphasis on the Second World War and the American Civil War;
- sexual/romantic drama, mostly focused on marriage;
- crime stories;
- speculative/fantastic fiction, including films and projects that feature supernatural elements and others that extrapolate from the present into the future or an alternative past.

War stories and sexual/romantic dramas are fairly evenly distributed across all of Kubrick's career, whereas crime stories are, with the exception of *A Clockwork Orange*, mainly to be found in the second half of the 1950s and the early 1960s, and speculative/fantastic fiction from the early 1960s onwards.

Here are some examples for each generic category, including both films and unrealized projects, from both early on and later in Kubrick's career (for details on the unrealized projects mentioned here and in the remainder of this chapter, see especially Ulivieri 2017a and Crawford 2018):

- war stories: *Fear and Desire* and *Full Metal Jacket*, *The Down Slope* (a 1956 story about an incident from the American Civil War), and the adaptation of Robert Marshall's 1988 book *All the King's Men* about a French double agent during the Second World War, which Kubrick was working on in 1989/90;
- crime stories: *Killer's Kiss* and *A Clockwork Orange*, *Cop Killer* (a story Kubrick wrote in 1955), a television series entitled *Three of a Kind* (outlined in 1959), and an account of the exploits of the Ned Kelly gang in Australia (considered in 1962);
- sexual/romantic drama: *Lolita* and *Eyes Wide Shut*, adaptations of Calder Willingham's 1952 novel *Natural Child* about the adventures of a young woman in New York (1956) and of Rosalind Erskine's 1962 novel *The Passion Flower Hotel* about girls setting up a brothel at their British boarding school (1963);
- speculative/fantastic stories: *Dr. Strangelove or: How I Learned to Stop Worrying and Love the Bomb* and *The Shining*, a film version of the multipart 1961 BBC radio drama *Shadow on the Sun* about an alien invasion (which Kubrick was interested in both in the early 1960s and in the late 1980s), and two supernatural, mythical tales that he considered adapting in the 1980s: Richard Wagner's 1876 opera cycle *Der Ring des Nibelungen* (The Ring of the Nibelung) and H. Rider Haggard's 1890 novel *Eric Brighteyes*.

One might also argue that Kubrick specialized in historical and epic fiction and in the procedural (Krämer 2017b), but it is perhaps more productive to point out that, in principle, war, crime, sexual/romantic and speculative/fantastic stories can be set in the past, present or future, can be told with a focus on organizations and procedures or not, and can have epic scope or not.

The tight focus of Kubrick's work becomes even more obvious when considering its main thematic concerns, which, once again, apply across both his features and his unrealized feature projects:

- male violence, which can be more or less physical, spontaneous or institutionalized, individual or collective, criminal or legitimated etc., with a strong emphasis on violence against women;
- dysfunctional heterosexual interaction, ranging from brief encounters to long-lasting marriages.

Both themes are jointly present in Kubrick's first two features, *Fear and Desire* (1953) and *Killer's Kiss* (1955), and also, for example, in Jim Thompson's 1952 novel *The Killer*

Inside Me, which Kubrick considered adapting in 1955. There is virtually no project Kubrick considered that does not explore at least one of these two themes.

Kubrick's features and unrealized feature projects often include minor themes closely connected to the two main themes: bonding among male adults and mother–child bonding, both for mutual support. While male bonding was already explored extensively in Kubrick's very first film, the short boxing documentary *Day of the Fight*, and in *The Seafarers*, a documentary about the Seafarers International Union, it seems that Kubrick first focused on the theme of mother–child bonding when in 1956 he worked on an adaptation of Stefan Zweig's 1911 novella *Brennendes Geheimnis* (published in English as *Burning Secret*) about an extramarital affair observed by the woman's young son. It then became a central concern of several of his films, starting with *Lolita*.

Historical Analysis: Overview

It is not unusual for filmmakers—whether they are producers, script writers, directors or, like Kubrick, hyphenates—to spend much of their time and energy researching and developing ideas for films that never get made. It is always difficult to find the right idea for a film project and to develop it in a satisfactory manner, and even more difficult to get funding for the actual production of a film. Thus, many ideas will have to be tested and rejected, many developments will be deemed failures and in most cases production funding will not be forthcoming. While this is common in the film industry, it is rarely examined in depth, whereas Kubrick's unrealized projects have received a lot of attention, which makes it seem that this is a distinctive aspect of his career, when it is not.

What is, however, quite distinctive (but by no means unique) about Kubrick's career is the dramatic—and ever worsening—reduction of his filmic output after 1964. The period from 1953 to 1964 saw the release of seven Kubrick features, whereas only six films were released in the thirty-five years after 1964. Such decline may well be characteristic of the careers of many filmmakers as they grow old, but in 1964 Kubrick was only 36, which, by industry standards at the time, was very young. It is remarkable, then, that the reduction of his filmic output set in so early in his life. What makes this even more remarkable is the fact that, during the first two phases of his career (up to 1962), there was a *necessity* for Kubrick to develop many projects because it was impossible to predict which ones might attract funding, whereas from *Dr. Strangelove* onwards Kubrick's status in the film industry was such that he was virtually guaranteed finance for any project he chose. And yet, it was during this third phase that his output went down while the amount of time he spent on projects that would not make it to the screen grew *larger* than it had been in the first two phases. Let's take a closer look at the three phases.

Historical Analysis: Phase 1—Formative Years

Information about the period from the late 1940s to 1955 is very sketchy (and exact dates are often difficult to establish), but what there is suggests that, as an extension of his employment at *Look*, Kubrick was initially mainly interested in working in the field of documentary and primarily as a cinematographer (on other people's films), but soon decided to develop scripts for feature films that he would direct himself (for this and the remainder of this section, see especially LoBrutto 1997: 45–106; Krämer 2013, 2015b; Ulivieri 2017a; Fenwick 2017: 48–68; Crawford 2018: 12–15). It is likely that he and his key collaborators (first Alexander Singer, then Howard Sackler) explored a range of possible themes and storylines before settling on what was to become *Fear and Desire*. For example, in 1950, Kubrick was offered a deal to work on an adaptation of Henrik Ibsen's 1882 play *An Enemy of the People* (Crawford 2018: 14).

Between then and 1955, the projects Kubrick considered included adaptations of Joseph Conrad novels (for several of which Kubrick took out film options), topical stories taken from newspapers, stories taken from history and original fictional stories Kubrick himself had come up with. The latter included at least one crime story (*Cop Killer*), but they generally seem to have focused on sexual and romantic relationships (e.g., jealousy in a marriage, an abusive relationship between a girl and her uncle). During the first phase of his career, then, Kubrick did not only make a war movie and a crime movie, both featuring intense acts of violence and disturbing, highly sexualized scenes, with *Killer's Kiss* being framed as a love story, but he also showed interest in several other projects along these lines.

Before ascribing the thematic concerns of these projects to Kubrick himself (as an expression of deeply rooted or emerging interests), it is necessary to ask who and what was driving the selection of topics and stories as well as the story development process. Kubrick's background was in photojournalism where he had had little control over the selection of topics or the shape of the final product (Mather 2013), and, as an extension of this, in documentary filmmaking where he might initiate projects but was unlikely to control the end product; in at least one case (*The Seafarers*), he was commissioned to make a film about a given topic. He also worked in subordinate roles on other people's projects. On his first two filmed scripts, he was working with Howard Sackler, who saw himself primarily as a writer, and may well have been the main creative force in developing the two stories. Furthermore, Kubrick had to keep in mind that his investors (a family member and a friend of the family) would want their money back, and that, for this to happen, he would have to be able to sell the film to a distributor, ideally a major studio. Thus, he had to consider which trends in the market for extremely low-budget productions he could follow with his projects.

Finally, there is the internal dynamic of career development, whereby the largely unpredictable outcomes of previous decisions inform future decision-making. From the outset, both Singer and Kubrick aimed at making films for the major studios. The failure of *Fear and Desire* to find a major distributor would therefore have strongly influenced which project(s) to focus on next, while the subsequent sale of *Killer's Kiss* to United Artists encouraged Kubrick to focus on crime movies. Indeed, when Kubrick teamed up with James B. Harris in 1955, Harris must have understood that the best way forward was another crime story, because it was Harris who brought Lionel White's 1955 novel *Clean Break* to Kubrick, and also commissioned Jim Thompson to write an original story (entitled *Lunatic at Large*) for yet another crime movie.

Historical Analysis: Phase 2—Harris-Kubrick Pictures

In 1955 James Harris brought substantial financial resources (both his own and those of his family) to Harris-Kubrick Pictures, which made it possible not only to option novels, as Kubrick had done earlier on with several Conrad books, but also to acquire the film rights for them, which was much more expensive (on this and the remainder of this chapter, see especially LoBrutto 1998: 109–226; Krämer 2015b, 2017b; Ulivieri 2017a; Fenwick 2017: 69–131). Other sources of finance became available through a development deal with MGM in 1956 and United Artists' commitment to invest in a suitable follow-up to *Killer's Kiss*. All of this meant that Harris and Kubrick, always with major studio deals in mind, were able to seriously pursue a wide range of projects, in some cases with the help of professional writers (Thompson, Calder Willingham, Shelby Foote, Martin Russ, Jules Feiffer) when they had the money to pay for their services.

The projects Harris and Kubrick pursued included numerous stories about crime and war as well as numerous sexual/romantic dramas, and there was hardly any project that did not fall into one (or more) of these three categories. Projects ranged from low-budget productions to star vehicles in the medium to big-budget range, and they seemed to be informed by several industry trends, most notably Hollywood's considerable output of low and medium-budget crime films and the success at the box office of many medium to big-budget films about war and of historical epics. Furthermore, in line with many other filmmakers and arguably both for artistic and for commercial reasons, Harris and Kubrick explored the boundaries of what it was possible to show in mainstream releases under the film industry's self-regulatory Production Code Administration (PCA), especially with regards to sex and violence. Several of their projects (notably an adaptation of Lionel White's 1955 novel *The Snatchers*) were rejected outright by the PCA, while others (most notably *Lolita*, which Harris and Kubrick started working on in 1958) required extensive negotiation between the producers and the PCA.

Given the large number of projects Harris and Kubrick considered from 1955 to the early 1960s, it is obvious that most of them would never go into production, but it is not easy to determine why some of them did get made. Of all the crime projects, only the adaptation of *Clean Break* was realized, under the title *The Killing*, as the second movie under the original deal with United Artists. As already mentioned, the PCA rejected several projects. An equally important role was played by the stars who wanted to work with Kubrick, a star's involvement being an important asset when looking for studio funding. Hence United Artists was willing to finance *Paths of Glory* once Kirk Douglas got involved. The urgent need to earn money so as to keep Harris-Kubrick Pictures afloat exerted a lot of pressure, which is why Kubrick was perfectly willing to work on other people's projects, namely Marlon Brando's *One-Eyed Jacks* (1961), which Kubrick was involved with in 1958, and Kirk Douglas's *Spartacus*. Negotiating skills also played an important role. For example, Harris and Kubrick overplayed their hand in demanding creative control of their *Lolita* adaptation and were initially rejected by both United Artists and Warner Bros. in 1959/60. Perhaps most importantly, it was a matter of good or bad timing and thus ultimately quite coincidental. For example, the firing of Anthony Mann from *Spartacus* in 1959 resulted in Kubrick's appointment at a time when he was more or less ready to shoot the Second World War combat movie *The German Lieutenant* in Germany.

This is not to say that Kubrick's output was random, because, as pointed out, the films he made shared generic characteristics and thematic concerns with the other projects he had been working on. In fact, there is a considerable degree of repetition (with both minor and major variations) across his films and unrealized projects not only from 1955 to 1962, but from the very beginnings of his film career to the early 1960s. For example, *Fear and Desire* and *The German Lieutenant* have much in common (soldiers operating in enemy-held territory, the glory of sacrifice, etc.); a female captive and an actual or implied sexual threat to her play an important role in both *Fear and Desire* and *Paths of Glory*; and a man coming between a mother and her child is the story of both *Burning Secret* and *Lolita*.

Historical Analysis: Phase 3—Power and Autonomy

The third phase began with the dissolution of Harris-Kubrick Pictures and the consolidation of Kubrick's status as a leading and very powerful Hollywood filmmaker, in both commercial and critical terms, following the release of *Lolita* in 1962 (on this and the remainder of this section, see LoBrutto 1998: 227–501; Krämer 2017c; Ulivieri 2017a; Fenwick 2017: 132–216). At this point, funding for *Dr. Strangelove* was already in place (because of the two-picture deal Harris-Kubrick Pictures had made with Seven Arts for *Lolita*). In fact, from this point onwards, Kubrick, making one hit after another (even *Barry Lyndon* was successful at the box office, although not as much as had been hoped), was able to get funding for almost any project he wanted to work on.

This exceptional level of autonomy would appear to be ideal for a filmmaker like Kubrick, insofar as it could facilitate a steady output of films that he found personally interesting and that he also thought could reach a large audience (an ambition he had throughout his whole career), and thus make money for the studios he was working with. So why did he spend an increasing amount of time on projects that he then did not realize?

Starting with *Dr. Strangelove* and continuing with *2001: A Space Odyssey*, Kubrick got used to spending more and more time on background research and story development for the films he was going to make—and also on preproduction, principal photography and postproduction (see, e.g., Krämer 2014b; Ulivieri and Odino 2019). He adopted what has been characterized as an "exploratory" approach to filmmaking (McAvoy 2015a; Krämer 2015a).

When, in the final stages of making *2001*, he embarked on *Napoleon*, he applied the same approach. There was always more research to be done, and also more work on different ways to tell the story. Highly unusually for the third phase of his career, on several occasions he was unable to secure studio funding for this project, so that after five years (1967–72) of often very intensive work, he had nothing to show for it, except that he managed to use some of his research as the basis for *Barry Lyndon*. Why Warners was willing to fund this commercially unpromising project when this studio, like the others, had been unwilling to invest in the Napoleon biopic is not easy to understand, nor is it obvious why Kubrick's later attempts to revive the project came to nothing.

From the moment in 1969 when he first ran into funding problems for *Napoleon*, Kubrick began to consider alternative projects, namely an adaptation of Arthur Schnitzler's 1926 book, *Traumnovelle* (which translates as "dream novella") and a film about Nazi Germany, but he only committed himself to another film after his wife Christiane suggested that he should consider Anthony Burgess's 1962 novel *A Clockwork Orange*. This film demonstrated that Kubrick was perfectly able to pick a project, write a script, do extensive preparations for the production, shoot, edit and score it in less than two years; the film was announced in February 1970 and released in December 1971. In this context it is intriguing to note that all the projects Kubrick realized after *2001*, with the exception of *Eyes Wide Shut*, the adaptation of *Traumnovelle* he made in the late 1990s, were suggested to him by someone else.

Once he had delivered *A Clockwork Orange*, Kubrick began to spend increasing amounts of time on researching sometimes very broadly defined topics that he might make a film about, often considering a wide range of possible storylines, without being able to decide on any one of them. A case in point is his extensive research on various aspects of Nazi Germany and on the Holocaust, with a view to make a film that might either try to illuminate the Third Reich's crimes from the point of view of perpetrators and bystanders, or explore the suffering it caused from the point of view of the victims. He came close (all the way to preproduction) to success only in the early 1990s, adapting, under the title *Aryan Papers*, Louis Begley's 1991 Holocaust novel *Wartime Lies*, which had been brought to his attention by Michael Herr.

Closely related to his interest in Nazi Germany and the Holocaust, across the 1970s, 1980s, and 1990s Kubrick carried out research on various wars, including the American Civil War, the Second World War, the Korean War and the Vietnam War, but only managed to make *Full Metal Jacket*, an adaptation of Gustav Hasford's 1979 novel *The Short-Timers*, which had also been suggested to him by Herr.

Following the success of *Dr. Strangelove*, *2001*, and *A Clockwork Orange*, Kubrick explored the possibility of another science fiction movie from the mid-1970s onwards, and also considered a film about the supernatural (apparent or real). The latter resulted in *The Shining*, an adaptation of Stephen King's 1977 bestseller, suggested to him by John Calley of Warner Bros., while the former led to many years across the 1980s and '90s of working, inconclusively, with several authors on *A.I.*, an adaptation of Brian Aldiss's 1969 short story "Supertoys Last All Summer Long."

Finally, going all the way back to the early 1950s, when several of the projects he envisioned were going to deal with jealousy in a marriage, and to the centrality of jealousy in *Killer's Kiss* (note the lethal "love" triangle of Davey, Gloria and Rapallo, also the traumatic relationship between Gloria, her sister and her father), from the late 1960s onwards Kubrick persistently returned to work on an adaptation of *Traumnovelle*. Even though he was truly committed to this project, it took him until 1999 to complete the film because he could not refrain from exploring many different approaches to its realization.

Conclusion

Stanley Kubrick explained his reduced output from the mid-1960s onwards with reference to the difficulty of finding a really good story that would be worth the effort of making a movie out of it (see Ulivieri 2017a: 110–11). Given the huge amount of money and energy that needs to be mobilized for the production of a movie, it is surely the case that most filmmakers have problems deciding on what projects to commit to. Yet, it is perfectly possible to combine preparatory work for numerous projects, most of which will never make it to the screen, with a regular output of movies, as Kubrick managed to do from the early 1950s to the early 1960s.

During this part of his career, there were all kinds of financial and contractual pressures, and there was considerable division of labor between Kubrick and key collaborators, notably James Harris, regarding the overall direction of his work. While one might consider all of this to be a hindrance, once Kubrick took full and exclusive control of his career, after the dissolution of Harris-Kubrick Pictures and, in the wake of two hit movies, with almost unconditional support from the major studios (in particular Warner Bros. from 1970 onwards), he found it increasingly difficult to make up his mind about anything, to stop the process of open-ended research and exploration of filmmaking options that he had become used to after 1962 (cf. Fenwick 2017: esp. 222). He spent more and more time before he was able to select and really commit to a project he would film, in the end relying on other people's suggestions. Once committed to a project, he took ever longer to realize it.

An examination of Kubrick's unrealized projects suggests that, despite the common belief that his cinema defies categorization, Kubrick was in fact consistent, if not limited, in terms of themes and genres across his entire career. This examination also offers a few hints as to the perils of power and autonomy.

Bibliography

Abramowitz, Rachel. 2001. "Regarding Stanley: Steven Spielberg Felt the Aura of Stanley Kubrick as He Brought an Idea of the Late Director's to the Screen." *LA Times* (May 6). http://articles.latimes.com/2001/may/06/entertainment/ca-59783 (accessed August 27, 2018).

Abrams, Jerold J. 2007. "The Logic of *Lolita*: Nabokov, Kubrick, Poe." In *The Philosophy of Stanley Kubrick*, edited by Jerold J. Abrams, 109–29. Lexington: University Press of Kentucky.

Abrams, Nathan. 2012. "'A Double Set of Glasses': Stanley Kubrick and the Midrashic Mode of Interpretation." In *De-Westernizing Film Studies*, edited by Saer Maty Ba and Will Higbee, 141–51. London and New York: Routledge.

Abrams, Nathan. 2014. "The Banalities of Evil: Polanski, Kubrick, and the Reinvention of Horror." In *Religion in Contemporary European Cinema: The Postsecular Constellation*, edited by Costa Bradatan and Camil Ungureanu, 145–64. New York: Routledge.

Abrams, Nathan. 2015a. "An Alternative New York Jewish Intellectual: Stanley Kubrick's Cultural Critique." In *Stanley Kubrick: New Perspectives*, edited by Tatjana Ljujić, Peter Krämer, and Richard Daniels, 62–80. London: Black Dog.

Abrams, Nathan. 2015b. "A Jewish American Monster: Stanley Kubrick, Anti-Semitism and *Lolita* (1962)." *Journal of American Studies* 49(3): 541–56.

Abrams, Nathan. 2015c. "Becoming a Macho Mensch: Stanley Kubrick, *Spartacus* and 1950s Jewish Masculinity." *Adaptation* 8(3): 283–96.

Abrams, Nathan. 2016. "Kubrick's Double: *Lolita*'s Hidden Heart of Jewishness." *Cinema Journal* 55(3): 17–39.

Abrams, Nathan. 2017. "What Was HAL? IBM, Jewishness and Stanley Kubrick's *2001: A Space Odyssey* (1968)." *Historical Journal of Film, Radio and Television* 37(3): 416–35.

Abrams, Nathan. 2018. *Stanley Kubrick: New York Jewish Intellectual*. New Brunswick, NJ: Rutgers University Press.

Acevedo-Muñoz, Ernesto R. 2002. "Don't Look Now: Kubrick, Schnitzler, and 'the Unbearable Agony of Desire.'" *Literature Interpretation Theory* 13(2): 117–37.

Adam, Ken. 2004. "For Him, Everything Was Possible." In *Stanley Kubrick*, edited by Hans-Peter Reichmann, 88–95. Frankfurt: Deutsches Filminstitut.

Adler, Renata. 1968. "*2001* Is Up, Up and Away." *New York Times* (April 4). https://archive.nytimes.com/www.nytimes.com/library/film/040468kubrick-2001.html (accessed August 25, 2020).

Agel, Jerome. 1970. *The Making of Kubrick's 2001*. New York: Signet.

Alberge, Dalya. 2018. "Stanley Kubrick Never Paid for My Early Work as a Composer, Childhood Friend Reveals." *Guardian* (October 20). https://www.theguardian.com/film/2018/oct/20/stanley-kubrick-refused-to-pay-composer-friend-gerald-fried (accessed August 25, 2020).

Albrecht, Donald and Sean Corcoran. 2018. "Through a Different Lens: Stanley Kubrick Photographs." In *Through a Different Lens: Stanley Kubrick Photographs*, edited by Donald Albrecht and Sean Corcoran, 8–13. Cologne: Taschen.

Alison, Jane. 2003. "Stanley Kubrick's *Eyes Wide Shut*: A Masque Disguise." *PostScript* 23(1): 3–13.

Allen, Graham. 2015. "'The Unempty Wasps' Nest: Kubrick's *The Shining*, Adaptation, Chance, Interpretation." *Adaptation* 8(3): 361–71.

Allen, Richard. 2004. "Psychoanalytic Film Theory." In *A Companion to Film Theory*, edited by Toby Miller and Robert Stam, 123–45. Malden, MA: Blackwell.

Altman, Rick. 1999. *Film/Genre*. London and New York: Bloomsbury.

Andrew, Geoff. 2017. "*Paths of Glory*: Stanley Kubrick's First Film of Genius." https://www. bfi.org.uk/news-opinion/news-bfi/features/paths-glory-stanley-kubricks-first-film-genius (accessed August 25, 2020).

Anon. 1962. "Herbert Humdrum and Lullita." *Time* (June 22). http://content.time.com/time/magazine/article/0,9171,870001,00.html (accessed August 25, 2020).

Anon. 2009. "Unfolding the Aryan Papers." http://animateprojectsarchive.org/films/by_date/2009/unfolding (accessed September 3, 2019).

Anon. "Novum." 2015. *The Encyclopedia of Science Fiction*. http://www.sf-encyclopedia.com/entry/novum (accessed August 25, 2020).

Ardrey, Robert. 1961. *African Genesis*. London: Collins.

Aristotle. 1984. *The Complete Works of Aristotle*. 2 vols (ed. Jonathan Barnes). Princeton, NJ: Princeton University Press.

Aristotle. 1988. *The Politics*. Cambridge: Cambridge University Press.

Aristotle. 2012. *Poetica. I classici del pensiero libero. Greci e latini – 11*. Milano: BUR Rizzoli, RCS Media Group Divisione Quotidiani.

Armstrong, Andy. 2011. "Interview by Jamey DuVall." The Kubrick Series. http://www.thekubrickseries.com/index.htm (accessed August 25, 2020).

Arnheim, Rudolf. 1969. *Visual Thinking*. Berkeley, LA and London: University of California Press.

Arthur, Paul. 2001. "*A.I.: Artificial Intelligence*." *Film Comment* 37 (July–August): 22–23.

Astruc, A. 1988. "The Birth of a New Avant-Garde: La Camera-Stylo" (trans. Peter Graham). Reprinted in Peter Graham (ed.), *The New Wave*, 17–23. New York: Doubleday.

Atunas, Jose. 2012. "From Kubrick to Anderson: One-Point Perspective." https://www. provideocoalition.com/from-kubrick-to-anderson-one-point-perspective/ (accessed June 10, 2019).

Bakhtin, M. 1981. *The Dialogic Imagination: Four Essays* (ed. Michael Holquist; trans. Caryl Emerson). Austin: University of Texas Press.

Ballinger, Alexander and Danny Graydon. 2007. *The Rough Guide to Film Noir*. London: Rough Guides.

Bane, Charles. 2008. "The Art of War (Films): *Fear and Desire* and *Paths of Glory*." In *Stanley Kubrick: Essays on His Films and Legacy*, edited by Gary D. Rhodes, 29–38. Jefferson, NC: McFarland.

Banks, Gordon. 1990. *Kubrick's Psychopaths, Society and Human Nature in the Films*. http://www.visual-memory.co.uk/amk/doc/0004.html (accessed May 30, 2019).

Barham, J. 2009. "Incorporating Monsters: Music as Context, Character and Construction in Kubrick's *The Shining*." In *Terror Tracks: Music, Sound and Horror Cinema*, edited by P. Hayward, 137–61. London: Oakville.

Baron, Cynthia and Sharon Carnicke. 2008. *Reframing Screen Performance*. Ann Arbor: University of Michigan Press.

Barr, Charles. 1972. "*Straw Dogs, A Clockwork Orange* and the Critics." *Screen* 13(2): 17–32.

Barshad, Amos. 2015. "Sex, Death, and Kubrick: How 'Eyes Wide Shut' Changed Tom Cruise's Career." Grantland (July 28). http://grantland.com/hollywood-prospectus/sex-death-and-kubrick-how-eyes-wide-shut-changed-tom-cruises-career/ (accessed January 25, 2019).

Barthes, Roland. 1977. *Image, Music, Text* (ed. and trans. Stephen Heath). London: Fontana Press.

Baxter, John. 1997. *Stanley Kubrick*. New York: Carroll & Graf.

Baxter, Peter. 1984. "The One Woman." *Wide Angle* 6(1): 34–41.

Beguiristain, Mario. 2006. *The Actors Studio and Hollywood in the 1950s*. Lewiston, NY: Edwin Mellen Press.

Bell-Meterau, Rebecca. 2008. "The Three Faces of *Lolita*, or How I Learned to Stop Worrying and Love the Adaptation." In *Authorship in Film Adaptation*, edited by Jack Boozer, 203–28. Austin: University of Texas Press.

Bell-Meterau, Rebecca. 2016. "An Actor's Director: Kubrick and Star Performances." In *Critical Insights: Stanley Kubrick*, edited by Peter J. Bailey, 176–90. Ipswich, MA: Salem Press.

Bender, J. 1999. "Farewell to the Master." *Film Score Monthly* 4(8): 24–7.

Benson, Michael. 2018. *Space Odyssey: Stanley Kubrick, Arthur C. Clarke, and the Making of a Masterpiece*. New York: Simon and Schuster.

Bergan, Ronald. 2008. "Leonard Rosenman: Obituary." *Guardian* (March 16). https://www.theguardian.com/music/2008/mar/17/film.obituaries (accessed August 26, 2020).

Berger, John. 1972. *Ways of Seeing*. London: BBC/Penguin.

Bernstein, Jeremy. 1966. Transcript of Kubrick interview with Jeremy Bernstein. http://kubrickarticles.blogspot.com/2017/07/sk-transcript-of-kubrick-interview-with.html (accessed August 25, 2020).

Bernstein, Jeremy. 2001. "Profile: Stanley Kubrick." In *Stanley Kubrick Interviews*, edited by Gene D. Phillips, 21–47. Jackson: University Press of Mississippi.

Bertram, John and Yuri Leving. 2013. *Lolita: The Story of a Cover Girl: Vladimir Nabokov's Novel in Art and Design*. Cincinnati, OH: F+W Publishers.

Bingham, Dennis. 1996. "The Displaced Auteur: A Reception of *The Shining*." In *Perspectives on Stanley Kubrick*, edited by Mario Falsetto, 284–306. New York: GK Hall.

Bingham, Dennis. 2004. "Kidman, Cruise, and Kubrick: A Brecthian Pastiche." In *More Than a Method: Trends and Traditions in Contemporary Film Performance*, edited by Cynthia L. Baron, Diane Carson, and Frank P. Tomasulo, 247–74. Detroit, MI: Wayne State University Press.

Bizony, Piers. 2014. *The Making of Stanley Kubrick's 2001: A Space Odyssey*. Cologne: Taschen.

Blakemore, Bill. 1987. "Kubrick's *Shining*'s Secret." *Washington Post* (July 12).

Bodde, G. 2002. *Musik in den Filmen von Stanley Kubrick*. Osnabruck: Der Andere Verlag.

Bogdanovich, Peter. 2000. "Foreword." In *The Complete Kubrick*, edited by David Hughes, xi–xii. London: Virgin.

Bond, J. 1999a. "A Clockwork Composer: Wendy Carlos." *Film Score Monthly* 4(3): 18–23.

Bond, J. 1999b. "Once in a Lifetime: Interview with Jocelyn Pook." *Film Score Monthly* 4(8): 24–5.

Bordwell, David. 1979. "The Art Cinema as a Mode of Film Practice." *Film Criticism* 4(1): 56–64.

Bordwell, David. 2001. *Narration in the Fiction Film*. New York: McGraw-Hill.

Bordwell, David. 2008. "Doing Film History." http://www.davidbordwell.net/essays/doing. php (accessed July 29, 2019).

Bordwell, David and Kristin Thompson. 2015. *Film Art: An Introduction*. New York: McGraw-Hill.

Bordwell, David, Thompson Kristin, and Jeff Smith. 2020. *Film Art: An Introduction*. 12th edn. New York: McGraw-Hill.

Borgna, Eugenio. 2015. *Il tempo e la vita*. Milano: Feltrinelli.

Bould, Mark. 2002. "Kubrick's Artistic Spectacle. Review of *Kubrick's Cinema Odyssey*, by Michel Chion." *Science Fiction Studies* 29(2): 279–82.

Boczar, Amanda Chapman. 2015. "Economics, Empathy, and Expectation. History and Representation of Rape and Prostitution in Late 1980s Vietnam War Films." *In Selling Sex on Screen: From Weimar Cinema to Zombie Porn*, edited by Catriona McAvoy and Karen A. Ritzenhoff, 69–93. Lanham, MD: Rowman and Littlefield.

Braae, Nick. 2015. "We'll Meet Again: Musical Design in the Films of Stanley Kubrick. Review of We'll Meet Again… by Kate McQuiston." *Popular Music & Society* 38(4): 536–8.

Bradshaw, Peter. 2000. "The Old Ultra-Violence." *Guardian* (March 3). https://www. theguardian.com/film/2000/mar/03/fiction (accessed August 25, 2020).

Bradshaw, Peter. 2001. "*A.I. Artificial Intelligence*." *Guardian* (September 21). https://www. theguardian.com/film/2001/sep/21/1 (accessed November 10, 2018).

Breckman, Warren. 2017. "The Fortunes of Freud." *New Republic* (June 1). https:// newrepublic.com/article/143027/fortunes-freud (accessed August 25, 2020).

Broderick, Mick. 2017a. *Reconstructing Strangelove: An Archaeology of Stanley Kubrick's "Nightmare Comedy"*. New York: Columbia University Press/Wallflower.

Broderick, Mick. 2017b. "Post-Kubrick: On the Filmmaker's Influence and Legacy." *Screening the Past* 42. http://www.screeningthepast.com/2017/09/post-kubrick-on-the-filmmakers-influence-and-legacy (accessed August 25, 2020).

Broderick, Mick. 2019a. *The Kubrick Legacy*. London: Routledge.

Broderick, Mick. 2019b. "Kubrick on Screen." In *The Kubrick Legacy*, edited by Mick Broderick, 88–105. London and New York: Routledge.

Bruner, Jerome. 1991. "The Narrative Construction of Reality." *Critical Inquiry* 18(1): 1–21.

Buckland, Warren. 2006. *Directed by Steven Spielberg: Poetics of the Contemporary Hollywood Blockbuster*. New York and London: Continuum.

Burdick, Eugene and Harvey Wheeler. [1962] 1999. *Fail Safe*. New York: HarperCollins.

Burlingame, Jon. 1999. "Her Avant-Garde Tunes Are Getting 'Wide' Notice." *L.A. Times* (July 26). http://articles.latimes.com/1999/jul/26/entertainment/ca-59637 (accessed August 26, 2020).

Burgess, Anthony. 2012. "The Clockwork Condition." *New Yorker* 4&11 (May 28). https:// www.newyorker.com/magazine/2012/06/04/the-clockwork-condition (accessed August 25, 2020).

Burgess, Anthony. 2013. *A Clockwork Orange* (ed. Andrew Biswell). London: Penguin

Burgess, Jackson. 1972. "Review: *A Clockwork Orange*." *Film Comment* 25(3): 33–6.

Burr, Ty. 1999. "Ty Burr on Stanley Kubrick." *Entertainment Weekly* (March 16).

Burton, Margaret. 2008. "Performances of Jewish Identity, *Spartacus*." *Shofar* 27(1): 1–15.

Buscombe, Edward. 1973. "Ideas of Authorship." *Screen* 14(3): 75–85.

Butler, Judith. 1988. "Performative Acts and Gender Constitution: An Essay in Phenomenology and Feminist Theory." *Theatre Journal* 40(4): 519–31.

Cahill, Tim. 1987. "The *Rolling Stone* Interview: Stanley Kubrick in 1987." https://www.rollingstone.com/movies/movie-news/the-rolling-stone-interview-stanley-kubrick-in-1987-90904/ (accessed August 25, 2020).

Canby, Vincent. 1971. "*A Clockwork Orange* Dazzles the Senses and Mind." *New York Times* (December 20). https://www.nytimes.com/1971/12/20/archives/a-clockwork-orange-dazzles-the-senses-and-mind.html (accessed August 25, 2020).

Canby, Vincent. 1987. "Kubrick's *Full Metal Jacket*, on Vietnam." *New York Times* (June 26). https://archive.nytimes.com/www.nytimes.com/library/film/062687kubrick-jacket.html (accessed August 25, 2020).

Carlos, Wendy. 2000. "Farewell, Stanley Kubrick" (February 2). http://www.wendycarlos.com/kubrick.html (accessed August 26, 2020).

Carnicke, Sharon Marie. 2006. "The Material Poetry of Acting: 'Objects of Attention,' Performance Style, and Gender in *The Shining* and *Eyes Wide Shut*." *Journal of Film and Video* 58(1): 21–30.

Castle, Alison. 2004. "Stanley Kubrick's 'A.I.'" In *The Stanley Kubrick Archives*, edited by Alison Castle, 504–8. Cologne: Taschen.

Castle, Alison (ed.). 2009. *Stanley Kubrick's "Napoleon": The Greatest Movie Never Made*. London: Taschen.

Castle, Alison (ed.). 2016. *The Stanley Kubrick Archives*. Cologne: Taschen/Bibliotheca Universalis.

Castle, Alison (ed.). 2018. *The Stanley Kubrick Archives*. Hohenzollernring: Taschen.

Castle, Robert and Stephen Donatelli. 1998. "Full Metal Jacket: Kubrick's Ulterior War." *Film Comment* (September/October): 24–8.

Cavell, Stanley. 1979. *The World Viewed: Reflections on the Ontology of Film*. Cambridge, MA: Harvard University Press.

Child, Ben. 2014. "Kubrick 'Did Not Deserve' Oscar for *2001* Says FX Master Douglas Trumbull." *Guardian* (September 4). https://www.theguardian.com/film/2014/sep/04/stanley-kubrick-did-not-deserve-oscar-2001-special-effects-douglas-trumbull (accessed August 25, 2020).

Chion, Michel. 2001. *Kubrick's Cinema Odyssey*. London: British Film Institute.

Chion, Michel. 2002. *Eyes Wide Shut*. London: British Film Institute.

Chion, Michel. 2006. *Eyes Wide Shut*. London: British Film Institute.

Chion, Michel. 2008. *Eyes Wide Shut*. London, British Film Institute.

Church, David. 2006. "The 'Cult' of Kubrick: Cult Cinema in the Land of the Auteur." *Offscreen* 10(5). http://offscreen.com/view/cult_kubrick (accessed September 30, 2018).

Ciment, Michel. 1982. *Kubrick on The Shining: An Interview with Michel Ciment*. http://www.visual-memory.co.uk/amk/doc/interview.ts.html (accessed May 30, 2019).

Ciment, Michel. 1983. *Kubrick*. London: William Collins.

Ciment, Michel. 2001. *Kubrick: The Definitive Edition*. New York and London: Faber and Faber.

Ciment, Michel. 2003a. *Kubrick* (trans. Gilbert Adair). New York: Holt, Rinehart, & Winston.

Ciment, Michel. 2003b. "The State of Cinema." http://unspokencinema.blogspot.com/2006/10/state-of-cinema-m-ciment.html (accessed June 18, 2019).

Clarke, Arthur C. 1951. *The Sentinel*. London: Voyager.

Clarke, Arthur C. 1953. *Childhood's End*. London: Ballantine Books.

Clarke, Arthur C. 1972. *The Lost Worlds of 2001*. New York: Signet Classics.

Clarke, Arthur C. 2009. "Back to *2001*." In *2001: A Space Odyssey*, edited by Arthur C. Clarke, ix–xix. London: Orbit.

Clarke, Arthur C. [1968] 2016. *2001: A Space Odyssey*. London: The Folio Society.

Clines, Francis X. 1987. "Stanley Kubrick's Vietnam." *New York Times*. https://www. nytimes.com/1987/06/21/movies/stanley-kubrick-s-vietnam.html (accessed August 25, 2020).

Cobb, Humphrey. 2010. *Paths of Glory* (ed. James H. Meredith). London: Penguin.

Cocks, Geoffrey. 2003. "Stanley Kubrick's Dream Machine: Psychoanalysis, Film, and History." *Annual of Psychoanalysis* 31: 33–45.

Cocks, Geoffrey. 2004. *The Wolf at the Door: Stanley Kubrick, History, and the Holocaust*. New York: Peter Lang.

Cocks, Geoffrey. 2006. "Death by Typewriter, Stanley Kubrick, the Holocaust, and *The Shining*." In *Depth of Field: Stanley Kubrick, Film, and the Uses of History*, edited by Geoffrey Cocks, James Diedrick, and Glen Perusek, 185–217. Madison: University of Wisconsin Press.

Cocks, Geoffrey. 2013. "Indirected by Stanley Kubrick." *Post Script* 32(2): 20–35.

Code, David. 2010. "Rehearing *The Shining*: Musical Undercurrents in the Overlook Hotel." In *Music in the Horror Film: Listening to Fear*, edited by Neil Lerner, 133–51. New York: Routledge.

Coëgnarts, Maarten. 2017. "Stanley Kubrick and the Art of Embodied Meaning-Making in Film." *Cinergie* 12: 53–71.

Cohen, Alexander. 1995. "*A Clockwork Orange* and the Aestheticization of Violence." http://www.visual-memory.co.uk/amk/doc/0025.html (accessed July 5, 2019).

Collins, R. 2014. "*A.I.* Revisited: A Misunderstood Classic." *Daily Telegraph* (October 28). https://www.telegraph.co.uk/culture/film/11189723/AI-revisited-a-misunderstood-classic.html (accessed September 4, 2018).

Combs, Richard. 1980. "Review of *The Shining*." *Monthly Film Bulletin* 47(562): 221–2.

Conard, Mark T. 2007. "Chaos, Order, and Morality: Nietzsche's Influence on *Full Metal Jacket*." In *The Philosophy of Stanley Kubrick*, edited by Jerold J. Abrams, 33–47. Lexington: University Press of Kentucky.

Conrich, Ian and Estella Tincknell. 2006. *Film's Musical Moments*. Edinburgh: Edinburgh University Press.

Cook, Brian. 2012. "Interview by Jamey DuVall." The Kubrick Series. http://www. thekubrickseries.com/index.htm (accessed August 25, 2020).

Cook, D. A. 2007. *Lost Illusions: American Cinema in the Shadow of Watergate and Vietnam, 1970–1979*. Berkeley: University of California Press.

Cook, Pam and Mieke Bernink. 1999. *The Cinema Book*. London: British Film Institute.

Cook, William. 2019. "Slow Burn: Why the Languid *Barry Lyndon* Is Kubrick's Masterpiece." *BBC Arts* (April 25). https://www.bbc.co.uk/programmes/articles/ 3lWVw91r3xlvZyN10rnhqqj/slow-burn-why-the-languid-barry-lyndon-is-kubrick-s-masterpiece (accessed August 25, 2020).

Cooke, Elizabeth F. 2007. "Understanding the Enemy: The Dialogue of Fear in *Fear and Desire* and *Dr. Strangelove*." In *The Philosophy of Stanley Kubrick*, edited by Jerold J. Abrams, 9–31. Lexington: University Press of Kentucky.

Corrigan, Timothy. 1991. *A Cinema without Walls: Movies and Culture after Vietnam*. London: Routledge.

Corrigan, Timothy. 2002. "The Commerce of Auteurism." In *Film and Authorship*, edited by Virginia Wright Wexman, 96–111. New Brunswick, NJ: Rutgers University Press.

Cossar, Harper. 2005. "The Revenge of the Repressed: Homosexuality as Other in *The Killing*." *Quarterly Review of Film and Video* 22(2): 145–54.

Coyle, Wallace. 1980. *Stanley Kubrick: A Guide to References and Resources*. Boston and London: G. K. Hall.

Crawford, Jane. 2018. "Childwickbury Box List for Researchers." Stanley Kubrick Archive, University of the Arts London.

Creed, Barbara. 1993. *The Monstrous-Feminine: Film, Feminism, Psychoanalysis*. New York: Routledge.

Croce, Arlene. 1962. "*Lolita*." *Sight and Sound* (Autumn): 191–2.

Crone, Rainer. 2005. *Stanley Kubrick: Drama & Shadows*. London: Phaidon Press.

Crowther, Bosley. 1953. "*Fear and Desire*, Tale of War Fashioned by Young Film Newcomers, at Guild." *New York Times* (April 1). https://archive.nytimes.com/www.nytimes.com/library/film/040153kubrick-fear.html (accessed August 25, 2020).

Crowther, Bosley. 1957. "Shameful Incident of War; *Paths of Glory* Has Premiere at Victoria." *New York Times* (December 26). https://www.nytimes.com/1957/12/26/archives/screen-shameful-incident-of-war-paths-of-glory-has-premiere-at.html (accessed August 25, 2020).

Crowther, Bosley. 1960. "*Spartacus* Enters the Arena: 3-Hour Production Has Premiere at DeMille." *New* York Times (October 7). https://www.nytimes.com/1960/10/07/archives/screen-spartacus-enters-the-arena3hour-production-has-premiere-at.html (accessed August 25, 2020).

Crowther, Bosley. 1962. "*Lolita*, Vladimir Nabokov's Adaptation of His Novel." *New York Times* (June 14). https://archive.nytimes.com/www.nytimes.com/library/film/061462kubrick-lolita.html (accessed August 25, 2020).

Cumming, Alan. 2013. "Alan Cumming on the First Time He Met Stanley Kubrick." https://www.youtube.com/watch?v=I_KA0gB13KU (accessed August 25, 2020).

Curtis, Tony. 1993. *The Autobiography*. New York: William Morrow.

D'Alessandro, Emilio. 2016. *Stanley Kubrick and Me*. New York: Arcade.

Dajka, Anna Friederike. 2019. "The Harfords' Relationship in Stanley Kubrick's *Eyes Wide Shut*." Paper delivered at the Behind *Eyes Wide Shut* Conference, London, December.

Daniels, Richard. 2015. "Selling the War Film: Syd Stogel and the *Paths of Glory* Press Files." In *Stanley Kubrick: New Perspectives*, edited by Tatjana Ljujić, Peter Krämer, and Richard Daniels, 81–97. London: Black Dog.

Danto, Arthur. 2009. *Andy Warhol*. New Haven, CT and London: Yale University Press.

Davis, Natalie Zemon. 2002. "Trumbo and Kubrick Argue History." *Raritan* 22(2): 173–90.

Davisson, Darrell D. 2009. *Art after the Bomb: Iconographies of Trauma in Late Modern Art*. Bloomington, IN: Author House.

Deaca, Mircea. 2020. "Coping with the Unknown." In *After Kubrick: A Filmmaker's Legacy*, edited by Jeremi Szaniawski, 231–41. London and New York: Bloomsbury.

Deana, Michele Pavan. 2017. "Epicentre of an Earthquake: The Literary Sources of *Full Metal Jacket* (1987)." *Historical Journal of Film, Radio and Television*. https://doi.org/10.1080/01439685.2017.1342331.

Decter, Midge. 1999. "The Kubrick Mystique." *Commentary* (September).

Deleyto, Celestino. 2006. "1999, A Closet Odyssey: Sexual Discourses in 'Eyes Wide Shut.'" *Atlantis* 28(1): 29–43.

Deleuze, Gilles. 1989. *Cinema 2: Time Image* (trans. Hugh Tomlinson and Robert Galeta). Minneapolis: University of Minnesota Press.

Deleuze, Gilles. 2003. *Cinema 2: The Time-Image* (trans. Hugh Tomlinson and Robert Galeta). Minneapolis: University of Minnesota Press.

Deleuze, Gilles. 2005. *Cinema 2: The Time-Image* (trans. Hugh Tomlinson and Robert Galeta). London: Continuum.

Deleuze, Gilles. 2014. *Cinema 1: The Movement Image* (trans. Hugh Tomlinson and Barbara Habberjam). London: Bloomsbury.

Dempsey, Michael. 1976. "Review: *Barry Lyndon* by Stanley Kubrick." *Film Quarterly* 30(1): 49–54.

Denby, David. 2001. "Face/Off." *New Yorker* (July 2): 86–7.

DeRosia, Margaret. 2003. "An Erotics of Violence: Masculinity and (Homo)sexuality in Stanley Kubrick's *A Clockwork Orange*." In *Stanley Kubrick's A Clockwork Orange*, edited by Stuart Y. McDougal, 61–84. Cambridge and New York: Cambridge University Press.

Dery, Mark. 2012. *I Must Not Think Bad Thoughts: Drive-by Essays on American Dread, American Dreams*. Minneapolis: University of Minnesota Press.

Desser, David and Lester D Friedman. 2003. *American Jewish Filmmakers*. Chicago: University of Illinois Press.

Dews, Peter. 2018. "The Idea of Hope." *New Left Review* 112 (July/August): 99–129.

Dickstein, Morris. 1984. "The Aesthetics of Fright." In *Planks of Reason: Essays on the Horror Film*, edited by Barry Keith Grant and Christopher Sharrett, 50–61. Lanham, MD: Scarecrow Press.

Didi-Huberman, Georges. 2008. *Images in Spite of All: Four Photographs from Auschwitz*. Chicago: University of Chicago Press.

Doherty, Thomas. 1996. "*Full Metal Jacket*: Stanley Kubrick's Combat Movie." In *Perspectives on Stanley Kubrick*, edited by Mario Falsetto, 307–16. New York: G. K. Hall.

Dombrowski, Lisa. 2014. "Postwar Hollywood, 1947–1967." In *Cinematography*, edited by Patrick Keating, 60–84. New Brunswick, NJ: Rutgers University Press.

Donhauser, Whitney W. 2018. "Preface." In *Through a Different Lens: Stanley Kubrick Photographs*, edited by Donald Albrecht and Sean Corcoran, 6. Cologne: Taschen.

Donnelly, Kelvin J. 2005. *The Spectre of Sound: Music in Film and Television*. London: British Film Institute.

Donnelly, Kevin. 2018. *The Shining*. New York: Columbia University Press/Wallflower.

Doss, Erika. 2009. *Twentieth-Century American Art*. New York: Oxford University Press.

Douglas, Kirk. 1988. *The Ragman's Son*. New York: Pocket Books.

Dovey, Lindiwe. 2008. "*Eyes Wide Shut*; Kubrick and the Representation of Gender." In *Stanley Kubrick: Essays on His Films and Legacy*, edited by Gary D. Rhodes, 170–81. Jefferson, NC: McFarland.

DSM-5. 2013. *Pedophilic Disorder DSM-5*. New York: American Psychiatric Publishing

Duffy, Martha and Richard Schickel. 2001. "Kubrick's Grandest Gamble: *Barry Lyndon*." In *Stanley Kubrick: Interviews*, edited by Gene D. Phillips, 159–70. Jackson: University Press of Mississippi.

Duncan, Paul. 2003. *Stanley Kubrick: The Complete Films*. Berlin and London: Taschen.

Dunne, Nathan. 2013. *Lichtenstein: A Retrospective*. https://www.tate.org.uk/context-comment/articles/wow (accessed June 25, 2020).

Durgnat, Raymond. 2011. *A Mirror for England*. 2nd edn. London: British Film Institute.

Eagleton, Terry. 2015. *Hope without Optimism*. New Haven and London: Yale University Press.

Eberl, Jason. 2007. "'Please Make Me a Real Boy': The Prayer of the Artificially Intelligent." In *The Philosophy of Stanley Kubrick*, edited by Jerold J. Abrams, 235–46. Lexington: University Press of Kentucky.

Ebert, Roger. 1972. *A Clockwork Orange*. https://www.rogerebert.com/reviews/a-clockwork-orange-1972 (accessed August 25, 2020).

Ebert, Roger. 1997. "*2001: A Space Odyssey*." *Chicago Sun-Times* (March 27). http://rogerebert.suntimes.com/apps/pbcs.dll/article?AID=/19970327/REVIEWS08/401010362/1023 (accessed August 27, 2020).

Edwards, Paul. 2013. "The Life and Myths of Stanley Kubrick." http://www.deathbyfilms.com/the-life-and-myth-of-stanley-kubrick (accessed August 25, 2020).

Egan, Kate. 2015. "Precious Footage of the Auteur at Work: Framing, Accessing, Using, and Cultifying Vivian Kubrick's 'Making the Shining.'" *New Review of Film and Television Studies* 13(1): 1–20.

Eisenstein, Sergei. 1942. *The Film Sense* (trans. Jay Leyda). New York: Harcourt.

Elsaesser, Thomas. 2004. "Evolutionary Imagineer: Stanley Kubrick's Authorship." In *Stanley Kubrick*, edited by Hans-Peter Reichmann, 136–48. Frankfurt: Deutsches Filminstitut.

Elsaesser, Thomas. 2018. *European Cinema and Continental Philosophy: Film as Thought Experiment*. London and New York: Bloomsbury.

Elsaesser, Thomas. 2020. "Stanley Kubrick's Prototypes: The Author as World-Maker." In *After Kubrick: A Filmmaker's Legacy*, edited by Jeremi Szaniawski, 29–50. London and New York: Bloomsbury.

Eugeni, Ruggero. 2017. *Invito al cinema di Kubrick*. Milano: Mursia.

Evangelista, Chris. 2018. "With 'A.I.' and 'Minority Report,' Steven Spielberg Redefined His Work for a New Century." https://www.slashfilm.com/spielberg-ai-and-minority-report/ (accessed September 4, 2018).

Eyes on Cinema. 2016. "Johanna ter Steege on Stanley Kubrick and His Unmade Film THE ARYAN PAPERS." https://www.youtube.com/watch?v=NfKw1Q_k5fc https://www.commentarymagazine.com/articles/the-kubrick-mystique/ (accessed August 25, 2020).

Falsetto, Mario. 2001. *Stanley Kubrick: A Narrative and Stylistic Analysis*. 2nd edn. Westport, CT: Praeger.

Fehr, R. 1977. Letter to J. Harlan, 12 December. Stanley Kubrick Archive, University of the Arts London.

Feldmann, Hans. 1976. "Kubrick and His Discontents." *Film Quarterly* 30(1): 12–19.

Fenwick, James. 2017. *Stanley Kubrick: Producers and Production Companies*. PhD thesis, De Montfort University. https://www.dora.dmu.ac.uk/bitstream/handle/2086/18210/Stanley%20Kubrick%20as%20Producer.pdf (accessed August 25, 2020).

Fenwick, James. 2018. *Understanding Kubrick's 2001 A Space Odyssey*. Bristol: Intellect.

Fenwick, James. 2020. "Kirk Douglas and Stanley Kubrick: Reconsidering a Creative and Business Partnership." In *A Critical Companion to Stanley Kubrick*, edited by Elsa Colombani. Lanham, MD: Lexington Books.

Fenwick, James, I.Q. Hunter, and Elisa Pezzotta. 2017a. "Stanley Kubrick: A Retrospective. Introduction." *Cinergie – Il cinema e le altre arti* 12: 1–7.

Fenwick, James, I.Q. Hunter, and Elisa Pezzotta. 2017b. "Introduction: The Stanley Kubrick Archive: A Dossier of New Research." *Historical Journal of Film, Radio and Television* 37(3): 367–72.

Fischer, Volker. 2004. "Designing the Future: On Pragmatic Forecasting in *2001. A Space* Odyssey." In *Stanley Kubrick*, edited by Hans-Peter Reichmann, 103–19. Frankfurt: Deutsches Filminstitut.

Foster, Hal. 1996. "Death in America." *October* 75: 36–59.

Foucault, Michel. 1977. "What Is an Author?". In *Language Counter-Memory Practice Selected Essays and Interviews*, edited and translated by D. F. Bouchard, 113–38. New York: Cornell University Press.

Frayling, Christopher. 2015. *The 2001 File: Harry Lange and the Design of the Landmark Science Fiction Film*. London: Reel Art Press.

Freedman, Carl. 1998. "Kubrick's *2001* and the Possibility of a Science-Fiction Cinema." *Science Fiction Studies* 25(2): 300–318.

Freedman, Carl. 2008. "Untitled Review of James Naremore, *On Kubrick*." *Science Fiction Film and Television* 1(1): 133–8.

Freud, Sigmund. 1922. "Some Neurotic Mechanisms in Jealousy, Paranoia and Homosexuality." In *The Standard Edition of the Complete Psychological Works of Sigmund Freud, Vol. 18*, edited and translated by J. Strachey, 221–4. London: Hogarth Press.

Frewin, Anthony. 2005. "Stanley Kubrick: Writers, Writing, Reading." In *The Stanley Kubrick Archives*, edited by Alison Castle, 514–19. London: Taschen.

Frewin, Anthony. 2015. *A Collection of Stanley Kubrick's Favorite Things*. http://flavorwire. com/529951/a-collection-of-stanley-kubricks-favorite-things/view-all (accessed May 30, 2019).

Frewin, Anthony. 2018. *2001: Beyond 50-Film Symposium*. https://www.youtube.com/ watch?v=hF2Y9A4_yAI (accessed August 25, 2019).

Fried, Gerald. 2003. Interview by Karen Herman, 26 June. https://interviews. televisionacademy.com/interviews/gerald-fried (accessed October 15, 2018).

Friedman, Lester D. 2007. *Citizen Spielberg*. Urbana: University of Illinois Press.

Frontiere, D. 1973. Letter to J. Harlan, 2 July. Stanley Kubrick Archive, University of the Arts London.

Fulford, R. 1974. *Marshall Delaney at the Movies: The Contemporary World as Seen on Film*. Toronto: Peter Martin.

Garcìa Mainar, Luis M. 1999. *Narrative and Stylistic Patterns in the Films of Stanley Kubrick*. New York: Camden House.

Gelmis, Joseph. 1970a. *The Film Director as Superstar*. New York: Doubleday.

Gelmis, Joseph. 1970b. "The Film Director as Superstar: Stanley Kubrick." In *Stanley Kubrick: Interviews*, edited by Gene D. Phillips, 80–104. Jackson: University Press of Mississippi.

Gelmis, Joseph. 1972. "What Is a Man?' Five Views of Stanley Kubrick's *A Clockwork Orange*." *Sound on Film* 18.

Gelmis, Joseph. 2001. "The Film Director as Superstar: Stanley Kubrick". In *Stanley Kubrick Interviews*, edited by Gene D. Phillips, 80–105. Jackson: University of Mississippi Press.

Gengaro, Christine Lee. 2013. *Listening to Stanley Kubrick: The Music in His Films*. Lanham, MD: Scarecrow Press.

Ghislotti, Stefano. 2012. *Film Time: le dimensioni temporali della visione*. Bergamo: Bergamo University Press.

Gilbey, Ryan. 2016. "Stanley Kubrick's *Barry Lyndon*: 'It Puts a Spell on People.'" *Guardian* (July 14). https://www.theguardian.com/film/2016/jul/14/stanley-kubrick-barry-lyndon-put-spell-on-people (accessed August 25, 2019).

Gilliatt, Penelope. 1968. "After Man", *New Yorker* (April 13).

Godard, J. L. 1968. *Godard on Godard* (ed. J. Narboni and T. Milne). London: Da Capo.

Gorbman, Claudia. 2006. "Ears Wide Open: Kubrick's Music." In *Changing Tunes: The Use of Pre-Existing Music in Film*, edited by Phil Powrie and Robynn Jeananne Stilwell, 3–18. Aldershot: Ashgate.

Gorchakov, Nikolai M. 1954. *Stanislavski Directs*. New York: Funk & Wagnalls.

Ginsberg, Merle. 2012. "Nicole Kidman on Life with Tom Cruise through Stanley Kubrick's Lens." *Hollywood Reporter* (October 24). https://www.hollywoodreporter.com/news/nicole-kidman-stanley-kubricks-lens-382186 (accessed January 25, 2019).

Gothard, J. Andrew. 2016. "Through the Looking Glass: Stanley Kubrick and Narratology." In *Critical Insights: Stanley Kubrick*, edited by Peter J. Bailey, 59–71. Ipswich, MA: Salem Press.

Grant, Barry Keith. 2006. "Of Men and Monoliths: Science Fiction, Gender, and *2001: A Space Odyssey*." In *2001: A Space Odyssey: New Essays*, edited by Robert Kolker, 69–86. New York: Oxford University Press.

Grant, Barry Keith. 2007. *Film Genre: From Iconography to Ideology*. London: Wallflower Press.

Grant, Barry Keith. 2008. *Auteurs and Authorship: A Film Reader*. Malden, MA: Blackwell.

Grant, Catherine. 2009. "Auteur Machines? Auteurism and the DVD." In *Film and Television after DVD*, edited by James Bennett and Tom Brown, 101–15. New York: Routledge.

Greene, Andy. 2014. *Stephen King: The Rolling Stone Interview* (October 30). https://www.rollingstone.com/culture/culture-features/stephen-king-the-rolling-stone-interview-191529/ (accessed May 30, 2019).

Gretton, Viveca. 1990. "Cracks in the King's Armour: Stephen King, Stanley Kubrick and *The Shining*." *Cineaction* 19–20: 62–73.

Grove, Lloyd. 1987. "Stanley Kubrick, at a Distance." *Washington Post* (June 28): F1, F5.

Hameiri, Avigdor. 1952. *The Great Madness*. New York: Vantage Press.

Hanson, Ellis. 1993. "Technology, Paranoia and the Queer Voice." *Screen* 34(2): 137–61.

Hare, Robert. 1999. *Without Conscience: The Disturbing World of the Psychopaths among Us*. New York: Guilford Press.

Hare, Robert. 2003. *Manual for the Revised Psychopathy Checklist*. 2nd edn. Toronto, ON: Multi-Health Systems.

Harlan, Jan. 1973. Letter to H. B. Eggers, 29 August. Stanley Kubrick Archive, University of the Arts London.

Harlan, Jan. 2004. "Foreword." In *Stanley Kubrick*, edited by Hans-Peter Reichmann, 7–8. Frankfurt: Deutsches Filminstitut.

Harlan, Jan. 2005. "From *Wartime Lies* to 'Aryan Papers.'" In *The Stanley Kubrick Archives*, edited by Alison Castle, 509. Cologne: Taschen.

Harlan, Jan. 2011a. "Stanley Kubrick's *Napoleon*." In *Stanley Kubrick's "Napoleon": The Greatest Movie Never Made*, edited by Alison Castle, 15–19. Cologne: Taschen.

Harlan, Jan. 2011b. Interview by Christine Gengaro, April 20, London.

Harlan, Jan. 2015. "Interview: Jan Harlan, Producer for Stanley Kubrick." *Film Ireland* (March 20). http://filmireland.net/2015/03/20/interview-jan-harland-producer/ (accessed June 13, 2019).

Harlan, Jan and Jane M. Struthers. 2009. *A.I.: Artificial Intelligence: From Stanley Kubrick to Steven Spielberg: The Vision Behind the Film*. London: Thames & Hudson.

Harris, James. B. 2010. Interviewed by Jamey DuVall. The Kubrick Series. http://www.thekubrickseries.com/index.htm (accessed August 25, 2019).

Hasford, Gustav. 1979. *The Short-Timers*. New York: Harper and Row.

Hasford, Gustav. 1980. *The Short-Timers*. New York: Bantam Books.

Heath, Stephen. 1999. "Cinema and Psychoanalysis: Parallel Histories." In *Endless Night: Cinema and Psychoanalysis: Parallel Histories*, edited by Janet Bergstrom, 25–56. Berkeley: University of California Press.

Henderson, Sanya Shoilevska. 2003. *Alex North: Film Composer*. Jefferson, NC: McFarland.

Heimerdinger, J. 2007. "'I Have Been Compromised. I Am Not Fighting against It': Ligeti vs. Kubrick and the Music for *2001: A Space Odyssey*." *Journal of Film Music* 3(2): 127–43.

Herr, Michael. 2000a. *Kubrick*. New York: Grove.

Herr, Michael. 2000b. "Completely Missing Kubrick." *Vanity Fair* (April). http://mentalfoto.tripod.com/herr/herr.html (accessed August 25, 2019).

Herr, Michael. 2010, "Kubrick." *Vanity Fair* (April). https://www.vanityfair.com/hollywood/2010/04/kubrick-199908 (accessed August 25, 2019).

Heymann, Danièle. 2005. "Stanley Kubrick's Vietnam." In *The Stanley Kubrick Archives*, edited by Alison Castle, 476–9. Hong Kong: Taschen.

Hibbert, S. 1974. Letter to Jan Harlan. Stanley Kubrick Archive, University of the Arts London.

Higgins, Scarlett. 2018. "Purity of Essence in the Cold War: *Dr. Strangelove*, Paranoia, and Bodily Boundaries." *Textual Practice* 32(5): 799–820.

Hilberg, Raul. 1961. *The Destruction of the European Jews*. Chicago: Quadrangle.

Hill, Rodney. 2016. "*Barry Lyndon*." In *The Stanley Kubrick Archives*, edited by Alison Castle, 562–601. Cologne: Taschen.

Hill, Rodney F. 2020. "Kubrick's Inheritors: Aesthetics, Independence, and Philosophy in the Films of Joel and Ethan Coen." In *After Kubrick: A Filmmaker's Legacy*, edited by Jeremi Szaniawski, 67–85. London: Bloomsbury.

Hiller, J. 1985. *Cahiers du Cinéma: The 1950s: Neo-Realism, Hollywood, New Wave*. Cambridge, MA: Harvard University Press.

Hobbs, Thomas. 2018. "How *Eyes Wide Shut*'s Uniquely Unsettling Score Was Made." http://www.dazeddigital.com/music/article/41996/1/eyes-wide-shut-stanley-kubrick-soundtrack-jocelyn-pook-interview (accessed August 25, 2019).

Hoberman, J. 2013. "*The Shining* Is about What?" *Tablet Magazine* (March 28).

Hofsess, John. 1968. "*2001*, Take One." In *The Making of Kubrick's 2001*, edited by Jerome Agel, 243. New York: Signet.

Hofsess, John. 1976. "How I Learned to Stop Worrying and Love *Barry Lyndon*." *New York Times* (January 11). https://archive.nytimes.com/www.nytimes.com/library/film/011176kubrick-lyndon.html (accessed August 25, 2019).

Hoffman, Karen. 2007. "Where the Rainbow Ends: *Eyes Wide Shut*." In *The Philosophy of Stanley Kubrick*, edited by Jerold J. Abrams, 59–84. Lexington: University Press of Kentucky.

Holdsworth, Nick. 2016. "Cary Fukunaga in Talks to Direct HBO Stanley Kubrick Mini 'Napoleon', from Steven Spielberg." *Hollywood Reporter* (May 20). https://www.hollywoodreporter.com/live-feed/cary-fukunaga-talks-direct-hbo-895382 (accessed August 25, 2019).

Holt, Jason. 2007. "Existential Ethics: Where the *Paths of Glory* Lead." In *The Philosophy of Stanley Kubrick*, edited by Jerold J. Abrams, 49–56. Lexington: University Press of Kentucky.

Homer. 1991. *The Odyssey of Homer* (trans. Richmond Lattimore). New York: HarperPerennial.

Hornbeck, Elizabeth Jean. 2016. "Who's Afraid of the Big Bad Wolf? Domestic Violence in *The Shining*." *Feminist Studies* 42(3): 689–719.

Houston, Penelope. 1976. "*Barry Lyndon*." *Sight and Sound* (Spring): 77–80.

Howard, J. 1999. *Stanley Kubrick Companion*. London: B.T. Batsford.

Hubbert, Julie. 2014. "The Compilation Soundtrack from the 1960s to the Present." In *The Oxford Handbook of Film Music Studies*, edited by David Neumeyer, 291–318. New York: Oxford University Press.

Hughes, David. 2000. *The Complete Kubrick*. London: Virgin.

Hunter, I.Q. 2011. "*A Clockwork Orange*, Exploitation and Art Film." In *British Science Fiction Film and Television: Critical Essays*, edited by Tobias Hochsherf and James Leggott, 96–103. Jefferson, NC: McFarland.

Hunter, I.Q. 2015. "Introduction: Kubrick and Adaptation." *Adaptation* 8(3): 277–390.

Hunter, I.Q. 2016. *Cult Film as a Guide to Life: Fandom, Adaptation and Identity*. New York and London: Bloomsbury.

Hutchinson, Sean. 2017. "*Fear and Desire*: The Movie Stanley Kubrick Didn't Want You to See." http://mentalfloss.com/article/93924/fear-and-desire-movie-stanley-kubrick-didnt-want-you-see (accessed August 25, 2019).

Ide, Wendy. 2016. "*Barry Lyndon* Review." *Observer* (July 31). https://www.theguardian.com/film/2016/jul/31/barry-lyndon-review-stanley-kubrick (accessed August 25, 2019).

IMDb. 2015. "The Best Movies about INSANITY." https://www.imdb.com/list/ls075057360/ (accessed May 30, 2019).

Ingui, Chris. 2004. "Recalling Kubrick: Interview with Sydney Pollack." *GW Hatchet* (April 8). https://www.gwhatchet.com/2004/04/08/recalling-kubrick/ (accessed August 25, 2019).

Jackson, Kathy Merlock. 1986. *Images of Children in American Film: A Sociocultural Analysis*. Metuchen, NJ and London: The Scarecrow Press.

Jacobs, Evan. 2007. "Jan Harlan Creates *Stanley Kubrick: A Life in Pictures* (Exclusive)." https://movieweb.com/exclusive-jan-harlan-creates-stanley-kubrick-a-life-in-pictures/ (accessed August 25, 2019).

Jaffe, Ira. 2008. *Hollywood Hybrids: Mixing Genre in Contemporary Films*. Lanham, MD: Rowman and Littlefield.

Jaffe, Ira. 2014. *Slow Movies: Countering the Cinema of Action*. New York: Columbia University Press/Wallflower.

Jameson, Fredric. 1990. *Signatures of the Visible*. London and New York: Routledge.

Jameson, Fredric. 1992. *The Geopolitical Aesthetic*. London and New York: Routledge.

Jameson, Richard T. 1999. "Ghost Sonata." *Film Comment* 35(5): 27–8.

Janes, Dominic. 2011. "Clarke and Kubrick's *2001*: A Queer Odyssey." *Science Fiction Film and Television* 4(1): 57–78.

Jaunas, Vincent and Jean François Baillon (eds). 2017. "Stanley Kubrick, Nouveaux Horizons." *Miranda* 15. https://journals.openedition.org/miranda/11266#quotation (accessed August 25, 2019).

Jenkins, Greg. 1997. *Stanley Kubrick and the Art of Adaptation, Three Novels, Three Films*. Jefferson, NC: McFarland.

Jones, James Earl. 2004. "A Bombardier's Reflection on *Strangelove*." *Wall Street Journal* (November 16).

Jordan, Miriam and Julian Jason Haladyn. 2008. "Carnivalesque and Grotesque Bodies in *Eyes Wide Shut*." In *Stanley Kubrick: Essays on His Films and Legacy*, edited by Gary D. Rhodes, 182–95. Jefferson, NC: McFarland.

Joyce, Paul. 1996. *Stanley Kubrick: The Invisible Man*. London: Lucida Productions/ Channel 4.

Kael, Pauline. 1962. "Movie Chronicle: Little Men." *Partisan Review* 29(4): 564–77.

Kael, Pauline. 1969. "Trash, Art and the Movies." *Harper's Magazine* (February).

Kael, Pauline. 1972a. "The Current Cinema: Stanley Strangelove." *New Yorker* (January 1): 50–53.

Kael, Pauline. 1972b. "Stanley Strangelove." *New Yorker* (January 1). http://www.visual-memory.co.uk/amk//doc/0051.html?LMCL=d699op (accessed August 25, 2019).

Kael, Pauline. 1975. "*Barry Lyndon*: Kubrick's Gilded Age." *New Yorker* (December 29).

Kael, Pauline. 1980. "*The Shining*: Devolution." *New Yorker* (June 9): 130.

Kael, Pauline. 1987. "*Full Metal Jacket*: Ponderosa." *New Yorker* (July 13).

Kagan, Norman. 1989. *The Cinema of Stanley Kubrick*. New York: Continuum.

Kagan, Norman. 2000. *The Cinema of Stanley Kubrick*. 3rd edn. New York and London: Continuum and Bloomsbury.

Kandel, Eric. 2016. *Reductionism in Art and Brain Science: Bridging the Two Cultures*. New York: Columbia University Press.

Kaplan, M. 2017. "How Stanley Kubrick Transformed the Modern Box-Office Report (By Accident)." https://www.huffingtonpost.com /mike-kaplan/stanley-kubrick-box-office_b_1195323.html?guccounter=1 (accessed October 9, 2018).

Karp, Mackenzie. 2015. *Ethic Lost: Brutalism and the Regeneration of Social Housing Estates in Great Britain*. Master's thesis, University of Oregon.

Karr, Rick. 2018. "Here's How the Score of 'Apocalypse Now' Originally Sounded" (February 3). https://www.wvtf.org/post/heres-how-score-apocalypse-now-originally-sounded#stream/0. (accessed September 28, 2020).

Kauffmann, Stanley. 1968. "Lost in the Stars." *New Republic* (May 4). https://newrepublic.com/article/132297/lost-stars (accessed August 25, 2019).

Kauffmann, Stanley. 1987. "*Full Metal Jacket*: Blank Cartridge." *New Republic* (July 27).

Keller, Cote. 2018. "Stanley Kubrick and the Evolution of Critical Consensus." *Global Tides* 12(1). https://digitalcommons.pepperdine.edu/cgi/viewcontent.cgi?article=1306&context=globaltides (accessed August 25, 2019).

Kiefer, Bernd. 2014. "Chess Games in the Boxing Ring: Stanley Kubrick's Early Work." In *Stanley Kubrick*, edited by Maja Keppler and Hans-Peter Reichmann, 28–43. Frankfurt am Main: Deutsches Filmmuseum.

Kilker, Robert. 2006. "All Roads Lead to the Abject: The Monstrous Feminine and Gender Boundaries in Stanley Kubrick's 'The Shining.'" *Literature/Film Quarterly* 34(1): 54–63.

King, Homay. 2008. "The Sadness of the Gaze: *Barry Lyndon*." In *Stanley Kubrick: Essays on His Films and His Legacy*, edited by Gary D. Rhodes, 123–35. Jefferson, NC: McFarland.

King, Stephen. 1977. *The Shining*. New York: Doubleday.

King, Stephen. 1989. "The *Playboy* Interview." In *The Stephen King Companion*, edited by George Beahm, 19–45. Kansas City: Andrews and McMeel.

Kirby, Jennifer. 2015. "A New Gang in Town: Kubrick's *A Clockwork Orange* as Adaptation and Subversion of the 1950's Juvenile Delinquent Cycle." *Literature/Film Quarterly* 43(4): 291–303.

Kiss, Miklós and Steven Willemsen. 2017. *Impossible Puzzle Films: A Cognitive Approach to Contemporary Complex Cinema*. Edinburgh: Edinburgh University Press.

Klinger, Barbara. 2010. "Becoming Cult: *The Big Lebowski*, Replay Culture and Male Fans." *Screen* 51(1): 19.

Kolker, Robert P. 1988. *A Cinema of Loneliness: Penn, Kubrick, Scorsese, Spielberg, and Altman*. Oxford: Oxford University Press.

Kolker, Robert P. 2000. *A Cinema of Loneliness: Penn, Stone Kubrick, Scorsese, Altman*. 3rd edn. Oxford: Oxford University Press.

Kolker, Robert P. (ed.). 2006. *Stanley Kubrick's 2001: A Space Odyssey: New Essays*. New York: Oxford University Press.

Kolker, Robert P. 2010. "Rage for Order." *Raritan* 30:1: 50–67.

Kolker, Robert P. 2011. *A Cinema of Loneliness: Penn, Stone Kubrick, Scorsese, Altman*, 4th edn. New York: Oxford University Press.

Kolker, Robert P. 2017. *The Extraordinary Image: Orson Welles, Alfred Hitchcock, Stanley Kubrick, and the Reimagining of Cinema*. Kindle ed. New Brunswick, NJ and London: Rutgers University Press.

Kolker, Robert P and Nathan Abrams. 2019. *Eyes Wide Shut: Stanley Kubrick and the Making of His Final Film*. New York: Oxford University Press.

Krämer, Peter. 2010. *2001: A Space Odyssey*. London: British Film Institute.

Krämer, Peter. 2011. *A Clockwork Orange*. Basingstoke and New York: Palgrave Macmillan.

Krämer, Peter. 2013a. "'Mein Führer, I Can Walk!' References to the Nazi Past in the Making and Reception of *Dr. Strangelove* (1964)." *Literatur in Wissenschaft und Unterricht* 46(2/3): 143–62.

Krämer, Peter. 2013b. "'To Prevent the Present Heat from Dissipating': Stanley Kubrick and the Marketing of *Dr. Strangelove*." *InMedia* 3. http://inmedia.revues.org/634 (accessed August 25, 2019).

Krämer, Peter. 2014a. "The Limits of Autonomy: Stanley Kubrick, Hollywood and Independent Filmmaking, 1950–53." In *American Independent Cinema: Indie, Indiewood and Beyond*, edited by Geoff King, Claire Molloy, and Yannis Tzioumakis, 153–64. London: Routledge.

Krämer, Peter. 2014b. *Dr. Strangelove or: How I Learnt to Stop Worrying and Love the Bomb*. London: British Film Institute.

Krämer, Peter. 2015a. "Adaptation as Exploration: Stanley Kubrick, Literature and *A.I. Artificial Intelligence*." *Adaptation: The Journal of Literature on Screen Studies* 18(3): 372–82.

Krämer, Peter. 2015b. "Complete Total Final Annihilating Artistic Control: Stanley Kubrick and Postwar Hollywood." In *Stanley Kubrick: New Perspectives*, edited by Tatjana Ljujić, Peter Krämer and Richard Daniels, 48–61. London: Black Dog.

Krämer, Peter. 2015c. "'What's It Going to Be, Eh?' Stanley Kubrick's Adaptation of Anthony Burgess' *A Clockwork Orange*." In *Stanley Kubrick: New Perspectives*, edited by Tatjana Ljujić, Peter Krämer, and Richard Daniels, 218–35. London: Black Dog.

Krämer, Peter. 2016. Video interview included on Eureka! Blu-ray edition of *Paths of Glory*. *Masters of Cinema* 155.

Krämer, Peter. 2017a. "Spielberg and Kubrick." In *A Companion to Steven Spielberg*, edited by Nigel Morris, 195–211. Oxford and Malden, MA: Wiley-Blackwell.

Krämer, Peter. 2017b. "Stanley Kubrick and the Internationalisation of Post-War Hollywood." *New Review of Film and Television Studies* 15(2): 250–69.

Krämer, Peter. 2017c. "Stanley Kubrick: Known and Unknown." *Historical Journal of Film, Radio and Television* 37(3): 373–95.

Kreider, Tim. 2000. "*Eyes Wide Shut*." *Film Quarterly* 53(3): 41–8.

Kreider, Tim. 2002. "*A.I. Artificial Intelligence.*" *Film Quarterly* 56(2): 32–9.

Kreider, Tim. 2006. "Introducing Sociology". In *Depth of Field: Stanley Kubrick, Film, and the Uses of History*, edited by Geoffrey Cocks, James Diedrick, and Glen Perusek, 280–97. Madison: University of Wisconsin Press.

Kuberski, Philip. 2012. *Kubrick's Total Cinema: Philosophical Themes and Formal Qualities.* London: Continuum.

Kubrick, Christiane. 2004. "Words of Greeting." In *Stanley Kubrick*, edited by Hans-Peter Reichmann, 6. Frankfurt: Deutsches Filminstitut.

Kubrick, Christiane. 2005. Interview with the author, April, Childwickbury.

Kubrick, Christiane. 2014. "Interview with Christiane Kubrick on Stanley Kubrick's "Voracious" Reading Habits." *Quill & Quire* (October 30). https://quillandquire.com/events/2014/10/30/qa-christiane-kubrick-on-stanley-kubricks-voracious-reading-habits/ (accessed August 25, 2019).

Kubrick, Katharina. 2016. "The Life and Legend of Stanley Kubrick: A Panel." Contemporary Jewish Museum, San Francisco, July 16. https://www.youtube.com/watch?v=tAeZhRwZwRM (accessed August 25, 2019).

Kubrick, Stanley. 1966. *The Other HAL.* London: The Kubrick Archive, SK/12/1/2/5. https://archiveshub.jisc.ac.uk/features/jul08d.shtml (accessed May 30, 2019).

Kubrick, Stanley. 1972. "Now Kubrick Fights Back." *New York Times* (February 27): D1.

Kubrick, Stanley. 1980. "Kubrick on *Barry Lyndon.*" Interviewed by Michel Ciment. http://www.visual-memory.co.uk/amk/doc/interview.bl.html (accessed October 15, 2018).

Kubrick, Stanley. 2005. "Words and Music." In *The Stanley Kubrick Archives*, edited by Alison Castle, 338–9. Cologne: Taschen.

Kubrick, Stanley. 2013. *Does IBM Know That HAL Is Psychotic?* http://www.lettersofnote.com/2013/01/does-ibm-know-that-hal-is-psychotic.html (accessed May 30, 2019).

Kubrick, Stanley 2016a. "Director's Notes." In *The Stanley Kubrick Archives*, edited by Alison Castle, 217–19. Cologne: Taschen.

Kubrick, Stanley. 2016b. "Words and Movies." In *The Stanley Kubrick Archives*, edited by Alison Castle, 272–5. Cologne: Taschen.

Kubrick, Stanley and Arthur C. Clarke. 1965. *2001: A Space Odyssey Script.* London: The Kubrick Archive, SK/12/1/2/2.

Labrecque, Jeff. 2014. "Malcolm McDowell on Stanley Kubrick: An All-Too-Human Artistic Genius." *Entertainment* (November 29). https://ew.com/article/2014/11/29/malcolm-mcdowell-stanley-kubrick-clockwork-orange/.

Lambert, Gavin. 1957–8. "*Paths of Glory* Reviewed." *Sight and Sound* (Winter): 144–5.

Latham, Rob. 2011. "'A Journey beyond the Stars': *2001* and the Psychedelic Revolution in 1960s Science Fiction." In *Science Fiction and the Prediction of the Future: Essays in Foresight and Fallacy*, edited by Gary Westfahl, Kim Yuen, and Amy Kit-sze Chan, 128–34. Jefferson, NC: McFarland.

Lehmann, Hans Thies. 2004. "Film/Theatre: Mask/Identities in *Eyes Wide Shut.*" In *Stanley Kubrick*, edited by Hans-Peter Reichmann, 232–43. Frankfurt: Deutsches Filminstitut.

Leibowitz, Flo and Lynn Jeffress. 1981. "Review of *The Shining.*" *Film Quarterly* 34(3): 45–51.

Levinson, Peter J. 2001. *September in the Rain: The Life of Nelson Riddle.* New York: Watson-Guptill.

Lewin, D. 1972. "Sex, Ultra Violence, Beethoven and Stanley Kubrick." *CinemaTV Today* (January 15): 8.

Lewis, Roger. 1994. *The Life and Death of Peter Sellers.* London: Arrow Books.

Lightman, Herb. A. 1980. "Photographing Stanley Kubrick's *The Shining*." *American Cinematographer* 61(9): 780–854.

Lionnet, L. 2004. "Mysteries of the Overlook." *Film Score Monthly* 9(1): 46–7.

Ljujić, Tatatjana. 2015. "Painterly Immediacy in Kubrick's *Barry Lyndon*." In *Stanley Kubrick: New Perspectives*, edited by Tatjana Ljujić, Peter Krämer, and Richard Daniels, 236–59. London: Black Dog.

Ljujić, Tatatjana, Peter Krämer, and Richard Daniels (eds). 2015. "Introduction." In *Stanley Kubrick: New Perspectives*, edited by Tatjana Ljujić, Peter Krämer, and Richard Daniels, 12–19. London: Black Dog.

LoBrutto, Vincent. 1995. *Stanley Kubrick: A Biography*. New York: Dutton.

LoBrutto, Vincent. 1997. *Stanley Kubrick: A Biography*. New York: Da Capo.

LoBrutto, Vincent 1999. *Stanley Kubrick: A Biography*. Cambridge, MA: Da Capo Press.

LoBrutto, Vincent. 2006. "The Written Word and the Very Visual Stanley Kubrick." In *Depth of Field, Stanley Kubrick, Film, and the Uses of History*, edited by Geoffrey Cocks, James Diedrick, and Glenn Perusek, 31–54. Madison: University of Wisconsin Press.

Loewy, Ronny. 2004. "'That Was about Success, Wasn't it?' Zum Projekt *Aryan Papers* (On the *Aryan Papers* project)." *Kinematograph* 19: 224–31.

Loren, Scott. 2008. "Mechanical Humanity, or How I Learned to Stop Worrying and Love the Android: The Posthuman Subject in *2001: A Space Odyssey* and *Artificial Intelligence: A.I.*" In *Stanley Kubrick: Essays on His Films and Legacy*, edited by Gary D. Rhodes, 211–31. Jefferson, NC: McFarland.

Luckhurst, Roger. 2013. *The Shining*. London: British Film Institute/Palgrave Macmillan.

Lucia, Cynthia. 2016. "Don't Ask, Don't Tell: Masculine Evasion and Crisis in Stanley Kubrick's *Eyes Wide Shut*." In *Critical Insights: Stanley Kubrick*, edited by Peter J. Bailey, 223–48. Ipswich, MA: Salem Press.

Lury, Karen. 2010. *The Child in Film: Tears, Fears and Fair Tales*. New York and London: Bloomsbury.

Ly, Lyn. 2017. "(Im)possible Futures: Liberal Capitalism, Vietnamese Sniper Women, and Queer Asian Possibility." *Feminist Formations* 29(1): 136–60.

Lyon, Peter. 1964. "The Astonishing Stanley Kubrick." *Holiday* 35(2): 147.

Lyons, Viktoria and Michael Fitzgerald. 2006. *Asperger Syndrome: A Gift or a Curse?* New York: Nova Science.

Macdonald, Dwight. 1962. "Of Nymphettes and Monsterettes." *Esquire* (September 1). https://classic.esquire.com/article/1962/9/1/of-nymphets-and-monsterettes (accessed August 25, 2019).

Macklin, F. Anthony. 1965. "Sex and *Dr. Strangelove*." *Film Comment* (Summer): 55–7.

Magid, Ron. 1999. "Quest for Perfection." *American Cinematographer* (October): 40–51. https://scrapsfromtheloft.com/2016/11/30/quest-for-perfection/ (accessed August 25, 2019).

Magistrale, Anthony. 2015. "Sutured Time, History and Kubrick's *The Shining*." In *Stanley Kubrick's The Shining: Studies in the Horror Film*, edited by Daniel Olson, 151–66. Lakewood, CO: Centipede Press.

Mainar, Louis M. Garcia. 1999. *Narrative and Stylistic Patterns in the Films of Stanley Kubrick*. Rochester, NY: Camden House.

Maitland, Sarah. 1999. "Arts: My Year with Stanley." *Independent* (March 12). https://www.independent.co.uk/arts-entertainment/arts-my-year-with-stanley-1079966.html (accessed August 25, 2019).

Maitland, Sarah. 2008. *In Full Metal Jacket: Between Good and Evil.* Documentary featurette for *Full Metal Jacket.* Deluxe Edition DVD. USA: Warner Bros.

Mamet, David. 2008. *Bambi vs. Godzilla: On the Nature, Purpose, and Practice of the Movie Business.* New York: Vintage.

Manchel, Frank. 1995. "What about Jack? Another Perspective on Family Relationships in Stanley Kubrick's *The Shining.*" *Literature/Film Quarterly* 23(1): 68–78.

Manes, Cara. 2012. "F-111, 1965." https://www.moma.org/explore/inside_out/2012/02/14/f-111-1965/ (accessed July 1, 2019).

Manon, Hugh S. 2008. "One Watches Sells: Kubrick's Films Noirs in Context." *In Stanley Kubrick: Essays on His Films and Legacy,* edited by Gary D. Rhodes, 47–64. Jefferson, NC: McFarland.

Martino, Caterina. 2018. "Negative/Positive, Metaphors of Photography in *2001: A Space Odyssey.*" In *Understanding Kubrick's 2001: A Space Odyssey: Representation and Interpretation,* edited by James Fenwick, 167–80. Bristol: Intellect.

Maslin, Janet. 1980. "Flaws Don't Dim *The Shining.*" *New York Times* (June 8). https://archive.nytimes.com/www.nytimes.com/library/film/060880kubrick-shining.html (accessed August 25, 2019).

Maslin, Janet. 1987. "Inside the 'Jacket': All Kubrick." *New York Times* (July 5). https://archive.nytimes.com/www.nytimes.com/library/film/070587kubrick-jacket.html (accessed August 25, 2019).

Mason, James. 1981. *Before I Forget.* London: Hamish Hamilton.

Mather, Philippe. 2013. *Stanley Kubrick at Look Magazine: Authorship and Genre in Photojournalism and Film.* Bristol: Intellect.

Mather, Philippe. 2015. "A Portrait of the Artist as a Young Man: The Influence of *Look* Magazine on Stanley Kubrick's Career as a Filmmaker." In *Stanley Kubrick: New Perspectives,* edited by Tatjana Ljujić, Peter Krämer, and Richard Daniels, 20–47. London: Black Dog.

Mayersberg, Paul. 1980–81. "The Overlook Hotel." *Sight & Sound* (Winter): 54–7.

McAvoy, Creion. 2010. Interview with Brian Cook (Assistant Director, *Barry Lyndon, The Shining, Eyes Wide Shut*), 19 September, London.

McAvoy, Catriona. 2015a. "The Uncanny, the Gothic and the Loner: Intertextuality in the Adaptation Process of *The Shining.*" *Adaptation* 8(3): 345–60.

McAvoy, Catriona. 2015b. "Creating *The Shining*: Looking beyond the Myths." In *Stanley Kubrick: New Perspectives,* edited by Tatjana Ljujić, Peter Krämer, and Richard Daniels, 280–307. London: Black Dog.

McAvoy, Catriona and Karen A. Ritzenhoff. 2015. "Machines, Mirrors, Martyrs, and Money: Prostitutes and Promiscuity in Steve McQueen's Shame and Stanley Kubrick's *Eyes Wide Shut.*" In *Selling Sex on Screen: From Weimar Cinema to Zombie Porn,* edited by Catriona McAvoy and Karen A. Ritzenhoff, 153–71. Lanham, MD: Rowman and Littlefield.

McDougal, Stuart Y. 2001. "*Eyes Wide Shut*: The Dream-Odyssey of Stanley Kubrick." *Cadernos De Tradução* 1(7): 189–202.

McDowell, Malcolm. 1973. "Interview with Malcolm McDowell on Stanley Kubrick's *A Clockwork Orange.*" https://www.youtube.com/watch?v=4gJvliX8W70 (accessed May 30, 2019).

McDowell, Malcolm. 1999. "He Was My Teacher and Tormentor." *Screen: The Observer* (March 14). http://www.visual-memory.co.uk/sk/memories/page2.htm (accessed May 30, 2019).

McDowell, Malcolm. 2011. *Commentary for A Clockwork Orange*. Anniversary edition Bluray. USA: Warner Bros.

McDowell, Malcolm. 2012. "Malcolm McDowell Shares His Stanley Kubrick Stories." https://www.youtube.com/watch?v=boQQRYMjLTc&t=6s (accessed May 30, 2019).

McEntee, Joy. 2015. "The End of Family in Kubrick's *A Clockwork Orange*." *Adaptation* 8(3): 321–9.

McEntee, Joy. 2016. "Paternal Responsibility and Bad Conscience in Adaptations of *The Shining*." *Journal of Adaptation in Film and Performance* 9(2): 175–86.

McGill, Hannah. 2019. "Eyes of the Beholder." *Sight and Sound* 29(12): 24–33.

McGowan, Todd. 2007. *The Real Gaze: Film Theory after Lacan*. Albany: State University of New York Press.

McGregor, C. 1972. "Nice Boy from the Bronx." *New York Times*. https://www.nytimes.com/1972/01/30/archives/article-1-no-title-kubrick-a-nice-boy-from-the-bronx.html (accessed August 25, 2019).

McQuiston, Kate. 2011. "'An Effort to Decide': More Research into Kubrick's Music Choices for *2001: A Space Odyssey*." *Journal of Film Music* 3(2): 145–54.

McQuiston, Kate. 2013. *We'll Meet Again: Musical Design in the Films of Stanley Kubrick*. New York and Oxford: Oxford University Press.

Mee, Laura. 2017. *The Shining*. Leighton Buzzard: Auteur.

Melia, Matt. 2017. "The Post-Kubrickian: Stanley Kubrick, Steven Spielberg, Adaptation and *A.I. Artificial Intelligence*." *Screening the Past* 42. http://www.screeningthepast.com/2017/09/the-post-kubrickian-stanley-kubrick-steven-spielberg-adaptation-and-a-i-artificial-intelligence/ (accessed August 25, 2019).

Merkley, Paul. 2007. "'Stanley Hates This But I Like It!': North vs. Kubrick on the Music for *2001: A Space Odyssey*." *Journal of Film Music* 2(1): 1–34.

Metlić, Dijana. 2019. "Stanley Kubrick: How Photography Shaped Film 'Reality.'" In *Interdisciplinary Companion to Photography*, edited by Dijana Metlić and Mia Cuk, 120–35. Novi Sad: Academy of Arts.

Metz, Walter. 2013. "Where Not to Hold Your Movie Class." *Contemporary Cinema* (April 7).

Michelson, Annette. 1969. "Bodies in Space: Film as Carnal Knowledge." *Artforum* 7(6): 54–63.

Miller, Mark. 1976. "Kubrick's Anti-Reading of *The Luck of Barry Lyndon*." *MLN* 91(6): 1360–79.

Milne, Tony. 1964. "*Dr Strangelove* Archive Review." *Sight and Sound* (Winter). https://www.bfi.org.uk/news-opinion/sight-sound-magazine/all/dr-strangelove-1964-stanley-kubrick-nuclear-cold-war-satire-tom-milne (accessed August 25, 2019).

Mills, Garry. 2015. "Leonard Rossiter: A Conviction in Comedy" (March 4). https://www2.bfi.org.uk/news-opinion/sight-sound-magazine/features/leonard-rossiter-conviction-comedy (accessed September 27, 2020).

Milsome, Douglas. 2011. Interviewed by Jamey DuVall. The Kubrick Series. http://www.thekubrickseries.com/index.htm (accessed August 25, 2019).

Minoff, Leon. 1963. "Nerve Center for a Nuclear Nightmare." *New York Times* (April 21). https://archive.nytimes.com/www.nytimes.com/library/film/042163kubrick-strange.html (accessed August 25, 2020).

Modine, Mathew. 2005. *Full Metal Jacket Diary*. New York: Rugged Land.

Modleski, Tania. 1988. "A Father Is Being Beaten: Male Feminism and the War Film." *Discourse* 10(2): 62–77.

Modleski, Tania. 2016. *The Women Who Knew Too Much: Hitchcock and Feminist Theory.* New York and Abingdon: Routledge.

Moholy-Nagy, Lázló. 1973. *Painting Photography Film* (trans. Janet Seligman). Cambridge, MA: MIT Press.

Molina Foix, Vicente. 1980. "An Interview with Stanley Kubrick." *El Pais*. http://www.archiviokubrick.it/english/words/interviews/1980mystery.html (accessed August 25, 2019).

Molina Foix, Vicente. 1999. "El artista maniático." *El País* (March 8). https://elpais.com/diario/1999/03/08/cultura/920847607_850215.html (accessed August 25, 2019).

Molina Foix, Vicente. 2005. "An Interview with Stanley Kubrick." In *The Stanley Kubrick Archives*, edited by Alison Castle, 460–64. Cologne: Taschen.

Molina Foix, Vicente. 2018. *Kubrick en casa*. Barcelona: Editorial Anagrama.

Morgenstern, J. 1962. "Really the Real Lolita?" *Sunday Herald Tribune*. http://www.archiviokubrick.it/english/words/interviews/1962really.html (accessed August 25, 2019).

Morrow, Justin. 2013. "It Was Nerve-Destroying: Legendary Set Designer Ken Adam Recalls Working with Kubrick." https://nofilmschool.com/2013/08/set-designer-sir-ken-adam-working-with-kubrick (accessed August 25, 2019).

Morrow, Justin. 2017. "Watch: Meet Stanley Kubrick's Beloved Cameras." http://nofilmschool.com/2017/06/stanley-kubrick-cameras-lenses-gear (accessed July 29, 2019).

Mulvey, Laura. 1972. "Death Gets a Kiss from Kubrick." *7 Days* (January 19): 21.

Mulvey, Laura. 1975. "Visual Pleasure and Narrative Cinema." *Screen* 16(3): 6–18.

Murphy, Robert. 1992. *Sixties British Cinema*. London: British Film Institute.

Musil, Robert. 1979. *The Man Without Qualities, Volume One* (trans. Eithne Wilkins and Ernst Kaiser). London: Picador.

Nabokov, Vladimir. 1964, "Nabokov's Interview." http://lib.ru/NABOKOW/Inter04.txt (accessed August 25, 2019).

Nabokov, Vladimir. [1955] 1970. *The Annotated Lolita* (ed. Alfred J. Appel). New York: McGraw-Hill.

Nabokov, Vladimir. 1997. *Lolita: A Screenplay*. New York: Vintage Books.

Naremore, James. 2007. *On Kubrick*. London: British Film Institute/Palgrave Macmillan.

Naremore, James. 2008. *More Than Night: Film Noir in Its Contexts*. Berkeley, LA and London: University of California Press.

Naremore, James. 2013. "No Other Country But the Mind." Booklet accompanying Eureka! Blu-ray edition of *Fear and Desire*. Masters of Cinema 51: 5–27.

Naremore, James. 2014. *An Invention without a Future: Essays on Cinema.* Berkeley: University of California Press.

Nashawaty, Chris. 2017. "Tom Cruise's Top 10 Best Movie Performances." *Entertainment Weekly* (October 2).

Neale, Steve. 1982. "Masculinity as Spectacle." *Screen* 24(6): 2–17.

Neale, Steve. 2000. *Genre and Hollywood*. New York and London: Routledge.

Nelson, Thomas Allen. 2000. *Kubrick: Inside a Film Artist's Maze*. Bloomington: Indiana University Press.

Nicholson, Amy. 2014. *Tom Cruise: Anatomy of an Actor*. London: Phaidon Press.

Nilsen, Hårvard Friis. 2011. "Desire and the Deterioration of Trust: The Political Warning in Stanley Kubrick's *Eyes Wide Shut*." In *Depoliticization: The Political Imaginary of Global Capitalism*, edited by Ingerid Straume and J. F. Humphrey, 261–78. Malmö: NSU Press.

Norden, Eric. 1968. "*Playboy* Interview: Stanley Kubrick." *Playboy* (September). https:// scrapsfromtheloft.com/2016/10/02/playboy-interview-stanley-kubrick/ (accessed August 25, 2019).

Norden, Eric. 2001. "*Playboy* Interview: Stanley Kubrick." In *Stanley Kubrick: Interviews*, edited by Gene D. Phillips, 47–74. Jackson: University Press of Mississippi.

Norden, Eric. 2016. "Stanley Kubrick Interview with *Playboy* Magazine." https:// scrapsfromtheloft.com/2016/10/02/playboy-interview-stanley-kubrick/ (accessed May 30, 2019).

Norman, Neil. 2003. "Alex's Most Treasured Reviews." *Evening Standard* (July 17).

Nornes, Abé Mark. 2007. *Cinema Babel—Translating Global Cinema*. Minneapolis: University of Minnesota Press.

Nowell-Smith, Geoffrey. 2003. *Visconti*. 3rd edn. London: British Film Institute.

O'Brien, G. 2001. "Very Special Effects." *New York Review of Books* 48(13). https://www. nybooks.com/articles/2001/08/09/very-special-effects/ (accessed November 13, 2018).

Odino, Simone. 2017. "'Dear Arthur, What Do You Think?' The Kubrick-Clarke Collaboration in Their Correspondence from the Smithsonian and London Archives." *Miranda* 15: 173–91.

OED. 2018. "OED 3: The Revisioning" (October). https://public.oed.com/blog/oed-3-the-revisioning-or-how-we-added-film-terms-in-the-september-2018-release/# (accessed November 10, 2018).

Ofengenden, Ari. 2015. "Agency, Desire, and Power in Schnitzler's Dream Novel and Kubrick's Adaptation *Eyes Wide Shut*." *CLCWeb: Comparative Literature and Culture* 17(2): 1–9.

Ollerman, Rick. 2017. "Crime à la White." In *The Snatchers/Clean Break*, edited by Rick Ollerman, 7–24. Eureka, CA: Stark House Press.

Ortner-Kreil, Lisa. 2014. "Eyes Wide Open: Stanley Kubrick als Fotografischer *Auteur*." In *Eyes Wide Open: Stanley Kubrick als Fotograf*, edited by Lisa Ortner-Kreil and Ingried Brugger, 6–13. Nuremberg: Verlag für moderne Kunst.

Osenlund, Kurt. 2018. "Stanley Kubrick's Apprentice Did Gay Film Research, Auditioned Dozens before Casting Alan Cumming in Eyes Wide Shut." https:// www.out.com/out-exclusives/2018/5/18/stanley-kubricks-apprentice-did-gay-film-research-auditioned-dozens-casting-alan-cumming-eyes-wide-shut (accessed May 30, 2019).

Owen, Wilfred. 1920. "The Parable of the Old Man and the Young." https://poets.org/ poem/parable-old-man-and-young (accessed August 25, 2019).

Palmer, R. Barton. 2006. "*2001*: The Critical Reception and the Generation Gap." In *Stanley Kubrick's 2001: A Space Odyssey: New Essays*, edited by Robert P. Kolker, 13–28. New York: Oxford University Press.

Palmer, R. Barton. 2007. "*The Shining* and Anti-Nostalgia: Postmodern Notions of History." *The Philosophy of Stanley Kubrick*, edited by Jerold J. Abrams, 201–18. Lexington: University Press of Kentucky.

Papson, Stephen. 2016. "Short-Circuiting Identification: The Pleasure and Displeasure of the Cinema of Stanley Kubrick." In *Critical Insights: Stanley Kubrick*, edited by Peter J. Bailey, 191–204. Ipswich, MA: Salem Press.

Paul, William. 1994. *Laughing Screaming: Modern Hollywood Horror and Comedy*. New York and Chichester: Columbia University Press.

Peldszus, Regina. 2015. "Speculative Systems: Kubrick's Interaction with the Aerospace Industry during the Production of *2001*." In *Stanley Kubrick: New Perspectives*, edited by Ljujić Tatjana, Peter Krämer, and Richard Daniels, 200–217. London: Black Dog.

Pérez-González, Luis. 2014. *Audiovisual Translation: Theories, Methods and Issues.* New York: Routledge.

Perko, Manca. 2019. *Voices and Noises. Collaborative Authorship in Stanley Kubrick's Films.* Doctoral thesis, University of East Anglia.

Peucker, Brigitte. 2001. "Kubrick and Kafka: The Corporeal Uncanny." *Modernism/Modernity* 8(4): 663–74.

Pezzotta, Elisa. 2013. *Stanley Kubrick: Adapting the Sublime.* Jackson and Atlanta: University Press of Mississippi.

Pezzotta, Elisa. 2015. "The Magic of Time in *Lolita*: The Time Traveller Humbert Humbert." *Adaptation* 8(3): 297–320.

Pezzotta, Elisa. 2017. "Slowness and Time Expansion in Long Takes: *2001: A Space Odyssey, Barry Lyndon,* and *Eyes Wide Shut*." *Cinergie* 12: 41–52.

Phillips, Gene D. 1977. *Stanley Kubrick: A Film Odyssey.* New York: Popular Library.

Phillips, Gene D. 2001. *Stanley Kubrick: Interviews.* Jackson: University Press of Mississippi.

Phillips, Gene D. 2005. "*Killer's Kiss*." In *The Stanley Kubrick Archives,* edited by Alison Castle, 278–87. Cologne: Taschen.

Phillips, Gene D and Rodney Hill. 2002. *The Encyclopedia of Stanley Kubrick.* New York. Checkmark.

Planka, Sabine. 2012. "Erotic, Silent, Dead: The Concept of Women in the Films of Stanley Kubrick." *Film International* 10(4–5): 52–67.

Polan, Dana. 1996. "Materiality and Sociality in *Killer's Kiss*." In *Perspectives on Stanley Kubrick,* edited by Mario Falsetto, 87–99. New York: G.K. Hall.

Polito, Robert. 1996. *Savage Art: A Biography of Jim Thompson.* New York: Vintage Books.

Poole, Robert. 2015. "*2001: A Space Odyssey* and the 'Dawn of Man.'" In *Stanley Kubrick: New Perspectives,* edited by Tatjana Ljujić, Peter Krämer, and Richard Daniels, 176–97. London: Black Dog.

Porter, Louis. 2017. "Clockwork Concrete." *'A' Magazine: For RIBA Friends of Architecture* (Spring): 18–23.

Pramaggiore, Maria. 2015a. *Making Time in Stanley Kubrick's Barry Lyndon: Art, History and Empire.* New York and London: Bloomsbury.

Pramaggiore, Maria . 2015b. "From Thackeray to the Troubles: The Irishness of Barry Lyndon." In *Stanley Kubrick: New Perspectives,* edited by Tatjana Ljujić, Peter Krämer, and Richard Daniels, 260–79. London: Black Dog.

Pringle, Peter. 1980. *SIOP, The Secret U.S. Plan for Nuclear War.* London: W.W. Norton.

Pritzer, Andrea. 2013. *The Secret History of Vladimir Nabokov.* New York: Pegasus.

Purić, Biljana. 2017. "Kubrick's Neobaroque Spectacle: An Aesthetic Analysis of Artificiality and Violence in *A Clockwork Orange*." *Etnoantropološki Problemi* 12(2): 489–503.

Pursell, Michael. 2001. "*Full Metal Jacket*: The Unravelling of Patriarchy." In *Perspectives in Stanley Kubrick,* edited by Mario Falsetto, 317–26. New York: G. K. Hall.

Rabinowitz, Peter T. 2003. "'A Bird of Like Rarest Spun Heavenmetal': Music in *A Clockwork Orange*." In *Stanley Kubrick's A Clockwork Orange,* edited by Stuart Y. McDougal, 109–30. Cambridge and New York: Cambridge University Press.

Radford, Fiona. 2015. "Having His Cake and Eating It Too: Stanley Kubrick and *Spartacus*." In *Stanley Kubrick: New Perspectives,* edited by Tatjana Ljujić, Richard Daniels, and Peter Krämer, 98–115. London: Black Dog.

Rafferty, Terrence. 1987. "Remote Control." *Sight and Sound* 56(4): 256–9.

Ramazani, Jahan and Jon Stallworthy. 2006. "The Twentieth Century and After." In *The Norton Anthology: English Literature*, edited by Stephen Greenblatt, 2293–829. New York and London: W.W. Norton.

Ransom, Amy J. 2010. "Opening *Eyes Wide Shut*: Genre, Reception, and Kubrick's Last Film." *Journal of Film and Video* 62(4): 31–46.

Raphael, Frederic. 1999. *Eyes Wide Open: A Memoir of Stanley Kubrick*. New York: Ballantine.

Raphael, Frederic. 2000. *Eyes Wide Open: A Memoir of Stanley Kubrick and Eyes Wide Shut*. London: Phoenix.

Raphael, Frederic. 2001. "Frederic Raphael, Screenwriter." In *Kubrick/The Definitive Edition*, edited by Michel Ciment, 269–71. New York: Faber and Faber.

Reichmann, Hans-Peter. 2004. *Stanley Kubrick*. Frankfurt: Deutsches Filminstitut.

Reilly, Nick. 2018. "'Lynchian,' 'Tarantinoesque' and 'Kubrickian' Lead New Film Words Added to *Oxford English Dictionary*." *NME* (October 5). www.nme.com/news/lm/lynchian-tarantinoesque-and-kubrickian-lead-new- lm-words-added-to-oxford-english-dictionary-definition-2387041 (accessed August 25, 2019).

Reynolds, Charles. 1960. "Interview with Stanley Kubrick." *Popular Photography* 46(6): 144–5, 149.

Reitz, Edgar. 2004. "'Our Work Was an Exception': Directing the Dubbing of *Eyes Wide Shut*. Interview with Edgar Reitz." In *Stanley Kubrick*, edited by Hans-Peter Reichmann and Ingeborg Flagge, 244–49. Frankfurt am Main: Detuchesfilmmuseum

Rice, Julian C. 1976. "Kubrick's *Barry Lyndon*: 'Like Father-Like Son.'" *Film Criticism* 1(2): 9–14.

Rice, Julian C. 2008. *Kubrick's Hope: Discovering Optimism from 2001 to Eyes Wide Shut*. Lanham, MD: Scarecrow Press.

Rice, Julian C. 2017. *Kubrick's Story, Spielberg's Film: A.I. Artificial Intelligence*. Lanham, MD: Rowman and Littlefield.

Rinke, H. 1975. Letter to J. Harlan. April 21. Stanley Kubrick Archive, University of the Arts London.

Ritzenhoff, Karen. 2015. "'UK Frost Can Kill Palms': Layers of Reality in *Full Metal Jacket*." In *Stanley Kubrick, New Perspectives*, edited by Ljujic Tatjana, Peter Krämer, and Richard Daniels, 326–41. London: Black Dog.

Robey, Tim. 2016. "Kubrick by Candlelight: How *Barry Lyndon* Became a Gorgeous, Period-Perfect Masterpiece." *Telegraph* (July 27). https://www.telegraph.co.uk/films/2016/07/27/kubrick-by-candlelight-how-barry-lyndon-became-a-gorgeous-period/ (accessed August 25, 2019).

Rodowick, David. 2001. *Reading the Figural or Philosophy after the New Media*. Durham, NC: Duke University Press.

Romi, Yvette. 1968. "Interview de Stanley Kubrick par Yvette Romi." *Le Nouvel Observateur* (September 23).

Romero Fresco, Pablo. 2013. "Accessible Filmmaking: Joining the Dots between Audiovisual Translation, Accessibility and Filmmaking." *Journal of Specialised Translation* 20: 201–23.

Romero Fresco, Pablo. 2019. *Accessible Filmmaking. Integrating Translation and Accessibility into the Filmmaking Process*. London and New York: Routledge.

Ronson, Jon. 2004. "Citizen Kubrick." *Guardian* (March 27). https://www.theguardian.com/film/2004/mar/27/features.weekend (accessed August 25, 2020).

Rosenbaum, Jonathan. 1976. 'The Pluck of *Barry Lyndon*'. *Film Comment* 12(2): 26–8.

Rosenbaum, Jonathan. 1995. "*Dr. Strangelove*, Review." *Chicago Reader* (February 1).

Rosenbaum, Jonathan. 2016. "In Dreams Begin Responsibilities." In *Depth of Field, Stanley Kubrick: Film, and the Uses of History*, edited by Geoffrey Cocks, James Diedrick, and Glenn Perusek, 245–54. Madison: University of Wisconsin Press.

Roud, Richard. 1968. "Review of *2001: A Space Odyssey*." *Guardian* (May 3). https://www.theguardian.com/film/2018/may/03/2001-a-space-odyssey-review-stanley-kubrick-1968 (accessed August 25, 2019).

Sanders, Steven. 2007. "The Big Score: Fate, Morality, and Meaningful Life in *The Killing*." In *The Philosophy of Stanley Kubrick*, edited by Jerold J. Abrams, 149–63. Lexington: University Press of Kentucky.

Sante, Luc. 2018. "Stanley Kubrick: Learning to Look." In *Through a Different Lens: Stanley Kubrick Photographs*, edited by Donald Albrecht and Sean Corcoran, 16–23. Cologne: Taschen.

Sarris, Andrew. 1962. "Movie Journal: Review of *Lolita*." *Village Voice* (July 5).

Sarris, Andrew. 1964. "*Dr. Strangelove Or, How I Learned to Stop Worrying and Love the Bomb*." *Village Voice* (February 13).

Sarris, Andrew. 1968a. *The American Cinema: Directors and Directions 1929–1968*. New York: E. P. Dutton.

Sarris, Andrew. 1968b. "Review of *2001: A Space Odyssey*." *New York Times* (April 11).

Sarris, Andrew. 1968c. "Review of *2001: A Space Odyssey*." *New York Times* (May 7).

Sarris, Andrew. 1971. "Films in Focus." *Village Voice* (December 30): 49.

Sarris, Andrew. 1975. "Review of *Barry Lyndon*." *Village Voice* (December 23). https://cinefiles.bampfa.berkeley.edu/cinefiles/DocDetail?docId=39020 (accessed November 9, 2018).

Sarris, Andrew. 1987. "*Full Metal Jacket*." *Washington Post* (August 7). https://www.washingtonpost.com/archive/lifestyle/tv/1988/08/07/full-metal-jacket/cdb75119-bc90-4f0f-901e-69687eca7ccb/ (accessed August 25, 2019).

Sarris, Andrew. 1996. *The American Cinema: Directors and Directions, 1929–1968*. New York: Da Capo Press.

Sarris, Andrew. 2001. "A.I. = (2001 + E.T.)2." *Observer* (June 25). https://observer.com/2001/06/ai-2001-et-2/ (accessed November 13, 2018).

Sarris, Andrew. 2009. "Notes on the Auteur Theory in 1962." In *Film Theory and Criticism: Introductory Readings*, edited by L. Braudy and M. Cohen, 561–4. Oxford: Oxford University Press.

Schatz, Thomas. 1981. *Hollywood Genres: Formulas, Filmmaking, and the Studio System*. New York: Random House.

Schatz, Thomas. 2015. *The Genius of the System: Hollywood Filmmaking in the Studio Era*. New York: Henry Holt.

Schickel, Richard. 1975. "Kubrick's Grandest Gamble." *Time Magazine* (December 15).

Schnitzler, Arthur. 1999. *Dream Story* (trans. J. M. Q. Davies). London: Penguin.

Schoenewolf, Gerald. 2017. "'What Do Women Want?' Revisited." *Psychoanalysis Now*. https://blogs.psychcentral.com/psychoanalysis-now/2017/05/what-do-women-want-revisited/ (accessed August 25, 2019).

Schrader, Paul. 1972. "Notes on Film Noir." *Film Comment* 8(1): 8–13.

Schwartz, Joan M. and Terry Cook. 2002. "Archives, Records, and Power: The Making of Modern Memory." *Archival Science* 2(1): 1–19.

Scott, A. O. 2001. "Do Androids Long for Mom?" *New York Times* (June 29). https://www.nytimes.com/2001/06/29/movies/film-review-do-androids-long-for-mom.html (accessed November 24, 2018).

Seed, David. 2011. *Science Fiction: A Very Short Introduction.* New York: Oxford University Press.

Seesslen, Georg. 2014. "'Shoot Me. Shoot Me.' On the Essence of War: *Full Metal Jacket.*" In *Stanley Kubrick*, edited by Maja Keppler and Hans-Peter Reichmann, 208–23. Frankfurt am Main: Deutsches Filmmuseum.

Seesslen, Georg and Jung Fernand. 1999. *Stanley Kubrick und seine Filme.* Marburg: Schüren.

Shaw, Daniel. 2007. "Nihilism and Freedom in the Films of Stanley Kubrick." In *The Philosophy of Stanley Kubrick*, edited by Jerold J. Abrams, 221–34. Lexington: University Press of Kentucky.

Shoard, Catherine. 2013. "Stephen King Damns Shelley Duvall's Character in Film of *The Shining.*" *Guardian* (September 19). https://www.theguardian.com/film/2013/sep/19/stephen-king-shining-shelley-duvall#:~:text=As%20played%20by%20Shelley%20Duvall,to%20scream%20and%20be%20stupid.%22 (accessed August 26, 2020).

Siddiquee, Imran. 2017. "Why Do We Let 'Genius' Directors Get Away With Abusive Behavior?" *BuzzFeed* (October 25). https://www.buzzfeednews.com/article/imransiddiquee/hollywood-abusive-auteur-problem (accessed August 26, 2020).

Singer, Irving. 2004. *Three Philosophical Filmmakers: Hitchcock, Welles, Renoir.* Cambridge: MIT Press.

Singer, Irving. 2008. *Cinematic Mythmaking: Philosophy in Film.* Cambridge: MIT Press.

Siskel, Gene. 2001. "Candidly Kubrick." In *Stanley Kubrick: Interviews*, edited by Gene D. Phillips, 177–89. Jackson: University Press of Mississippi.

Smith, Greg M. 1999. "Local Emotions, Global Moods, and Film Structure." In *Passionate Views: Film, Cognition, and Emotion*, edited by Carl Plantinga and Greg M. Smith, 103–26. Baltimore, MD: The Johns Hopkins University Press.

Smith, P. D. 2007. *Doomsday Men.* London: Penguin.

Smith, Richard J. 2016. "Darwin, Freud, and the Continuing Misrepresentation of the Primal Horde." *Current Anthropology* 57(6): 838–43.

Sobchack, Vivian. 1997. *Screening Space: The American Science Fiction Film.* Rutgers, NJ: Rutgers University Press.

Sobchack, Vivian. 2008. "Love Machines: Boy Toys, Toy Boys and the Oxymorons of *A.I.: Artificial Intelligence.*" *Science Fiction Film and Television* 1(1): 1–13.

Sontag, Susan. 1988. *AIDS and Its Metaphors.* New York: Farrar, Straus and Giroux.

Sperb, Jason. 2004. "The Country of the Mind in Kubrick's *Fear and Desire.*" *Film Criticism* 29(1): 23–37.

Spiegel, Alan. 1979. "Kubrick's *Barry Lyndon.*" *Salmagundi* 38(39): 194–208.

Stanley Kubrick Archive. SK Box–1950–53. "Brown Wallet E & K."

Stackhouse, Margaret. 2016. "Interpretations of *2001: A Space Odyssey.*" In *The Stanley Kubrick Archives*, edited by Alison Castle, 466–71. Cologne: Taschen.

Staiger, Janet. [1997] 2003. "Hybrid or Inbred: The Purity Hypothesis and Hollywood Genre History." In *Film Genre Reader 3*, edited by Barry Keith Grant, 185–99. Austin: University of Texas Press.

Stam, Robert. 2000. *Film Theory: An Anthology.* Oxford: Blackwell.

Stein, Jack Medison. 1960. *Richard Wagner and the Synthesis of the Arts*. Detroit: Wayne University Press.

Sternberg, Meir. 1978. *Expositional Modes and Temporal Ordering in Fiction*. Bloomington and Indianapolis: Indiana University Press.

Strick, Philip. 1972a. "*A Clockwork Orange*." *Sight and Sound* (Winter). https://www.bfi. org.uk/news-opinion/sight-sound-magazine/features/clockwork-orange-stanley-kubrick-anthony-burgess-raucous-perfection (accessed August 25, 2019).

Strick, Philip. 1972b. "Interview with Stanley Kubrick." *Sight and Sound* 41(2). Reprinted in *Stanley Kubrick: Interviews*, edited by Gene D. Phillips, 126–40. Jackson: University Press of Mississippi, 2001.

Strick, Philip and Penelope Houston. 1972. "Interview with Stanley Kubrick Regarding *A Clockwork Orange*." *Sight and Sound* (January). http://visual-memory.co.uk/amk/doc/ 0070.html?LMCL=l5lZ56 (accessed August 25, 2019).

Stuckey, Karyn. 2015 "Re-writing Nabokov's *Lolita*: Kubrick, the Creative Adaptor." In *Stanley Kubrick: New Perspectives*, edited by Tatjana Ljujic, Peter Krämer, and Richard Daniels, 116–35. London: Black Dog.

Suvin, Darko. 2015. "Metaphoricity and Narrativity in Fiction: The Chronotope as the Differentia Generica." https://darkosuvin.com/2015/05/24/metaphoricity-and-narrativity-in-fiction-the-chronotope-as-the-differentia-generica/ (accessed August 25, 2019).

Swenson, Gene. 1963. "What Is Pop Art? Answers from 8 Painters, Part I." *ARTnews* 62(7): 24–7, 60–64.

Tanner, Michael. 1979. "The Total Work of Art." In *The Wagner Companion*, edited by Peter Burbridge and Richard Sutton, 140–224. New York: Cambridge University Press.

Taylor, Steven. 1964. "*Dr Strangelove Or, How I Learned to Stop Worrying and Love the Bomb*." *Film Comment* 2(1): 40–43.

Telotte, J. P. 1989. *Voices in the Dark: The Narrative Patterns of Film Noir*. Urbana and Chicago: University of Illinois Press.

Telotte, J. P. 2006a. "The Gravity of *2001: A Space Odyssey*." In *2001: A Space Odyssey: New Essays*, edited by Robert Kolker, 43–58. Oxford and New York: Oxford University Press.

Telotte, J. P 2006b. "The New Hollywood Musical: From *Saturday Night Fever* to *Footloose*." In *Genre and Contemporary Hollywood*, edited by Steve Neale, 48–61. London: British Film Institute.

Thackeray, W. M. 1984. *The Memoirs of Barry Lyndon, Esq*. (ed. Andrew Sanders). Oxford: Oxford University Press.

Thissen, Rolf. 1999. *Stanley Kubrick: Der Regisseur als Architekt*. Munich: Heyne.

Thomas, T. 1979. *Film Score: View from the Podium*. South Brunswick: A.S. Barnes.

Thompson, Kristin. 1981. *Eisenstein's Ivan the Terrible: A Neoformalist Analysis*. Princeton: Princeton University Press.

Thompson, Kristin. 1988. *Breaking the Glass Armor: Neoformalist Film Analysis*. Princeton, NJ: Princeton University Press.

Titterington, P. L. 1981. "Kubrick and *The Shining*." *Sight and Sound* 50(2): 120–21.

Toles, George. 2006. "Double Minds and Double Binds in Stanley Kubrick's Fairy Tale." In *Stanley Kubrick's 2001: A Space Odyssey: New Essays*, edited by Robert Kolker, 147–76. Oxford: Oxford University Press.

Trilling, Lionel. 1958. "The Last Lover: Vladimir Nabokov's *Lolita*." *Encounter* 11: 4.

Truffaut, François. 1975. *The Films in My Life* (trans. L. Mayhew). New York: Simon and Schuster.

Truffaut, François. 2008. "A Certain Tendency of the French Cinema." In *Auteurs and Authorship: A Film Reader*, edited by Barry K. Grant, 9–18. Malden, MA: Blackwell.

Trumbo, Dalton. 1991. "Report on *Spartacus*." *Cinéaste* 18(3): 30–33.

Tully, David. 2010. *Terry Southern and the American Grotesque*. Jefferson, NC: McFarland.

Turing, Alan M. 1950. "Computing Machinery and Intelligence." *Mind* 49(236): 433–60.

TV Store Online. 2014. "Rachel Elkind, Producer/Co-Composer of the Scores for the Stanley Kubrick Films *A Clockwork Orange* (1971) and *The Shining* (1980) Talks with TV Store Online about Kubrick and the Haunting Images of *The Shining*." *Cinephilia and Beyond*. http://5cinephiliabeyond.tumblr.com/post/96638220455/rachel-elkind-producerco-composer-of-the-scores (accessed August 25, 2019).

Ulivieri, Filippo. 2016. *Stanley Kubrick and Me: Thirty Years at His Side*. New York: Arcade.

Ulivieri, Filippo. 2017a. "Waiting for a Miracle: A Survey of Stanley Kubrick's Unrealized Projects." *Cinergie; Il Cinema e le altri Alpe* 12: 95–115.

Ulivieri, Filippo 2017b. "From "Boy Genius" to "Barking Loon": An Analysis of Stanley Kubrick's Mythology." Stanley Kubrick Nouveaux Horizons. *Essais: Revue Interdisciplinaire d'Humanités*, 221–42.

Ulivieri, Filippo. 2017c. "Writing and Rewriting Kubrick: Or, How I Learned to Stop Worrying about the Kubrickian Memoirs and Love Emilio D'Alessandro." *Screening the Past* 42. http://www.screeningthepast.com/issue-42/ (accessed August 25, 2019).

Ulivieri, Filippo and Simone Odino. 2019. *2001 Between Kubrick and Clarke. The Genesis, Making and Authorship of a Masterpiece*. Loreto: Streetlib.

Ustinov, Peter. 1977. *Dear Me*. London: Heinemann.

Varela, Jay. 2016. "Conversation with Stanley Kubrick." In *The Stanley Kubrick Archives*, edited by Alison Castle, 166–71. Cologne: Taschen.

Variety. 1954. "*Killer's Kiss*." https://variety.com/1954/film/reviews/killer-s-kiss-1200417893/ (accessed August 25, 2019).

Variety. 1961. "*Lolita*." https://variety.com/1961/film/reviews/lolita-1200420145/ (accessed August 25, 2019).

Vernet, Marc, Jacques Aumont, Alain Bergala, and Michel Marie. 1992. *Aesthetics of Film* (trans. Richard Neupert). Austin: University of Texas Press.

Walker, Alexander. 1972. *Stanley Kubrick Directs*. New York: Harcourt Brace Jovanovich.

Walker, Alexander. 1964. "How Mr. Kubrick Learned to Stop Worrying." *Evening Standard* (December 11).

Walker, Alexander. 1985. *National Heroes: British Cinema in the Seventies and Eighties*. London: Harrap.

Walker, Alexander. 2000. *Stanley Kubrick, Director*. New York: W.W. Norton.

Walker, Alexander, Sybil Taylor, and Ulrich Ruchti. 1999. *Stanley Kubrick, Director: A Visual Analysis*. Revised and expanded edition. New York: W.W. Norton.

Warhol, Andy. 1975. *The Philosophy of Andy Warhol (From A to B and Back Again)*. Orlando: A Harvest Book.

Warner, Rick. 2020. "Kubrickian Dread: Echoes of *2001: A Space Odyssey* and *The Shining* in Works by Jonathan Glazer, Paul Thomas Anderson, and David Lynch." In *After Kubrick: A Filmmaker's Legacy*, edited by Jeremi Szaniawski, 125–45. London and New York: Bloomsbury.

Watson, Ian. 1999. "My Adventures with Stanley Kubrick." *Playboy* (August): 82–159.

Webster, Patrick. 2011. *Love and Death in Kubrick: A Critical Study of the Films from Lolita through Eyes Wide Shut*. Jefferson, NC: McFarland.

Wells, Ira. 2015. "Forgetting Lolita: How Nabokov's Victim Became an American Fantasy." *New Republic* 246(7/8): 70–73. https://newrepublic.com/article/121908/lolita-cultural-icon (accessed January 25, 2019).

Weiler, A. H. 1956. "*The Killing*: Film at the Mayfair Concerns a Robbery." *New York Times* (May 21). https://archive.nytimes.com/www.nytimes.com/library/film/052155kubrick-killing.html (accessed August 25, 2019).

Weintraub, Bernard. 1972. "Kubrick Tells What Makes *A Clockwork Orange* Tick." *New York Times*. http://www.archiviokubrick.it/english/words/interviews/1972clockworktick.html (accessed August 25, 2019).

Welsh, James M. 2002. "Walker, Alexander." In *The Encyclopedia of Stanley Kubrick*, edited by Gene D. Phillips and Rodney Hill, 396. New York: Checkmark Books.

White, Lionel. 1955. *The Snatchers* / *Clean Break*. Eureka, CA: Stark House.

White, Susan. 1988. "Male Bonding, Hollywood Orientalism, and the Repression of the Feminine in Kubrick's *Full Metal Jacket*." *Arizona Quarterly* 44(3): 120–44.

White, Susan M. 2006. "Kubrick's Obscene Shadows." In Stanley Kubrick's 2001: A Space Odyssey, New Essays, edited by Robert Kolker, 127–46. New York: Oxford University Press.

Whitehouse, Charles. 1999. "Eyes without a Face." *Sight and Sound* (September): 38–9.

Whitinger, Raleigh and Susan Ingram. 2003. "Schnitzler, Kubrick, and 'Fidelio.'" *Mosaic: An Interdisciplinary Critical Journal* 36(3): 55–71.

Whitlock, Pope. 2019. "Book Review: *Eyes Wide Shut* by Nathan Abrams and Robert Philip Kolker." https://whitlockandpope.com/2019/09/23/book-review-eyes-wide-shut-by-nathan-abrams-and-robert-phillip-kolker/ (accessed August 25, 2019).

Wierzbicki, James. 2003. "Banality Triumphant: Iconographic Uses of Beethoven's Ninth Symphony in Recent Films." *Beethoven-Forum* 10(2): 113–38.

Wild, Mary. 2019. "Stanley Kubrick's *Eyes Wide Shut*: Mary Wild and Nathan Abrams in Conversation." *Freud Museum* (September 11).

Williams, Linda. 2017a. "*Blue Is the Warmest Color*: Or the After-life of 'Visual Pleasure and Narrative Cinema.'" *New Review of Film and Television Studies* 15(4): 465–70.

Williams, Linda Ruth. 1991. "Film Bodies: Gender, Genre, and Excess." *Film Quarterly* 44(4): 2–13.

Williams, Linda Ruth. 2005. *The Erotic Thriller in Contemporary Cinema*. Edinburgh: Edinburgh University Press.

Williams, Linda Ruth. 2017b. "'Who Am I, David?': Motherhood in Spielberg's Dramas of Family Dysfunction." In *A Companion to Steven Spielberg*, edited by Nigel Morris, 243–57. Oxford and Malden, MA: Wiley-Blackwell.

Williams, Tony. 2008. "The Dream Landscape of *Killer's Kiss*." In *Stanley Kubrick: Essays on His Films and Legacy*, edited by Gary D. Rhodes, 39–46. Jefferson, NC: McFarland.

Willoquet-Maricondi, Paula. 1994. "Full-Metal-Jacketing, or Masculinity in the Making." *Cinema Journal* 33(2): 5–21.

Willoquet-Maricondi, Paula. 2006. "Full-Metal Jacketing, or Masculinity in the Making." In *Depth of Field: Stanley Kubrick, Film, and the Uses of History*, edited by Geoffrey Cocks, James Diedrick, and Glen Perusek, 218–41. Madison: University of Wisconsin Press.

Wiseman, Andreas. 2019. "Stanley Kubrick Screenplay Ideas Unearthed with Focus On Marriage, Jealousy & Adultery." *Deadline* (July 12). https://deadline.com/2019/07/stanley-kubrick-screenplay-ideas-discovered-uk-1202645403/ (accessed August 25, 2019).

Wollen, Peter. 1972. *Signs and Meaning in the Cinema*. 3rd edn. London: British Film Institute.

Wood, Michael. 1976. "No, But I Read the Book." *New York Review of Books* (February 5). https://www.nybooks.com/articles/1976/02/05/no-but-i-read-the-book/ (accessed August 26, 2020).

Wood, Robin. 2003. *Hollywood from Vietnam to Reagan ... and Beyond*. 2nd edn. New York: Columbia University Press.

Wright, Jarrell D. 2008. "Reconsidering Fidelity and Considering Genre in (and with) *The Shining*." In *Stanley Kubrick: Essays on His Films and Legacy*, edited by Gary D. Rhodes, 136–48. Jefferson, NC and London: McFarland.

Yacavone, Daniel. 2008. "Towards a Theory of Film Worlds." *Film-Philosophy* 12(2): 83–108.

Yaoi, Junichi. 2018. "*The Shining*: Unseen Interviews with Stanley Kubrick & Vivian Kubrick." https://www.youtube.com/watch?v=fVlXbS0SNqk (accessed May 30, 2019).

Zabalbeascoa, Patrick, Natália Izard, and Laura Santamaria. 2001. "Disentangling Audiovisual Translation". In *(Multi)media Translation: Concepts, Practices, and Research*, edited by Yves Gambier and Henrik Gottlieb, 101–12. Amsterdam and New York: Benjamins.

Zanotti, Serenella. 2019a. "Investigating the Genesis of Translated Films: A View from the Stanley Kubrick Archive." *Perspectives: Studies in Translation Theory and Practice* 27(2): 201–17.

Zanotti, Serenella. 2019b. "Auteur Dubbing: Translation, Performance and Authorial Control in the Dubbed Versions of Stanley Kubrick's Films." In *Reassessing Dubbing: Historical Approaches and Current Trends*, edited by Irene Ranzato and Serenella Zanotti, 79–100. Amsterdam and Philadelphia: Benjamins.

Zanotti, Serenella. Forthcoming. "Translaboration in a Film Context: A Study of Stanley Kubrick's Collaborative Approach to Translation." *Target* 32. Special issue on Translaboration: Exploring Collaboration in Translation and Translation in Collaboration, edited by Alexa Alfer and Cornelia Zwischenberger.

Žižek, Slavoj. 2000. *The Ticklish Subject*. London: Verso.

Žižek, Slavoj. 2001. *The Fright of Real Tears: Krzysztof Kieslowski between Theory and Post Theory*. London: British Film Institute.

Filmography

1951 *Day of the Fight* (Documentary)

Script: Robert Rein
Direction, cinematography (b&w): Kubrick, Alex Singer
Music: Gerald Fried
Editing: Julian Bergman, Stanley Kubrick
Cast: Walter Cartier, Vincent Cartier, Bobby James, Dan Stampler, Nat Fleischer
Produced by Stanley Kubrick, Jay Bonafield for RKO-Pathe, 16 min

1951 *Flying Padre* (Documentary)

Direction, cinematography (b&w): Kubrick
Editing: Isaac Kleinerman
Music: Nathaniel Shilkret
Cast: Fred Stadtmueller, Pedro
Produced for RKO, 8 min

1953 *The Seafarers*

Direction, cinematography (color), editing: Kubrick
Script: Will Chasen
Cast: Don Hollenbeck, Paul Hall
Produced by Lester Cooper for Lester Cooper Productions, Pietrzak Filmways, Seafarers International Union, Atlantic & Gulf Coast District, American Federation of Labor, 29 min

1953 *Fear and Desire*

Script: Howard O. Sackler
Direction, cinematography (b&w), editing: Kubrick
Cast: Frank Silvera (*Mac*), Kenneth Harp (*Corby*), Virginia Leith (*The Girl*), Paul Mazursky (*Sidney*), Steve Coit (*Fletcher*)
Produced by Stanley Kubrick, Joseph Perveler for Joseph Burstyn, 68 min

1955 *Killer's Kiss*

Script: Kubrick, Howard O. Sackler
Direction, cinematography (b&w), editing: Kubrick
Music: Gerald Fried
Choreography: David Vaughan
Cast: Frank Silvera (*Vincent Rapallo*), Jamie Smith (*Davy Gordon*), Irene Kane (*Gloria Price*), Jerry Jarret (*Albert*), Ruth Sobotka (*Iris*), Mike Dana, Felice Orlandi, Ralph Roberts, Phil Stevenson (*Hoodlums*), Julius Adelman (*Mannequin Factory Owner*), David Vaughan, Alec Rubin (*Conventioneers*)
Produced by Stanley Kubrick, Morris Bousel for Minotaur, United Artists, 61 min

1956 *The Killing*

Script: Kubrick, based on the novel *Clean Break* by Lionel White
Additional dialogue: Jim Thompson
Direction: Kubrick
Cinematography (b&w): Lucien Ballard
Art direction: Ruth Sobotka Kubrick
Editing: Betty Steinberg
Music: Gerald Fried
Cast: Sterling Hayden (*Johnny Clay*), Jay C. Flippen (*Marvin Unger*), Marie Windsor (*Sherry Peatty*), Elisha Cook (*George Peatty*), Coleen Gray (*Fay*), Vince Edwards (*Val Cannon*), Ted de Corsia (*Randy Kennan*), Joe Sawyer (*Mike O'Reilly*), Tim Carey (*Nikki*), Kola Kwariani (*Maurice*).
Produced by James B. Harris for Harris-Kubrick Productions, United Artists, 83 min

1957 *Paths of Glory*

Script: Kubrick, Calder Willingham, and Jim Thompson, based on the novel by Humphrey Cobb
Direction: Kubrick
Cinematography (b&w): George Krause
Art direction: Ludwig Reiber
Editing: Eva Kroll
Music: Gerald Fried
Cast: Kirk Douglas (*Colonel Dax*), Ralph Meeker (*Corporal Paris*), Adolphe Menjou (*General Broulard*), George Macready (*General Mireau*), Wayne Morris (*Lieutenant Roget*), Richard Anderson (*Major Saint-Auban*), Joseph Turkel (*Private Arnaud*), Timothy Carey (*Private Ferol*), Peter Capell (*Colonel Judge*), Susanne Christian (*German Girl*), Bert Freed (*Sergeant Boulanger*), Emile Meyer (*Priest*), John Stein (*Captain Rousseau*)

Produced by James B. Harris, Kirk Douglas for Bryna Productions, United
Artists, 86 min

1960 *Spartacus*

Script: Dalton Trumbo, based on the novel by Howard Fast
Direction: Kubrick
Cinematography (Super Technirama-70): Russell Metty
Additional cinematography: Clifford Stine
Production design: Alexander Golitzen
Editing: Robert Lawrence, Robert Schultz, Fred Chulack
Music: Alex North
Cast: Kirk Douglas (*Spartacus*), Laurence Olivier (*Marcus Crassus*), Jean Simmons
(*Varinia*), Charles Laughton (*Gracchus*), Peter Ustinov (*Batiatus*), John Gavin
(*Julius Caesar*), Tony Curtis (*Antoninus*), Nina Foch (*Helena*), Herbert Lom
(*Tigranes*), John Ireland (*Crixus*), John Dall (*Glabrus*), Charles McGraw
(*Marcellus*), Joanna Barnes (*Claudia*), Harold J. Stone (*David*), Woody Strode
(*Draba*)
Produced by Kirk Douglas, Edward Lewis for Bryna, Universal Pictures, 196 min

1962 *Lolita*

Script: Vladimir Nabokov, based on his novel
Direction: Kubrick
Cinematography (b&w): Oswald Morris
Art direction: William Andrews
Editing: Anthony Harvey
Music: Nelson Riddle, Bob Harris
Cast: James Mason (*Humbert Humbert*), Sue Lyon (*Lolita Haze*), Shelley Winters
(*Charlotte Haze*), Peter Sellers (*Clare Quilty*), Diana Decker (*Jean Farlow*), Jerry
Stovin (*John Farlow*), Suzanne Gibbs (*Mona Farlow*), Gary Cockrell (*Dick*),
Marianne Stone (*Vivian Darkbloom*), Cec Linder (*Physician*), Lois Maxwell (*Nurse
Mary Lore*), William Greene (*Swine*)
Produced by James B. Harris for MGM, Seven Arts, Anya/Transworld, A.A.
Productions, Ltd., Transworld Pictures, 153 min

1964 *Dr. Strangelove, Or How I Learned to Stop Worrying and Love the Bomb*

Script: Kubrick, Terry Southern, and Peter George, based on George's novel *Red Alert*
Direction: Kubrick

Cinematography (b&w): Gilbert Taylor
Production design: Ken Adam
Editing: Anthony Harvey
Special effects: Wally Veevers
Music: Laurie Johnson
Cast: Peter Sellers (*Group Captain Lionel Mandrake, President Merkin Muffley,
    Dr. Strangelove*), George C. Scott (*General Buck Turgidson*), Sterling Hayden
    (*General Jack D. Ripper*), Keenan Wynn (*Colonel Bat Guano*), Slim Pickens
    (*Major Kong*), Peter Bull (*Ambassador de Sadesky*), Tracy Reed (*Miss Scott*),
    James Earl Jones (*Lieutenant Lothar Zogg, Bombardier*), Jack Creley (*Mr. Staines*),
    Frank Berry (*Lieutenant H. R. Dietrich, D.S.O.*), Glenn Beck (*Lieutenant W. D.
    Kivel, Navigator*), Shane Rimmer (*Captain Ace Owens, Co-pilot*), Paul Tamarin
    (*Lieutenant B. Goldberg, Radio Operator*), Gordon Tanner (*General Faceman*)
Produced by Kubrick for Hawk Films, Columbia, 94 min

1968 *2001: A Space Odyssey*

Script: Kubrick, Arthur C. Clarke
Direction: Kubrick
Cinematography (Super Panavision): Geoffrey Unsworth
Additional cinematography: John Alcott
Production design: Tony Masters, Harry Lange, Ernie Archer
Special cinematographic effects design and direction: Kubrick
Special cinematographic effects supervision: Wally Veevers, Douglas Trumbull, Con
    Pederson, Tom Howard
Editing: Ray Lovejoy
Music: Richard Strauss, Johann Strauss, Aram Khachaturian, György Ligeti
Costumes: Hardy Amies
Cast: Keir Dullea (*David Bowman*), Gary Lockwood (*Frank Poole*), William Sylvester
    (*Dr. Heywood Floyd*), Daniel Richter (*Moonwatcher*), Douglas Rain (*Voice of
    HAL 9000*), Leonard Rossiter (*Smyslov*), Margaret Tyzack (*Elena*), Robert Beatty
    (*Halvorsen*), Sean Sullivan (*Michaels*), Frank Miller (*Mission Control*), Penny
    Brahms (*Stewardess*), Alan Gifford (*Poole's Father*)
Produced by Stanley Kubrick for MGM, Polaris, Stanley Kubrick Productions,
    141 min

1971 *A Clockwork Orange*

Script: Kubrick, from the novel by Anthony Burgess
Direction: Kubrick
Cinematography: John Alcott
Production design: John Barry

Editing: Bill Butler
Music: Walter Carlos
Cast: Malcolm McDowell (*Alex*), Patrick Magee (*Mr. Alexander*), Anthony Sharp
(*Minister of the Interior*), Godfrey Quigley (*Prison Chaplain*), Warren Clarke
(*Dim*), James Marcus (*Georgie*), Aubrey Morris (*Deltoid*), Miriam Karlin (*Cat
Lady*), Sheila Raynor (*Mum*), Philip Stone (*Dad*), Carl Duering (*Dr. Brodsky*), Paul
Farrell (*Tramp*), Michael Gover (*Prison Governor*), Clive Francis (*Lodger*), Madge
Ryan (*Dr. Branom*), Pauline Taylor (*Psychiatrist*), John Clive (*Stage Actor*), Michael
Bates (*Chief Guard*)
Produced by Si Litvinoff, Max L. Raab, Stanley Kubrick for Warner Bros., Hawk
Films, 137 min

1975 *Barry Lyndon*

Script: Kubrick, from the novel by William Makepeace Thackeray
Direction: Kubrick
Cinematography: John Alcott
Production design: Ken Adam
Editing: Tony Lawson
Music: J. S. Bach, Frederick the Great, Handel, Mozart, Paisiello, Schubert, Vivaldi,
The Chieftains
Music adaptation: Leonard Rosenman
Costumes: Ulla-Britt Soderlund, Milena Canonero
Cast: Ryan O'Neal (*Barry Lyndon*), Marisa Berenson (*Lady Lyndon*), Patrick Magee
(*The Chevalier*), Hardy Kruger (*Captain Potzdorf*), Marie Kean (*Barry's Mother*),
Gay Hamilton (*Nora*), Murray Melvin (*Reverend Runt*), Godfrey Quigley (*Captain
Grogan*), Leonard Rossiter (*Captain Quinn*), Leon Vitali (*Lord Bullingdon*), Diana
Koerner (*German girl*), Frank Middlemass (*Sir Charles Lyndon*), André Morell
(*Lord Wendover*), Arthur O'Sullivan (*Highwayman*), Philip Stone (*Graham*),
Michael Hordern (*Narrator*)
Produced by Stanley Kubrick, Jan Harlan for Warner Bros., Peregrine, Hawk Films,
185 min

1980 *The Shining*

Script: Kubrick and Diane Johnson, from the novel by Stephen King
Direction: Kubrick
Cinematography: John Alcott
Production design: Roy Walker
Editing: Ray Lovejoy
Music: Béla Bartók, Wendy Carlos, Rachel Elkin, György Ligeti, Krzysztof Penderecki

Cast: Jack Nicholson (*Jack Torrance*), Shelley Duvall (*Wendy Torrance*), Danny Lloyd (*Danny Torrance*), Scatman Crothers (*Hallorann*), Barry Nelson (*Stuart Ullman*), Joe Turkel (*Lloyd*), Philip Stone (*Delbert Grady*), Anne Jackson (*Doctor*), Tony Burton (*Larry Durkin*), Lia Beldam (*Young Woman in Bath*), Billie Gibson (*Old Woman in Bath*), Lisa Burns, Louise Burns (*The Grady Girls*)
Produced by Jan Harlan, Stanley Kubrick for Warner Bros., Hawk Films, Peregrine, Producer's Circle, 145 min

1987 *Full Metal Jacket*

Script: Kubrick, Michael Herr, Gustav Hasford, based on Hasford's novel, *The Short-Timers*
Direction: Kubrick
Cinematography: Douglas Milsome
Production design: Anton Furst
Editing: Martin Hunter
Music: Abigail Mead
Cast: Matthew Modine (*Private Joker*), Lee Ermey (*Gunnery Sergeant Hartman*), Vincent D'Onofrio (*Private Pyle*), Arliss Howard (*Cowboy*), Adam Baldwin (*Animal Mother*), Dorian Harewood (*Eightball*), Kevyn Major Howard (*Rafterman*), Ed O'Ross (*Lieutenant Touchdown*)
Produced by Jan Harlan, Stanley Kubrick, Philip Hobbs for Warner Bros., Stanley Kubrick Productions, Natant, 118 min

1999 *Eyes Wide Shut*

Script: Kubrick and Frederic Raphael, based on Arthur Schnitzler's *Traumnovelle*
Direction: Kubrick
Cinematography: Larry Smith
Production design: Leslie Tomkins and Roy Walker
Editing: Nigel Galt
Music: Jocelyn Pook, György Ligeti, Dmitri Shostakovich
Cast: Tom Cruise (*Dr. William Harford*), Nicole Kidman (*Alice Harford*), Sydney Pollack (*Victor Ziegler*), Marie Richardson (*Marion*), Rade Serbedzija (*Milich*), Leelee Sobieski (*Milich's Daughter*), Todd Field (*Nick Nightingale*), Vinessa Shaw (*Domino*), Alan Cumming (*Desk Clerk*), Carmela Marner (*Waitress at Gillespie's*), Sky Dumont (*Sandor Szavost*), Fay Masterson (*Sally*), Thomas Gibson (*Carl*), Louise J. Taylor (*Gayle*), Stewart Thorndike (*Nuala*), Julienne Davis (*Mandy*), Madison Eginton (*Helena Harford*), Leon Vitali (*Man in Red*)
Produced by Jan Harlan, Stanley Kubrick, Brian W. Cook for Warner Bros., 165 min

Index

Note: Page numbers in **bold** denote Illustrations.

CPSIA information can be obtained
at www.ICGtesting.com
Printed in the USA
LVHW080108230722
724192LV00011B/240

9 781501 373954